Same-Sex Dynamics among
Nineteenth-Century Americans

D. MICHAEL QUINN

Same-Sex Dynamics among Nineteenth-Century Americans

A MORMON EXAMPLE

UNIVERSITY OF ILLINOIS PRESS URBANA AND CHICAGO

© 1996 by the Board of Trustees of the University of Illinois
Manufactured in the United States of America

C 5 4 3 2 1

This book is printed on acid-free paper.

Library of Congress Cataloging-in-Publication Data
Quinn, D. Michael, 1944–
Same-sex dynamics among nineteenth-century Americans :
a Mormon example / D. Michael Quinn.
p.   cm.
Includes bibliographical references and index.
ISBN 0-252-02205-X (acid-free paper)
1. Homosexuality—Religious aspects—Church of Jesus Christ
of Latter-day Saints—History of doctrines—19th century.
2. Mormons—United States—Sexual behavior. 3. Mormon gays—
United States—History—19th century. 4. Church of Jesus Christ
of Latter-day Saints—Doctrines—History—19th century.
5. Mormon Church—Doctrines—History—19th century. I. Title.
BX8643.H65Q55 1996
305.9'0664—dc20 95-32473
CIP

To Mary, my firstborn, for her empathy, to Lisa, Adam, and Paul for their love, to Mom for her compassion, to Dad for his Catholic toleration, to my ex-wife, Jan, for her understanding and continued friendship, to Mr. Roeloff for introducing high school students to the life of the mind, to Duff for his Mormon inspiration, to Leonard for his encouragement, to Uncle Frank and George for their support, to Juanita Brooks for her example. And to those long-gone men who loved me more than I understood: Grampa, my stepfathers Wayne and Vaude, and Vincent.

Contents

Preface and Acknowledgments ix

Introduction 1

1 Cross-Cultural Perspectives on Same-Sex Dynamics 33

2 The Homosocial 66

3 The Homopastoral and the Homotactile 84

4 The Homoemotional and the Homoromantic 107

5 The Homomarital, Gender Roles, and Cross-Dressing 130

6 Same-Sex Couples, Homoenvironmental Subcultures, and the Census 152

7 The Earliest Community Study of Lesbians and Gay Men in America: Salt Lake City 195

8 The Coming Out of Three Prominent Mormons in 1919 231

9 Homoeroticism and Sex Crimes in Early Mormonism and Pioneer Utah 265

10 Utah's Judicial and Medical Responses: The Wilde Case to 1918 314

11 From Relative Tolerance to Homophobia in Twentieth-Century Mormonism 366

Conclusion 401

Appendix: Chronology of Same-Sex Issues in American and Mormon Culture 405

Index 445

Illustrations follow p. 230

Preface and Acknowledgments

LIKE MANY SOCIAL HISTORIANS of recent decades, I prefer to write about the silences in traditional history. And in the writing of Mormon history there have been many silences. Although one person's definition of a significant topic in human experience is another's irrelevance, most silences in Mormon history writing are the results of public relations and defensive self-censorship.[1] That observation also holds true for traditional American history's silence about sexuality.[2]

Because of a long dispute over my academic freedom to publish controversial Mormon history, I resigned in 1988 as full professor and director of the graduate history program at Brigham Young University. Officially charged with "apostasy" (heresy) in 1993 for my historical writings, I was excommunicated from the LDS Church.[3] Nevertheless, by heritage (through my mother) I remain a seventh-generation Mormon. And I define myself as a believing Mormon outside the church toward which I feel genuine affection and for which I have fond hopes.[4]

I am indebted to Richard Fernandez and his life's partner, Henry Miller, for first encouraging me to give a presentation about the same-sex relationships of early Mormons. I express special appreciation to the following persons who gave critiques and helpful suggestions on preliminary versions of this study: Lavina Fielding Anderson, Maureen Ursenbach Beecher, Gary James Bergera, Martha Sonntag Bradley, Bonnie Bullough, Vern L. Bullough, Robert Dawidoff, Elizabeth G. Dulany, Sarah Barringer Gordon, Maxine Hanks, David Knowlton,

Rocky O'Donovan, Marybeth Raynes, and Allen D. Roberts. Also I am grateful to Dean H. Hamer and Duane E. Jeffery for conversations about this study and about the need for even a historical work to give attention to the scientific and therapeutic debates about the origins of same-sex desire. However, I alone am responsible for the content and interpretations of this study.

NOTES

1. For a longer statement of that view see "Editor's Introduction," in D. Michael Quinn, ed., *The New Mormon History: Revisionist Essays on the Past* (Salt Lake City: Signature Books, 1992), vii–xx.

2. Martin Bauml Duberman, Martha Vicinus, and George Chauncey Jr., eds., *Hidden from History: Reclaiming the Gay and Lesbian Past* (New York: New American Library, 1989), 1; Martin Duberman, *About Time: Exploring the Gay Past,* rev. ed. (New York: Meridian Books/Penguin, 1991), 54, 121; John D. Wrathall, "Provenance as Text: Reading the Silences around Sexuality in Manuscript Collections," *Journal of American History* 79 (June 1992): 165–78.

3. See also "Apostles vs. Historians," *Newsweek,* 15 Feb. 1982, 77; D. Michael Quinn, "On Being a Mormon Historian (And Its Aftermath)," in George D. Smith, ed., *Faithful History: Essays on Writing Mormon History* (Salt Lake City: Signature Books, 1992); "Apostasy Investigation Launched against Historian," *Salt Lake Tribune,* 13 Feb. 1993, A-6, A-7; "Six Facing Censure Accuse Mormon Church of Purge," *Los Angeles Times,* 18 Sept. 1993, B-5; "Verdict in Trials of Six Mormon Scholars: Guilty in Each Case," *Salt Lake Tribune,* 2 Oct. 1993, C-2; "As Mormon Church Grows, So Does Dissent from Feminists and Scholars," *New York Times,* 2 Oct. 1993, 7; "Elders Banishing Dissidents in Struggle over Mormon Practices," *Washington Post,* 26 Nov. 1993, A-3; "Mormon Church Ousts Dissidents," *Los Angeles Times,* 30 Dec. 1993, E-2.

4. For a longer statement of my postexcommunication views, see D. Michael Quinn, "Dilemmas of Feminists and Intellectuals in the Contemporary LDS Church," *Sunstone* 17 (June 1994): 67–73; Quinn, "The Rest Is History," *Sunstone* 18 (Dec. 1995).

Introduction

IN NINETEENTH-CENTURY AMERICA, same-sex friends of all ages held hands while walking down the streets of cities and towns. Few people regarded it as remarkable when same-sex friends kissed each other "full on the lips" in public or private. Fewer still saw anything unusual in the common American practice of same-sex friends sleeping in the same bed, sometimes for years at a time. Rather than regarding this sleeping arrangement as a grim necessity of overcrowded houses, American teenagers and married persons of that era indicated that they looked forward to their next opportunity to share a bed with a same-sex friend. Whether in privileged society or working-class culture, letters between same-sex friends in the nineteenth century had emotional intensity and passionate references. These are manifestations of what I call the "homocultural orientation" of nineteenth-century America.

To twentieth-century ears, these sound like sexual activities we associate with romantic love. However, the intimate same-sex dynamics of most nineteenth-century Americans did not involve homoeroticism. Although some writers acknowledged that there *could* be an erotic dimension in such same-sex friendships, publications like the YMCA's official magazine simply cautioned against genital contact while continuing to encourage the emotional intimacy and physical closeness of same-sex friends. In many respects, nineteenth-century America's response to same-sex relationships was closer to the response in tribal societies than to contemporary America's homophobic concerns.

The Mormons of the nineteenth century, however, have often been regarded as an exception to the social patterns prevalent in the United

States, due to their clannish adherence to a social order molded by "living prophets" in the Old Testament mold.[1] In fact, twentieth-century Mormons still cling to that self-perception, as expressed by the nationally acclaimed science fiction writer Orson Scott Card: "Those of us who grew up in Mormon society and remain intensely involved are only nominally members of the American community."[2]

Mormon history began with Joseph Smith Jr.'s publication of the Book of Mormon in 1830 as an ancient record of God's actions in the Western Hemisphere. To believers it is as true as the Bible. As Smith moved from New York to Ohio to Missouri to Illinois, his followers, a tightly knit community known as Mormons, exerted increasing social and political power in their communities. After an anti-Mormon mob murdered Smith in 1844, Brigham Young led the majority of Mormons to Utah.[3] By 1890 the federal government had disincorporated the Church of Jesus Christ of Latter-day Saints, confiscated all its financial assets, and was preparing to deprive every Mormon of the rights of citizenship. These sanctions resulted from polygamous marriages that a minority of Mormon men contracted in violation of American laws and against the social expectations of all other Americans.[4]

Ironically, while Mormons departed radically from the opposite-sex relationships common among nineteenth-century Americans, Mormon same-sex dynamics reflected national patterns. Because Mormons have been exceptional record keepers, it is easy to demonstrate that same-sex intimacy was normative in nineteenth-century America, even within one of the nation's most self-consciously religious communities. In other words, nineteenth-century Mormon culture confirms what scattered sources indicate for the United States as a whole: there was an extensive homocultural orientation among Americans generally. In fact, Mormons at times were even more tolerant than other Americans of sexual activities between persons of the same gender.

However, rather than focusing on the erotic, this study emphasizes the full range of same-sex dynamics among Mormons born in the nineteenth century. Also included are relevant statements and actions by leaders of the LDS Church who reached adulthood in the nineteenth century. This study also describes same-sex dynamics of nineteenth-century non-Mormons who lived in the "Mormon culture region"[5] and whose experiences were often described by Latter-day Saints. Although sexual activities are a necessary part of the story, this study's primary emphasis is on the social, emotional, and cultural dynamics of behaviors between females and between males.

This study avoids the common approach of seeing the Mormon experience in isolation. I emphasize cross-cultural comparisons and the American social context. Because those contexts are interconnected, most of this study interweaves the related dynamics of world cultures, U.S. society, and Mormon experiences. I describe Mormon patterns that reflected nineteenth-century American society, as well as those LDS experiences that departed from the national culture at that time. In that regard I comment on trends but acknowledge exceptions. Although my emphasis is on persons of the distant past, the narrative text and source notes include current perspectives that seem relevant. Because of the diverse topics and disciplines in this study, I assume no specialized knowledge on the part of readers and provide careful explanations of subjects that may be obvious to some. The notes also give detailed sources for the benefit of readers who wish to explore particular topics.

There are many things about nineteenth-century American and Mormon culture that are familiar to most Americans and to most Mormons. However, the pervasiveness of nineteenth-century America's "homo-culture" of same-sex dynamics would be somewhat alien to many of us. Nevertheless, if it is not obvious from the following study, I must emphasize that the nineteenth century was neither a "Dark Age" nor a "Golden Age" of America, of Mormonism, of gender relationships, or of sexual dynamics. The concept of any so-called Golden Age selectively emphasizes what we regard as good, while conveniently ignoring what we regard as bad. Likewise, in reverse, for the concept "Dark Age."

Because the nineteenth century is relatively close to our own time period, we are also influenced by what historians call the "presentist bias." In other words, we expect that during an earlier time in our own religion, culture, society, or nation, all people basically shared our present behaviors, attitudes, and definitions. To the contrary, life does not stay the same for long in dynamic societies that have experienced war; transitions in religion, politics, education, economics, and technology; internal migration; immigration; or minority-majority interaction within the population. For that reason, an English historian once coined a great title for a book about what his own society was like three centuries earlier: *The World We Have Lost.*[6] Paradoxically, our presentist expectations coexist with our search for Golden and Dark Ages in the past.

My presentation is also shaped by several biases of belief. First, I accept the empirical, historical, and anecdotal evidence that the vast majority of females feel their primary sexual attraction for males and that the vast majority of males feel their primary sexual attraction for females. Correspondingly, I reject the view of some theorists that same-sex attraction is the primary orientation of both males and females, against which all societies have constructed "the institution of heterosexuality."[7]

Second, I accept current research that indicates that (like left-handedness) genetic or pre-birth factors determine whether some persons have primary sexual attraction for their same gender. Thus, even in the absence of written records, homoerotic desire has undoubtedly existed as long as humans have existed in sufficient numbers to allow a sexual minority.[8] Third, from the above I conclude that heterosexuality is no more moral than right-handedness and that homosexuality is no less moral than left-handedness. Homosexuality is simply left-handed sexuality, and bisexuality is simply ambidextrous sexuality.[9]

Therefore, physical orientation and sexual orientation are not moral issues, and majority/minority phenomena in nature do not involve "natural" versus "unnatural" categories. The exceptional in nature is still "natural," whether the exception is left-handedness or the homosexual orientation of erotic desire. In addition, the concept of sexual activities being natural or unnatural apparently did not exist before the fifth century B.C.[10]

Nevertheless, I acknowledge the twentieth-century fact that much of the world's 90 percent of heterosexually oriented people regard the remainder as unnatural. Similarly, right-handed people gave us definitions of the left as "sinister" and "gauche," while defining the right as "righteous" and "dexterous."

Fourth, I also accept the research that indicates that human environment (including early childhood experiences, family, culture, socialization, social class, and religion) "constructs" how people recognize, define, experience, and express their inherent sexuality.[11] However, I reject the claim of some therapists that male homosexuality is caused by a poor relationship between son and father,[12] because such assertions are based on fallacies of evidence or interpretation.

For sixty years, various studies have demonstrated that a significant percentage, perhaps a majority, of American males have always felt estranged from the fathers who raised them. As early as 1928 Meyer F.

Nimkoff found that 60 percent of the 1,336 males he studied (average age twenty-two) did not feel close enough to their fathers to confide in them, and the father-son relationship was distant in other significant ways. He concluded: "If sons withhold trust from their fathers, it appears they deny his leadership and limit association with him, also."[13] Researchers have also noted that one-third to one-half of American teenage boys and adult men regard their fathers as "distant," unaccepting, "cold or indifferent."[14] The psychiatrist Irving Bieber found that 37 percent of the heterosexual males he studied even said they "hated" their fathers, which was paralleled by a study that 21 percent of male heterosexuals at the University of Utah disliked their fathers.[15]

As indirect evidence of this widespread father-son emotional dysfunction, studies of thousands of American adolescents since the 1930s have shown that only 5–22 percent of the young men "preferred" their fathers. In contrast, 34–76 percent of young men listed their mother as the preferred parent, even though the surveys also allowed sons to indicate equal preference or no preference. These statistics apply to young men in families without divorce.[16] In addition, 82 percent of males in a 1978 study felt alienated from their fathers, while a 1985 study reported that only 8 percent of 500 male adolescents felt "loved" by their fathers.[17]

Thus, claiming father-son emotional distance as the explanation for male homosexuality is similar to claiming that right-handedness causes homosexuality merely because most homosexuals are right-handed.[18] The equation "abdicating fathers, homosexual sons" is a theory based on isolating homosexual experiences from human experiences generally.[19] Typically, authors whose "reparative therapy" of male homosexuals depends on "a failed relationship to father" do not acknowledge such well-known studies of father-son "failure" among American males generally.[20] As the psychiatrist Richard Green, whose own research was originally based on the assumption of parental causation, has observed: "A gnawing question in these studies is what percent of heterosexuals answer all items [concerning father-son relationships] in the 'homosexual direction' and what percent of homosexuals answer all items in the 'heterosexual direction.'" Because of such inconsistencies, Green returned to genetic or other biological determinants for homosexuality.[21]

Another fallacy involves attaching great significance to the finding of many studies that homosexual men are "more likely" to describe their fathers as "distant, hostile, or rejecting" than heterosexual sons are.[22] Such a pattern is unsurprising in a culture that has negative judgments about homosexuality. In other words, since both heterosexual and homosexual American males report unsatisfactory relationships with their fathers, the higher incidence of strain between homosexual sons and their fathers is more likely a result of the sons' "homosexual tendencies" rather than the cause.[23]

In fact, a cross-cultural study of 148 heterosexual sons and 151 homosexual sons in families from the United States, Guatemala, Brazil, and the Philippines described this as a "culturally invariable" pattern from early childhood: "the father of a homosexual son becomes distant, detached, and hostile because he is disappointed in the effeminate son."[24] Even when fathers attempted to be close, accepting, and nurturing to sons who were effeminate or who seemed to be homosexually oriented, an American psychiatrist found that it was the boys themselves (aged six to sixteen) who had withdrawn emotionally and socially from their supportive fathers. As adults the homosexual sons blamed the fathers for this childhood estrangement.[25] Nevertheless, many of these studies acknowledge that a large proportion of male homosexuals have exhibited no effeminate behavior as children or as adults.

However, for the purposes of this study, it is irrelevant whether homoerotic desire originates biologically, environmentally, or through a combination of both factors. "The real problem [of existential sexuality] does not lie in whether homosexuality is inborn or learned," Jeffrey Weeks has written. "It lies instead in the question: what are the meanings this particular culture gives to homosexual behavior, however it may be caused, and what are the effects of those meanings on the way in which individuals organize their sexual lives?"[26] Even my use of "sexuality" is a product of my culture. The historian David M. Halperin observes: "Far from being a necessary or intrinsic constituent of human life, 'sexuality' seems indeed to be a uniquely modern, Western, even bourgeois production."[27]

Fifth, my use of this culturally defined term *sexuality* must also be understood within my conviction that a person's sexuality involves far more than sexual activities. Blanche Wiesen Cook's classic statement concerning lesbians can apply equally well to male homosexuals:

It may seem elementary to state here that lesbians cannot be defined simply as women who practice certain physical rites together. Unfortunately, the heterosexual image—and sometimes even the feminist image—of the lesbian is defined by sexual behavior alone and sexual in the most limited sense. It therefore seems important to reiterate that physical love between women is one expression of a whole range of emotions and responses to each other that involves all the mysteries of our human nature. Woman-related women feel attraction, yearning, and excitement with women. Nobody and no theory has yet explained why for some women, despite all cultural conditioning and social penalties, both intellectual and emotional excitement are aroused in response to women.[28]

People who define themselves as lesbians or as male homosexuals ("gays") consistently describe a whole range of responses (besides the erotic) to those of their same gender. They share many of those responses with persons who define themselves as heterosexuals (or "straights").[29]

Sixth, I nevertheless believe there is a gulf between those who have experienced erotic desire for a person of their same sex and those who have *never* experienced erotic desire for a person of their same sex.[30] That gulf is as real, as gut-wrenching, and as potentially antagonistic as any other gulf that divides humanity into us-them camps—gender, race, ethnicity, and a host of others that have estranged people. That gulf cannot be papered over with slogans that end up marginalizing people or with platitudes that try to obscure fundamental differences or with theories that do not touch the lives of people the theories are supposed to persuade. In my view, that gulf of same-sex desire is unbridgeable for those who feel themselves on either side of it. We can (and often do) choose to ignore those on the other side, to feel superior or inferior, to call out insults, to throw rocks at each other. Or we can communicate with each other, even across that gulf of same-sex desire. In the effort to gain an understanding of the humanity on the other side of the gulf, we better understand our own humanity. That is why I have written this study.

Seventh, I approach these topics with several theological biases. I believe Mormon theology's affirmation that every human has a pre-mortal, individual spirit that is "innocent" at its birth into whatever kind of body (and physiology) the innocent spirit receives as a human being. I regard behavior as a moral issue and make personal judgments constantly, but I am not confident that I understand God's sense of morality. Finally, I believe that every human being (even those whose values or behavior I reject) is of value to God and to me.

Nevertheless, this study does not overstate what I wish had occurred in the past or brush over what I wish had not occurred. I have done my best to maintain the historian's balance of rigorous inquiry and sensitivity while examining controversial experiences of persons and institutions for whom current readers may have strong loyalties. Likewise, I seek to maintain that same balance in my discussion of sexual matters about which people have various judgments.

This study is not designed to be politically correct or religiously correct. It does not aim to please a particular group or to offend a particular group. It seeks neither heroes, nor role models, nor villains. I describe and analyze social attitudes, cultural values, community standards, legislative acts, judicial decisions, church policies, and individual attitudes and behavior, but this study does not try to endorse, to criticize, to recommend, or to change any of them. Within my own limits, I have done my best to describe and analyze the historical evidence as I am aware of it.

I recognize that some members of the LDS Church wish there was no evidence of any same-sex experiences among early Mormons and prefer to ignore such evidence that does exist. For example, one Mormon historian (whom I do not identify here in any way) strenuously recommended against the publication of this study and argued that it "does not address important historical issues. Certainly it is not surprising to know that homosexual men and women have existed in Mormon society at all periods." That is the same argument that some have used against the historical study of various minorities, and such an attitude contains a philosophy that I reject: that some humans are irrelevant because they differ from the majority in a fundamental way.

Other readers may welcome the evidence of "positive" relationships between persons of the same gender in the distant past, but prefer less "negative" evidence in this study. Still others may regard the "negative" evidence as validating their own point of view, while dismissing the "positive" evidence as mere exceptions. Those are not hypothetical reactions, and I have listened respectfully to such advocates.

Instead, I have chosen to present all the relevant evidence I have found, without attempting to change the proportions to please my own preferences or those of others. A lot of the past we will never know because it occurred without leaving traces for us to examine in the present. And the most conscientious researchers have honest differences about the significance and meaning of the historical evidence that does exist.

NOTES

1. Howard Roberts Lamar, *The Far Southwest, 1846–1912: A Territorial History* (New Haven: Yale University Press, 1966), 324, 377, 410–11.

2. Orson Scott Card, "Author's Note: On Sycamore Hill," in *The Folk of the Fringe* (New York: Tom Doherty Associates, 1989), 284.

3. For general studies of Mormonism and its largest church, the Church of Jesus Christ of Latter-day Saints, headquartered in Utah, see the following: Leonard J. Arrington and Davis Bitton, *The Mormon Experience: A History of the Latter-day Saints* (New York: Alfred A. Knopf, 1979); Klaus J. Hansen, *Mormonism and the American Experience* (Chicago: University of Chicago Press, 1981); Jan Shipps, *Mormonism: The Story of a New Religious Tradition* (Urbana: University of Illinois Press, 1985); James B. Allen and Glen M. Leonard, *The Story of the Latter-day Saints,* 2d ed., rev. (Salt Lake City: Deseret Book, 1992); D. Michael Quinn, *The Mormon Hierarchy: Origins of Power* (Salt Lake City: Signature Books/Smith Research Associates, 1994); and Quinn, *The Mormon Hierarchy: Extensions of Power* (Salt Lake City: Signature Books/Smith Research Associates, 1995).

For biographies of the principal leaders of nineteenth-century Mormonism, see Donna Hill, *Joseph Smith: The First Mormon* (Garden City, N.Y.: Doubleday, 1977); Leonard J. Arrington, *Brigham Young: American Moses* (New York: Alfred A. Knopf, 1985); Samuel W. Taylor, *The Kingdom or Nothing: The Life of John Taylor, Militant Mormon* (New York: Macmillan, 1976); Thomas G. Alexander, *Things in Heaven and Earth: The Life and Times of Wilford Woodruff, a Mormon Prophet* (Salt Lake City: Signature Books, 1991). There is no scholarly biography of Lorenzo Snow, who served as LDS president from 1898 to 1901, but for a recent summary of his life from a devotional perspective, see Francis M. Gibbons, *Lorenzo Snow: Spiritual Giant, Prophet of God* (Salt Lake City: Deseret Book, 1982).

4. To the extent that there have been studies of early Mormon sexuality, authors have emphasized primarily the married, heterosexual dynamics of polygamous husbands and plural wives. See especially Lawrence Foster, *Religion and Sexuality: Three American Communal Experiments of the Nineteenth Century* (New York: Oxford University Press, 1981); Joan Iversen, "Feminist Implications of Mormon Polygyny," *Feminist Studies* 10 (Fall 1984): 505–22; Julie Dunfey, "'Living the Principle' of Plural Marriage: Mormon Women, Utopia, and Female Sexuality in the Nineteenth Century," *Feminist Studies* 10 (Fall 1984): 523–36; Kahile Mehr, "Women's Response to Plural Marriage," *Dialogue: A Journal of Mormon Thought* 18 (Fall 1985): 84–97; Jessie L. Embry, *Mormon Polygamous Families: Life in the Principle* (Salt Lake City: University of Utah Press, 1987); Kathryn M. Daynes, "Plural Wives and the Nineteenth-Century Mormon Marriage System: Manti, Utah, 1849–1910"

(Ph.D. diss., Indiana University, 1991); Lawrence Foster, *Women, Family, and Utopia: Communal Experiments of the Shakers, the Oneida Community, and the Mormons* (Syracuse: Syracuse University Press, 1991). Both monogamists and polygamists were included in Vicky Burgess-Olson's "Family Structure and Dynamics in Early Mormon Families, 1847–1885" (Ph.D. diss., Northwestern University, 1976).

For studies of monogamous, heterosexual dynamics among twentieth-century Mormons, see Nels Anderson, "The Mormon Family," *American Sociological Review* 2 (Oct. 1937): 601–8; Harold T. Christensen, "A Comparative Study of the Time Interval between the Marriage of Parents and the Birth of Their First Child, Based on 1670 Couples in Utah County, Utah, 1905 to 1935" (M.S. thesis, Brigham Young University, 1937); G. Byron Done, "A Study of Mormon-Gentile Intermarriages in Los Angeles" (M.A. thesis, University of Southern California, 1937); Roy A. West, "The Mormon Village Family," *Sociology and Social Research* 23 (Mar.–Apr. 1939): 353–59; Vivian H. Grindstaff, "A Study of the Marriage Patterns of One Hundred Five Members of the Church of Jesus Christ of Latter-day Saints Residing in Springville, Utah, 1949" (M.S. thesis, Brigham Young University, 1949); Fred L. Strodtbeck, "A Study of Husband-Wife Interaction in Three Cultures" (Ph.D. diss., Harvard University, 1950); Fred L. Strodtbeck, "Husband-Wife Interaction over Revealed Differences," *American Sociological Review* 16 (Aug. 1951): 469–73; Fred L. Strodtbeck, "The Interaction of a 'Henpecked' Husband with His Wife," *Marriage and Family Living* 14 (Nov. 1952): 305–8; Ernest Cameron McKay, "A Study of Husband-Wife Authority Patterns in Two Generations of Selected Rural Mormon Families" (M.S. thesis, Utah State Agricultural College, 1952); Lorenzo Hess Snow, "A Study of Mixed vs. Non-Mixed Marriages among a Mormon Group" (M.A. thesis, Northwestern University, 1955); Charles M. Woolf, "An Investigation of the Frequency of Consanguineous Marriages among the Mormons and Their Relatives in the United States," *American Journal of Human Genetics* 8 (Dec. 1956): 236–52; Paul Everett Nuttall, "Comparison of Latter-day Saint Couples Married in the Temple and Latter-day Saint Couples Not Married in the Temple: In Respect to Marital Adjustment, Feelings of Security, and Empathy" (M.S. thesis, Brigham Young University, 1959); Charles F. Taylor, "Mormon Marriage and Its Canonical Consequences" (Doctor in Canon Law diss., Pontifica Universitas Lateranensis, 1959); Duane Marvin Laws, "Comparison of the Religious Orthodoxy and Marital Adjustment of Individuals with Temple and Non-Temple Marriages" (M.A. thesis, Brigham Young University, 1959); Phillip Ray Kunz, "The Faith of Their Fathers: A Study of the Religious Influence on Child-Rearing" (M.S. thesis, Brigham Young University, 1962); Marilyn Jean Blaycock, "An Analysis of the Marriages of a Selected Group of High School Students in Utah County, September 1, 1958 to September 1, 1960" (M.S. thesis,

Brigham Young University, 1963); Blaine R. Porter, ed., *Selected Readings in the Latter-Day Saint Family* (Dubuque, Iowa: Wm. C. Brown Book, 1963); Harold T. Christensen and Kenneth L. Cannon, "Temple versus Nontemple Marriage in Utah: Some Demographic Considerations," *Social Science* 39 (Jan. 1964): 26–33; Phillip R. Kunz, "Mormon and Non-Mormon Divorce Pattern," *Journal of Marriage and the Family* 26 (May 1964): 211–13; Harold Daniel Bywater, "The Relationship of Occupation and Marital Adjustment of a Sample of Latter-day Saint Couples Registered in Utah County in 1955" (M.S. thesis, Brigham Young University, 1965); Carole Irene Crismon Cook, "The Crisis of Parenthood as Experienced by LDS Couples with One Child" (M.S. thesis, Brigham Young University, 1966); Roy H. Marlow, "Development of Marital Dissatisfaction of Mormon College Couples over the Early Stages of the Family Life Cycle" (M.S. thesis, Brigham Young University, 1968); Seymour Paul Steed, "A Study of Divorce Rates for Temple and Non-Temple Marriages according to Occupational Status and Age at Marriage" (M.S. thesis, Brigham Young University, 1969); Jack Harold Peterson, "A Study of Selected Family Background Factors Influencing Women to Marry outside the L.D.S. Church" (M.S. thesis, Brigham Young University, 1969); Sydney Mitchell and Evan T. Peterson, *A Longitudinal Study of Factors Associated with Divorce among Mormons* (Provo: Brigham Young University Institute of Genealogical Studies, 1972); Ronald Shill Jones, "Factors Associated with Marital Adjustment of Young Mormon Married College Students" (M.S. thesis, Utah State University, 1973); Lina Flake Hatch, "The Relationship between Religious Endogamy and Marital Happiness when Similarity of Religious Beliefs and Subjectively Perceived Importance of Religious Beliefs Are also Taken into Account" (M.S. thesis, Brigham Young University, 1973); Gilbert Craig Orme, "Marriage Role Expectations and Religiosity" (M.S. thesis, Utah State University, 1974); Bruce L. Campbell and Eugene E. Campbell, "The Mormon Family," in Charles H. Mindel and Robert W. Habenstein, eds., *Ethnic Families in America* (New York: Elsevier, 1976), 379–416; Brent A. Barlow, "Notes on Mormon Interfaith Marriages," *Family Coordinator* 20 (Apr. 1977): 143–50; Ernst G. Beier and Daniel P. Sternberg, "Marital Communication: Subtle Clues between Newlyweds," *Journal of Communication* 27 (Summer 1977): 92–100; Phillip R. Kunz and Stan L. Albrecht, "Religion, Marital Happiness, and Divorce," *International Journal of Sociology of the Family* 7 (July/Dec. 1977): 227–32; Albert Dean Byrd, "LDS Parents of Normal and Emotionally Disturbed Children: Differences in Personality Characteristics, Values, and Attitudes" (Ph.D. diss., Brigham Young University, 1978); Stan L. Albrecht, Howard M. Bahr, and Bruce A. Chadwick, "Changing Family and Sex Roles: An Assessment of Age Differences," *Journal of Marriage and the Family* 41 (Feb. 1979): 41–50; Richard A. Heaps and Karen M. Walker, "Marital Adjustment in Mormon and Non-Mormon Marriages," *AMCAP: Journal of the*

Association of Mormon Counselors and Psychotherapists 5 (Oct. 1979): 16–18; Melvin L. Wilkinson and William C. Tanner III, "The Influence of Family Size, Interaction, and Religiosity on Family Affection in a Mormon Sample," *Journal of Marriage and the Family* 42 (May 1980): 297–303; A. Dean Byrd, "MMPI Differences between LDS Parents of Disturbed and Nondisturbed Children," *AMCAP: Journal of the Association of Mormon Counselors and Psychotherapists* 7 (July 1981): 14–16, 23; Howard M. Bahr, "Religious Intermarriage and Divorce in Utah and the Mountain States," *Journal for the Scientific Study of Religion* 20 (Sept. 1981): 251–61; D. Corydon Hammond and Robert F. Stahman, "Sex Therapy with LDS Couples," *AMCAP: Journal of the Association of Mormon Counselors and Psychotherapists* 8 (Jan. 1982): 13–16; Howard M. Bahr, "Religious Contrasts in Family Role Definitions and Performance: Utah Mormons, Catholics, Protestants, and Others," *Journal for the Scientific Study of Religion* 21 (Sept. 1982): 200–217; Howard M. Bahr, Spencer J. Condie, and Kristen L. Goodman, *Life in Large Families: Views of Mormon Women* (Washington, D.C.: University Press of America, 1982); Gayleen Wayman Thalman, "Religious Activity and Time Use of 149 Utah Husbands" (M.S. thesis, Utah State University, 1982); Darwin L. Thomas, "Family in the Mormon Experience," in William V. D'Antonio and Joan Aldous, eds., *Families and Religions: Conflict and Change in Modern Society* (Beverly Hills: Sage, 1983), 267–88; Robert W. Reynolds, "Level of Marital Adjustment and Spiritual Well-Being among Latter-day Saints" (M.S. thesis, Brigham Young University, 1984); Larry Kent Langlois, "Mormons and the Family" (Ph.D. diss., University of Southern California, 1984); Richard Miller, "Selected Aspects of Family Change in Provo, Utah: A Replication of Canning's 1955 Survey" (M.S. thesis, Brigham Young University, 1984), summarized in "Trends in Marital Happiness in Provo, Utah: 1955 to 1983," *Sociology and Social Research* 71 (July 1987): 294–97; Robert W. Reynolds, "Level of Marital Adjustment and Spiritual Well-Being among Latter-day Saints" (M.S. thesis, Brigham Young University, 1984); Michael L. Elliott, "Marital Intimacy and Satisfaction as a Support System for Coping with Police Officer Stress," *Journal of Police Science and Administration* 14 (Mar. 1986): 40–44; William G. Dyer and Phillip R. Kunz, "Successful Mormon Families," *AMCAP: Journal of the Association of Mormon Counselors and Psychotherapists* 12, no. 1 (1986): 73–87; William G. Dyer and Phillip R. Kunz, *Effective Mormon Families: How They See Themselves* (Salt Lake City: Deseret Book, 1986); O. Kendall White Jr., "Ideology of the Family in Nineteenth Century Mormonism," *Sociological Spectrum* 6, no. 3 (1986): 289–306; Tim B. Heaton, "Four Characteristics of the Mormon Family: Contemporary Research on Chastity, Conjugality, Children, and Chauvinism," *Dialogue: A Journal of Mormon Thought* 20 (Summer 1987): 101–14; Marybeth Raynes, "Mormon Marriages in an American Context," in Maureen Ursenbach Beecher and Lavina Fielding Anderson, eds., *Sisters in the Spirit: Mormon Women in Historical and Cultural Perspective* (Urbana: University of Illinois Press, 1987), 227–48; Paul Keith Browning, "Mormon Marital Satisfaction: A Perceived Congruence of Expectation and Outcomes and Factors Related to Satisfaction and Expectations" (Ph.D. diss., University of California at Los Angeles, 1987); Joe Edgar Glenn, "Cohesion in a Utah Sample of Latter-day Saint Couples" (M.S. thesis, Brigham Young University, 1988); Colleen Margaret Peterson, "Couple Cohesion: Differences between Clinical and Non-Clinical Mormon Couples" (M.S. thesis, Brigham Young University, 1988); Thomas R. Lee, N. Jean Kobayashi, and Gerald R. Adams, "Family Influences on Adolescent Development in Non-Problematic L.D.S. Families," *AMCAP: Journal of the Association of Mormon Counselors and Psychotherapists* 14, no. 1 (1988): 15–29; Barry L. Johnson, Susan Eberley, James T. Duke, and Deborah Hunt Sartain, "Wives' Employment Status and Marital Happiness of Religious Couples," *Review of Religious Research* 29 (Mar. 1988): 259–70; Pamela J. Sapyta, "Agreement in Conjugal Decision-Making among Non-Metropolitan Utah Spouses" (M.S. thesis, Utah State University, 1988); Ted M. Bair, "The Effect of Religiosity on the Marital Satisfaction of Utah Husbands and Wives Who Are Members of the Church of Jesus Christ of Latter-day Saints" (Ph.D. diss., Utah State University, 1989); Bron Ingoldsby, "Mormon Marriage: A Review of Family Life and Social Change," *Family Science Review* 2 (Nov. 1989): 389–96; Lisa Tensmeyer Hansen, "Gender Differences in Marital Satisfaction: Communication and Commitment" (B.A. honors thesis, Brigham Young University, 1990); Ken R. Canfield, "Factorial Validity of Brief Satisfaction Scales in Surveys of Mormon, Roman Catholic, and Protestant Fathers," *Psychological Reports* 67 (Dec. 1990): 1319–22; Marie Cornwall and Darwin L. Thomas, "Family, Religion, and Personal Communities: Examples from Mormonism," in Donald G. Unger and Marvin B. Sussman, eds., *Families in Community Settings: Interdisciplinary Perspectives* (New York: Haworth Press, 1990), 229–52; Marguerite Irene Adams, "Family Stress and the Role of the Mormon Bishop's Wife" (M.S. thesis, Brigham Young University, 1991); Romel W. Mackelprang, "'And They Shall Be One Flesh': Sexuality and Contemporary Mormonism," *Dialogue: A Journal of Mormon Thought* 25 (Spring 1992): 49–67; Janet Lyn Samuelson Sharman, "Qualitative Study of Relationship Issues in Church of Jesus Christ of Latter-day Saints Blended Families" (Ph.D. diss., University of Utah, 1992), summarized in Sharman, "Relationship Issues in LDS Blended Families, *AMCAP: Journal of the Association of Mormon Counselors and Psychotherapists* 20, no. 1 (1994): 15–38.

Useful for examining the experience of unmarried Mormons are Rulon Squires McCarrey, "Premarital Orientation and Expectations of College Youth" (Ph.D. diss., University of Utah, 1958); Charles W. Martain, "A Study of the Degrees of Affectional Response in Dating of a Selected Group of High

School Students" (M.S. thesis, Utah State University, 1959); Gary Phil McBride, "Marriage Role Expectations of Latter-day Saint Adolescents in Utah County" (M.S. thesis, Brigham Young University, 1963); Homer Duncan Capener, "An Analysis of Dating Attitudes and Frequency Patterns of Coeds Residing in Helaman Halls, Heritage Halls, and Wymount Terrace of Brigham Young University" (M.S. thesis, Brigham Young University, 1967); Paul Eugene Dahl, "Some Factors which Differ between Married and Never-Married L.D.S. Males and Females Who Attended 1969 Summer School at Brigham Young University in Relationship to Their Families of Orientation" (Ph.D. diss., Brigham Young University, 1971); Ramah P. Mortenson, "Affectional Attitudes and Behavior Patterns of Selected L.D.S. Students at Universities and Colleges in Utah" (M.S. thesis, Brigham Young University, 1972); Glen Orvil Jenson, "Antecedents and Consequences of Non-Marriage in a Select Mormon Population" (Ph.D. diss., Utah State University, 1974); Gilbert Craig Orme, "Marriage Role Expectations and Religiosity" (M.S. thesis, Utah State University, 1974); Marshall Rowland Huff, "The Relationship between Emotional Maturity, Engagement Adjustment, and Premarital Counseling Attitude of Engaged Individuals" (M.S. thesis, Brigham Young University, 1976); John Thomas Hill, "Romanticism and Friendship Levels of Engaged BYU Couples Related to Similarity Perception and Understanding of Partner's Values" (M.S. thesis, Brigham Young University, 1978); Joseph William Larkin, "A Correlation Study: Attitude, Communicative Willingness, and Frequency of Dating" (M.A. thesis, Brigham Young University, 1978); Frank Edward Burke, "A Demographic Study of a Singles' Branch in the Church of Jesus Christ of Latter-day Saints" (M.S. thesis, University of Utah, 1980); Wesley W. Craig Jr., "Counseling the LDS Single Adult Masturbator: Successful Application of Social Learning Theory: A Case Study," *AMCAP: Journal of the Association of Mormon Counselors and Psychotherapists* 6 (Jan. 1980): 2–5; Jeffery Ogden Johnson, "On the Edge: Mormonism's Single Men," *Dialogue: A Journal of Mormon Thought* 16 (Autumn 1983): 48–58; Lavina Fielding Anderson, "Ministering Angels: Single Women in Mormon Society," *Dialogue: A Journal of Mormon Thought* 16 (Autumn 1983): 59–72; Beverly L. Shaw, "Sexual Value-Behavior Congruence or Discrepancy: Coping of the Single Adult Mormon" (Ph.D. diss., United States International University, 1987); Lawrence A. Young, "Being Single, Mormon, and Male," *Dialogue: A Journal of Mormon Thought* 23 (Spring 1990): 146–51; Carol Markstrom Adams, "Attitudes on Dating, Courtship, and Marriage by Religious Minority and Majority Adolescents," *Family Relations* 40 (Jan. 1991): 91–96; Sally Emery, "A Four-Dimensional Analysis of Sex-Role Attitudes in a Mormon Population: Personal Control, Self-Esteem, Dogmatism, and Religious Affiliation" (Ph.D. diss., California School of Professional Psychology, 1991), for 88 LDS singles and 103 Protestant singles; Beverly L. Shaw, "A Chronic Identity Issue: Singleness and Divorce," *AMCAP: Journal of the Association of Mormon Counselors and Psychotherapists* 17, no. 1 (1991): 69–84; Jane Rutledge, "Coping with Intimacy: A Problem for Single Adult Mormons" (Ph.D. diss., University of Denver, 1993); Marybeth Raynes and Erin Parsons, "Single Cursedness: An Overview of LDS Authorities' Statements about Unmarried People," in Brent Corcoran, ed., *Multiply and Replenish: Mormon Essays on Sex and Family* (Salt Lake City: Signature Books, 1994), 217–30.

5. Geographers and social scientists have defined "the Mormon culture region" as that large area of LDS population and Mormon communities emanating in all directions from Salt Lake City, Utah. It includes the entire state of Utah, the southeastern counties of Idaho, the western counties of Wyoming and Colorado, the southern tip of Nevada (including Las Vegas), the northern counties of Arizona as far south as Phoenix, and the northwestern counties of New Mexico. See Wilbur Zelinsky, "An Approach to the Religious Geography of the United States: Patterns of Church Membership in 1952," *Annals of the Association of American Geographers* 51 (June 1961): 163–64, 193; D. W. Meinig, "The Mormon Culture Region: Strategies and Patterns in the Geography of the American West, 1847–1964," *Annals of the Association of American Geographers* 55 (June 1965): 191–220; Samuel S. Hill, "Religion and Region in America," *Annals of the American Academy of Political and Social Science* 480 (July 1985): 137; D. Michael Quinn, "Religion in the American West," in William Cronon, George Miles, and Jay Gitlin, eds., *Under an Open Sky: Rethinking America's Western Past* (New York: W. W. Norton, 1992), 146, 160.

"Mormon culture region" is also a useful term for the non-Utah enclaves of Mormons or Mormon-oriented groups centering on Palmyra, New York (1827–31); Kirtland, Ohio (1831–present); northern Missouri (1831–39); Nauvoo, Illinois (1839–46); Voree, Wisconsin ("Strangites," 1846–49); Council Bluffs, Iowa (1846–69); Beaver Island, Michigan ("Strangites," 1849–56); San Bernardino, California (1849–57); Laie, Hawaii (1851–present); Independence, Missouri (Reorganized Church of Jesus Christ of Latter Day Saints, 1873–present), Lamoni, Iowa (RLDS, 1881–present); Colonia Juarez, Chihuahua, Mexico (1885–present); Cardston, Alberta, Canada (1885–present); North Island, New Zealand (esp. 1889–present); Baker City, Oregon (1889–present); American Samoa and Western Samoa (esp. 1914–present); and Tonga (esp. 1926–present). For "Strangites," see Roger Van Noord, *King of Beaver Island: The Life and Assassination of James Jesse Strang* (Urbana: University of Illinois Press, 1988); for the RLDS see Paul M. Edwards, *Our Legacy of Faith: A Brief History of the Reorganized Church of Jesus Christ of Latter Day Saints* (Independence, Mo.: Herald, 1991); for smaller groups see Albert J. Van Nest, *A Directory to the "Restored Gospel" Churches: A Survey of Churches and Groups that Have Based Their Beliefs and Teachings on the "Restored*

Gospel" as Brought Forth by Joseph Smith (Evanston, Ill.: Institute for the Study of American Religions, 1983); Steven L. Shields, *The Latter Day Saint Churches: An Annotated Bibliography* (New York: Garland, 1987); Steven L. Shields, *Divergent Paths of the Restoration: A History of the Latter Day Saint Movement,* 4th ed., rev. (Los Angeles: Restoration Research, 1990); Roger D. Launius and Linda Thatcher, eds., *Differing Visions: Dissenters in Mormon History* (Urbana: University of Illinois Press, 1994).

   6. Peter Laslett, *The World We Have Lost* (New York: Scribners, 1966).

   7. That is Adrienne Rich's famous phrase concerning women, but this post-Freudian concept was articulated earlier concerning men by Jean Lipman-Blumen. In "Changing Sex Roles in American Culture: Future Directions for Research," *Archives of Sexual Behavior* 4 (July 1975): 439–40, Lipman-Blumen wrote: "Contrary to the frequent accusation that men have turned women into sex objects, women are forced by the structural situation into the role of sex objects in order to distract men [from other men] into entering and developing heterosexual relationships." The flip side of that revisionist theory was Adrienne Rich's revisionist essay five years later, "Compulsory Heterosexuality and Lesbian Existence," *Signs: Journal of Women in Culture and Society* 5 (Summer 1980): 631–60, reprinted in Ann Snitow, Christine Stansell, and Sharon Thompson, eds., *Powers of Desire: The Politics of Sexuality* (New York: Monthly Review Press, 1983), and in Henry Abelove, Michele Aina Barale, and David M. Halperin, eds., *The Lesbian and Gay Studies Reader* (New York: Routledge, 1993). More widely known than Lipman-Blumen, Rich argued: "If we think of heterosexuality as the 'natural' emotional and sensual inclination for women, [then lesbian] lives as these are seen as deviant, as pathological, or as emotionally and sensually deprived" (652).

   However, Rich did not seem to recognize that she retained the pathological-natural dichotomy and simply exchanged the positions of lesbianism and heterosexuality on it. As a man, I venture to assert that it is no more helpful to their self-images for women to regard themselves as pathological if they feel an exclusively heterosexual orientation. Rich argued: "The assumption that 'most women are innately heterosexual' stands as a theoretical and political stumbling block for many women" (648). However, I think a far larger number of women would regard as a stumbling block the statement: "most women are innately lesbian." As Esther Newton has written, such a redefinition of lesbianism is "a model that, not incidentally, puts heterosexual feminists at a disadvantage." See Newton, "The Mythic Mannish Lesbian: Radclyffe Hall and the New Woman," *Signs: Journal of Women in Culture and Society* 9 (Summer 1984): 573.

   Although Rich acknowledged the nonsexualized term *homosocial,* she insisted on using the sexualized and politicized term *lesbian* throughout the essay. However, Rich structured her argument in such a way that it cannot be tested (and therefore cannot be challenged) by any historical, empirical, or anecdotal evidence.

Paradoxically, Rich eroticized all relationships between women into a "lesbian continuum," by de-eroticizing the word *erotic*: "we begin to discover the erotic in female terms: as that which is unconfined to any single part of the body or solely to the body itself, as an energy not only diffuse but . . . omnipresent . . . whether physical, emotional, psychic" (650).

One could make an identical statement about "the erotic in male terms," which is what Lipman-Blumen essentially did in her earlier essay: "males have a predisposition to be interested in, excited by, or stimulated by other males. . . . Men can turn to other men for the satisfaction of most of their needs: intellectual, physical, emotional, social, and sexual stimulation, as well as power" (439–40).

Lipman-Blumen and later Rich postulated that homosexuality and lesbianism are the natural conditions of humanity against which all societies have constructed a "compulsory heterosexual orientation" (Rich's phrase on page 632) in order to perpetuate the species. Postulates do not require proof, but I find the views of Lipman-Blumen and Rich to be both provocative and unconvincing.

Without directly naming Adrienne Rich or Lipman-Blumen, Lillian Faderman, in *Surpassing the Love of Men: Romantic Friendship and Love between Women from the Renaissance to the Present* (New York: Columbia University Press, 1981), 173, criticized unnamed writers who used *lesbianism* as the term to describe such common nineteenth-century situations as "two women holding one another in bed, breast to breast." That critique certainly applies to Rich's essay: "If we consider the possibility that all women—from the infant suckling at her mother's breast, to the grown woman experiencing orgasmic sensations while suckling her own [female] child . . . to the woman dying at ninety, touched and handled by women—exist on a lesbian continuum, we can see ourselves moving in and out of this continuum, whether we identify ourselves as lesbian or not" (650–51). Faderman's critique of the unnamed writers continued: "To provide a label ["lesbianism"] which has been charged with connotations of sickness or sin and then to apply that label to a particular situation renders that situation sick or sinful regardless of its innate attributes" (173).

Likewise, it is futile (if not disingenuous) to claim one is rejecting conventional definitions of such highly charged terms as *erotic* and *lesbian* and then apply those redefined terms to "acceptable" behaviors that are being subtly employed to legitimize the conventional meanings of *erotic* and *lesbian*. That seems to be the agenda of Adrienne Rich's essay. Thus, Rich's "all-inclusive definitions of lesbianism" were central in the criticism by Bonnie Zimmerman in "What Has Never Been: An Overview of Lesbian Feminist Literary Criticism," in Elaine Showalter, ed., *The New Feminist Criticism: Essays on Women, Literature, Theory* (New York: Pantheon, 1985), 218. Although personally favorable to Rich's essay, Deborah Cameron has listed the objections of "many feminists" to Rich's essay and its assumptions, in "Ten Years On: 'Compulsory Heterosexuality and Lesbian Existence,'" in Stevi Jackson, et al., eds., *Women's Studies: Essential Readings* (New York: New York University Press, 1993), 246–48.

8. However, for decades I unquestioningly accepted the explanation that homosexuality was caused by neurotic or dysfunctional relationships with parents, which was the position of every book I had read and which was consistent with the family background of the one homosexual I knew well. Useful sources concerning biological-genetic origins are Franz J. Kallman, "Comparative Twin Study on the Genetic Aspects of Male Homosexuality," *Journal of Nervous and Mental Disease* 115 (Apr. 1952): 283–98, and Kallman, "Twin and Sibling Study of Overt Male Homosexuality," *American Journal of Human Genetics* 4 (June 1952): 136–46. In Kallman's study of identical twins, in every case if one identical twin was homosexual the other twin was also homosexual. See also Theo Lang, "Studies on the Genetic Determination of Homosexuality," *Journal of Nervous and Mental Disease* 92 (July 1940): 55–64; Emil Witschi and William F. Mengert, "Endocrine Studies on Human Hermaphrodites and Their Bearing on the Interpretation of Homosexuality," *Journal of Clinical Endocrinology* 2 (May 1942): 279–86; Roy A. Darke, "Heredity as an Etiological Factor in Homosexuality," *Journal of Nervous and Mental Disease* 107 (Jan.–June 1948): 251–68; John D. Rainer, Alvin Mesnikoff, Lawrence C. Kolb, and Arthur C. Carr, "Homosexuality and Heterosexuality in Identical Twins," *Psychosomatic Medicine* 22 (July–Aug. 1960): 251–59; Leonard L. Heston and James Shields, "Homosexuality in Twins: A Family Study and a Registry Study," *Archives of General Psychiatry* 18, no. 2 (1968): 149–60; Barry M. Dank, "Six Homosexual Siblings," *Archives of Sexual Behavior* 1, no. 3 (1971): 193–204; Charlotte C. Taylor, "Identical Twins: Concordance for Homosexuality?" *American Journal of Psychiatry* 129 (Oct. 1972): 486–87; M. Sydney Margolese and Oscar Janiger, "Androsterone/Etiocholanolone Ratios in Male Homosexuals," *British Medical Journal* 3 (28 July 1973): 207–10; "Homosexuality: Origin of Sexual Drive," *Nature* 244 (10 Aug. 1973): 329; Muriel Wilson Perkins, "Homosexuality in Female Monozygotic Twins," *Behavior Genetics* 3 (Dec. 1973): 387–88; Guenther Doerner, Wolfgang Rohde, Fritz Stahl, Lothar Krell, and Wolf-Guenther Masius, "A Neuroendocrine Predisposition for Homosexuality in Males," *Archives of Sexual Behavior* 4 (Jan. 1975): 1–8; Frederick L. Whitam, "Childhood Indicators of Male Homosexuality," *Archives of Sexual Behavior* 6 (Mar. 1977): 89–96; John L. Fuller and William Robert Thompson, *Foundations of Behavior Genetics* (St. Louis: C. V. Mosby, 1978), 415–18; John Money, "Genetic and

Chromosomal Aspects of Homosexual Etiology," in Judd Marmor, ed., *Homosexual Behavior: A Modern Reappraisal* (New York: Basic Books, 1980), 51–72; Michael Ruse, "Are There Gay Genes?" *Journal of Homosexuality* 6 (Summer 1981): 5–34; Alan P. Bell, Martin S. Weinberg, and Sue Kiefer Hammersmith, "Biology?" *Sexual Preference: Its Development in Men and Women* (Bloomington: Indiana University Press, 1981), 212–20; Richard C. Pillard, Jeannette Poumadere, and Ruth A. Carretta, "A Family Study of Sexual Orientation," *Archives of Sexual Behavior* 11 (Dec. 1982): 511–20; James D. Weinrich, "Is Homosexuality Biologically Natural?" in William Paul, James D. Weinrich, John C. Gonsiorek, and Mary E. Hotvedt, eds., *Homosexuality: Social, Psychological, and Biological Issues* (Beverly Hills: Sage, 1982), 197–208; Douglas J. Futuyma and Stephen J. Risch, "Sexual Orientation, Sociobiology, and Evolution," *Journal of Homosexuality* 9 (Winter 1983–Spring 1984): 157–67; Joseph Harry, "Sexual Orientation as Destiny," *Journal of Homosexuality* 10 (Winter 1984): 111–24; Michael Ruse, "Nature/Nurture: Reflections on Approaches to the Study of Homosexuality," *Journal of Homosexuality* 10 (Winter 1984): 141–51; David M. Seaborg, "Sexual Orientation, Behavioral Plasticity, and Evolution," *Journal of Homosexuality* 10 (Winter 1984): 153–58; Thomas J. Bouchard, "Twins Reared Together and Apart: What They Tell Us about Human Diversity," in Sidney W. Fox, ed., *Individuality and Determinism: Chemical and Biological Bases* (New York: Plenum, 1984); Elke D. Eckert, Thomas J. Bouchard, Joseph Bohlen, and Leonard L. Heston, "Homosexuality in Monozygotic Twins Reared Apart," *British Journal of Psychiatry* 148 (Apr. 1986): 421–25; Richard C. Pillard and James D. Weinrich, "Evidence of Familial Nature of Male Homosexuality," *Archives of General Psychiatry* 43 (Aug. 1986): 808–12; Richard Green, *The "Sissy Boy Syndrome" and the Development of Homosexuality* (New Haven: Yale University Press, 1987), 372, 384; James D. Weinrich, *Sexual Landscapes: Why We Are What We Are, Why We Love Whom We Love* (New York: Charles Scribner's Sons, 1987), 211–23; John Money, *Gay, Straight, and In-Between: The Sexology of Erotic Orientation* (New York: Oxford University Press, 1988); Bernard Zuger, "Homosexuality in Families of Boys with Early Effeminate Behavior: An Epidemiological Study," *Archives of Sexual Behavior* 18 (Apr. 1989): 155–66; Geoff Puterbaugh, ed., *Twins and Homosexuality: A Casebook* (New York: Garland, 1990); Louis Govern, "Biomedical Theories of Sexual Orientation: A Critical Examination," in David P. McWhirter, Stephanie A. Sanders, and June Machover Reinisch, eds., *Homosexuality/Heterosexuality: Concepts of Sexual Orientation* (New York: Oxford University Press, 1990), 71–87; John Bancroft, "Commentary: Biological Contributors to Sexual Orientation," in McWhirter, Sanders, and Reinisch, eds., *Homosexuality/Heterosexuality,* 101–11; "S.L. Psychiatrist to Talk on Homosexual Origins," *Deseret News,* 6 June 1991, B-10; Marcia Barinaga,

"Is Homosexuality Biological?" *Science,* 30 Aug. 1991, 956–57; Carol Ezzell, "Brain Feature Linked to Sexual Orientation," *Science News,* 31 Aug. 1991, 134; "Are Gay Men Born That Way?" *Time,* 9 Sept. 1991, 60–61; J. Michael Bailey and Richard C. Pillard, "A Genetic Study of Male Sexual Orientation," *Archives of General Psychiatry* 48 (Dec. 1991): 1089–96; "Among Twin Men," *U.S. News and World Report,* 30 Dec. 1991, 32; John A. W. Kirsch and James D. Weinrich, "Homosexuality, Nature, and Biology: Is Homosexuality Natural? Does It Matter?" in John C. Gonsiorek and James D. Weinrich, eds., *Homosexuality: Research Implications for Public Policy* (Newbury Park, Calif.: Sage, 1991), 13–31; Constance Holden, "Twin Study Links Genes to Homosexuality," *Science,* 3 Jan. 1992, 33; "Born or Bred?" *Newsweek,* 24 Feb. 1992, 46–53; "Genes May Affect Homosexuality," *Deseret News,* 8 Apr. 1992, A-9; Laura S. Allen and Roger A. Gorski, "Sexual Orientation and the Size of the Anterior Commissure in the Human Brain," *Proceedings of the National Academy of Sciences of the United States* 89 (1 Aug. 1992): 7199–202; Bruce Bower, "Genetic Clues to Female Homosexuality," *Science News,* 22 Aug. 1992, 117; Darrell Yates Rist, "Are Homosexuals Born That Way?: Sex on the Brain," *The Nation,* 19 Oct. 1992, 424–29; "Gay Men Were 'Wired' Differently," *Deseret News,* 28 Dec. 1992, A-7; Jay P. Paul, "Childhood Cross-Gender Behavior and Adult Homosexuality: The Resurgence of Biological Models of Sexuality," *Journal of Homosexuality* 24 (Jan.–Feb. 1993): 41–54; J. Michael Bailey and Deana S. Benishay, "Familial Aggregation of Female Sexual Orientation," *American Journal of Psychiatry* 150 (Feb. 1993): 272–77; "Lesbian Study Shows Gender Preferences Run in the Family," *Deseret News,* 9 Feb. 1993, 3; Chandler Burr, "Homosexuality and Biology," *Atlantic Monthly,* Mar. 1993, 47–65; J. Michael Bailey, Richard C. Pillard, Michael C. Neale, and Yvonne Agyei, "Heritable Factors Influence Sexual Orientation in Women," *Archives of General Psychiatry* 50 (Mar. 1993): 217–23; William Byne and Bruce Parsons, "Human Sexual Orientation: The Biological Theories Reappraised," *Archives of General Psychiatry* 50 (Mar. 1993): 228–39; "Few Gays Can Change, Expert Says," *Deseret News,* 25 Apr. 1993, B-3; "Keynoter Explores Differences in Behavior of Males and Females," *Deseret News,* 26 Apr. 1993, B-2; Frederick G. Whitam, Milton Diamond, and James Martin, "Homosexual Orientation in Twins: A Report on Sixty-One Pairs and Three Triplet Sets," *Archives of Sexual Behavior* 22 (June 1993): 187–206; J. Michael Bailey, "Heritable Factors Influence Sexual Orientation in Women," *Journal of the American Medical Association* 269 (2 June 1993): 2729; Duane Jeffery, "How Is Homosexuality Determined?" *Provo Daily Herald,* 28 June 1993, C-1; J. Michael Bailey and Alan P. Bell, "Familiality of Female and Male Homosexuality," *Behavior Genetics* 23 (July 1993): 313–22; "Gays Born That Way, Professor's Study Says: Lengthy Study of Twins Backs Theory," *Phoenix Gazette,* 5 July 1993, B-1; Dean H. Hamer, Stella Hu,

Victoria L. Magnuson, Nan Hu, and Angela M. L. Pattatucci, "A Linkage between DNA Markers on the X Chromosome and Male Sexual Orientation," *Science,* 16 July 1993, 321–27; "Gene Pattern Linked to Homosexuality," *Deseret News,* 16 July 1993, A-5; Bruce Bower, "Genetic Clue to Male Homosexuality Emerges," *Science News,* 17 July 1993, 37; "Male Homosexuality May Be Linked to a Gene," *New York Times,* 18 July 1993, E-2; "Sexual Orientation and the X," *Nature,* 22 July 1993, 288–89; "Born Gay?: Studies of Family Trees and DNA Make the Case that Male Homosexuality Is in the Genes," *Time,* 26 July 1993, 36–38; "Does DNA Make Some Men Gay?" *Newsweek,* 26 July 1993, 59; William Byne, "Interview: The Biological Evidence for Homosexuality Reappraised," *AMCAP: Journal of the Association of Mormon Counselors and Psychotherapists* 19, no. 1 (1993): 17–27; Duane Jeffery, "New Report Aids Gender Discussion," *Provo Daily Herald,* 11 Oct. 1993, C-1; Neil Risch, Elizabeth Squires-Wheeler, and Broyna J. B. Keats, "Male Sexual Orientation and Genetic Evidence," *Science,* 24 Dec. 1993, 2063–65; Dean H. Hamer, Stella Hu, Victoria L. Magnuson, Nan Hu, and Angela M. L. Pattatucci, "Response," *Science,* 24 Dec. 1993, 2065; Simon Le Vay, *The Sexual Brain* (Cambridge, Mass.: MIT Press, 1993), 111–30; John Money, "Sin, Sickness, or Status?: Homosexual Gender Identity and Psychoneuroendocrinology," in Linda D. Garnets and Douglas C. Kimmel, eds., *Psychological Perspectives on Lesbian and Gay Male Experiences* (New York: Columbia University Press, 1993), 130–67; William J. Turner, "Comments on Discordant Monozygotic Twinning in Homosexuality," *Archives of Sexual Behavior* 23 (Feb. 1994): 115–19; Simon LeVay and Dean H. Hamer, "Evidence for a Biological Influence in Male Homosexuality," *Scientific American,* May 1994, 43–49; William Byne, "The Biological Evidence Challenged," *Scientific American,* May 1994, 50–55; "Study Links Brain Traits to Sexual Orientation," *Salt Lake Tribune,* 18 Nov. 1994, A-5; "Brain Study Points to Biological Variation in Gays," *Deseret News,* 24 Nov. 1994, 12; "Study Links Genetics, Male Homosexuality: Canadian Scientists Say Gay Men Have More Ridges in Fingerprints," *Los Angeles Times,* 26 Dec. 1994, A-32; "Finger Print Ridges Linked to Homosexuality," *Deseret News,* 26 Dec. 1994, A-3; Dean Hamer and Peter Copeland, *The Science of Desire: The Search for the Gay Gene and the Biology of Behavior* (New York: Simon and Schuster, 1994); "Geneticist Will Discuss Sexuality Meet at U," *Deseret News,* 27 Apr. 1995, B-7; "'Science of Desire' Is Topic for 'Gay Gene' Finder: Origins of Sexuality Concern Researcher Speaking Tonight," *Salt Lake Tribune,* 28 Apr. 1995, B-3; William J. Turner, "Homosexuality, Type 1: An Xq28 Phenomenon," *Archives of Sexual Behavior* 24 (Apr. 1995): 109–34.

However, even though the LDS Church–owned newspaper has reported some of the above stories, the LDS First Presidency recently denounced "the false belief of inborn homosexual orientation." On behalf of the full Presidency,

Second Counselor James E. Faust wrote in 1995: "No scientific evidence demonstrates absolutely that this is so. Besides, if it were so, it would frustrate the whole plan of mortal happiness." James E. Faust, "First Presidency Message: Serving the Lord and Resisting the Devil," *Ensign* 25 (Sept. 1995): 5. At the risk of compromising the neutral analysis of my presentation in this book, I will observe that it is difficult for many fair-minded persons to understand how the marital success or "mortal happiness" of 90 percent of the world's population can be jeopardized by accepting as a fact the scientific evidence that "inborn homosexual orientation" is a reality for a small percentage of humanity. Likewise, the continued right-handedness of the world's population is not threatened by the existence of left-handedness in a small minority. As the Roman Catholic church once learned about its doctrinal insistence on a flat earth at the center of the universe, religious leaders are ill-advised to deny statements about earthly realities that can be verified with a telescope, brain-scan technology, or increasingly sophisticated genetic analysis.

9. See chap. 1 for the historical development and cultural significance of these terms.

10. John J. Winkler, "Laying Down the Law: The Oversight of Men's Sexual Behavior in Classical Athens," in David M. Halperin, John J. Winkler, and Froma I. Zeitlin, eds., *Before Sexuality: The Construction of Erotic Experience in the Ancient Greek World* (Princeton: Princeton University Press, 1990), 172, expressing this as B.C.E. (Before the Common Era or Before the Christian Era).

11. In addition to this emphasis in chap. 1 and its notes, see also Thomas S. Weinberg, *Gay Men, Gay Selves: The Social Construction of Homosexual Identities* (New York: Irvington, 1983); Celia Kitzinger, *The Social Construction of Lesbianism* (London: Sage, 1987); Edward Stein, ed., *Forms of Desire: Sexual Orientation and the Social Constructionist Controversy* (New York: Garland, 1990); John P. DeCecco and John P. Elia, "A Critique and Synthesis of Biological Essentialism and Social Constructionist Views of Sexuality and Gender," *Journal of Homosexuality* 24, nos. 3–4 (1993): 1–26.

12. This discussion emphasizes male homosexuality rather than female homosexuality because the former has been the primary emphasis of the behavioral science literature, which has often claimed direct parental causation of male homosexuality, while acknowledging ambiguous evidence for the parental role as a cause of lesbianism. See John Nash's "The Father in Contemporary Culture and Current Psychological Literature," *Child Development* 36 (Mar. 1965): 277, for "paternal insufficiency as a causal factor" of male homosexuality because "homosexual case histories reveal that in the male there is characteristically a lack of warm, affectionate relationships with the father," although his bibliographic essay did not mention the similar findings for American males in general; Lewis Yablonsky's *Fathers and Sons* (New York:

Simon and Schuster, 1982), 175, regarding his male homosexual patients, although there is no comparison to the "unrequited love for their fathers" among the 564 "normal" men he also surveyed (10); Charles W. Socarides's "Abdicating Fathers, Homosexual Sons: Psychoanalytical Observations on the Contributions of the Father to the Development of Male Homosexuality," in Stanley H. Cath, Alan R. Gurwitt, and John Munder Ross, eds., *Father and Child: Developmental and Clinical Perspectives* (Boston: Little, Brown, 1982), 509–21, based on his therapy with 214 homosexual males, although there is no reference to the experience of heterosexual males with their fathers; see also Victor L. Brown Jr., "Male Homosexuality: Identity Seeking a Role," *AMCAP: Journal of the Association of Mormon Counselors and Psychotherapists* 7 (Apr. 1981): 4; Elizabeth R. Moberly, *Homosexuality: A New Christian Ethic* (Cambridge: James Clarke, 1983), 2–11; Thomas E. Pritt and Ann F. Pritt, "Homosexuality: Getting beyond the Therapeutic Impasse," *AMCAP: Journal of the Association of Mormon Counselors and Psychotherapists* 13, no. 1 (1987): 41–42, 49; Joseph Nicolosi, *Reparative Therapy of Male Homosexuality: A New Clinical Approach* (Northvale, N.J.: Jason Aronson, 1991), 43–44, 45, 49; and Joseph Nicolosi, *Healing Homosexuality: Case Stories of Reparative Therapy* (Northvale, N.J.: Jason Aronson, 1993), 130.

I make these assessments from the perspective of the historical evidences of these interpretations and relevant studies, but I claim no expertise as a clinician or behavioral scientist. The following paragraphs in the text constitute a brief history of ideas and methodologies. However, just as I regard the "compulsory heterosexuality" view of some homosexual theorists as fundamentally flawed, I likewise see essential flaws in the assumptions and methodology of certain clinical approaches toward homosexuality. I do not question the sincerity of those who promote "reparative therapy" for homosexuality, and I feel only compassion for the desperation of those who seem willing to do anything to experience such a "cure."

13. Meyer F. Nimkoff, "Parent-Child Intimacy: An Introductory Study," *Social Forces* 7 (Dec. 1928): 248, 249.

14. L. Pearl Gardner, "An Analysis of Children's Attitudes toward Fathers," *Journal of Genetic Psychology* 70 (Mar. 1947): 5, 11, for a study of 182 boys (37 percent "wished the father to show more love toward them"); Jerome Kagen, "The Child's Perception of the Parent," *Journal of Abnormal and Social Psychology* 53 (Sept. 1956): 257, for a study of 111 boys ages 6–10 (a "majority" said their fathers were "less friendly" than their mothers); Irving Bieber, Harvey J. Dain, Paul R. Dince, Marvin G. Drellich, Henry G. Grand, Ralph H. Gundlach, Malvina W. Kremer, Alfred H. Rifkin, Cornelia B. Wilbur, Toby B. Bieber, *Homosexuality: A Psychoanalytic Study* (New York: Basic Books, 1962), 86–87, for a study of 100 heterosexual males (54 percent feared their fathers and only 47 percent felt accepted by their fathers); Leif J.

Braatan and C. Douglas Darling, "Overt and Covert Homosexual Problems among Male College Students," *Genetic Psychology Monographs* 71 (May 1965): 273–74, 281, 294, for a study of 50 heterosexual men (25 percent had "detached-hostile father," 43 percent "did not feel accepted and respected by father," and 19 percent "expressed hatred for father"); W. W. Meissner, "Parental Interaction of the Adolescent Boy," *Journal of Genetic Psychology* 107 (Dec. 1965): 226–27, for a study of 1,278 male high school students (35 percent "felt that their fathers were cold or indifferent"), reprinted in Alvin E. Winder, ed., *Adolescence: Contemporary Studies,* 2d ed. (New York: D. Van Nostrand, 1974), 247, 250; Morris Rosenberg, *Society and the Adolescent Self-Image* (Princeton, N.J.: Princeton University Press, 1965), 44, for a study of 441 boys (32 percent of "lower class" boys, 24 percent of middle-class boys, and 15 percent of upper-class boys said they were "not close" to their fathers); Richard Melvin Smith, "The Impact of Fathers on Delinquent Males" (Ed.D. diss., Oklahoma State University, 1974), 41, for a study of 183 nondelinquent white males (18.6 percent denied they were close with their fathers and 26.8 percent were undecided, which findings were paralleled at higher percentages for male residents of reform schools); Alan P. Bell, Martin S. Weinberg, and Sue Kiefer Hammersmith, *Sexual Preference: Its Development in Men and Women: Statistical Appendix* (Bloomington: Indiana University Press, 1981), 22–26, for a study of 265 white heterosexual men (38 percent felt distant from their fathers, 35 percent described their fathers as emotionally detached, 31 percent regarded the relationship with their fathers as generally negative, 20 percent felt anger or hostility toward their fathers, and 19 percent felt rejected by their fathers) and for a study of 50 black heterosexual men (20 percent felt distant from their fathers, 30 percent described their fathers as emotionally detached, 18 percent regarded the relationship with their fathers as generally negative, 10 percent felt anger or hostility toward their fathers, and 14 percent felt rejected by their fathers); James Youniss and Jacqueline Smollar, *Adolescent Relations with Mothers, Fathers, and Friends* (Chicago: University of Chicago Press, 1985), 22, 68, for a study of 500 male adolescents (39 percent reported their fathers as "withdrawn," and 39 percent described fathers as "distant"); Samuel Oshershon, in *Finding Our Fathers: The Unfinished Business of Manhood* (New York: Free Press/Macmillan, 1986), 4–5, calls this pattern of father-son estrangement "one of the great underestimated tragedies of our times"; Ralph Keyes, in *Sons on Fathers: A Book of Men's Writings* (New York: HarperCollins, 1992), xix, describes this "father hunger" as lifelong for most American males rather than as only an early developmental stage, which is how others characterize this impulse. Despite their emphasis on parent-child relationships, many well-known studies have not separately analyzed father-son relationships. For example, see Alice Sowers, "Parent-Child Relationships from the Child's Point of View," *Journal of Experimental Education* 6 (Dec.

1937): 205–31; Theodore Caplow, Howard M. Bahr, Bruce A. Chadwick, Reuben Hill, and Margaret Holmes Williamson, *Middletown Families: Fifty Years of Change and Continuity* (Minneapolis: University of Minnesota Press, 1982), 145–46, 374; George Gallup Jr., *The Gallup Poll: Public Opinion, 1989* (Wilmington, Del.: Scholarly Resources, 1990), 155.

15. Bieber, *Homosexuality,* 86–87; see Thomas Elwood Pritt, "A Comparative Study between Male Homosexuals' and Heterosexuals' Perceived Parental Acceptance-Rejection, Self-Concepts, and Self-Evaluation Tendencies" (Ph.D. diss., University of Utah, 1971), 52, 72, for a study of 42 heterosexual male students. Bieber and Pritt reported findings that were two or three times higher than the later study by Bell, Weinberg, and Hammersmith, *Statistical Appendix,* 25, which found that 12 percent of 265 white heterosexual men disliked or hated their fathers, and 14 percent of 50 black heterosexual men disliked or hated their fathers.

16. See Margaret Simpson, *Parent Preferences of Young Children* (New York: Teachers College, Columbia University, 1935), 25, a study of hundreds of nine-year-old boys that found that only 10 percent preferred their fathers, as compared to 76 percent who preferred their mothers, as reported in Robert L. Griswold, "'Ties That Bind and Bonds That Break': Children's Attitudes toward Fathers, 1900–1930," in Elliott West and Paula Petrik, eds., *Small Worlds: Children and Adolescents in America, 1850–1950* (Lawrence: University Press of Kansas, 1992), 257; a study of approximately 6,500 "public school" boys in White House Conference on Child Health and Protection, *The Adolescent in the Family* (New York: D. Appleton and Century, 1934), xiii, 133, 142–44 ("the Father—An Outsider"), 357, and report (142), which found that only 5 percent of urban "white" boys "preferred the father," as compared to 40 percent who preferred their mothers; H. Meltzer, "Sex Differences in Parental Preference Patterns," *Character and Personality* 10 (Dec. 1941): 119–20, a study that found that 17.9 percent of 76 boys preferred their fathers, compared to 50 percent who preferred their mothers; Meyer F. Nimkoff, "The Child's Preference for Father or Mother," *American Sociological Review* 7 (Aug. 1942): 517, reporting that 22 percent of several hundred boys (ages 5 to 10) preferred their fathers as compared to 70 percent who stated a preference for their mothers; L. Pearl Gardner, "An Analysis of Children's Attitudes toward Fathers," *Journal of Genetic Psychology* 70 (Mar. 1947): 5, 11, 23, a study that found that 15 percent of 182 boys preferred their fathers as compared with 34 percent who stated a preference for their mothers; Marvin O. Nelson, "The Concept of God and Feelings toward Parents," *Journal of Individual Psychology* 27 (May 1971): 47–48, a study that found that 14 percent of 37 men (ages 15 to 44) preferred their fathers, compared to 59 percent who preferred their mothers.

17. Daniel J. Levinson, Charlotte Darrow, Edward B. Klein, Martha H.

Levinson, and Broxton McKee, *Seasons of a Man's Life* (New York: Alfred A. Knopf, 1978), 74; Youniss and Smollar, *Adolescent Relations,* 68, concerning 500 male adolescents; see also Judith Arcana, *Every Mother's Son: The Role of Mothers in the Making of Men* (Seattle: Seal Press, 1986), 143, who reported that "about 1 percent of the sons described only good relations with their fathers," while the rest had distant or troubled relationships with fathers. Since her study involved sixty sons (xi), only one son reported this positive relationship with his father.

18. However, as further evidence of the genetic/biological origin of homosexuality, homosexuals are more likely to be left-handed than heterosexuals, three or four times more likely according to some studies. See James Lindesay, "Laterality Shift in Homosexual Males," *Neuropsychologia* 25, no. 6 (1987): 965–69; Cheryl M. McCormick, Sandra F. Witelson, and Edward Kingstone, "Left-Handedness in Homosexual Men and Women: Neuroendocrine Implications," *Psychoneuroendocrinology* 15, no. 1 (1990): 69–76; "Homosexuals Likely to Be Left-Handed, Study Shows," *Deseret News,* 26 July 1990, A-10; Nora Underwood, "The Hands Have It: A Study Provides a Clue to the Mystery of Sexuality," *Maclean's,* 6 Aug. 1990, 51; S. E. Marchant-Haycox, I. C. McManus, and G. D. Wilson, "Left-Handedness, Homosexuality, HIV Infection, and AIDS," *Cortex: A Journal Devoted to the Study of the Nervous System and Behavior* 27 (Mar. 1991): 49–56. Those findings are consistent with other studies that indicate that the brain structure and mental processes of homosexuals are different from the brain structure and cognitive processes of heterosexuals, as in Brian A. Gladue, William W. Beatty, Jan Larson, and R. Dennis Staton, "Sexual Orientation and Spatial Ability in Men and Women," *Psychobiology* 18 (Mar. 1990): 101–8; D. F. Swaab and M. A. Hofman, "An Enlarged Suprachiasmatic Nucleus in Homosexual Men," *Brain Research* 537 (24 Dec. 1990): 141–48; Cheryl M. McCormick and Sandra F. Witelson, "A Cognitive Profile of Homosexual Men Compared to Heterosexual Men and Women," *Psychoneuroendocrinology* 16, no. 6 (1991): 459–73; Simon LeVay, "A Difference in Hypothalamic Structure between Heterosexual and Homosexual Men," *Science,* 30 Aug. 1991, 1034–37; Carol Ezzell, "Brain Feature Linked to Sexual Orientation," *Science News,* 31 Aug. 1991, 134; Allen and Gorski, "Sexual Orientation and the Size of the Brain," 7199–202; LeVay, *Sexual Brain,* 111–30; Cheryl M. McCormick and Sandra F. Witelson, "Functional Cerebral Asymmetry and Sexual Orientation in Men and Women," *Behavioral Neuroscience* 108 (June 1994): 525–31.

19. That same methodological fallacy has been common in published studies of other "deviant" groups, such as schizophrenics, whose family relationships have been analyzed without comparison to findings concerning the families of noninstitutionalized persons or of the "normal" population. The classic example is the comparative analysis in Louise Behrens Apperson and W. George

McAddoo Jr., "Parental Factors in the Childhood of Homosexuals," *Journal of Abnormal Psychology* 73 (June 1968): 201–6. Instead of comparing homosexuals to a "normal" heterosexual sample, Apperson and McAddoo used hospitalized schizophrenics as the "control group" for understanding the experience of homosexuals. As an LDS example of interpreting homosexual experience in isolation, Pritt and Pritt, in "Homosexuality," 53, referred to "homosexuals' unnatural and immoral physical transactions," explaining that male homosexuals "become highly responsive to [male] genitalia, the primary insignia" of a man. That observation ignored the fact that heterosexual men also "become highly responsive" to a woman's breasts, which most men regard as "the primary insignia" of a woman. Either both equivalent behaviors are pathological or neither is, but it is fallacious to identify one as pathological while assuming that the equivalent behavior is not.

20. The phrases are Nicolosi's, whose *Reparative Therapy* cites Bieber and Bell, Weinberg, and Hammersmith about difficulties in father-son relationships for homosexual males, without acknowledging the significant percentages of "father failure" for heterosexual sons in those two studies. Moreover Nicolosi's bibliography (317–40) does not list the well-known studies of heterosexual estrangement from fathers, which I cite in note 14. Such omissions are extraordinary in a book whose central framework is father-son dysfunction. This same pattern of citing only studies of homosexual son-father difficulties and omitting standard sources about heterosexual son-father "failure" is observable in the citations of Socarides, "Abdicating Fathers," 509–16, and in the bibliographies of Albert Ellis, *Homosexuality: Its Causes and Cure* (New York: Lyle Stuart, 1965), 57–58, 280–88; Lawrence J. Hatterer, *Changing Homosexuality in the Male: Treatment for Men Troubled by Homosexuality* (New York: McGraw-Hill, 1970), 19, 485–86; Charles W. Socarides, *Homosexuality* (New York: Jason Aronson, 1978), 183–84, 603–26; Charles W. Socarides, "The Psychoanalytical Theory of Homosexuality with Special Reference to Therapy," in Ismond Rosen, ed., *Sexual Deviation*, 2d ed. (Oxford: Oxford University Press, 1979), 267, 275–77; Charles W. Socarides, *The Preoedipal Origin and Psychoanalytic Therapy of Sexual Perversions* (Madison, Conn.: International Universities Press, 1988), 263–67, 587–614; Charles W. Socarides and Vamik D. Volkan, eds., *The Homosexualities and the Therapeutic Process* (Madison, Conn.: International Universities Press, 1991), 293–303; and Yablonsky, *Fathers and Sons*, 217–18.

21. Green, *"Sissy Boy Syndrome,"* 372, 384, quotation from 59.

22. The phrases are from Nicolosi, *Reparative Therapy*, 43–44, who depends primarily on Bieber, *Homosexuality*, and Yablonsky, *Fathers and Sons*, 175–77. On this matter Yablonsky did not provide any statistical comparison of his 564 surveyed heterosexuals and his unspecified number of homosexual clients. Bieber, in *Homosexuality*, 86–87, shows that for 106 homosexual

males, 66 percent feared their fathers, 60 percent hated their fathers, and only 23 percent felt accepted by their fathers, compared with 100 heterosexual males, of which 54 percent feared their fathers, 37 percent hated their fathers, and only 47 percent felt accepted by their fathers. However, Bieber ignored the obvious question of why this same factor did not produce homosexuality in the nearly half of heterosexual males who had equally troubled relationships with their fathers. Green, in *"Sissy Boy Syndrome,"* 58, observed that "this overlap weakens the significance of the finding" in Bieber's study.

Nevertheless, a much higher rate of father-son antagonism for homosexual males than for heterosexual males has also been reported by Carl H. Jonas, "An Objective Approach to the Personality and Environment in Homosexuality," *Psychiatric Quarterly* 18 (Oct. 1944): 626, 629, 633; D. J. West, "Parental Figures in the Genesis of Male Homosexuality," *International Journal of Social Psychiatry* 5 (Autumn 1959): 92–93, 95; Leif J. Braatan and C. Douglas Darling, "Overt and Covert Homosexual Problems among Male College Students," *Genetic Psychology Monographs* 71 (May 1965): 273–74, 281, 294; Ray B. Evans, "Childhood Parental Relationships of Homosexual Men," *Journal of Consulting and Clinical Psychology* 33 (Apr. 1969): 129, 133; John R. Snortum, James F. Gillespie, John E. Marshall, John P. McLaughlin, and Ludwig Mosberg, "Family Dynamics and Homosexuality," *Psychological Reports* 24 (June 1969): 767; Pritt, "Comparative Study," 52, 72, 78; Norman L. Thompson Jr., David M. Schwartz, Boyd R. McCandless, and David A. Edwards, "Parent-Child Relationships and Sexual Identity in Male and Female Homosexuals and Heterosexuals," *Journal of Consulting and Clinical Psychology* 41 (Aug. 1973): 121, 123; Walter Stephan, "Parental Relationships and Early Social Experiences of Activist Male Homosexuals and Male Heterosexuals," *Journal of Abnormal Psychology* 82 (Dec. 1973): 507–8; Marcel T. Saghir and Eli Robins, *Male and Female Homosexuality: A Comprehensive Investigation* (Baltimore: Williams and Wilkins, 1973), 146; Brenda H. Townes, William D. Ferguson, and Sandra Gillam, "Differences in Psychological Sex, Adjustment, and Familial Influences among Homosexual and Nonhomosexual Populations," *Journal of Homosexuality* 1 (Spring 1976): 270; Bell, Weinberg, and Hammersmith, *Statistical Appendix,* 22–26; Johanna H. Milic and Douglas P. Crowne, "Recalled Parent-Child Relations and Need for Approval of Homosexual and Heterosexual Men," *Archives of Sexual Behavior* 15 (June 1986): 239–46; and publications and doctoral dissertations on this matter in Europe and the United States summarized by Marvin Siegelman, "Kinsey and Others: Empirical Input," in Louis Diamant, ed., *Male and Female Homosexuality: Psychological Approaches* (New York: Hemisphere/Taylor and Francis Group, 1987), 51–57.

However, Marvin Siegelman, in "Parental Background of Male Homosexuals and Heterosexuals," *Archives of Sexual Behavior* 3 (Jan. 1974): 16, "seriously question[ed] the existence of any association between family relations and homosexuality vs. heterosexuality" in his study of 445 cases. He repeated that assessment in a separate study of British samples, "Parental Backgrounds of Homosexual and Heterosexual Men: A Cross National Replication," *Archives of Sexual Behavior* 10 (Dec. 1981): 509–10. A similar finding appeared in Michael D. Newcomb, "The Role of Perceived Relative Parent Personality in the Development of Heterosexuals, Homosexuals, and Transvestites," *Archives of Sexual Behavior* 14 (Apr. 1985): 156: "The homosexual males did not perceive their relative parent personalities differently than did the heterosexual males."

23. Thompson, Schwartz, McCandless, and Edwards, "Parent-Child Relationships," 125, and Green, *"Sissy Boy Syndrome,"* 377, both suggested this interpretation of data, which indicated that "nonmasculine" behavior and attitudes of young sons had actually preceded the estrangement and rejection by their fathers from early childhood onward. Moberly, in *Homosexuality: A New Christian Ethic,* 5, acknowledged this pattern of rejection by fathers, but insisted that such findings were no basis for concluding "that homosexuality is not caused by [parental] relational difficulties in the first place." However, the LDS psychotherapist Jan Stout has stated that some male homosexuals "haven't been able to make good bonds with father because of the way they feel inside. It's the effect of the biology, not the other way around." See "Going Straight?" *Deseret News,* 3 May 1990, C-1.

24. Frederick L. Whitam and Michael Zent, "A Cross-Cultural Assessment of Early Cross-Gender Behavior and Familial Factors in Male Homosexuality," *Archives of Sexual Behavior* 13 (Oct. 1984): 432.

25. These are the findings of Bernard Zuger, who began a longitudinal study in the mid-1960s of 25 boys (ages 6–16) whose parents regarded them as effeminate or homosexually oriented, and 25 noneffeminate boys of similar ages. He discovered that 23 fathers (92 percent) had been rebuffed in their efforts to be affectionate, nurturing, and socially involved with their effeminate or homosexually oriented sons. He did not mention the probability that this situation caused a cycle of reciprocal antagonism: distancing by the homosexual son led to emotional frustration of the father whose frustrated irritation caused fear and hostility in the son who withdrew further from the father. Ten years later Zuger followed up with 16 of the original group of effeminate boys, finding that 8 were homosexual, 2 were "probably homosexual," 1 was heterosexual, 1 was "probably heterosexual," 1 was transsexual, 1 was a transvestite, and 2 were uncertain of their sexual orientation. See Bernard Zuger, "The Role of Familial Factors in Persistent Effeminate Behavior in Boys," *American Journal of Psychiatry* 126 (Feb. 1970): 1153, 1168, 1169; Zuger, "Effeminate Behavior Present in Boys from Childhood: Ten Additional Years of Follow-Up," *Comprehensive Psychiatry* 19 (July–Aug. 1978): 363, 366;

Zuger, "Homosexuality and Parental Guilt," *British Journal of Psychiatry* 137 (July 1980): 55–56, in which Zuger denies parental causation and assumes inborn causality.

26. Jeffrey Weeks, "History, Desire, and Identities," in Richard G. Parker and John H. Gagnon, eds., *Conceiving Sexuality: Approaches to Sex Research in a Postmodern World* (New York: Routledge, 1995), 34.

27. David M. Halperin, "Is There a History of Sexuality?" in Abelove, Barale, and Halperin, eds., *Lesbian and Gay Studies Reader,* 424.

28. Blanche Wiesen Cook, "Female Support Networks and Political Activism: Lillian Wald, Crystal Eastman, Emma Goldman," in Nancy F. Cott and Elizabeth H. Pleck, eds., *A Heritage of Her Own: Toward a New Social History of American Women* (New York: Touchstone/Simon and Schuster, 1979), 420.

29. Although I use these terms according to their meaning in general usage today, I recognize that some religious leaders, physicians, and psychotherapists reject the concept of "homosexual" as a type of person. In their view, everyone is heterosexual, but a heterosexual may experience what need be no more than temporary confusion about the object of one's erotic desire. In their view, the term and concept of "homosexual" can actually block a person's reorientation of desire. Such advocates speak or write with contempt for anyone who gives sexual-orientation meaning to the word *gay,* because in their view *gay* is a political term. For Mormon examples, see "'Gay' Label Misapplied on Basis of a Few Traits," *Brigham Young University Daily Universe,* 8 Mar. 1978, 14; Victor L. Brown Jr., "Male Homosexuality: Identity Seeking a Role," *AMCAP: Journal of the Association of Mormon Counselors and Psychotherapists* 7 (Apr. 1981): 3, which indicates that "the label 'homosexuality' is inappropriate and misleading." I acknowledge here those objections, but this study uses *homosexual* in its traditional meaning and *gay* in its more recent, general application to those who acknowledge their homoerotic orientation. Nevertheless, *AMCAP: Journal of the Association of Mormon Counselors and Psychotherapists* 19, no. 1 (1993): 131, reviewed Robert A. Rees, *No More Strangers and Foreigners,* and claimed that Rees, an LDS bishop, had been "recruited" by the "strident voices of the gay and lesbian community," because "consistently throughout his discussion Rees identifies the subjects of his presentation as 'homosexuals' or 'lesbians' rather than, for example, 'individuals with homosexual problems.'"

30. "Homosexual Attraction Is Found in One of Five," *New York Times,* 4 Sept. 1994, A-14, which summarizes the findings of Nathaniel McConaghy, Neil Buhrich, and Derrick Silove, "Opposite Sex-Linked Behaviors and Homosexual Feelings in the Predominantly Heterosexual Male Majority," *Archives of Sexual Behavior* 23 (Oct. 1994): 565–77. This also reflects the findings of Samuel S. Janus and Cynthia L. Janus in *The Janus Report on Sexual*

Behavior (New York: John Wiley and Sons, 1993), 69. In other words, approximately 80 percent of men and women today report that they have never felt sexual attraction for someone of their same gender. Even if statistically representative, these findings are undoubtedly influenced ("constructed") by cultural taboos against admitting homosexual attraction and against conscious awareness of same-sex attraction. For example, in sexually permissive Denmark during the 1970s, 29 percent of men and 42 percent of women reported sexual interest in persons of their same gender. See Borge Alf Borgesen, "A Comparison of Danish and Intermountain Sexual Attitudes and Behavior" (M.A. thesis, University of Utah, 1975), 69.

CHAPTER I

Cross-Cultural Perspectives on Same-Sex Dynamics

ALTHOUGH *homosexuality, bisexuality, gay,* and *lesbian* are terms we all use, *same-sex dynamics* is a better way to discuss these concepts in other cultures or earlier periods of American society. The concept of homosexuality as a state of being or personal identity did not even exist in European-American culture until the late nineteenth century. Jonathan Katz notes that in reality, "heterosexuality is as recent a concept in Euro-American culture as homosexuality, since the former depends on the latter as the frame of reference."[1]

The German physician Karoly Maria Benkert coined the term *Homosexualität* in 1869, but it took decades for the concept and term *homosexuality* to enter Anglo-American discourse.[2] For example, the word *lesbianism* first appeared in English in 1870 as the female equivalent of *sodomy*—an act, not a human condition. By 1884, an American medical article equated "Perverted Sexual Instinct" with "Lesbian loves (from Lesbos, an old Greek city)." The concept *homosexual* similarly did not appear as a term in American writings until 1892, when *heterosexual* also appeared for the first time.[3] Before the late nineteenth century, European-American society regarded all males as having the same "sexuality" (our term), but acknowledged that it was possible for every male to have genital contact with another male, which was "unnatural" (their term). Society held the same views of females.[4]

Coexisting with this lack of a concept of homosexual identity in Judeo-Christian society were laws against same-sex activities dating back to biblical times.[5] For that reason, a British author has written that "there is plenty of evidence of homosexual groups being targeted by the authorities." In support of his claim that "homosexual identity" is centuries old, A. D. Harvey cites executions for anal sex in Venice in the early 1400s, in Geneva in the mid-1500s, and 250 such cases in Valencia from the mid-1500s to 1700. However, Harvey's slippery use of the term *homosexual coteries* includes groin groping by "layabouts indulging in drunken pranks." Even published references in the mid-1720s to London's "Sodomitical Clubs" identified places where men met to commit illegal acts rather than describing the inherent nature of those persons.[6]

European-American culture called men "Sodomites" because they had engaged in sodomy, not because they felt a sexual attraction toward other men. Likewise, age-old references to houses of prostitution and prostitutes did not define a subclass of humanity that existed independent of specific acts. Disapproved behaviors were the focus of attention for millennia, rather than our modern concept of sexuality, which exists within a person long before that person engages in sexual activities of any kind. In her study of the "passions between women" in England during the same period as Harvey's study, Emma Donoghue comments that "the change from a concept of sex acts between women to a concept of lesbian identity was very gradual, and that these ideas overlapped for several centuries."[7]

This was also part of American jurisprudence before there was even a United States of America. In 1610, the colony at Jamestown, Virginia, decreed the death penalty for any man who committed sodomy, and several were executed there and in other colonies. In 1636 the Puritan minister John Cotton also recommended the death penalty for "carnal fellowship of . . . woman with woman." The Massachusetts Bay Colony did not adopt the death penalty for female-female sexual acts, but did sentence a woman in 1642 "to be severely whipped . . . for unseemly practices between her and another maid." Seven years later, the colony at Plymouth, Massachusetts, gave only a stern warning to Sarah Norman (married, age unknown) and Mary Hammon (age fifteen, recently married) "for lewd behavior each with [the] other upon a bed." In 1656, the colony at New Haven, Connecticut, enacted the first American law to require the death penalty for any woman who committed "Sodomitical filthiness" with another woman. However, thereafter the American judiciary gave almost no attention to "unnatural" sexual activities between women.[8] On the other hand, even such a liberally minded American revolutionary as Thomas Jefferson wrote the Virginia law of 1779 that decreed castration as the punishment for all men convicted of rape, sodomy, bestiality (sex with animals), or polygamy.[9]

However, in the 1790s one visitor to the recently formed United States remarked that in Philadelphia some women were "willing to seek unnatural pleasure with persons of their own sex."[10] Still, not until the 1920s did *lesbian* describe a female whose sexual orientation was different from most females.[11] For example, in a study that began before 1922 a Utah researcher used *homosexual* rather than *lesbian* to describe the same-sex experiences and relationships of herself and her female friends.[12]

Although sexual behavior did not divide males into separate categories or females into separate categories until the last hundred years in European-American culture, gender behaviors did. From earliest times, people in all known cultures have regarded males who act in ways considered traditionally "feminine" as distinct—a different breed, so to speak—from all other males. Similarly, "masculine-acting" females have been considered different from all other females. Some cultures have regarded those male-male and female-female behavioral differences with derision, yet other cultures have regarded feminine-acting males and masculine-acting females with honor, even deference.[13] In addition, some cultures do not limit their concept of gender to the male-female binary system, and these cultures recognize what we might call a "third gender" or "third sex."[14] As a further complication, some cultures define all "effeminate" males as homosexual and "noneffeminate" males as nonhomosexual, no matter which gender the males have sex with.[15]

While masculinity or femininity in gender behavior is not an emphasis here, they have influenced customs, cultural definitions, and self-definitions of relationships between persons of opposite genders as well as relationships between persons of the same gender. Even "Wild Bill" Hickok in the 1870s seemed "effeminate," "feminine," and "sissy" to an adolescent neighbor who later commented on this Western folk hero's "hermaphroditism" in behavior.[16] Not surprisingly, by 1900 American medical journals were discussing "effeminate men and masculine women."[17] Therefore, this study occasionally makes reference to effeminate behavior in males and masculine behavior in females, but even those observations are culturally defined.

In fact, cultural bias and individual bias are major problems in any discussion of same-sex dynamics. Unlike prejudices, biases are not simply decisions we make about people that we can change when our experiences help us to outgrow prejudice. Instead, we all see reality through biases of who we are and what we have experienced.

Those of us who are female understand reality through the interaction of hormones and the imprinting of cultural femaleness. Likewise, those of us who are male understand reality through the interaction of hormones and the imprinting of cultural maleness. Those who were born intersexual and those who are emotionally or surgically transsexual (transgendered) see reality in ways different from those who have had an exclusively female or exclusively male gender identity.[18] Through communication we can gain understanding, even empathy, for an identity or experience that is not ours. However, we cannot see the world in the same way as someone with a different self-identity or experience.

Without entering the nature-versus-nurture controversy,[19] it is safe to say that a person's sexual attractions also affect that person's worldview. If people feel sexual attraction only for their opposite sex, it is impossible for them to really "understand" those who feel sexual attraction only for their same sex, and vice versa. Also, a person with either of those exclusive sexual attractions is unable to really understand those "bisexuals" who feel nearly equal attraction for both genders.[20]

In fact, it was the well-known bisexual behaviors in ancient Greece[21] that prejudiced European-American culture for two thousand years against the concept of homosexuals or homosexuality. The prominence of ancient bisexuals like Alexander the Great led to Western culture's blind spot about the possibility that there were ancient Greeks and prenineteenth-century European Americans who felt erotic desire only for persons of their same gender. By extrapolating backward from the research findings of the last century, one can assume that persons with exclusively same-sex desires have always existed. Undoubtedly since prehistoric times, these persons have sensed their own difference from those who manifested only opposite-sex erotic interest. Nevertheless, until the midnineteenth century, European-American culture did not acknowledge the existence of people whose erotic drives were only same-sex oriented.

The culture we know and the time period we live in both define reality for us. These are environmental biases, but they make it difficult, sometimes impossible, for us to imagine different realities. Our culture and time period overshadow the biases of gender, sexual orientation, social class, nationality, religion, family, education, and personal experience.

Culture and time period determine if others have concepts that are even roughly equivalent to our contemporary concepts of "homosexual," "lesbian," "bisexual," "homosexuality," "lesbianism," or "bisexuality." European-American culture now defines a person in one of the above categories if that person engages in same-gender sexual activities frequently or exclusively for a period of time. In fact, both "gays" and "straights" in America seem obsessed with asking "is he?" or "is she?" questions about sexual "identity."

Such questions, categories, and concepts of sexual identity are products of our twentieth-century culture, not of the collective human experience. Even in our own culture, we often regard our individual experience as too complex for someone else to compartmentalize into neat categories. The problems with this "compartmental bias"[22] become clear in cross-cultural examinations of erotic encounters between persons of the same gender. The same act can be erotic or nonerotic.

In that regard, the anthropologist Carole S. Vance's description fits my approach as a social historian: "At minimum all social construction approaches adopt the view that physically identical sexual acts may have varying social significance and subjective meaning depending on how they are defined and understood in different cultures and historical periods."[23] This study gives examples that have existed in both present and past, but mostly beyond our own experience and culture.

Among some South American Indian peoples, it is customary for males to greet each other by gently squeezing each other's penis. If engaged in extended conversation, these males customarily sit side by side or lie together holding each other's penis throughout the conversation. Do we regard that as offensive? Do we regard that as erotic? Do we regard that as homosexual? Do they even have our concepts of the homoerotic or of homosexuality? An interesting twist on this custom is that one group's men became embarrassed when this conversational mode caused an American anthropologist to get an erection.[24]

Even my upcoming discussion of the "right" words to use for same-sex activities is a bias of my culture. Among some Indian peoples of

South America, same-gender sex to orgasm is so common that their native languages do not have words for the activity. Although that absence seems strange to our word-oriented society, such a silence is similar to the silence in diaries when Americans write routine statements like "did the chores" or "worked as usual," but never mention if they kissed their parents or spouse good-bye upon leaving the house.

In his discussion of the marriage practices among Amazon peoples in the mid-1980s, the anthropologist Arthur P. Sorensen observed in passing: "Homosexual activity represents a relatively uncharged item [of sexual behavior] in the culture of the Northwest Amazon. It is not thought of as unusual or perverse. In fact, there is no direct name for it in the Indian language of the area. If anything it is regarded as normal, occasional behavior."[25] In contrast, during his famous trial for sodomy, the Englishman Oscar Wilde said he was being punished for "the Love that dare not speak its name."[26]

The first Anglo-American explorers of the Hawaiian Islands also described same-sex relations among the indigenous leaders and their *Aikane*. John Ledyard's 1779 diary gave the most detailed account of this practice "of sodomy, which is very prevalent if not universal among the chiefs." This American continued: "The cohabitation is between the chiefs and the most beautiful males they can procure about 17 years old. These they call Kikuana [*sic*], which in their language signifies a relation. These youths follow them wherever they go, and . . . [the chiefs] are extremely fond of them, and by a shocking inversion of the laws of nature, they bestow all those affections upon them that were intended for the other sex." Robert J. Morris, a Mormon specialist on Hawaiian language and folklore, has examined these early accounts and explained the special status of those young male "consorts."[27]

The *Aikane* sometimes had wives of their own in addition to their erotic relationships with older men. They were not effeminate males or cross-dressers,[28] both of whom traditionally have a different name in the Hawaiian language. There is no evidence that these young men were limited to the passive role in their homoerotic activities with Hawaii's chiefs, and they were the honored emissaries from the chiefs to visitors. As political protégés, these sexual companions of the chiefs could also attain the stature of King Kamehameha the Great, a former *Aikane*.[29] Such sexual relationships of young men with chiefs in Tahiti also "appeared to be identical with the rites of marriage."[30]

Without the bluntness of Ledyard's earlier reference to sodomy,

American writers in the 1840s described their own special friendships with Hawaiian and Tahitian young men. Richard Henry Dana's *Two Years before the Mast* referred in 1840 to his young Hawaiian "friend and *aikane*" who "adopt[ed]" him. He explained that this young man considered "himself bound to do everything" for his older companion, but Dana did not refer to the sexual intimacy that was traditionally involved in this intergenerational relationship.[31] Seven years later, Herman Melville described Tahiti's "extravagant friendships, unsurpassed by the story of Damon and Pythias: in truth, much more wonderful." He wrote: "Mine was Poky, a handsome youth, who never could do enough for me."[32] Other accounts indicated that in such cases the Polynesian young man himself chose or "adopted" the Anglo-American visitor. The relationship began with the teenager's abrupt invitation for the man to sleep at his family's house where the teenager wore no clothes "after dark."[33]

Apparently, the first Mormon missionaries in Hawaii unknowingly interacted with these *Aikane*. William Farrer recorded in his 1851 diary that while eating dinner with one native Hawaiian family, "a young man invited me to go & sleep at his house [—] I accepted the invitation & accompanied him to the house of his father." At this time, Farrer, a thirty-year-old bachelor, had no LDS missionary "companion" (a same-gender co-missionary who never leaves the presence of the other missionary). He wrote that the next "evening after dark," the young Hawaiian "came in & told me that his father wanted me to leave in the morning . . . because I was not a Catholic." Farrer's diary did not specify that he shared a bed with the "young man" on either of these two nights, and the last entry referred to him only by the oddly distant phrase: "the person who had invited me to go there."[34]

In February 1851, the president of this first LDS mission to Hawaii also baptized as Mormonism's first native convert a sixteen-year-old boy who spoke English.[35] President Hiram Clark had already complained that the Hawaiians were "guilty of all kinds of whoredoms and abominations," and his first convert may have been the *Aikane* of a previous Anglo-American visitor. In any event, within days of the teenager's baptism, Clark abandoned the Hawaiian Islands in disgust and traveled to the Society Islands (which included Tahiti) to look for better prospects as converts.[36] Whatever the background of Hawaii's first LDS convert or his reasons for letting Hiram Clark baptize him, this teenager made no contact with the Mormon missionaries Clark left behind. The young man disappeared from their view as quickly as the older missionary did.

In September 1869 the respected San Francisco literary journal *Overland Monthly* published a detailed account of a young Tahitian's love relationship with Charles Warren Stoddard. This male-male romance included Stoddard's erotic experiences in a bed "big enough for a Mormon" with "my beloved" sixteen-year-old Tahitian, after "an immense amount of secrecy and many vows."[37]

The LDS Church's *Deseret News* had frequently encouraged its Mormon subscribers to read this magazine's articles. A month before the publication of Stoddard's "South-Sea Idyl," the *News* praised "*The Overland Monthly,* which, as usual, is full of good things." The editor at that time was George Q. Cannon, who had been a missionary in Hawaii. Cannon was then an apostle in the Quorum of the Twelve (the second highest decision-making body in the LDS Church).[38] Although some American critics immediately recognized the subtext of homoeroticism in Stoddard's story, most did not. "South-Sea Idyl" appeared in at least nineteen book anthologies during the next fifty years, sometimes by its alternate title: "Chumming with a Savage."[39]

Stoddard's story was apparently not reprinted in Utah publications, but he had Mormon and Utah connections. He was the close friend of Ina Coolbrith, a California poet who confided to him that she was a niece of the Mormon founder Joseph Smith.[40] Stoddard also visited Utah, to which he referred briefly in a book he dedicated to a young American ("in Memory of Our Home-Life In the Bungalow") who was fifteen when he began a long-term sexual relationship with Stoddard.[41]

A Mormon leader referred directly to the Hawaiian *Aikane* tradition at least early as 1879. Joseph F. Smith (Ina Coolbrith's first cousin) was a counselor in the First Presidency (the highest decision-making body in the LDS Church).[42] He had been a young missionary in Hawaii and sometimes used Hawaiian words in his diary to conceal sensitive topics. In November 1879 Counselor Smith had a "long discussion" with twenty-six-year-old Bruce Taylor and wrote that he was "acane!" Despite his misspelling, the exclamation point demonstrated Smith's surprise at learning that Utah's leading family had the equivalent of an *Aikane*. A son of English-born LDS Church president John Taylor, Arthur Bruce Taylor (b. 1853) had served a mission in England. Following this private conversation with Counselor Smith, Bruce Taylor moved to Oregon, where he remained unmarried for the rest of his life. Nothing is known about the personal associations of this Anglo-Mormon *Aikane*.[43]

By European-American standards, the same-sex indoctrination of males in Melanesia is even more extraordinary than Hawaii's nearly forgotten *Aikane* tradition. In one New Guinea society an initiation ceremony instructs all young boys to "suck the penis" and swallow all the ejaculated semen they can "if they wish to grow big and live a long life." The boys perform oral sex on any willing male who is sexually mature, except close relatives. From the age of seven until puberty, these boys swallow "semen every night." From puberty to their late teens or early twenties, males strictly avoid sex with females yet provide semen to prepubescent boys every day. Nevertheless, nearly all of the men marry women by the time they reach their midtwenties.[44]

The only males regarded as "deviant" by these Melanesians are the 5 percent who prefer exclusively homoerotic or heteroerotic sexual activities throughout their lives. However, Melanesians regard exclusively heterosexual males as odd, not repulsive. They feel the same way about the few exclusively homosexual males.[45] It is also noteworthy that effeminacy and cross-dressing are unknown among these Melanesian males—even by those who prefer same-gender sexual activities throughout their lives.[46]

Among the peoples of Papua New Guinea and Melanesia, the first decade of every young man's sexual activity is exclusively homoerotic.[47] This usually involves oral sex between males, but among some Melanesian groups "anal intercourse is believed to be necessary for boys' physical development."[48] This long-term homoerotic activity was inevitably practiced by some of the thousands of Mormons converted and baptized in Papua New Guinea since 1980 by LDS missionaries in "remote villages where many were interested in learning about the gospel." Half or more of these converts are men.[49]

According to the current assumptions of many European Americans, these young Melanesian men went into psychological "denial" or into a social-sexual "closet"[50] when they married women. If not, then that suggests our psychological concepts of denial and sexual repression are also cultural constructs.

Are such cultures "homosexual"? Since all Melanesian males have exclusively homoerotic experiences daily for ten or more years, does this "mean" that they are homosexual or bisexual?

With less detail, two anthropologists have examined the homoerotic dynamics among two widely separated peoples in Africa. Barry D. Adams describes the Nyakyusa males living in the Lake Nyasa region of east Africa. At the age of ten all boys leave their parents and move to villages comprised entirely of male youths. Until they marry women at about age twenty-five, these young men "engage in reciprocal homosexual relations, including sleeping and dancing together erotically." Walter Cline also tersely assessed one of the Berber-speaking peoples of Libya: "All normal Siwan men and boys practice sodomy."[51] Can our concepts of homosexuality or of bisexuality apply to such cultures? The anthropologist Gilbert Herdt concludes that "homosexuality as a term can no longer be used as an uncritical concept across cultures."[52]

Comparative sex surveys in Salt Lake City and Copenhagen also raise other questions. At the University of Utah, only 1 percent of surveyed men reported having engaged in sex with another man, and only another 3 percent were interested in doing so. By contrast, in a Copenhagen study with the same questions, 13 percent of men reported that they had engaged in sex with another man, and an additional 16 percent were interested in doing so.[53] If sexual orientation is genetically based, does this mean that 29 percent of Danish men were born homosexually oriented, whereas only 4 percent of Utah men were born gay oriented? Or does it mean that 25 percent of men at the University of Utah lied on the survey?

If sexual orientation is environmental, that raises interesting questions about sex surveys conducted at Brigham Young University at the same time as the University of Utah study. While only 1 percent of male students at the state school reported having sex with another man, 10 percent of men at the Mormon school reported having sex with other men.[54] Does that mean University of Utah students were ten times more likely to lie about their homosexual experiences? Does it mean that BYU students were ten times more likely to tell the truth about their homosexual experiences? Or if the surveys were representative of Utah's college-age population, do the findings mean that homosexually oriented men were more likely to choose to attend BYU? Or does it mean that something in the childhood environment of men attending religiously sponsored BYU made them ten times more likely to be homosexually oriented than male students at the secular University of Utah?

Even more interesting, female-female eroticism was significantly higher for respondents in both Salt Lake City and Copenhagen. Three percent of female students surveyed at the University of Utah reported that they had engaged in sex with another woman, and an additional 6 percent were interested in doing so. That was triple the rate of homosexual activity reported by the university's male students and double the interest in homosexual activity reported by men on that campus. However, 9 percent of Copenhagen's women reported that they had engaged in sex with another woman, and an additional 33 percent of the surveyed Danish women were interested in having sex with another woman.[55]

Just ponder the further questions posed by these findings for women. Did the data really indicate that women in both locations were two to three times more same-sex oriented than men? Or is it possible that surveyed women in both locations were two to three times more honest in their survey answers than the surveyed men in both locations? Again, if sexual orientation is determined by genetics, does this mean that 42 percent of Danish women were born with a lesbian orientation, while only 9 percent of University of Utah women were? Assuming that there were few siblings in the Utah and Danish samples, do the surveys indicate that about 10 percent of Utah families and about 40 percent of Danish families either bred or nurtured homosexuality in their male and female children? When considering the disparities between the Salt Lake City and Copenhagen samples, one must remember that both are Judeo-Christian, urbanized, and literate cultures.

Cross-cultural comparisons demonstrate that similar behaviors of gender and sexuality can have vastly different meanings to different peoples at different times. Can we find historical evidence of males and females adopting the dress and behaviors of their opposite gender? Yes. Did they and their cultures regard cross-dressing and cross-gender behaviors in the same way our culture presently does? No. Can we find historical evidence of males and females having homoerotic relationships in various cultures? Yes. Did they and their cultures regard these homoerotic behaviors in the same way our culture presently does? No. Did cultures throughout history have our present concepts of "sexual identity," in other words, heterosexuality and homosexuality as states of being? No.[56]

If our present European-American concepts of heterosexuality, homosexuality, and bisexuality do not apply to even one human society, can we be sure that those concepts apply to everyone in our own society and time period? If "homosexuality" means different things according to time and place, then "heterosexuality" in one culture may contain same-sex dynamics that are defined as "homosexual" in another culture. Also, "homophobia"[57] may not exist in some cultures or may be very different over time in the same culture.

Moreover, does everyone at a particular time in a society accept that society's conventional definitions of sexuality? For example, in a survey of 7,000 American men during the 1970s, 46 percent had experienced a sexual act with another male, yet only 9 percent defined themselves as homosexual or gay and an additional 2 percent defined themselves as bisexual. Thus, 35 percent of the men considered themselves heterosexual despite having had sex with other males. Would the rest of America's heterosexual men agree? For that matter, would self-defined gay men in America agree? For the women of the study, 10 percent had experienced a sexual act with another female, yet only 4.8 percent defined themselves as lesbian and an additional 2.8 percent defined themselves as bisexual.[58] Again, would the rest of America's heterosexual women agree? Would self-defined lesbians in America agree?

Even within a culture that has categories of heterosexuality and homosexuality, there is a crucial "difference between sexual orientation/ identity and sexual behavior," as the anthropologist Gilbert Herdt wrote in an American journal of psychiatry. "That someone engages in a sexual act does not necessarily mean that he or she has the characteristics associated with the general category of such acts. Thus, a woman may marry and have children but regard her sexual orientation as lesbian; or a man may engage in sexual activity with males but regard himself as heterosexual." These are not superficial distinctions but are verifiable as fundamental self-definitions for many males and females in today's European-American culture, which tries to make inflexible distinctions between heterosexuality and homosexuality. Herdt concludes: "We must therefore distinguish homosexuality as a state of being from same-sex acts and transient relationships, which may not involve homoerotic sex-object choice and intentionality in the same way."[59]

Aside from the cultural biases in the use of the adjective *homosexual,* there is also a common tendency to limit its meaning to the erotic. Jonathan Katz observes: "The term *homosexual,* with its emphasis on same-sex genital contact directed toward orgasm, is particularly inadequate as a means of encompassing and understanding the historical variety of same-sex relations."[60]

To better describe that "historical variety," the feminist historian Carroll Smith-Rosenberg used different terminology. Her path-breaking essay in social history, "The Female World of Love and Ritual," examined the "homosocial" in the personal dynamics of nineteenth-century America. She used this as a nonerotic term to describe same-sex social behaviors that were decades-long among persons whose erotic experiences were primarily or exclusively with opposite-sex persons.[61] My study also uses the terms *homocultural, homoenvironmental, homopastoral, homotactile, homoemotional, homoromantic, homomarital,* and finally the more familiar *homoerotic.*[62]

Although I discuss these dynamics separately, they obviously overlap in numerous ways. Problems may remain, but I believe these terms and concepts more accurately describe diverse personal experiences, various cultures, and different time periods. Nevertheless, the perceived meaning of those dynamics will differ widely according to one's own self-identity, experience, culture, and time period. I also prefer to use *same-sex* as an adjective, rather than *homosexual, gay,* or *lesbian.* I generally use the latter three terms to refer to people's self-definitions rather than to their behaviors. Readers should always understand my occasional use of *gay, homosexual, lesbian,* or *bisexual* within the culturally defined context I have described in this chapter.[63]

NOTES

1. Jonathan Ned Katz, "The Invention of Heterosexuality," *Socialist Review* 20 (Jan.–Mar. 1990): 7–34; George Chauncey, *Gay New York: Gender, Urban Culture, and the Making of the Gay Male World, 1890–1940* (New York: Basic Books/HarperCollins, 1994), 26–27, 100, 111–27; Linda Dowling, *Hellenism and Homosexuality in Victorian Oxford* (Ithaca: Cornell University Press, 1994), 134; Jonathan Ned Katz, *The Invention of Heterosexuality* (New York: Dutton, 1995).

2. Jonathan Ned Katz, *Gay/Lesbian Almanac: A New Documentary* (New York: Harper and Row, 1983), 6, 153; George H. Wiedeman, "Survey of Psychoanalytic Literature on Overt Male Homosexuality," *Journal of the American Psychoanalytic Association* 10 (Apr. 1962): 386n.

3. *Oxford English Dictionary,* 2d ed., 20 vols. (Oxford: Clarendon Press, 1989), 8:839; James G. Kiernan, "Insanity. Lecture XXVI.—Sexual Perversion," *Detroit Lancet* 7 (May 1884): 481–84, and Kiernan, "Responsibility in Sexual Perversion," *Chicago Medical Reporter* 3 (May 1892): 185–210, both

as quoted in Katz, *Gay/Lesbian Almanac,* 195, 232, and 232n. Despite the existence of homosexual and heterosexual categories in medical literature in Europe by 1869 and in the United States by 1892, respectable journalism has recently created a new homosexual myth that the Oscar Wilde sodomy trials of 1895 "can justifiably lay claim to producing the 'category' of the homosexual," as Will Eaves states in "Theoretically Gay: Tracing the History of Effeminacy," *New York Times Literary Supplement,* 20 Jan. 1995, 24. A similar overstatement occurs as the first lines of Robert Atkins's "Very Queer Indeed," *Village Voice,* 31 Jan. 1995, 69: "When a British court branded Oscar Wilde a pervert, it also gave birth to the modern homosexual. Homosexual acts were transformed into homosexual identity." The Wilde case *popularized* the category of homosexual, which the medical community had defined only a few years earlier. For Oscar Wilde's influence in transforming the self-identity of many male homosexuals since 1895, see Alan Sinfield, *The Wilde Century: Effeminacy, Oscar Wilde, and the Queer Movement* (New York: Columbia University Press, 1994).

    4. Vern L. Bullough, *Sexual Variance in Society and History* (New York: John Wiley and Sons, 1976), 636–45; Vern L. Bullough, "Challenges to Societal Attitudes toward Homosexuality in the Late Nineteenth and Early Twentieth Centuries," *Social Science Quarterly* 58 (June 1977): 29–44; "The Modern United States: The Invention of the Homosexual, 1880–1950," in Katz, *Gay/Lesbian Almanac,* 135–74; David F. Greenberg, *The Construction of Homosexuality* (Chicago: University of Chicago Press, 1988), 407–17; Bert Hansen, "American Physicians' Earliest Writings about Homosexuals, 1880–1900," *Milbank Quarterly* 67, supp. 1 (1989): 92–108; Martha Vicinus, "'They Wonder to Which Sex I Belong': The Historical Roots of the Modern Lesbian Identity," in Dennis Altman, et al., *Homosexuality, Which Homosexuality?: International Conference on Gay and Lesbian Studies* (Amsterdam: Schorer; London: GMP, 1989); Randolph Trumbach, "Gender and the Homosexual Role in Modern Western Culture: The Eighteenth and Nineteenth Centuries Compared," in Altman, et al., *Homosexuality, Which Homosexuality?*

    5. Lev. 18:22, 20:13. For revisionist views, see Martin Samuel Cohen, "The Biblical Prohibition of Homosexual Intercourse," *Journal of Homosexuality* 19, no. 4 (1990): 3–20; Saul M. Olyan, "'And with a Male You Shall Not Lie the Lying Down of a Woman': On the Meaning and Significance of Leviticus 18:22 and 20:13," *Journal of the History of Sexuality* 5 (Oct. 1994): 179–206; also Robin Scrogg, *The New Testament and Homosexuality* (Philadelphia: Fortress Press, 1984); George Edward, *Gay/Lesbian Liberation: A Biblical Perspective* (New York: Pilgrim Press, 1984); John J. McNeill, "Scripture and Homosexuality," *The Church and the Homosexual,* 4th ed. (Boston: Beacon Press, 1993), 36–64; Michael L. Satlow, "'They Abused Him like a Woman': Homoeroticism, Gender Blurring, and the Rabbis in Late Antiquity," *Journal of the History of Sexuality* 5 (July 1994): 1–25.

6. A. D. Harvey, *Sex in Georgian England: Attitudes and Prejudices from the 1720s to the 1820s* (New York: St. Martin's Press, 1994), 130, 132–33. A more careful reconstruction of the evolution of ideas concerning sodomy from the 1600s to the 1890s is a study that preceded Harvey's book, Richard Davenport-Hines, *Sex, Death, and Punishment: Attitudes toward Sex and Sexuality in Britain since the Renaissance* (London: Collins, 1990), 55–155.

7. Emma Donoghue, *Passions between Women: British Lesbian Culture, 1668–1801* (New York: HarperCollins, 1995), 20.

8. For the American colonial laws and punishments for same-sex intercourse, see Katz, *Gay/Lesbian Almanac*, 66–133, and for those activities specifically cited here see 68–69, 85–86, 92–93, 101–2; see Jonathan Katz, *Gay American History: Lesbians and Gay Men in the U.S.A.* (New York: Thomas Y. Crowell, 1976), 20 for John Cotton's proposal, and 127–28 for the only known imprisonment in the modern United States (in 1967) of women for consensual same-sex acts.

9. Cited in Katz, *Gay American History*, 23–24.

10. Kenneth Roberts and Anna M. Roberts, eds., *Moreau de St. Mery's American Journey (1793–1798)* (Garden City, N.Y.: Doubleday, 1947), 286, also quoted in Bullough, *Sexual Variance*, 592; Katz, *Gay American History*, 25–26.

11. *Oxford English Dictionary*, 8:839, and sources cited in note 3.

12. Mildred J. Berryman, "The Psychological Phenomena of the Homosexual," rough-typed on the back of stationery of the American Red Cross, Salt Lake City, Utah, with the last page of the study dated 13 November 1938, in the June Mazer Lesbian Collection, West Hollywood, Calif.; see also chap. 7 for analysis of this study and chap. 7, notes 3 and 5 for its dating.

13. Wayne R. Dynes, ed., *Encyclopedia of Homosexuality*, 2 vols. (New York: Garland, 1990), 1:346–49; see also chap. 5 for discussions of Siberian and Aleut "soft men," as well as the Native American berdache and amazons.

14. W. W. Hill, "The Status of the Hermaphrodite and Transvestite in Navajo Culture," *American Anthropologist* 37 (Apr.–June 1935): 273–79; Robert B. Edgerton, "Pokot Intersexuality: An East African Example of the Resolution of Sexual Incongruity," *American Anthropologist* 66 (Dec. 1964): 1288–99; Robert I. Levy, "The Community Function of Tahitian Male Transsexualism: A Hypothesis," *Anthropological Quarterly* 44 (Jan. 1971): 12–21; Unni Wikan, "Man Becomes Woman: Transsexualism in Oman as a Key to Gender Roles," *Man: The Journal of the Royal Anthropological Institute* 12 (Aug. 1977): 304–19; Ian Stevenson, "The Southeast Asian Interpretation of Gender Dysphoria: An Illustrative Case Report," *Journal of Nervous and Mental Disease* 165 (Sept. 1977): 201–8; Bengt Danielsson and Marie Therese, "Polynesia's Third Sex: The Gay Life Starts in the Kitchen," *Pacific Islands Monthly* 49 (Aug. 1978): 10–13; Serena Nanda, "The Hijras of India: A Preliminary Report," *Medicine and Law* 3, no. 1 (1984): 59–75; Serena Nanda,

"The Hijras of India: Cultural and Individual Dimensions of an Institutionalized Third Gender Role," *Journal of Homosexuality* 11 (Summer 1985): 35–54; Walter L. Williams, *The Spirit and the Flesh: Sexual Diversity in American Indian Culture* (Boston: Beacon Press, 1986), 81–86; James D. Weinrich, *Sexual Landscapes: Why We Are What We Are, Why We Love Whom We Love* (New York: Charles Scribner's Sons, 1987), 344–45; Serena Nanda, *Neither Man nor Woman: The Hijras of India* (Belmont, Calif.: Wadsworth, 1990); Charlotte Furth, "Androgynous Males and Deficient Females: Biology and Gender Boundaries in Sixteenth- and Seventeenth-Century China," in Henry Abelove, Michele Aina Barale, and David M. Halperin, eds., *The Lesbian and Gay Studies Reader* (New York: Routledge, 1993), 479–97; and relevant essays in Gilbert Herdt, ed., *Third Sex, Third Gender: Beyond Sexual Dimorphism in Culture and History* (New York: Zone Books, 1994). For a Jungian interpretation of "third sex" cultural constructs and their application to European Americans, see June Singer, *Androgyny: Toward a New Theory of Sexuality* (Garden City, N.Y.: Anchor Press/Doubleday, 1976).

15. Sue-Ellen Jacobs and Jason Cromwell, "Visions and Revisions of Reality: Reflections on Sex, Sexuality, Gender, and Gender Variance," *Journal of Homosexuality* 23, no. 4 (1992): 58; Michael L. Tan, "From *Bakla* to Gay: Shifting Gender Identities and Sexual Behaviors in the Philippines," in Richard G. Parker and John H. Gagnon, eds., *Conceiving Sexuality: Approaches to Sex Research in a Postmodern World* (New York: Routledge, 1995), 88–89.

16. Stuart Henry, *Conquering Our Great American Plains: A Historical Development* (New York: E. P. Dutton, 1930), 271, 275–76, 288.

17. William Lee Howard, "Effeminate Men and Masculine Women," *New York Medical Journal* 77 (5 May 1900): 686–87, quoted in Katz, *Gay/Lesbian Almanac*, 302–3.

18. For intersexuality (or hermaphroditism), see David J. B. Ashley, *Human Intersex* (Baltimore: Williams and Wilkins, 1962); Claus Overzier, ed., *Intersexuality* (New York: Academic Press, 1963); C. N. Armstrong and Alan J. Marshall, eds., *Intersexuality in Vertebrates Including Man* (New York: Academic Press, 1964); Virginia V. Weldon, Robert M. Blizzard, and Claude J. Migeon, "Newborn Girls Misdiagnosed as Bilaterally Cryptorchid Males," *New England Journal of Medicine* 274 (14 Apr. 1966): 829–33; David C. Hefelfinger, Kenneth R. T. Tyson, Dieter Assor, and George T. Bryan, "True Hermaphroditism Unassociated with a Common Urogenital Sinus," *Pediatrics* 43 (May 1969): 896–900; John Money, *Errors of the Body: Dilemmas, Education, Counseling* (Baltimore: Johns Hopkins University Press, 1968); Jan E. Jirasek, *Development of the Genital System and Male Pseudohermaphroditism* (Baltimore: Johns Hopkins University Press, 1971); John Money and Anke A. Ehrhardt, *Man and Woman, Boy and Girl: The Differentiation and*

Dimorphism of Gender Identity from Conception to Maturity (Baltimore: Johns Hopkins University Press, 1972); John Money and Jean Dalery, "Iatrogenic Homosexuality: Gender Identity in Seven 46,XX Chromosomal Females with Hyperadrenocortical Hermaphroditism Born with a Penis, Three Reared as Boys, Four Reared as Girls," *Journal of Homosexuality* 1 (Summer 1976): 357–71; Deborah Heller Feinbloom, *Transvestites and Transsexuals: Mixed Views* (New York: Delacorte Press, 1976), 129–253; Duane E. Jeffery, "Intersexes in Humans: An Introductory Exploration," *Dialogue: A Journal of Mormon Thought* 12 (Fall 1979): 107–13; Duane E. Jeffery, "Intersexes Illuminate Gender Issue," *Provo Daily Herald,* 24 May 1993, C-1; Duane E. Jeffery, "Intersexes' Biology Is Complex," *Provo Daily Herald,* 31 May 1993, D-1; Duane E. Jeffery, "Humans May Need Five Sexes," *Provo Daily Herald,* 7 June 1993, C-1.

In addition to physically intersexual persons, there are emotional transsexuals who regard themselves as having the gender opposite to their physical genitalia. Emotional transsexualism can exist even if the person never becomes surgically transsexual or transgendered. Although it has become an insensitive cliché, presurgical transsexuals literally feel that they are men "trapped" in female bodies or women "trapped" in male bodies. For studies of emotional and surgical transsexualism, see Ira B. Pauly, "Male Psychosexual Inversion: Transsexualism," *Archives of General Psychiatry* 13 (Aug. 1965): 172–81; Harry Benjamin, *The Transsexual Phenomenon* (New York: Julian Press, 1966); Richard Green and John Money, eds., *Transsexualism and Sex Reassignment* (Baltimore: Johns Hopkins University Press, 1969); Jon K. Meyer, Norman J. Knorr, and Dietrich Blumer, "Characterization of a Self-Designated Transsexual Population," *Archives of Sexual Behavior* 1, no. 3 (1971): 219–30; Jan Walinder, "Incidence and Sex Ratio of Transsexualism in Sweden," *British Journal of Psychiatry* 119 (Aug. 1971): 195–96; B. D. Hore, F. V. Nicolle, and J. S. Calnan, "Male Transsexualism: Two Cases in a Single Family," *Archives of Sexual Behavior* 2 (Dec. 1973): 317–21; Robert J. Stoller and Howard J. Baker, "Two Male Transsexuals in One Family," *Archives of Sexual Behavior* 2 (Dec. 1973): 323–28; Thomas Kando, *Sex Change: The Achievement of Gender Identity among Feminized Transsexuals* (Springfield, Ill.: Charles C. Thomas, 1973); Ethel Person and Lionel Ovesey, "The Transsexual Syndrome in Males," *American Journal of Psychotherapy* 28 (Jan.–Apr. 1974): 4–20, 174–93; Lawrence E. Newman and Robert J. Stoller, "Nontranssexual Men Who Seek Sex Reassignment," *American Journal of Psychiatry* 131 (Apr. 1974): 437–41; Ira B. Pauly, "Female Transsexualism," *Archives of Sexual Behavior* 3 (Nov. 1974): 487–526; Jon K. Meyer, "Clinical Variants among Applicants for Sex Reassignment," *Archives of Sexual Behavior* 3 (Nov. 1974): 527–58; Richard Green, *Sexual Identity Conflict in Children and Adults* (New York: Basic Books, 1974); B. D. Hore, F. V. Nicolle, and J. S. Calnan, "Male

Transsexualism in England: Sixteen Cases with Surgical Intervention," *Archives of Sexual Behavior* 4 (Jan. 1975): 81–88; Elliott M. Heiman and Cao Van Le, "Transsexualism in Vietnam," *Archives of Sexual Behavior* 4 (Jan. 1975): 89–95; Vern L. Bullough, "Transsexualism in History," *Archives of Sexual Behavior* 4 (Sept. 1975): 561–71; Edward M. Levine, Doris Gruenewald, and Charles H. Shaiova, "Behavioral Differences and Emotional Conflict among Male-to-Female Transsexuals," *Archives of Sexual Behavior* 5 (Jan. 1976): 81–86; Peter M. Bentler, "A Typology of Transsexualism: Gender Identity Theory and Data," *Archives of Sexual Behavior* 5 (Nov. 1976): 567–84; R. Langevin, D. Paitich, and B. Steiner, "The Clinical Profile of Male Transsexuals Living as Females vs. Those Living as Males," *Archives of Sexual Behavior* 6 (Mar. 1977): 143–54; John Money and A. Russo, "Homosexual Outcome of Discordant Gender Identity/Role in Childhood: Longitudinal Follow-Up," *Journal of Pediatric Psychology* 4 (Mar. 1979): 29–41; P. J. Huxley, J. C. Kenna, and S. Brandon, "Partnership in Transsexualism. Part I. Paired and Nonpaired Groups," *Archives of Sexual Behavior* 10 (Apr. 1981): 133–42, and "Part II. The Nature of the Partnership," *Archives of Sexual Behavior* 10 (Apr. 1981): 143–60; Michael Flemming, Deborah Cohen, Patricia Salt, David Jones, and Sharon Jenkins, "A Study of Pre- and Postsurgical Transsexuals: MMPI Characteristics," *Archives of Sexual Behavior* 10 (Apr. 1981): 161–70; Thorkil Sorensen and Preben Hertoft, "Male and Female Transsexualism: The Danish Experience with Thirty-Seven Patients," *Archives of Sexual Behavior* 11 (Apr. 1982): 157–70; Dwight B. Billings and Thomas Urban, "The Socio-Medical Construction of Transsexualism: An Interpretation and Critique," *Social Problems* 29 (Feb. 1982): 266–82; Ethan C. O'Gorman, "A Retrospective Study of Epidemiological and Clinical Aspects of Twenty-Eight Transsexual Patients," *Archives of Sexual Behavior* 11 (June 1982): 231–45; Lesie Martin Lothstein, *Female-to-Male Transsexualism: Historical, Clinical, and Theoretical Issues* (Boston: Routledge and Kegan Paul, 1983); Michael Z. Fleming, Bradford R. MacGowan, and Patricia Self, "Female-to-Male Transsexualism and Sex Roles: Self and Spouse Ratings on the PAQ," *Archives of Sexual Behavior* 13 (Feb. 1984): 51–58; D. F. MacFarlane, "Transsexual Prostitution in New Zealand: Predominance of Persons of Maori Extraction," *Archives of Sexual Behavior* 13 (Aug. 1984): 301–10; Ray Blanchard, "Typology of Male-to-Female Transsexualism," *Archives of Sexual Behavior* 14 (June 1985): 247–62; John Hoenig, "Etiology of Transsexualism," in Betty W. Steiner, ed., *Gender Dysphoria: Development, Research, Management* (New York: Plenum Press, 1985), 33–73; Kenneth J. Zucker, "Cross-Gender Identified Children," in Steiner, ed., *Gender Dysphoria,* 75–174; Gunnar Lindemalm, Dag Koerlin, and Nils Uddenberg, "Long-Term Follow-Up of 'Sex Change' in Thirteen Male-to-Female Transsexuals," *Archives of Sexual Behavior* 15 (June 1986): 187–210; Holly Devor, "Gender Blending Females: Women and Sometimes Men,"

American Behavioral Scientist 32 (Sept.–Oct. 1987): 12–40; Anne Bolin, "Transsexualism and the Limits of Traditional Analysis," *American Behavioral Scientist* 32 (Sept.–Oct. 1987): 41–65; David E. Grimm, "Toward a Theory of Gender: Transsexualism, Gender, Sexuality, and Relationships," *American Behavioral Scientist* 32 (Sept.–Oct. 1987): 66–85; Richard F. Docter, *Transvestites and Transsexuals: Toward a Theory of Cross-Gender Behavior* (New York: Plenum, 1988); Holly Devor, *Gender Blending: Confronting the Limits of Duality* (Bloomington: Indiana University Press, 1989); Sandra L. Johnson and D. Daniel Hunt, "The Relationship of Male Transsexual Typology to Psychosocial Adjustment," *Archives of Sexual Behavior* 19 (Aug. 1990): 349–60; Ray Blanchard and Betty W. Steiner, eds., *Clinical Management of Gender Identity Disorders in Children and Adults* (Washington, D.C.: American Psychiatric Press, 1990); Marjorie Garber, "Spare Parts: The Surgical Construction of Gender," in Abelove, Barale, and Halperin, eds., *Lesbian and Gay Studies Reader,* 321–36; Anne Bolin, "Transcending and Transgendering: Male to Female Transsexuals, Dichotomy, and Diversity," in Herdt, ed., *Third Sex, Third Gender,* 447–86; Eli Coleman, Walter O. Bockting, and Louis Gooren, "Homosexual and Bisexual Identity in Sex-Reassigned Female-to-Male Transsexuals," *Archives of Sexual Behavior* 22 (Feb. 1993): 37–50; Heino F. L. Meyer-Bahlburg, "Intersexuality and the Diagnosis of Gender Identity Disorder," *Archives of Sexual Behavior* 23 (Feb. 1994): 21–40; C. D. Doorn, J. Poortinga, and A. M. Verschoor, "Cross-Gender Identity in Transvestites and Male Transsexuals," *Archives of Sexual Behavior* 23 (Apr. 1994): 185–201.

19. At its most extreme, the nature-nurture controversy of homosexuality centers on the religious claim "God does not create homosexuals or allow babies to be born with abnormal sexual orientation." However, it is generally acknowledged that God "creates" left-handedness (which the Bible consistently equates with evil). Also, people who claim that God does not create homosexuals seem to acknowledge that God allows babies to be born color blind, RH negative, deaf, hemophiliac, mentally diminished, or with hundreds of other kinds of "abnormal" characteristics of prenatal origin. For sources concerning the biological-genetic origins of homosexuality and lesbianism, see introduction, note 8. Nevertheless, *Homosexuality,* 2d ed. (Salt Lake City: First Presidency and Council of the Twelve Apostles of the Church of Jesus Christ of Latter-day Saints, 1981), 2, stated: "It is inconceivable that—as some involved in homosexual behavior claim—he [God] would permit some of his children to be born with desires and inclinations which would require behavior contrary to the eternal plan." Most advocates of inborn homosexuality are heterosexual geneticists, neurologists, and endocrinologists.

20. At the turn of the twentieth century, *bisexual* (like *intersex* or *intermediate sex*) was a common Anglo-American term to explain "homosexuals" who had the sex organs of one gender but "belong *mentally* and *emotionally* to the

other." See Edward Carpenter, *The Intermediate Sex: A Study of Some Transitional Types of Men and Women* (New York: Mitchell Kennerley, 1912), 19, emphasis in original; see also Xavier Mayne [Edward Irenaeus Prime Stevenson], *The Intersexes: A History of Similisexualism as a Problem in Social Life* (Rome: n.p., [1909?]; reprint, New York: Arno Press/New York Times, 1975); Chauncey, *Gay New York,* 48–49, 387n7. My study and the following sources use *bisexual* in its post-1920s (and now universally understood) denotation of the condition of feeling sexual desire and erotic interest for both genders, rather than for only one gender: Preston Harriman, *Bi-Sexuality: Normal or Not?* (North Hollywood, Calif.: Dominion, 1969); Colin MacInnes, *Loving Them Both: A Study in Bisexuality and Bisexuals* (London: Martin Brian and O'Keefe, 1973); Duane E. Spiers, "The No-Man's-Land of the Bisexual," *Corrective and Social Psychiatry and Journal of Behavior Technology, Methods, and Therapy* 22, no. 3 (1976): 6–11; Janet Bode, *View from Another Closet: Exploring Bisexuality in Women* (New York: Hawthorn Books, 1976); Martin B. Duberman, "The Bisexual Debate," in John H. Gagnon, ed., *Human Sexuality in Today's World* (Boston: Little, Brown, 1977); David A. I. Harris, "Social-Psychological Characteristics of Ambisexuals" (Ph.D. diss., University of Tennessee, 1977); Michael Ross, "Bisexuality: Fact or Fallacy?" *British Journal of Sexual Medicine* 6 (Feb. 1979): 49–50; Charlotte Wolff, *Bisexuality: A Study,* rev. ed. (London: Quartet Books, 1979); Jay P. Paul, "The Bisexual Identity: An Idea without Social Recognition," *Journal of Homosexuality* 9 (Spring 1984): 45–63; Gilbert H. Herdt, "A Comment on Cultural Attributes and Fluidity of Bisexuality," *Journal of Homosexuality* 10 (Winter 1984): 53–61; Michael W. Ross, "Beyond the Biological Model: New Directions in Bisexual and Homosexual Research," *Journal of Homosexuality* 10 (Winter 1984): 63–70; Gisela T. Kaplan and Lesley J. Rogers, "Breaking Out of the Dominant Paradigm: A New Look at Sexual Attraction," *Journal of Homosexuality* 10 (Winter 1984): 71–75; John P. DeCecco, ed., *Bisexual and Homosexual Identities: Critical Clinical Issues* (New York: Haworth Press, 1984); John P. DeCecco and Michael G. Shively, eds., *Bisexual and Homosexual Identities: Critical Theoretical Issues* (New York: Haworth Press, 1984); the special issue "Bisexualities: Theory and Research," *Journal of Homosexuality* 11 (Spring 1985): 1–234; Fritz Klein and Timothy J. Wolf, eds., *Two Lives to Lead: Bisexuality in Men and Women* (New York: Harrington Park Press, 1985); Weinrich, "Limerance, Lust, and Bisexuality: A New Theory," in *Sexual Landscapes,* 108–34; Ivan Hill, ed., *The Bisexual Spouse* (New York: Harper and Row, 1989); Rosalie F. Zoltano, *Sex and Bisexuality: Index of Modern Information with Bibliography* (Washington, D.C.: ABBE Publishers Association, 1990); Loraine Hutchins and Lani Kaahumanu, eds., *BI Any Other Name: Bisexual People Speak Out* (Boston: Alyson, 1991); Elizabeth Daumer, "Queer Ethics, or the Challenge of Bisexuality to Lesbian Ethics,"

Hypatia: A Journal of Feminist Philosophy 7 (Fall 1992): 91–105; Elizabeth Reba Weise, ed., *Closer to Home: Bisexuality and Feminism* (Seattle: Seal Press, 1992); Sue George, *Women and Bisexuality* (London: Scarlet Press, 1993); Philip W. Blumenstein and Pepper Schwartz, "Bisexuality: Some Social Psychological Issues," in Linda Garnets and Douglas C. Kimmel, eds., *Psychological Perspectives on Lesbian and Gay Male Experiences* (New York: Columbia University Press, 1993), 168–83; Peter J. Snyder, James D. Weinrich, and Richard D. Pillard, "Personality and Lipid Differences Associated with Homosexual and Bisexual Identity in Men," *Archives of Sexual Behavior* 23 (Aug. 1994): 433–51; Martin S. Weinberg, Colin J. Williams, and Douglas W. Pryor, *Dual Attraction: Understanding Bisexuality* (New York: Oxford University Press, 1994), which is a detailed study of 800 bisexual women and men; Gilbert Herdt and Andrew Boxer, "Bisexuality: Toward a Comparative Theory of Identities and Culture," in Parker and Gagnon, eds., *Conceiving Sexuality,* 69–83; "Bisexuality Is the Wild Card of Our Erotic Life," *Newsweek,* 17 July 1995, 44–50; Marjorie Garber, *Vice Versa: Bisexuality and the Eroticism of Everyday Life* (New York: Simon and Schuster, 1995).

21. Kenneth J. Dover, *Greek Homosexuality* (Cambridge, Mass.: Harvard University Press, 1978); David M. Halperin, *One Hundred Years of Homosexuality, and Other Essays on Greek Love* (New York: Routledge, 1989); John J. Winkler, "Laying Down the Law: The Oversight of Men's Sexual Behavior in Classical Athens," and relevant sections of other essays in David M. Halperin, John J. Winkler, and Froma I. Zeitlin, eds., *Before Sexuality: The Construction of Erotic Experience in the Ancient Greek World* (Princeton: Princeton University Press, 1990); Eva Cantarella, *Bisexuality in the Ancient World,* trans. Cormac O'Cuillean'ain (New Haven: Yale University Press, 1992); Wayne R. Dynes and Stephen Donaldson, eds., *Homosexuality in the Ancient World* (New York: Garland Press, 1992); John Maxwell O'Brien, *Alexander the Great: The Invisible Enemy, a Biography* (London: Routledge, 1992), 57–59, 112–13.

22. Marybeth Raynes, a clinical social worker, suggested this term while discussing with me a preliminary version of this study.

23. Carole S. Vance, "Social Construction Theory: Problems in the History of Sexuality," in Altman, Vance, Vicinus, and Weeks, eds., *Homosexuality, Which Homosexuality?* 18.

24. Christine Hugh-Jones, *From the Milk River: Spatial and Temporal Processes in Northwest Amazonia* (Cambridge: Cambridge University Press, 1979), 110; also reported in Dr. C. A. Tripp, *The Homosexual Matrix* (New York: McGraw Hill, 1975), 50, referring to the work of the anthropologist Kenneth M. Kensinger among a different group, the Cashinahua of Peru, in the early 1970s.

25. Arthur P. Sorensen Jr., "Linguistic Exogamy and Personal Choice in the

Northwest Amazon," in Kenneth M. Kensinger, ed., *Marriage Practices in Lowland South America* (Urbana: University of Illinois Press, 1984), 185.

26. Richard Ellman, *Oscar Wilde* (New York: Vintage Books, 1988), 463; Richard Ellman, "A Late Victorian Love Affair," *Oscar Wilde: Two Approaches* (Los Angeles: William Andrews Clark Memorial Library, University of California at Los Angeles, 1977), 9. Although Wilde's use of this phrase is well known, he was quoting from the already published poem "Two Loves" by his younger male lover, Alfred Lord Douglas. The phrase was part of the prosecution's examination of Wilde and Douglas's poem was reprinted in Byrne R. S. Fone, ed., *Hidden Heritage: History and Gay Imagination, An Anthology* (New York: Avocation, 1980), 194–96.

27. Robert J. Morris, "*Aikane*: Accounts of Hawaiian Same-Sex Relationships in the Journals of Captain Cook's Third Voyage (1776–80)," *Journal of Homosexuality* 19, no. 4 (1990): 23–24, 27, 34–44, quotation from 32.

28. *Cross-dresser* and *cross-dressing* are the common English translations of the traditional Latinate terms *transvestite* and *transvestism*. See also the discussion in chap. 5.

29. See note 27 and Robert J. Morris, "Same-Sex Friendships in Hawaiian Lore: Constructing the Canon," in Stephen O. Murray, ed., *Oceanic Homosexualities* (New York: Garland, 1992), 71–102; Curt Sanburn, "'Men of the First Consequence': The Aikane Tradition, Homosexuality in Old Hawaii," *Honolulu Weekly,* 12 May 1993, 4–6; Robert J. Morris, "Same-Sex Unions Were Accepted in Hawaii," *Honolulu Advertiser,* 13 June 1993, B-3; recent statement of the distinction between the cross-dressing *Mahu* (sometimes spelled "Mahoo") and the *Aikane* in "Hawaii Weighing Gay Marriages and Same-Sex Benefits," *New York Times,* 25 Apr. 1994, B-8.

30. Niel Gunson, "Great Women and Friendship Contract Rites in Pre-Christian Tahiti," *Journal of the Polynesian Society* 73 (Mar. 1964): 66.

31. Richard Henry Dana, *Two Years before the Mast* (New York: Harper and Brothers, 1840; reprint, New York: Signet Classics, New American Library, 1964), 231, also 140.

32. Herman Melville, *Omoo: A Narrative of Adventures in the South Seas* (New York: Harper and Brothers, 1847), 178, 180. Consistent with Melville's well-known sexual wordplays and innuendoes in *Moby Dick* (e.g., the "Cassock" chapter), the name of this story's accommodating boyfriend ("Poky") was a playful reference to anal sex. For Melville's homosexual subtexts, see Newton Arvin, *Herman Melville* (New York: William Sloan Associates, 1950), 128–30; Edwin Haviland Miller, *Melville* (New York: George Braziller, 1975), 234–30; Georges-Michel Sarotte, *Like a Brother, Like a Lover: Male Homosexuality in the American Novel and Theater from Herman Melville to James Baldwin,* trans. Richard Miller (Garden City, N.Y.: Anchor Press/Doubleday, 1978), 12–13, 73, 78–83; Robert K. Martin, *Hero, Captain, and Stranger: Male*

Friendship, Social Critique, and Literary Form in the Sea Novels of Herman Melville (Chapel Hill: University of North Carolina Press, 1986), 6–7, 14–16, 26, 51–58, 63–64, 73–74, 105; Zan Dale Robinson, *Semiotic and Psychoanalytical Interpretation of Herman Melville's Fiction* (San Francisco: Mellon Research University Press, 1991), 53, 100.

33. For example, see Charles Warren Stoddard, "A South-Sea Idyl," *Overland Monthly* 3 (Sept. 1869): 258, 260. See note 37 for the details of Stoddard's story in which he used the less conventional spelling "idyl" as a closer play on the words "idle" (for his unproductive behavior there in the judgment of his father) and "idol" (for his teenage sexual companion).

34. William Farrer, "Biographical Sketch, Hawaiian Mission Report, and Diary of William Farrer, 1821–1906," typescript, 66–67 (29–30 Apr. 1851), Department of Special Collections and Manuscripts, Harold B. Lee Library, Brigham Young University, Provo, Utah. This was the first and only report in Farrer's diary of such an encounter with a Hawaiian boy. Following his return to Utah from this mission, Farrer married just days before his thirty-fifth birthday and fathered eight children.

35. R. Lanier Britsch, *Moramona: The Mormons in Hawaii* (Laie, Hawaii: Institute for Polynesian Studies, Brigham Young University–Hawaii, 1989), 16; Farrer diary, 56 (14 Feb. 1851).

36. Hiram Clark to "Dear Brethren," 27 Jan. 1851, *Deseret News,* 26 July 1851, 301; Donald Robert Shaffer, "A Forgotten Missionary: Hiram Clark, Mormon Itinerant, British Emigration Organizer, and First President of the L.D.S. Hawaiian Mission, 1795–1853" (M.A. thesis, California State University at Fullerton, 1990), 178–84; Donald Robert Shaffer, "Hiram Clark and the First LDS Hawaiian Mission: A Reappraisal," *Journal of Mormon History* 17 (1991): 94–96, 105, 106.

37. The *Overland Monthly* is available in the Library of American Civilization microfiche collection at university libraries. Homoromantic and erotic dimensions appear in several passages of Charles Warren Stoddard's three-part story about the Tahitian boy Kana-ana. In "A South-Sea Idyl," *Overland Monthly* 3 (Sept. 1869): 258, Stoddard writes: "he placed his two hands on my two knees, and declared, 'I was his best friend, as he was mine; I must come at once to his house, and there live always with him.' What could I do but go?" Page 259: "There was an immense amount of secrecy and many vows, and I was almost crying." Page 260: Asleep in a bed "big enough for a Mormon," the naked teenager "never let loose his hold on me. . . . His sleek figure, supple and graceful in repose, was the embodiment of free, untrammeled youth." Page 261: "If it is a question how long a man may withstand the seductions of nature, and the consolations and conveniences of the state of nature, I have solved it in [this] one case; for I was as natural as possible in about three days." Page 263: "Again and again he would come with a delicious banana to the

bed where I was lying, and insist upon my gorging myself. . . . He would mesmerize me into a most refreshing sleep with a prolonged manipulation." After returning to Boston, Stoddard told his father about the Tahitian boy because "more than any one else ever can, he loved your Prodigal [son]" (264). In "How I Converted My Cannibal: The Sequel To 'A South-Sea Idyl,'" *Overland Monthly* 3 (Nov. 1869): 459, Stoddard spoke of his absent boyfriend: "I can see you, my beloved—sleeping, naked, in the twilight of the west." In "Barbarian Days: Revealing the Fate of My Cannibal," *Overland Monthly* 4 (Apr. 1870): 334, upon his return to Tahiti after the death of his boyfriend at about age eighteen, Stoddard said that Kana-ana was "the only boy I ever truly loved—dead now in his blossoming prime!" Most of my excerpts from the September 1869 story appear in the more available Katz, *Gay American History*, which did not refer to the two sequels of the initial story. This was autobiography, not fiction, and when Stoddard first landed in Tahiti, he wrote the following diary entry: "I find myself in a foreign land with no one to love and none to love me. But I may do as I please in consequence, and it is nobody's business save my own." That quotation first appeared in Stoddard's "A Prodigal in Tahiti," *Atlantic Monthly,* Nov. 1872, 613, which was reprinted in William Dean Howells, ed., *The Great Modern American Stories: An Anthology* (New York: Boni and Liveright, 1921), 129.

38. "The Overland Monthly" in "Local and Other Matters" section, *Deseret Evening News,* 11 July 1868, [3], 21 Dec. 1868, [3], quotation from "Books Received," in "Local and Other Matters" section, *Deseret Evening News,* 7 Aug. 1869, [3]. For Cannon, see Andrew Jenson, *Latter-day Saint Biographical Encyclopedia,* 4 vols. (Salt Lake City: Deseret News Press and Andrew Jenson History, 1901–36), 1:42–51; *Deseret News 1995–1996 Church Almanac: The Church of Jesus Christ of Latter-day Saints* (Salt Lake City: Deseret News, 1994), 45. For the Quorum of the Twelve Apostles, see Daniel H. Ludlow, ed., *Encyclopedia of Mormonism: The History, Scripture, Doctrine, and Procedure of the Church of Jesus Christ of Latter-day Saints,* 5 vols. (New York: Macmillan, 1992), 3:1185–89; D. Michael Quinn, *The Mormon Hierarchy: Origins of Power* (Salt Lake City: Signature Books/Smith Research Associates, 1994), 57–67, 245–63.

39. *National Union Catalog of Pre-1956 Imprints* 754 vols. (London: Mansell, 1968–81), 570:407–9, including the 1887 multivolume collection *Little Classics,* published in Boston. For early reactions to Stoddard's story about his Tahitian boyfriend and for his later relationships with young men in the United States, see Roger Austen, "Stoddard's Little Tricks in *South Sea Idyls,*" *Journal of Homosexuality* 8 (Spring–Summer 1983): 73–81, which quotes from the 1899 edition; John W. Crowley, "Howells, Stoddard, and Male Homosocial Attachment in Victorian America," in Harry Brod, ed., *The Making of Masculinities: The New Men's Studies* (Boston: Allen and Unwin, 1987),

310; Roger Austen, *Genteel Pagan: The Double Life of Charles Warren Stoddard*, ed. John W. Crowley (Amherst: University of Massachusetts Press, 1991), 61–64, 67–82, 87–88, 95, 99, 132–34.

40. Austen, *Genteel Pagan*, 19; Josephine DeWitt Rhodehamel, *Ina Coolbrith: Librarian and Laureate of California* (Provo, Utah: Brigham Young University Press, 1973). Ina Coolbrith was the pen name of Josephine Smith, daughter of Agnes Coolbrith and Don Carlos Smith, brother of Mormonism's first prophet.

41. For his undated visit as a college undergraduate to Salt Lake City, see Charles Warren Stoddard, *Over the Rocky Mountains to Alaska* (St. Louis: B. Herder, 1899), dedication page and 45; see also Austen, *Genteel Pagan*, 132–34, 142–43. Stoddard was born in 1843.

42. For Smith, see biographies in Jenson, *Latter-day Saint Biographical Encyclopedia*, 1:66–74; Joseph Fielding Smith, *The Life of Joseph F. Smith, Second President of the Church of Jesus Christ of Latter-day Saints* (Salt Lake City: Deseret News Press, 1938); Francis M. Gibbons, *Joseph F. Smith: Patriarch and Preacher, Prophet of God* (Salt Lake City: Deseret Book, 1984). For the First Presidency, see Ludlow, ed., *Encyclopedia of Mormonism*, 1:512–13; Quinn, *Origins of Power*, 40–46.

43. Joseph F. Smith diary, 16 Nov. 1879, Archives, Historical Department of the Church of Jesus Christ of Latter-day Saints, Salt Lake City, Utah; Nellie T. Taylor, "John Taylor, His Ancestors and Descendants," *Utah Genealogical and Historical Magazine* 21 (July 1930): 105; entry for Arthur Bruce Taylor in Journal History of the Church of Jesus Christ of Latter-day Saints, 25 May 1873, page 6, 5 Nov. 1874, page 1, Special Collections, J. Willard Marriott Library, University of Utah, Salt Lake City, Utah; entry for Arthur Bruce Taylor in U.S. 1900 Census of Baker City, Baker County, Oregon, enumeration district 163, sheet 19, microfilm, Family History Library of the Church of Jesus Christ of Latter-day Saints, Salt Lake City, Utah (hereafter LDS Family History Library); entry for Arthur Bruce Taylor in U.S. 1920 Census of Rainier, Columbia County, Oregon, enumeration district 100, sheet 12, microfilm, LDS Family History Library.

44. Gilbert H. Herdt, *Guardians of the Flutes: Idioms of Masculinity* (New York: Columbia University Press, 1981), 204, 233–34, 236, quotations from 233 and 235; Gilbert H. Herdt, "Fetish and Fantasy in Sambia Initiation," in Herdt, ed., *Rituals of Manhood: Male Initiation in Papua New Guinea* (Berkeley: University of California Press, 1982), 62–79; Robert J. Stoller, *Presentations of Gender* (New Haven: Yale University Press, 1985), 188–99; Gilbert H. Herdt, *Sambia: Ritual and Gender in New Guinea* (New York: Holt, Reinhart, and Winston, 1987), 102–69; Theodore Lidz and Ruth Wilmanns Lidz, *Oedipus in the Stone Age: A Psychoanalytical Study of Masculinization in Papua New Guinea* (Madison, Conn.: International Universities Press, 1989),

90–103; Gilbert H. Herdt and Robert J. Stoller, *Intimate Communications: Erotics and the Study of Culture* (New York: Columbia University Press, 1990), 57–84; Gilbert H. Herdt, "Semen Transactions in Sambia Culture," in David N. Suggs and Andrew W. Miracle, eds., *Culture and Human Sexuality: A Reader* (Pacific Grove, Calif.: Brooks/Cole, 1993), 298–327.

45. Herdt, *Guardians of the Flutes,* 252n60.

46. Greenberg, *Construction of Homosexuality,* 39; Herdt and Stoller, *Intimate Communications,* 425–26n7.

47. Gerald W. Creed, "Sexual Subordination: Institutionalized Homosexuality and Social Control in Melanesia," *Ethnology* 23 (July 1984): 157–76, reprinted in Jonathan Goldberg, ed., *Reclaiming Sodom* (New York: Routledge, 1994), 66–94; Gilbert H. Herdt, ed., *Ritualized Homosexuality in Melanesia* (Berkeley: University of California Press, 1993); J. Patrick Gray, "Growing Yams and Men: An Interpretation of Kimam Male Ritualized Homosexual Behavior," *Journal of Homosexuality* 11 (Summer 1985): 55–68, reprinted in Evelyn Blackwood, ed., *The Many Faces of Homosexuality: Anthropological Approaches to Homosexual Behavior* (New York: Harrington Park Press, 1986), 55–68; the chapter "Homosexual Relations in Kinship-Structured Societies" in Greenberg, *Construction of Homosexuality,* 25–88; Bruce M. Knauft, "The Question of Ritualised Homosexuality among the Kiwai of South New Guinea," *Journal of Pacific History* 25 (Oct. 1990): 188–211; Thomas M. Ernst, "Onabasulu Male Homosexuality: Cosmology, Affect, and Prescribed Male Homosexual Activity among the Onabasulu of the Great Papuan Plateau," *Oceania* 62 (Sept. 1991): 1–12.

48. Mark William Busse, "Sister Exchange among the Wamek of the Middle Fly" (Ph.D. diss., University of California at San Diego, 1987), 318; Jan Van Baal, *Dema: Description and Analysis of Marind-Anim Culture* (The Hague: Martinus Nijhoff, 1966), 118, 147, 151–52, 495; Lidz and Lidz, *Oedipus in the Stone Age,* 149.

49. *Deseret News 1995–1996 Church Almanac,* 271, which reported 3,300 Mormons in Papua New Guinea as of 31 December 1993; see also Varsel Jenks and Minnie Woods Jenks, "Saints in Kuriva, Papua New Guinea," *Ensign* 20 (Apr. 1990): 76–77, for more than half of village converts being males over age twelve.

50. Dynes, *Encyclopedia of Homosexuality,* 1:244–46; Eve Kosofsky Sedgwick, *Epistemology of the Closet* (Berkeley: University of California Press, 1990).

51. Barry D. Adams, "Age, Structure, and Sexuality: Reflections on the Anthropological Evidence on Homosexual Relations," in Blackwood, ed., *Many Faces of Homosexuality,* 21; Walter Cline, *Notes on the People of Siwah and El Garah in the Libyan Desert,* General Series in Anthropology, no. 4 (Menasha, Wisc.: George Banta, 1936), 43. Although anal sex was univer-

sal among these Siwan males from about age seven to old age, it was an individual choice that was not ritualized as a rite of passage or as a ceremony of same-sex marriage.

52. Herdt, "Introduction to the Paperback Edition," *Ritualized Homosexuality in Melanesia,* xiii; Gilbert H. Herdt, "Cross-Cultural Forms of Homosexuality and the Concept of 'Gay,'" *Psychiatric Annals* 18 (Jan. 1988): 37–39; Peter Fry, "Male Homosexuality and Spirit Possession in Brazil," *Journal of Homosexuality* 11 (Summer 1985): 142; Gilbert H. Herdt, "Developmental Discontinuities and Sexual Orientations across Cultures," in David P. McWhirter, Stephanie A. Sanders, and June Machover Reinisch, eds., *Homosexuality/Heterosexuality: Concepts of Sexual Orientation* (New York: Oxford University Press, 1990), 208–36; John Boswell, "Sexual and Ethical Categories in Premodern Europe," in McWhirter, Sanders, and Reinisch, eds., *Homosexuality/Heterosexuality,* 15–31. However, the English anthropologist Daryl K. Feil defines these as "homosexual societies" in his *The Evolution of Highland Papua New Guinea Societies* (Cambridge: Cambridge University Press, 1987), 177.

53. Borge Alf Borgesen, "A Comparison of Danish and Intermountain Sexual Attitudes and Behavior" (M.A. thesis, University of Utah, 1975), 69. However, a survey of 200 single men (median age: 19) enrolled in marriage-preparation courses at the University of Utah during 1949 showed that 16.5 percent of them reported "active participation in some kind of homosexual practice." Sixty-nine percent of the total sample were LDS, with 80 percent reporting active attendance in church. See John Albert Pennock, "A Study of the Sexual Attitudes and Behavior of Two Hundred Single College Men" (M.S. thesis, University of Utah, 1949), 22, 24, 50. Also, two years before Borgesen's study, a survey of 519 students at the University of Utah found that 7.4 percent of the 300 men reported that they had "caressed a man's penis." See Kenneth Langeland Nyberg, "Homosexual and Homoerotic Behavior Differences in Men and Women" (Ph.D. diss., University of Utah, 1973), 76.

54. Wilford E. Smith, "Mormon Sex Standards on College Campuses, Or Deal Us out of the Sexual Revolution," *Dialogue: A Journal of Mormon Thought* 10 (Autumn 1976): 77. This was the finding of questionnaires that Professor Smith distributed during a twenty-year period to BYU sociology students whom he identified on page 77 as "Mormons in a large church university." While I was enrolled in a BYU sociology course during those years, I took this survey, which was identified as Wilford E. Smith's on the day my class received it. By contrast, in a face-to-face survey at BYU during one day in 1991, only 5 percent of all surveyed students defined themselves as "gay" and none as "lesbian." However, this 1991 survey did not break down the responses by gender, which indicated that the male "gay" response was actually 6–10 percent of responding BYU males. In addition, 22 percent of surveyed BYU stu-

dents in 1991 said they knew "gay men or lesbian women who are attending or have attended BYU." See "Everything You Wanted to Know about BYU but Were Afraid to Ask: SR Surveys the Campus," *Student Review* (Provo, Utah), 13 Mar. 1991, 6. However, a face-to-face survey concerning sexual behavior does not carry the statistical significance of Smith's decades-long study that guaranteed anonymity to participants. For other relevant sources about homosexual issues at BYU, see also Brigham Young University Board of Trustees Minutes, 6 Dec. 1972, 8–9, regarding homosexuality; Brigham Young University Board of Trustees Minutes, 2 May 1973, 6–7, regarding homosexuality, photocopies in my possession; Robert McQueen, "BYU Inquisition," *Advocate*, 13 Aug. 1975, 14; "Homosexuality" section of minutes, Executive Committee, Brigham Young University Board of Trustees, 15 Sept. 1977, 6–7, photocopy in my possession; "The Misery and Suffering of Homosexuals at BYU," *Daily Utah Chronicle*, 7 Feb. 1978, 5; "'Gay' Label Misapplied on Basis of a Few Traits," *Brigham Young University Daily Universe*, 8 Mar. 1978, 14; "KBYU: Gays Rejected," *Brigham Young University Daily Universe*, 30 Mar. 1978, 5; Richard Johnson report, 3 Aug. 1979, that of 95 males treated by Brigham Young University Counseling Center in the winter 1979 semester a total of 47.4 percent mentioned homosexuality, with 29 (30.6 percent) having participated in homoerotic activities with other males and an additional 16 (16.8 percent) experiencing "fears and fantasies only" of homosexuality, photocopy in my possession; "Brigham Young U. Admits Stakeouts on Homosexuals," *New York Times*, 27 Sept. 1979, A-16; "BYU Security Personnel Can Operate Off Campus: Gays Protest Power," *Salt Lake Tribune*, 23 Oct. 1979, D-2; BYU president Jeffrey Holland memorandum, 7 Oct. 1980, to take action against four male students at BYU who were identified as sexually active homosexuals ("all returned missionaries") during a bishop's interview in New Mexico with a young man who was "apparently trying to put his life in order and prepare for a mission," photocopy in my possession; "Homosexuality at BYU," *Seventh East Press* (Provo, Utah), 27 Mar. 1982, 1, 13, and 12 Apr. 1982, 1, 12–13; "Homosexual Series Cancelled: Disagreement Ensues at KBYU-TV," *Brigham Young University Daily Universe*, 12 Aug. 1982, 1; "KBYU Cancels Gay Documentary," *Sunstone Review* 2 (Sept. 1982): 9; Gary James Bergera and Ronald Priddis, *Brigham Young University: A House of Faith* (Salt Lake City: Signature Books, 1983), 83–89, 122, 126–27, 324, 422n71; "Homosexuals Endure at BYU Despite a Strict Code of Honor," *Salt Lake Tribune*, 15 Nov. 1986, C-3; John David Wolverton, "The Smiling Man," *Inscape: A Brigham Young University Student Journal* (Winter 1987): 87–103; Brent Pace, "Mensonge," *Inscape: A Brigham Young University Student Journal* (Spring/Summer 1988): 17; Timothy Liu, "Fisherman's Wharf," *Inscape: A Brigham Young University Student Journal* (Spring/Summer 1988): 45; Brent C. Pace, "Noon Bathers," *Inscape: On the Farm* (1988): 61; Debra A. Fairchild, "An Exploratory Study of Women Divorced from Homosexual Men Compared to Women Divorced from Heterosexual Men" (M.S. thesis, Brigham Young University, 1988); *The Legacy Foundation and Brigham Young University* (Provo, Utah: Legacy Foundation, 1990); "Focusing on Homosexuality at Brigham Young University," *Student Review* (Provo, Utah), 28 Nov. 1990, 1–6; "Gay and Lesbian Mormons Seek Spiritual Center," *Student Review* (Provo, Utah), 28 Oct. 1992, 12, 14; "Why's a Nice Mormon Girl Like Me Married to a Gay Man?" *Student Review* (Provo, Utah), 28 Oct. 1992, 12, 15; "Abandoning Homophobia," *Student Review* (Provo, Utah), 28 Oct. 1992, 13; "On Being a Homosexual at BYU," *Brigham Young University Daily Universe,* 21 Jan. 1993, 4; "Appalling Values," *Brigham Young University Daily Universe,* 26 Jan. 1993, 4; "Lift Military Ban," *Brigham Young University Daily Universe,* 2 Feb. 1993, 4; "Fear and Loathing in Colorado," *Student Review* (Provo, Utah), 10 Feb. 1993, 8, 15; "More on Colorado," *Student Review* (Provo, Utah), 24 Feb. 1993, 3; "A Night at the (Gay) Theater," *Student Review* (Provo, Utah), 10 Mar. 1993, 5; "Prejudicial Policy: The Need to Lift the Military Gay Ban," *Student Review* (Provo, Utah), 10 Mar. 1993, 8, 10; Earl Kofoed, "Memories of Being Gay at BYU," *Affinity: Official Publication of Affirmation/Gay and Lesbian Mormons* (Apr. 1993): 9; "Thoughts From a BYU Lesbian," *Student Review* (Provo, Utah), July 1993, 9; "SR Brings Distress," *Student Review* (Provo, Utah), Aug. 1993, 3. "UVSC Homosexual Club Faces Opposition, Encourages Education, *Brigham Young University Daily Universe,* 21 Nov. 1994, 17; "Tuesday Lecture on Homosexuality Questioned by Students and Faculty," *Brigham Young University Daily Universe,* 25 Jan. 1995, 6; "LDS Church's Actions in Hawaii Appropriate," *Brigham Young University Daily Universe,* 28 Feb. 1995, 4; "Stance on Same-Sex Unions Not Appropriate, Painful," *Brigham Young University Daily Universe,* 9 Mar. 1995, 4; "Same-Sex Viewpoint Ignores Counsels of Living Prophets," *Brigham Young University Daily Universe,* 30 Mar. 1995, 4; "Ignorance Is Not Bliss," *Student Review* (Provo, Utah), 12 Apr. 1995, 4; "Homosexuality and the Mormon Community," *Student Review* (Provo, Utah), 12 Apr. 1995, 5; "BYU May Face Decision on Gay, but Celibate Language Professor," *Salt Lake Tribune,* 22 July 1995, C-3.

55. Borgesen, "Danish and Intermountain Sexual Attitudes," 69. These findings mirrored Nyberg's 1973 study at the University of Utah, in which 2.3 percent of 218 surveyed women reported that they had "caressed a woman's vagina." See Nyberg, "Homosexual and Homoerotic," 76. Nyberg also found that more women engaged in homoerotic activities on a regular basis than men did. Nearly 6 percent of the women reported having regular "sexual experiences with a woman," while barely 4 percent of surveyed men at the University of Utah reported having regular "sexual experiences with a man" (76–77).

56. See also James D. Weinrich and Walter L. Williams, "Strange Customs,

Familiar Lives: Homosexualities in Other Cultures," in John C. Gonsiorek and James D. Weinrich, eds., *Homosexuality: Research Implications for Public Policy* (Newbury Park, Calif.: Sage, 1991), 59.

57. Gregory M. Herek, "Beyond Homophobia: Social Psychological Perspective on Attitudes toward Lesbians and Gay Men," *Journal of Homosexuality* 10 (Fall 1984): 1–21; John Wayne Plasek and Janicemarie Allard, "Misconceptions of Homophobia," *Journal of Homosexuality* 10 (Fall 1984): 23–37; Joseph E. Aguero, Laura Bloch, and Donn Byrne, "The Relationships among Sexual Beliefs, Attitudes, Experience, and Homophobia," *Journal of Homosexuality* 10 (Fall 1984): 95–107; Thomas J. Ficarotto, "Racism, Sexism, and Erotophobia: Attitudes of Heterosexuals toward Homosexuals," *Journal of Homosexuality* 19, no. 1 (1990): 111–16; Dynes, *Encyclopedia of Homosexuality*, 1:552–55; Barbara Smith, "Homophobia: Why Bring It Up?" in R. Jeffrey Ringer, ed., *Queer Words, Queer Images: Communication and the Construction of Homosexuality* (New York: New York University Press, 1994), 99–102; Vern L. Bullough and Bonnie Bullough, *Human Sexuality: An Encyclopedia* (New York: Garland, 1994), 275–76. Other interpreters have emphasized *heterosexism* as related to homophobia, but not identical with it. Patricia Beattie Jung and Ralph F. Smith, *Heterosexism: An Ethical Challenge* (Albany: State University of New York Press, 1993), 13: "*Heterosexism* is a reasoned system of bias regarding sexual orientation. It denotes prejudice in favor of heterosexual people and connotes prejudice against bisexual and, especially, homosexual people." They add: "Heterosexism is analogous to racism and sexism. Homophobia finds appropriate analogies in racial bigotry and misogynism" (14); also Gregory M. Herek, "The Context of Antigay Violence: Notes on Cultural and Psychological Heterosexism," in Linda D. Garnets and Douglas C. Kimmel, eds., *Psychological Perspectives on Lesbian and Gay Male Experience* (New York: Columbia University Press, 1993), 89–107. Likewise "hegemonic masculinity" is part of this interpretative mix, as in Tim Carrigan, Bob Connell, and John Lee's "Hard and Heavy: Toward a New Sociology of Masculinity," in Michael Kaufman, ed., *Beyond Patriarchy: Essays by Men on Pleasure, Power, and Change* (Toronto: Oxford University Press, 1987), 166; and Annelies Knoppers's "A Critical Theory of Gender Relations," in Mary Stewart Van Leeuven, Annelies Knoppers, Margaret L. Koch, Douglas J. Schurman, and Helen M. Sterk, eds., *After Eden: Facing the Challenges of Gender Reconciliation* (Grand Rapids, Mich.: William B. Eerdmans, 1993), 249–54.

58. Shere Hite, *The Hite Report on Male Sexuality: How Men Feel about Love, Sex, and Relationships* (New York: Knopf/Random House, 1981; reprint, New York: Ballantine Books, 1990), xxviii, 36, 822; Shere Hite, *The Hite Report: A Nationwide Study on Female Sexuality* (New York: Macmillan, 1976), xxii, 278. For reasons I do not understand, Hite cited higher percent-

ages for the 3,019 women of her study. Nevertheless, the percentages of my text reflect the total of 301 women from her sample who had sexual experiences with other women, the 144 women of her sample who said they preferred sex with women, the 73 who defined themselves as bisexual, and the 84 who had sex with both men and women but did not define themselves as either lesbian or bisexual. Because the survey respondents were self-selected by their decision to participate, the Hite reports have been criticized as nonrepresentative of the general population. However, my point here is the contrast between reported sexual experience and the self-definition of those who participated in her survey. In that respect, it is irrelevant whether or not these findings are representative of the total U.S. population. Hite's findings are paralleled (at lower percentages) by Samuel S. Janus and Cynthia L. Janus, *The Janus Report on Sexual Behavior* (New York: John Wiley and Sons, 1993), 4, 69–70. In their national survey of 1,300 men from 1988 to 1992, 22 percent reported engaging in sex with another man at least once, yet only 4 percent defined themselves as homosexual and 5 percent defined themselves as bisexual. For the 1,400 surveyed women (1988–92), 17 percent reported having sex with another woman at least once, while 2 percent defined themselves as homosexual or lesbian, and 3 percent defined themselves as bisexual. Again, to me the significance of the Janus findings in this respect is not the issue of applicability to the national population but how those in the Janus study defined themselves with regard to homoerotic behaviors they had engaged in.

59. Gilbert H. Herdt, "Cross-Cultural Forms of Homosexuality and the Concept 'Gay,'" *Psychiatric Annals* 18 (Jan. 1988): 38.

60. Katz, *Gay American History*, 446.

61. Carroll Smith-Rosenberg, "The Female World of Love and Ritual: Relations between Women in Nineteenth-Century America," originally published in *Signs: Journal of Women in Culture and Society* 1 (Autumn 1975): 1–29, reprinted in Nancy F. Cott and Elizabeth H. Pleck, eds., *A Heritage of Her Own: Toward a New Social History of American Women* (New York: Simon and Schuster, 1979) and in Smith-Rosenberg, *Disorderly Conduct: Visions of Gender in Victorian America* (New York: Alfred A. Knopf, 1987); John H. Gagnon and William Simon, in *Sexual Conduct: The Social Sources of Human Sexuality* (Chicago: Aldine, 1973), 68, coined the term "homosociality, that is, a period in life when valuation of the self is more keyed to those of like gender than it is to those of opposite gender." However, Gagnon and Simon seemed to limit this to a transitional period, i.e., "the existence of a male alliance (a *homosocial* world) in early puberty" (72). Unlike Smith-Rosenberg, Gagnon and Simon did not use their term *homosociality* to describe decades-long or lifelong relationships between same-sex persons.

62. I recognize that my terms are subject to the kind of criticism that some have directed at Smith-Rosenberg's use of *homosocial*. For example, Robert

K. Martin, in *Hero, Captain, and Stranger: Male Friendship, Social Critique, and Literary Form in the Sea Novels of Herman Melville* (Chapel Hill: University of North Carolina Press, 1986), 13, described *homosocial* as "a linguistic monster, [which] seems to me best reserved, if at all, for institutions and situations. Thus prisons may be said to be homosocial institutions, but prisoners remain heterosexual or homosexual, according to their principal sexual orientation." Martin's objection seems more of a resistance to jargon no matter how useful it may be. Although it has not yet entered standard dictionaries, *homosociality* has become the standard term for describing social interaction between same-gender persons without implying that these relationships are erotic. See Jessie Bernard, "Homosociality and Female Depression," *Journal of Social Issues* 32 (Fall 1976): 213–38; Suzanna M. Rose, "Same- and Cross-Sex Friendships and the Psychology of Homosociality," *Sex Roles: A Journal of Research* 12 (Jan. 1985): 63–74; Cheris Kramarae and Paula A. Treichler, *A Feminist Dictionary* (Boston: Pandora Press, 1985), 195–96; Robert T. Francoeur, ed., *A Descriptive Dictionary and Atlas of Sexology* (New York: Greenwood Press, 1991), 283–84.

However, to turn Martin's objection on its head, he ironically suggested another useful category when he observed that some social environments allow only same-sex interaction. In such gender-segregated situations, the human dynamics are vastly different from those environments in which homosociality is simply an option, not a requirement. Therefore, I use *homoenvironmental* to describe environments in which persons have no social or sexual access to the opposite gender. See chap. 6.

63. Quite apart from cultural considerations, official LDS psychotherapists make a strict distinction between *homosexual* and *gay*. According to A. Dean Byrd, the assistant commissioner of LDS Social Services, "Homosexual refers to same-sex attraction which, in many cases, has become eroticized. Gay refers to a social, political identity." Thus, P. Scott Richards, director of counseling psychology at Brigham Young University, has written that "non-gay homosexual people . . . reject the gay or lesbian lifestyle." See A. Dean Byrd, "Interview: An LDS Reparative Therapy Approach for Male Homosexuality," *AMCAP: Journal of the Association of Mormon Counselors and Psychotherapists* 19, no. 1 (1993): 92; and P. Scott Richards, "The Treatment of Homosexuality: Some Historical, Contemporary, and Personal Perspectives," *AMCAP: Journal of the Association of Mormon Counselors and Psychotherapists* 19, no. 1 (1993): 41.

However, in matters of self-definition concerning sexuality, nothing is simple. For example, in reaction against the "stereotypes about ourselves that are just as clichéd as anything the religious right might dream up," a former activist with Queer Nation has announced: "I'm not gay." Although "for most of my adult life I have insisted on being thought of as a gay man," John Weir now writes that "I just want to say right now that I'm over it. Big deal, I'm homosexual." He explains: "I don't mean I don't still fall in love with guys, or that I wouldn't go to a gay rights demonstration if I thought it would enhance someone's civil liberties. I never said I was straight." See John Weir, "Sexual Politics: Queer and Loathing," *Details,* May 1995, 81–82.

CHAPTER 2

The Homosocial

THE HISTORIAN PETER GAY has written that nineteenth-century Britain and America "fostered, even institutionalized, the segregation of young men and women in dress, in general appearance, in clubs, in sports, at work and play—and idealized the differences. The two sexes lived distinct lives, occupied distinct spheres, seemed to have distinct natures."[1]

Mormon males associated closely with other males in the homosocial environment of the nineteenth century. They did so in priesthood quorums; as missionary companions after the publication of the Book of Mormon in 1830; in the 1833 School of the Prophets at church headquarters in Kirtland, Ohio; in the 1834 military expedition to Missouri called Zion's Camp; in the paramilitary organization called the Danites in Missouri just prior to the violent expulsion of Mormons from that state in 1838; in the Masonic lodges of the transplanted church headquarters at Nauvoo, Illinois, during the 1840s; in the Nauvoo Lyceum; in the Nauvoo Legion; in the theocratic Council of Fifty from 1844 onward; in the Utah School of the Prophets at the new Mormon headquarters, which Brigham Young established at Salt Lake City in 1847; in youth auxiliary programs; and in pioneer Utah's baseball teams.[2] As Mormonism's second president and Utah's first governor, Brigham Young was so homosocial that he preached in 1857: "There are probably but few men in the world who care about the private society of women less than I do."[3]

Likewise, Mormon females associated closely with other females socially in the charitable and educational Relief Society from 1842 onward, in cultural organizations, in female-only "testimony meetings" (often with glossolalia, or "speaking in tongues"), and sometimes in polygamy as plural wives living under one roof with their husband.[4] However, not until 1898 did unmarried Mormon women serve as full-time missionaries. Prior to then female missionaries accompanied their mission-president husbands or sometimes accompanied their husbands whose regular missionary assignments lasted as long as six years. Therefore, very few nineteenth-century women experienced LDS missionary companionship with each other.[5]

On the other hand, in the nineteenth century many of the male missionaries were married men who left the company of their wives for two or more years. For the duration of this unpaid LDS missionary service, each male missionary (whether sixteen or sixty) was expected to be sexually celibate and to remain in the constant company of a male missionary companion. Nineteenth-century Mormon leaders regarded this as a sufficient substitute for opposite-sex associations. In their view, a full-time missionary's "loneliness, homesickness, and the desire to seek the companionship of women are considerably lessened" by this male companionship.[6]

Throughout most of the nineteenth century, Mormon congregations were also segregated by gender. After he spoke to Nauvoo's citywide Sunday meeting in 1843, Mormon founder Joseph Smith criticized the fact that there were "men among women, and women among men" in the congregation.[7] In 1859, Brigham Young proclaimed the Salt Lake Tabernacle's seating arrangement as the standard for all Mormon congregations: women sitting to the north (or right) of the center aisle, and men sitting to the south (or left), with children on the front benches. That seating pattern continued for decades in LDS congregations.[8]

However, the nearly equal participation of men and women in nineteenth-century Mormon worship distinguished it from American Protestantism of the time. The virtual absence of significant male participation in Protestant congregational life resulted in what Barbara Welter called "the feminization of American religion," which included the same-sex character of Protestant voluntary work during the nineteenth century.[9] By contrast Mormon congregations in the American West were about equally divided between participating men and women, even if they were segregated by gender.

Despite all the structures and encouragement for homosociality in nineteenth-century Mormon culture, some faithful Mormons lived in social isolation. For example, the diary of Henri Edouard Desaules from

1882 to 1892 is a testament of the abject solitude an LDS bachelor could experience in Mormon Utah.[10] Completely fluent in English, this Swiss convert chose to isolate himself from everybody else in the small Mormon communities in which he lived. Friendly married couples and pairs of single women of the community occasionally visited him. He expressed his appreciation of this in his diary, but did not return their visits. After declining to attend every community social and celebration for nine years, the fifty-seven-year-old Desaules went to the Utah pioneer day celebration on 24 July 1891: "I staid but a little while & then went back home, to rest and read."

Aside from LDS meetings, Desaules associated with other men only in his business as a carpenter. He wrote on 5 February 1889 that these men were "friends only in so far as they require my help." There was one man whom Desaules called "friend," yet they saw each other only once during these ten years when the man with his wife and children visited Desaules. Otherwise, the two men corresponded sporadically with each other. The bachelor went to the home of an elderly widower on Christmas day of 1889, but merely because the man had first "brought me some pies and cake." That night Desaules wrote: "Except the visit of Father Syrett I have not seen a soul all day. I feel at times wretched and unhappy. May the Good Lord Father in Heaven pity me a little. I have not, I feel, a single friend in the whole world but Him to look to. Yet at times I feel very despondent." However, a week later, on New Year's Eve, he acknowledged that his loneliness was "more of my fault than otherwise."

Not surprisingly, Desaules experienced sexual tension in late nineteenth-century Utah. On 4 July 1885, at age fifty-one, he complained that he had "tried over and over again to overcome" masturbation since he was fourteen, but had "never been able to be fifteen days without succumbing to it." A week later he wrote: "Ellen Mar McCullough kissed me, but would not let me kiss her again."[11] During the ten years of his extant diary, he referred only once (5 February 1889) to the possibility that he might marry, and then only in the context that such an event would prevent him from traveling to visit his niece.

Desaules did not indicate the gender involved when he wrote that he "lay awake early dreaming lasciviously," but did specify in June 1884 that this occurred while he was reading a boy's magazine, *Youth's Companion*. Whatever his sexual orientation, Desaules complained that people in his Mormon community circulated "hidden slurs & innuendoes" about him. "I have not got very clear conscience," this faithful Mormon bachelor wrote at age fifty-eight concerning masturbation: "it is very hard to break off bad habits."[12] Still socially isolated, Henri Edouard Desaules died at age seventy as an exception to the homosocial attachments and activities of nineteenth-century Mormons—both female and male, married and unmarried.[13]

Homosociality in American and Mormon culture was a widespread phenomenon in the nineteenth century and rarely involved homoerotic interest or desire. However, contrary to currently popular assumptions, there was also an early American subculture of people who interacted socially because they shared an erotic interest in persons of their same gender.[14] For example, an American physician wrote in 1889 that there was "in every community of any size a colony of male sexual perverts; they are usually known to each other, and are likely to congregate together."[15] At the turn of the century, Salt Lake City not only had such a "colony," or subculture, of self-defined gay men but it also had a similar group of self-defined lesbians.

The Mormon capital even had a club that provided a social haven for those who regarded themselves as gay men and lesbians, according to the definitions of their time. During her attendance at Westminster College in Salt Lake City from 1916 to 1922, lesbian Mildred J. Berryman (b. 1901) began a sociological study of lesbians and gay males in her acquaintance. She ended the study in 1938.[16] Many of these thirty-three persons were members of the Salt Lake Bohemian Club "with which many of the homosexuals in the city, male and female, had some affiliation," and many of them were born in the nineteenth century.[17] Her study probably did not include the Bohemian Club's total membership during that time period, since her case studies included so few gay men as compared with the number of lesbians. That study's author was a Utah photographer with a lesbian lover also of Mormon background. Berryman received her LDS patriarchal blessing (a lengthy pronouncement about one's present and future life) in 1921, after she had begun this study.[18]

Rocky O'Donovan, a contemporary researcher of Utah's lesbian and gay history, dates the beginning of this homosexually oriented Salt Lake Bohemian Club as early as 1886. In October of that year, its published purpose was to "furnish instruction and entertainment for the young men of this city."[19] In the religiously polarized Utah of that year, the roster of officers and committee members shows that Utah's Bohemian Club was originally restricted to men who were either non-Mormons, anti-Mormons, or LDS apostates. The club's members were both married and unmarried.[20] Without the kind of verification that Berryman's study later provided, it is difficult to determine whether Salt Lake City's Bohemian Club provided a social haven for self-defined gay men as early as 1886. However, this Utah club of men owed its name to San Francisco's famous all-male Bohemian Club, whose annual publications during this time celebrated the presence of "slender young Bohemians, clad in economical bathing suits" at the secret retreats of the San Francisco Bohemians by the Russian River.[21]

At its legal incorporation as "a social club" in November 1891, the Salt Lake Bohemian Club became gender inclusive and its central figure was Katherine Young Schweitzer. She was a granddaughter of Brigham Young, the sister of one of the male incorporators, the wife of one of the other incorporators, and the sister-in-law of another. Katherine personally paid for all but $50 worth of the $10,000 in capital shares of Bohemian Club stock. However, she remained only a director, while her husband was president. Her sister's husband, William W. Macintosh, was also a director. In view of the Bohemian Club's later history, its married officers may have provided a heterosexual cover for the club's unmarried members. Katherine's twenty-year-old brother Bryant S. Young was a director and never married. Two other directors, forty-one-year-old Isaac "Ike" Woolf and his brother Simon, also remained bachelors. Katherine's husband, Henry, and the Woolf brothers were Jewish, while Katherine and her brother were Mormons, and Macintosh was apparently Protestant.[22] With this incorporation, Utah's Bohemian Club ceased being a male-only club of anti-Mormons. Despite their prominent Mormon origins, the female and male leaders of Utah's Bohemian Club were not closely identified with the LDS Church in 1891.

Within fifteen years, some prominent Mormon members of the Bohemian Club associated themselves publicly with the organization. In the 1905 *Salt Lake City Directory* Willard E. Weihe announced himself as president of the Bohemians, with Calvin S. Carrington as vice president, Willard J. Flashman as treasurer, and Henry Klenke as secretary.[23] Forty-nine-year-old Weihe had been the violin soloist for the Mormon Tabernacle Choir since the 1880s. When he was publicly listed as president of the Bohemian Club, Weihe had been married twenty-nine years, had no children, and was apparently not very close to his wife. At Weihe's death, the *Deseret News* published two long articles that made no mention of his marriage or his wife.[24] Twenty-year-old Flashman was a Mormon founder of the Salt Lake Philharmonic Orchestra, married a year after this listing as a Bohemian officer, and fathered two children. Still unmarried in 1905 at age thirty-five, Klenke was director of the Utah State Band and defined himself as the domestic "partner" of the two-years-older male musician with whom he lived. However, Klenke also later married and fathered two children.[25]

The Bohemian's vice president in 1905 was the forty-three-year-old son of Mormon apostle Albert Carrington. After the death of his wife in 1897, Calvin S. Carrington remained unmarried until his own death thirty-three years later. From 1900 until after 1903, Carrington lived with a former bartender of his same age. It is unknown, however, if Carrington was living with another man in 1905.[26] By 1905 the leadership of Utah's Bohemian Club had shifted from primarily married descendants of Brigham Young to nineteenth-century musicians—several of whom were living with same-sex partners.

The same 1905 city directory also announced the organization of the Athenian Bachelors' Club, whose name echoed popular conceptions of Greek homosexuality.[27] Its officers were between nineteen and twenty-eight years old. Half were students and half were newspaper carriers. These Mormon bachelors met weekly, and the organization joined once a month with its "ladies' auxiliary." Most of these men later married and fathered several children each.[28] It is possible that no self-defined gay men were members of the Athenian Bachelors' Club, but the organization was typical of the many homosocial fraternities, sororities, and gender-exclusive clubs to which nineteenth-century Americans and Utahns belonged.[29]

For example, in 1905, Salt Lake City's women belonged to at least twelve gender-exclusive, secular organizations. These were the Cleophan Society, Daughters of the American Revolution of Utah, Gamma Phi, James B. McKean Women's Relief Corps No. 1 and George R. Maxwell Women's Relief Corps No. 3 of the Grand Army of the Republic, Ladies Aid Society, Ladies Literary Club, Reapers' Club, Utah Federation of Women's Clubs, Utah State Mother's Assembly, Utah Women's Press Club, Women's Christian Temperance Union, Women's Club, and the Ladies' Auxiliary of the Young Men's Christian Association.[30]

For men, the *Salt Lake City Directory, 1905* listed twenty-four gender-exclusive organizations, aside from the separately listed secret societies. These male-only clubs and societies were the Alta Club, Amici Fidessimi Fraternity, Athenian Bachelors' Club, Cambrian Association of Salt Lake City, Commercial Club, Delta Sigma, Exchange Club, Franklin Club, Grand Army of the Republic, Norden Literary Society, Original Order of Owls, Salt Lake Caledonian Club, Salt Lake Horticultural Society, Salt Lake Rifle Association, Salt Lake Sportmen's Club, Shamrock Athletic Club, Thistle Club, University Club, Utah Sons of the American Revolution, Varsity Club, Young Men's Christian Association, Young Men's Democratic Club, Young Men's League of Westminster Church, and Young Men's Republican Club.

By 1908, leadership of the Salt Lake Bohemians had shifted to still another group. As were the Bohemian officers in 1891 and 1905, Louis C. Shaw Jr. was related to a former general authority of the LDS Church.[31] He was a grandnephew of First Presidency Counselor George Q. Cannon. None of these new leaders were professional musicians; all worked in clerical positions. Unlike the primarily middle-aged Bohemian officers of the past, the 1908 leaders were between twenty and twenty-six years old. All later married, but the twenty-year-old waited until he was fifty-seven to do so. In the last publicized description of the Bohemian Club its meeting place was the Constitution Building in downtown Salt Lake City.[32] These were also the last nineteenth-century Mormons specifically identified as leaders of the Salt Lake Bohemian Club.

In addition, among the 1908 officers there was one significant continuation of the musical affiliation of the Bohemian officers three years earlier. Club president Louis Shaw had been in the Male Glee Club at the LDS high school of Salt Lake City while Evan Stephens was the music teacher there. Stephens was also director of the Mormon Tabernacle Choir. The middle-aged Stephens had a lifelong pattern of falling in love with teenage male singers who then became his bedmates. Unlike Tabernacle Choir violinist Weihe, Stephens never publicly affiliated with the Bohemian Club. However, less than a year after seventeen-year-old Shaw joined the Glee Club, Stephens announced a same-sex love song to an assembly of the LDS high school in which Stephens invited his unnamed "friend" to "conspire" and rebel against "the established order," which made it difficult to "love if we dared to do so." In 1904, another LDS high school student began living with Stephens, and the young man was still sharing the Tabernacle Choir director's bed when Shaw became president of the Bohemian Club of Salt Lake City in 1908.[33]

By the time Mildred Berryman began her study a decade later, the Bohemian Club was no longer a public enterprise, even though many of her one hundred gay and lesbian friends were members.[34] This suggests that after 1908 the discussions and social interaction at the Bohemian Club's meetings became more obviously homosexual. Thus, there were disadvantages to advertising the meeting place of Salt Lake City's Bohemians. Likewise, during the years of the Bohemian Club's high profile, some of its participants had no homosexual interests, having discovered it through the city directories rather than through a homosexual network. Unfortunately, there are no known details about this transition in Salt Lake City's Bohemian Club, which continued to 1942.[35]

However, there are significant details about the marital status of Utah's Bohemians. In Mildred Berryman's study, six self-defined lesbians had been married (25 percent of the study's women), and two continued to live with their husbands. Of the nine self-defined gay men in her study, only one (11.1 percent) had been married, yet two gay men planned to marry women. Thus, one-third of the gay men in her study had either married or planned to marry women.[36]

Therefore, Utah's Bohemian Club demonstrates again that marital status is an inconclusive way to identify either heterosexuals or self-defined homosexuals. As John D. Wrathall writes:

> Marriage, even "happy" marriage (however we choose to define "happy"), is not proof that homoeroticism did not play an important and dynamic role in a person's relationships with members of the same sex. Nor is evidence of strong homoerotic attachments proof that a man's marriage was a sham or that a man was incapable of marriage. It is clear, however, that while strong feelings toward members of both sexes can co-exist, the way in which such feelings are embodied and acted out is strongly determined by culture.

He adds that lifelong bachelorhood also "should not be interpreted as a suggestion that these men were 'gay,' any more than marriage allows us to assume that they were 'heterosexual.'"[37] Nevertheless, because marital status is a significant dimension of one's adult life, this study indicates the marital status of persons mentioned in discussions of same-sex dynamics.

NOTES

1. Peter Gay, *The Bourgeois Experience: Victoria to Freud,* vol. 2, *The Tender Passion* (New York: Oxford University Press, 1986), 215; see also Nancy F. Cott, *The Bonds of Womanhood: "Woman's Sphere" in New England, 1780–1835* (New Haven: Yale University Press, 1977).

2. Leon M. Strong, "A History of the Young Men's Mutual Improvement Association, 1877–1938" (M.S. thesis, Brigham Young University, 1939); Klaus J. Hansen, *Quest for Empire: The Political Kingdom of God and the Council of Fifty in Mormon History* (East Lansing: Michigan State University Press, 1967); Warren A. Jennings, "The Army of Israel Marches into Missouri," *Missouri Historical Review* 62 (Jan. 1968): 107–35; John R. Patrick, "The School of the Prophets: Its Development and Influence in Utah Territory" (M.A. thesis, Brigham Young University, 1970); Kenneth W. Godfrey, "Joseph Smith and the Masons," *Journal of the Illinois State Historical Society* 64 (Spring 1971): 79–90; Peter Crawley and Richard L. Anderson, "The Political and Social Realities of Zion's Camp," *Brigham Young University Studies* 14 (Summer 1974): 406–20; Leland H. Gentry, "The Danite Band of 1838," *Brigham Young University Studies* 14 (Summer 1974): 421–50; Thurmon Dean Moody, "Nauvoo's Whistling and Whittling Brigade," *Brigham Young University Studies* 15 (Summer 1975): 480–90; Stanley B. Kimball, "Zion's Camp March from Ohio to Missouri," *Ensign* 9 (Apr. 1979): 45–49; D. Michael Quinn, "The Council of Fifty and Its Members, 1844 to 1945," *Brigham Young University Studies* 20 (Winter 1980): 163–97; Andrew F. Ehat, "'It Seems like Heaven Began on Earth': Joseph Smith and the Constitution of the Kingdom of God," *Brigham Young University Studies* 20 (Spring 1980): 253–79; William P. McIntire Minute Book of the Nauvoo Lyceum (1841–42), in Andrew F. Ehat and Lyndon W. Cook, eds., *The Words of Joseph Smith: The Contemporary Accounts of the Nauvoo Discourses of the Prophet Joseph* (Provo, Utah: Religious Studies Center, Brigham Young University, 1980); Milton V. Backman Jr., *The Heavens Resound: A History of the Latter-day Saints in Ohio, 1830–1838* (Salt Lake City: Deseret Book, 1983), 264–68; Kenneth L. Cannon II, "Deserets, Red Stockings, and Out-of-Towners: Baseball Comes of Age in Salt Lake City, 1877–79," *Utah Historical Quarterly* 52 (Fall 1984): 136–57; Roger Launius, *Zion's Camp: Expedition to Missouri, 1834* (Independence, Mo.: Herald, 1984); John E. Thompson, "A Chronology of Danite Meetings in Adam-ondi-Ahman, Missouri, July to September, 1838," *Restoration* 4 (Jan. 1985): 12; Stephen C. LeSueur, *The 1838 Mormon War in Missouri* (Columbia: University of Missouri Press, 1987); Bruce A. VanOrden, "Zion's Camp: A Refiner's Fire," in Larry C. Porter and Susan Easton Black, eds., *The Prophet Joseph: Essays on the Life and Mission of Joseph Smith* (Salt Lake City: De-

seret Book, 1988), 192–207; George W. Givens, *In Old Nauvoo: Everyday Life in the City of Joseph* (Salt Lake City: Deseret Book, 1990), 170.

3. *Journal of Discourses,* 26 vols. (Liverpool, England: Latter-day Saints Book Depot, 1854–86), 5:99 (Young/1857). In a later sermon, Young said: "Ever since I knew that my mother was a woman I have loved the sex." See *Journal of Discourses,* 12:194 (Young/1868); see also the discussion of Young's emotional distance from women in chap. 4.

4. Susa Young Gates, *History of the Young Ladies Mutual Improvement Association* (Salt Lake City: Deseret News, 1911); Marba C. Josephson, *History of the YWMIA* (Salt Lake City: Young Women's Mutual Improvement Association of the Church of Jesus Christ of Latter-day Saints, 1955); Chris Rigby Arrington, "The Finest of Fabrics: Mormon Women and the Silk Industry in Early Utah," *Utah Historical Quarterly* 46 (Fall 1978): 376–96; Jill Mulvay Derr and Ann Vest Lobb, "Women in Early Utah," in Richard D. Poll, Thomas G. Alexander, Eugene E. Campbell, and David E. Miller, eds., *Utah's History* (Provo, Utah: Brigham Young University Press, 1978); Carol Cornwall Madsen and Susan Staker Oman, *Sisters and Little Saints: One Hundred Years of Primary* (Salt Lake City: Deseret Book, 1979); Carol Cornwall Madsen, "Mormon Women and the Struggle for Definition: The Nineteenth Century Church," *Sunstone* 6 (Nov.–Dec. 1981): 7–11, reprinted in *Dialogue: A Journal of Mormon Thought* 14 (Winter 1981): 40–47; Maureen Ursenbach Beecher, "The 'Leading Sisters': A Female Hierarchy in Nineteenth Century Mormon Society," *Journal of Mormon History* 9 (1982): 25–39; Linda Thatcher and John R. Sillito, "'Sisterhood and Sociability': The Utah Women's Press Club, 1891–1928," *Utah Historical Quarterly* 53 (Spring 1985): 144–56; Jill Mulvay Derr, "'Strength in Our Union': The Making of Mormon Sisterhood," in Maureen Ursenbach Beecher and Lavina Fielding Anderson, eds., *Sisters in the Spirit: Mormon Women in Historical and Cultural Perspective* (Urbana: University of Illinois Press, 1987), 153–207; Jessie L. Embry, *Mormon Polygamous Families: Life in the Principle* (Salt Lake City: University of Utah Press, 1987); Leonard J. Arrington, "Modern Lysistratas: Mormon Women in the International Peace Movement," *Journal of Mormon History* 15 (1989): 89–104; Jill Mulvay Derr, Janath D. Cannon, and Maureen Ursenbach Beecher, *Women of Covenant: The Story of Relief Society* (Salt Lake City: Deseret Book, 1992).

5. Andrew Jenson, *Church Chronology: A Record of Important Events Pertaining to the History of the Church of Jesus Christ of Latter-day Saints,* 2d ed., rev. (Salt Lake City: Deseret News, 1914), for 21 Apr. 1898; Calvin S. Kunz, "A History of Female Missionary Activity in the Church of Jesus Christ of Latter-day Saints, 1830–1898" (M.A. thesis, Brigham Young University, 1976); Diane Mangum, "The First Sister Missionaries," *Ensign* 10 (July 1980): 62–65; Maxine Hanks, "Sister Missionaries and Authority," in Hanks, ed.,

Women and Authority: Re-Emerging Mormon Feminism (Salt Lake City: Signature Books, 1992), 315–34.

6. Heber J. Grant, J. Reuben Clark, David O. McKay, the First Presidency of the Church of Jesus Christ of Latter-day Saints, *The Missionary's Hand Book* (Independence, Mo.: Zion's Printing and Publishing, 1937), 16, for the requirement of celibacy, quotation from 26. These instructions emphasized only men, despite the existence of female missionaries. For the role of married men as missionaries in the nineteenth century, see James B. Allen and Glen M. Leonard, *The Story of the Latter-day Saints,* 2d ed., rev. (Salt Lake City: Deseret Book, 1992), 390; Daniel H. Ludlow, ed., *Encyclopedia of Mormonism: The History, Scripture, Doctrine, and Procedure of the Church of Jesus Christ of Latter-day Saints,* 5 vols. (New York: Macmillan, 1992), 2:911, 918.

7. Brigham H. Roberts, ed., *History of the Church of Jesus Christ of Latter-day Saints,* 7 vols., 2d ed., rev. (Salt Lake City: Deseret Book, 1978), 6:34.

8. Hosea Stout diary, 2 Jan. 1859, in Juanita Brooks, ed., *On the Mormon Frontier: The Diary of Hosea Stout, 1844–1861,* 2 vols. (Salt Lake City: University of Utah Press, 1964), 2:675, 675n44.

9. Barbara Welter, "The Feminization of American Religion, 1800–1860," in Mary S. Hartman and Lois Banner, eds., *Clio's Consciousness Raised: New Perspectives on the History of Women* (New York: Harper Colophon Books, 1974), 137–57, which acknowledged (149–50) the LDS Church as an exception to this pattern; Ann Douglas, *The Feminization of American Culture* (New York: Alfred A. Knopf, 1977), 98; Betty A. DeBerg, *Ungodly Women: Gender and the First Wave of American Fundamentalism* (Minneapolis: Fortress Press, 1990), 20–21.

10. Jeffery Ogden Johnson, in "On the Edge: Mormonism's Single Men," *Dialogue: A Journal of Mormon Thought* 16 (Autumn 1983): 54–55, referred to the experience of Desaules (b. 27 Oct. 1833); my citations here are from the Henri Edouard Desaules diary (7 Jan. 1882–18 Dec. 1892), Archives, Historical Department of the Church of Jesus Christ of Latter-day Saints, Salt Lake City, Utah.

11. Johnson, in "On the Edge," 55, also quoted these passages from the diary about the "solitary vice" and McCullough.

12. Desaules diary, 20 June 1884, 4 July 1886, "May 1890" (actually 1892).

13. Johnson, "On the Edge," and Lavina Fielding Anderson, "Ministering Angels: Single Women in Mormon Society," *Dialogue: A Journal of Mormon Thought* 16 (Autumn 1983): 48–58, 59–72.

14. George Chauncey, in *Gay New York: Gender, Urban Culture, and the Making of the Gay Male World, 1890–1940* (New York: Basic Books/HarperCollins, 1994), 2, observes that the currently popular "*myth of isolation* holds that anti-gay hostility prevented the development of an extensive gay subculture and forced gay men to lead solitary lives in the decades before the

rise of the gay liberation movement" at New York City's Stonewall Bar in 1969, as examined in Martin Duberman, *Stonewall* (New York: Dutton

15. G. Frank Lydston, "Sexual Perversion, Satyriasis, and Nymp *Medical and Surgical Reporter* 61 (7 Sept. 1889): 254, quoted in Bullough, *Sexual Variance in Society and History* (New York: John Wiley and Sons, 1976), 590.

16. Vern Bullough and Bonnie Bullough, "Lesbianism in the 1920s and 1930s: A Newfound Study," *Signs: Journal of Women In Culture and Society* 2 (Summer 1977): 896, wrote: "The author of the manuscript, M. B., had been gathering data for some twenty years. She had started the project as an honor's thesis while in college, had been discouraged from pursuing it by her adviser, but nonetheless had continued to gather data." Mildred Berryman enrolled as a first-year student at Westminster College on 11 October 1916 at age fifteen and continued at Westminster until her final year as a "special" student in 1921–22. Because Westminster had no formal graduate program, its graduate students had the designation "special." See statement of Helen Olpin, Alumni Coordinator, Westminster College, photocopy in "History—Utah" Folder, Vertical Files, Library, Stonewall Center, Salt Lake City, Utah; *Westminster College Bulletin* 3 (May 1917): 51; *Westminster College Bulletin* 8 (May 1922): 51. Berryman's original study is "The Psychological Phenomena of the Homosexual," rough-typed on the back of stationery of the American Red Cross, Salt Lake City, Utah, with the last page of the study dated 13 November 1938, in the June Mazer Lesbian Collection, West Hollywood, California. See chap. 7 for my analysis of her study's findings and notes 3 and 5 of that chapter for a detailed discussion of the question about dating the start of Berryman's study.

17. Bullough and Bullough, "Lesbianism in the 1920s and 1930s," 896. Berryman's study itself does not refer to the Bohemian Club in any way, but the Bulloughs obtained that information through their personal contact with her during the decades Berryman was living with Bonnie Bullough's mother. Vern Bullough specifically identified the homosexually oriented club cited in their article as the Salt Lake Bohemian Club in an interview with Rocky O'Donovan on 26 Aug. [1989], "History—Utah" Folder, Stonewall Center. O'Donovan donated the materials in this Stonewall Center file about lesbian and gay history in Utah. He summarized both the club and Berryman's study in "Historian's Research Aimed at Learning about Living in Utah," *Salt Lake Tribune*, 5 May 1990, A-10.

18. Bullough and Bullough, in "Lesbianism in the 1920s and 1930s," 896–97, identified the study's author as a woman named "M.B." who was a Salt Lake City photographer and who entered into a lesbian relationship with "the mother of one of the authors of this present paper (B.B.) . . . and moved to a small town outside Salt Lake City." Concerning the manuscript study of les-

bianism in the 1920s, the authors noted that "when M.B. died (at the age of seventy-two), the manuscript arrived in our mail, complete with summaries of her interviews, most of them over forty years old" (898). Also see chap. 7, notes 3 and 5 for discussion of the year Berryman began this study.

As of the 1917 city directory, Mildred J. Berryman (b. 22 Sept. 1901; d. 7 Nov. 1972) was living with her father and her photographer brother, but she was listed as a photographer herself only from 1928 through 1942. As female case number 23 (page 61) in her study, Berryman said that she married twice briefly (first at age sixteen, ca. 1917–18, and then at age twenty or twenty-one, ca. 1921–22). However, there is no record of a marriage for Mildred Berryman in LDS genealogical records, in the Salt Lake County Marriage License Index (1914–28), Family History Library of the Church of Jesus Christ of Latter-day Saints, Salt Lake City, Utah (hereafter LDS Family History Library), in her attendance records at Westminster College, or in her obituary. See *Westminster College Bulletin* 3 (May 1917): 51; *Salt Lake City Directory, 1917* (Salt Lake City: R. L. Polk, 1917), 121; *Westminster College Bulletin* 8 (May 1922): 51; *Salt Lake City Directory, 1928* (Salt Lake City: R. L. Polk, 1928), 246; *Salt Lake City Directory, 1942* (Salt Lake City: R. L. Polk, 1942), 98; and Berryman's obituary in *Deseret News*, 8 Nov. 1972, E-4.

Bonnie Bullough's mother was Ruth Uckerman (b. 7 Oct. 1909; md. Francis E. Larsen in 1926, with child Bonnie; divorced in 1928; md. Harry I. Dempsey in 1929, with two children; separated in 1942 after which she lived as Mildred Berryman's lover). See entries for Berryman and Uckerman in LDS Patriarchal Blessing Index (1833–1963); for Andrew Uckerman family (including Ruth) in 1914 LDS Church Census of Beaver West Ward, Utah, and (including Ruth) in 1920 LDS Church Census of Beaver West Ward; for Ruth Uckerman and Francis Larsen in Salt Lake County Marriage License Index for 1926; for Ruth Uckerman in Beaver West Ward membership record (early to 1945), 389; for Ruth Uckerman in Delta First Ward membership record (1924–41), 790; for Ruth Uckerman in Manti Center Ward membership record (1923–41), 1021; for Ruth "Ockerman" Dempsey in 1935 LDS Church Census for Fort Wayne, Indiana; and for unexplained "Harry Dempsey Family" in 1940 LDS Census entry for an Uckerman family in Manti North Ward, all in LDS Family History Library; see also Vern L. Bullough to D. Michael Quinn, 22 Aug. 1995, page 4 for the Berryman-Uckerman relationship in the 1940s and his reason for denying Uckerman's Mormon background: "Bonnie's mother was also not a Mormon although she certainly was born one and was raised one until she abandoned the church at 18 when she got her divorce" (1). See chap. 7, notes 5, 6, 11, and 17 for further affirmations and denials by the Bulloughs as of 1995.

Midway through her study, Mildred Berryman's lover was Edith Mary Chapman, a school teacher who was sixteen years older than Mildred. A year or two before she ended the study in 1938, Berryman began a relationship with female case 24, a woman twelve years younger than Mildred. Berryman's only reference to this woman's occupation was that she "has aspirations to an operatic career" (63). However, Bullough and Bullough in "Lesbianism in the 1920s and 1930s: A Newfound Study," 897, 898, claimed that she was a "young social worker." Four years after Berryman concluded the study, she began a thirty-year relationship with Ruth Uckerman, eight years her junior. Chapman and Uckerman were of Mormon background, and Berryman's unidentified second lover was probably also.

Ruth Uckerman was not one of the women Berryman met in Salt Lake City and described in her study. Uckerman lived hundreds of miles away in Delta, Utah, with her parents until 1925, then with her first husband in equally distant Manti, Utah, until 1928, then with her family in Manti until 1929, and then with her second husband in Indiana until after Berryman ended her study. The two women met in 1942 after Ruth Uckerman Dempsey had returned to Utah with her second husband and children. For Berryman's relationship with Edith Chapman, see chap. 6.

19. "The Bohemian Club," *Salt Lake Tribune*, 28 Oct. 1886, [4]; "Historian's Research," A-10; Rocky O'Donovan, "Utah Gay and Lesbian History," official audiotape of paper presented at Conference on Sexuality and Homosexuality, 24 Apr. 1993, University of Utah; Rocky O'Donovan, "Historical Highlights of Mormon Attitudes toward Homosexuality," entry for 1886–1942, typed document in Utah State Historical Society, Salt Lake City. According to "City and Neighborhood," *Salt Lake Tribune*, 27 Oct. 1886, [4], the Bohemian Club first organized on that date.

I am not aware of the sources O'Donovan used for the 1880s history of the homosexually oriented Bohemian Club in Salt Lake City. However, he is mistaken in identifying the lawyer Harry Edwards as the founder of an 1886 social group of gays in Utah. The only Utah lawyer by that name was Harry C. Edwards, who married in 1888, "moved to Utah in 1890," and was not admitted to the practice of law until 1891, according to C. C. Goodwin, *History of the Bench and Bar of Utah* (Salt Lake City: Interstate Press Association, 1913), 132. Harry C. Edwards, the lawyer, did not appear in available city directories through 1893, but was listed in *Salt Lake City Directory, 1896* (Salt Lake City: R. L. Polk, 1896), 275.

The Harry Edwards who did live in Salt Lake City during 1886–93 was Harry E. Edwards, an "artist," bartender, and liquor dealer. See *Salt Lake City Directory, for the Year Commencing August 1, 1885* (New York: U.S. Directory, 1885), 128; *Salt Lake City Business Directory, 1885–86* (Salt Lake City: George A. Crofutt, 1885), 63; *Utah Gazetteer and Directory of Salt Lake, Ogden, Provo, and Logan Cities, for 1888* (Salt Lake City: Lorenzo Stenhouse, 1888), 131; *Salt Lake City Directory for 1889* (Salt Lake City: Kelly, 1889),

66; *Utah Gazetteer . . . 1892–93* (Salt Lake City: Stenhouse, 1892), 276. It is possible that O'Donovan confused the two men named Harry Edwards. Also, Edwards was not among the many officers and committeemen of the exclusively male Bohemian Club that publicly organized in Salt Lake City during 1886. See note 20. This small correction aside, O'Donovan's contributions to gay and lesbian Utah history cannot be overstated. See "Historian's Research," A-10.

20. "The Bohemians," *Salt Lake Tribune*, 2 Nov. 1886, [4], which listed fifteen of the twenty-two total members as follows: officers M. S. Pendergast, William Nelson (editor of the anti-Mormon *Salt Lake Tribune* and former U.S. marshal), Robert J. Hilton, Alma H. Winn, William C. Browe (U.S. postmaster of Salt Lake City), Arthur L. Thomas (secretary and later governor of Utah), John A. Marshall (attorney and later probate judge), S. C. Nash, R. L. Scannell, and committeemen Charles L. Stevenson (U.S. mineral surveyor), Bolivar Roberts Jr. (prominent member of the anti-Mormon Liberal party), Harry T. Duke (Salt Lake City treasurer in the non-Mormon administration of the city), John M. Zane (son of a federally appointed judge in Utah), H. P. Mason, and Joseph Oberndorfer (member of the local Jewish congregation). In addition, Edward Pike was listed as a Bohemian in "City and Neighborhood," *Salt Lake Tribune*, 30 Oct. 1886, [4]. For their backgrounds, see *Salt Lake City Directory, Aug. 1, 1885; The Annual Message of the Mayor with the Annual Reports of the Officers of Salt Lake City, Utah, for the Year 1892* (Salt Lake City: Salt Lake Lithographing, 1893), 6; Goodwin, *History of the Bench and Bar of Utah*, 173–74; Orson F. Whitney, *History of Utah*, 4 vols. (Salt Lake City: George Q. Cannon and Sons, 1892–1904), 3:23; Jenson, *Church Chronology*, 5 Feb. 1886, 13 May 1886, 15 Mar. 1887, 16 Feb. 1888, 6 May 1889, 11 Mar. 1904; O. N. Malmquist, *The First 100 Years: A History of the Salt Lake Tribune, 1871–1971* (Salt Lake City: Utah State Historical Society, 1971), 125, 245; Minutes of the Board of Directors of Congregation B'nai Israel, Salt Lake City, Utah (1881–89), 154, film A-859, Utah State Historical Society.

21. Quoted in Mary W. Blanchard, "Boundaries and the Victorian Body: Aesthetic Fashion in Gilded Age America," *American Historical Review* 100 (Feb. 1995): 38; see also Marjorie Garber, *Vested Interests: Cross-Dressing and Cultural Anxiety* (New York: Routledge, 1992), 66; Kevin Starr, *Americans and the California Dream, 1850–1915* (New York: Oxford University Press, 1973), 246–47.

22. Incorporation documents executed by H[enry]. B. Schweitzer, K[atherine]. Y. Schweitzer, "Ike" Woolf, Simon Woolf, B[ryant]. S. Young, W[illiam]. W. "Mackintosh" as incorporators, and L[ouis]. Schweitzer and L[eopold]. Schweitzer as witnesses for the Bohemian Club, filed 9 Nov. 1891, file 832, Corporation Records, Salt Lake County Clerk, Utah State Archives, Salt Lake City, Utah; *Utah Gazetteer . . . 1892–3* (Salt Lake City: Stenhouse,

1892), 486, 632, 769, 775; Susa Young Gates and Mabel Young Sanborn, "Brigham Young Genealogy," *Utah Genealogical and Historical Magazine* 12 (Jan. 1921): 31; entry for William Wallace Macintosh (b. 15 Mar. 1858; proxy LDS baptism after death) in Ancestral File, LDS Family History Library (hereafter LDS Ancestral File); entry for Ike Woolf (b. May 1850) in U.S. 1900 Census of Salt Lake City, Salt Lake County, Utah, microfilm, LDS Family History Library. This unmarried Ike Woolf was different from the Isaac Woolf (b. Feb. 1841) who was a married Mormon also in Utah's 1900 census and in *An Index of the Descendants of John Anthony Woolf and Sarah Ann Devoe* (n.p.: Woolf Family Organization, n.d.), 181–82. Like his brother Ike, Simon Woolf was a member of Salt Lake City's Congregation B'nai Israel and was listed without a wife in meetings in which other men were listed with their wives. Katherine's husband, Henry B. Schweitzer, did not join the Jewish congregation, but his brother Louis did. See Minutes of the Board of Directors of Congregation B'nai Israel, Salt Lake City, Utah (1881–89), 64, 75, 183.

23. *Salt Lake City Directory, 1905* (Salt Lake City: R. L. Polk, 1905), 79. I have found no reference to the Bohemian Club in Utah documents from 1891 to 1905. It was not in the listing of social clubs in the annual city directories until 1905, and Katherine Young Schweitzer was last listed as a city resident in *Salt Lake City Directory, 1897* (Salt Lake City: R. L. Polk, 1897), 582.

24. J. Spencer Cornwall, *A Century of Singing: The Salt Lake Mormon Tabernacle Choir* (Salt Lake City: Deseret Book, 1958), 59, 65, 72, 77; "Tabernacle Choir in Readiness for Tour of Eastern States," *Deseret Evening News,* 21 Oct. 1911, sect. 3, p. 1; photo of "Willard E. Weihe: Solo Violinist with Tabernacle Choir," *Improvement Era* 47 (Dec. 1912): 693; also Weihe's biographies in *Men of Affairs in the State of Utah: A Newspaper Reference Work* (Salt Lake City: Press Club of Salt Lake, 1914), [241]; Anthon H. Lund, Andrew Jenson, J. M. Sjodahl, and C. A. F. Orlob, eds., *Scandinavian Jubilee Album: 1850–1900* (Salt Lake City: Deseret News Press, 1913), 234; W. E. Ellsworth, *Musicians: Comprising Photogravures and Biographies of Prominent Utah Musicians* (Salt Lake City: Magazine Printing, 1917), 26; "Prof. Weihe to Be Buried Today," *Deseret News,* 7 June 1926, sect. 2, p. 1; "Hundreds Honor Willard E. Weihe," *Deseret News,* 8 June 1926, sect. 2, p. 1; and entry for Willard E. Weihe (b. 17 Oct. 1856; md. 1876, no children; d. 1926) in LDS Ancestral File.

25. Entries for Willard J. Flashman (b. 20 Aug. 1885; md. 1906; d. 1943) in LDS Ancestral File, in International Genealogical Index, LDS Family History Library, and his obituary in *Deseret News,* 12 July 1944, 14. Flashman and Weihe were in the LDS Church census for 1914, LDS Family History Library; U.S. 1900 Census of Salt Lake County, Utah, enumeration district 21, sheet 3–A, microfilm, LDS Family History Library, for Major E. Dearing (b. Feb. 1869) and Heinrich Klenke (b. 5 Oct. 1870) and Henry Klenke's obitu-

ary in *Deseret News* (5 July 1943): 12. Although the city directories did not show their co-residence, the census showed that Klenke and Dearing lived together in the same house with two other male "partner" couples, also in their thirties. See chap. 6 for a discussion of same-sex domestic partners in the U.S. census.

26. Entry for Calvin S. Carrington (b. 28 Oct. 1865; md. 1887–97; remained an unmarried widower; d. 1930) in LDS Ancestral File; U.S. 1900 Census of Salt Lake County, Utah, enumeration district 28, sheet 9, for Calvin S. Carrington and Charles H. Fowler; Charles H. Fowler as bartender and clerk in *Salt Lake City Directory, 1899* (Salt Lake City: R. L. Polk, 1899), 296; *Salt Lake City Directory, 1900* (Salt Lake City: R. L. Polk, 1900), 178, 287; *Salt Lake City Directory, 1903* (Salt Lake City: R. L. Polk, 1903), 218, 356.

27. Bullough, in *Sexual Variance,* 106, discussed ancient Greek men's clubs.

28. *Salt Lake City Directory, 1905,* 77. The Bohemian Club's officers in 1905 were Ralph O. Hanson as president, Burton G. Settle as vice president, Henry Leclyde Steed (b. 1886; md. 1907, 3 children; d. 1916) as secretary, Francis E. M. Settle (b. Dec 1876) as treasurer, Lehi Eggersten Cluff (b. 1886; md. 1915, 3 children) as judge; Percy H. Field (b. abt. 1879) as librarian, and Hyrum F. Syndergaard (b. 1883; md. 1907, no children; d. 1951) as sergeant-at-arms. For the above men, see J. Cecil Alter, *Utah: The Storied Domain,* 3 vols. (Chicago: American Historical Society, 1932), 2:67; and LDS Ancestral File.

29. Karen J. Blair, *The Clubwoman as Feminist: True Womanhood Defined, 1868–1914* (New York: Holmes and Meier, 1980); Theodora Penny Martin, *The Sound of Our Own Voices: Women's Study Clubs, 1860–1910* (Boston: Beacon Press, 1987); Karen J. Blair, *The History of American Women's Voluntary Organizations, 1810–1960* (Boston: G. K. Hall, 1989); Mary Ann Clawson, *Constructing Brotherhood: Class, Gender, and Fraternalism* (Princeton: Princeton University Press, 1989); Mark C. Carnes, *Secret Ritual and Manhood in Victorian America* (New Haven: Yale University Press, 1989); Mark C. Carnes, "Middle-Class Men and the Solace of Fraternal Ritual," in Carnes and Clyde Griffin, eds., *Meanings for Manhood: Constructions of Masculinity in Victorian America* (Chicago: University of Chicago Press, 1990), 37–67; Anne Firor Scott, *Natural Allies: Women's Associations in American History* (Urbana: University of Illinois Press, 1991); Karen J. Blair, *The Torchbearers: Women and Their Amateur Arts Associations in America, 1890–1930* (Bloomington: Indiana University Press, 1994).

30. For these female and male clubs and societies, see *Salt Lake City Directory, 1905.*

31. In Mormon parlance, *general authority* refers to a man serving in the offices of the Mormon hierarchy that have churchwide jurisdiction. Usually of life tenure, these offices of the LDS Church have been the church president,

the president's counselors, the Patriarch to the Church (until the office was abolished in 1979), members of the Quorum of the Twelve Apostles, the Assistants to the Twelve (from 1941 to 1976), the Seventy, the Presiding Bishop, and the counselors to the Presiding Bishop. See "Assistants to the Twelve," "General Authorities," and "Patriarch to the Church," in Ludlow, ed., *Encyclopedia of Mormonism,* 1:81–82, 2:539, 3:1065–66; see also D. Michael Quinn, *The Mormon Hierarchy: Origins of Power* (Salt Lake City: Signature Books/Smith Research Associates, 1994), 39–77.

32. *Salt Lake City Directory, 1908* (Salt Lake City: R. L. Polk, 1908), 83, 135, 832, 985; entries for James H. Anson (b. 1882; md. 1914, 4 children; d. 1937), Louis Casper Lambert Shaw Jr. (b. 1884; md. 1909, 2 children; wife died; md. 1926, no children; d. 1962), and James Z. Oviatt (b. 1888; md. 1945; d. 1974) in LDS Ancestral File, and in *Salt Lake Tribune,* 2 Apr. 1937, 12. Oviatt was not in the 1910 or 1920 census of Utah, so it is unclear who he was living with during the years after his public association with the Bohemian Club and before his marriage. Only Shaw was in the LDS Church census for 1914.

33. *Gold and Blue* 2 (1 Mar. 1902): 11, (June 1902): 5; "Stephens' Day at School," *Gold and Blue* 3 (14 Jan. 1903): 5; See chap. 8 for Stephens and his live-in "boy chums," including his 1904–9 relationship with Noel Pratt of the LDS high school and LDS University; entry for Louis Casper Lambert Shaw Jr. (b. 17 May 1884) in LDS Ancestral File. However, this homosexual Bohemian Club was different from a social club by the same name that organized at the University of Utah in 1920 and continued for several years.

34. Bullough and Bullough, "Lesbianism in the 1920s and 1930s," 896; Berryman, "Psychological Phenomena, 64; see also chap. 7.

35. O'Donovan, "Historical Highlights," entry for 1886–1942.

36. Bullough and Bullough, "Lesbianism in the 1920s and 1930s," 899; see female cases 10, 17, 18, 19, 22, 23 and male case 9, with intentions of marriage in male cases 2 and 3, in Berryman, "Psychological Phenomena," 49–71. See chap. 7, note 10 for a discussion of the number of women and men in Berryman's study.

37. John Donald Wrathall, "American Manhood and the Y.M.C.A., 1868–1920" (Ph.D. diss., University of Minnesota, 1994), 127–28. Wrathall places "gay" and "heterosexual" in quotation marks because (128) "the entire concept of sexual orientation is culturally contingent." I am pleased to acknowledge the important work of this former student who was enrolled as an undergraduate in my introductory course in American social history at Brigham Young University.

CHAPTER 3

The Homopastoral
and the Homotactile

IN EVERY PATRIARCHAL religious organization, men administer the religion's most sacred ordinances to other males. In the early LDS Church this included blessing newborn sons with their officially recorded names, baptizing by immersion, ordaining to priesthood (ecclesiastical) offices, offering healing blessings, giving patriarchal blessings, washing the feet and anointing the head with consecrated oil in 1836, and conferring the temple endowment (instructions and covenants) from 1842 on.[1] Less known is that Mormon women did many of the same things—women blessing women prophetically, women anointing women with consecrated oil, women blessing women for health, women assisting in other women's childbirth, women administering the endowment ceremonies to women, and Utah female physicians caring for women with the encouragement of LDS leaders.[2] Nineteenth-century Mormons (both leaders and the rank and file) also regarded LDS women as "priestesses, prophetesses, seers and revelators."[3] In its homosocial culture, Mormonism provided homopastoral opportunities for both genders throughout the nineteenth century and into the twentieth.

Mormon men and women clearly had close physical contact with persons of their same sex. Some ordinances of the LDS Church required men and women to touch the bodies of same-gender persons. From 1833 to 1836 and again in 1883, Mormon men washed and anointed the feet of other men during meetings of the School of the Prophets.[4] Since 1842 men have washed with water and have anointed with olive oil various parts of the naked bodies of other men during the Mormon endowment ceremony.[5] Like men, women have washed and anointed the bodies of women during the LDS endowment ordinance since 1843.[6] Also, in healing ordinances and prior to childbirth, a nineteenth-century Mormon woman would directly wash and anoint with oil the back, hips, breasts, abdomen, thighs, and genital area of another woman. These were religious ordinances, not medical treatments.[7]

In addition to religious rituals, close physical interaction of men with men characterized social events of early Mormonism. Moreover, both females and males experienced close physical touch by sleeping with persons of their same gender. In fact, same-sex sleeping arrangements were nearly a requirement for Mormon men in church leadership positions that involved extensive travel. However, very few people regarded such homotactile experiences as erotic, despite the physical intimacy involved.

As a social activity, Mormon men danced with other men at church headquarters in Nauvoo—often in the LDS temple there. On 29 November 1845, Mormon general authorities Brigham Young, Heber C. Kimball, Joseph Young, and Levi W. Hancock "danced a French four together" accompanied by the Nauvoo Brass Band. Several weeks later, in the Nauvoo temple, "President B. Young then invited some one to join him in the dance and found a partner in Brother Chase."[8] Until all Mormons abandoned Nauvoo in mid-1846, priesthood quorums met for late-night dances in the temple. Sometimes men danced with their wives in the Nauvoo temple, but more often men danced with men in the temple, "drinking Wine &c until 2 Oclock in the Morning."[9] Dancing in an LDS temple was limited to Nauvoo, Illinois, in 1845–46, and there are no known references to female-female dancing.

Throughout the rest of nineteenth-century America, same-sex dancing occurred primarily where a gender imbalance in the local community made opposite-sex partners scarce. This was especially true in mining camps and other male-dominant populations of the frontier West. A surviving painting and a photograph from the nineteenth-century West show dance floors with male couples and teenage boys dancing as couples. Similar scenes occurred in mining camps throughout the world, as demonstrated by an illustration of male couples dancing in the Transvaal, South Africa, during the nineteenth century.[10] Some Americans even wore feminine apparel over their cowboy clothes while dancing all evening with male partners.[11]

However, the dancing in pioneer Mormon society was unique in America because Brigham Young and other LDS Church leaders sometimes organized male-only dances that excluded available women, even their own wives. In January 1847, Apostle Wilford Woodruff described three male couples of dancers: "The persons that took the floor to set the pattern were as follows: Brigham Young, Heber C. Kimball, Wilford Woodruff & Ezra Taft Benson of the Twelve, & Joseph Young & A. P. Rockwood of the Seventies." At the time of this male-male dance, these men were living with their wives at Winter Quarters (near Omaha, Nebraska). In Salt Lake City during 1860, Woodruff recorded that the "the Twelve [apostles] and others" danced together until two in the morning, when they returned home to their wives. Brigham Young's close physical contact with fellow apostles was reflected in an 1857 photograph of his twenty-one-year-old son Brigham Jr. and twenty-nine-year-old James Ferguson. The younger Brigham held his companion's knee while Ferguson rested his hand on his friend's shoulder.[12]

Outside LDS headquarters in Salt Lake City, all-male dances apparently continued into the late 1880s in Utah's small Mormon communities. For example, in Grass Valley, Henri Edouard Desaules lived in a schoolhouse that also served as the dance hall. After describing several conventional dances for males and females, he referred to one that was apparently for males only. "The boys had a Dance last night, on the occasion of young Johny Wilcox leaving for a trip to Colorado," Desaules wrote in July 1885. He added: "I let them dance till half past twelve oclock. They wanted to dance longer, but I protested, & reminded them that the agre'ment was that they were to quit at twelve oclock. So they were shamed and left."[13]

Beyond same-sex dancing in the West, nineteenth-century American culture generally endorsed physical intimacy between persons of the same gender. The historians John D'Emelio and Estelle B. Freedman observed: "Physical intimacy—though not genital stimulation—among women was, to an extent, normative within Victorian culture." As an example, they referred to Eliza Ware Farrar's *The Young Lady's Friend*. Published in seven editions from 1836 to 1849, this "advice book accepted the customs of girls holding hands, kissing, and caressing, explaining that these practices should be reserved for 'hours of privacy, and never indulged in before gentlemen.'"[14] For example, one American woman wrote her friend in 1832: "I wish I could be with you present in the body as well as the mind & heart—I would turn your *good husband out of bed*—and snuggle into you."[15]

Likewise, twenty-seven-year-old Elizabeth Haven put a Mormon perspective on this common practice of same-sex snuggling between females. After describing recent LDS events, she wrote her second cousin Elizabeth Bullard in 1839: "If I could sleep with you one night, [I] think we should not be very sleepy," and added, "at least I could converse all night and have nothing but a comma between the sentences, now and then." The two young Mormon women had previously roomed together at Amherst College in Massachusetts. Haven married a year after writing this letter; her cousin married exactly two years after that. A family history later asked: "Was her marriage date being the same as Elizabeth Haven's a mere coincidence?" The family left that question unanswered.[16]

In fact, the Mormon prophet Joseph Smith enjoyed bedtime snuggling with male friends throughout his life. Early in 1826, the twenty-year-old bachelor boarded with the Knight family, whose eighteen-year-old son later wrote: "Joseph and I worked together and slept together."[17] In an 1843 sermon, Smith (then the husband of many wives) preached that "two who were vary friends indeed should lie down upon the same bed at night locked in each other['s] embrace talking of their love & should awake in the morning together. They could immediately renew their conversation of love even while rising from their bed." That was how Apostle Wilford Woodruff recorded his prophet's words.[18] The official *History of the Church* still renders Smith's words this way: "it is pleasing for friends to lie down together, locked in the arms of love, to sleep and wake in each other's embrace and renew their conversation."[19] The night before he was murdered by a mob in 1844, Smith shared a bed with thirty-two-year-old Dan Jones, "and lay himself by my side in a close embrace."[20]

Smith's successor, Brigham Young, even dreamed of sleeping with non-Mormon men as a way of resolving conflict. In 1858 the church historian wrote: "Prest. Young said he dreamed last night, of seeing Gov. [Alfred] Cumming. He appeared exceedingly friendly, and said to Prest. Young we must be united, we must act in concert; and commenced undressing himself to go to bed with him."[21]

There were few bedrooms in nineteenth-century Mormon homes, and this often required same-sex persons to share a bed. In the early pioneer era of Utah, as many as eight children shared a single room with their parents, and one mother with three children shared a single room "with two newly married Danish couples."[22] Twentieth-century expectations of privacy were impossible in the residential patterns of early Mormons.

Although Mormon families typically had large numbers of children, single-room and two-room houses predominated in Utah to at least the mid-1870s. Even the two-story homes of the late nineteenth century usually had only three bedrooms at the most.[23] For example, the Utah Mormon home of a "wealthy farmer" in the 1870s had three bedrooms for a family with "thirteen children (twelve of whom lived in the house at one time)."[24] In 1892, the *Deseret News* advertised the floor plan for a two-story house which was "Suitable for a Genteel Family." However, this ideal home for upper-class Mormon families had only three small bedrooms at a time when Mormons had double or triple that number of children. During that same year, for example, thirty-two-year-old Lorenzo Robinson, his wife, and six children shared a two-room log cabin in Beaver, Utah. Six more children soon joined their siblings in the cabin.[25]

Such cramped housing required Mormon families to allow two or more children (usually of the same sex) to sleep in a single bed. Adult visitors sometimes slept with children of their same gender, but more often shared a bed with the parent of their same sex. Even the parents' bed was narrow, which meant that any shared bed literally required sleeping in the arms of one's bedmate in nineteenth-century Mormon culture. However, same-sex LDS siblings spoke fondly of their physical closeness in bed. For example, Brent F. Cahoon, a twenty-year-old student at the University of Utah, described how he and his brother had recently responded to their father's morning knock on the bedroom door. "Then suddenly we both made a plunge for the middle of the bed and I grabbed Jack and Jack grabbed me—but we did not try to kick each other out at all; we just huddled down and held each other in." Instead of getting up early to study for school, the two brothers continued snuggling in bed.[26]

On at least some occasions, these sleeping arrangements resulted in homoerotic encounters between siblings. For that reason, a physician's book warned American parents in the 1860s about "the common practice" of allowing "boys of the same family [to] sleep together, and girls the same." Specifically, this popular family reference book observed that if sleeping brothers "are of the age when puberty arrives . . . their sexual functions are more than ordinarily active." Therefore, brothers sleeping together "more likely than not, [will] awaken in them desires which are prurient." This physician said it was "pathological" for same-sex siblings to have erotic encounters as "bedfellows," and he recommended that everyone sleep alone. American families purchased three editions of this book during the 1860s.[27] A shared bed did result in homoerotic encounters between brothers in a Mormon family and with an overnight guest (see chap. 9).

However, for the vast majority of Americans, such same-sex sleeping arrangements were nonerotic, yet affectionate experiences of physical closeness. As Robert Brain asserted in his cross-cultural study of friendship: "It is maligning friendship always to associate it with sex, and silly to assume that physical contact is in itself evidence of homosexuality."[28] Nevertheless, it is true that the phrase "sleeping with" had a sexual meaning for Mormons as early as the 1840s.[29] Still, most nineteenth-century Americans wrote that they "slept with" someone of the same gender in the literal sense of sharing a bed, without the erotic meaning that phrase now has.[30] Therefore, due to necessity or personal preference, Mormon culture and LDS leaders both continued to encourage same-sex sleeping arrangements.

In addition, it was LDS Church practice until the midtwentieth century for a visiting general authority to share a bed with his traveling companion or with the father or older son in homes the LDS leader visited. As early as 1845, a twenty-three-year-old unmarried man at Nauvoo wrote that Apostle William Smith "slept with me last night and will to night." The young man was renting a single room at the time.[31] Apostles such as Erastus Snow sometimes had a favorite sleeping companion during long journeys. John D. Lee wrote in 1858: "Bro. E. Snow Said that he wantd me to Stay with him where ever he tarried."[32]

By the mid-1870s, general authorities were visiting every quarterly conference in each Mormon stake (diocese) of the western United States, and they sometimes even visited conferences in local wards (congregations). During an ecclesiastical trip in October 1879, Apostle Wilford Woodruff wrote: "Brother Hatch . . . Staid & slept with me over night."[33]

By the mid-1890s these church-speaking trips included stakes in Canada and in Mexico. LDS leaders also stayed with families along the way to and from conferences that were distant from Salt Lake City. Although Mormonism's founder had encouraged same-sex friends to sleep in "the same bed at night locked in each other['s] embrace talking of their love," I have found no similar descriptions in Mormon diaries of loving pillow talk between males or between females.

Until at least the 1940s, however, general authorities continued the practice of sleeping with local leaders and having religious discussions in bed. For example, S. Dilworth Young wrote about his official visit in 1945 with an LDS mission president in northern California: "I slept in the same bed with him for three weeks, nearly, and he told me a lot of things about the brethren, good and bad of his own experiences." This general authority shared a bed with a Mormon man only because of his church assignment, not because he wanted to be close with another man. Young later wrote: "I have never had in my life a man in whom I confided. So I guess I'm a loner."[34]

Cold weather was another reason why LDS general authorities slept with other men while away from their wives on church assignments. "After going home with [stake president] Orson Smith we sat up for about two hours talking," Apostle Abraham H. Cannon wrote in January 1895. He added: "He slept with me at night, as it was extremely cold."[35] Winter nights in unheated houses also caused Mormons of the same gender to follow their prophet's counsel about sleeping "locked in each other['s] embrace."

Some LDS leaders even complained about this necessity of physical closeness with a male bedmate. Upon sharing a bed with one Mormon leader, local LDS leader Francis M. Lyman wrote in 1876: "he was so dirty that it made me crawl whenever he touched me."[36] During one of his church-speaking trips, Apostle David O. McKay wrote that he would rather sleep on the floor than sleep with another man.[37]

However, most general authorities shared beds during trips, if they did not sleep with other Mormons. For example, Apostle Anthon H. Lund noted in 1891 that he "slept with" Apostle John Henry Smith during a trip from Salt Lake City to nearby Ogden, Utah.[38]

In fact, some LDS leaders slept with one another when it was not necessary to do so. As an apostle, Francis M. Lyman overcame his earlier dislike of sharing a bed with another man. While in Salt Lake City during the spring of 1891, L. John Nuttall, official secretary of the First Presidency, noted: "I found Bro F.M. Lyman in my bed at the Gardo [House, owned by the First Presidency] & we slept together." At the time, wives of both men were living in Salt Lake City. During the next several months, sixty-three-year-old Nuttall wrote the same words frequently: "Bro F M Lyman slept with me."[39] He left no explanation of why the two Mormon men often slept together while their wives were also in the city. In the spring there was no cold weather to require sharing a bed.

Nuttall described still another custom of same-sex sleeping among early Utah Mormons. In Salt Lake City during May 1893, Nuttall wrote: "At [my wife] Sophia's Brother & Sister R also staid with us. He slept with me."[40] Therefore, early Mormons did not follow what seems to current Mormon families the obvious thing to do when a married couple visits: let the visiting couple sleep in a bed in one bedroom, while the host couple sleeps in another. Instead, the First Presidency's secretary indicated that early Mormons followed a different pattern when a married couple visited a family: the two husbands slept together in one bedroom and the two wives slept together in another. As with most customary practices, Nuttall did not think to explain why this was the sleeping arrangement, even among the Mormon elite, during the nineteenth century.

In 1835, outside church headquarters, some Mormon men routinely kissed whenever they met. An LDS apostle visiting an overly "enthusiastic" branch of nineteen members in New York state found that "the Elders seemed to want almost every quality except Zeal and that they had abundantly—even to the saluting with a kiss." However, such pro forma greetings did not take place at church headquarters in Ohio, where Joseph Smith had revised the New Testament text to rephrase "holy kiss" into a verbal greeting of "holy salutation."[41]

Nevertheless, same-sex kissing was common among Mormon women and men in the nineteenth century as a spontaneous expression of their religious devotion and personal affection. At Kirtland headquarters in 1837, Mary Fielding Smith wrote: "Some of the Sisters while engaged in conversing in toungues their countenances beaming with joy, clasped each others hands & kissd in the most affectinate manner."[42] Although they did not usually specify it, this same-sex kissing between adults was probably "full on the lips," which one Mormon said was the practice of brothers in his family.[43]

Several nineteenth-century Mormons who became LDS presidents were accustomed to kissing other men. After a long dispute with Presidency Counselor George Q. Cannon, Apostle Heber J. Grant wrote in 1891: "he leaned over and kissed me and I felt the tears of gratitude coming to my eyes as I returned the kiss."[44] In 1898, as soon as a fellow apostle returned from a trip, "Brother Grant kissed me when he saw me."[45] After they had traveled together for several weeks, Apostle David O. McKay wrote in 1907 that he "kissed Elder John Henry [Smith] good bye, after a mutual expression of pleasure at each other's company."[46] Raised in pioneer Utah, Joseph F. Smith and Heber J. Grant kissed their counselors good-bye during their service as LDS presidents in the twentieth century.[47] This reflected the common practice of kissing among nineteenth-century American men, especially if these men shared strong religious views.[48]

Some Mormon leaders even had ardent dreams of same-sex kissing. For example, in 1847 Brigham Young dreamed that he met the deceased Joseph Smith and "kissed him many times."[49] In 1896 stake president Charles O. Card recorded: "I dreamed that president Woodruff & I met & embraced each other & Kissed each other in a very affectionate manner & I remarked he was the sweetest man I ever kissed. I thought in our embraces it was from the pure love of the Gospel."[50] Despite the homotactile dimension of this dream, Card was a polygamist who had no known homoerotic experiences.

Was Card's dream itself "homosexual" by the definitions of our society? More important, was it homoerotic by the nineteenth-century definitions of his Mormon society? It is impossible to know exactly what Card's own definitions were, but he recorded this homotactile dream without any self-doubt in an era when Mormon diary writers rarely referred to their sexual thoughts or experiences.[51] Charles O. Card's dream of kissing his beloved leader was typical of male friends in the nineteenth century who "spoke of a physical component that may or may not have been explicitly sexual, but at least included hugs, kisses, and sleeping together."[52]

Other middle-class Americans of that era were very candid about physical intimacy. In 1804, before he became one of the most famous U.S. senators, Daniel Webster wrote: "I don't see how I can live any longer without having a friend near me, I mean a male friend." The twenty-two-year-old Webster explained what "near me" meant by telling his twenty-three-year-old friend: "Yes, James, I must come; we will yoke together again; your little bed is just wide enough."[53] In 1817, twenty-six-year-old Anne Lister began a diary of her emotional and intimate relations with women, including a nightly tabulation of their shared orgasms.[54]

This openness of some middle-class Americans persisted throughout the period when English Victorianism dominated American culture. The eastern intellectual Mabel Loomis Todd kept a diary in which she recorded every sexual activity and orgasm she experienced with her husband from their marriage in 1879 onward. She and other women of nineteenth-century America did not acquiesce to the sexual repressiveness advocated by many (but not all) Victorian writers.[55] Some middle-class American women of that period were even willing to describe their sexual feelings and experiences to a female researcher.[56]

With nearly equal detail, at the age of twelve Frederick S. Ryman started a diary in New York State that recorded his every sexual encounter with same-age girls and later with women. Ryman seemed a typically American young man, yet his diary also referred to his intense same-sex experiences. For example, at age twenty-eight in 1886, he began recording his experiences with a nineteen-year-old friend: "I confess I like the Oriental custom of men embracing & kissing each other if they are indeed dear friends. When we went to bed Rob put his arms around me & lay his head down by my right shoulder in the most loving way & then I put my arms around his neck & thus clasped in each others arms we talked for a long time till we were ready to go to sleep." When young Rob left in the morning, "he came to the bed & threw his arms around my neck & we kissed each other good bye."

However, the affectionate twenty-eight-year-old Ryman drew a clear line between the homotactile and the homoerotic: "Now in all this I am certain there was no sexual sentiment on the part of either of us. We both have our mistresses whom we see with reasonable regularity [for sexual intercourse] & I am certain that the thought of the least demonstration of unmanly & abnormal passion would have been as revolting to him as it is & ever has been to me." Then the young man added: "yet I do love him & love to hug & kiss him." Martin Duberman, the historian who edited this diary, describes Ryman's male friendship as same-sex "intimacy without orgasm."[57] In this study's terms, the two young men's experiences were homotactile and homoemotional without being homoerotic. My research in Mormon sources indicates that Ryman's attitudes were also typical of same-gender bedmates in nineteenth-century Mormon culture, even though Mormons did not express themselves as pointedly as Ryman did.

On the other hand, nineteen-year-old Albert Dodd, a student at Yale, did not find it necessary to make that kind of disclaimer about a same-sex friendship. In his 1837 diary Dodd wrote about a fellow student, Anthony: "Often too he shared my pillow—or I his, and then how sweet to sleep with him, to hold his beloved form in my embrace, to have his arms around my neck, to imprint upon his face sweet kisses!" Dodd had a young lady as his fiancee, yet Dodd joined with Anthony in making a mutual pact of love with her during the same month Anthony "shared my pillow."[58]

Even the experience of homoerotic pleasure in the nineteenth century did not cause middle-class American men to define themselves in a separate category from other men. In 1826, twenty-two-year-old Jeffrey Withers (signing himself "the old Stud") asked if his former college roommate, James H. Hammond, was still "poking and punching a writhing Bedfellow with your long fleshen pole?" These young men had clearly crossed the line from the homotactile to the homoerotic. However, after acknowledging his fond memory of those "exquisite touches," Withers lightheartedly recommended that his friend turn more of his attentions to women. Both young men eventually married and had distinguished careers in the political and judicial life of South Carolina and the Confederacy.[59] Unfortunately, there is no evidence to demonstrate whether or not early Mormon men with homoerotic experience had attitudes similar to the lighthearted views of these young men in South Carolina.

Other analysts have explained that there were specific reasons why nineteenth-century American men did not regard their manhood as threatened by physical intimacy with other men or even by homoerotic encounters. For example, E. Anthony Rotundo has commented:

> To the extent that they did have ideas—and a language—about homosexuality, they thought of particular sexual acts, not of a personal disposition or social identity that produced such acts. . . . In a society that had no clear concept of homosexuality, young men did not need to draw a line between right and wrong forms of contact, except perhaps at genital play. . . . Middle-class culture drew no clear line of division between homosexual and heterosexual. As a result young men (and women, too) could express their affection for each other physically without risking social censure or feelings of guilt.[60]

Of women in that era who wrote passionate love letters and lived together, a recent article in *U.S. News and World Report* also observes: "But Ruth Cleveland [sister of the U.S. president] and Evangeline Whipple loved in the waning years of another time, when the lines were drawn differently, the urge to categorize and dissect not so overpowering. Belonging to the 19th century, they were not yet initiated into the idea of 'sexual identity.'" This is evident in a 1911 photograph of a women's physical education class at Brigham Young University, in which the young women's reclining bodies were almost intertwined.[61]

When society, culture, and religion impose no stigma, individuals feel no personal guilt for activities that seem natural to them.

For example, an official photograph of a YMCA baseball team in 1900 showed two young men holding hands while surrounded by their teammates, and a 1906 photo of a YMCA basketball team showed one young man with his hand on the bare thigh of his seated teammate. This was reflected in Mormon culture by an 1878 photograph of Utah's territorial baseball champions, including Heber J. Grant, whose knee was being held by a teammate. By 1920, YMCA leaders had a homophobic view of such images, which disappeared from athletic team photographs thereafter.[62]

Until the 1940s, however, some Mormon male teenagers continued to hold each other with apparent affection in the posed photographs of school athletic teams. This was particularly true of one young man on the track team of Salt Lake City's East High School in 1923. Seated in the front row, he held the bare leg of one teammate with his right hand, his left hand rested on the bare knee of another, while his own shoulders were embraced by a third teammate kneeling above him. Aside from these four, several of their teammates were also holding each other affectionately in this track team photo. From 1922 to 1930 the yearbooks of the Latter-day Saint University in Salt Lake City also showed members of the basketball team holding hands and male swimmers with their hands on the bare knees of fellow teammates. In the track team's posed photographs at Salt Lake City's Protestant Westminster College in the early 1940s, bare-chested young men in shorts also held one another close, with one arm around a teammate's waist and the other around his shoulders.[63] Longer than in American culture generally, young men continued to publicly hold hands and touch the bare legs of other young men in Utah and Mormon culture. Despite newspaper reports of sexual activities among Mormon students since the early 1900s,[64] for decades some LDS administrators and Mormon teenagers showed no homophobia.

Nevertheless, these athletic team photographs also demonstrate that by the 1920s such homotactile displays in team photographs were exceptional in Mormon culture. In fact, 90 percent of the photographs indicate a concerted effort to avoid any physical contact—young men are standing with arms folded tightly across their chests, with several inches of space separating their bodies. This is evident in the yearbooks of Brigham Young University and LDS University (which was primarily a high school), in the yearbooks of the University of Utah as well as of the public high schools in the major urban centers of Salt Lake City and Ogden. There clearly was widespread discomfort at showing homotactile contact in photos of athletic teams, even to the extent of preventing any young man's arm from brushing against his teammates.

In those Utah college and high school photographs that did show some physical contact (even affectionate touching), there was obviously an individual choice on the part of the young men who maintained a careful distance from their teammates. However, in the dozens of photographs showing every young man avoiding even the touch of shoulders with a teammate, the physical distancing was clearly required by the adult coaches or the photographers. Since affectionate touching was allowed in some team photographs, it was more likely a homophobic coach who regulated the pose of his athletes. Physical touch occurred where the team's coach was either not present for the photograph or not homophobic.

To the end of the nineteenth century most Americans thought of friendship and affection when they observed homotactile situations. By the 1920s most Americans wondered about "sexuality" and feared the possibility of homoeroticism when they saw homotactile situations, especially males affectionately touching other males. Physical distancing between males became the hallmark of American homophobia.

Although not to the same extent as in contemporary Melanesia, nineteenth-century American society either endorsed or tolerated a high degree of same-sex physical intimacy. This was also true of Mormon culture, and apparently for a longer time. Nevertheless, by the 1920s both national culture and Mormon culture demonstrated a homophobic concern about physical closeness between those of the same gender. The awkward physical distancing in photographs of young men during the 1920s was the outward symptom of an inner retreat from emotional intimacy between males. By contrast, intense homoemotionalism had characterized America's same-sex relationships before the twentieth century.

NOTES

1. For the meaning and significance of these ordinances, see relevant entries in Daniel H. Ludlow, ed., *Encyclopedia of Mormonism: The History, Scripture, Doctrine, and Procedure of the Church of Jesus Christ of Latter-day Saints,* 5 vols. (New York: Macmillan, 1992).

2. Claudia Lauper Bushman, "Mystics and Healers," in Bushman, ed., *Mormon Sisters: Women in Early Utah* (Salt Lake City: Olympus, 1976), 1–23; Chris Rigby Arrington, "Pioneer Midwives," in Bushman, ed., *Mormon Sisters,* 383–97; Cheryll Lynn May, "Charitable Sisters," in Bushman, ed., *Mormon Sisters,* 399–413; Susan Sessions Rugh, "Patty B. Sessions," in Vicky Burgess-Olson, ed., *Sister Saints* (Provo, Utah: Brigham Young University Press, 1976), 304–22; Ann Gardner Stone, "Ellen B. Ferguson," in Burgess-Olson, ed., *Sister Saints,* 327–39; Christine Croft Waters, "Romania P. Penrose," in Burgess-Olson, ed., *Sister Saints,* 343–60; Gail Farr Casterline, "Ellis R. Shipp," in Burgess-Olson, ed., *Sister Saints,* 365–81; Jean Bickmore White, "Martha H. Cannon," in Burgess-Olson, ed., *Sister Saints,* 385–97; Vicky Burgess-Olson, "Margaret Ann Freece," in Burgess-Olson, ed., *Sister Saints,* 401–13; Linda King Newell, "A Gift Given, a Gift Taken: Washing, Anointing, and Blessing the Sick among Mormon Women," *Sunstone* 6 (Sept.–Oct. 1981): 16–25, reprinted in D. Michael Quinn, ed., *The New Mormon History: Revisionist Essays on the Past* (Salt Lake City: Signature Books, 1992), 101–20; Linda King Newell, "Gifts of the Spirit: Women's Share," in Maureen Ursenbach Beecher and Lavina Fielding Anderson, eds., *Sisters in the Spirit: Mormon Women in Historical and Cultural Perspective* (Urbana: University of Illinois Press, 1987), 111–50; Betina Lindsey, "Woman as Healer in the Modern Church," *Dialogue: A Journal of Mormon Thought* 23 (Fall 1990): 39–61, reprinted in Maxine Hanks, ed., *Women and Authority: Re-emerging Mormon Feminism* (Salt Lake City: Signature Books, 1992), 439–60. For Mormon women administering religious ordinances to women, see also note 6.

3. *Journal of Discourses,* 26 vols. (Liverpool: Latter-day Saints Book Depot, 1854–86), 1:312 (Young/1853), 6:45 (Young/1857), 18:171 (O. Pratt/1865); Joseph F. Smith sermon, 14 Apr. 1913, at the residence of Alfred W. McCune, Salt Lake City, Archives, Historical Department of the Church of Jesus Christ of Latter-day Saints, Salt Lake City, Utah (hereafter LDS Archives); Vella Neil Evans, "Woman's Image in Authoritative Mormon Discourse: A Rhetorical Analysis" (Ph.D. diss., University of Utah, 1985), 187; see also Linda King Newell, "The Historical Relationship of Mormon Women and Priesthood," in Hanks, ed., *Women and Authority,* 23–48; Ian G. Barber, "Mormon Women as 'Natural' Seers: An Enduring Legacy," in Hanks, ed., *Women and Authority,* 167–84; D. Michael Quinn, "Mormon Women Have Had the Priesthood Since 1843," in Hanks, ed., *Women and Authority,* 365–409.

4. Brigham H. Roberts, ed., *History of the Church of Jesus Christ of Latter-day Saints,* 7 vols., 2d ed., rev. (Salt Lake City: Deseret Book, 1978), 1:312, 323; Milton V. Backman Jr., *The Heavens Resound: A History of the Latter-day Saints in Ohio, 1830–1838* (Salt Lake City: Deseret Book, 1983), 264–68; Merle H. Graffam, ed., *Salt Lake School of the Prophets: Minute Book, 1883* (Palm Desert, Calif.: ULC Press, 1981), 50–51.

5. Roberts, *History of the Church,* 2:431, 475–76, 5:2; William Clayton diary, 10 Dec., 11 Dec. 1845, in George D. Smith, ed., *An Intimate Chronicle: The Journals of William Clayton* (Salt Lake City: Signature Books/Smith Research Associates, 1991), 203, 207.

6. Carol Cornwall Madsen, "Mormon Women and the Temple: Toward a New Understanding," in Beecher and Anderson, eds., *Sisters in the Spirit,* 87–88; Alma P. Burton, "Endowment," in Ludlow, ed., *Encyclopedia of Mormonism,* 2:454–56; Allen Claire Rozsa, "Temple Ordinances," in Ludlow, ed., *Encyclopedia of Mormonism,* 4:1444.

7. Newell, "A Gift Given," 112. Because of this touching of intimate body parts during the healing ordinance, a Mormon leader preached in 1884 that it was inappropriate for men to perform such ordinances for women. See Quinn, "Mormon Women Have Had the Priesthood," 378–79.

8. Clayton diary, 29 Nov. 1845, 2 Jan. 1846, in Smith, ed., *An Intimate Chronicle,* 191, 250.

9. Samuel W. Richards diary, 9 Feb., 9 May, 27 May 1846, LDS Archives, with copy in Henry E. Huntington Library, San Marino, Calif.; see also John D. Lee diary, 17 Dec. 1845, Huntington Library; Jacob Gates diary, 9 Feb. 1846, LDS Archives; Franklin D. Richards diary, 9 Feb., 28 Feb. 1846, LDS Archives; William G. Hartley, *My Best for the Kingdom: History and Autobiography of John Lowe Butler, a Mormon Frontiersman* (Salt Lake City: Aspen Books, 1993), 182.

10. Jonathan Katz, *Gay American History: Lesbians and Gay Men in the U.S.A.* (New York: Thomas Y. Crowell, 1976), 509–10 for photographs and painting of American cowboys dancing; Richard Davenport-Hines, *Sex, Death, and Punishment: Attitudes toward Sex and Sexuality in Britain since the Renaissance* (London: Collins, 1990), 109 for illustration of South African miners dancing as male couples; see also chap. 6 for a discussion of the "homoenvironmental" situations in society.

11. Edgar Beecher Bronson, *Reminiscences of a Ranchman* (New York: McClure, 1908), 269–70; see also Neil Miller, *Out of the Past: Gay and Lesbian History from 1869 to the Present* (New York: Vintage/Random House, 1995), 41.

12. Scott G. Kenney, ed., *Wilford Woodruff's Journal, 1833–1898 Typescript,* 9 vols., plus index (Midvale, Utah: Signature Books, 1983–91), 3:123 (23 Jan. 1847), 5:433 (13 Feb. 1860); William W. Slaughter, *Life in Zion: An Intimate Look at the Latter-day Saints, 1820–1995* (Salt Lake City: Deseret Book, 1995), 38.

13. Henri Edouard Desaules diary, 19 July 1885, LDS Archives.

14. John D'Emelio and Estelle B. Freedman, *Intimate Matters: A History of Sexuality in America* (New York: Harper and Row, 1988), 126; John S. Haller Jr. and Robin M. Haller, *The Physician and Sexuality in Victorian*

America (Urbana: University of Illinois Press, 1974), 106. This referred to Eliza Ware Farrar's *The Young Lady's Friend* published in various editions from 1836 through 1880 under the name Mrs. John Farrar. See *National Union Catalog of Pre-1956 Imprints,* 754 vols. (London: Mansell, 1968–81), 164:234–35. The above studies quoted pages 241–42 in the 1860 edition of Farrar's book, without noting its earlier popularity.

15. Mary Black Couper to Sophie M. DuPont, 5 Mar. 1832, quoted in Carroll Smith-Rosenberg, "The Female World of Love and Ritual," in Nancy F. Cott and Elizabeth H. Pleck, eds., *A Heritage of Her Own: Toward a New Social History of American Women* (New York: Touchstone/Simon and Schuster, 1979), 330.

16. Elizabeth Haven to Elizabeth H. Bullard, 24 Feb. 1839, in Ora H. Barlow, *The Israel Barlow Story and Mormon Mores* (Salt Lake City: Publishers Press, 1968), 144, 231n1, also 140–41, 179. The quoted phrase was reprinted with the full letter in Kenneth W. Godfrey, Audrey M. Godfrey, and Jill Mulvay Derr, eds., *Women's Voices: An Untold History of the Latter-day Saints, 1830–1900* (Salt Lake City: Deseret Book, 1982), 109.

17. Joseph Knight Jr. (b. 22 June 1808) manuscript autobiography, quoted in William G. Hartley, *"They Are My Friends": A History of the Joseph Knight Family, 1825–1850* (Provo, Utah: Grandin Book, 1986), 18–19.

18. Kenney, *Wilford Woodruff's Journal,* 2:227 (16 Apr. 1843).

19. Roberts, *History of the Church,* 5:361, which is a slight variation on the original minutes of apostle and historian Willard Richards as reproduced in Andrew F. Ehat and Lyndon W. Cook, eds., *The Words of Joseph Smith: The Contemporary Accounts of the Nauvoo Discourses of the Prophet Joseph Smith* (Provo, Utah: Religious Studies Center, Brigham Young University, 1980), 195, and in Scott H. Faulring, ed., *An American Prophet's Record: The Diaries and Journals of Joseph Smith* (Salt Lake City: Signature Books/Smith Research Associates, 1987), 366, both of which show that *History of the Church* failed to reprint a repetition of the word "locked" before "in each others embrace." However, in his review of the book by Ehat and Cook, Dean C. Jessee claimed that the omitted word was actually "rocked," which intensifies the tenderness of same-sex bedmates as described by the prophet. See *Brigham Young University Studies* 21 (Fall 1981): 531. Smith used sleeping friends to illustrate the doctrine of resurrection, as he used other common experiences to illustrate salvation and spiritual growth (*History of the Church,* 5:387, 401).

20. Dan Jones (b. 4 Aug. 1811) to Thomas Bullock, 20 Jan. 1855, in Ronald D. Dennis, ed., "The Martyrdom of Joseph and Hyrum Smith," *Brigham Young University Studies* 24 (Winter 1984): 101.

21. Church Historian's Office Journal, 20 May 1858, LDS Archives.

22. Marilyn Higbee, ed., "'A Weary Traveler': The 1848–50 Diary of Zina D. H. Young," *Journal of Mormon History* 19 (Fall 1993): 92; Kathryn M.

Daynes, "Plural Wives and the Nineteenth-Century Mormon Marriage System: Manti, Utah, 1849–1910" (Ph.D. diss., Indiana University, 1991), quotation from 70.

23. Leon Sidney Pitman, "A Survey of Nineteenth-Century Folk Housing in the Mormon Culture Region" (Ph.D. diss., Louisiana State University, 1973), 138, 151, 157–75; Austin E. Fife, "Stone Houses of Northern Utah," *Utah Historical Quarterly* 40 (Winter 1972): 9–11.

24. Keith Bennett and Thomas Carter, "Houses with Two Fronts: The Evolution of Domestic Architectural Design in a Mormon Community," *Journal of Mormon History* 15 (1989): 50.

25. "A $1,400 House: Make a Pretty Dwelling Suitable for a Genteel Family," *Deseret Evening News,* 28 Jan. 1892, 7; file on Jeremiah L. Robinson house and log cabin (deeded to his son Lorenzo Robinson in 1884), Historic Preservation Office, Utah State Historical Society, Salt Lake City; caption of Photo 728 ("Residences: Robinson, Lorenzo"), Utah State Historical Society; Lorenzo Robinson (b. 14 June 1860), Ancestral File, Family History Library of the Church of Jesus Christ of Latter-day Saints, Salt Lake City, Utah (hereafter LDS Family History Library). At its highest level of occupancy nine children lived continuously in the Robinson cabin during the two decades after 1899, as the older three children left and were replaced by newborns.

26. Brent Cahoon, "We Both Agreed," *University of Utah Pen* 5 (Dec. 1913): 82; obituary in *Deseret News,* 19 June 1963, for Brent F. Cahoon (b. 23 Aug. 1893; md. 1919; 1 child). Photographs of nineteenth-century "double" beds do not adequately communicate their narrowness to the viewer. However, readers will understand the text description if they have visited the furnished "master bedrooms" of plantation houses in the American South or similar beds in the nineteenth-century houses of wealthy Americans throughout the United States. In Utah, one can gain this perspective by touring Brigham Young's Beehive House in Salt Lake City, located one block east of the Salt Lake Temple.

27. The "Bedfellows" discussion in James C. Jackson, *The Sexual Organism and Its Healthful Management* (Boston: B. Leverett Emerson, 1861; reprint, New York: Arno Press, 1974), 41, 42, 43; *National Union Catalog,* 274:673.

28. Robert Brain, *Friends and Lovers* (New York: Basic Books, 1976), 65. To demonstrate his own lack of homophobia, Brain dedicated this book to his "many friends and lovers of both sexes," yet he used the term "homosexuality" as though it had only an erotic meaning (26). Likewise, the openly gay historian John Donald Wrathall, in "American Manhood and the Y.M.C.A., 1868–1920" (Ph.D. diss., University of Minnesota, 1994), 282n5, stated that "the word 'gay' implies a self-conscious identity, while 'homosexual' connotes any same-sex sexual activity." Those are examples of why Smith-Rosenberg's nonerotic term "homosocial" is necessary in this discourse.

29. Nauvoo High Council Minutes, 6 Feb. 1841, transcript, Folder 10, Box 76, H. Michael Marquardt Papers, Manuscripts Division, J. Willard Marriott Library, University of Utah, Salt Lake City, Utah (hereafter Marriott Library); Strangite High Council Minutes, 16 Dec. 1846, Voree, Wisc., in "Chronicles of Voree," 130–31, Historical Society of Wisconsin, Madison; Hosea Stout diary, 11 Mar. 1848, in Juanita Brooks, ed., *On the Mormon Frontier: The Diary of Hosea Stout, 1844–1861,* 2 vols. (Salt Lake City: University of Utah Press, 1964), 1:304; as well as non-Mormon usage of "sleep with" as a sexual term in U.S. Army lieutenant Sylvester Mowry to Edward J. ("Ned") Bicknall, 27 Apr. 1855, Utah State Historical Society. This is the most extraordinary example of the delay (114 years) between conventional usage and the dating of a slang phrase in a dictionary. According to Harold Wentworth and Stuart Berg Flexner, eds., *Dictionary of American Slang* (New York: Thomas Y. Crowell, 1967), 486, the year 1955 is the earliest known use of the phrase "sleep with" as meaning "to have sexual intercourse with."

30. E. Anthony Rotundo, "Romantic Friendship: Male Intimacy and Middle-Class Youth in the United States, 1800–1900," *Journal of Social History* 23 (Fall 1989): 10.

31. James M. Monroe diary, 15 May 1845, Western Americana Collection, Beinecke Rare Book and Manuscript Library, Yale University, New Haven, Conn., with microfilm copies at the Huntington Library and at Utah State Historical Society; entry for James M. Monroe (b. 22 Jan. 1822) in Susan Easton Black, *Membership of the Church of Jesus Christ of Latter-day Saints, 1830–1848,* 50 vols. (Provo, Utah: Religious Studies Center, Brigham Young University, 1984–88), 31:376–77.

32. John D. Lee diary, 5 Aug. 1858, in Robert Glass Cleland and Juanita Brooks, eds., *A Mormon Chronicle: The Diaries of John D. Lee, 1848–1876,* 2 vols. (San Marino, Calif.: Huntington Library, 1955), 1:179.

33. Kenney, *Wilford Woodruff's Journal,* 7:524 (24 Oct. 1879).

34. Benson Y. Parkinson, *S. Dilworth Young: General Authority, Scouter, Poet* (American Fork, Utah: Covenant Communications, 1994), 223, 301.

35. Abraham H. Cannon diary, 27 Jan. 1895, Utah State Historical Society.

36. Francis M. Lyman diary, 8 Feb. 1876, LDS Archives. At that time, Lyman was a stake president. He later became a member of the Quorum of the Twelve Apostles.

37. Undated letter from David O. McKay to his wife Emma Ray McKay after his appointment as an apostle in 1906, private possession, Salt Lake City, Utah.

38. Anthon H. Lund diary, 2 Apr. 1891, microfilm, LDS Archives. The Lund diary microfilm is unrestricted to all researchers at LDS Archives by stipulation of its donor, and will be published in edited form by Signature Books, Salt Lake City.

39. L. John Nuttall diary, 19 July, 25 Aug., 13 Oct., 15 Oct. 1891, Department of Special Collections and Manuscripts, Harold B. Lee Library, Brigham Young University, Provo, Utah (hereafter Lee Library), with photocopy of typescript in Manuscripts Division, Marriott Library; Andrew Jenson, *Latter-day Saint Biographical Encyclopedia,* 4 vols. (Salt Lake City: Deseret News Press and Andrew Jenson History, 1901–36), 1:355.

40. Nuttall diary, 16 May 1893.

41. William E. McLellin diary, 8 June 1835, in Jan Shipps and John W. Welch, eds., *The Journals of William E. McLellin, 1831–1836* (Provo, Utah: BYU Studies, Brigham Young University; Urbana: University of Illinois Press, 1994), 183, 205n47.

42. Mary Fielding Smith to Mercy R. Fielding Thompson, 8 July 1837, in Godfrey, Godfrey, and Derr, eds., *Women's Voices,* 61.

43. Ralph G. Smith (b. 1899) interview, 17 June 1977, page 17, transcript in my possession, and also my handwritten notes of interview at his apartment in Salt Lake City. Smith referred specifically to his oldest brother, who was born in 1879.

44. Heber J. Grant letterbook-journal, 29 Jan. 1891, LDS Archives.

45. Lund diary, 10 Sept. 1898.

46. David O. McKay diary, 1 Aug. 1907, copy in LDS Archives.

47. Lund diary, 17 Feb. 1909, 20 Dec. 1920.

48. Donald Yacovone, "Abolitionists and the 'Language of Fraternal Love,'" in Mark C. Carnes and Clyde Griffen, eds., *Meanings for Manhood: Constructions of Masculinity in Victorian America* (Chicago: University of Chicago Press, 1990), 88, 93.

49. Elden J. Watson, ed., *Manuscript History of Brigham Young, 1846–1847* (Salt Lake City: by the author, 1971), 528; see also Young's statement as recorded in Willard Richards diary, 28 Feb. 1847, LDS Archives; see also the statement in John D. Lee diary, 28 Feb. 1847, which added "embrased in his arms," in Charles Kelley, ed., *Journals of John D. Lee, 1846–47 and 1859* (Salt Lake City: Western, 1938), 105.

50. Charles Ora Card diary, 24 Jan. 1896, in Donald Y. Godfrey and Brigham Y. Card, eds., *The Diaries of Charles Ora Card: The Canadian Years, 1886–1903* (Salt Lake City: University of Utah Press, 1993), 325. This published version accidentally dropped the final *t* from *thought,* which is in the original diary entry.

51. While Card's diary expressed male intimacy in the unselfconscious terms of a culture lacking concepts of sexuality, his great-grandson depicted male-male intimacy in the multifaceted view of contemporary American society. Charles Ora Card and Orson Scott Card are familial examples of a major difference between nineteenth- and twentieth-century Mormons. Nationally acclaimed as a science fiction writer, Orson Scott Card has written in conflicting

ways about sexual identity and the consequences of same-sex intimacy that did not seem to concern his great-grandfather. The modern Card's negative portrayals appeared in several publications between 1978 and 1993, yet co-existed with his positive portrayals of male-male intimacy and homoeroticism.

Beginning as installments in 1978, Card's *Songmaster* (New York: Dial, 1980; New York: Tor, 1987) introduced homophobia with a nine-year-old boy's complaint about a security guard who "held my penis as if he wanted to own it" (125). In fact the first half of the book homophobically acknowl-edged only one kind of homoerotic desire—the lust of men for a prepubescent boy (46, 105, 120–21, 122–23, 125, 127–28, 143, 145, 164, 210). This boy had only one homoerotic experience at age seventeen, which was followed by the castration and suicide of his male lover and resulted in lifelong impotency for the boy (298–301, 312, 319–20). In "Notes from a Guardian Angel," *Seventh East Press* (Provo, Utah), 22 July 1982–8 Mar. 1983, Card described the traumatic experience of a sixteen-year-old Mormon. After the young Mormon and a recently returned LDS missionary declared their mutual love one night, a "wrestling match soon turned to something else . . . an act he had barely been aware existed in the world" (8 Feb. 1983, 16). Because he "en-joyed" this sexual act, Card's hero reluctantly told himself: "I am a homosex-ual." His guardian angel countered: "God does not make such creatures, they make themselves! Like murderers, adulterers, shoplifters, liars, and traffic scofflaws, you are only what you choose" (16). The last words that the six-teen year old said to the young man he had "loved" and now rejected as re-pulsive: "But you don't want to be happy. You just want to be ----ed" (16). In "Lost Boys," *Magazine of Fantasy and Science Fiction*, Oct. 1989, 12–76, Orson Scott Card related a case of homosexual pedophilia and child murder as if his own son had been one of several victims of "the old man" (reprinted in 1990, 1992). Later Card replied to "the argument by the hypocrites of homosexuality that homosexual tendencies are genetically ingrained" in his essay "A Changed Man: The Hypocrites of Homosexuality," *Sunstone* 14 (Feb. 1990): 44. He answered that "the average fifteen-year old teenage boy is ge-netically predisposed to copulate with anything that moves." This statement was revised in Card, *A Story Teller in Zion* (Salt Lake City: Bookcraft, 1993), 183. Speaking on behalf of all "the Saints," Card wrote that "we expect them to meet a higher standard of behavior than the one their own body teaches them" (44). This essay was reviewed by fellow Mormon Paul Swenson in the *Salt Lake Tribune*, 12 Sept. 1993, E-4.

Contemporaneous with these negative assessments, nonjudgmental accounts of homoeroticism and self-defined homosexuals appeared in Card's writing. In addition to having emotionally intense, nonerotic relationships with older males, *Songmaster*'s teenage hero began his first homoerotic act by telling his married friend: "But why shouldn't you have what you want?" (297). Before his marriage, this man had told his future wife: "I'm sixty-two percent attracted to men, thirty-one percent attracted to women, and seven percent attracted to sheep" (231). She "understood something that nobody had ever bothered to explain to her in all the explanations of homosexuality that she had heard. That when [his male lover] Bant left it was the end of the world for Josif, because when he attached to somebody he didn't know how to let go" (230). Card writes about another homoerotic experience: "Josif's touch was not like the touch of the guard who had lusted for Ansset. . . . His eyes were not like the eyes of the pederasts. . . . Josif's lips on his skin spoke more eloquently than they had ever spoken when only air could receive their touch" (298).

Card's *Wyrms* (New York: Arbor House, 1987) included a nonjudgmental description of a homoerotic relationship (198–99, 201). The older male's name, derived from "Christ," was Kristiano, whose "boyok" partner "had a way of brushing ever-so-gently across the crotch of a rich-looking customer" (194).

In *Ships of Earth* (New York: Tor, 1994) gay bashing and homophobia are condemned in the scene revealing the homosexuality of Zdorab. Zdorab describes grisly castration-murders of two young men (138–39) and speaks of heterosexual males: "imagine what they'd do if they learned I was the monstrous thing, the crime against nature, the unmanly thing, the perfect image of what they fear they are" (142). In a marriage of necessity, "even though his body had had no particular joy from [his wife's] . . . there was joy in it on another level." Although he "merely acted out of duty while desperately trying to fantasize another love . . . I acted out of pure love, and not out of some inborn instinct that captured me. Indeed, I acted *against* my instinct" (225). In the sequel *Earthfall* (1995), this happy couple has a son and a daughter.

Like most nineteenth-century Americans, Charles Ora Card expressed no concern that kissing another man had homoerotic potential. Like most twentieth-century Americans, Orson Scott Card shows a concern in his writings that close physical contact with a same-sex friend could lead to a homoerotic experience. However, few nineteenth-century Americans regarded male-male sexual relationships with the diversity of views found in Card's writings.

52. Karen V. Hansen, "'Helped Put in a Quilt': Men's Work and Male Intimacy in Nineteenth-Century New England," *Gender and Society* 3 (Sept. 1989): 347.

53. Daniel Webster to J. Hervey Bingham, 3 Apr. 1804, in Charles M. Wiltse and Harold D. Moser, eds., *The Papers of Daniel Webster: Correspondence*, 7 vols. (Hanover, N.H.: University Press of New England, 1974–86), 1:51, and 24n for Bingham's age; this letter is also in Kenneth E. Shewmaker, ed., *Daniel Webster: "The Completest Man"* (Hanover, N.H.: University Press of New England, 1990), 159.

54. Helena Whitbread, ed., *I Know My Own Heart: The Diaries of Anne Lister, 1791–1840* (New York: New York University Press, 1992); Helena

Whitbread, ed., *No Priest but Love: The Journals of Anne Lister from 1824–1826* (New York: New York University Press, 1992).

55. Carl N. Degler, "What Ought to Be and What Was: Women's Sexuality in the Nineteenth Century," *American Historical Review* 79 (Dec. 1974): 1467–90; Peter Gay, *The Bourgeois Experience: Victoria to Freud,* vol. 1, *Education of the Senses* (New York: Oxford University Press, 1984), 72–89, 461–62; see also Karen Lystra, *Searching the Heart: Women, Men, and Romantic Love in Nineteenth-Century America* (New York: Oxford University Press, 1989); Michael Mason, *The Making of Victorian Sexual Attitudes* (Oxford: Oxford University Press, 1994), 13, 141, 216–17, 218–22; see also Michael Mason, *The Making of Victorian Sexuality* (Oxford: Oxford University Press, 1994), 199–204, 218–19. See chap. 4, note 4 and chap. 7, note 28 for sources on the widespread encouragement of women's sexual repression in nineteenth-century America.

56. Celia Duel Mosher, *The Mosher Survey: Sexual Attitudes of Forty-Five Victorian Women,* ed. James MaHood and Kristine Wenburg (New York: Arno Press/New York Times, 1980); Carl N. Degler, *At Odds: Women and the Family in America from the Revolution to the Present* (New York: Oxford University Press, 1980), 262–65. Mosher's first survey was dated 11 Apr. 1892. She was also a speaker at the first International Conference of Women Physicians in 1919. See chap. 8 for a discussion of that conference's presentations about homosexuality.

57. F[rederick]. S. Ryman diary, Aug. 1886, printed in full in Martin Duberman, *About Time: Exploring the Gay Past,* rev. ed. (New York: Meridian Books/Penguin, 1991), 63; for Frederick S. Ryman (b. Apr. 1858) see 1900 U.S. Census of Boston, Suffolk County, Massachusetts, enumeration district 1481, sheet 3, microfilm, LDS Family History Library.

58. Albert Dodd diary, Mar. 1837, quoted in Peter Gay, *The Bourgeois Experience: Victoria to Freud,* vol. 2, *The Tender Passion* (New York: Oxford University Press, 1986), 210; see also E. Anthony Rotundo, *American Manhood: Transformations in Masculinity from the Revolution to the Modern Era* (New York: Basic Books, 1993), 81.

59. Martin Bauml Duberman, "'Writhing Bedfellows': 1826, Two Young Men from Antebellum South Carolina's Ruling Elite Share 'Extravagant Delight,'" *Journal of Homosexuality* 6 (Fall 1980–Winter 1981): 85–101, esp. 87–88, reprinted in Salvatore J. Licata and Robert P. Petersen, eds., *The Gay Past: A Collection of Historical Essays* (New York: Harrington Park Press, 1985), 85–101, reprinted as "'Writhing Bedfellows' in South Carolina: Historical Interpretation and the Politics of Evidence," in Martin Bauml Duberman, Martha Vicinus, and George Chauncey Jr., eds., *Hidden from History: Reclaiming the Gay and Lesbian Past* (New York: New American Library, 1989), 153–68.

60. Rotundo, "Romantic Friendship," 10–12; see also Rotundo's other statement of this view in his *American Manhood,* 83–84, and in Karen V. Hansen, "'Our Eyes Behold Each Other': Masculinity and Intimate Friendship in Antebellum New England," in Peter M. Nardi, ed., *Men's Friendship: Research on Men and Masculinities* (Newbury Park, Calif.: Sage, 1992), 45; see also Wrathall, "American Manhood and the Y.M.C.A.," 3.

61. "Intimate Friendships: History Shows That the Lines Between 'Straight' and 'Gay' Sexuality Are Much More Fluid Than Today's Debate Suggests," *U.S. News and World Report,* 5 July 1993, 49; Slaughter, *Life in Zion, 1820–1995,* 124; see also William R. Taylor and Christopher Lasch, "Two 'Kindred Spirits': Sorority and Family in New England, 1839–1846," *New England Quarterly* 36 (Mar. 1963): 23–41.

62. Wrathall, "American Manhood and the Y.M.C.A.," 205, 209–10; Slaughter, *Life in Zion,* 67.

63. Track team photograph in *Eastonia* (Salt Lake City: East High School, 1923), 87; basketball's "Southern Team" photograph in *The S Book, 1922* (Salt Lake City: Latter-day Saints University, 1922), unnumbered page; track team photograph in *Etosian* (Salt Lake City: Students of Westminster College and Collegiate Institute, 1923), 118; swimming team photograph in *The Anniversary "S" Book* (Salt Lake City: Latter-day Saints University, 1927), 118; see also *The "S" Book, 1930* (Salt Lake City: Latter-day Saints College, 1930), 172, for a photo of the swimming team in which three young men in the front row (out of twelve total) hold the knees of teammates; basketball team photograph in *The Etosian* (Salt Lake City: Sophomore Class of Westminster College, 1930), 55; track team photograph in *The 1941 Etosian* (Salt Lake City: Associated Students of Westminster College, 1941), 46; track team photograph in *1942 Etosian* (Salt Lake City: Associated Students of Westminster College, 1942), [49]. During this period many school yearbooks, especially at Westminster College, had photographs of athletes individually rather than in groups, which prevents any analysis of physical touch or lack of it in photographs of athletic teams. The first and only such photograph in the yearbooks of Brigham Young University to 1930 was in *Banyan, 1912,* 71.

64. See chap. 10.

CHAPTER 4

The Homoemotional
and the Homoromantic

THE HOMOEMOTIONAL CONTENT of nineteenth-century America is startling to many Americans today. For example, the official history of the Young Men's Christian Association (YMCA) stated that it was formed in the midnineteenth century in response to "the craving of young men for companionship with each other."[1] Rather than using the term *homoaffectionalism,* which other authors have used to describe such intense feelings,[2] I prefer the concept *homoemotionalism,* which implies a broader range of responses, including grief, jealousy, anger, and mutual admiration.

Like Mormonism, nineteenth-century American culture was extremely homosocial, homotactile, and homoemotional. In other words, most American males looked to other males for intense emotional bonding as well as for social activity and physical touch.[3] Such intense friendships were even more common among middle-class females in Victorian America, which rigorously encouraged females to have a separate sphere of life from males, to conceal their sexual interest in men, and to suppress their enjoyment of sexual intimacy with males.[4]

On the female side of nineteenth-century homoemotional expression are the letters of the American poet Emily Dickinson. In 1846, at age fifteen, she wrote a girlfriend: "I long to see you once more, to clasp you in my arms." In 1855, she wrote another young woman: "How I wish you were mine, as you once were, when I had you in the morning, and when the sun went down, and was sure I should never go to sleep without a moment from you." Then Emily added: "Let us love with all our might, Jennie, for who knows where our hearts go, when this world is done?" To an absent female friend in 1860, Emily wrote: "I touch your hand—my cheek, your cheek—I stroke your vanished hair." Emily Dickinson typically used such physical terms to express her emotional connection with women. She remained unmarried, but most of her female correspondents were married.[5]

A public expression of homoemotionalism among Mormon females first appeared in April 1873. "Perhaps you do not know it, but there are women who fall in love with each other," began a brief essay reprinted in the Mormon suffragist periodical *Woman's Exponent*. Published originally in a New York newspaper by "Fanny Fern," the non-Mormon author Grata P. Willis (Eldredge Parton), the essay lightheartedly described the woman "who does the courting" with the warning: "She will flirt with women by the score." In addition to these references to female-female courtship and flirting Willis titled this essay "Women Lovers." The editor of the *Woman's Exponent* at this time was twenty-four-year-old Louise L. Greene, who married two months after this essay appeared in the LDS publication. Greene's decision to reprint the essay indicates her assumption that "Women Lovers" was of interest to Mormon women.[6]

Two years later, editor "Lula" Greene Richards printed in the *Woman's Exponent* one reader's explanation of why some "women lovers" in Utah remained unmarried. Under the name "Old Maid," this woman wrote: "I have such an utter detestation for the whole [male] sex that it is with the greatest difficulty that I can treat the men with common civility." She added: "And don't think I have been crossed in love either, for I haven't." Unlike the non-LDS author of "Women Lovers," this anti-male author was a Utah woman and probably Mormon. A later article referred to her recent attendance at a lecture by a Mormon artist.[7] Maxine Hanks, a feminist researcher of Mormon lesbianism, regards this 1875 essay as an example of Mormon women for whom "female bonding and lesbianism are the only escape from the pattern of male dominance." Hanks indicates that Mormon lesbian experience is female bonding, which is the *only* possible escape from or resistance against the "coding of male perspective onto female bodies and lives within a patriarchal or male-dominant context."[8]

However, Leila J. Rupp has warned against applying the twentieth-century's narrowly defined category *lesbian* to such relationships in either the twentieth century or the nineteenth. She suggests that there is and was "a broader category of woman-committed women who would not identify as lesbians but whose primary commitment, in emotional and practical terms, was to other women." Although people have commonly denied any erotic component in the emotionally intimate and physically close relationships between nineteenth-century women, the truth was probably more complex. Rather than assuming that all or none were what we in the twentieth century think of as lesbians, Rupp adds: "There are lesbians who have never had a sexual relationship with another woman and there are women who have had sexual experiences with women but do not identify as lesbians."[9]

The male-male emotional bonding that was common in the nineteenth century appears in Albert Dodd's Connecticut diary. Only days after writing about his friend Anthony's "arms around my neck" and Dodd's desire "to hold his beloved form in my embrace," this Yale student wrote in 1837: "what is love?" He answered: "All I know is that there are three persons in this world whom I have loved, and those are, Julia, John, & Anthony. Dear, beloved trio." The historian Peter Gay comments that the young man "loved men and women indiscriminately without undue self-laceration, without visible private guilt or degrading public shame. His bisexual inclinations seemed innocent to Dodd, and apparently to others, because his bearing and behavior, including his emotional attachments to others of his sex, did not affront current codes of conduct."[10]

The historian Donald Yacovone has observed that emotional intimacy between nineteenth-century men was especially intense when they were united in a holy cause, such as abolishing American slavery (or, for that matter, building the Mormon "Zion"). Charles Stuart wrote fellow abolitionist Theodore Dwight Weld in 1838: "You are mine and I am yours. God made us one from the beginning." Nearly thirty years younger than his friend, Weld told his own fiancee: "I can hardly trust myself to speak or write of him: so is my whole being seized with love and admiration of his most worthy character."[11] That same year, another young abolitionist wrote "My Dear Bro. Weld" and confessed: "the gushings of my soul have prompted me to throw my arms around your neck and kiss you." Neither they, nor their wives, saw any impropriety in such same-sex feelings and acts.[12]

However, there was one group in the early nineteenth century who defined such intense same-sex friendships as "unnatural," "improper," or "disease[d]." Phrenologists provided "scientific" descriptions of people's personalities after examining the contours of their heads. The two phrenological categories of significance with regard to personal relationships were "Adhesiveness" (friendship) and "Amativeness" (amorous love between male and female). As early as 1836, the British phrenologist Robert Macnish described an "unnatural" same-sex friendship. "ADHESIVENESS.—I knew two gentlemen whose attachment to each other was so excessive, as to amount to a disease. When the one visited the other, they slept in the same bed, sat constantly alongside of each other at table, spoke in affectionate whispers, and were, in short, miserable when separated. The strength of their attachment was shown by the uneasiness, amounting to jealousy, with which one surveyed any thing approaching to tenderness and kindness, which the other might show to a third party." The historian Michael Lynch explains that phrenologists like Macnish and Orson S. Fowler, an American, believed that such "same-sex passions resulted from high Adhesiveness and low Amativeness (which involved exclusively opposite-sex relationships)."[13]

Those views were significant to Mormonism because phrenology was very popular among nineteenth-century Mormons. It was so popular that some Utah congregations used phrenological publications as Sunday School class textbooks, and individual Mormons praised Fowler's writings.[14] The official *History of the Church* still publishes Joseph Smith's 1842 phrenological chart based on a 12–point scale. It described his amativeness and adhesiveness as follows: "Amativeness—11, [V.] L[arge]. . . . passionately fond of the company of the other sex," and "Adhesiveness—8, F[air]. Solicitous for the happiness of friends." This official history also continues to acknowledge that a score of 11 on the scale (such as the Mormon prophet had) indicated "V.L.," or an "extreme liability to perversion" in the trait.[15]

Although Smith had a moderate score for male friendship, his score was extremely high for opposite-sex relationships. His contemporaries nodded in agreement with that assessment of the Mormon prophet, who secretly married more than forty wives, including several teenagers as young as fourteen. Some of these plural wives testified that they "roomed" with him "as a wife," and expressed their adoration for him.[16]

However, it is significant that some prominent Mormons had phrenological charts with higher scores for same-sex Adhesiveness than for opposite-sex Amativeness. This was the ratio that phrenologists regarded as potentially "unnatural." For example, in 1842 the front page of Nauvoo's *Wasp* printed Brigham Young's phrenological chart, which showed his scores were "Amativeness—7 [Fair]" and "Adhesiveness—10 [Large]."[17] Since Mormons were familiar with phrenological interpretations, they were not surprised by Brigham's public statement that he was less interested in "the private society of women" than most men were.[18] In fact, despite fathering fifty-seven children, Young had a reputation for ignoring the emotional and sexual needs of his wives, as several of them attested.[19] One of his daughters even wrote that Brigham Young's sexual neglect caused a plural wife's emotional problems due to "her gnawing desire."[20]

Although phrenology's cranial examination and personality scores may sound ludicrous to twentieth-century ears, nineteenth-century Mormons seemed to take these charts seriously.[21] However, there is no evidence that Mormons expressed any concern about having higher phrenological scores for same-sex Adhesiveness than for opposite-sex Amativeness. Despite phrenology's popularity among nineteenth-century Mormons, they valued the intensity of same-sex friendships more than phrenology's warnings about "excessive," "unnatural," "improper," or "disease[d]" friendships between persons of the same gender.

However, apparently unaware of the decades-old warning of male phrenologists about same-sex friendships, by the 1880s some American women were expressing similar concern. After an investigation of the private colleges for women, Alice Blackwell reported: "One thing which damaged the health of the girls seriously was 'smashes'—an extraordinary habit which they have of falling violently in love with each other, and suffering all the pangs of unrequited attachment, desperate jealousy etc. etc., with as much energy as if one of them were a man." Blackwell regarded this as an unfortunate result of the gender segregation in the "Seven Sisters" colleges: "The coeducational colleges don't suffer much from 'smashes.' The natural attraction between young men & young women is pretty sure to be stronger than this unnatural & fantastic one between girl & girl."[22] Like the warnings of phrenologists, there is no evidence that any Mormons of the late nineteenth century shared this concern about overly intense friendships between females.

This was most clearly indicated in the tribute Emmeline B. Wells, editor of the Mormon *Woman's Exponent,* wrote for the recently deceased Frances E. Willard, national president of the Woman's Christian Temperance Union (WCTU). Nine years before her death, the never-married suffragist devoted a section of her widely circulated autobiography to her "heart affair[s]" with fifty women during the previous forty years. Willard's biographer has noted: "From time to time circumstances made one intimate friend more important to Willard than others, but her relationships with women were never exclusive."[23] The *Exponent*'s editor knew her personally and emphasized the last same-sex relationship in Frances Willard's life: "She has lived much of the time with Lady [Isabel] Somerset . . . a congeniality between these two women has held them fast in a sublime and sacred friendship."[24] Emmeline B. Wells was a thrice-married woman who expressed passionate love for each of her husbands, yet she had nothing but praise for a woman who had "heart affair[s]" with women rather than men.[25]

Likewise, despite his well-earned reputation of emotional intimacy with women, Joseph Smith also shared love of similar intensity with young men. In the autumn of 1838, Smith stayed two weeks with the family of John W. Hess, who later wrote: "I was a boy then about fourteen years old. He used to take me up on his knee and caress me as he would a little child." As a result, Hess wrote: "I became very much attached to him, and learned to love him more dearly than any other person I ever met, my father and mother not excepted."[26]

Even more profound was the lifelong effect of a three-week visit Smith made to the Taylor home in 1842, beginning on the nineteenth birthday of William Taylor (a younger brother of LDS president John Taylor). "It is impossible for me to express my feelings in regard to this period of my life," William Taylor began. "I have never known the same joy and satisfaction in the companionship of any other person, man or woman, that I felt with him, the man who had conversed with the Almighty." That was an extraordinary statement in view of Taylor's marriage at age twenty-two and his four subsequent plural marriages. Decades later, Taylor explained: "Sometimes in our return home in the evening after we had been tramping around in the woods, he [Joseph Smith] would call out: 'Here, mother, come David and Jonathan.'"[27]

In that way Mormonism's founding prophet referred to the most famous male friendship in the Bible. David said of his boyhood mentor Jonathan: "thy love to me was wonderful, passing the love of women" (2 Sam. 1:26). Jonathan and David already had wives when the two young men "kissed one another, and wept one with another" (20:41). Consistent with Smith's David-and-Jonathan reference to young Taylor, a Mormon woman described the Mormon prophet's last words to forty-two-year-old George W. Rosecrans as Smith was traveling to his certain death in Carthage Jail in June 1844: "If I never see you again, or if I never come back, remember that I love you."[28]

For more than a thousand years, David and Jonathan have been revered as sexual lovers by Jews and Christians who valued homoeroticism.[29] However, because David was a teenage polygamist and Jonathan fathered at least one child, most Bible readers and scholars regard David and Jonathan as platonic (or nonerotic) lovers.[30] Likewise, many regard the Bible's Song of Solomon as spiritual allegory rather than sexual imagery.[31]

First Presidency counselor George Q. Cannon paraphrased David's expression of male-male love during a sermon on Utah Pioneer Day in 1881: "Men may never have beheld each other's faces and yet they will love one another, and it is a love that is greater than the love of woman." Cannon, like other nineteenth-century Americans, then emphasized the platonic dimension of this male-male love: "It exceeds any sexual love that can be conceived of, and it is this love that has bound the [Mormon] people together."[32] As an example of such instant love between Mormon men, Apostle Abraham Owen Woodruff told a newly appointed stake president in 1898 that "he had learned to love me from our first meeting."[33]

Love for LDS leaders bordered on adoration by those Mormons who rarely, if ever, saw the men they regarded as prophets, seers, and revelators. For example, a young Tongan husband, born in 1889, wrote a letter to Apostle David O. McKay "to show my love for you," shortly after meeting McKay, who was the first general authority to visit Tonga. The letter continued: "And I thank the Lord that I have lived to see you, to hear your voice and to touch your hand."[34]

Because it was common for male-male friendships to be emotionally intense in the nineteenth century, it did not occur to LDS leaders to instruct full-time missionaries to make an effort to love each other. They assumed that would happen naturally within days after missionary companions met. For example, in 1899 the first published guide for prospective LDS missionaries expected love would develop between missionary companions even before their arrival at their mission assignment: "During the short time they have traveled together they have become quite attached to each other."[35] After American males generally became emotionally distant from other males in the midtwentieth century, then it became necessary for Mormon leaders to teach young missionaries to feel love for other young men.[36]

However, in keeping with the nineteenth century's valuation of male-male love, in 1902 Apostle Heber J. Grant cited David and Jonathan to describe his love for General Authority J. Golden Kimball. "The people of the world know not the love which fills the hearts of faithful and devoted servants of God," Grant wrote. Kimball described their next meeting, where Grant "not only shook me by the hand, but kissed me."[37]

Twentieth-century Mormon publications have also praised Mormon leaders for sharing a David-and-Jonathan love. For example, Apostle (and later church president) David O. McKay was the center of two relationships in which his friend was defined as a Jonathan. McKay's son referred to this modern apostle David's "beloved 'Jonathan,' Orson F. Whitney." Apostle Whitney sometimes signed his letters "Jonathan" when writing to his friend David O. McKay.[38] Nicknaming one another "David" and "Jonathan" was common among nineteenth-century friends, including Protestant ministers.[39] In 1951, Gordon B. Hinckley (later appointed an apostle and LDS president) wrote that in their late twenties, church president McKay and his counselor Stephen L Richards "commenced a David-and-Jonathan friendship which has lasted and strengthened . . . [and] their love and appreciation for one another has grown steadily over the years."[40]

There has never been a suggestion of a homoerotic dimension in the deep friendship David O. McKay shared with either apostle he called his "Jonathan." I find no evidence whatever of sexual intimacy or homoerotic interest among these LDS leaders. On the other hand, physical intimacy was part of the relationship between two prominent nineteenth-century Mormon women who were also described as David and Jonathan.[41]

The Homoromantic

The line separating emotional attachment from romantic love is often unclear—even to the person who experiences the emotions. Love letters and love poetry are traditional indicators of the romantic love of one person for another. However, nineteenth-century Anglo-American literature was also filled with such effusive phrasing by men as the poet

Shelley's "I fall upon the thorns of life! I bleed!"[42] The social historian Vern L. Bullough has called this "the breast-heaving literary style of the day."[43]

The overheated romanticism of nineteenth-century literary conventions complicates our current evaluation of apparently romantic exchanges between persons of the same gender during that period. Yacovone writes: "We must not misunderstand the purposes or befuddle the context of this language and the nature of such intimacies. The nineteenth century understood and rejected what we would call homosexual acts but had no consciousness of a homosexual persona."[44] However, it would be simplistic to deny there was an erotic dimension in every romantic exchange between male friends and between female friends in the nineteenth century.

Mormons left many literary expressions of their feelings. There were romantic (even passionate) love letters between Mormon husbands and wives of the nineteenth century, including correspondence with plural wives.[45] However, I know of no similar examples of same-sex romance among Mormon letter writers of the nineteenth century.

As for poetry, no Mormon rivaled the same-sex romanticism of Walt Whitman and Emily Dickinson.[46] Despite his openly homoerotic poetry, Whitman specifically denied that he was homosexual in a letter to John Addington Symonds, who was a homosexual, yet Whitman acknowledged his sexual interest in men during a conversation with Oscar Wilde.[47] Thirty years before that admission, Whitman recorded in his diary that he took to bed several young men he met on the streets of New York City or in the Turkish baths there.[48] Whitman demonstrated that a person's public and private denials of homoerotic interest cannot be accepted at face value in a culture that disapproves of the homoerotic.

A prominent LDS poet of the Dickinson-Whitman era wrote about both male-male love and female-female romance. Born in 1871, Kate Thomas contributed many short stories and poems to the LDS Church's *Young Woman's Journal*. She never married.[49] Lavina Fielding Anderson has observed that Kate Thomas "actually preferred using a male point of view" in the stories and poems she published in the LDS magazine. For example, Thomas adopted the persona of a boy named Tom for a story that began: "And I was madly in love with my big-bodied English chum, Ashford, summering in the same village."[50]

However, in her love poetry Thomas wrote by her own name and assumed no male persona as she expressed love for women, whom she often named in the poems. Her readers may have assumed that a male was speaking in her love poetry, but Kate Thomas's by-line indicated the voice was hers in all but one love poem directed to women. The *Young Woman's Journal* also published some of Kate's love poetry addressed to women, including one that began: "I have a little boat of Love, moored where the lilies grow" and continued: "O exquisite white maiden, come in my boat with me!" Whether Thomas intended it or not, those words and images suggested eroticism according to the language usage of her time.[51]

Those lines in the Thomas poem also echoed the concluding stanza of Emily Dickinson's controversial "Wild Nights." In 1891 Dickinson's devoted editor hesitated to publish that poem "lest the malignant read into it more than that virgin recluse ever dreamed of putting there."[52] Dickinson's "Wild Nights" concluded: "Rowing in Eden— / Ah, the Sea! / Might I but moor—Tonight— / In Thee!" Those words were less explicit than the phrasing in Thomas's poem yet Dickinson's nineteenth-century editor recognized a sexual meaning that he did not want to admit she had intended.[53] Their poetry indicates that both Dickinson and Thomas "dreamed of" far more than some have been willing to acknowledge. They, like all poets, carefully chose each word and its nuances and were clearly aware of the erotic subtext in their work.[54]

Kate Thomas also frequently used the word *gay* in its common meaning of "happy" or "light-hearted" in her love poetry. On the surface that seems insignificant. However, the appearance of *gay* in several of Thomas's same-sex love poems also echoed its century-old reference to sensuality and the specific use of *gay* since the 1880s as a slang word for males who had sex with other males.[55] Concerning *gay* as a code word in early twentieth-century America, the historian George Chauncey observes: "Because the word's use in gay environments had given it homosexual associations that were unknown to people not involved in the gay world, more circumspect gay men [and women] could use it to identify themselves secretly to each other in a straight setting."[56]

For example the *Young Woman's Journal* published one of Kate Thomas's same-sex love poems about "the one in all the world I love best." The next line used the word *gay* and continued: "From her lips I take Joy never-ceasing."[57] Thomas published this in the LDS journal for young women in 1903 while she was living in New York City's

Greenwich Village, where the word *gay* meant homosexual.[58] By then, the Village area below Fourteenth Street was a sexually ambiguous mix of working-class immigrants (primarily unmarried men), cultural bohemians, political radicals, avant-garde writers, street prostitutes (both female and male) living in a neighborhood of coffee houses, restaurants, small businesses, warehouses, hotels, tenements, and dance halls, as well as female and male houses of prostitution. This was where "New York's first substantial lesbian enclaves developed."[59]

Nevertheless, literary historians have warned that the homoerotic elements in such poetry should not obscure other dimensions of the poet's craft. For example, Ronald A. Sharp has written concerning Whitman's poetry about men: "But must we rescue the poems' homosexual dimensions by denying—or at least ignoring—their concern with friendship?"[60] Certainly not.

Still, Kate Thomas chose not to publish her poems that expressed "an almost sensual passion for women," according to the archivist of her private papers.[61] For example, the unpublished poem "A Gay Musician" seemed to describe Kate's gentle seduction of a female friend:

> That dear white hand within my own I took.
> "Illa," I whispered, "may I keep it so?"
> My eager blood its anxious cheek forsook.
> Fearing my love that loved me might say no.
>   Oh foolish fear! My dear love's heart rebelled
> That I should doubt & seeking to reprove,
> She raised her eyes. There looking I beheld
> The soul of Music through the eyes of love.[62]

Another unpublished poem by Thomas referred to an aggressive female-female seduction: "With the rose I gave her fastened in her hair; / And her eyes o'errun with laughter— / Well she knows what I am after / . . . I must storm her if I take her!" Had the words been more explicit, the poem would have bordered on pornography by her society's standards. In an unpublished poem addressed to "Margaret," Kate also wrote: "And the kiss you gave me, sweet-heart, it burned into my heart."[63]

Kate Thomas is the only known writer of same-sex romantic poetry of such raw emotion among nineteenth-century Mormons. However, other Mormons have links to same-sex poetry. As director of the Mormon Tabernacle Choir, Evan Stephens wrote at least two romantic poems to celebrate the many same-sex relationships he "dared" to enter with male teenagers who shared his bed. In addition, the LDS actress Ada Dwyer Russell was the inspiration for same-sex poetry by the American poet Amy Lowell.[64]

NOTES

1. Laurence L. Doggett, *History of the Y.M.C.A.* (New York: Association Press, 1896), quoted in John Donald Wrathall, "American Manhood and the Y.M.C.A., 1868–1920" (Ph.D. diss., University of Minnesota, 1994), 13.

2. Paul D. Hardman, *Homoaffectionalism: Male Bonding from Gilgamesh to the Present* (San Francisco: GLB, 1993).

3. Ben Barker-Benfield, "The Spermatic Economy: A Nineteenth-Century View of Sexuality," *Feminist Studies* 1 (Summer 1972): 45–74; Elizabeth H. Pleck and Joseph H. Pleck, *The American Man* (Englewood Cliffs, N.J.: Prentice-Hall, 1980), 13; Leonard Harry Ellis, "Men among Men: An Exploration of All-Male Relationships in Victorian America" (Ph.D. diss., Columbia University, 1982); E. Anthony Rotundo, "Romantic Friendship: Male Intimacy and Middle-Class Youth in the United States, 1800–1900," *Journal of Social History* 23 (Fall 1989): 1–25, esp. 4; Karen V. Hansen, "'Our Eyes Behold Each Other': Masculinity and Intimate Friendship in Antebellum New England," in Peter M. Nardi, ed., *Men's Friendship: Research on Men and Masculinities* (Newbury Park, Calif.: Sage, 1992), 153–68. For a broader survey, see Hardman, *Homoaffectionalism*.

4. On repression of female sexuality in Victorian America, see Michael Gordon, "From an Unfortunate Necessity to a Cult of Mutual Orgasm: Sex in American Marital Education Literature, 1830–1940," in James Heslin, ed., *Studies in the Sociology of Sex* (New York: Appleton, Century, Crofts, 1971), 53–77; Peter T. Cominos, "Innocent Femina Sexualis in Unconscious Conflict," in Martha Vicinus, ed., *Suffer and Be Still* (Bloomington: Indiana University Press, 1972); Charles E. Rosenberg, "Sexuality, Class, and Roles in Nineteenth-Century America," *American Quarterly* 25 (May 1973): 131–53; Ronald G. Waters, *Primers for Prudery: Sexual Advice to Victorian America* (Englewood Cliffs, N.J.: Prentice-Hall, 1974); J. G. Barker-Benfield, *The Horrors of the Half-Known Life: Male Attitudes toward Women and Sexuality in Nineteenth-Century America* (New York: Harper and Row, 1976); Nancy F. Cott, "Passionless: An Interpretation of Victorian Sexual Ideology, 1790–1850," *Signs: Journal of Women in Culture and Society* 4 (Winter 1978): 219–36, reprinted in Nancy F. Cott and Elizabeth H. Pleck, eds., *A Heritage of Her Own: Toward a New Social History of American Women* (New York: Touchstone/Simon and Schuster, 1979), 548–49; Steven Seidman, "The Power of Desire and

the Danger of Pleasure: Victorian Sexuality Reconsidered," *Journal of Social History* 24 (Fall 1990): 47–67, esp. 49; Robert M. Ireland, "Frenzied and Fallen Females: Women and Sexual Dishonor in the Nineteenth-Century United States," *Journal of Women's History* 3 (Winter 1992): 96; Michael Mason, *The Making of Victorian Sexual Attitudes* (Oxford: Oxford University Press, 1994), 13, 218–22, with exceptional encouragement of female sexual pleasure by such writers as William Thompson (141) and Sylvia Pankhurst (216–17); see also Michael Mason, *The Making of Victorian Sexuality* (Oxford: Oxford University Press, 1994), 199–204, 218–19, which examines medical and popular writings that emphasized female pleasure in marital sex, the female orgasm, and the need for mutual orgasm.

On female-female friendships, see Judith Becker Ranlett, "Sorority and Community: Women's Answer to a Changing Massachusetts, 1865–1895" (Ph.D. diss., Brandeis University, 1974); Carroll Smith-Rosenberg, "The Female World of Love and Ritual: Relations between Women in Nineteenth-Century America," *Signs: Journal of Women in Culture and Society* 1 (Autumn 1975): 1–29; Carol Lasser, "'Let Us Be Sisters Forever': The Sororal Model of Nineteenth-Century Female Friendship," *Signs: Journal of Women in Culture and Society* 14 (Autumn 1988): 158–81; Neil Miller, *Out of the Past: Gay and Lesbian History from 1869 to the Present* (New York: Vintage/Random House, 1995), 55–63. For a historical survey of female-female friendship, see Lillian Faderman, *Surpassing the Love of Men: Romantic Friendship and Love between Women from the Renaissance to the Present* (New York: Columbia University Press, 1981).

5. Emily Dickinson to Abiah Root, 8 Sept. 1846, Dickinson to Jane Humphrey, 16 Oct. 1855, and Dickinson to Catherine Scott Turner (Anton), summer 1860, in Thomas H. Johnson and Theodora Ward, eds., *The Letters of Emily Dickinson,* 3 vols. (Cambridge, Mass.: Belknap Press/Harvard University Press, 1958), 1:38, 2:320, 365; see also John Cody, *After Great Pain: The Inner Life of Emily Dickinson* (Cambridge, Mass.: Belknap Press/Harvard University Press, 1971), 107–28; Lillian Faderman, "Emily Dickinson's Letters to Sue Gilbert," *Massachusetts Review* 18 (Summer 1977): 197–225; and Judith Farr, *The Passions of Emily Dickinson* (Cambridge, Mass.: Harvard University Press, 1992), 101–3.

6. Fanny Fern [Grata P. Willis Eldredge Parton], "Women Lovers," *Woman's Exponent* 1 (15 Apr. 1873): 175, and for Greene as editor, 172; Andrew Jenson, *Latter-day Saint Biographical Encyclopedia,* 4 vols. (Salt Lake City: Deseret News Press and Andrew Jenson History, 1901–36), 4:295; Sherilyn Cox Bennion, "Lula Greene Richards: Utah's First Woman Editor," *Brigham Young University Studies* 21 (Spring 1981): 155–74. For a biography of the original essayist (who died six months before the Utah reprinting of her essay), see E. Addie Heath, "Fanny Fern," *Woman's Exponent* 8 (15 May 1880):

191–92. Heath's article indicated that Fanny Fern's essays appeared originally in the *New York Ledger.*

7. "An Old Maid's Protest," *Woman's Exponent* 4 (15 Oct. 1875): 79, reprinted in Maxine Hanks, ed., *Women and Authority: Re-emerging Mormon Feminism* (Salt Lake City: Signature Books, 1992), 80. The reference to the Salt Lake City artist George M. Ottinger was in "Fourth Epistle of Hal to the 'Old Maid,'" *Woman's Exponent* 5 (1 Sept. 1876): 49. For Ottinger, see Frank Esshom, *Pioneers and Prominent Men of Utah* (Salt Lake City: Utah Pioneers Book Publishing, 1913), 1080. Many writers, even during her own lifetime, have spelled her nickname "Lulu," but "Lula" is how it appeared on the editorial page of the above issue of *Woman's Exponent,* as well as in Bennion's brief biography.

8. Maxine Hanks, "Toward a Mormon Lesbian History: Female Bonding as Resistance to Patriarchal Colonization," audiotape of paper presented at Conference on Sexuality and Homosexuality, 24 Apr. 1993, University of Utah; Hanks to D. Michael Quinn, 8 Aug. 1995. Hanks's views are similar to some of those expressed by Adrienne Rich in "Compulsory Heterosexuality and Lesbian Existence," *Signs: Journal of Women in Culture and Society* 5 (Summer 1980): 631–60, especially Rich's statements on pages 653 and 657: "Heterosexuality has been both forcibly and subliminally imposed on women, yet everywhere women have resisted it. . . . Woman-identification is a source of energy, a potential springhead of female power, violently curtailed and wasted under the institution of heterosexuality . . . [which is] the lie of compulsory female heterosexuality."

Mildred J. Berryman's study provides the only available test for the applicability of what I call the "Hanks Thesis" to nineteenth-century lesbians in Mormon culture. Berryman's interviews, which are examined in chap. 7, did not demonstrate there was an antipatriarchal or "escape" motivation for the lesbian experiences of her informants. However, Berryman reported anti-male feelings in several of the Mormon lesbians and also that several LDS women had their first same-sex experiences after unhappy relationships with men. Those findings were consistent with the Hanks Thesis, even though resistance to patriarchy is not identical with anti-male feelings. Still, most nineteenth-century lesbians in Berryman's study explained their same-sex experiences as the result of their feeling erotic interest in other women since childhood. That does not seem to support the Hanks Thesis, at least at the conscious level, for the lesbians in Berryman's study.

I know of two contemporary cases that support the Hanks Thesis. I became acquainted with one Mormon woman who was a student at Brigham Young University and who later entered a long-term lesbian relationship after a bitterly unhappy "time and eternity" LDS marriage to a man. She told me that her lesbian relationship was simply a postdivorce "feminist choice" (which she assured me was permanent) and that she had never previously felt erotic interest in a woman. She expressed gratitude that her sexual responses cooperated with her feminist decision to enter a lesbian relationship. This was also the experience described by the Mormon feminist Sonia Johnson in her *Going Out of Our Minds: The Metaphysics of Liberation* (Freedom, Calif.: Crossing Press, 1987), 95–124.

Nevertheless, I regard those cases as exceptional for contemporary feminists and for lesbians. According to my research and my personal acquaintances, only a minority of feminists are lesbian and only a minority of those in lesbian relationships have chosen that lifestyle as a feminist option, rather than as a sexual imperative. The vast majority of contemporary lesbians and female bisexuals report early childhood feelings of erotic interest in females.

Moreover, Adrienne Rich would regard as irrelevant and misleading the Berryman study's examples and the BYU student example I cited above. She also argued: "Another layer of the lie is the frequently encountered implication that women turn to women out of hatred for men" (658). Ultimately, the "Rich Thesis" (and possibly the Hanks version of it) is beyond either verification or refutation because it asserts that resistance against "woman-hatred" and "compulsory female heterosexuality" is universally unconscious and consciously inconsistent, especially on the part of many "lifelong sexual lesbians" who have aligned their "social, political, and intellectual allegiances with men" (645). Likewise, I regard as both unverifiable and irrefutable the claim for some polygamous marriage arrangements as "heroic acts of Lesbian resistance" by early Mormon women as asserted by Rocky O'Donovan in "'The Abominable and Detestable Crime against Nature': A Brief History of Homosexuality and Mormonism, 1840–1980" in Brent Corcoran, ed., *Multiply and Replenish: Mormon Essays on Sex and Family* (Salt Lake City: Signature Books, 1994), 125 (for which he cited Rich's essay). In contrast, I find the interpretation of Leila J. Rupp as persuasive and subject to historical verification (see note 9).

9. Leila J. Rupp, "'Imagine My Surprise': Women's Relationships in Historical Perspective," *Frontiers: A Journal of Women's Studies* 5 (Fall 1980): 67, and on the historical denial of lesbianism, 61–62, which is both an affirmation of and revision of Blanche Wiesen Cook's "The Historical Denial of Lesbianism," *Radical History Review* 20 (Spring–Summer 1979): 60–65.

10. Albert Dodd diary, Mar. 1837, quoted in Peter Gay, *The Bourgeois Experience: Victoria to Freud,* vol. 2, *The Tender Passion* (New York: Oxford University Press, 1986), 210, and Gay's commentary on 211–12.

11. Quotations from Donald Yacovone, "Abolitionists and the 'Language of Fraternal Love,'" in Mark C. Carnes and Clyde Griffen, eds., *Meanings for Manhood: Constructions of Masculinity in Victorian America* (Chicago: University of Chicago Press, 1990), 87–88, 91–92.

12. James A. Thome to Theodore Dwight Weld, 17 Apr. 1838, in Gilbert H. Barnes and Dwight L. Dumond, eds., *Letters of Theodore Dwight Weld, Angelina Grimke Weld, and Sarah Grimke, 1822–1844,* 2 vols. (Gloucester, Mass.: Peter Smith, 1965), 2:642, also quoted without exact date in Vern L. Bullough, *Sexual Variance in Society and History* (New York: John Wiley and Sons, 1976), 605.

13. Michael Lynch, "'Here Is Adhesiveness': From Friendship to Homosexuality," *Victorian Studies* 29 (Autumn 1985): 83 (for phrenologist references to "unnatural" or "improper"), 84 (for Macnish quotation), 82 (for Lynch quotation), 87 (for Fowler).

14. Davis Bitton and Gary L. Bunker, "Phrenology among the Mormons," *Dialogue: A Journal of Mormon Thought* 9 (Spring 1974): 42–61, esp. 45–46.

15. Brigham H. Roberts, ed., *History of the Church of Jesus Christ of Latter-day Saints,* 7 vols., 2d ed., rev. (Salt Lake City: Deseret Book, 1978), 5:53. The text explains that scores of 1 or 2 were V.S. ("very small or almost wholly wanting"), of 3 or 4 were S. ("small, or feeble, inactive"), of 5 or 6 were M. ("moderate or active only in a subordinate degree"), 7 or 8 were F. ("fair, and a little above par"), 9 or 10 were L. ("large, or quite energetic"), and 11 or 12 were V.L. ("very large, or giving a controlling influence, and extreme liability to perversion") (55).

16. Lawrence Foster, *Religion and Sexuality: Three American Communal Experiments of the Nineteenth Century* (New York: Oxford University Press, 1981), 155–66; Richard S. Van Wagoner, *Mormon Polygamy: A History* (Salt Lake City: Signature Books, 1986), 38–58; Lawrence Foster, *Women, Family, Utopia: Communal Experiments of the Shakers, the Oneida Community, and the Mormons* (Syracuse: Syracuse University Press, 1991), 137–55; Linda King Newell and Valeen Tippets Avery, *Mormon Enigma: Emma Hale Smith,* 2d ed. (Urbana: University of Illinois Press, 1994), 65–67, 95–101, 111, 125, 128–29, 134–47, 151–54.

17. *Wasp* (Nauvoo, Ill.), 16 July 1842, 1.

18. *Journal of Discourses,* 26 vols. (Liverpool: Latter-day Saints Book Depot, 1854–86), 5:99 (Young/1857).

19. Dean C. Jessee, ed., *Letters of Brigham Young to His Sons* (Salt Lake City: Deseret Book, 1974), xxiii, and for the names of his fifty-seven children, listed with each mother, 357–58. This is misstated as forty-six (which is actually the number who lived to adulthood) in Leonard J. Arrington's *Brigham Young: American Moses* (New York: Alfred A. Knopf, 1985), 223. For Young's emotional and sexual distance from his wives, see Ann-Eliza Young, *Wife No. 19 . . .* (Hartford, Conn.: Dustin, Gilman, 1875), 457, 460, 488, 489, 490, 491, 493, 494, 500, 512, 513, 514; Augusta Cobb Young to Brigham Young, 22 Jan., 20 July 1850, and 24 Mar. 1852 reference to "Emily [D. Partridge Young]

who is much in the Same condition," Theodore Schroeder Papers, Manuscript and Rare Book Division, New York Public Library, New York City, New York; Mary Ann Clark Powers Young to Brigham Young, 18 June 1851, Brigham Young Papers, Archives, Historical Department of the Church of Jesus Christ of Latter-day Saints, Salt Lake City, Utah (hereafter LDS Archives); Emily D. Partridge Young diary, 16 Apr. 1874, 1 Feb. 1875, 29 July 1881, typescript, Department of Special Collections and Manuscripts, Harold B. Lee Library, Brigham Young University, Provo, Utah (hereafter Lee Library).

20. Susa Young Gates, "My Father's Wives," typescript, page 2, Folder 1, Box 12, Gates Collection, Utah State Historical Society, Salt Lake City. The plural wife was Harriet Cook Young, who was not Gates's mother. Gates was not as specific about other plural wives she acknowledged her father had neglected.

21. Bitton and Bunker, "Phrenology among the Mormons."

22. Alice Blackwell to Kitty Blackwell, 12 Mar. 1882, quoted in Jonathan Ned Katz, *Gay/Lesbian Almanac: A New Documentary* (New York: Harper and Row, 1983), 178, also in Miller, *Out of the Past,* 60–61. See the discussion of these homoenvironmental schools in chap. 6.

23. Frances E. Willard, *Glimpses of Fifty Years: The Autobiography of an American Woman* (Chicago: H. J. Smith for the Woman's Temperance Publication Association, 1889), 637–49, esp. 638–39; Ruth Bordin, *Frances Willard: A Biography* (Chapel Hill: University of North Carolina Press, 1986), 45.

24. Emmeline B. Wells, "Frances Elizabeth Willard," *Woman's Exponent* 26 (1 May 1898): 273–74; for the relationship between Willard and Somerset, see Bordin, *Frances Willard,* 198–200, 225–26.

25. Emmeline B. Woodward Harris Whitney [unsigned] to Newel K. Whitney ("Father Guardian Husband"), 16 Oct. 1847, Document 205, Newel K. Whitney Papers, Department of Special Collections and Manuscripts, Lee Library, with full transcription in Carol Cornwall Madsen, "A Mormon Woman in Victorian America" (Ph.D. diss., University of Utah, 1985), 45, with further discussion of her passionate/emotional relationships with her husbands on pages 57–60.

26. John W. Hess, "Recollections of the Prophet Joseph Smith," *Juvenile Instructor* 27 (15 May 1892): 302, quoted in Hyrum L. Andrus and Helen Mae Andrus, comps., *They Knew the Prophet* (Salt Lake City: Bookcraft, 1974), 101.

27. "Joseph Smith, the Prophet," *Young Woman's Journal* 17 (Dec. 1906): 548, quoted in Andrus and Andrus, *They Knew the Prophet,* 161; Jenson, *Latter-day Saint Biographical Encyclopedia,* 1:564.

28. Mary Ellen Abel Kimball statement, quoted in Andrus and Andrus, *They Knew the Prophet,* 182; for Rosecrans see Susan Easton Black, *Membership of the Church of Jesus Christ of Latter-day Saints, 1830–1848,* 50 vols. (Pro-

vo, Utah: Religious Studies Center, Brigham Young University, 1984–88), 37:730. His name has sometimes been spelled Rosecrantz or Rosecraus.

29. John Boswell, *Christianity, Social Tolerance, and Homosexuality: Gay People in Western Europe from the Beginning of the Christian Era* (Chicago: University of Chicago Press, 1980), 238–39, 252, 299; Gladys Schmitt, *David the King* (New York: Dial Press, 1946), 67–69, 114–16, 156–58; Tom Horner, *Jonathan Loved David: Homosexuality in Biblical Times* (Philadelphia: Westminster Press, 1978); Wayne R. Dynes, ed., *Encyclopedia of Homosexuality*, 2 vols. (New York: Garland, 1990), 1:296–99.

30. George Arthur Buttrick, ed., *The Interpreter's Dictionary of the Bible*, 4 vols. (New York: Abingdon Press, 1962), 1:772–73, 2:969; David Lyle Jeffrey, ed., *A Dictionary of Biblical Tradition in English Literature* (Grand Rapids, Mich.: William B. Eerdmans, 1992), 411. As in *Webster's Ninth New Collegiate Dictionary* (Springfield, Massachusetts: Merriam-Webster, 1985), 901, I use the phrase *platonic love* in its conventional meaning of love where "sexual desire has been suppressed or sublimated." However, Plato's concept of ideal love included (rather than excluded) sexual expression between men, as explained in Paul Edwards, ed., *The Encyclopedia of Philosophy*, 8 vols. (New York: Macmillan Company and the Free Press, 1967), 5:90. Plato's most detailed expression of this was his *Symposium*.

31. Buttrick, *The Interpreter's Dictionary of the Bible*, 4:420, 422. The page headings in the King James Bible version of the Song of Solomon read as follows: "Christ calleth the church: she glorieth in him, Graces of the church: Christ's love to her, The graces of Christ, and of the church, The church's graces, and her love to Christ." A translation in poetic stanzas with a brief commentary that emphasizes the erotic is Marcia Falk's *The Song of Songs: Love Poems from the Bible, Translated from the Original Hebrew* (New York: Harcourt, Brace, Jovanovich, 1977). The exhaustive and definitive version is the more than 700 page study by Marvin H. Pope, *Song of Songs: A New Translation with Introduction and Commentary*, Anchor Bible Series, vol. 7 (Garden City, N.Y.: Doubleday, 1977).

32. *Journal of Discourses*, 22:365 (Cannon/1881); see also Jeffrey Richards, "'Passing the Love of Women': Manly Love and Victorian Society," in J. A. Mangan and James Walvin, eds., *Manliness and Morality: Middle-Class Masculinity in Britain and America, 1800–1940* (Manchester: Manchester University, 1987), 92–122.

33. Andrew Kimball diary, 3 Jan. 1898, LDS Archives. For his son Spencer W. Kimball's attitudes toward same-sex love and homoeroticism, see chap. 11.

34. Jione Ma'u to David O. McKay, at Nuku'alofa, Tonga, 30 June 1921, translation in 1921 from Tongan original (translator unknown), photocopies of both letters in private possession, Salt Lake City; entry for "Jone" Ma'u and

wife Mele in LDS Church 1925 census, Family History Library of the Church of Jesus Christ of Latter-day Saints, Salt Lake City, Utah; *Deseret News 1995–1996 Church Almanac: The Church of Jesus Christ of Latter-day Saints* (Salt Lake City: Deseret News, 1994), 292, which shows that in 1994 Tonga's population was one-third Mormon.

35. Edwin F. Parry, *Sketches of Missionary Life* (Salt Lake City: George Q. Cannon and Sons, 1899), 41.

36. E. Anthony Rotundo, *American Manhood: Transformations in Masculinity from the Revolution to the Modern Era* (New York: Basic Books, 1993), 278, 292; see also chap. 11 for the new emphasis of teaching missionaries to love their companions.

37. Heber J. Grant to J. Golden Kimball, 3 Mar. 1902, from Tokyo, copied in Kimball diary, 27 Mar. 1902, Manuscripts Division, J. Willard Marriott Library, University of Utah, Salt Lake City, and see entry for 28 Sept. 1903 for their reunion upon Grant's return from his mission to Japan.

38. David Lawrence McKay, *My Father, David O. McKay,* ed. Lavina Fielding Anderson (Salt Lake City: Deseret Book, 1989), 172; "Jonathan" [Orson F. Whitney] to "Dear Brother David" [O. McKay], 19 October 1918, identified as Whitney by a notation in McKay's handwriting, photocopy in private collection, Salt Lake City.

39. Yacovone, "Abolitionists," 88.

40. Gordon B. Hinckley, "An Appreciation of Stephen L Richards," *Improvement Era* 54 (July 1951): 499; see also chap. 11 for the lenient response of Richards toward homoeroticism and for McKay's disgust at such conduct.

41. "The 'David and Jonathan' of the General Board," photo caption in "Mary and May," *Children's Friend* 18 (Oct. 1919): 421, concerning Sarah Louise "Louie" Felt and her counselor May Anderson; see also chap. 8.

42. Percy Bysshe Shelley, "Ode to the West Wind," in Alfred H. Miles, ed., *The Poets and the Poetry of the Nineteenth Century,* 12 vols. (London: George Routledge and Sons, 1905), 2:541. Dead at age thirty, he was married to Mary Wollstonecraft Shelley.

43. Bullough, *Sexual Variance,* 606.

44. Yacovone, "Abolitionists," 93–94; see also William R. Taylor and Christopher Lasch, "Two 'Kindred Spirits': Sorority and Family in New England, 1839–1846," *New England Quarterly* 36 (Mar. 1963): 31.

45. Joseph Smith to Emma Hale Smith, 12 Nov. 1838, in Dean C. Jessee, ed., *The Personal Writings of Joseph Smith* (Salt Lake City: Deseret Book, 1984), 368–69; Augusta Adams Cobb Young ("Annie") to Brigham Young, 11 Mar. 1846, Schroeder Papers, Manuscript Division, New York Public Library; Heber C. Kimball to Vilate Murray Kimball, 16 Apr. 1847, in Stanley B. Kimball, *Heber C. Kimball: Mormon Patriarch and Pioneer* (Urbana: University of Illinois Press, 1981), 152–53; Emmeline Whitney to Newel Whit-

ney, 16 Oct. 1847; Artimesia Beaman Snow to Erastus Snow, 27 July 1851, and Erastus Snow to Julia Josephine Spencer Snow, 10 Aug. 1886, in Andrew Karl Larson, *Erastus Snow: The Life of a Missionary and Pioneer for the Early Mormon Church* (Salt Lake City: University of Utah Press, 1971), 712–13; Martha Hughes Cannon ("Maria") to Angus M. Cannon ("My Dear Lover"), 9 July 1886, Martha Hughes Cannon ("Emma J. Quick") to Angus M. Cannon ("My Own Loved James"), 13 Feb. 1887, Martha Hughes Cannon ("Maria") to Angus M. Cannon ("My Own Loved One"), 12 July 1887, and Angus M. Cannon ("AM") to "My Own Dear Martha," 13 Feb. 1888, in Constance L. Lieber and John Sillito, eds., *Letters from Exile: The Correspondence of Martha Hughes Cannon and Angus M. Cannon, 1886–1888* (Salt Lake City: Signature Books/Smith Research Associates, 1989), 30, 97, 145, 261–62.

46. For the homoromantic and homoerotic in Whitman's poetry, see Gustav Bychowski, "Walt Whitman: A Study in Sublimation," in Hendrik Ruitenbeek, ed., *Homosexuality and Creative Genius* (New York: Astor-Honor, 1967), 140–81; Walter Lowenfels, ed., *The Tenderest Lover: The Erotic Poetry of Walt Whitman* (New York: Dell, 1972); Robert K. Martin, "Whitman's Song of Myself: Homosexual Dream and Vision," *Partisan Review* 42, no. 1 (1975): 80–96; John Snyder, *The Dear Love of Man: Tragic and Lyric Communion in Walt Whitman* (The Hague: Mouton, 1975); Robert K. Martin, *The Homosexual Tradition in American Poetry* (Austin: University of Texas Press, 1979), 3–89; Calvin Bedient, "Walt Whitman: Overruled," *Salmagundi: A Quarterly of the Humanities and the Social Sciences,* nos. 58–59 (Fall 1982–Winter 1983): 326–46; Stephen Coote, ed., *The Penguin Book of Homosexual Verse* (London: Penguin Books, 1983), 203–5; Joseph Cady, "Drum-Taps and Nineteenth-Century Male Homosexual Literature," in Joann P. Krieg, ed., *Walt Whitman Here and Now* (Westport, Conn.: Greenwood Press, 1985), 49–59; M. Jimmie Killingsworth, *Whitman's Poetry of the Body: Sexuality, Politics, and the Text* (Chapel Hill: University of North Carolina Press, 1989), 98–111; Edwin Haviland Miller, ed., *Walt Whitman's "Song of Myself": A Mosaic of Interpretations* (Iowa City: University of Iowa Press, 1989); Byrne R. S. Fone, *Masculine Landscapes: Walt Whitman and the Homoerotic Text* (Carbondale: Southern Illinois University Press, 1992); David S. Reynolds, *Walt Whitman's America: A Cultural Biography* (New York: Alfred A. Knopf, 1995), 323–24, 391–402, 575–76; Byrne R. S. Fone, *A Road to Stonewall, 1750–1969: Male Homosexuality and Homophobia in English and American Literature* (New York: Twayne, 1995), 57–83.

For Dickinson's female-female love poems, see examples and discussion in Vivian R. Pollak, *Dickinson: The Anxiety of Gender* (Ithaca: Cornell University Press, 1984), 134–56; Sandra Gilbert, "The American Sexual Poetics of Walt Whitman and Emily Dickinson," in Sacvan Bercovitch, ed., *Reconstructing American Literary History* (Cambridge, Mass.: Harvard University Press,

1986), 123–54; see also discussions in Cody, *After Great Pain*, 135–52, 176–84; Richard Sewall, *The Life of Emily Dickinson*, 2 vols. (New York: Farrar, Straus, and Giroux, 1974), 2:605; Paula Bennett, "The Pea That Duty Locks: Lesbian and Feminist-Heterosexual Readings of Emily Dickinson's Poetry," in Karla Jay and Joanne Glasgow, eds., *Lesbian Texts and Contexts: Radical Revisions* (New York: New York University Press, 1990), 104–25. Coote, in *The Penguin Book of Homosexual Verse*, 207–11, gives nearly twice the space to Dickinson poems as to examples of Whitman's poetry.

47. Lynch, in "'Here Is Adhesiveness,'" 93, pointed out the irony that "Whitman was trying to disprove his homosexuality by claiming paternity in an argument [written] to a homosexual [Symonds] who had a wife and four children." Reynolds, in *Walt Whitman's America*, 577–78, examines the complexities of this Symonds-Whitman exchange. For Whitman's verbal acknowledgment of his homoerotic interests, see Richard Ellman, *Oscar Wilde* (New York: Vintage Books, 1988), 171; Reynolds, *Walt Whitman's America*, 540.

48. Edward F. Grier, ed., *Walt Whitman: Notebooks and Unpublished Manuscripts*, 6 vols. (New York: New York University Press, 1984), esp. 2:480, 481, 496, 497; Jonathan Katz, *Gay American History: Lesbians and Gay Men in the U.S.A.* (New York: Thomas Y. Crowell, 1976), 337–40, 349–50, 499–500.

49. Kate Thomas (b. 2 July 1871; d. 1950); LeNae Peavey, "Kate Thomas (1871–1950)," graduate paper for Vicky Burgess-Olson's course on Women in Mormon Culture, History 579R, University of Utah, Fall 1988, copy in Utah State Historical Society. Lavina Fielding Anderson credits Thomas as a member of the LDS Young Women's general board, but she was not a board member. See Marba C. Josephson, "Appointments and Releases of YMMIA Board Members," *History of the YWMIA* (Salt Lake City: Young Women's Mutual Improvement Association of the Church of Jesus Christ of Latter-day Saints, 1955), 350–78. Kate Thomas was not related to Thomas S. Thomas, discussed in chap. 8, nor to Evan S. Thomas, discussed in chap. 9, nor to Heber H. Thomas, discussed in chap. 10.

50. Kate Thomas, "A Romance of Bedruthen Steps," *Young Woman's Journal* 27 (Aug. 1916): 471. Lavina Fielding Anderson's "Ministering Angels: Single Women in Mormon Society," *Dialogue: A Journal of Mormon Thought* 16 (Autumn 1983): 68–69, was the first published study to observe these dimensions in the writings of Kate Thomas.

51. Kate Thomas, "Song," *Young Woman's Journal* 12 (May 1901): 202. The invitation for a "maiden" to "come" in Kate's "little boat of Love," which was moored in the place where "the lilies grow" had sexual overtones when she published the poem. In well-established English usage by that time, a woman's "flower(s)" referred to her pubic area or to menstruation (Lev. 15: 24, 33), and the first slang meaning of the verb "come" was "to experience

the sexual spasm." John S. Farmer and W. E. Henley, *Slang and Its Analogues,* 7 vols. (London: Routledge and Kegan Paul, 1890–1904), 2:159, 3:3; Eric Partridge, *A Dictionary of Slang and Unconventional English: Colloquialisms and Catch-Phrases, Solecisms and Catachreses, Nicknames, and Vulgarisms,* 8th ed., ed. Paul Beale (London: Routledge and Kegan Paul, 1984), 410. Although slang dictionaries do not record "little boat of Love," in the early 1900s "boat" alone was a slang reference to the labia of the female genitalia. By 1916, "boy in the boat" was published slang for clitoris. See J. E. Lighter, ed., *Random House Historical Dictionary of American Slang,* 3 vols. (New York: Random House, 1994–96), 1:357. Other examples of female-female love poems published by Kate Thomas are "Irish Love Song," *Young Woman's Journal* 11 (Nov. 1900): 506; "Song," *Young Woman's Journal* 14 (Nov. 1903): 488; "Irish Love Song," *Young Woman's Journal* 20 (July 1909): 348–51; untitled poem, *Young Woman's Journal* 24 (Feb. 1913): 129; "Lines," *Young Woman's Journal* 25 (June 1914): 366; and "A Glad New Year," *Young Woman's Journal* 15 (Jan. 1904): 8, which was published under the name Max and which was also clipped in Red Scrapbook, Folder 6, Box 3, Kate Thomas Papers, Utah State Historical Society.

52. Thomas Wentworth Higginson to Mrs. Mabel P. (Loomis) Todd, 21 Apr. 1891, in Millicent Todd Bingham, *Ancestor's Brocades: The Literary Debut of Emily Dickinson* (New York: Harper and Brothers, 1945), 127. The prudish Higginson didn't realize he was writing to a woman whose diary described her every sexual experience. See Carl N. Degler, "What Ought to Be and What Was: Women's Sexuality in the Nineteenth Century," *American Historical Review* 79 (Dec. 1974): 1467–90; Peter Gay, *The Bourgeois Experience: Victoria to Freud,* vol. 1, *Education of the Senses* (New York: Oxford University Press, 1984), 72–89, 461–62.

53. For a summary of literary criticism of "Wild Nights" and the consensus about its eroticism, see Joseph Duchac, *The Poems of Emily Dickinson: An Annotated Guide to Commentary Published in English, 1890–1977* (Boston: G. K. Hall, 1979), 608–11.

54. John Ciardi, *How Does a Poem Mean?* (Boston: Houghton Mifflin, 1975).

55. For example, Kate Thomas wrote about "Gay Narcissus" in *Young Woman's Journal* 18 (June 1907): 243. By 1903, *gay boy* was American slang for "a man who is homosexual." See Lighter, *Random House Historical Dictionary of American Slang,* 1:872. This slang use of *gay* to describe the emerging concept of homosexuality can be specifically dated to 1889. In the so-called "Cleveland Street Scandal," a male prostitute used the word *gay* to describe his fellow residents at a male house of prostitution in London. See Hugh Rawson, *Wicked Words: A Treasury of Curses, Insults, Put-Downs, and Other Formerly Unprintable Terms from Anglo-Saxon Times to the Present* (New York: Crown,

1989), 171, and Geoffrey Hughes, *Swearing: A Social History of Foul Language, Oaths, and Profanities in English* (Oxford: Blackwell, 1991), 232; see also Katz, *Gay/Lesbian Almanac,* 215–16, for the scandal's background.

Gay was probably associated with homoeroticism several years prior to this courtroom use of the slang word in 1889. For a possible use of *gay* to refer to male effeminacy as early as 1868, see Katz, *Gay/Lesbian Almanac,* 315. For *gay* as a nineteenth-century adjective meaning erotic or immoral, see Farmer and Henley, *Slang and Its Analogues,* 3:126, which also cited its sexual usage in an ambiguous phrase from Leech's 1854 *Pictures of Life and Character:* "How long have you been gay?" See also, Partridge, *Dictionary of Slang and Unconventional English,* 304.

56. George Chauncey, *Gay New York: Gender, Urban Culture, and the Making of the Gay Male World, 1890–1940* (New York: Basic Books/HarperCollins, 1994), 18.

57. Kate Thomas, "Song," *Young Woman's Journal* 14 (Jan. 1903): 34. The word *gay* appeared in love poems on pages 20, 25, 36, 53, 79, and 80 of Kate Thomas, "Record" book (1896–1904), Folder 5, Box 3, Thomas Papers.

58. Sterne McMullen, "Biographical Notes," 2, Register of the Kate Thomas Collection, Utah State Historical Society, 19 Mar. 1979; LeNae Peavey, "Kate Thomas (1871–1950)," 7; Chauncey, *Gay New York,* 18; Lighter, *Random House Historical Dictionary of American Slang,* 1:872.

59. Chauncey, *Gay New York,* 67–68, 190, 228–29, 232, 243, 293, quotation from 228; see also Miller, *Out of the Past,* 137–40; Judith Schwarz, Kathy Peiss, and Christina Simmons, "'We Were a Little Band of Willful Women': The Heterodoxy Club of Greenwich Village," in Kathy Peiss, Christina Simmons, and Robert A. Padug, eds., *Passion and Power: Sexuality in History* (Philadelphia: Temple University Press, 1989), 118–37.

60. Ronald A. Sharp, *Friendship and Literature: Spirit and Form* (Durham, N.C.: Duke University Press, 1986), 75. He added the obviously anachronistic and (in my view) polemical statement: "Must the desire to legitimize homosexuality force us to read these lines [by Walt Whitman] . . . mainly as a call for gay liberation?"

61. McMullen, "Biographical Notes," 2.

62. Thomas, "Record" book, 79, also quoted in McMullen, "Biographical Notes," 15–16, and in O'Donovan, "'Abominable and Detestable Crime,'" 130–31, who referred to her as "Mormon Lesbian poet Kate Thomas" (128).

63. Thomas, "Record" book, 15, 38. Additional love poems specifically addressed to women appear in her ninety-two-page "Record" book on 4, 13, 20–21, 26, 34, 35, 36, 37–40, 43, 46, 53, 57, 76, 82, 83, 84–85, and in other poems in which the gender of the lover is unstated.

64. See chap. 8 for a discussion of Evan Stephens and chap. 6 for a discussion of Ada Dwyer Russell.

CHAPTER 5

The Homomarital,
Gender Roles, and
Cross-Dressing

ALTHOUGH HOMOSOCIAL, homopastoral, homotac-
tile, homoemotional, and homoromantic dynamics occur in cultures
throughout the world, less common are ceremonies that formally unite
same-sex couples into marriage-like relationships. In the western European tradition, however, the Yale historian John Boswell found evidence of same-sex marriages in pre-Roman and pre-Christian Greece.
Homosexual marriages in the Roman Empire included public ceremonies and dowries. Even the early Christian church performed marriage
ceremonies for same-sex couples.[1]

In China there were two separate traditions of same-sex marriages.
During the medieval Ming dynasty from the mid-1300s to the mid-
1600s Chinese men entered into same-sex marriages that included
dowries and formal ceremonies. For almost a century after 1865, nearly
100,000 women also entered into same-sex marriages in one province
of China.[2]

In eastern Siberia during the 1890s, the Russian anthropologist
Waldemar Bogoras observed the courtship and marriage relations of
"soft men," shamans who were revered (and feared) for their metaphys-
ical insights. "Thus he has all the young men he could wish for striv-
ing to obtain his favor. From these he chooses his lover, and after a time
takes a husband. The marriage is performed with the usual rites, and I

must say that it forms quite a solid union, which often lasts till the death of one of the parties."[3] For a century, Europeans had also described two types of male-male polygamous marriage among the Inuit and Aleuts on both sides of the Bering Strait. Shamans could be "male concubines" or "wives" of an already married man. Also, some "androgynous Kodiak males" (who adopted female dress and behavior) had two husbands each—a ménage à trois or a kind of male-male polyandry.[4] This gender arrangement was typical of male-male marriage in several cultures—one partner was a masculine-acting man, while the other was a feminine-acting, cross-dressing man. Such marriages preserved traditional gender roles even though both husband and wife were of the same biological gender.

On one island in the New Hebrides (now Vanuatu) in the South Pacific, the other common form of male-male marriage is performed in which a masculine-acting man formally "marries" a male teenager (often also masculine-acting). As each boy reaches puberty, his father selects a male adult as a "guardian" who becomes the boy's "husband" and "has complete sexual rights over his boy." Until the boy is old enough to be a husband in his own marriage, the man and boy are inseparable. If one dies, the other goes into formal mourning. The elite men among these people have both female wives and formally arranged "boy-lovers." The anthropologist A. Bernard Deacon observed that some of the husbands "seldom have intercourse with their wives, preferring to go with their boys." Unlike other kinds of mentor-protégé relationships, these were formally solemnized unions of same-sex persons who were sexually intimate.[5] Fifty years after Deacon's publication, LDS missionaries began baptizing converts in those islands, but the local government soon stopped Mormon proselytizing there.[6]

Some sub-Saharan African peoples also have man-boy marriage ceremonies. Azande warriors paid the traditional "bridewealth" for "boy-wives." One boy-wife told an anthropologist that the "relatives of a boy escorted him (when he was married) in the same way as they escorted a bride (on her marriage) to her husband." The anthropologist E. E. Evans-Pritchard noted that this man-boy "relationship was, for so long as it lasted, a legal union on the model of a normal marriage."

These African boy-wives were "between about twelve and twenty years of age. When they ceased to be boys they joined the companies of warriors to which their at-one-time husbands belonged and took boys to wife on their own account." As part of this nonjealous transition, the first warrior-husband then married a different boy-wife as a sexual partner. Some warriors married several boys in succession, as each boy-wife chose at about age twenty to become the husband of his own marriage. Although they performed marital duties that were traditional for women, these boy-wives did not wear female clothes or exhibit feminine behavior. Also, unlike males in Melanesian cultures, participants in these man-boy relationships avoided both oral and anal sex.[7]

However, the same options did not exist for female-female marriage in Africa. Among the Azande, there was no female-female marriage ceremony even for those who engaged in homoerotic behaviors. Those women lovers were usually wives of the same husband. Many members of the community ridiculed homoerotic behaviors between these females, in contrast to the honor given to homoeroticism within male-male marriage.[8]

In a double irony, as many as 37 percent of married women among various sub-Saharan peoples are currently in female-female marriages, and yet the "female husband does not engage in sexual interaction with her wife." These female-female marriages throughout Africa, though formally solemnized, confer all the social obligations and privileges of marriage except sexual intimacy. These same-sex unions are usually mentor-protégé relationships between older women and teenagers or young women prior to their marriage with a man.[9] Predominant, but not universal, celibacy also characterizes the female-female relationships in Lesotho.[10]

Celibacy is also a feature of some male-male marriages currently solemnized in Africa. For example, the men of the Nzema of southern Ghana "fall in love, form bond friendships, share their beds, and even marry, but they do not have sex." There is similar celibacy in the male-male marriages of the Banguia in Cameroon.[11]

Some of these celibate and noncelibate marriages of same-sex persons probably involve African Mormons. By January 1994, there were more than three hundred Mormon converts in Lesotho, more than twelve thousand in Ghana, and more than forty thousand other sub-Saharan Africans who joined the LDS Church in previous years.[12]

However, whether sexually intimate or celibate, these same-sex marriages have had one thing in common among the various peoples and traditional cultures that honored them. These same-sex marriages preserved the subordination of one marriage partner to the other that was traditional in heterosexual marriage within those cultures. Either the dominant marriage partner was significantly older than the subordinate same-sex partner[13] or one same-sex partner took the masculine role of husband while the other took the feminine role of wife. In the latter case, the female husband and male wife were usually cross-dressers.[14]

Likewise, directly in the path of millions of European-American explorers and pioneers were dozens of Native American tribes that celebrated same-sex marriages. In these male-male marriages, the wife was a feminine-acting male "berdache" who dressed as other females did or wore mixtures of male and female clothing. In Native American female-female marriages, the husband was an "amazon" who dressed like other males and served as a female hunter-warrior with them. Amazons often participated in such otherwise male-only activities as the sweat baths and sweat lodges. Among Native American peoples, these same-sex marriages were relationships of honor, and the berdache were often shamans and called "seers." Polygamy was the one area in which there was gender discrimination in these same-sex marriages among Native Americans—a male husband could have a female spouse and a male spouse at the same time, but female husbands could have only female spouses. Whether polygamous or monogamous, however, women in female-female marriages among these Native American peoples had the same rights of sexual intimacy as men in male-male marriages.[15]

Some nineteenth-century Mormons observed berdache male wives and amazon female husbands among the western Native Americans. From the 1840s to the 1890s, Mormons proselytized and lived among twenty-seven tribes that had berdache and amazons—Apache, Bannock, Chickasaw, Choctaw, Creek, Fox, Gosiute, Hopi, Iowa, Isleta, Laguna, Maricopa, Navajo, Nez Perce, Omaha, Oto, Paiute, Papago, Pawnee, Pima, Ponca, Potawatomi, Seminole, Shoshone, Sioux, Ute, and Zuni.[16] During the decades in which nineteenth-century Mormons visited these Native Americans, the berdache interacted openly with visitors.

In fact, a non-Mormon took photographs of a Zuni berdache named We'Wha in 1885, nine years after Mormons began proselytizing among that Pueblo group in New Mexico.[17] In 1876–78, LDS missionaries baptized more than two hundred Zunis, including the pueblo's chief, and performed a "miraculous healing" of four hundred more. Thus Mormons had won over nearly half the Zuni population within two

years, either through baptism or by the trust and good feelings gener-
ated from this healing experience. The Zuni mission was of sufficient
interest to LDS leaders that Apostle Wilford Woodruff visited in 1879.[18]

Mormon missionaries were certainly aware of this Zuni berdache
who was twenty-seven years old when they first arrived. Six feet tall,
We'Wha towered over all similarly dressed women and over most men
in the Zuni population of only 1,500. As a preserver of traditional Zuni
religious beliefs, he was among the traditionalists who eventually turned
against Mormonism in the early 1880s and persuaded his people to
reject LDS missionaries as well as their Presbyterian competitors. In
1886, We'Wha traveled to Washington, D.C., and is the only berdache
who has shaken hands with a U.S. president.[19]

Most Mormon missionaries were more interested in describing proselytizing activities than in recording observations of Native American
life and customs. However, some LDS missionaries learned Native
American languages and their diaries occasionally referred to native
customs in the nineteenth century.[20] Careful research may find that some
Mormon diaries contain obscure references to the berdache, the amazons, and the same-sex marriages among these twenty-seven tribes.

It is also significant that these cross-dressing Native Americans were
interacting with "white" Americans during the same time that thousands of Anglo-American women and men were cross-dressing. However, these Anglo-American women differed significantly from men in
their reasons for cross-dressing and in its duration.

Thousands of women in Victorian America chose to dress and live
as men for years at a time. During the Civil War, Union military surgeons discovered that more than four hundred wounded soldiers were
actually cross-dressing women (one of whom died in battle).[21] In nineteenth-century America, women were literally willing to risk their lives
in order to live as men with the privileges of men.[22] Only one female
cross-dresser, however, is known to have entered pioneer Utah. On her
way to California in 1855, "Mountain Charley" came only close
enough to the Mormon settlements of northern Utah to see the Great
Salt Lake in the distance from a mountain pass.[23]

On the other hand, most of the thousands of Anglo-American male
cross-dressers during the same period were only temporarily engaging
in a form of entertainment. Female impersonation began on the American stage in 1828, and male impersonation in the 1860s.[24] Both became popular during the last half of the nineteenth century. "In effect,

transvestism on stage and in real life was regarded as a lark," observes the historian Vern Bullough. Among the general population, "there was as yet no real understanding of the sexual implications of the imper-sonation of either men or women."[25]

Even in Utah society, surrounded by Native American peoples whose cross-dressing had a clear sexual meaning, most Mormons recognized no sexual significance (or potential) in cross-dressing for special occa-sions. Thus, Brigham Young's thirty-fifth child, Brigham Morris Young (1854–1913), frequently appeared in the dress and make-up of a wom-an during performances in LDS wards and stakes from the 1880s to the 1900s. In writing a biography of Brigham Morris Young, his son Galen wrote that "Father was called to many of the Wards of the Church in this area as an entertainer when he posed as a great Italian lady singer dressed in costume and representing and calling himself, 'Madam Pattirini.'" Next to a photograph of his cross-dressing father in full costume and wig, the son added: "He would sing in a high fal-setto voice. He fooled many people."[26] Likewise, in 1904 LDS photog-rapher George E. Anderson photographed his fifteen-year-old daugh-ter dressed as boy and taking "the part of the boy" while dancing with her teenage girlfriend, who dressed as a girl for the pose.[27]

Utah's Maude Adams (b. 1872, LDS) performed on Broadway as a male. A year after she starred as Napoleon's son her beloved compan-ion Lillie Florence died in 1901. Adams was the first *Peter Pan* in 1905 and the first woman to star in *Chantecler* in 1911. From 1905 to 1951 her "lifelong love" was Louise Boynton. They are buried side by side.[28]

However, for some Mormon actors, female impersonation was a sly (and safe) way to express their homosexuality publicly. An example in Mildred Berryman's study was male case number 5, a thirty-year-old bachelor at the time she described him in Salt Lake City, sometime be-fore 1938. She wrote that "L" was a self-defined homosexual and was a "clever female impersonator and delights in the role. [He] is an all-around clever actor and has pursued acting as a career."[29]

Even though cross-dressing had become common in the United States among male prostitutes and at homosexual "drag dances" during the late nineteenth century,[30] this did not stigmatize cross-dressing on spe-cial occasions for the general population. Unlike traditional cultures that had same-sex marriages, cross-dressing did not signal a changed gender role for most Americans. In fact, occasional cross-dressing was perceived to have no sexual significance despite the increasing awareness in the twentieth century that some self-defined homosexuals also cross-dressed to signal their sexual interests. Ironically, since there is no generally accepted form of same-sex marriage in modern European-American culture, the occasional switching of gender roles is viewed without criticism.[31]

Same-Sex Ceremonies in Mormonism

Joseph Smith's published revelations[32] contained no reference to same-sex marriages. However, one revelation did give the words for a ceremony of friendship between men. This December 1832 revelation instructed the presiding officer or teacher in the School of the Prophets to greet the students in this manner: "Art thou a brother or brethren? I salute you in the name of the Lord Jesus Christ, in token or remembrance of the everlasting covenant, in which covenant I receive you to fellowship, in a determination that is fixed, immovable, and unchangeable, to be your friend and brother through the grace of God in the bonds of love, to walk in the commandments of God blameless, in thanksgiving, forever and ever. Amen" (Doctrine and Covenants 88: 133). This formal covenant "to be your friend . . . forever and ever" was officially implemented only during the periods in which the School of the Prophets was operational: in Ohio from 1833 to 1837, and in Utah from 1867 to 1874 and again in 1883.[33]

Joseph Smith also once referred figuratively to himself as married to a male friend. Beginning in 1840, twenty-nine-year-old Robert B. Thompson became the prophet's scribe and personal secretary. Their relationship was so close that Smith told his friend's wife, "Sister Thompson, you must not feel bad towards me for keeping your husband away from you so much, for I am married to him." She added that "they truly loved each other with fervent brotherly affection."[34] Concerning Thompson's death in 1841 Smith made this unusual explanation to his next secretary during a discussion of "loose conduct" and sexual transgressions: "He said [Robert B.] Thompson professed great friendship for him but he gave away to temptation and he had to die."[35]

In 1954, the sociologist Kimball Young first suggested that Mormon marriage "sealing" ceremonies (which began in 1843 and bind husband and wife for "time and eternity") included same-sex marriage. For example Brigham Young preached in 1862: "I will here refer to a principle that has not been named by me for years. With the introduction of the Priesthood upon the earth was also introduced the sealing ordinance." Although modern readers would expect to hear next about eternal marriage, Young did not mention marriage or women. Instead, he said: "By this power men will be sealed to men back to Adam." In another sermon he preached that "we can seal women to men [without a temple], but not men to men, without a Temple."[36]

Such statements caused his sociologist grandson to observe: "Here is evidence of deep, psychological *Bruederschaft* [brotherhood]. There are obviously latent homosexual features in this idea and its cultural aspect has many familiar parallels in other religions." Kimball Young added that Mormonism "had strong homosexual components" but acknowledged: "Most Saints, including Brigham himself, would have been much shocked by such an interpretation." The grandson regarded homosexuality as unappealing as the Mormon practice of polygamy that was the topic of his book.[37]

However, this sociologist misunderstood Brigham Young's statements about "sealing men to men," which referred to the nineteenth-century LDS practice of spiritual adoption. By this ordinance, a man (usually an apostle) became the spiritual father of the adopted man and of the adopted man's wife and children (if any). In social terms, this was an institutionalized form of mentor-protégé relationships between Mormon men. In its early stages under Brigham Young's direction, this adoptive sealing of men to men also involved obligations of financial support. One of Brigham Young's adopted sons was John D. Lee. As was customary in the first adoption ceremonies of 1846, Lee temporarily added the surname of his adopted father to his own.[38] In these respects, this early Mormon ordinance is very similar to the celibate same-sex marriages of sub-Saharan Africa today.

However, Brigham Young also indicated that some pioneer Mormon men had made special covenants with each other, independent of the adoption ordinance. "No man had a right to make a covenant to bind men together," Young said in 1848. He added that "God only had that right and by his commandment to the person holding the keys of revelation could any man legally make a covenant & all covenants otherwise made were null & of no effect."[39] It is unclear whether pioneer Mormons who entered into this unauthorized "covenant to bind men together" intended it as a substitute for the mentor-protégé adoption ceremony or as a covenant for male-male friendship/companionship in which neither man was subordinate. Either way, Young disapproved of this ordinance-like covenant between men who had acted independent of the Mormon hierarchy.

A generation after Kimball Young, Antonio A. Feliz wrote: "I found that Joseph began a practice of sealing men to men during the last two years of his life in Nauvoo." Feliz concluded that Joseph Smith secretly provided for a same-sex ordinance of companionship or sealing, which Brigham Young later changed to the father-son adoption ordinance. His evidence involves the funeral service for missionary Lorenzo D. Barnes in which all notetakers said Joseph Smith referred to an unidentified "Lover" of Barnes, rather than to a wife. Feliz elaborated on this in a 1985 article in the newsletter of Affirmation, the society of Mormon lesbians, gays, and bisexuals; in his 1988 autobiography *Out of the Bishop's Closet;* in a 1992 story by the *Salt Lake Tribune;* and in his 1993 paper at Salt Lake City's Stonewall Center, a community resource for lesbians, gays, and bisexuals.[40]

Barely two years after Barnes's death, Apostle Wilford Woodruff visited his English grave site and commented that Lorenzo's "fidelity was stronger than death towards his Lover." Woodruff added: "I thought of his Lover, his Mother, his Father, his kindred & the Saints for they all loved him." From this, Feliz concluded that "we can only speculate on the identity of the person with whom he shared an intimate relationship in Nauvoo prior to his mission to England."[41]

However, there are aspects of the Lorenzo Barnes case that undermine Feliz's assertions. Woodruff's diary also quoted from love poetry and love letters that Barnes wrote in January 1842 to Susan Conrad, "his intended." Sixteen years old when Barnes left her in Nauvoo for his English mission in 1841, Susan Conrad was "the friend" and "Lover" of whom Joseph Smith spoke in the 1843 funeral service for Barnes. She later married a man named Wilkinson and moved from Nauvoo to Utah, where Apostle Woodruff sometimes reminisced with her about Barnes.[42] Even less known is that Barnes had returned to his hometown in Ohio while en route to his mission assignment. There in October 1841 another Mormon performed the civil marriage ceremony for Barnes and Amanda Wilson, who may have been one of his former students.[43] Thus, Barnes was already married when he wrote the 1842 love poetry and letters to his sixteen-year-old "Lover" Susan Conrad. Lorenzo D. Barnes may have been a polygamist at heart, but his experience had nothing to do with homoromantic attachments or a homomarital ceremony.

Still, it is true that Joseph Smith's 1843 funeral sermon for Barnes never once mentioned husband-wife relationships. That was remarkable in a sermon on loving relationships in this life and in the resurrection during which the prophet repeatedly spoke of "brothers and friends," fathers and sons, mothers, daughters, and sisters. Smith's silence concerning husbands and wives was deafening in this sermon about attachments of love.[44] Feliz appropriately asked why. I do not agree that the answer involved same-sex ceremonies, but I do see this as the first Mormon expression of male bonding. George Q. Cannon forty years later called it "greater than the love of woman."[45]

I know of no historical evidence that Mormonism's founding prophet ever said an officiator could perform a marriage-like ordinance for a same-sex couple. Nevertheless, I realize that some believing Mormons regard it as emotionally appealing or spiritually inspiring for there to be a priesthood ordinance to seal same-sex couples similar to Mormonism's opposite-sex ordinance of marriage "for time and all eternity." Because of the personal interest that some have expressed, I will explore the historical evidence for an alternative marriage ceremony that could apply to Mormon same-sex couples.

There is a crucial example from Nauvoo Mormonism that shows that it is legitimate for a couple to mutually covenant to each other for time and eternity, without the aid of an officiator to perform this as an ordinance. In fact, the written wording for this covenant has existed since December 1845. These are the words Apostle Willard Richards recorded in his diary, as the couple holds each other by the hand: "of our own free will and avow[, we] mutually acknowledge each other [as] husband & wife, in a covenant not to be broken in time or Eternity for time and for all Eternity, to all intents & purposes as though the seal of the covenant had been placed upon us for time & all Eternity." The apostle and his bride entered into this mutual covenant without other witnesses. They did not have it reperformed as a sealing ordinance in the Nauvoo temple, as they could have within a few days.[46]

It is crucial that it was Willard Richards who recorded the text of this mutual covenant of eternal companionship. Joseph Smith had appointed him as the official recorder for temple ordinances in 1841 and as the "Recorder of the Kingdom" in 1844.[47] Richards knew that Smith's 1843 revelation on the eternity of marriage specifically denied the validity of a mutual covenant of eternal marriage "if that covenant is not by me or by my word, which is my law, and is not sealed by the

Holy Spirit of promise, through him whom I have anointed and appointed unto this power" (Doctrine and Covenants 132:18).

However, two years later, Richards recorded this mutual covenant of eternal marriage that he obviously regarded as legitimate. Richards could have had an officiator perform his marriage sealing ceremony by simply asking his first cousin, senior apostle Brigham Young, to do so. Instead, Richards and his prospective wife exchanged the words of this mutual covenant just days before the Nauvoo temple began performing marriage sealings.

I can think of only one logical reason why Richards performed this ceremony outside the temple and only one reason why he privately recorded its exact wording. As church historian and recorder, Richards wanted to demonstrate that such a private covenant was legitimate, and he wanted to be sure that there was a record of its wording somewhere. Because this mutual covenant of eternal marriage was not an ordinance involving the official church, the official church historian chose to record it in his private diary instead of on the records of the LDS Church. However, for this 1845 mutual covenant to apply to same-sex persons, it would be necessary to drop the husband-and-wife reference. Richards obviously did not intend this ceremony for same-sex couples.

That is the most that Mormon history has to offer for even the possibility of a homomarital LDS ordinance. Aside from the 1833 covenant of friendship in the School of the Prophets and Brigham Young's possible reference in 1848, I have no evidence that there were any same-sex covenants of eternal companionship among nineteenth-century Mormons.[48] However, as previously indicated, nineteenth-century Mormon missionaries may have unknowingly baptized *Aikane* boys in Hawaii (or their equivalent in Tahiti) who had previously entered same-sex marriages. Also, tens of thousands of twentieth-century converts to the LDS Church in sub-Saharan Africa have come from areas in which celibate same-sex marriage ceremonies are common.

NOTES

1. John Boswell, *Christianity, Social Tolerance, and Homosexuality: Gay People in Western Europe from the Beginning of the Christian Era* (Chicago: University of Chicago Press, 1980), 26n47, 82–83; John Boswell to D. Michael Quinn, 14 Sept. 1993, letter in author's possession; Boswell, *Same-Sex Unions in Premodern Europe* (New York: Villard/Random House, 1994).

2. Bret Hinsch, *Passions of the Cut Sleeve: The Male Homosexual Tradition in China* (Berkeley: University of California Press, 1990), 127–33; Andrea Sankar, "Sisters and Brothers, Lovers and Enemies: Marriage Resistance in Southern Kwangtung," *Journal of Homosexuality* 11 (Summer 1985): 69–81, reprinted in Evelyn Blackwood, ed., *The Many Faces of Homosexuality: Anthropological Approaches to Homosexual Behavior* (New York: Harrington Park Press, 1986), 69–81; Wayne R. Dynes, ed., *Encyclopedia of Homosexuality*, 2 vols. (New York: Garland, 1990), 1:218–20. For same-sex "marriages" with no apparent ceremony, see also Dynes, *Encyclopedia of Homosexuality*, 1:46, 128, 2:941.

3. Waldemar Bogoras, "The Chukchee," *Memoirs of the American Museum of Natural History* 11 (1904–9): 451, with his full discussion of "soft men" on 449–57.

4. Ibid., 449–57; George H. Von Langsdorff, *Voyages and Travels in Various Parts of the World during the Years 1803, 1804, 1805, 1806, and 1807*, 2 vols. (London: Henry Colburn, 1813–14), 2:47–48, 64; Walter L. Williams, *The Spirit and the Flesh: Sexual Diversity in American Indian Culture* (Boston: Beacon Press, 1986), 255.

5. A. Bernard Deacon, in *Malekula: A Vanishing People in the New Hebrides* (London: George Routledge and Sons, 1934), 260, 261, 267, described these practices among the inhabitants of the Big Nambas.

6. R. Lanier Britsch, *Unto the Islands of the Seas: A History of the Latter-day Saints in the Pacific* (Salt Lake City: Deseret Book, 1986), 514–15.

7. E. E. Evans-Pritchard, "Sexual Inversion among the Azande," *American Anthropologist* 72 (Dec. 1970): 1428–29. The latter page also explains: "With regard to the sexual side, at night the boy slept with his lover [husband], who had intercourse with him between his thighs (Azande expressed disgust at the suggestion of anal penetration). The boys got what pleasure they could by friction of their organs on the husband's belly or groin." Compare with the discussion in chap. 1.

8. Ibid., 1431.

9. Eileen Jensen Krige, "Woman-Marriage, with Special Reference to the Lovendu: Its Significance for the Definition of Marriage," *Africa* 44 (Jan. 1974): 11–37, esp. 25, 34; Denise O'Brien, "Female Husbands in Southern Bantu Societies," in Alice Schlegal, ed., *Sexual Stratification: A Cross Cultural View* (New York: Columbia University Press, 1977), 109; also Regina Smith Oboler, "Is the Female Husband a Man?: Woman/Woman Marriage among the Nandi of Kenya," *Ethnology* 9 (Jan. 1980): 69–88, esp. 69; Ifi Amadiume, *Male Daughters, Female Husbands: Gender and Sex in an African Society* (London: Zed Books, 1987).

10. Judith Gay, "'Mummies and Babies' and Friends and Lovers in Lesotho," in David N. Suggs and Andrew W. Miracle, eds., *Culture and Human Sexuality: A Reader* (Pacific Grove, Calif.: Brooks/Cole, 1993), 341–55.

11. Robert Brain, *Friends and Lovers* (New York: Basic Books, 1976), 62–63, 32–34.

12. *Deseret News 1995–1996 Church Almanac: The Church of Jesus Christ of Latter-day Saints* (Salt Lake City: Deseret News, 1994), 201, 206–7, 215, 220, 227, 228, 233, 236, 247, 250, 253, 254, 263, 267, 283, 285, 288, 291, 292, 303–4, lists the numbers of Mormons in these sub-Saharan countries of Africa as of 31 December 1993: Botswana (300), Burundi (100), Cameroon (100), Central Africa Republic (100), Congo (800), Equatorial Guinea (100), Ethiopia (100), Gabon (100), Ghana (12,000), Ivory Coast (1,500), Kenya (1,400), Lesotho (300), Liberia (1,400), Namibia (100), Nigeria (22,000), Sierra Leone (1,900), South Africa (23,000 primarily white, although conversions "in townships and other areas in South Africa progressed significantly in the 1980s"), Swaziland (700), Tanzania (100), Uganda (800), Zaire (4,600), Zambia (200), and Zimbabwe (5,300). In the three years since those statistics were compiled, LDS membership among sub-Saharan peoples has increased substantially. Compared with the statistics as of December 1991, those countries experienced LDS growth rates of 10 percent to 50 percent in two years. See *Deseret News 1993–1994 Church Almanac: The Church of Jesus Christ of Latter-day Saints* (Salt Lake City: Deseret News, 1992).

13. Gilbert Herdt, in "Cross-Cultural Forms of Homosexuality and the Concept 'Gay,'" *Psychiatric Annals* 18 (Jan. 1988): 38, refers to such intergenerational relationships as "age-structured homosexuality." Nevertheless, the dominance-subordination description does not apply to the actual dynamics of all intergenerational relationships involving sexual intimacy between two males or between two females. Even with decades of age difference, the older partner may be emotionally dependent on the younger, the two may be sharing expenses and household duties if they are in co-residence, the younger partner may actually be controlling and dominant in the relationship, and the "who's on top" question may reflect personal preferences rather than issues of age, wealth, or social class. However, egalitarian dynamics in such same-sex relationships are less likely in cultures that venerate the elderly, expect the young to always be deferential to their elders, or have strict expectations of dominance-subordination in heterosexual relationships. Correspondingly, during the past fifty years, two factors have encouraged equality in intergenerational same-sex relationships in Northern Europe and North America. First, the feminist emphasis on "partnership" and criticism of subordination in heterosexual marriages has provided a model for same-sex relationships as well. Second, European-American culture's recent devaluation of the elderly and emphasis on and envy of youth have encouraged young adults to be neither deferential nor subordinate to older people in any type of relationship.

14. Gilbert Herdt, "Developmental Discontinuities and Sexual Orientation across Cultures," in David P. McWhirter, Stephanie A. Sanders, and June

Machover Reinisch, eds., *Homosexuality/Heterosexuality: Concepts of Sexual Orientation* (New York: Oxford University Press, 1990), 221–23.

15. Dr. William A. Hammond, "The Disease of the Scythians (Morbus Feminarum) and Certain Analogous Conditions," *American Journal of Neurology and Psychiatry* 1 (Aug. 1882): 343–51, concerning his 1851 examination of two men acting as women among the Pueblo peoples of New Mexico, quoted in Jonathan Ned Katz, *Gay/Lesbian Almanac: A New Documentary* (New York: Harper and Row, 1983), 181–82; A. B. Holder, "The Bote: Description of a Peculiar Sexual Perversion Found among North American Indians," *New York Medical Journal* 50 (7 Dec. 1889): 623–25, concerning his physical examination of a "burdash" male who had "lived constantly two years as the female party to a marital partnership with a well-known male Indian"; O. B. Sperlin, "Two Kootenay Women Masquerading as Men? Or Were They One?" *Washington Historical Society* 21 (Apr. 1930): 120–30; George Devereaux, "Institutionalized Homosexuality of the Mohave Indians," *Human Biology* 9 (Dec. 1937): 498–527; W. W. Hill, "Note on the Pima Berdache," *American Anthropologist* 40 (Apr.–June 1938): 338–40; Oscar Lewis, "The Manly-Hearted Women among the North Piegan," *American Anthropologist* 43 (Apr.–June 1941): 173–87; Nancy Oestreich Lurie, "Winnebago Berdache," *American Anthropologist* 55 (Dec. 1953): 708–12; Edwin Thompson Denig, "Biography of Woman Chief" (1855), in John C. Ewers, ed., *Five Indian Tribes of the Upper Missouri,* (Norman: University of Oklahoma Press, 1961), 195–200, esp. 199 ("she took to herself a wife"); Claude E. Schaeffer, "The Kutenai Female Berdache: Courier, Guide, Prophetess, and Warrior," *Ethnohistory* 12 (Summer 1965): 193–236; Donald G. Forgey, "The Institution of Berdache among the North American Plains Indians," *Journal of Sex Research* 11 (Feb. 1975): 1–15; Jonathan Katz, *Gay American History: Lesbians and Gay Men in the U.S.A.* (New York: Thomas Y. Crowell, 1976), 281–334; Harriet Whitehead, "The Bow and the Burden Strap: A New Look at Institutionalized Homosexuality in Native North America," in Sherry B. Ortner and Harriet Whitehead, eds., *Sexual Meanings: The Cultural Construction of Gender and Sexuality* (Cambridge: Cambridge University Press, 1981), 80–115, also in Henry Abelove, Michele Aina Barale, and David M. Halperin, eds., *The Lesbian and Gay Studies Reader* (New York: Routledge, 1993), 498–527; Beatrice Medicine, "'Warrior Women'—Sex Role Alternatives for Plains Indian Women," in Patricia Albers and Beatrice Medicine, eds., *The Hidden Half* (Lanham, Md.: University Press of America, 1983), 267–77; Evelyn Blackwood, "Sexuality and Gender in Certain Native American Tribes: The Case of Cross-Gender Females," *Signs: Journal of Women in Culture and Society* 10 (Autumn 1984): 27–42; Walter L. Williams, "Persistence and Change in the Berdache Tradition among Contemporary Lakota Indians," *Journal of Homosexuality* 11 (Summer 1985): 191–200, reprinted in Linda Garnets and

Douglas C. Kimmel, eds., *Psychological Perspectives on Lesbian and Gay Male Experiences* (New York: Columbia University Press, 1993), 339–47; Judy Grahn, "Strange Country This: Lesbianism and North American Indian Tribes," *Journal of Homosexuality* 12 (May 1986): 43–57; Paula Gunn Allen, *The Sacred Hoop: Recovering the Feminine in American Indian Traditions* (Boston: Beacon Press, 1986), 196–99; Williams, *The Spirit and the Flesh;* Will Roscoe, "We'Wa and Klah: The American Indian Berdache as Artist and Priest," *American Indian Quarterly* 12 (Spring 1988): 127–50; Paula Gunn Allen, "Lesbians in American Indian Culture," in Martin Bauml Duberman, Martha Vicinus, and George Chauncey Jr., eds., *Hidden from History: Reclaiming the Gay and Lesbian Past* (New York: New American Library, 1989), 106–17; Will Roscoe, "'That Is My Road': The Life and Times of a Crow Berdache," *Montana: The Magazine of Western History* 40 (Winter 1990): 46–55; Raymond E. Hauser, "The Berdache and the Illinois Indian Tribe during the Last Half of the Seventeenth Century," *Ethnohistory* 37 (Winter 1990): 45–66; Neil Miller, *Out of the Past: Gay and Lesbian History from 1869 to the Present* (New York: Vintage/Random House, 1995), 29–40.

Williams, in *The Spirit and the Flesh*, explains that several Native American tribes regard berdache as a third gender (81–86) and why "female berdache" (although sometimes used by European-American writers such as Schaeffer) is an inappropriate term for the Native American women whom Williams calls "amazons" (11, 233–35). Williams described the berdache and amazons as shamans and seers (31–43). Williams also points out that sex between masculine-acting males outside berdache marriage also occurs among Native American Indians: "When I was living on reservations in the Dakotas, several masculine Lakota men made sexual advances to me. They clearly wanted to take the active role. . . . Since they did not consider me to be *winkte* [berdache], they were interacting as one male to another" (92–93).

The anthropologist Sabine Lang has also written that some Native Americans and anthropologists now object to the use of *berdache* in this discourse, because of its differing meaning in the Arabic cultures from which the term was borrowed in the nineteenth century. Sabine recommends instead the use of "two-spirit" when referring to both genders of Native Americans in this gender-blending category and "womanly man" or "manly female" when referring to specific genders. See Sabine Lang, "Traveling Woman: Conducting a Fieldwork Project on Gender Variance and Homosexuality among North American Indians," in Ellen Lewin and William L. Leap, eds., *Out in the Field: Reflections on Lesbian and Gay Anthropologists* (Urbana: University of Illinois Press, 1996). While Lang's terminology may one day become widespread in anthropological studies of Native Americans, my text discussion uses the *berdache* term that has been standard in scholarly literature for decades. Because that term is Arabic in origin, European-American scholars have had the advantage of defining this term in a nonjudgmental way for the general readership in Europe and North America, where relatively few people have any other perception of the word *berdache*.

16. Daniel W. Jones, *Forty Years among the Indians* (Salt Lake City: Juvenile Instructor Office, 1890), 37–43, 90–95, 318–31, 363–72; Lawrence George Coates, "A History of Indian Education by the Mormons, 1830–1900" (Ph.D. diss., Ball State University, 1969); Charles S. Peterson, *Take Up Your Mission: Mormon Colonizing along the Little Colorado River, 1870–1900* (Tucson: University of Arizona Press, 1973), 192–211; George S. Tanner and J. Morris Richards, *Colonization on the Little Colorado: The Joseph City Region* (Flagstaff: Northland Press, 1977), 64–72; Bruce A. Chadwick and Thomas Garrow, "Native Americans," in Daniel H. Ludlow, ed., *Encyclopedia of Mormonism: The History, Scripture, Doctrine, and Procedure of the Church of Jesus Christ of Latter-day Saints*, 5 vols. (New York: Macmillan, 1992), 3:982–83; Richard E. Bennett, *Mormons at the Missouri, 1846–1852: "And Should We Die . . ."* (Norman: University of Oklahoma Press, 1987), 47, 93–100; Ronald W. Walker, "Toward a Reconstruction of Mormon and Indian Relations, 1847–1877," *Brigham Young University Studies* 29 (Fall 1989): 25; and compare the above-listed Native American groups with Charles Callender and Lee M. Kochems, "The North American Berdache," *Current Anthropology* 24 (Aug.–Oct. 1983): 445, for a list of 113 tribes with berdache; Will Roscoe, "Bibliography of Berdache and Alternative Gender Roles among North American Indians," *Journal of Homosexuality* 14, nos. 3–4 (1987): 88–112, for a list of 137 tribes with berdache; Will Roscoe, ed., "North American Tribes with Berdache and Alternative Gender Roles," *Living the Spirit: A Gay American Indian Anthology* (New York: St. Martin's Press, 1988), 217–22; and Williams, *The Spirit and the Flesh*, 70, 198, for Seminole and Sioux berdache. Mormons also proselytized and lived among other Native American tribes that had no berdache.

17. Williams, *The Spirit and the Flesh*, photographic plates 9–11; Will Roscoe, *The Zuni Man-Woman* (Albuquerque: University of New Mexico Press, 1991), 42; Peterson, *Take Up Your Mission*, 204–7.

18. Lorenzo Hill Hatch diary, 8 Sept., 22 Oct. 1876, typescript, pages 89, 92, Folder 3, Box 9, Collection of Mormon Settlements on the Little Colorado, Manuscripts Division, J. Willard Marriott Library, University of Utah, Salt Lake City, Utah; Llewellyn Harris, "Miraculous Healing among the Zunis," *Juvenile Instructor* 14 (15 July 1879): 160; Irving Trilling, "Ramah, New Mexico, 1876–1900: An Historical Episode with Some Value Analysis," *Utah Historical Quarterly* 21 (Apr. 1953): 118–21; C. Gregory Crampton, *The Zunis of Cibola* (Salt Lake City: University of Utah Press, 1977), 116–17; Scott G. Kenney, ed., *Wilford Woodruff's Journal, 1833–1898 Typescript*, 9 vols., plus index (Midvale, Utah: Signature Books, 1983–91), 7:503–4 (19–20 Aug.

1879). Woodruff mistakenly estimated the Zuni population as twice the actual number. See note 19.

19. John R. Swanton, *The Indian Tribes of North America,* Bureau of American Ethnology Bulletin no. 145 (Washington, D.C.: GPO, 1952), 348, for Zuni population of 1,530 in 1889 (up from 1,470 in 1871); Crampton, *Zunis of Cibola,* 117, and Trilling, "Ramah, New Mexico," 20–21, for the Zuni rejection of Mormonism in the early 1880s; see also Roscoe, *Zuni Man-Woman,* 29, 52, 69–71, 98–99, 120–21, 126; and Matilda Coxe Stevenson, "The Zuni Indians: Their Mythology, Esoteric Fraternities, and Ceremonies," *Bureau of American Ethnology Annual Report* 23 (1901–2): 20, and page 416 for photograph of "We'Wha Weaving Belt."

20. D[imick]. B. Huntington, *Vocabulary of the Utah and Sho-Sho-Ne or Snake Dialects, with Indian Legends and Traditions* (Salt Lake City: Salt Lake Herald Office, 1872); Jones, *Forty Years among the Indians;* James S. Brown, *Life of a Pioneer: Being the Autobiography of James S. Brown* (Salt Lake City: George Q. Cannon and Sons, 1900), 304–78, 457–76; Howard Egan, *Pioneering the West, 1846 to 1878: Major Howard Egan's Diary, Also Thrilling Experiences of Pre-Frontier Life among Indians, Their Traits, Civil and Savage,* ed. William M. Egan (Richmond, Utah: Howard R. Egan Estate, 1917), esp. 226–79; Ronald W. Walker, "Native Women on the Utah Frontier," *Brigham Young University Studies* 32 (Fall 1992): 87–124; my interview on 18 May 1994 with S. Lyman Tyler, emeritus professor of American history at the University of Utah, with a research interest in Native Americans.

21. Mary A. Livermore, in *My Story of the War: A Woman's Narrative of Four Years Personal Experience as Nurse in the Union Army . . .* (Hartford, Connecticut: A. D. Worthington, 1876), 120, commented on the estimate of less than four hundred such women: "I am convinced that a larger number of women disguised themselves and enlisted in the service, for one cause or other, than was dreamed of"; and Richard Hall, *Patriots in Disguise: Women Warriors of the Civil War* (New York: Marlow, 1994), 197–200, for a list of fifty-six cross-dressing soldiers by name, including the fatally wounded Frances Day, alias Frank Mayne. See also Rosanne Smith, "Women Who Wanted to Be Men," *Coronet* 42 (Sept. 1957): 62–66; Lillian Faderman, *Odd Girls and Twilight Lovers: A History of Lesbian Life in Twentieth-Century America* (New York: Penguin, 1991), 43; and Vern L. Bullough and Bonnie Bullough, *Cross Dressing, Sex, and Gender* (Philadelphia: University of Pennsylvania Press, 1993), 157–58; see also Gen. Philip Sheridan's description of two of these cross-dressing soldiers in Katz, *Gay American History,* 227–28; see also the personal accounts by Loreta Janeta Velazquez in *The Woman in Battle: A Narrative of the Exploits, Adventures, and Travels of Madame Loreta Janeta Velazquez, Otherwise Known as Lieutenant Harry T. Buford, Confederate States Army* (Richmond, Va.: Dustin, Gilman, 1876); by Sarah Edmunds Seelye, who cross-

dressed as Frank Thompson during the Civil War, as related in her 1883 newspaper interview reprinted in Katz, *Gay/Lesbian Almanac*, 191–94, and in Sylvia G. L. Dannett, *She Rode with the Generals: The True and Incredible Story of Sarah Emma Seelye, alias Franklin Thompson* (New York: Thomas Nelson, 1960); and by Elsa J. Guerin in *Mountain Charley; or, The Adventures of Mrs. E. J. Guerin, Who Was Thirteen Years in Male Attire* (Dubuque, Ia.: by the author, 1861; reprint, Norman: University of Oklahoma Press, 1968), xi, 82–112, on her service as Lt. Charles Hatfield in the Iowa Cavalry of the Union Army.

22. See the San Francisco Lesbian and Gay History Project, "'She Even Chewed Tobacco': A Pictorial Narrative of Passing Women in America," in Duberman, Vicinus, and Chauncey, eds., *Hidden from History*, 183–94; Mary Chaney Hoffman, "Whips of the Old West," *American Mercury* 84 (Apr. 1957): 107–10, about the stagecoach driver Charles Durkee Parkhurst who, at his death in 1879, was discovered to be a woman; and Louis Sullivan, *From Female to Male: The Life of Jack Bee Garland* (Boston: Alyson Publications, 1990), concerning the complex sexual orientation of Elvira Virginia Mugarrieta (b. 1869) who lived as a man and preferred relationships with men who thought she was a man.

23. Guerin, *Mountain Charley*, 48–49.

24. Bullough and Bullough, *Cross Dressing*, 228, 233.

25. Vern L. Bullough, *Sexual Variance in Society and History* (New York: John Wiley and Sons, 1976), 624–25; see also Mary W. Blanchard, "Boundaries and the Victorian Body: Aesthetic Fashion in Gilded Age America," *American Historical Review* 100 (Feb. 1995): 45 and 45n51.

26. Galen Snow Young, "Brief History of Brigham Morris Young," 31, Department of Archives and Special Collections, Harold B. Lee Library, Brigham Young University, Provo, Utah; see also photograph of Brigham Morris Young as Madam Pattirini, photo 157, negative 3, Archives, Historical Department of the Church of Jesus Christ of Latter-day Saints, Salt Lake City, Utah (hereafter LDS Archives). On both photos, the word *Pattirini* is typeset on what was apparently a mass-produced handbill for Brigham Morris Young's female impersonation. Dean C. Jessee, in *Letters of Brigham Young to His Sons* (Salt Lake City: Deseret Book, 1974), 243, referred to Brigham Morris Young's performances as Madam Pattirini, and Jessee cited a surviving announcement of the performance in 1889. Young apparently began this entertainment cross-dressing after 1885, when he, his wife, and their children returned from an LDS mission in Hawaii.

27. Rell G. Francis, *Utah Photographs of George Edward Anderson* (Lincoln: University of Nebraska Press, 1979), 53.

28. Phyllis Robbins, *Maude Adams: An Intimate Portrait* (New York: G. P. Putnam's Sons, 1956), 35, 62–63, 143, 284; Keith Melville, *The Mormon*

Drama and Maude Adams (Provo, Utah: Extension Publications, Brigham Young University, 1965).

29. Mildred J. Berryman, "The Psychological Phenomena of the Homosexual," page 68, with corrections in spelling and punctuation, rough-typed on the back of stationery of the American Red Cross, Salt Lake City, Utah, with the last page of the study dated 13 Nov. 1938, in the June Mazer Lesbian Collection, West Hollywood, Calif. See chap. 7 for my analysis of Berryman's findings for all the lesbians and gay men in her study.

30. C. H. Hughes, "Postscript to a Paper of 'Erotopathia,'" *Alienist and Neurologist* 14 (Oct. 1893): 731–32, quoted in Bullough and Bullough, *Cross Dressing,* 191; Katz, *Gay American History,* 40, 43; George Chauncey, *Gay New York: Gender, Urban Culture, and the Making of the Gay Male World, 1890–1940* (New York: Basic Books/HarperCollins, 1994), 40–42, 293.

31. Bullough and Bullough, *Cross Dressing,* 228–52; see Marjorie Garber, *Vested Interests: Cross-Dressing and Cultural Anxiety* (New York: Routledge, 1992), 60–66, 165–85, 267–303, for the long tradition and continued acceptance of cross-dressing in the United States as entertainment and "the male-bonding rituals provided by institutionalized transvestite theaters in privileged spaces like universities and millionaires' clubs" (60). The recent legalization of same-sex marriages in Denmark, Norway, and the Netherlands is beyond the time period of this study.

32. Joseph Smith (b. 1805) proclaimed that he was a prophet in the manner of ancient Moses—able to speak with God face-to-face, to utter statements or revelations as "thus saith the Lord," to give new commandments to God's people on earth, and to write the words of God. These claims transcended (but did not repudiate) the text and authority of the Bible, and Joseph Smith's first published example of his prophetic role was the 1830 Book of Mormon. For scholarly Mormon views of Joseph Smith's prophetic claims, see Leonard J. Arrington and Davis Bitton, *The Mormon Experience: A History of the Latter-day Saints* (New York: Alfred A. Knopf, 1979), 5–17; James B. Allen and Glen M. Leonard, *The Story of the Latter-day Saints,* 2d ed., rev. (Salt Lake City: Deseret Book, 1992), 29–53; Richard L. Bushman, *Joseph Smith and the Beginnings of Mormonism* (Urbana: University of Illinois Press, 1984). For the interpretative views by non-Mormon specialists on Joseph Smith, see Jan Shipps, "The Prophet Puzzle: Suggestions Leading toward a More Comprehensive Interpretation of Joseph Smith," in D. Michael Quinn, ed., *The New Mormon History: Revisionist Essays on the Past* (Salt Lake City: Signature Books, 1992), 53–74; and Lawrence Foster, "The Psychology of Religious Genius: Joseph Smith and the Origins of New Religious Movements," *Dialogue: A Journal of Mormon Thought* 26 (Winter 1993): 1–22.

33. Brigham H. Roberts, ed., *History of the Church of Jesus Christ of Latter-day Saints,* 7 vols., 2d ed., rev. (Salt Lake City: Deseret Book, 1978), 1:312,

323; Milton V. Backman Jr., *The Heavens Resound: A History of the Latter-day Saints in Ohio, 1830–1838* (Salt Lake City: Deseret Book, 1983), 264–68; John R. Patrick, "The School of the Prophets: Its Development and Influence in Utah Territory" (M.A. thesis, Brigham Young University, 1970); Minutes of the Salt Lake City School of the Prophets (1870–74), LDS Archives; Merle H. Graffam, ed., *Salt Lake School of the Prophets: Minute Book, 1883* (Palm Desert, Calif.: ULC Press, 1981); Leonard J. Arrington, *Great Basin Kingdom: An Economic History of the Latter-day Saints, 1830–1900* (Cambridge, Mass.: Harvard University Press, 1958), 245–51; Allen and Leonard, *Story of the Latter-day Saints,* 107, 338.

34. Andrew Jenson, *Latter-day Saint Biographical Encyclopedia,* 4 vols. (Salt Lake City: Deseret News Press and Andrew Jenson History, 1901–36), 1:253–54; "Recollections of the Prophet Joseph Smith," *Juvenile Instructor* 27 (1 July 1892): 398, quoted in Hyrum L. Andrus and Helen Mae Andrus, comps., *They Knew the Prophet* (Salt Lake City: Bookcraft, 1974), 199.

35. William Clayton diary, 23 June 1843, in George D. Smith, ed., *An Intimate Chronicle: The Journal of William Clayton* (Salt Lake City: Signature Books/Smith Research Associates, 1991), 108.

36. *Journal of Discourses,* 26 vols. (Liverpool: Latter-day Saints Book Depot, 1854–86), 9:269 (Young/1862), 16:186 (Young/1873). For the 1843 beginning of the marriage sealing ceremony, see Andrew F. Ehat, "Joseph Smith's Introduction of Temple Ordinances and the 1844 Mormon Succession Question" (M.A. thesis, Brigham Young University, 1982), 62–63.

37. Kimball Young, *Isn't One Wife Enough?* (New York: Henry Holt, 1954), 280.

38. Gordon Irving, "The Law of Adoption: One Phase of the Development of the Mormon Concept of Salvation, 1830–1900," *Brigham Young University Studies* 14 (Spring 1974): 291–314, esp. 296–303; see also Robert Glass Cleland and Juanita Brooks, eds., *A Mormon Chronicle: The Diaries of John D. Lee, 1848–1876,* 2 vols. (San Marino, Calif.: Huntington Library, 1955), 1:ix; Juanita Brooks, *John Doyle Lee: Zealot, Pioneer Builder, Scapegoat* (Glendale, Calif.: Arthur H. Clark, 1962), 73. When he was adopted to Apostle Willard Richards, Thomas Bullock also recorded that he changed "his name to Thomas Bullock Richards." See Thomas Bullock Apr. 1845–Feb. 1846 diary (25 Jan. 1846), LDS Archives, and Greg R. Knight, ed., *Thomas Bullock Nauvoo Journal* (Orem, Utah: Grandin Book., 1994), 44–45. However, within two years, this name-adoption practice ended, and men such as Lee and Bullock stopped referring to themselves by their adopted surnames. Male-male adoption itself continued with regularity in LDS temples until publicly ended in 1894, after which such spiritual adoptions (in contrast to legal adoptions) occurred only sporadically. Irving's article describes the decline of this once-popular ordinance of Mormonism.

39. Hosea Stout diary, 5 Jan. 1848, in Juanita Brooks, ed., *On the Mormon Frontier: The Diary of Hosea Stout, 1844–1861,* 2 vols. (Salt Lake City: University of Utah Press, 1964), 1:295.

40. Antonio A. Feliz, "The Law of Adoption and the Homosexual Saint," *Affinity: Official Publication of Affirmation, Gay and Lesbian Mormons* (July 1985): [2–3]; Feliz, *Out of the Bishop's Closet* (San Francisco: Aurora Press, 1988), 85; "Gay Ex-Mormon Renews Faith in Joseph Smith," *Salt Lake Tribune,* 17 Oct. 1992, B-2; Feliz, "Cultural Transformation Theory: A Radical Reconciliation of Early Mormon Social Innovations and Today's Changing Social Values: In Celebration of the Sesquicentennial of the Joseph Smith Funeral Sermon for Lorenzo D. Barnes Delivered on Apr. 16, 1843 in Nauvoo, Illinois," paper presented at the Stonewall Center, Salt Lake City, Utah, 15 Apr. 1993, copy at Library, Stonewall Center. I first disputed the claims of Feliz in "Gay Ex-Mormon Renews Faith in Joseph Smith," *Salt Lake Tribune,* 17 Oct. 1992, B-2.

41. Kenney, *Wilford Woodruff's Journal,* 2:511 (20 Feb. 1845); Feliz, *Out of the Bishop's Closet,* 214. Feliz claimed that Wilford Woodruff's shorthand entries referred to this person as "priesthood Lover," or "kingdom Lover," or "sealed Lover" (213). There are no such adjectives preceding Woodruff's descriptions of Lorenzo's "Lover" as found in Woodruff's published diary (which includes transcriptions of his shorthand entries). See Kenney, *Wilford Woodruff's Journal,* 2:226–27 (16 Apr. 1843), 2:510–15 (20 Feb. 1845). The wording of page 214 seemed to imply that Woodruff was actually Barnes's "Lover," but Feliz informed me on 23 March 1994 that he did not intend to make such a suggestion.

42. Kenney, *Wilford Woodruff's Journal,* 2:512–13 (20 Feb. 1845). On 9 Feb. 1864, Woodruff wrote: "I visited . . . Sister Susan Conrad or Wil(conson). I conversed with her about Elder Lorenzo D. Bar[nes]" (6:156). Born in 1825, Susan Conrad first married Samuel Thomas in 1849 and later married William B. Wilkinson. See entries for the above in Ancestral File, Family History Library of the Church of Jesus Christ of Latter-day Saints, Salt Lake City, Utah (hereafter LDS Family History Library). Feliz, in *Out of the Bishop's Closet,* 213, questioned the claim concerning Conrad, but overlooked Woodruff's 1864 statement and was unaware of her marriage to Wilkinson.

43. See entries for Lorenzo D. Barnes and William S. Johnson in Susan Easton Black, *Membership of the Church of Jesus Christ of Latter-day Saints, 1830–1848,* 50 vols. (Provo, Utah: Religious Studies Center, Brigham Young University, 1984–88), 3:810–11, 25:278; marriage of Lorenzo D. Barnes and Amanda Wilson, 3 Oct. 1841, performed by William Johnson in Medina County, Ohio Marriage Record (1818–44), 257, microfilm, LDS Family History Library.

44. Roberts, *History of the Church,* 5:361–63.

45. *Journal of Discourses,* 22:365 (Cannon/1881); see also chap. 4.

46. Willard Richards diary, 23 Dec. 1845, in D. Michael Quinn, "LDS Church Authority and New Plural Marriages, 1890–1904," *Dialogue: A Journal of Mormon Thought* 18 (Spring 1985): 55.

47. Roberts, *History of the Church,* 4:470; Clayton diary, 13 Mar. 1844, in Smith, ed., *An Intimate Chronicle,* 127.

48. However, the Restoration Church (organized in 1985, by Antonio Feliz originally) proclaimed that part of its mission was to perform same-sex sealings for "all loving relationships for time and eternity as the inspirations of God may direct." See Steven L. Shields, "The Restoration Church of Jesus Christ," *Divergent Paths of the Restoration: A History of the Latter Day Saint Movement,* 4th ed., rev. (Los Angeles: Restoration Research, 1990), 274–76. In addition, Feliz, in *Out of the Bishop's Closet,* 182, recommends a same-sex rewording of the covenant of marriage in the 1845 diary of Willard Richards, and Feliz notes that two gay men used that reworded covenant for their own ceremony.

CHAPTER 6

Same-Sex Couples, Homoenvironmental Subcultures, and the Census

SAME-SEX PERSONS could not marry in the United States of the nineteenth century despite the favorable climate for same-sex dynamics. Still, a few American cross-dressers (primarily women) entered into civil marriages (under false pretenses) with same-sex spouses.[1]

There is no known example of that among nineteenth-century Utahns. However, during 1994 in Salt Lake City a female cross-dresser sexually cohabited with another female under false pretenses. In 1995 a Utah man discovered that the sexually shy woman he had married three years earlier was actually a man who still had a penis despite partial transsexual surgery. Their marriage had been ratified in the LDS temple.[2]

On the other hand, there were tens of thousands of same-sex couples of the nineteenth century who simply lived together for companionship, emotional support, financial cooperation, physical closeness, and sometimes for sexual fulfillment. In sum, they did so for all of the reasons people enter into heterosexual marriages, except procreation.[3] In fact, heterosexual couples who married after the woman passed child-bearing age had the same reasons for establishing a relationship as did same-sex couples. Same-gender couples who also wanted sexual intimacy had one major advantage in nineteenth-century America—few thought it unusual for persons of the same sex to share a single bed—either for a night or for years.[4]

A male-male couple first came to Mormon attention in 1856. Among the English converts on their way to Utah were Luke Carter (age forty-five) and Charles Edmonds (age fifty-six). Carter had been an unmarried widower for ten years, and Edmonds was a bachelor. They traveled on the same ship to America, and during the overland journey "they slept in the same tent, cooked and bunked together." Another Mormon in their emigrant group noted that one was "a tall, loosely built and tender man physically," while the other was "more stocky and sturdy." Carter, the more "tender" of the two, died "on the plains," despite his companion's effort to ease his burdens. Aside from their description as traveling and sleeping companions, there is no evidence that Carter and Edmonds had romantic or erotic attachments. Nevertheless, the two men's association was sufficiently impressive to be singled out in another man's reminiscence fifty-seven years later.[5]

During the American Civil War, a male couple in the Confederate Army was also the subject of comment without criticism. A few years after the battlefield death of Maj. Gen. Patrick Ronayne Cleburne, a fellow officer wrote a biographical sketch of this unmarried Irishman: "Among his attachments was a very strong one for his adjutant, General Captain Irving A. Buck, a boy in years, but a man in all soldierly qualities, who for nearly two years of the war, shared Cleburne's labours during the day and his blankets at night." Because there was no provable homoeroticism (or perhaps none at all), their fellow officer saw nothing wrong about this male-male relationship. Nor did the author of the 1868 book *The Irish in America*, which included this account.[6] However, male couples and homoerotic intimacy were both common in America's male subcultures.

These subcultures were homoenvironmental. In other words, there were (and continue to be) entire living environments that lack the presence of the opposite sex for weeks, months, or years at a time. As a term, *homoenvironmental* would exaggerate the homosocial experiences of Mormon missionary companions or of same-sex persons in co-residence, both of whom have daily opportunities to interact socially with persons of the opposite sex. On the other hand, *homoenvironmental* is a useful term for describing the living situation of prison populations, gender-segregated reform schools and boarding schools, convents and monasteries, cowboys during a cattle drive, the populations of mining camps and logging camps in nineteenth-century America, and the traditional shipboard life of sailors for months at a time.

The military was the source of the earliest evidence of sexual relations in the homoenvironmental subcultures of America. In March 1778 George Washington ordered the court-martial of a German lieutenant in the Continental Army for attempted sodomy.[7] However, General Washington was unaware that General von Steuben, who had recently arrived to train the Continental Army, had already been accused of engaging in sex with young males. He left Europe because of a complaint in August 1777 that he had "taken familiarities with young boys which the laws forbid and punish severely." A German newspaper described his conduct as "a crime" that had been common "formerly among the Greeks." When forty-eight-year-old General von Steuben reported for duty with the American Continental Army in 1778, his companion was a seventeen-year-old Frenchman to whom the general had been "strongly attracted" at their first meeting. They lived together for the first two years of von Steuben's vital service to the Continental Army. During the remainder of the Revolution the general began "one of the closest and tenderest ties in all human relations" with a twenty-four-year-old American man.[8]

A century later, there was a same-sex scandal in the U.S. Seventh Cavalry. When "Mrs. Nash" died in 1878, the attending physician at the fort discovered that this army wife was actually a man.[9] The military physician William A. Hammond knew an army officer in another far western fort who was allowed to resign after he was discovered having sex with an enlisted man. A U.S. soldier was also involved in the first sodomy scandal of pioneer Mormon Utah.[10] A man who served in the U.S. Marines from 1846 to 1869 wrote in his diary that "ninety percent of the white boys in the Navy of this day" were "sodomites." Only one of the sailors/marines he knew "did not engage in sex with shipmates."[11]

Sexual activities were common in the homoenvironmental culture of prisons as well. In 1826 Louis Dwight reported on the condition of various men's prisons from Massachusetts to Georgia: "THE SIN OF SODOM IS THE VICE OF PRISONS AND BOYS ARE THE FAVORITE PROSTITUTES."[12] In 1886, a physician also published a study of the consensual anal sex engaged in by most young men at a reform school in Baltimore. Similar sexual activity among the young men at Utah's reform school became the source of extensive newspaper publicity at the turn of the twentieth century.[13]

By end of the nineteenth century, thousands of upper-class American teenagers had attended all-male boarding schools in military academies, prep schools, and colleges. In 1826, two young Southerners peppered their correspondence with light-hearted references to their erotic experiences as "writhing Bedfellows" at college.[14] However, no American of that era chronicled the erotic dimension of this environment as graphically as John Addington Symonds described his experiences at Harrow, the elite English school, during the 1850s: "Here and there one could not avoid seeing acts of onanism, mutual masturbation, the sports of naked boys in bed together." Although Symonds already recognized his own homoerotic desires as a teenager, he added: "There was no refinement, no sentiment, no passion; nothing but animal lust in these occurrences. They filled me with disgust and loathing."[15]

However, contrary to Symonds's experience, intimate relationships at the all-male boarding schools were not limited to impersonal sex. As a member of Parliament in 1844, Benjamin Disraeli published a remarkable description of the "passionate admiration and affection" of schoolboys at Eton:

> At school, friendship is a passion. It entrances the being; it tears the soul. All loves of after-life can never bring its rapture, or its wretchedness; no bliss so absorbing, no pangs of jealousy or despair so crushing and so keen! What tenderness and what devotion; what illimitable confidence, infinite revelations of inmost thoughts; what ecstatic present and romantic future; what bitter estrangements and what melting reconciliations; what scenes of wild recrimination, agitating explanations, passionate correspondence; what insane sensitiveness, and what frantic sensibility; what earthquakes of the heart and whirlwinds of the soul are confined in that simple phrase, a schoolboy's friendship.

By twentieth-century definitions, far more than "friendship" was involved here, but no one regarded Disraeli's widely circulated statement as inappropriate, and he eventually became prime minister.[16]

The earliest Mormon to attend an American college's boarding school was Albert Carrington, who graduated from Dartmouth College in 1834. It is unknown whether his experience reflected Symonds's or Disraeli's. Carrington left no descriptions of his roommates or dormitory life there.[17]

Unlike the men's schools, there were no explicit references to sexual activities in American women's colleges during the early nineteenth century. There were, however, references to female homoeroticism in British schools for girls and young women in the early 1800s.[18] Both students and administrators commented about intimacy between female students at American boarding schools in the later part of the century.

Two Mormon women roomed together at Amherst College in the 1830s, and when separated from each other in 1839, Elizabeth Haven wrote of her wish to "sleep with you one night."[19] At age twenty in 1877, non-Mormon Carey Thomas described the beginning of her ongoing relationship with a fellow student in the Sage College for women at Cornell University. While reading together in bed, Carey "turned to her and asked, 'Do you love me?' She threw her arms around me and whispered, 'I love you passionately.'" Although she did not specify that their relationship was erotic, Carey Thomas wrote in her diary during 1877: "Often I prayed that I might stop loving her."[20]

In 1882, there was an official investigation of this widespread occurrence of female students "falling violently in love with each other" at American women's colleges, "as if one of them were a man."[21] Nevertheless, female-female romance continued at such schools as Wellesley College where Mary Woolley and Jeannette Marks made "a mutual declaration of ardent love," exchanged rings, and eventually lived together the rest of their lives at Mount Holyoak, where Woolley was college president and Marks was a teacher.[22] Passion at female boarding schools was not simply an Anglo-American phenomenon, since investigators in 1905 found "an epidemic" of female-female sexual activities in Argentina's schools for girls and young women.[23]

The male subculture to receive the first sociological (rather than medical) study of this intimacy was America's hobo, or tramp, population. In 1897, Josiah Flynt published his study "Homosexuality among Tramps," based on ten years of interviewing and eight months of living as a hobo among American tramps, including those in Utah. "Every hobo in the United States knows what 'unnatural intercourse' means," Flynt wrote, "and, according to my finding, every tenth man practises it, and defends his conduct."[24] Flynt may have been the first American researcher to cite 10 percent as an estimate of men who preferred same-gender sex.[25] "Boys are the victims of this passion," Flynt affirmed, but he did not claim that force was involved, and observed that among American tramps, "nothing is more severely judged than rape."[26] Nevertheless, tramps were involved in several cases of homosexual rape in Utah just before Flynt published his essay.[27]

Flynt's 1897 study was the first analysis of the dynamics in sexual relationships between intergenerational males in America.[28] He reported that tramp boys told him "they get as much pleasure out of the affair as the jocker [the boy's adult companion] does." He added: "The majority of the prushuns [boys with a "jocker"] are between ten and fifteen years of age, but I have known some under ten and a few over fifteen." Despite his dislike for "this perversion," Flynt (who remained unmarried) acknowledged: "Such attachments frequently last for years." The relationship usually ended when the younger tramps reached their late teens, and could "have a boy and use him as they have been used." His article estimated the total number of tramps at about sixty thousand, and therefore concluded that there were up to six thousand homosexual hobos in the United States in the 1890s: "this includes men and boys."[29]

Curiously, Flynt's full-length book on tramps did not refer to homoeroticism in his discussion of the adult "jocker" and his "prushun" boys. However, it gave prominent attention to Salt Lake City in his section on the characteristics of tramps in the American West during the late nineteenth century: "The blanket-stiffs are men (or sometimes women) who walk, or 'drill,' as they say, from Salt Lake City to San Francisco about twice a year begging their way from ranch to ranch, and always carrying their blankets with them. The ex-prushuns are young fellows who have served their apprenticeship as kids in the East, and are in the West 'looking for revenge,' *i.e.*, seeking some kid whom they can press into their service and compel to work for them. The gay-cats are men who will work for 'very good money.'" The homoerotic dimensions of that passage are obscure without reading Flynt's essay in *Sexual Inversion* or knowing that there was a homosexual meaning of *gay-cat*. In his book he added that Salt Lake City was a "hang-out" for tramps.[30]

A generation later, the sociologist Nels Anderson (a graduate of Brigham Young University) interviewed hundreds of hobos and tramps in the American West, including Utah. He likewise found that "there are attachments between [hobo] men and between men and [hobo] boys that 'surpass the love of woman.'" Of approximately two million hobos nationally in 1921, Anderson gave no percentage estimate for homosexuality except to say that "one-fourth of the tramp class in the United States are boys under twenty-one," and that "sex perversion is very prevalent among the tramp population."[31] Midway between the Flynt and Anderson publications, a study of New York City's tramps "reported that twenty-four of the hundred men were perverts."[32]

Cowboy life was the male subculture of the American West where personal accounts of male coupling were not filtered through sociological studies. A lifelong bachelor, Charles Badger Clark (b. 1883) was a cowboy in Arizona from age twenty-one to twenty-five. After the death of his "Pardner," Clark grieved: "we loved each other... more than any woman's kiss could be," and yet, "he's gone—and left me here!" Clark wrote that he longed to "feel his knee rub mine the good old way." Of the nearly universal bachelorhood among cowboys, he discreetly commented: "We never count a wife. Each has a reason why he's lone, but keeps it 'neath his hat."[33] Despite Clark's candid admissions, most American cowboys referred to their homoerotic experiences only in limericks.[34]

However, an Oklahoma cowboy of the early 1900s explained that men on the cattle range were attracted to each other because of "admiration, infatuation, a sensed need of an ally, loneliness and yearning, but it regularly ripened into love." He said that cowboy couples practiced mutual masturbation and "the ecstatically comforting 69." Although the 1900 census listed 1,946 cowboys in Utah, there are no similar accounts from its cowboys of the period. A Utah cowboy later wrote:

> A cowboy needs a closer tie,
> It's a partnership with another guy.
> To city folks it may seem queer,
> To want another man so near.

By the time of this Utah poem, "queer" had only one meaning in America, homosexual.[35]

Of his teenage experiences during the early twentieth century in logging camps of the Northwest, another man wrote: "Out of the 55 men in camp, conservatively over half were getting relief from one another.... My time was pretty well monopolized in the evenings by first one and then another of those inclined towards homosexuality." Although the young man had no sexual commitment with another lumberman, he envied one male couple: "two of the most masculine of the crew (a tram operator and a jackhammer man) soon started pairing off exclusively, moving into a cabin together."[36] The co-residence of such same-gender couples can be precisely located nationwide, but sources generally do not exist for identifying whether sexual intimacy was involved in their co-residence.

For several years, social historians have used the manuscript census to study heterosexual couples who were cohabiting without formal marriage in the United States.[37] Within certain limits, the same can be done for same-sex couples who were cohabiting. Co-residence does not prove sexual cohabitation, either for same-gender couples or for childless heterosexual couples. Nor for that matter did previous or subsequent marriage prove that same-gender household members had a platonic relationship. For example, Oscar Wilde was married with two children at the time of his imprisonment for sodomy.[38] Several of Utah's sodomy cases also involved married men, and some of the defendants were Mormon polygamists who were simultaneously living with their plural wives.[39]

The likelihood of uncovering an intimate relationship increases with the expanded information each census provided about same-gender co-residents. Nevertheless, Walter L. Williams, an ethnohistorian in the Program for the Study of Women and Men in Society at the University of Southern California, has observed: "The 'proof' of genital contact that is wanted to confirm a male marriage [or sexual relationship] is not asked of historians discussing the heterosexuality of women and men who live together for many years, or even of women and men who have ephemeral love relations [with each other]."[40] Sheila Jeffreys adds: "Men and women who simply take walks together are assumed to be involved in some sort of heterosexual relationship."[41] Because some historians and biographers go to extraordinary lengths to deny there is a homoerotic dimension in the otherwise intimate relationships between famous women, Blanche Wiesen Cook has written that this demand for absolute proof of same-sex genital contact equals the "historical denial of lesbianism."[42]

In addition, census rules obscured the existence of many same-sex couples who were in co-residence. Same-sex couples occupying the same bed in a hotel or the same room in a boarding house were listed only as "lodger," "renter," or "boarder" in the census. That was the relationship of these people to the "head" of the hotel or boarding house. There is no way to verify from these census lists which lodgers were cohabiting a single room or single bed in hotels and boarding houses.

For example, thousands of males (both same-aged and intergenerational) shared rooms and sometimes beds in YMCA dormitories in cities throughout the United States from the midnineteenth century onward, yet the census enumerated them as though they were individual lodgers without acknowledging they were at least roommates. In fact, many regarded their roommates as "intimate" friends, such as one of the YMCA's national leaders who shared a room in New York City with a young man for five years, "a fellowship growing in intimacy and tenderness until the end of his life on earth." Remarkably, the periodical of the Young Men's Christian Association simply assumed that sexual desire was part of the "friendship" between men in YMCA dormitories: "Let this man burn with a fierce desire toward that man, but let him not evidence that desire except by the action of his eyes, his hands, and his heart. Let the other man keep his distance in the same way."[43] For some same-sex roommates at the YMCA and elsewhere, keeping their distance erotically was more difficult than for others.

Since the 1830s Mormons had also frequently boarded with other Mormons. For example, Hyrum Smith had nine boarders in succession at his Ohio house during the last six months of 1835.[44] Because boarders and lodgers were common in the late nineteenth century and the early twentieth,[45] the U.S. census underreported same-sex couples. Same-sex couples staying with families or living in boarding houses and hotels may have equalled or exceeded the number of same-sex couples whom the census identified in co-residence in the cities. Also, the census can provide no evidence of those same-sex, intimate couples who lived separately, rather than in co-residence.

In the 1880 census of Salt Lake City there was a total of sixteen same-sex couples who were not relatives. The stated relationship of the second person to the household head was typically that of servant, boarder, lodger, or roomer. These sixteen couples were not even .5 percent of the 4,207 families in the city that year.[46]

For convenience, I will provide percentages for various characteristics of same-sex couples in Salt Lake City in the census of 1880 and 1900 (since a fire destroyed the census of 1890), although their numbers are too small to be statistically significant. In other words, I do not suggest that the percentage findings here are representative of same-sex couples in urban co-residence for the West or for the nation. Also, because the total number of same-sex couples is so small in the census data examined here, the percentages would change dramatically if one or two couples had been on one side of the comparison instead of the other. Keeping those limits in mind, I will examine the census data with regard to various areas of interest to social historians. The significance of these Salt Lake City findings can be known only by examining the thousands of other same-sex couples in the manuscript census for cities throughout the West and throughout the United States. Examination of such a large population would be statistically significant.

Eleven of these same-sex couples in Salt Lake City in 1880 were female and five were male. The census described all of them as "white." There was no same-sex couple in which both persons were in their twenties or late teens. The only couple close to that age relationship was twenty-seven-year-old Shamira Rossiter, who was a plural wife, but was listed only with her fourteen-year-old servant, Minnie. The census did not list Shamira's newborn daughter.[47]

In fact, age disparities greater than ten years were characteristic of the same-sex couples of Salt Lake City in 1880. Eleven couples (68.8 percent) had age disparities varying from thirteen years to fifty-four years. Women accounted for all same-sex couples with age disparities greater than twenty-four years—five of the eleven couples. Moreover, gender determined the kind of age disparity that existed in these same-sex couples of 1880. Of the eight female couples with significant age disparities, the older woman was between fifty-eight and eighty years old in all but one case (Shamira Rossiter, cited above). That supports the hypothesis that these female couples were in renter relationships that had no erotic dimension.

However, in the three male couples of significant age disparity in 1880, the older was always middle-aged (ages forty-five, forty-two, and thirty-nine) and cohabiting with a young man, respectively aged twenty-eight, twenty-five, and fifteen. That pattern supports (but cannot prove) the hypothesis that a sexual relationship is likely when a middle-aged man is living with a significantly younger male who is not a relative. The greatest age disparity of these co-resident males in 1880 involved a thirty-nine-year-old non-Mormon patent-medicine salesman and his fifteen-year-old live-in "assistant," a Mormon immigrant from Scotland.[48]

European immigrants were prominent in Salt Lake City's same-sex couples of 1880. Twelve couples (75.0 percent) included at least one European immigrant. Six couples (37.5 percent) comprised only European immigrants. That reflects the European immigrants' 36.6 percent share of the city's population in 1880.[49] Three couples (18.8 percent) were composed of a European immigrant and an American born outside Utah. Three domestic partnerships (18.8 percent) were formed between a European immigrant and a Utah native.

The 1880 census of Utah was unique in the history of the American census. Because of the contemporary conflict with Mormons, the federal census takers identified individual Utahns by their religious affiliation. Four of the same-sex couples (25 percent) were composed of two "Gentiles" (non-Mormons) each. That percentage was slightly more than the non-Mormon percentage of Salt Lake City's population in 1880.[50]

In 1900, for the first time, census instructions specified that members of a household—even if it consisted of only two unrelated persons—could describe themselves as domestic "partners." The U.S. government acknowledged in 1900 that "the word 'family,' for census purposes, has a somewhat different application from what it has in popular usage."[51] It is impossible to know how many of these domestic partners in the census were sexually intimate or regarded themselves as homosexual. However, the U.S. government in effect defined lesbian and gay couples as families and allowed them to identify themselves as domestic partners. For example, the 1900 census indicated that there were more than two thousand same-sex partner households in the combined New York City boroughs of the Bronx and Manhattan.[52] That included Greenwich Village's homosexual "Fairyland."[53]

In 1995, the *Salt Lake Tribune* used similar census data to illustrate a front-page article about the ban on same-sex marriage in Utah. The article noted that there were 401 "Unmarried Partner Same Sex" households in Utah as of the 1990 census and implied that these were sexually intimate couples.[54]

Census takers were flexible in 1900 and allowed the second person in a co-residence couple to define their relationship to the head of household in any way they wished. For example, the Salt Lake City census listed one person as "companion" and another as "friend" to their respective heads of household.[55] However, the other one hundred same-sex persons defined themselves as in a "partner" relationship. Despite the value-neutral approach of the census takers in 1900, many self-defined lesbian, gay, or bisexual couples probably declined to use the term *partner*, even if they were living together intimately. After all, Utah judges were giving long sentences to men convicted of sodomy that year.[56]

It is important to keep in mind, however, that even years of co-residence by same-sex domestic partners does not prove sexual intimacy. Nevertheless, the historian Lillian Faderman has written that such same-sex living arrangements were so "pervasive" for middle-class women in nineteenth-century America that these relationships were popularly called "Boston marriages." She observes: "They afforded a woman companionship, nurturance, a communion of kindred spirits, romance (and undoubtedly, in some but not all such relationships, sex)—all the advantages of having a 'significant other' in one's life and none of the burdens that were concomitant with heterosexuality."[57] At a minimum, these co-resident persons were in a prolonged homosocial relationship with each other, whether in Boston or in Salt Lake City.

Recognizing these limits, I will first present a statistical profile of the 52 same-sex couples who listed themselves as "partner," "companion," or "friend" in Salt Lake City in 1900. I use the term *domestic partnership* to describe the relationship of those 104 persons. Next I will provide a statistical profile of 21 same-sex couples living together in Salt Lake City who did not define themselves as partners in 1900. In each case, I will compare the findings for the total of 146 same-sex persons in the 1900 census of Salt Lake City to the findings for the 32 same-sex persons in the 1880 census. And remember that for Salt Lake City and other cities, the actual number of same-sex couples was probably more than the census can demonstrate. Again my term *domestic partnership* reflects the census description of these households and is not an assertion of sexual intimacy, which is impossible to prove from the census alone.[58]

To be conservative in this discussion of domestic partnerships, I have excluded business partners who lived in co-residence. I also have excluded couples in which the "partner" had the same surname as the "head," which suggested they were close relatives.[59] However, one domestic partnership I have included merits special mention. This 1900 household combined a marital relationship with a male domestic partnership that did not seem to be business oriented.

In 1900, thirty-eight-year-old James Storey (a recent LDS convert) began living with fifty-four-year-old James Gibson, an Irish Mormon, and with Gibson's ten-years-younger Irish wife and two children (aged nine and three). Although Storey, who was unmarried, defined himself as the "partner" of the Irish husband, their relationship did not seem to be business oriented. Gibson was a laborer, while his younger partner owned his own business. Storey, his domestic partner Gibson, and Gibson's wife continued living together at a succession of residences in Salt Lake City from 1900 until Storey died in 1908.[60]

At the least, this was a domestic triangle based on mutual friendship. There is also the possibility that the Gibson-Storey household was a romantic ménage à trois involving both marital and same-sex relationships centering on the husband. However, the U.S. census was not constructed to reveal the dynamics of the household relationships it defines. The triangular dynamics of this household may have been only social.

Demographically, there is one interesting characteristic of Salt Lake City's same-sex partners in 1900 compared with the city's same-sex couples in the 1880 census. Male domestic partnerships in 1900 outnumbered female domestic partnerships by 5.5 to 1—forty-four male couples to eight female couples. Involving more than one hundred persons, this lopsided proportion seems significant (qualitatively, if not quantitatively).

In contrast, there were only half as many male couples in 1880 as female couples in Salt Lake City. Yet males slightly outnumbered females in Salt Lake County's total population of 1880, whereas males made up less than half of Salt Lake City's total population in 1900.[61] Thus, while there had been a decrease in the male percentage of the total population, the proportion of male couples had virtually skyrocketed in Salt Lake City by 1900.

Occupation and age are possible explanations for the increase of male domestic partnerships in Salt Lake City after 1880. Utah's growing mining industry could partially account for the increase of male couples in Salt Lake City. However, only eight of the eighty-eight men in domestic partnerships were employed in the mining industry, and in only two domestic partnerships were both men in mining.

Another socioeconomic explanation for the fivefold dominance of male couples could be that men in their twenties were simply sharing expenses in the transition from the parental home to the marital home, while women preferred to stay in the parental home until marriage. However, even if that were true, it would not explain why the proportion of women sharing expenses prior to marriage declined so dramatically from 1880 to 1900, when there was no corresponding decline in the number of females in the city.

Moreover, age analysis does not support parental-marital transition as an explanation for the overwhelming male dominance in domestic partnerships in 1900 Salt Lake City. Four male couples and four female couples were composed of partners in their twenties or late teens, the typical age of transition. There is no way to determine if these eight couples were merely sharing expenses or if they were sexual partners. Despite these small numbers, the percentages do reflect the gender ratio of the entire city's population. However, these eight couples do not reflect the gender ratio of same-sex couples in 1900.

On the other hand, the age disparity in the other domestic partnerships suggests that many of them were mentor-protégé relationships. There may have been a few instances of "kept boys,"[62] such as thirteen-year-old Peter who was living in an apartment as the "partner" of twenty-five-year-old Sam.[63] Historically, it is more defensible to acknowledge the possibility of a "kept boy" relationship in such co-residence of intergenerational males than to simply assume there was no sexual dynamic involved.

For example, the Young Men's Christian Association's publication matter-of-factly acknowledged the erotic dimension of intergenerational friendships at the YMCA in the late nineteenth century and the early twentieth. "The friend of boys should be a lover of boys—should have suffered because of boys until he has purged himself without pity of the lustful desires that come storming, whether he will or not, to take possession of him." The YMCA publication advised the older "lover of boys" to "sublimate his friendship so that it moves on grandly, unrequited, like the friendship of a god."[64]

Twenty-four (46.2 percent) of all the same-sex domestic partnerships in 1900 Salt Lake City involved age differences greater than ten years, and all but one of those couples was male. In other words, over half (52.3 percent) of male domestic partnerships in Salt Lake City during 1900 had age differences of eleven to forty-two years.[65]

Perhaps because they involved only forty-six men, these intergenerational domestic partnerships did not represent Salt Lake City's demographics very well. There was only one native Utahn, twenty-three-year-old Oliver Due. He was the domestic partner of sixty-five-year-old Aaron Post of Minnesota.[66] Nearly 46 percent of these intergenerational domestic partnerships included European immigrants to Utah, which was double their percentage of Salt Lake City's population. Moreover, 20 percent of these intergenerational couples were Chinese, who composed less than 1 percent of the city's male population.[67]

In fact, five out of the six total Chinese domestic partnerships had age differences greater than ten years. Despite the small numbers, these partnership couples were consistent with China's cultural expectation that "deep and lasting Chinese friendship bound together old men and young men."[68] However, in China such male friendships existed where there was the possibility of sexual fulfillment through marriage with women.

In the United States, there was an enormous gender imbalance among Chinese immigrants. Many Chinese men came to America to work in the nineteenth century and rarely saw a Chinese woman again. Census records demonstrate that more than 90 percent of Chinese men in America remained unmarried or permanently separated from their wives. In 1890, there were nearly twenty-seven Chinese men for every Chinese woman in the United States, resulting in what the historian Stanford M. Lyman called the "womanless condition of the Chinese in America."[69] In a discussion of the "Friendship and Sexuality" of these womanless men, the historian Francis Hsu observed that Chinese men felt no "fear of homosexuality" in living with a male friend for years at a time.[70]

In nineteenth-century Utah, as elsewhere in America, the only opportunity a Chinese man had for sexual expression was either with a female prostitute or with the Chinese man who was his domestic partner.[71] In his study of sexual practices in China, R. H. Van Gulik commented about the modern "immigrant communities outside China, where there was a scarcity of Chinese women and hence an abnormal tendency towards homosexuality."[72]

Because of their linguistic and racial isolation, there is less evidence about the domestic experiences of the Chinese than other immigrant groups. However, Chauncey's history of New York City in the early 1900s notes that "slender oral history hints at homosexual activity among some of the [Chinese] bachelors" in co-residence there.[73] During his 1893 visits to Boston, New York City, Philadelphia, Chicago, and Denver, the German physician Magnus Hirschfeld (a prominent homosexual writer and activist) made a similar observation about the reputation for homoeroticism among Asian immigrants in those cities.[74]

Interracial marriage was illegal in Utah, and in 1898 the Salt Lake County clerk refused to allow a Chinese man to marry an African-American woman.[75] Chinese men accounted for six (11.5 percent) of the same-sex domestic partnerships of Salt Lake City in 1900. This was more than ten times the proportion of Chinese males to the city's total male population.

Along with the age discrepancy previously mentioned, unmarried men constituted four of the six Chinese domestic partnerships in Salt

Lake City. Another couple was twenty-nine-year-old bachelor Lee Let and fifty-five-year-old John M. Yee, who was married, but far from his wife. The last couple was made up of two married Chinese men, ages thirty-nine and twenty-eight, whose wives were in China.[76] Lyman's history noted that "most of the Chinese remained absentee husbands while in America."[77]

People of color were involved in 26.9 percent of the total number of Salt Lake City's same-sex domestic partnerships, regardless of age. However, African Americans, Asians, and Native Americans account- ed for barely 1 percent of the city's population in 1900.[78] The only people of color in these domestic partnerships of Salt Lake City were African Americans of both sexes and Asian men born in China.

European immigrants were about half as prominent in Salt Lake City's domestic partnerships of 1900 as they were among the same-sex couples of 1880. Twenty domestic partnerships (38.5 percent) includ- ed at least one European immigrant in 1900. This compares to the European immigrants' 23.4 percent share of Salt Lake City's popula- tion in 1900.[79] Twelve couples (23.1 percent of the total partnership couples) were made up of only European immigrants, which was al- most exactly their share of the city's population in 1900. Seven cou- ples (13.5 percent) were composed of a European immigrant and an American born outside Utah. Only one couple (1.9 percent) comprised a European immigrant and a Utah native. Even by adding the Asian immigrants among the 1900 domestic partnerships, the total immigrant representation in these couples was 50.0 percent. That was one-third less than the immigrant representation in Salt Lake City's few same- sex couples of 1880.

African Americans were involved in eight (15.4 percent) of Salt Lake City's domestic partnerships in 1900. By comparison, African Americans accounted for less than 1 percent of the city's total population.[80] Although twentieth-century readers might expect that during this period in Utah the African Americans involved in relationships with whites would be subordinate, three of these same-sex domestic partnerships do not fulfill this expectation. Steven Williams was a seventy-year-old African-Amer- ican head of household whose occupation was "whitewasher." His white partner was thirty-seven-year-old James Orbison, a bachelor and team- ster from Pennsylvania.[81] Raffella Lee was a twenty-five-year-old Afri- can-American head of household whose partner was twenty-three-year- old Austrian immigrant Jennette Henry.[82]

Salt Lake City's last same-sex couple of mixed race involved a thirty-four-year-old Scotsman and his "partner" who were lodging with a thirty-seven-year-old African-American widower from Alabama. The head and three other black male partners in this household were also paired by age. All the African-American men in this household were either unmarried, widowed, or divorced, and all were from the American South.[83]

Not surprisingly, none of the "white" partners in these same-sex interracial domestic partnerships were Utah-born. Beginning with Brigham Young, nineteenth-century Utah Mormons had inflexible views about the inferiority of anyone with black African ancestry.[84] In fact, there were no Utah-born African Americans in any of these same-sex domestic partnerships in Salt Lake City in 1900.

The most prominent Mormon among the same-sex domestic partnerships in Salt Lake City's 1900 census was twenty-eight-year-old Estelle Neff. Lillian Estelle Neff, born in 1871, had been the business manager and assistant editor for the *Young Woman's Journal* since 1897. Her domestic partner in 1900 was twenty-one-year-old Marian Adams, a student at the University of Utah. They had started living together in 1899, after Adams's sister stopped living with Neff. Adams and Neff remained together until 1902. That was the year Neff became a member of the general board of the LDS Church's Young Women's Mutual Improvement Association. Neff married at age thirty-three.[85] Another prominent Mormon, Evan Stephens, did not have a same-sex partner in the June 1900 census because he was traveling in Europe with his longtime male companion.[86]

The longest domestic partnership of this Salt Lake City group was between two young Jewish men. It was also a domestic partnership that most clearly involved same-sex persons who chose to be together for reasons other than business or sharing the expenses of an apartment. William Graupe was related to the Watters family of Salt Lake City and his brother moved in with that family in 1892. At that time, twenty-five-year-old William Graupe helped organize the city's first lodge of B'nai Brith. His nephew William G. Watters was then fifteen, and William Graupe soon moved in with the boy's family. The two Williams lived with the young man's parents for the next fifteen years, and it would be easy for neighbors to regard the older man as simply a boarder. The Jewish parents may also have thought the two young men were merely friendly relations.[87]

However, William Graupe and William Watters regarded themselves as having a closer relationship. While living at the Watters family home during the 1900 census, the two men defined themselves as a separate family, with thirty-three-year-old Graupe as the "head" and twenty-three-year-old Watters as his domestic "partner." They remained together until 1907, when the younger partner (then age thirty) moved to New York City. His uncle later married, fathered no children, and his obituary listed his nephew William Watters as a survivor.[88]

In addition to the fifty-two domestic partnerships of the same gender in 1900 Salt Lake City, there were also twenty-one same-sex couples who did not describe themselves as partners. Instead, the stated relationship of the other person to the household head was that of servant, boarder, lodger, or roomer.[89] I use the term *nonpartnership couple* to describe this kind of household, which involved forty-two persons in Salt Lake City in 1900.

The gender ratio alone indicates that the personal dynamics in these nonpartnership couples differed from the dynamics of the same-sex domestic partnerships. About an equal number of men and woman composed these same-gender couples who did not define themselves as domestic partners. Eleven couples were male and ten couples were female. That near equality of numbers was close to the gender ratio of Salt Lake City's population, in contrast to the more than five to one advantage of male domestic partnerships in 1900.

These nonpartnership couples showed age disparity that was both similar and different from the partnership couples. First, 38.1 percent of these nonpartnership couples showed an age difference greater than ten years, as compared to 46.2 percent of domestic partnerships. In view of the small numbers involved, this difference is negligible. Possibly more significant is that the gender ratio was reversed in these intergenerational couples. Seventy-five percent of these intergenerational nonpartnership couples were female. That was consistent with the pattern of older women obtaining income by renting out a room of their home and reflected the findings of the Salt Lake City 1880 census. For example, 40 percent of heads of these female nonpartnership couples in 1900 were widows.

By contrast, men accounted for 95.8 percent of the intergenerational couples who defined themselves as domestic partners in 1900. Those lopsided gender ratios add support to the assumption that a different dynamic (i.e., sexual intimacy) may have existed in the domestic partnerships of the same gender. However, even if there were thousands of these same-sex couples in Salt Lake City, the kind of numerical consistency described here would not prove a sexual dimension in their co-residence.

Nevertheless, there are indications that sexual intimacy may have been involved in one of these nonpartnership couples. The census listed twenty-eight-year-old Mormon immigrant Thomas Hughes as the "servant" to the twenty-four-year-old head of household "Will" Howe. However, "servant" Hughes was actually William C. Howe's employer. Both the census and city directories listed Hughes as a railroad "depot master," whereas Howe was only a "ticket-agent." "Servant" did not describe the actual social relationship between the men, but that description may have been this couple's way of letting the census describe their personal relations. More significant, Hughes concealed the two men's co-residence for four years by publicly listing his residence as the depot of the Denver and Rio Grande Railroad instead of his home with the younger Howe.[90] Such secrecy would be unnecessary in same-sex co-residence that was nonerotic.

There were also different ethnic dimensions to the same-sex couples who did not define themselves as partners. First, only one such couple (4.8 percent) was African American, and there were no mixed-race persons in the nonpartnership couples. Second, Asians were one-third of Salt Lake City's same-sex couples in which one person was a servant or renter in 1900. One such couple involved Japanese women, and Chinese men made up the other six couples.

Thus, the Chinese men accounted for 28.6 percent of nonpartnership couples in Salt Lake City in 1900. This was more than double the percentage of Chinese people in domestic partnerships. However, not a single nonpartnership couple of Chinese men had an age disparity over nine years, and most of these paired men were within three years of age. In other words, a Chinese man in Salt Lake City would accept a male renter who was about his same age, but Chinese men in Salt Lake City preferred a significant age disparity for their same-sex domestic partners. Again, this indicates that Chinese immigrants also regarded the "partner" option of the 1900 census as way of describing a special domestic relationship for same-gender members of a household. Only through extensive research in the census returns can it be known if this age and residence pattern was typical of the "womanless" Chinese throughout the American West.

Even when combining both kinds of same-sex couples, the total number of both Asian and European immigrants in 1900 was far less than the corresponding number in 1880. In Salt Lake City in 1900, there was a total of seventy-three partnership and nonpartnership same-sex couples. Asian and European immigrants accounted for a total of thirty-five (47.9 percent) of these. That was about one-third less than the number of immigrants in Salt Lake City's 1880 same-sex couples. Still, that 47.9 percent in 1900 was double the immigrant portion of Salt Lake City's population. The seventy-three same-sex couples (both partner and nonpartner) amounted to little more than .5 percent of Salt Lake City's 11,797 families in the 1900 census.[91]

Two decades later, some nineteenth-century Mormon lesbians established joint households in Salt Lake City. One lesbian was Caroline ("Carline") Monson (b. 1859), a great-aunt of Thomas S. Monson, a counselor in the LDS First Presidency in 1996.[92] The 1920 census listed sixty-one-year-old Caroline as the live-in "servant" of recently widowed Sarah Ann Briggs Chapman (b. 1851). One indication that the two older women were actually domestic partners is that Caroline did not notify the city directories of her co-residence in the Chapman home until after Sarah Chapman's death in 1923.[93] A second piece of evidence was Monson's subsequent relationships in the Chapman household.

In 1924, twenty-three-year-old Mildred Berryman moved into the home as the lesbian lover of Sarah's daughter, thirty-nine-year-old Edith Mary Chapman, who was an instructor at the University of Utah. Although she concealed her own age and identity, Berryman's study described her relationship with female case number 9, whose occupation, age, and parental descriptions matched that of Edith Chapman: "At 39 years of age [female case 9] fell desperately in love with a young woman of 20 [actually twenty-three-year-old Mildred]."[94]

In 1925, the city directory finally showed Caroline Monson as a resident of the Chapman home. She listed herself as "Mrs." Monson, even though that was her maiden name. That same year, twenty-five-year-old Dorothy Graham joined Caroline, Edith, and Mildred in this Ninth South Street house. Their friends nicknamed it "Casa Lesbiana."[95]

The four women were residents of Casa Lesbiana until 1929, when Mildred Berryman left the house due to the break-up of her relationship with Edith Chapman. "This attachment lasted but a short time and the younger woman pulled away," Berryman wrote years later. Mildred was "unhappy in the relationship and possessiveness of Z. who wanted a lover and child in one individual and made the object of her attentions wretched with heavy attention, jealous rages and amorous demands."[96]

The three other women remained at Casa Lesbiana until the latter part of 1931, when Edith Chapman moved to Oakland, California, and Dorothy Graham moved to Seattle. In the 1932 city directory, Caroline Monson was alone at the Ninth South house, but no member of the Chapman family resided there. This indicated that Monson had rights to the house greater than simply being the "servant" of its previous owner, Sarah Briggs Chapman. For several years Caroline Monson rented out the house to someone different every year before her death in 1941.[97] Shortly after that, Mildred Berryman, the last resident of Casa Lesbiana still in Utah, began a thirty-year lesbian relationship that only death ended.[98]

Two LDS women born in nineteenth-century Utah also became involved in same-sex living arrangements outside Utah with famous American lesbians. Their non-Mormon contemporaries and non-LDS biographers were fully aware of the Utah-Mormon heritage of these two women who attained recognition as performing artists in New York City.

Ada Dwyer Russell (b. 1863) became an actress in the Salt Lake Theatre, on Broadway, and on the London stage. Her Mormon biographer observed that Russell and her husband had separated "for unknown reasons" shortly after the birth of her only child. She never remarried.[99] In March 1912 she met the poet Amy Lowell, who was eleven years younger. Russell and Lowell felt an immediate attraction ("Between us lept a gold and scarlet flame"), and the two women lived together that summer.[100] Lowell was a well-known lesbian who once said that "no verses can equal the poetry of a young girl's naked body."[101]

By apparent coincidence, the same summer that Utah's well-known actress began living with a famous lesbian, the first allusion to lesbianism appeared in an LDS Church magazine. In September 1912, the *Young Woman's Journal* paid tribute to "Sappho of Lesbos," who was widely known for her love poetry addressed to young women in ancient times. This LDS publication opened with an illustration depicting Sappho entertaining five women. A separate article by the Mormon artist and poet Alfred Lambourne referred to her "extreme emotions" and alluded to this poet of ancient Lesbos as the source for the term *lesbianism:* "The name of Sappho has been tarnished through many a century . . . [but] the clouds of calumny and reproach have been cleared away."[102] An example of such "calumny" was the 1884 article about the "Perverted Sexual Instinct" of two women who had legally married in Illinois, which a medical journal classified as an example of "Lesbian loves (from Lesbos the Greek city)."[103]

As far as Lowell and Russell were concerned, Russell's Mormon biographer noted that "the criticism leveled at the [two] women's personal lives did not seem important" to them. Russell soon ended all affiliation with Mormonism.[104] A year after she began living with Lowell, LDS leaders learned that Russell's father, James Dwyer, had been advocating sodomy to young men in Utah.[105]

In June 1914, Ada finally accepted the poet's repeated requests to give up acting and live permanently together. Typical of her well-known brashness, Amy Lowell nicknamed her "Peter," then-current slang for penis. Lowell's biographer compared these two domestic partners to Gertrude Stein and Alice B. Toklas and wrote that Lowell "loved, and was loved by, someone [Ada] who was not only worthy of love but who was also a continuous inspiration and an object of adoration."[106]

Mormon-raised Ada Dwyer Russell was the subject of Amy Lowell's same-sex love poetry from 1912 until Lowell's death in 1925. Of these poems, Lowell's biographer writes: "Probably no other woman poet of her time described the female nude body as often or as sensuously as Amy Lowell."[107] More cautious in his assertions about their relationship than Amy's biographer, the Lowell family historian concluded: "Whether Amy and Ada had sex together remains an open-ended and perhaps irrelevant question. Ada, responding to the inevitable gossip, insisted always that they were only friends." She continued those denials until her own death in 1952, twenty-seven years after her beloved companion died.[108]

More flamboyant than Ada Dwyer Russell, Natacha Rambova was born as Winifred Kimball Shaughnessy in 1897 in Salt Lake City. She was a granddaughter of Heber P. Kimball (a member of the theocratic Council of Fifty) and a great-granddaughter of Heber C. Kimball (one of Mormonism's first ordained apostles and Brigham Young's first counselor). Although her Irish father had her christened at birth in the Cathedral of the Madeleine, her LDS mother divorced him when Winifred was three. After that, the young girl lived with her actively Mormon aunt, who probably arranged for an LDS baptism when her niece turned eight.[109]

Shaughnessy moved to Europe later that year and lived each summer in a household of lesbians. Her host was the interior decorator Elsie de Wolfe, sister of Shaughnessy's stepfather. Also sharing the home were the literary agent Elisabeth Marbury and Anne Morgan, a daughter of the financier J. P. Morgan. Shaughnessy's biographer wrote that these women "were grooming her for membership in their lesbian clique." Just before the guns of August 1914, seventeen-year-old "Wink" left for the United States to begin the dancing career for which the three women had prepared her.[110]

Utah-born Winifred Kimball Shaughnessy changed her name to Natacha Rambova while she was the lover of Theodore Kosloff and principal dancer in his Imperial Russian Ballet in America. Soon her life was a complex set of same-sex and opposite-sex relationships. Rambova became the close friend (and alleged lesbian lover) of Alla Nazimova, star of silent films *Salome* and *Camille* for which Rambova designed her costumes and stage sets. Nazimova's longtime male lover said Nazimova "preferred women most of the time," yet he and her costar Rudolph Valentino were also "occasional roommates." Valentino's first wife was one of Nazimova's lesbian lovers. Then Rambova replayed her Mormon heritage by marrying Valentino as a bigamous wife in 1922. While a Los Angeles court sorted out the legalities, Rambova returned to Utah. For a few years the Valentinos were an "ideal" Hollywood couple, and Natacha told friends, "I detest lesbians!" Some regard that as proof of Rambova's heterosexuality, while others view such statements as her self-hating homophobia and psychological denial.[111]

NOTES

1. See Jonathan Katz, *Gay American History: Lesbians and Gay Men in the U.S.A.* (New York: Thomas Y. Crowell, 1976), 231, for the civil marriage of Anna Morris (alias Frank Blunt) to Gertrude Field in Wisconsin; 232–38 for the marriages of Mary Anderson (alias Murray Hall) in New York City; 248 for the thirty-five-year marriage of female "George" Green and wife in Virginia; 248–49 for the civil marriage of "William" C. Howard and Miss Dwyer in Canandaigua, New York; 250–51 for the civil marriages and one civil divorce of "Nicholas" de Raylan in Arizona; and 254 for the civil marriage of Cora Anderson (alias Ralph Kerwinieo) and Dorothy Klenowski; Jonathan

Ned Katz, *Gay/Lesbian Almanac: A New Documentary* (New York: Harper and Row, 1983), 194–95, for the civil marriage of Lucy Ann Lobell and her wife in Illinois; and 323–24 for Katherine Vosbaugh and her wife in Colorado. Some of these cases appeared in Havelock Ellis, *Sexual Inversion*, vol. 2 of *Studies in the Psychology of Sex* (Philadelphia: F. A. Davis, 1915), 246–49, and in Vern L. Bullough, *The Subordinate Sex: A History of Attitudes toward Women* (Urbana: University of Illinois Press, 1973), 318–22, and in Vern L. Bullough and Bonnie Bullough, *Cross Dressing, Sex, and Gender* (Philadelphia: University of Pennsylvania Press, 1993), 164–65; Neil Miller, *Out of the Past: Gay and Lesbian History from 1869 to the Present* (New York: Vintage/Random House, 1995), 71–74; see also the San Francisco Lesbian and Gay History Project, "'She Even Chewed Tobacco': A Pictorial Narrative of Passing Women in America," in Martin Bauml Duberman, Martha Vicinus, and George Chauncey Jr., eds., *Hidden from History: Reclaiming the Gay and Lesbian Past* (New York: New American Library, 1989), 183–94.

2. "W. V. Woman Was Not Your Ordinary Joe," *Salt Lake Tribune*, 27 Aug. 1994, D-2, concerning criminal charges filed by a legal minor against twenty-year-old Tasha "Joe" Montalvo: "The girl told police that sometime last month she had sex with 'Joe' and believed she had become pregnant. The incident happened in a West Valley home during a party. A 16–year-old boy who was in the same room making out with his girlfriend told police he watched 'Joe' and the 12–year-old girl have sex. . . . Later, the 16–year-old boy was looking through 'Joe's' gym bag and found a plastic phallus, according to charging documents." See also "Marital Masquerade: Man Posing as Wife Is Jailed for Fraud," *Salt Lake Tribune*, 14 July 1995, C-7, about Felix Urioste, who "had his testicles surgically removed and was taking female hormones that gave him slight breasts." This deceived his LDS husband, Bruce Jensen, who "never saw him nude" as his wife, "Leasa Jensen."

In 1993 there was a more tragic conclusion to a young woman's three-year masquerade as the boyfriend of several young women in Nebraska. Since nothing comparable occurred in nineteenth-century America (even in small towns where cross-dressing women lived with their legal wives), this case demonstrates the homophobic differences between the two centuries. From age nineteen, Brandon Teena was the sexually fulfilling "boyfriend" to six girlfriends in succession during the early 1990s. Although Brandon regarded herself as male, she feared transsexual surgery and wore a strap-on penis by which she had sexual intercourse with her female lovers. However, Brandon avoided lesbians and told her girlfriends, "I'm not gay!" and "We're not in a gay relationship." After public disclosure of Brandon's true gender in a small town, she was raped, beaten, and later murdered in December 1993 by the former boyfriend of Brandon's last girlfriend. The small-town police captain referred to the murder victim as "an it." In addition, the director of Nebraska's Gay and Lesbian Resource Center declined to publicize or champion this murder case "because the victim adamantly didn't consider herself a lesbian" or bisexual. See Donna Minkowitz, "Love Hurts: Brandon Teena Was a Woman Who Lived and Loved as a Man; She was Killed for Carrying It Off," *Village Voice*, 19 Apr. 1994, 24–30; see also chap. 1, note 18 for sources on emotional transsexualism.

3. On same-sex couples and long-term relationships, see Joseph Harry, "Marriages among Gay Males," in Scott G. McNall, ed., *The Sociological Perspective: Introductory Readings*, 2d ed. (Boston: Little, Brown, 1977), 330–40; Donna M. Tanner, *The Lesbian Couple* (Lexington, Mass.: D. C. Heath, 1978); Randall W. Jones and John E. Bates, "Satisfaction in Male Homosexual Couples," *Journal of Homosexuality* 3 (Spring 1978): 217–24; Neil R. Tuller, "Couples: The Hidden Segment of the Gay World," *Journal of Homosexuality* 3 (Summer 1978): 331–43; Alan P. Bell and Martin S. Weinberg, *Homosexualities: A Study of Diversity among Men and Women* (New York: Simon and Schuster, 1978), 81–105; Joseph Harry and Robert Lovely, "Gay Marriages and Communities of Sexual Orientation," *Alternative Lifestyles* 2 (May 1979): 177–200; Michael Denneny, *Lovers: The Story of Two Men* (New York: Avon, 1979); Sharon M. Raphael and Mina K. Robinson, "The Older Lesbian: Love Relationships and Friendship Patterns," *Alternative Lifestyles* 3 (May 1980): 207–29; Mary Mendola, *The Mendola Report: A New Look at Gay Couples* (New York: Crown, 1980); Letitia Anne Peplau and Susan D. Cochran, "Value Orientations in the Intimate Relationships of Gay Men," *Journal of Homosexuality* 6 (Spring 1981): 1–19; Charles Silverstein, *Man to Man—Gay Couples in America* (New York: William Morrow, 1981); Joseph Harry, "Decision-Making and Age Differences among Gay Male Couples," *Journal of Homosexuality* 8 (Winter 1982): 9–21; Letitia Anne Peplau, Christine Padesky, and Mykol Hamilton, "Satisfaction in Lesbian Relationships," *Journal of Homosexuality* 8 (Winter 1982): 23–35; Jeanne Marecek, Stephen E. Finn, and Mona Cardell, "Gender Roles in the Relationships of Lesbians and Gay Men," *Journal of Homosexuality* 8 (Winter 1982): 45–49; Victoria A. Vetere, "The Role of Friendship in the Development and Maintenance of Lesbian Love Relationships," *Journal of Homosexuality* 8 (Winter 1982): 51–65; Paul C. Larsen, "Gay Male Relationships," in William Paul, James D. Weinrich, John C. Gonsiorek, and Mary E. Hotvedt, eds., *Homosexuality: Social, Psychological, and Biological Issues* (Beverly Hills: Sage, 1982), 219–32; Letitia Anne Peplau and Hortensia Amaro, "Understanding Lesbian Relationships," in Paul, Weinrich, Gonsiorek, and Hotvedt, eds., *Homosexuality*, 233–47; Philip Blumstein and Pepper Schwartz, *American Couples: Money, Work, Sex* (New York: William Morrow, 1983), esp. 448–545; Joseph Harry, "Gay Male and Lesbian Relationships," in Eleanor D. Macklin and Roger H. Rubin, eds., *Contemporary Families and Alternative Lifestyles* (Beverly Hills:

Sage, 1983), 216–34; Mayta A. Caldwell and Letitia Anne Peplau, "The Balance of Power in Lesbian Relationships," *Sex Roles: A Journal of Research* 10 (Apr. 1984): 587–99; David P. McWhirter and Andrew M. Mattison, *The Male Couple: How Relationships Develop* (Englewood Cliffs, N.J.: Prentice-Hall, 1984); Joseph Harry, *Gay Couples* (New York: Praeger, 1984); David Blasband and Letitia Anne Peplau, "Sexual Exclusivity versus Openness in Gay Male Couples," *Archives of Sexual Behavior* 14 (Oct. 1985): 395–412; Sally M. Duffy and Caryl E. Rusbult, "Satisfaction and Commitment in Homosexual and Heterosexual Relationships," *Journal of Homosexuality* 12 (Winter 1985–86): 1–23; Jean M. Lynch and Mary Ellen Reilly, "Role Relationships: Lesbian Perspectives," *Journal of Homosexuality* 12 (Winter 1985–86): 53–69; Lawrence A. Kurdek and J. Patrick Schmitt, "Relationship Quality of Gay Men in Closed or Open Relationships," *Journal of Homosexuality* 12 (Winter 1985–86): 85–99; Elizabeth H. Kassoff, "The Diverse Nature of Nonmonogamy for Lesbians: A Phenomenological Investigation" (Ph.D. diss., University of California at Berkeley, 1985), 110–50; Lawrence A. Kurdek, "Relationship Quality of Gay and Lesbian Cohabiting Couples," *Journal of Homosexuality* 15, nos. 3–4 (1988): 93–118; Monika Kehoe, "Lesbian Relationships and Homosexuality," *Journal of Homosexuality* 16, nos. 3–4 (1988): 43–62; John P. DeCecco, ed., *Gay Relationships* (New York: Haworth Press, 1988); Carol S. Becker, *Unbroken Ties: Lesbian Ex-Lovers* (Boston: Alyson, 1988); Cherry Kittredge and James Mitulski, "Committed Couples in the Gay Community," *Christian Century* 107 (28 Feb. 1990): 218–21; Natalie S. Eldridge and Lucia A. Gilbert, "Correlates of Relationship Satisfaction in Lesbian Couples," *Psychology of Women Quarterly* 14 (Mar. 1990): 43–62; Mary Ellen Reilly and Jean M. Lynch, "Power-Sharing in Lesbian Partnerships," *Journal of Homosexuality* 19, no. 3 (1990): 1–30; Raymond M. Berger, "Men Together: Understanding the Gay Couple," *Journal of Homosexuality* 19, no. 3 (1990): 31–49; Richard Steinman, "Social Exchanges between Older and Younger Gay Male Partners," *Journal of Homosexuality* 20, nos. 3–4 (1990): 179–206; Susan E. Johnson, *Staying Power: Long Term Lesbian Couples* (Tallahassee: Naiad Press, 1990); Becky Butler, ed., *Ceremonies of the Heart: Celebrating Lesbian Unions* (Seattle: Seal Press, 1990); Suzanne Sherman, ed., *Lesbian and Gay Marriage: Private Commitments, Public Ceremonies* (Philadelphia: Temple University Press, 1992); Elizabeth DePoy and Sandy Noble, "The Structure of Lesbian Relationships in Response to Oppression," *Affilia: Journal of Women and Social Work* 7 (Winter 1992): 49–64; Ina Russell, ed., *Jeb and Dash: A Diary of Gay Life, 1918–1945* (Boston: Faber and Faber, 1993); A. A. Deenen, L. Gijs, and A. X. van Naerssen, "Intimacy and Sexuality in Gay Male Couples," *Archives of Sexual Behavior* 23 (Aug. 1994): 421–31; Rod Jackson-Paris and Bob Jackson-Paris, *Straight from the Heart: A Love Story* (New York: Warner Books, 1994); Mary Anne Fitzpatrick, Fred E. Jandt,

Fred L. Myrick, and Timothy Edgar, "Gay and Lesbian Couple Relationships," in R. Jeffrey Ringer, ed., *Queer Words, Queer Images: Communication and the Construction of Homosexuality* (New York: New York University Press, 1994), 265–77; John Preston and Michael Lowenthal, eds., *Friends and Lovers: Gay Men Write about the Families They Create* (New York: Dutton, 1995); see also chaps. 7 and 8 about same-sex relationships of nineteenth-century Utahns and Mormons.

4. E. Anthony Rotundo, "Romantic Friendship: Male Intimacy and Middle-Class Youth in the United States, 1800–1900," *Journal of Social History* 23 (Fall 1989): 10–11; Karen V. Hansen, "'Our Eyes Behold Each Other': Masculinity and Intimate Friendship in Antebellum New England," in Peter M. Nardi, ed., *Men's Friendship: Research on Men and Masculinities* (Newbury Park, Calif.: Sage, 1992), 35, 44; E. Anthony Rotundo, *American Manhood: Transformations in Masculinity from the Revolution to the Modern Era* (New York: Basic Books, 1993), 84–85; Donald Yacovone, "Abolitionists and the 'Language of Fraternal Love,'" in Mark C. Carnes and Clyde Griffen, eds., *Meanings for Manhood: Constructions of Masculinity in Victorian America* (Chicago: University of Chicago Press, 1990), 94.

5. My text discussion reconciles some contradictions between original sources and Josiah Rogerson's reminiscence, "Strong Men, Brave Women, and Sturdy Children Crossed the Wilderness Afoot," *Salt Lake Tribune,* 14 Jan. 1914, n.p. Rogerson's memory confused several elements of this incident nearly fifty-eight years earlier. First, he identified the wrong English branch for the LDS membership of one man and called him a bachelor instead of a widower. Second, he gave the wrong name to the other man. Third, he misidentified the one who died. Rogerson described them as "Two bachelors named Luke Carter, from the Clitheroe branch, Yorkshire, England, and William Edwards from Manchester, England, each about 50 to 55 years of age."

Luke Carter (b. 18 Oct. 1810) was a member of the LDS branch at Blackburn, near Preston, England, not of the branch at Clitheroe, also near Preston. Luke Carter married Hannah Pye, who died in 1846. He traveled aboard ship to America in 1856 with his fifteen-year-old daughter, Nancy. Contrary to Rogerson's memory, it was Carter who "died on the plains," not Edwards. See passenger list for the steamship *Horizon,* 25 May 1856, page 173, LDS Emigration Registers of the British Mission (1849–1925), Family History Library of the Church of Jesus Christ of Latter-day Saints, Salt Lake City, Utah (hereafter LDS Family History Library); entries for Luke Carter (b. 18 Oct. 1810) and Hannah Pye in Ancestral File (hereafter LDS Ancestral File) and International Genealogical Index, both in LDS Family History Library; entries for Luke Carter (b. 15 [*sic*] Oct. 1810), Hannah Pie (Pye) Carter (d. 10 Mar. 1846), and Nancy Carter (b. 5 Apr. 1840) in LDS Membership Card Index (Minnie Margetts File), and in Blackburn Branch (Preston Conference) Record, page

25, both in LDS Family History Library; LeRoy R. Hafen and Ann W. Hafen, *Handcarts to Zion: The Story of a Unique Western Migration, 1856–1860* (Glendale, Calif.: Arthur H. Clark, 1960), 296.

William Edwards was actually a twenty-eight year old (not fifty to fifty-five) who was traveling with sixteen-year-old Harriet Edwards. According to the ship register and branch records in England, they were both single and apparently brother and sister. Contrary to Rogerson, Edwards was not from Manchester. Due to these discrepancies, I believe Rogerson mistakenly remembered the name "Edwards" when he was describing someone from this journey fifty-eight years earlier. See entries for William Edwards (b. 15 Mar. 1828) and for Harriet Edwards (b. 2 June 1839) in LDS Membership Card Index (Minnie Margetts File); in Brighton Branch Record (1849–57), page 17; in passenger list for the steamship *Horizon*, 25 May 1856, page 156; and in LDS Emigration Registers of the British Mission; Hafen and Hafen, *Handcarts to Zion*, 297 (which mistakenly identified them as husband and wife).

Rogerson's reminiscence apparently referred to the similarly surnamed Charles Edmonds, who was a fifty-six-year-old bachelor from Manchester. This corresponds with the age and English residence that Rogerson remembered for Carter's male companion in the Martin emigrant company. See entry for Charles Edmonds (b. 17 Oct. 1799) in LDS Membership Card Index (Minnie Margetts File); passenger list for the steamship *Horizon*, 25 May 1856, page 187; LDS Emigration Registers of the British Mission; Hafen and Hafen, *Handcarts to Zion*, 297. In contrast to this note and my narrative discussion, Rocky O'Donovan, in "'The Abominable and Detestable Crime against Nature': A Brief History of Homosexuality and Mormonism, 1840–1980" in Brent Corcoran, ed., *Multiply and Replenish: Mormon Essays on Sex and Family* (Salt Lake City: Signature Books, 1994), 140–41, accepts Rogerson's memory that the second man was William Edwards.

6. General W. T. Hardee, "Biographical Sketch of Major-General P.R. Cleburne," written on 1 May 1867 and published in John Francis Maguire, *The Irish in America* (London: Longmans, Green, 1868; reprint, New York: Arno Press/New York Times, 1969), 651. On the basis of Hardee's statement alone, Randy Shilts, in *Conduct Unbecoming: Lesbians and Gays in the U.S. Military, Vietnam to the Persian Gulf* (New York: St. Martin's Press, 1993), 14, concluded that General Cleburne was "a celebrated gay general." I regard that as an overstatement of the slender evidence in this case of a physically close, but not necessarily erotic, friendship of two men.

7. Katz, *Gay American History*, 24; Shilts, *Conduct Unbecoming*, 8–9.

8. John McAuley Palmer, *General von Steuben* (New Haven: Yale University Press, 1937), 92, 93, 100, 208. Pierre Etienne Duponceau and William North both married, fathered children, and maintained lifelong friendships with von Steuben, who adopted North as a son. However, if their earlier live-

in relationships with von Steuben were nonerotic, this would have been a departure from his reported behavior only months before he met these two young men.

9. Katz, *Gay American History,* 509–10.

10. A. B. Holder, "The Bote: Description of a Peculiar Sexual Perversion Found among North American Indians," *New York Medical Journal* 50 (7 Dec. 1889): 623. See the Frederick Jones case of 1864 in chap. 9.

11. B. R. Burg, *An American Seafarer in the Age of Sail: The Erotic Diaries of Philip C. Van Buskirk, 1851–1870* (New Haven: Yale University Press, 1994), xi, 81.

12. Louis Dwight broadside, 25 Apr. 1826, reprinted in Katz, *Gay American History,* 27.

13. Randolph Winslow, "An Epidemic of Gonorrhea Contracted from Rectal Coition," *Medical News* 49 (14 Aug 1886): 180–82, described and partially quoted in Katz, *Gay/Lesbian Almanac,* 202; "KNEASS TELLS TORTURE STORIES: Industrial School Boys Whipped until Unconscious—Others Wore Oregon Boots," *Salt Lake Herald,* 24 June 1909, 3; "Close of Inquiry at Ogden School," *Salt Lake Herald,* 26 June 1909, 3; "Investigation at State Industrial School Ends," *Ogden Morning Examiner,* 30 June 1909, 8; see also chap. 10.

14. Martin Bauml Duberman, "'Writhing Bedfellows': 1826, Two Young Men from Antebellum South Carolina's Ruling Elite Share 'Extravagant Delight,'" *Journal of Homosexuality* 6 (Fall 1980–Winter 1981): 85–101, reprinted in Salvatore J. Licata and Robert P. Petersen, eds., *The Gay Past: A Collection of Historical Essays* (New York: Harrington Park Press, 1985), and reprinted as "'Writhing Bedfellows' in South Carolina: Historical Interpretation and the Politics of Evidence," in Duberman, Vicinus, and Chauncey, eds., *Hidden from History.*

15. Phyllis Grosskurth, ed., *The Memoirs of John Addington Symonds* (London: Hutchinson, 1984), 94; see also Grosskurth, *The Woeful Victorian: A Biography of John Addington Symonds* (New York: Holt, Rinehart, and Winston, 1964), 32–34. For less explicit references to homoeroticism at other English schools for males in the early 1800s, see Vern L. Bullough and Bonnie Bullough, "Homosexuality in Nineteenth Century English Public Schools," in Joseph Harry and Man Singh Das, eds., *Homosexuality in International Perspective* (New Delhi: Vikas, 1980), 123–31; A. D. Harvey, *Sex in Georgian England: Attitudes and Prejudices from the 1720s to the 1820s* (New York: St. Martin's Press, 1994), 117–18.

16. Benjamin Disraeli, *Coningsby; or, The New Generation,* 2 vols. (New York: M. Walter Dunne, 1904), 1:60–61, reprinted in *The Works of Benjamin Disraeli, Earl of Beaconsfield,* 20 vols. (New York: AMS Press 1976), 12: 60–61; also quoted from an 1881 edition in Eve Kosofsky Sedgwick, *Between Men: English Literature and Male Homosocial Desire* (New York: Columbia Uni-

versity Press, 1985), 176. For Disraeli's own boy's school experience, his long-term friendship with William Meredith, and the reactions in 1844 to this publication, see Stanley Weintraub, *Disraeli: A Biography* (New York: Truman Talley Books/Dutton, 1993), 33, 45–49, 211–29.

17. Andrew Jenson, *Latter-day Saint Biographical Encyclopedia*, 4 vols. (Salt Lake City: Deseret News Press and Andrew Jenson History, 1901–36), 1:126; Folder 21, Box 4, Albert Carrington Papers, Manuscripts Division, J. Willard Marriott Library, University of Utah, Salt Lake City, Utah.

18. Harvey, *Sex in Georgian England*, 117–18.

19. Elizabeth Haven to Elizabeth H. Bullard, 24 Feb. 1839, in Ora H. Barlow, *The Israel Barlow Story and Mormon Mores* (Salt Lake City: Publishers Press, 1968), 144, 231n1, also 140–41, 179. The quoted phrase was reprinted with the full letter in Kenneth W. Godfrey, Audrey M. Godfrey, and Jill Mulvay Derr, eds., *Women's Voices: An Untold History of the Latter-day Saints, 1830–1900* (Salt Lake City: Deseret Book, 1982), 109; see also my discussion of this friendship in chap. 3.

20. M. Carey Thomas diary, 12 June 1877, in Marjorie Housepain Dobkin, ed., *The Making of a Feminist: Early Journals and Letters of M. Carey Thomas* (Kent, Ohio: Kent State University Press, 1979), 118.

21. Alice Blackwell to Kitty Blackwell, 12 Mar. 1882, quoted in Katz, *Gay/Lesbian Almanac*, 178, and in Miller, *Out of the Past*, 60–61; see also the discussion in chap. 4.

22. Leila J. Rupp, "'Imagine My Surprise': Women's Relationships in Historical Perspective," *Frontiers: A Journal of Women's Studies* 5 (Fall 1980): 63; Anna Mary Wells, in *Miss Marks and Miss Woolley* (Boston: Houghton Mifflin, 1978), ix, explained that as their biographer she discovered their "ardent love letters [which were] expressed in terms that both shocked and embarrassed me."

23. Jorge Salessi, "The Argentine Dissemination of Homosexuality, 1890–1914," *Journal of the History of Sexuality* 4 (Jan. 1994): 342.

24. Josiah Flynt [Josiah Flint Willard], "Homosexuality among Tramps," in Havelock Ellis and John Addington Symonds, *Sexual Inversion* (London: Wilson and Macmillan, 1897; reprint, New York: Arno Press/New York Times, 1975), 253–54. This coauthored book was an early version of what later appeared as a volume by the same title in multiple editions of *Studies in the Psychology of Sex* with Ellis as sole editor and author. After his death, Symonds's heirs withdrew permission to use his name. Before publishing about hobos and tramps under the name of Flynt, Josiah Flint Willard studied at the University of Berlin. See *Dictionary of American Biography*, 22 vols. (New York: Charles Scribner's Sons, 1928–58), 21:706–7.

25. Edward O. Laumann, John H. Gagnon, Robert T. Michael, and Stuart Michaels, in *The Social Organization of Sexuality: Sexual Practices in the*

United States (Chicago: University of Chicago Press, 1994), interviewed 1,749 women and 1,410 men and asserted that "over 4 percent of the women and 9 percent of the men reported they engaged in at least one of these sexual practices with a person of their own gender since puberty" (294–95). However, they discuss the evidence (contrary to common assumptions in recent decades) that less than 10 percent actually *prefer* having sex with persons of their same gender.

26. Flynt, "Homosexuality among Tramps," 253–54.

27. "BRUTAL TRAMPS: They Make a Beastly Assault on Little Boys," *Provo Daily Enquirer*, 1 May 1896, 1; "BEASTLY TRAMPS: Crime Committed by Them against Nature," *Provo Daily Enquirer*, 16 Sept. 1896, 1; see also chap. 10.

28. Gilbert Herdt, in "Cross-Cultural Forms of Homosexuality and the Concept 'Gay,'" *Psychiatric Annals* 18 (Jan. 1988): 38, uses the term *age-structured* to describe "institutionalized same-sex acts between males of unequal ages" that existed in ancient Greece, China, Japan, and Islamic countries, and in modern Africa, lowland South America, and the Pacific. See also Herdt, "Developmental Discontinuities and Sexual Orientations across Cultures," in David P. McWhirter, Stephanie A. Sanders, and June Machover Reinisch, eds., *Homosexuality/Heterosexuality: Concepts of Sexual Orientation* (New York: Oxford University Press, 1990), 221–22. *Age-structured* is particularly useful when the culture virtually requires such relationships, but is less useful as a term where a man-boy or woman-girl relationship is a private choice of the younger partner, sometimes entered into despite cultural prejudices against age differences in all intimate relationships. For that reason I consistently use *intergenerational* to describe the voluntary relationships of same-sex couples with significant age differences in America.

29. Flynt, "Homosexuality among Tramps," 254–56. His exact phrase was "sexually perverted tramps."

30. Josiah Flynt [Josiah Flint Willard], *Tramping with Tramps: Studies and Sketches of Vagabond Life* (New York: Century, 1893; reprint, College Park, Md.: McGrath, 1969), 57–58 (on relations of the jocker with his prushun), 104 (on western American hobos), and 106 (on Salt Lake City); Eric Partridge, *A Dictionary of the Underworld, British and American* (London: Routledge and Kegan Paul, 1961), 281.

31. Nels Anderson, "The Juvenile and the Tramp," *Journal of the American Institute of Criminal Law and Criminology* 14 (1923–24): 290, 293, 301, 307. His article examined social, emotional, and sexual dimensions of the companionships between tramp boys and their men. Anderson's better known *The Hobo: The Sociology of the Homeless Man* (Chicago: University of Chicago Press, 1923) discussed homosexual relations only on pages 147–49, but the book's introduction referred to his longer analysis in the legal journal.

32. Frank Charles Laubach, "Why There Are Vagrants: Based upon an

Examination of One Hundred Men" (Ph.D. diss., Columbia University, 1916), 13–14, cited in George Chauncey, *Gay New York: Gender, Urban Culture, and the Making of the Gay Male World, 1890–1940* (New York: Basic Books/HarperCollins, 1994), 397n56.

33. See "The Lost Pardner," and "Bachin'" in [Charles] Badger Clark, *Sun and Saddle Leather: A Collection of Poems by Badger Clark* (Boston: R. G. Badger, 1915; Tucson: Westerners International, 1983), 11–18 (for his biography), 76–77 (for his deceased partner), and 66 (for cowboy bachelorhood).

34. Clifford P. Westermeier, "Cowboy Sexuality: A Historical No-No?" *Red River Valley Historical Review* 2 (Spring 1975): 101, reprinted in Charles W. Harris and Buck Rainey, eds., *The Cowboy: Six-Shooters, Songs, and Sex* (Norman: University of Oklahoma Press, 1976), 101.

35. Manuel Boyfrank Papers, International Gay and Lesbian Archives, West Hollywood, Calif., as quoted in Walter L. Williams, *The Spirit and the Flesh: Sexual Diversity in American Indian Culture* (Boston: Beacon Press, 1986), 159–60, and page 158 quoted a portion of the previously cited writings by Badger Clark; U.S. Department of the Interior, Census Office, *Twelfth Census of the United States, Taken in the Year 1900, Population,* 2 vols. (Washington: United States Census Office, 1901–2), 2:541; J'Wayne "Mac" McArthur (b. 31 Oct. 1935), "Pardners," in Carol A. Edison, ed., *Cowboy Poetry from Utah: An Anthology* (Salt Lake City: Utah Folklife Center, 1985), 100.

36. Williams, *Spirit and the Flesh,* 160.

37. For example, see Richard Griswold del Castillo, *The Los Angeles Barrio, 1860–1890: A Social History* (Berkeley: University of California Press, 1979), 67–68; Susan L. Johnson, "Sharing Bed and Board: Cohabitation and Cultural Difference in Central Arizona Mining Towns, 1863–1873," in Susan Armitage and Elizabeth Jameson, eds., *The Women's West* (Norman: University of Oklahoma Press, 1987), 77–91.

38. Wilde's wife and two sons changed their names after his conviction. See Richard Ellman, *Oscar Wilde* (New York: Vintage Books, 1988), 266, 492, 499; Anne Clark Amor, *Mrs Oscar Wilde: A Woman of Some Importance* (London: Sedgwick and Jackson, 1983); see also chap. 9, note 132.

39. See especially the Thomas Taylor case of 1886 and the Abraham Hunsaker case of 1893 discussed in chap. 9.

40. Williams, *Spirit and the Flesh,* 162.

41. Sheila Jeffreys, "Does It Matter If They Did It?" in Lesbian History Group, *Not a Passing Phase: Reclaiming Lesbians in History, 1840–1985* (London: Woman's Press, 1993), 23.

42. Blanche Wiesen Cook, "The Historical Denial of Lesbianism," *Radical History Review* 20 (Spring–Summer 1979): 60–65; see also Leila J. Rupp, "'Imagine My Surprise': Women's Relationships in Historical Perspective," *Frontiers: A Journal of Women's Studies* 5 (Fall 1980): 61–62, 67.

43. John Donald Wrathall, "American Manhood and the Y.M.C.A., 1868–1920" (Ph.D. diss., University of Minnesota, 1994), 58 (quoting Richard C. Morse, *My Life with Young Men*), 65 (quoting from Arthur Gordon, "Friendship," *Association Men*, July 1920), and 66 (for an example of sharing a single bed). Although the census takers identified the YMCA's roomers as simply "lodger," it is possible that the manuscript census listed them in order of the rooms they occupied. For example, in the 1910 census of Salt Lake City's YMCA, there were thirty-two lodgers listed after the YMCA's minister-manager. The assumption that they were listed by their occupancy of two-man rooms is supported by the similar birthplaces of several pairs: two native Utahns (ages thirty-eight and sixteen) apparently rooming together, also a native Utahn and Idahoan (ages twenty-nine and eighteen), two Illinoisans (ages twenty-five and twenty-one), two Englishmen (ages twenty-three and twenty), and two more Utahns (ages eighteen and twenty-one). See U.S. 1910 Census of Salt Lake City, Salt Lake County, Utah, enumeration district 144, sheet 13–A, microfilm, LDS Family History Library. There was no YMCA in the 1900 Utah census.

44. Hyrum Smith 1835 account book, pages 6–11, Joseph Smith Sr. Family Collection, Department of Special Collections and Archives, Harold B. Library, Brigham Young University, Provo, Utah. Some boarded at Hyrum's house only three days; others stayed for several weeks.

45. John Modell and Tamara Hareven, "Urbanization and the Malleable Household: An Examination of Boarding and Lodging in American Families," *Journal of Marriage and the Family* 35 (Aug. 1973): 467–79; Paul Erling Groth, "Forbidden Housing: The Evolution and Exclusion of Hotels, Boarding Houses, Rooming Houses, and Lodging Houses in American Cities, 1880–1930" (Ph.D. diss., University of California at Berkeley, 1983); Mark Peel, "On the Margins: Lodgers and Boarders in Boston, 1860–1900," *Journal of American History* 72 (Mar. 1986): 813–34.

46. U.S. 1880 Census of Salt Lake City, Salt Lake County, Utah, microfilm, LDS Family History Library, compared with U.S. Department of the Interior, Census Office, *Statistics of the Population of the United States at the Tenth Census (June 1, 1880)* ... (Washington, D.C.: GPO, 1883), 671. I dropped all same-sex couples whose relationship was defined as mother-daughter, father-son, brothers, sisters, same-gender cousins, aunt-niece, uncle-nephew, grandfather-grandson, or grandmother-granddaughter.

47. U.S. 1880 Census of Salt Lake City, enumeration district 49, sheet 159–A; Frank Esshom, *Pioneers and Prominent Men of Utah, Comprising Photographs-Genealogies-Biographies* (Salt Lake City: Utah Pioneers Book, 1913), 1142.

48. U.S. 1880 Census of Salt Lake City, enumeration district 42, sheet 41–A; see entry for Robert Moffatt (b. 8 Oct. 1864) in LDS Membership Card Index (Minnie Margetts File), with no entry for him in LDS Obituary Index

(1839–1970), LDS Family History Library. The LDS Ancestral File has an entry for a Robert Moffatt who married in Salt Lake City in 1892, but it is not clear that this is the same one, since the assumed birth year of this man is simply the year of the wife's birth.

49. *Tenth Census.* Salt Lake City's total population was 20,768 and its total immigrant population was 7,673 (see 456). I obtained the total European immigrant population by subtracting the city's total Asian immigrant population of 82 (see 425).

50. In 1880, Salt Lake City's non-Mormon population was midway in its growth from 17 percent in 1874 to 25 percent in 1887. See Paul A. Wright, "The Growth and Distribution of the Mormon and Non-Mormon Populations in Salt Lake City" (Ph.D. diss., University of Chicago, 1970), 14, 16.

51. "Instructions to Enumerators," from *Two Hundred Years of U.S. Census Taking: Population and Housing Questions, 1790–1990* (Washington, D.C.: Bureau of the Census, U.S. Department of Commerce, 1989), 41, 50. The term *partner* was also not a census substitute for a single head of household who had a single boarder or roomer. For example in the U.S. 1900 Census of Salt Lake City, Salt Lake County, Utah, enumeration district 5, sheet 2–A, microfilm, LDS Family History Library, "M. Nasholds," a female head of household, had a single female "boarder" as the only other member of the household. Also in Salt Lake City enumeration district 5, sheet 2–B, "C. Fraaks," a female head of household had a single female "roomer" as the only other member of the household.

52. *Twelfth Census,* 2:607. This is a conservative estimate, based on the published total of 3,793 "other" families in the two boroughs of Manhattan and the Bronx. The census defined "other" to include "miscellaneous groups of persons lodging together but having no family relationship in common," but "other" did not include persons in a hotel, boarding house, resident school, or institution. The published census report did not separately tabulate the number of same-sex and opposite-sex "partners" in the total of "other" households. However, the total of "other" families in Salt Lake City was 69, of which I found 52 (75.4 percent) were same-sex "partner" couples. That proportion would yield 2,860 of the "other" families in the two New York City boroughs, which I conservatively round down to 2,000 same-sex domestic partnerships. In the Bronx and Manhattan, "other" families were .87 percent of the 433,953 total families in the two boroughs in the 1900 census, whereas in Salt Lake City, "other" families were .58 percent of its 11,797 total families in 1900.

53. Lyrics of a 1914 song, quoted in Steven Watson, *Strange Bedfellows: The First American Avant-Garde* (New York: Abbeville Press, 1991), 114; see also Chauncey, *Gay New York,* 67–68, 190, 228–29, 232, 243, 293.

54. "Bill Drafted to Bolster Ban on Homosexual Marriages," *Salt Lake Tribune,* 9 Feb. 1995, B-1.

55. For example of a "friend," see U.S. 1900 Census of Salt Lake City, enumeration district 34, sheet 1–B; for example of "companion," see enumeration district 47, sheet 8–B. These were the only examples in Salt Lake City.

56. "The Two Found Guilty," *Ogden Standard,* 20 July 1900, 5; "Billings Found Guilty," *Salt Lake Tribune,* 20 Sept. 1900, 3; see also chap. 10 for a discussion of sentencing patterns for sodomy during this period.

57. Lillian Faderman, "Nineteenth-Century Boston Marriages as a Possible Lesson for Today," in Esther D. Rothblum and Kathleen A. Brehony, eds., *Boston Marriages: Romantic but Asexual Relationships among Contemporary Lesbians* (Amherst: University of Massachusetts Press, 1993), 31.

58. I recognize the redundancy of my qualification in this regard, but prepublication reviewers indicated that such emphatic restatements were necessary in my discussion of the census data on same-sex persons in co-residence.

59. For example, I excluded Isabella Stevenson and Emily Cottrell, her domestic "partner" in the 1900 census, who had lived together since the late 1890s. The city directory showed that they were business partners in the firm of "Stevenson & Cottrell." I also excluded partnership households because the persons listed as "partner" by the census were probably business partners to the head of household. For example, I excluded one household of three Chinese men, all of whom worked in a laundry. I also excluded a similar household of five Chinese men. For the same reason of probable business partnership rather than domestic partnership, I excluded a household of three "white" women, where the head was a saleswoman and the two partners were seamstresses. Also, to be conservative, regardless of occupation, I defined as business-related any household where two persons were listed as "partner" to the head of household. However, I did not exclude households comprised of only two persons merely because the "partner" had the same or related occupation as the head of household.

I also need to explain some variations in the partnership couples included within these calculations. There were several three-person households in which two same-sex persons were listed as partners, and another person (sometimes of the opposite sex) was a servant in the house or a relative of one of the partners. I defined that kind of household as comprising one partnership couple of unrelated persons. In one case, I counted six men in one household as three separate partnership couples, where five were listed as partners of the "head." The six men seemed to be listed in age partnerships: two in their forties, two in their thirties, and one fifty-year-old man combined with one sixty-two-year-old man. Only two of the six shared the same occupation, and I therefore included this as a household of multiple domestic partnerships, rather than excluding this household as comprised of business partnerships. Even though a domestic partnership existed for nonbusiness reasons, this does not mean the reasons were sexual.

60. U.S. 1900 Census of Salt Lake City, enumeration district 37, sheets 2–A

and 2–B; entries for James Gibson in LDS European Emigration Index (1849–1925) and in LDS Ancestral File; entry for James Storey in LDS Membership Card Index (Minnie Margetts File); *Salt Lake City Directory, 1901* (Salt Lake City: R. L. Polk, 1901), 316, 713; *Salt Lake City Directory, 1903* (Salt Lake City: R. L. Polk, 1903), 377, 877; *Salt Lake City Directory, 1908* (Salt Lake City: R. L. Polk, 1908), 449, 1047. The city directory claimed that Storey was "age 54" at his death in May 1908, but the 1900 census listed his birth as September 1861, which made him forty-six years old at death.

61. *Tenth Census*, 664; *Twelfth Census*, 1:644. The 1880 census report listed the sex ratio for Utah's counties only, not for its cities.

62. *Little hustlers* and *kept boys* have been slang phrases in vernacular English for male prostitutes since at least the twelfth century, when Richard of Devizes first used these words as equivalent definitions in his discussion of London's underworld. His *Chronicle of the Times of Richard the First* appeared in six modern English editions from 1848 to 1892, including American printings. See Wayne R. Dynes, ed., *Encyclopedia of Homosexuality*, 2 vols. (New York: Garland, 1990), 1:741; *National Union Catalog of Pre-1956 Imprints*, 754 vols. (London: Mansell, 1968–81), 492:599. Although originally meaning a male prostitute who moved in with one of his clients, *kept boy* has evolved to include the less negative meaning of any sexual relationship in which an older man pays most of a younger man's expenses. For example, in Mildred Berryman's study of Salt Lake City's homosexuals, a twenty-three-year-old gay man was "self-supporting," but had "expressed a desire to find someone who would keep him and allow him to pursue a feminine role." See male case 4 in Mildred J. Berryman, "The Psychological Phenomena of the Homosexual," 68, roughtyped on the back of stationery of the American Red Cross, Salt Lake City, Utah, with the last page of the study dated 13 Nov. 1938, in the June Mazer Lesbian Collection, West Hollywood, Calif.

63. U.S. 1900 Census of Salt Lake City, enumeration district 52, sheet 3–B.

64. Wrathall, "American Manhood and the Y.M.C.A.," 65–66, quoting from Arthur Gordon, "Friendship," *Association Men* (July 1920): 498.

65. However, in three of these domestic partnerships the head of household was younger than his partner.

66. U.S. 1900 Census of Salt Lake City, enumeration district 54, sheet 2–B.

67. *Twelfth Census*, 1:644, 2:143. Although not specifically itemized, the total European immigrant population can be verified in two ways: First by subtracting the Asian immigrants from Salt Lake City's total immigrant population, and second by the total "Foreign White" population (2:143). The Chinese population was 214 (predominantly male), the city's male population was 25,849, and its total population was 53,531.

68. Francis L. K. Hsu, *The Challenge of the American Dream: The Chinese in the United States* (Belmont, Calif.: Wadsworth, 1971), 73.

69. Stanford M. Lyman, *The Asian in North America* (Santa Barbara, Calif.:

ABC-Clio, 1977), 178, 71. He added that this enormous gender imbalance was "one of the most profound and least discussed factors affecting Chinese communities and acculturation." Chinese males continued to greatly outnumber Chinese females in the United States until the midtwentieth century. Before the 1890 census accidentally burned, the U.S. government published a statistical summary of its findings.

70. Hsu, *Challenge of the American Dream,* 72–73. However, Hsu dismissed even the possibility of an erotic dimension in these long-term living relationships between Chinese men in America: "But the well-defined boundaries of sexuality gave the Chinese their capacity for forming deeper and therefore more lasting friendships with members of the same sex than white Americans. They [Chinese men] do not have to fear homosexuality." Such a categorical denial of male-male sexual intimacy among the Chinese immigrants on the basis of cultural norms is not supportable in view of the male-male marriages once common in China. See Bret Hinsch, *Passions of the Cut Sleeve: The Male Homosexual Tradition in China* (Berkeley: University of California Press, 1990), 127–33.

71. Lucie Cheng Hirata, "Free, Indentured, Enslaved: Chinese Prostitutes in Nineteenth-Century America," *Signs: Journal of Women in Culture and Society* 5 (Autumn 1979): 3–29. For example, Don C. Conley, in "The Pioneer Chinese of Utah," in Helen Z. Papanikolas, ed., *The Peoples of Utah* (Salt Lake City: Utah State Historical Society, 1976), 258, observed that in the town of Terrace, Utah, there were fifty-four Chinese men and only one Chinese woman (a prostitute). These sources identify prostitution as the only sexual outlet for Chinese male immigrants in the United States. Failing to acknowledge even the possibility of homoerotic experiences among these "womanless men" is another example of the previously discussed "historical denial" of homosexuality.

72. R. H. Van Gulik, *Sexual Life in Ancient China* (Leiden: E. J. Brill, 1961), 49n. He consistently used the term *homosexuality* as the equivalent of homoeroticism, and his note contrasted this high incidence of homoeroticism among immigrant Chinese men with the evidence for a low incidence of homoeroticism among Chinese men in ancient times.

73. Chauncey, *Gay New York,* 392n12.

74. Katz, *Gay American History,* 51.

75. "Woman of Mixed Blood Desirous of Marrying a Chinaman—License Refused," *Deseret Evening News,* 16 Sept. 1898, 2.

76. U.S. 1900 Census of Salt Lake City, enumeration district 24, sheet 10–A, enumeration district 32, sheet 1–B, enumeration district 54, sheet 3–B, enumeration district 55, sheet 1–B, enumeration district 55, sheet 4–A.

77. Lyman, *The Asian in North America,* 69.

78. *Twelfth Census,* 1:682, 2:143. Peoples of color totaled 514 of Salt Lake City's population of 53,531.

79. Ibid., 1:644, 2:143. See note 67 for the tabulation of European immigrants.

80. Ibid., 1:644, 682.

81. U.S. 1900 Census of Salt Lake City, enumeration district 52, sheet 5–A.

82. Ibid., enumeration district 54, sheet 2–A. The census failed to list an occupation for either woman, but they were prostitutes. See Salt Lake City Police Arrest Register 1896–99 Book (15 Apr., 15 June 1897, 23 July, 22 Aug., 22 Sept., 22 Oct. 1898, 21 Jan., 21 Feb., 23 Feb., 21 Mar., 20 Apr., 20 May, 20 June, 19 July, 19 Aug., 19 Sept., 18 Oct., 18 Nov., 19 Dec. 1899), Series 4611, Utah State Archives, Salt Lake City, Utah, for arrests and fines of Jennette Henry and Raffella Lee, with various ages given, for prostitution.

83. U.S. 1900 Census of Salt Lake City, enumeration district 52, sheet 5–B.

84. However, that was not true of Mormonism's founding prophet, who taught that social opportunities were all that separated the poorest black person from the most eminent white person. Joseph Smith also authorized the priesthood ordination of an African American, Elijah Abel, who was the only free black at LDS Church headquarters during Smith's presidency. On the other hand, three slaves were the only African Americans who were among the pioneers Brigham Young led to Utah in July 1847. See Kate B. Carter, comp., *The Story of the Negro Pioneer* (Salt Lake City: Daughters of Utah Pioneers, 1965); Dennis L. Lythgoe, "Negro Slavery in Utah," *Utah Historical Quarterly* 39 (Winter 1971): 40–54; Margaret Judy Maag, "Discrimination against the Negro in Utah and Institutional Efforts to Eliminate It" (M.S. thesis, University of Utah, 1971); Klaus J. Hansen, "The Millennium, the West, and Race in the Antebellum Mind," *Western Historical Quarterly* 3 (Oct. 1972): 373–90; Lester E. Bush Jr., "Mormonism's Negro Doctrine: An Historical Overview," *Dialogue: A Journal of Mormon Thought* 8 (Spring 1973): 11–68; Ronald K. Esplin, "Brigham Young and Denial of the Priesthood to Blacks: An Alternative View," *Brigham Young University Studies* 19 (Spring 1979): 394–402; Ronald Gerald Coleman, "A History of Blacks in Utah, 1825–1910" (Ph.D. diss., University of Utah, 1980); Newell G. Bringhurst, *Saints, Slaves, and Blacks: The Changing Place of Black People within Mormonism* (Westport, Conn.: Greenwood Press, 1981); Armand L. Mauss, "The Fading of the Pharaoh's Curse: The Decline and Fall of the Priesthood Ban against Blacks in the Mormon Church," *Dialogue: A Journal of Mormon Thought* 14 (Fall 1981): 10–45. Several of the above articles appeared in Lester E. Bush Jr. and Armand Mauss, eds., *Neither White nor Black: Mormon Scholars Confront the Race Issue in a Universal Church* (Midvale, Utah: Signature Books, 1984). For Brigham Young's announcement of a policy to exclude those of black African descent from the LDS priesthood, even "if no other Prophet ever spake it before," see Brigham Young's speech to the Joint Session of the Utah Legislature in Scott G. Kenney, ed., *Wilford Woodruff's Journal, 1833–1898 Type-*

script, 9 vols., plus index (Midvale, Utah: Signature Books, 1983–91), 4:97–99 (5 Feb. 1852).

85. *Salt Lake City Directory, 1899* (Salt Lake City: R. L. Polk, 1899), 78, 604; *Salt Lake City Directory, 1900* (Salt Lake City: R. L. Polk, 1900), 88, 536; *Salt Lake City Directory, 1901,* 87, 548; *Salt Lake City Directory, 1902* (Salt Lake City: R. L. Polk, 1902), 86, 606; U.S. 1900 Census of Salt Lake City, enumeration district 22, sheet 4–A; Jenson, *Latter-day Saint Biographical Encyclopedia,* 4:225.

86. "Prof. Stephens' European Trip: Will Begin Next Month and Last for about One Year," *Deseret Evening News,* 2 Jan. 1900, 1; see also chap. 8 for a discussion of the relationship between this director of the Mormon Tabernacle Choir and Willard Christopherson, a member of the choir.

87. Leon L. Watters, *The Pioneer Jews of Utah* (New York: American Jewish Historical Society, 1952), 97, 142–43, 143n6, 153–54; *Utah Gazetteer, 1892–93* (Salt Lake City: Stenhouse, 1892), 329–30, 736; *Salt Lake City Directory, 1893* (Salt Lake City: R. L. Polk, 1893), 349, 834 (which erroneously gave Watters's first name as "Willard" for the first and only time).

88. *Salt Lake City Directory, 1900,* 313, 743; U.S. 1900 Census of Salt Lake City, enumeration district 51, sheet 1–B; *Salt Lake City Directory, 1907* (Salt Lake City: R. L. Polk, 1907), 457, 1099; "Ex-Salt Laker Dies in L.A.: Illness Fatal to William Graupe," *Salt Lake Tribune,* 13 June 1938, 9. Thus far, I have no evidence that William G. Watters ever married. The *New York Times,* 26 May 1956, 17, listed the death of a William Watters of New Jersey, age eighty-one, who had six children; he and his family were in the U.S. 1920 Census of Essex County, New Jersey, enumeration district 7, sheet 10, microfilm, LDS Family History Library. However, the census showed that this married William Watters was Irish-born, and his obituary said he had lived in New Jersey for "sixty years" (since 1896), whereas Utah-born William G. Watters did not move to New York City until 1907.

89. With one exception, these numbers omit all same-sex couples that I could determine were relatives. The Graupe-Watters partners were uncle-nephew, but I kept them in the calculations for the reasons indicated in the text.

90. U.S. 1900 Census of Salt Lake City, enumeration district 16, sheet 5–A; *Salt Lake City Directory, 1900,* 372, 376; *Salt Lake City Directory, 1904* (Salt Lake City: R. L. Polk, 1904), 435, 439; entry for Thomas Hughes in LDS European Emigration Index (1849–1925).

91. *Twelfth Census,* 2:143, 607.

92. Information given in an interview by a neighbor of Caroline Monson in the notes of an interview with J—— M—— (name withheld by her request), and also the unsigned, undated, handwritten talk [by Rocky O'Donovan], "Gay History of Utah," 10–13, with a dedication to his then-lover Robert on its first page, photocopies in "History—Utah" Folder, Ver-

tical Files, Library, Stonewall Center, Salt Lake City, Utah. Caroline Monson (b. 7 Apr. 1859 in Sweden; endowed 22 June 1887; d. 26 Dec. 1941), her brother Nels N. Monson (b. 1867), his son George Spencer Monson (b. 1901), his son Thomas S. Monson (b. 1927), in LDS Ancestral File; also *Deseret News 1995–1996 Church Almanac: The Church of Jesus Christ of Latter-day Saints* (Salt Lake City: Deseret News, 1994), 15. Caroline Monson may have been female case 22 in Berryman's study, "Psychological Phenomena," 60–61, which began about 1918–22 and listed her age as fifty-six. Although Caroline Monson turned fifty-nine in Apr. 1918, she had a pattern of understating her age. For example, in the June 1920 census, she stated her age as sixty, when she was actually sixty-one. It would have been consistent for her to give her age as fifty-six in early 1918, rather than fifty-eight. It is often unclear at what point in Berryman's two-decade study she estimated the ages that appeared in the 1938 draft, and she indicated that she had not seen some of these people for years. For the starting date of Berryman's study, see chap. 7, notes 3 and 5.

93. Entries for Chapman and Monson in U.S. 1920 Census of Salt Lake City, Salt Lake County, Utah, enumeration district 79, sheet 8, microfilm, LDS Family History Library; entry for Sarah Ann Briggs (b. 1851; LDS endowment in 1866; widowed twice; d. 1923) in LDS Ancestral File; *Salt Lake City Directory, 1920* (Salt Lake City: R. L. Polk, 1920), 196, 627; *Salt Lake City Directory, 1925* (Salt Lake City: R. L. Polk, 1925), 812. The LDS Ancestral File mistakenly lists a third husband, "Dr. Chatwin," for Sarah Ann Briggs. This was a misspelling of the name of her dentist-husband, Arvis Scott Chapman. See *Salt Lake City Directory, 1918* (Salt Lake City: R. L. Polk, 1918), 202.

94. *Salt Lake City Directory, 1924* (Salt Lake City: R. L. Polk, 1924), 119, 202; [O'Donovan], "Gay History of Utah," 10–13; description of female case 9 and her parents in Berryman, "Psychological Phenomena," 49; entries for Mary E[dith]. Chapman (b. Nov 1885) and her father Arvis Scott Chapman (b. Aug 1839) in U.S. 1900 Census of Salt Lake City, enumeration district 2, sheet 1; entries for George Handley (b. 1826 in England; d. 1879) and his plural wife Sarah Ann Briggs in LDS Ancestral File; obituary for Sarah's second husband, "Dr. Arvis Scott Chapman Is Suddenly Summoned," *Deseret Evening News*, 13 May 1919, sect. 2, p. 7; "Called by Death: Sarah Ann Chapman," *Deseret News*, 16 Apr. 1923, 8; Ralph V. Chamberlin, *The University of Utah: A History of Its First Hundred Years, 1850 to 1950* (Salt Lake City: University of Utah Press, 1960), 572; also Vern L. Bullough to D. Michael Quinn, 22 Aug. 1995, 2, refers to Berryman "living at the boarding house with the English professor."

95. Entry for "Dorothey" Graham (b. 6 Oct. 1899) in LDS Church census for 1920, LDS Family History Library; *Salt Lake City Directory, 1925*, 283, 363, 538, 812; statements by a neighbor of Edith Chapman, Mildred Berry-

man, Caroline Monson, and Dorothy Graham while the four were living to-gether, as contained in notes of interview with J—— M—— (name withheld by her request), and also [O'Donovan], "Gay History of Utah," 10–13. I give Graham's age as twenty-five because her listing in the 1925 directory was before her October birthday.

If Caroline Monson was female case 22 in the Berryman study (see note 92), her use of "Mrs." with her maiden name would be consistent with Berryman's description of female case 22 in "Psychological Phenomena," 60: "She liked her husband and they were on friendly terms. She treated him more as a pal than a husband." There is no marriage entry for Caroline Monson in the Salt Lake County Marriage Indexes (1887–1923), LDS Family History Library, but it is possible she entered into this nonsexual marriage in another county of Utah.

96. *Salt Lake City Directory, 1929* (Salt Lake City: R. L. Polk, 1929), 226, 314, 508, 803; Berryman, "Psychological Phenomena," 49, for female case 9.

97. *Salt Lake City Directory, 1932* (Salt Lake City: R. L. Polk, 1932), 220, 362, 592, 1172; *Salt Lake City Directory, 1933* (Salt Lake City: R. L. Polk, 1933), 998; *Salt Lake City Directory, 1934* (Salt Lake City: R. L. Polk, 1934), 1204; *Salt Lake City Directory, 1935* (Salt Lake City: R. L. Polk, 1935), 1218; *Salt Lake City Directory, 1936* (Salt Lake City: R. L. Polk, 1936), 1119; *Salt Lake City Directory, 1937* (Salt Lake City: R. L. Polk, 1937), 1183; *Salt Lake City Directory, 1938* (Salt Lake City: R. L. Polk, 1938), 1189; *Salt Lake City Directory, 1939* (Salt Lake City: R. L. Polk, 1939), 1232; "Carline Monson," *Deseret Evening News,* 27 Dec. 1941, 12; [O'Donovan], "Gay History of Utah," 10–13.

98. See chap. 2, note 18 for information about the relationship of Mildred Berryman and Ruth Uckerman.

99. Chris Rigby, "Ada Dwyer: Bright Lights and Lilacs," *Utah Historical Quarterly* 43 (Winter 1975): 44–45.

100. Rigby, "Ada Dwyer," 46; quotation from Thomas Cowan, *Gay Men and Women Who Enriched the World* (New Canaan, Conn.: Mulvey Books, 1988), 131. Lillian Faderman, in *Chloe Plus Olivia: An Anthology of Lesbian Literature from the Seventeenth Century to the Present* (New York: Viking, 1994), 460, explains why she concluded that Russell and Lowell met in 1909. However, in his authorized *Amy Lowell: A Chronicle* (Boston: Houghton Mifflin, 1935), S. Foster Damon noted (xix) that Russell "has read and commented on the entire manuscript of this book," which stated (182–83) that Lowell and Russell first met in March 1912.

101. Jean Gould, *Amy: The World of Amy Lowell and the Imagist Movement* (New York: Dodd, Mead, 1975), 282.

102. *Young Woman's Journal* 23 (Sept. 1912): 487 for illustration, and 498–99 for Alfred Lambourne's article, "Sappho of Lesbos and Marie Bashkirtseff."

For Sappho and her poetry, see John J. Winkler, *The Constraints of Desire: The Anthropology of Sex and Gender in Ancient Greece* (New York: Routledge, 1990), 162–87; Christine Downing, *Myths and Mysteries of Same-Sex Love* (New York: Continuum, 1991), 216–36, and John J. Winkler, "Double Consciousness in Sappho's Lyrics," in Henry Abelove, Michele Aina Barale, and David M. Halperin, eds., *The Lesbian and Gay Studies Reader* (New York: Routledge, 1993), 577–94. See Dynes, *Encyclopedia of Homosexuality*, 2: 1153–54, for the differences in cultural concepts about Sappho's same-sex relationships and about contemporary lesbianism. Lambourne was an unmarried LDS widower, but his own published love poems were clearly directed toward the opposite sex. See entry for Alfred Lambourne in LDS Ancestral File; "Lambourne, of Wide Fame as Artist, Is Dead," *Deseret News,* 7 June 1926, sect. 2, p. 1; Lambourne, *A Lover's Book of Sonnets* (Salt Lake City: by the author, 1917).

103. James G. Kiernan, "Insanity. Lecture XXVI—Sexual Perversion," *Detroit Lancet* 7 (May 1884): 481–84, and "Chicago Medical Society," *Chicago Medical Journal and Examiner* 48 (Mar. 1884): 264, quoted in Katz, *Gay/ Lesbian Almanac*, 195.

104. Rigby, "Ada Dwyer," 48, 50. Ada was buried as an Episcopalian.

105. Anthon H. Lund diary, 9 May 1913, microfilm, Archives, Historical Department of the Church of Jesus Christ of Latter-day Saints, Salt Lake City, Utah. The Lund diary microfilm is unrestricted to all researchers at LDS Archives by stipulation of its donor, and will be published in edited form by Signature Books, Salt Lake City. See also chap. 11 for a discussion of the James Dwyer case.

106. Gould, *Amy,* 123 (for "Peter" nickname), 194–95, quotation from 258; Rigby, "Ada Dwyer," 47, 49–50 (for "Pete"); Damon, *Amy Lowell,* 225–26. For *Peter* as slang for penis since the midnineteenth century, see John S. Farmer and W. E. Henley, *Slang and Its Analogues,* 7 vols. (London: Routledge and Kegan Paul, 1890–1904), 5:177, and Eric Partridge, *A Dictionary of Slang and Unconventional English: Colloquialisms and Catch-Phrases, Solecisms and Catachreses, Nicknames, and Vulgarisms,* 8th ed., ed. Paul Beale (London: Routledge and Kegan Paul, 1984), 872. For a biography that emphasizes the relationship between Stein and Toklas, see Diana Souhami, *Gertrude and Alice* (San Francisco: Pandora/Harper, 1991).

107. Gould, *Amy,* 181, with examples of Lowell's poetic descriptions of Ada Dwyer Russell and of poetry dedicated to her on 146–47, 258–59, 273–83, 356–57, in the "Two Speak Together" section of Amy Lowell, *Pictures of the Floating World* (Boston: Houghton Mifflin, 1919), 39–99, in the "Ada Russell" section of G. R. Ruihley, ed., *A Shard of Silence: Selected Poems of Amy Lowell* (New York: Twayne, 1957), 9–20, and in Faderman, *Chloe Plus Olivia,* 462–70.

108. C. David Heymann, *American Aristocracy: The Lives and Times of James Russell Lowell, Amy, and Robert Lowell* (New York: Dodd, Mead, 1980), 211; Rigby, "Ada Dwyer," 50.

109. Michael Morris, *Madam Valentino: The Many Lives of Natacha Rambova* (New York: Abbeville Press, 1991), 19, 23–32; D. Michael Quinn, "The Council of Fifty and Its Members, 1844 to 1945," *Brigham Young University Studies* 20 (Winter 1980): 193–94, for her grandfather and great-grandfather; entry for her aunt Teresa Kimball Werner in LDS Church census for 1914, LDS Family History Library.

110. Morris, *Madam Valentino*, 37–39; John William Leonard, ed., *Woman's Who's Who of America: A Biographical Dictionary of Contemporary Women of the United States and Canada, 1914–1915* (New York: American Commonwealth, 1914), 244, 539; *Who Was Who in America: A Companion Biographical Reference Work to Who's Who in America, Vol. 3, Sketches of Who's Who in America Biographies, as Last Published in Volumes 27 to 31 Inclusive (1951–1960)* (Chicago; A. N. Marquis, 1963), 616.

111. Morris, *Madam Valentino*, 47, 66–93, 112–40, 246–47, 263–64, quotation of Nazimova's male lover from 66, and quotation of Rambova from 246. After several years, she and Valentino divorced amid claims that their marriage was never sexually consummated. Her biographer disputed that allegation as well as the claim that Rambova was sexually intimate with any of her lesbian mentors and friends. However, Natacha Rambova has been identified as bisexual or lesbian in Kenneth Anger, *Hollywood Babylon* (San Francisco: Straight Arrow Books, 1975), 108–13; Vito Russo, *The Celluloid Closet: Homosexuality in the Movies* (New York: Harper and Row, 1981), 27; *The Alyson Almanac: A Treasury of Information for the Gay and Lesbian Community* (Boston: Alyson, 1989), 155; Dell Richards, *Lesbian Lists: A Look at Lesbian Culture, History, and Personalities* (Boston: Alyson, 1990), 176; Donald Spoto, *Blue Angel: The Life of Marlene Dietrich* (New York: Doubleday, 1992), 105, 105n; and Terry Castle, *The Apparitional Lesbian: Female Homosexuality and Modern Culture* (New York: Columbia University Press, 1993), 17–18. Rocky O'Donovan was the first Mormon to publicize Rambova's Utah-Mormon background in "Historian's Research Aimed at Learning about Living In Utah," *Salt Lake Tribune*, 5 May 1990, A-10, but the first published account was a kiss-and-tell lesbian autobiography by Mercedes de Acosta, *Here Lies the Heart* (New York: Reynal, 1960; reprint, New York: Arno Press, 1975), 144–45.

CHAPTER 7

The Earliest Community Study of Lesbians and Gay Men in America: Salt Lake City

MILDRED J. BERRYMAN'S study is the only source for the views and experiences of early Utahns and Mormons who regarded themselves as homosexual. She indicated that she knew one hundred homosexuals of whom there were "about an equal number of men and women."[1] However, without explanation, Berryman limited her study to twenty-four women and nine men. That was disproportionate of the gender ratio in Salt Lake City's homosexual population by her own statement, and was only one-third of the Utah homosexuals she knew. Many homosexual participants in her study were members of Salt Lake City's Bohemian Club, which was incorporated in 1891.[2]

Berryman was the first woman and the first lesbian to study an American community of women and men who were lesbian and gay in their self-concepts. In their published summary of the study, Vern Bullough and Bonnie Bullough described how Berryman began it: "She had started the project as an honor's thesis while in college, had been discouraged from pursuing it by her adviser, but nonetheless had continued to gather data." The school was Salt Lake City's Westminster College where Mildred Berryman attended from age fifteen in October 1916 to age twenty in May 1922.[3]

Although she did not give a precise date, Berryman described the circumstances that caused her to study homosexuality at such an early age. Westminster College had a dormitory for its female students, and in describing herself as female case 23 Berryman wrote that her "first discovery of [homosexual] tendency wakened in girl's school at age of about fourteen. Was shocked by the discovery and did everything to break from the attraction for other girls" (61). After an unhappy marriage at age sixteen (ca. 1917–18), Berryman "had first homosexual relationship at age of nineteen [ca. 1920–21]. This lasted about a year and a half, then through jealousy of the companion they became estranged," and Berryman married a man briefly.[4] Noting that the final version of her study "dates from 1938," the Bulloughs's article stated that Berryman "had been gathering data for some twenty years."[5]

These were urban homosexuals, but Salt Lake City's culture and social life reflected America's heartland, rather than the bohemian enclaves and migrant anonymity of New York City or San Francisco at the same time. That is undoubtedly the reason Berryman gave her study a misleading subtitle that implied she had conducted it in Seattle, rather than in Salt Lake City.[6] In fact, her work remained unpublished throughout her life, apparently due to her concern about possible identification of the lesbians and gay men she described.

Although Berryman began the first lesbian research project of its kind (the Bulloughs called it a study of "the Salt Lake lesbians"), there were precedents. The first female researcher of the sexual experiences of American women was Dr. Celia Mosher, who began her interviews of forty-five women in 1892, but did not emphasize same-sex experiences.[7] In 1895, Havelock Ellis published separate articles in U.S. medical journals on "Sexual Inversion" in women and in men. Ellis criticized previous studies that depended on "inverts" in asylums, prisons, and police records because such sampling caused earlier researchers "to overestimate the morbid or vicious elements in such cases."[8] Ellis was a friendly outsider to his gay and lesbian subjects, while Berryman was a lesbian studying lesbians and gay men of her acquaintance.

Because the Mosher and Berryman studies remained unpublished and unknown for many years, the first woman to achieve recognition in studies of sexuality was Katharine Bement Davis in 1929. Her book *Factors in the Sex Life of Twenty-Two Hundred Women* found that 26 percent of unmarried college graduates "admitted overt homosexual practices" with other women, and 31.7 percent of married college graduates had engaged in same-sex acts with other women.[9]

Berryman's study also used the words *homosexual* or *inter-sex* for both females and males, but my analysis follows the current practice of referring to female homosexuals as *lesbians* and male homosexuals as *gay men* or *gays*. The age range for her twenty-four anonymous lesbians (including herself) was from 19 to 56, with an average (mean) age of 30.9 years. The study's nine gay men were ages 20 to 39, with an average (mean) age of 26.9 years.[10] However, Berryman's twenty-year study did not indicate whether the stated ages were at the beginning of the study, at its end, or at the time she met each individual.

Berryman included many dimensions of self-definition and interpersonal dynamics regarding the same-sex orientation of the thirty-three Utahns. Sometimes Berryman quoted the people she interviewed, but more often she paraphrased their words. Routinely she gave evaluative descriptions of each individual—which revealed as much about her as about the persons in her survey. In fact, Berryman's tone and judgmental statements are sometimes jarring, and readers should not assume that I share the views I quote from her study.

Because their own words provide an extraordinary view of a previously unknown social world in early Utah, I will emphasize the personal narratives of these lesbians and gay men. A mere statistical summary would be an inadequate description of the data for these thirty-three persons.

For each topic of discussion here, I will present these various perspectives according to her numerical arrangement of the case studies. This preserves whatever significance Berryman intended for that ordering of her cases. Statements about a particular topic often appear for only a portion of her respondents. Nevertheless, in total, Berryman's study gives an unparalleled insight into the self-concepts of a sexual minority that was otherwise hidden from the late nineteenth-century and early twentieth-century history of America.

Like Mildred Berryman herself,[11] many (possibly all) the persons in her study were of Mormon background. Nevertheless, her only direct reference to a church was the comment that female case 2 was "reared in L.D.S. faith" (35). Berryman's other allusions to religion were in the unspoken context of Salt Lake City's Mormon society. The ancestors of female case 3 were "pioneers and strict adherents to their religion" (39). Female case 5 "has been more or less a source of worry to her father because she could not accept the chosen faith" for which the parents had immigrated to Utah from Europe (44). Regarding female case 8, her "father was [a] polygamist," her "fiance went on a mission," and her "family [is] well-known and prominent in church circles" (47, 48).

The father of female case 9 "took another wife in polygamy" (49). Female case 11 "comes from a splendid family, has two talented sisters, both married to important men" (50). Female case 21 "was an off-spring of a polygamist and was one of many children. All of her brothers and sisters were . . . socially prominent" (60). And finally male case 9 came "from fine old pioneer stock," a common phrase among Utah Mormons (71).

Although these lesbians and gay men came from "prominent" and "splendid" families at Mormon headquarters, Berryman's study gave no attention to any informant's church activity, attitudes about Mormonism, or toward religion in general. Her study even ignored the obvious issues involved with sexual orientation and sexual behaviors in regard to one's Mormon beliefs, church activity, and the expectations of LDS leaders. Berryman also gave no hint of the process by which her friends stopped participating in the LDS Church, if (in fact) they did become "inactive" as Mormons. Nevertheless, during her study's twenty-year duration, Mildred Berryman had two lesbian lovers in succession, and at least one was also Mormon.

The study made a specific reference to only one lesbian's religious beliefs, then implied religious cynicism on the part of another, and referred only indirectly to the religious conflict experienced by one gay man. She wrote that twenty-three-year-old female case 5 was "a cold and calculating thinker, almost an agnostic in regard to religion and principles of life" (44). Twenty-nine-year-old female case 12 was "radical in opinions and arrogant" (51). As a teacher, this lesbian had been criticized "for expressing personal opinions of politics and church in the class room. Thinks democracy a joke and thinks our civilization isn't much to shout about" (51). However, Berryman only implied that this lesbian's views of religion were equally cynical. Concerning twenty-six-year-old male case 7 Berryman wrote: "His personality shows definite effects of poor integration due to the conflict between his conventional social attitude and his sexual variance" (69). One can only assume that his "conventional social attitude" included religion. Aside from her statements about these three persons, Berryman ignored the religious beliefs, disbeliefs, activities, and religious conflicts (if there were any) of the thirty-three people in her study.

Apparently Berryman thought religious data would leave the impression that her findings were too focused in Mormon culture to have relevance to the national population of lesbians and gay men. Typical of many sociologists, Berryman implied national applicability of her findings by not identifying the location of the fieldwork. Likewise, sociologists in the 1920s identified their famous study as "Middletown, U.S.A.," rather than by its actual location in Muncie, Indiana.[12]

Due to the Mormon background of these lesbians and gay men, a larger perspective is necessary concerning their sexual experiences. Berryman's study showed that all of these Utah lesbians and gay men had engaged in at least one homoerotic encounter. In addition, nearly half of the gay men and nearly half of the lesbians had also had premarital sex with opposite-sex partners. Without a historical perspective, these data leave the impression that early Mormon lesbians and gays were sexual athletes by comparison to assumptions about the strict morality of early Mormon heterosexuals.

To the contrary, early Mormon heterosexuals were also sexually active before marriage. From the 1890s to the early 1900s, LDS apostles reported that premarital sex occurred prior to 58 percent to 80 percent of Mormon marriages in Utah.[13] For example, in Provo (home of Brigham Young University) from 1905 to 1915, as many as 14.8 percent of new brides were already pregnant, and bridal pregnancy is a very conservative measure of the total incidence of premarital sex.[14] In 1914, the Quorum of the Twelve Apostles also received mission president reports indicating that 15 percent of LDS young men were "guilty of immoral practices" during their full-time missions.[15] Therefore, despite the LDS Church's long tradition of emphasizing strict chastity for both males and females, premarital sexual intercourse seemed to be the majority's experience at least as early as the 1890s and probably throughout nineteenth-century Mormon culture.

Aside from the fact that all persons in her study had had at least one homoerotic experience, Berryman gave only one clue about the adherence of her friends to the LDS Church. For twenty-two of her cases, she referred to their use or avoidance of alcohol and tobacco. These were forbidden by the LDS Church's increased emphasis on the revelatory Word of Wisdom in the early decades of the twentieth century.[16] Twenty of these gay men and lesbians (90.9 percent) used either alcohol, tobacco, or both. The study described only one lesbian (age twenty-four) and one gay man (age thirty-nine) who refrained from both alcohol and tobacco.

Private sexual activities did not equal public rebellion against LDS expectations, but the use of alcohol and tobacco had become a litmus test in Mormon culture. Therefore, Berryman's study indicated that 90 percent of Salt Lake City's lesbians and gays in the 1920s and 1930s openly distanced themselves from the LDS Church's expectations of behavior. It is likely that about the same percentage had stopped attending LDS meetings, but neither LDS records nor Berryman's study can verify that assumption. Within a few years of completing her study, Mildred Berryman identified herself as a lifelong Episcopalian and "her hatred of the Mormons grew with every passing year."[17]

However, her study did not claim that these lesbians and gay men began smoking or drinking as acts of rebellion. For example, from age sixteen to age twenty-two, female case 6 "did some very heavy drinking, as a means of escape from family and her [homosexual] problem" ("44," should be p. 45). Female case 13 "started drinking . . . because of an unhappy attachment for a girl friend who did not return her affection" (53). And female case 17 began drinking after being injured in an automobile accident (56).

Two related questions that were of interest to Berryman were how early these persons realized they were sexually attracted to persons of their same gender and how soon they acted upon that sexual awareness. Twenty-year-old female case 3 reported: "At sixteen she manifested an active tendency toward homosexuality" (37–38). Twenty-three-year-old female case 5 said that "when she first discovered her preference for girls, she accepted it quite naturally, although she did not close the possibilities of a normal relationship out of her life" (44).

Twenty-three-year-old female case 6 had "preferred members of her own sex since early childhood . . . [and] always had a crush on some little girl playmate" (45). Thirty-five-year-old female case 10 "always had homosexual leanings" (49). Nineteen-year-old female case 16 had "always been homosexual" (55). Twenty-nine-year-old female case 17 also had "always been homosexual, [and] had first relation when she was fifteen" (55). Twenty-nine-year-old female case 20 "always preferred girls . . . [and] had first homosexual relation when about fifteen years of age" (58). Fifty-six-year-old female case 22 "had first [female] sex relation when in early teens. Lived with companion over a long period of time" (60).

Female case 23 (Mildred Berryman herself) had "always been homosexual" and upon discovering her lesbian attraction "at age of about fourteen," she "felt deeply humiliated and disgraced by it" (61). In contrast to the early awareness in other lesbians of their same-sex desires, female case 24 was twenty-two years old before she "began to doubt the strict normalcy of her own sexual reactions" (62).

Although fewer in numbers, most men in Berryman's study responded to the inquiry about earliest homosexual awareness and experience. Twenty-five-year-old male case 1 said: "The first experience of homosexual relations were youthful pranks or rather considered so at the time. . . . I also experienced a definite hatred of myself for years of the (only occasional) homosexual relations" (65–66). Twenty-year-old male case 2 had his "first [homosexual] experience at age of 17" (66). Twenty-three-year-old male case 3 had "always shown homosexual tendencies since a small child" (67). Thirty-year-old male case 5 had "always been homosexual" (68). Of twenty-nine-year-old male case 8, Berryman wrote: "Since his early teens he has been actively homosexual" (70). Thirty-nine-year-old male case 9 began a long-term homosexual relationship when he was a teenager (71).

Related to the early evidence of homosexuality in these people's lives, Berryman was also interested in homosexuality among other family members. Of the thirty-three people in her study, only one referred to homosexuality among immediate family members. Female case 5 "suspects her brother . . . of being a homosexual," and "her eldest sister of having homosexual leanings. The sister, however, seems to have fought her tendency and has no patience with" her openly lesbian sister (44). Female case 3 also implied, but did not specify, that her brother was homosexually oriented. He "was by far more effeminate than his sister, [and] people often remarked that he should have been the girl" (39).

Only two persons in the study commented specifically about parental reactions to their sexual orientation. Regarding female case 14 Berryman explained: "Her family feel she is a disgrace to them" (54). Of female case 17, Berryman wrote that "the father knew and understood. He tried to be a pal to this unhappy daughter" (56). However, "her mother looked upon her sexual variance with horror and disgust" and Berryman was inclined to believe "she [the mother] hated her" (57). This made her daughter suicidal (56).

Suicide was an issue for a minority of these gay men and lesbians in the early 1900s, but it was a real problem. Three lesbians (12.5 percent) reported their own suicide attempts. Female case 1 attempted suicide once (34), and female cases 17 and 19 made two attempts each

(56, 57). Female case 5 (a twenty-three-year-old nurse "in her second year [of] training") also reported that she knew a young "probationary" nurse who attempted suicide: "It was generally known [at the hospital] that the cause was due to her homosexuality, which she could not accept and had been unable to make any adjustment to a normal mode of living" (44).

One gay man (11.1 percent of the study's men) reported that he "at one time had a suicidal mania." This male case 1 indicated that he became suicidal because someone mocked his effeminate way of walking (65). His humiliation was not an isolated case in Utah of the early 1900s. In 1909, the LDS University in Salt Lake City even published a caricature of effeminate men. On an illustration of a woman in evening dress, the student publication put the photograph of a young man's head, with this caption: "A dandy is a thing that would / Be a young lady if he could, / But since he can't, does all he can / To let you know he's not a man."[18]

In fact, among the topics for which Berryman showed special interest were the masculine/feminine behaviors and orientation of participants. Researchers Vern L. Bullough and Bonnie Bullough (who knew Berryman because Bonnie's mother was her long-term lover) commented that Mildred Berryman took "the husbandly role" and "viewed herself as having a masculine psychology." The Bulloughs observed that Berryman's "masculine psychology" predisposed her to be "somewhat hostile" to all but one of the men in her study because "these men were feminine."[19] One indication of that hostility is the fact that Berryman identified three of her male cases by the first initial of their names (male case 1 as *J*, male case 2 as *T*, male case 5 as *L*), whereas she maintained strict anonymity for her female cases whom she named either *X* or *Z*. I will return to the significance of Berryman's bias about masculinity after demonstrating her descriptions of the participants in this regard.

Berryman described polarized behaviors and characteristics among the lesbians. She used the word *masculine* six times in describing female case 1, who "carries her liquor more like a man" (33). On the other hand, twenty-nine-year-old female case 2 "to all appearances is a very femininely normal girl, sexually and psychologically" (36). Berryman evaluated twenty-year-old female case 3: "Her psychology grows more masculine with each year. It is deep and could not be up-rooted" (39). Twenty-year-old female case 4 "has [a] strong masculine swagger in walk and [her] entire bearing is aggressively masculine" (40). She "hates the idea of her feminine body, although she loves all of the feminine qualities in another person" (41).

Twenty-three-year-old female case 5 said: "Sometimes I feel definitely masculine and dominating toward [my lesbian lover] and at other times the reverse" (43). Twenty-three-year-old female case 6 "is hyper sexed and dominating, [and] loves feminine types of girls" (45). Female case 7 had a "feminine" appearance with a "voice, feminine and soft" (46). Female case 8, age forty-three, had a "deep-rooted feminine psychology—passive" and was "attracted to dominating mas[culine]-type women" (48). Concerning female case 9 (actually Berryman's former lover), she wrote that her "entire make-up—mental and physical—[is] positively feminine" (49).

In contrast, thirty-five-year-old female case 10 "is definitely masculine in her psychology and has more physical[ly] masculine traits than feminine" (50). Female case 11, age forty-eight, had "deep-rooted masculine psychology," with a "deep voice, powerful masculine gait and [was] decisive in movement and actions" (50). Twenty-nine-year-old female case 12 "had many boy companions, but those were always as feminine as she was masculine" (51). Again by contrast, twenty-three-year-old female case 13 "is feminine and she is attracted to very masculine types of girls" (52).

On the other hand, Berryman said that female case 14 "has a husky masculine voice, walks with a swagger and has a very masculine attitude" (53). Berryman noted that despite the "masculine psychology" of this twenty-two-year-old woman, she was "powerfully attracted to masculine types of women" (54). Concerning twenty-one-year-old female case 15 Berryman wrote: "When I was first introduced to X I was sure I was talking with a man and the name was masculine" (54). Berryman described nineteen-year-old female case 16's appearance as "masculine" (55), but twenty-nine-year-old female case 17's psychology as "a mixture of masculine and feminine" (55). Berryman characterized twenty-nine-year-old female case 18 thus: "Build, feminine, psychology deep-rooted feminine, [and] attracted to masculine women," while twenty-nine-year-old female case 19 was a "true feminine type" (57).

Female case 20, age twenty-nine, had "masculine psychology" and "prefers blond, feminine types of women" (58). Berryman also perceived "a tendency toward a masculine psychology" in female case 21, even though this forty-one-year-old-woman was "very feminine in build and appearance" (58). Female case 22, age fifty-six, "was masculine and aggressive, practical and capable. She was a direct antithesis of her companion who was frail and delicate and artistic" (60). Interestingly, Berryman did not use the term *masculine* in describing herself as case 23, but acknowledged this dimension in herself only through the description of her own partner, case 24, who "runs the domestic part and her consort assumes the masculine responsibility" (63).

Of twenty-five-year-old male case 1, Berryman wrote: "Father and mother have been at a loss to understand the youth and there has always been considerable unhappiness for him in his home life, the father always holding up the masculine brother as an example. J. has met with opposition and scorn because of his desire to dance and his interest in art and, as his father terms them, 'sissy things'" (66). Berryman added that male case 1 "likes to sew, cook and keep a house, loves to buy vases and silks—all the things which delight the feminine heart" (66). In contrast, she wrote that twenty-year-old male case 2 was "masculine in type . . . [and had a] Bass voice. [He was] virile and extremely masculine in appearance" (66). He was the study's only man whom she seemed to like.

There was a definite edge in Berryman's descriptions of the other male participants. Of twenty-three-year-old male case 3, she wrote: "This young man is of a decided[ly] feminine type, face almost lacking in hair growth, round face and a light voice. . . . [He] Enjoys cooking and the type of things most enjoyed by women. . . . Attitude, feminine" (67). Twenty-three-year-old male case 4 "is powerfully attracted to virile types of men. Is passive and feminine in his emotional relationship," and his "walk is more feminine" (67, 68). Thirty-year-old male case 5 "Is of a petulant and feminine temperament . . . [and] Likes very virile and masculine types of men" (68). Twenty-seven-year-old male case 6 has "the temperament of a badly integrated female personality" (69). Twenty-six-year-old male case 7 is "an apparently feminine, passive type himself, [and] most of his associates are of a like type" (70). Twenty-nine-year-old male case 8 is "very feminine in mannerisms, [and] affected. . . . Enjoys knitting and feminine housework. . . . Enjoys the companionship of men who are nearly his own prototype" (70). And of thirty-nine-year-old male case 9, she wrote that his "walk is not especially masculine and strident, although firm and not mincing" (71).

Berryman never described her lesbian acquaintances with such phrases as "[her] own prototype" or "of a like type." Nor did she use the negative word *petulant* for any lesbian whom she described with equivalent phrases of softer tone: "a quick temper" (female case 3), "quick tempered" (female case 4), and "easily upset" (female case 6). In fact, her study demonstrated an idealization of masculinity in the hostile descriptions of effeminate men and her enthusiastic descriptions of masculine lesbians.

There is a historical perspective for Mildred Berryman's idealization of masculinity during these first decades of the twentieth century. "The mannish lesbian," the anthropologist Esther Newton has written, "came to dominate the discourse about female homosexuality. . . . Because sexual desire was not considered inherent in women, the lesbian was thought to have a trapped male soul that phallicized her and endowed her with active lust."[20] Berryman gave a precise demonstration of that view in her description of female case 21's lesbian "companion," who "was masculine and virile and without a doubt made sex demands which were met" (60).

A similar discourse was occurring at the same time regarding effeminate gay men. "The effeminate 'fairy,'" observes the historian George Chauncey about *Gay New York* in the early 1900s, "represented the primary role model available to men forming a gay identity." Chauncey adds that the cultural "belief that desire for a man was inherently a woman's desire led even many of those queers who regarded themselves as normally masculine in all other respects to regard their homosexual desire as a reflection of a feminine element in their character." Chauncey uses the term *queer* according to the perspective of one of his gay male sources: "'Queer wasn't derogatory,' one man active in New York's gay world in the 1920s recalled. 'It . . . just meant you were different.'"[21]

Nevertheless, her idealization of masculinity was a serious bias in Mildred J. Berryman's study of lesbians and gay men. As the feminist Kathleen Barry has written: "Male identification is the act whereby women place men above women, including themselves."[22] Berryman placed masculinity above femininity as the preferred type of behavior for both lesbians and gay men. She was a historical example of Adrienne Rich's classic observation that "male identification" can "exist among lifelong sexual lesbians."[23]

Berryman's personal bias was so intrusive that it raises obvious (but unanswerable) questions about how representative her participants were of her community's lesbians and gay men at the time. This is a special concern since her study included only half of the lesbians she knew and less than one-fifth of the gay men she knew, and she did not describe her reasons for omitting the others. Berryman's female cases demonstrated only the extremes of Esther Newton's anthropological observation: "Many lesbians *are* masculine; most have composite styles; many are emphatically feminine."[24] Only three of Berryman's female cases had the "composite style," whereas thirteen lesbians were very masculine and eight were very feminine. On the other hand, 90 percent of the gay men in her study were effeminate.

By contrast, Chauncey's research indicates that noneffeminate men "constituted the majority of gay-oriented men in New York in the early decades of the century." However, he also notes that many male homosexuals "embraced the style of the fairies before rejecting it," and that "the style of the fairy was more likely to be adopted by young men."[25] That last observation was consistent with the fact that seven of Berryman's nine male cases were under age thirty. However, unlike Berryman, Chauncey found gay men in their twenties who made such statements as: "I like gentleness in a youth or man, but effeminacy repels me."[26] There is no way to know if, as Berryman's study indicates, effeminacy was actually more common among gay men in Salt Lake City during the 1900s than it was among New York City's gay men at the same time.

Although social critique was not her purpose, Berryman's male identification may also explain why her study gave no hint of criticizing the male patriarchy in the Mormon culture region or in American society. Kathleen Barry has written that male identification "means taking on the values of masculinist ideology, surely the path of least resistance for women in patriarchy."[27] Nevertheless, despite the bias of her male identification and the unexplained sampling design in her study, Mildred J. Berryman stands alone as an early interpreter of an American homosexual community.

An extension of her interest in masculine women and effeminate men was the emphasis on cross-dressing, both subtle and overt. She remarked that thirty-seven-year-old female case 1 had "no desire for masquerade, although [she] preferred shirts, blouses, tailored suits, riding breeches and boots to more feminine apparel" (34). Female case 3 "despises the more feminine dress" (37). Female case 11 had "no patience with feminine frills and prefers tailored suits and blouses" (51). Female case 22, age fifty-six, also "wore severe tailored clothes and had a strong masculine gait" (60). In fact, Berryman described only one lesbian with an enthusiasm for "feminine" apparel. Female case 24 "loves pretty feminine clothes, frills and accouterments" (63).

Berryman's study expressed a kind of awe for the success of two lesbian cross-dressers. Twenty-one-year-old female case 15 had "broad shoulders, narrow masculine pelvis and no hips," with breasts "so small they were not visible." Her hair was "close cropped and [she] wore a cap and overalls, the Levi type." Some of Berryman's friends thought that this female case and her girlfriend "were man and girl" (54). However, the most convincing cross-dresser was nineteen-year-old female case 16, who "has masqueraded as a boy and worked [a]round on farms as a farm hand. Always wears man's clothing and hob-nobs with men. . . . [She] seems to manage herself into fist fights quite regularly and always seems to come out the victor. She worked upon one farm for over a year before the farmers made the discovery she was a girl, and this was accidental" (55).

Berryman also commented on the dressing preferences of several gay men. She noted that twenty-three-year-old male case 4 "loves wearing feminine clothes" (67), and that twenty-six-year-old male case 7 "likes the more feminine pastel colors in clothes, strange as it may seem" (69). She also observed that twenty-nine-year-old male case 8 "uses make-up" and "likes extreme clothes (large checks, light baggy trousers and light pointed shoes)" (70). Also, concerning thirty-nine-year-old male case 9, Berryman wrote that the "one betraying factor in his appearance is the careful use of face make-up" (71). However, she made only one specific comment about male cross-dressing. Thirty-year-old male case 5 was a "clever female impersonator and delights in the role" (68).

Four lesbians (16.7 percent of the women) had avoided close relationships with males. Thirty-seven-year-old female case 1 "never cared for boys other than as playmates" (35). Twenty-year-old female case 4 has had "positively no heterosexual experience. Shudders at the very thought of allowing anyone to touch her intimately. [However, she] Does go about with boy friends. This is done as a shield" (41). Twenty-nine-year-old female case 20 "has never had heterosexual experience. The idea is repugnant to her and she expressed her distaste for coitus with a man" (58). A forty-one-year-old mining engineer, female case 21, reported that she "never cared for masculine companionship and preferred the company of other women" (58).

Five of the female cases (20.8 percent) had been in relationships with men, but these were without sexual intimacy. Female case 7 only "considered marriage from an economic point of view" (46). As teenagers, female cases 8 and 9 were both engaged to be married to young men, but had not had sex with them (47, 49). The men broke the engagements, and thereafter both young women turned to women for love and intimacy. Twenty-nine-year-old female case 12 had "thought about marrying for convenience and then shunted the idea aside" (51). Twenty-three-year-old female case 13 "was engaged to a young man [but] [could not] reconcile herself to marriage" and had "never had heterosexual relations" (52). There was no reference to men in the reports of three of the female cases.

Exactly half of the lesbians reported they had had sexual intercourse with men, some in marriage and some outside wedlock. Twenty-nine-year-old female case 2 had "known heterosexual relationship and could not be happy with any one except her [female] companion" (36). Concerning the experiences of female case 3 from the age of sixteen onward, Berryman wrote: "Throughout these years she has had all kinds of love-adventures, even experimenting in heterosexual relationships" (38). However, at the age of twenty, this young woman said, "There is something about [sexual intercourse] that is repulsive to me." Twenty-three-year-old female case 5 had "heterosexual experience but [she] did not find satisfaction in it. . . . [She] went on until she had assured herself she could not escape her homosexuality by indulging in heterosexual relationship" (43–44).

Using more details, Berryman explained that twenty-three-year-old female case 6 "was seduced when very young, in early teens, and has a definite dislike for men, although after a few years she overcame this feeling. . . . She has been engaged several times and each time has broken her engagement. She admits she would make a mess of her life if she married and only wants a girl companion with whom she could be happy" (45).

Berryman next described three lesbians who were unhappy in their intimate relationships with men. Thirty-five-year-old female case 10 reported: "I have tried to cure myself, to make myself fall in love with a man and [I] even married, but I was unhappy and so was my husband. I could not love him as I should, and the only way it was possible for me to tolerate his embraces was to imagine he was a beloved woman" (53). Of twenty-two-year-old female case 14 Berryman wrote: "She hated the act of coitus in the heterosexual relation and said she could not live under such an arrangement. Her attitude toward her very beautiful little daughter is more like a man's attitude than a woman's" (53). She added that this woman liked "men as friends, but not as lovers" (54). Concerning twenty-nine-year-old female case 17 Berryman related: "Once during her second matrimonial venture her husband asserted his [sexual] rights and she suffered seriously from the effects. Upon making another attempt, he was smashed over the head with a bottle and nearly killed. He also knew of her sex variance" (56).

By contrast, Berryman reported that twenty-nine-year-old female case 18 had "been married for about five years and seems quite happy." This woman said: "I can be perfectly happy in one person's arms and imagine he is some one else." However, Berryman regarded this woman's marriage as a callous exploitation of the husband: "She is ruthless in her ambitions and would think nothing of using anyone for a stepping stone to accomplish her aims. In fact, the said husband has proven very convenient to further her ambitions" (57). That devastating assessment of a lesbian was as vicious as any of Berryman's frequent criticisms of the gay men in her study.

Nevertheless, that was a specific assessment of female case 18 and was not a general indictment of lesbians who married men. For example, Berryman gave a positive description of twenty-nine-year-old female case 19, who "lived in homosexual relations for three years or more, then companion left and married. Shortly after, she [herself] married, has two children and seems quite happy in her heterosexual relationship" (57). Berryman added: "I have talked to her of her [lesbian] friend with whom she keeps in close contact and her eyes never fail to light up when her name is mentioned" (58). This was the one woman who had been happy in both homosexual and heterosexual relationships, but chose to remain in a heterosexual one. The study would later describe a woman who chose to remain in a homosexual relationship, despite her previously fulfilling heterosexual relationship.

Two other lesbians responded to their marriages in divergent ways. Fifty-six-year-old female case 22: "Had first [lesbian] sex relations when in early teens. Lived with [female] companion over a long period of time. Something caused a rift and she [case 22] married. . . . She liked her husband and they were only [on] friendly terms. She treated him more as a pal than a husband" (60). Berryman added: "She was a child of the Victorian age."[28] Of thirty-six-year-old female case 23 (Berryman herself), the study noted: "Ran away and married at the age of sixteen to try to escape her homosexuality. The experience proved disastrous and [she] has since had a horror of coitus. . . . [She] married a second time, but never had relations with husband and left him right after the ceremony, trying to explain to him somehow that they could not be happy together and it was better this way" (61).

Berryman described the last lesbian, female case 24, as "one of the most unusual cases I have ever encountered." The reason? "To all appearances this young woman is the most 'normal' of human beings, [and] has experienced heterosexual relations over a period of about three years" with personal enjoyment. "Her first homosexual relationship [at age twenty-two] occurred long after a 'conditioned' heterosexual life. At the same time, she felt that something was lacking in her heterosexual relationship." Then the young woman "became infatuated with a member of her own sex, despite the fact that she [herself] was living in a comparatively congenial heterosexual relationship. . . . She felt obliged to give up any further heterosexual relationship and since has found complete happiness in her homosexual life" (62).

The nine gay men reported slightly less (44.4 percent) sexual experience with their opposite gender during the early 1900s. Because of the small numbers involved, this was equivalent to that half of the study's lesbians who had also experienced heterosexual intercourse. Twenty-five-year-old male case 1 had sexual intercourse at age nineteen, which he described as "a poor substitute for the relationship I wanted but dreaded at this period" (65). Later he had his first sexual experience with a man. On the other hand, twenty-year-old male case 2 reported that he felt apparently equal "satisfaction" in sexual intercourse with a young woman when he was seventeen, as he did in having sex with a man shortly afterward (66). Therefore, this gay man "would try and live congenially in a conventional [heterosexual] relationship for comfort and social reasons." The study did not continue long enough to report whether this young man's marriage plans were successful.

Male case 3 vacillated between the responses of the first two gay men. This twenty-three-year-old reported that he had sexual intercourse with a female when he was seventeen and then had sex with a male later: "Reaction to heterosexual relationship—at first apathetic, [but] after homosexual experience, [he felt] revulsion" for sex with women (67). Nevertheless, this young man "has considered a permanent heterosexual relationship," yet he "enjoys the companionship of the more masculine types of girls upon an impersonal basis" only. Berryman added that this young man's "attitude is feminine. Would like to find someone who would want to provide the living while he kept house." Again, her study did not follow up on whether this young man married a woman or became the "kept boy"[29] of another man.

The next two men took different social approaches toward their similar sexual orientation. Twenty-six-year-old male case 7 "consorts a great deal with girls in order to hide his true interests. . . . He became engaged to a girl for obvious social and conventional reasons, although those who knew him never expected to see a marriage consummated" (69–70). In contrast, twenty-nine-year-old male case 8 "definitely has an aversion to the very idea" of heterosexual intercourse and he socialized only with men (70).

The last gay men, thirty-nine-year-old male case 9 demonstrated the dilemma of homosexuals who felt emotional ties and sexual attraction for both women and men. He "married in his early twenties and very shortly his wife left him. He was apparently heart-broken over this for many years and grieves over it. . . . However, he was living in a homosexual relation for many years before this marriage and apparently this was the true cause of the break with his wife." Berryman added that "it is believed the real reason for his marriage was his desire to conform to society and the wishes of his family who were anxious to see him married and settled down. . . . [He] enjoys feminine company . . . and often takes girl friends out to teas and legitimate social functions." The man admitted: "the girl I married just wasn't for me. It wasn't to be. I loved her, but I shouldn't have married her and I will never marry again" (71).

Berryman also provided some extraordinary insights into the emotional and sexual response of her lesbian and gay friends in the early decades of the twentieth century. Of twenty-year-old female case 3 she wrote: "The sex libido of this individual is very mild and the affection and companionship [are] the important factor[s] in her relationship with a [female] companion" (39). In stark contrast, twenty-year-old female case 4 was the only one of the twenty-four women and nine men who demonstrated "even a hint of sadism" (40). This was the basis of Berryman's harsh assessment that this young woman was "not a credit to society, yet cannot be classed as a menace" (42).

Berryman explained that this twenty-year-old lesbian "delights in rough abusive treatment of the [female] consort. Never allows consort to touch her person, even upon the breast. If one should be so indiscreet, [s]he might . . . [be] dealt a smashing blow. Quick tempered and highly sexed, yet the only means of [her] sexual satisfaction seems to come through producing orgasm in the [female] consort" (40). In contrast, without any physical abusiveness, twenty-three-year-old female case 5 described her own lesbian relationship: "At times my friend is definitely the aggressor in our sexual relationship, but mostly I suppose I dominate" (43).

Forty-eight-year-old female case 11 "accepts her [own] sexual demands and satisfies them quite as a man takes his sexual demands for granted" (51), but "is only happy when she is able to support a companion and make a home through her own earning capacity" (50). This woman "likes attractive, intelligent women and chooses only that type for companionship," and she "is living quite happy with a companion" (51). Twenty-nine-year-old female case 12 "must absorb a companion mentally and physically in order to be happy. If the companion resists she is abusive and quarrelsome" (52). Twenty-three-year-old female case 13 "is attracted to very masculine types of girls. [She] is passive in a homosexual relation" (52). Twenty-two-year-old female case 14 "stated she could be perfectly happy with the love of a person of her own sex if she could find that person" (54). Twenty-one-year-old female case 15 "had completed her training and felt that she would be able to support her companion [and therefore] she was returning for her" (55). Twenty-nine-year-old female case 20 is "aggressive and demanding with a companion," and "wants a home with a girl companion and would prefer to furnish the support for both" (58).

Berryman gave brief descriptions for the same-sex intimacy of most of her other lesbian friends. Twenty-three-year-old female case 6 "is hyper sexed and dominating, loves feminine types of girls and is most happy when she can champion some girl friend" (45). Female case 7, age twenty-seven, "is hyper-sexed and often is nervous because of her suppressed sexual needs" (46). Fifty-year-old female case 9 had ruined all her lesbian relationships with "jealous rages and amorous demands" (49). Thirty-five-year-old female case 10 "Is hyper-sexed and often lives in bi-sexual relations," left her young son "with her deceased husband's parents, [and she has] never expressed a loneliness or desire to see the boy" (49).

Mildred Berryman saved until the last the most detailed and positive account of a lesbian relationship, the one between herself (female case 23) and her partner (female case 24). For Berryman, it was a welcome change from a succession of unhappy lesbian relationships (61). Of her own relationship with female case 24, Berryman wrote: "She has found her first real contentment in her homosexual relationship and there is every reason to believe this love will last throughout the lifetime of the two people" (63).

By contrast, the study gave negative (or faint praise) descriptions of the intimate dynamics in nearly all of the male relationships. Male case 1 "would be happy making a home for another male of the definitely masculine type" (65). Instead, however, this twenty-five-year-old gay man "lavishes all his love and affection on his younger [five-year-old] brother, and calls him 'SON.' He watches him for hours and tends him like a woman" (66). Male case 3 is "emotionally unstable and vacillating in his affections" and "exploit[s] his [intimate male] friends without a qualm of conscience" (67). Berryman added: "This is characteristic in many cases of male homosexuals. They are less stable and sincere in their attachments and transfer their affections lightly." She wrote that twenty-three-year-old male case 4 had "expressed a desire to find someone who would keep him and allow him to pursue a feminine role" (68). She described that as a "feminine romance complex." Thirty-year-old male case 5 is "selfish and ruthless where his desires are involved, although his cruelty is of the spiteful, feminine type, [with] petty retaliation" (68).

Twenty-seven year-old male case 6 is "given to fits of jealous rage and abusive language toward his friend if crossed. . . . Prefers male company exclusively—likes virile types of men—[He] will exploit anyone who shows any interest in him, if possible" (69). Male case 7 was "dependent upon others for his happiness" (70). "Under favorable conditions," male case 8 "might become parasitic" (70). Mildred Berryman reserved her only favorable comment about male relationships for thirty-nine-year-old male case 9: "The companion with whom he was living at the time worried him a great deal, and despite the fact he was unhappy in this relationship he seemed unable to break with it" (71).

In fact, Berryman dismissed gay male relationships in general:

It is worthy of note [that] constancy is much more in evidence among homosexual women than among homosexual men. Often they [lesbians] love but once, and if their union is broken they seldom try further but remain true to the one love. While among men homosexuals, their affections seem fleeting and they are vacillating in their friendships. They form cliques and groups, and just as suddenly as these groups are formed they are dispersed and each member forms the nucleus of a new group. There is evidenced in the male homosexual all the [negative] characteristics which are absent in the female homosexual. (48)

Berryman's phrase about remaining "true to the one love" referred to a pattern of celibacy she found only among the lesbians. Female case 8 had her first "homosexual experience when in [her] early twenties. The affair broke up and this was the only known relationship. X has spent her life since [then] in her work and has never cared for any one since" (47). The study later specified that this had been the forty-three-year-old lesbian's "one and only sex experience" (48). Concerning fifty-year-old female case 9 Berryman wrote: "For several years after the fracture with [her] woman companion, Z made no further amatory attachments and devoted her time and attention to study and teaching" (49).

Twenty-nine-year-old female case 12 "had one [lesbian] love which proved to be a failure. The companion she chose could not tolerate her possessiveness and domination. They quarreled constantly for about two years and separated. Miss X went east and took her Master's in Latin and Greek. She has never had another companionship to my knowledge, that is, an intimate companionship" (51–52). Twenty-three-year-old female case 13 had "only one experience in homosexuality, although for several years [she] had a violent crush upon another girl, secretly" (52). Twenty-two-year-old female case 14 "has only had one intimate homosexual relationship and thinks she will remain celibate because of her frustrated love" (54).

Berryman summarized the celibacy of female case 21: "When in her early teens, [she] met her first and only [lesbian] love. They were inseparable for many years, then something caused a breach between them, and her companion married and they were estranged definitely" (58–59). Of this Utah lesbian who died at age forty-one, Berryman continued: "She had never had any other sex experience and did not desire it. She said she could not be happy in any other relationship and after she lost her companion she remained celibate and true to the one love" (60). Because of her age at death and the date of the study's final draft, this woman was definitely one of nineteenth-century Utah's lesbians.

The last lesbian with prolonged celibacy was fifty-six-year-old case 22: "There was only this one woman in her life and she married because she said she would never again be able to love another [woman]" (60). In all, seven lesbians in this study (29.2 percent of the total) lived celibate lives after their first and only lesbian relationship. This included the woman who later entered a heterosexual marriage that was either unconsummated or became celibate.

There were significant age differences (from eight years to sixteen years or more) only in the lesbian relationships. Female case 1 was "eight or nine" years older than her companion (34). "At 39 years of age" female case 9 "fell desperately in love with a young woman of 20 [Berryman, who was actually twenty-three]" (49). Twenty-nine-year-old female case 17 "met a woman many years her senior whom she grew to love dearly" (56). Concerning female case 23 (herself at age thirty-six), Berryman wrote: "Over a year ago X met a woman twelve years her junior who was powerfully attracted to X. They formed a permanent relationship which embodies all the things X sought and now they have an ideal home" (61). Thus, including her own relationships with the older female case 9 and with the younger female case 24, five (20.8 percent) of the lesbians had been in relationships with significant age differences. Since Berryman's study gave little attention to male-male relationship dynamics, there is no necessary significance to the lack of reference to age differences in the relationships of the gay men.

The study reported both sexual fidelity and "philandering" in the committed relationships of these lesbians in the early twentieth century. Of thirty-seven-year-old female case 1, Berryman wrote: "Except for a short interim, in which time X did some philandering, she has been faithful to this companion" for ten years (34). Berryman described the relationships of twenty-three-year-old female case 5: "A year ago Miss Z met a girl with whom she fell in love. Since then her entire attention is centered upon this companion. . . . Miss Z. confessed this is the first time she has really been seriously involved. Inclined to be hyper-sexed and up until the meeting with [her new companion] X, [Miss Z] admitted the fact she had played around. Felt that sexual desire should not be suppressed at the expense of nervous disturbance and had found expression when necessary" (43). In an added reference to this female case 5, Berryman stated that she "had many fleeting affairs [with women] altho she frankly admits that she has never been deeply in love with anyone" (unnumbered page, dated 13 Nov. 1938).

Likewise, thirty-five-year-old female case 10 "is not constant in her loves and has had innumerable affairs. Fears being dominated" (50). Thus, three (12.5 percent) of the lesbians reported "philandering" or "innumerable affairs." By contrast, twenty-two-year-old female case 14 "doesn't believe in promiscuity between either homosexual or heterosexual individuals. Believes that the sexual expression is merely an expression of the love one feels to another" (54).

Of lesbian constancy despite parental interference, Berryman described the teenage experience of female case 17. She "fell in love with a [female] cousin and for years this love lasted. [Her] mother discovered her homosexual relations with the cousin and from then on forbid them staying together. When X finished school and started working, the cousin moved to a distant city and they spent their vacations together" (55–56). Of her own relationship with female case 24, Mildred Berryman observed: "Both regard their relationship in the light of marriage and hold it just as sacred. Neither ever go[es] with anyone else" (64).

Contrary to her own expectations, Berryman found both fidelity and "philandering" among the gay men. Thirty-year-old male case 5 "had many affairs with men." She wrote that he was "unstable emotionally and vacillating in his affections," the exact phrase she used to describe male case 3 (68). With somewhat more sympathy, she added: "When a boy in high school, [he] fell in love with a school-mate and for many years after made himself ill over his failure to gain the love of this individual. This seemed to be the one person to whom he might have been faithful had it worked out that way" (68). Likewise, she found that twenty-seven-year-old male case 6 "is unreliable in his affections and cannot be trusted to be sincere in an attachment. [He] breaks appointments, [and] philanders around" (69). However, Berryman acknowledged what she regarded as the exception among male couples in thirty-nine-year-old male case 9: "He is one of the rare cases in which there seemed to be a depth of sincere affection and a need for fidelity. He is not the vacillating type" (71).

Related to her emphasis on fidelity, Berryman commented on the longevity of both lesbian and gay male relationships. Concerning thirty-seven-year-old female case 1 Berryman wrote: "For ten years now X has lived with a young woman at least eight or nine years her junior and they have lived very happily" (34). Twenty-nine-year-old female case 2 "gave up teaching contract, after finishing college, to go to the girl friend with whom she has lived for several years. . . . They have lived in perfect harmony for about ten years or more" (35). Twenty-year-old female case 3 began a lesbian relationship at age sixteen "with a girl who stayed with her for about two years and then went to someone else" (37). Forty-eight-year-old female case 11 "was constant and true to one woman for a period of eight or nine years. Then they separated and since then she has had relations with about three different women" (50). Female case 17 remained with her first lover "for years" (55). Twenty-nine-year-old female case 18, married to a man, had previously "been living in a homosexual relationship for three or more years," after which she had another lesbian relationship "which only lasted a very short time" (57). Female case 19, also age twenty-nine, had "lived in homosexual relationship for three years or more, then companion left and married" a man (57).

In her "early teens," female case 21 had a lesbian relationship and "they were inseparable for years" (58). Female case 22 began a lesbian relationship "in early teens, [and] lived with companion over a long period of time" (60). As female case 23, Berryman described her own "first homosexual relationship at age of nineteen, [and] this lasted for about a year and a half" (61). Female case 24 had been in a relationship with female case 23 for more than a year at the time of the study's conclusion (62). Therefore, eleven (45.8 percent) of the lesbians reported long-term relationships.

Berryman had both positive and negative comments about the longevity of male relationships. Concerning twenty-nine-year-old male case 8, she wrote: "For a period of about two years [he] remained constant to one person. . . . Since that time [he] has been vacillating and more the coquette in his relations which are ephemeral, fleeting and frequent" (70). Also, as a teenager, thirty-nine-year-old male case 9 entered into "a homosexual relationship [which lasted] for many years" (71). Although the numbers are too small to be statistically significant, 22.2 percent of the gay men reported that they had been in long-term relationships with other men during the early 1900s. In other words, twice as many lesbians entered long-term relationships as did gay men.

As a variation on fidelity in couple relationships, Berryman also described "one of the most unique cases which I have encountered, a case of polygamous homosexuality" (54–55). In this ménage à trois of lesbians, twenty-one-year-old female case 15 "intended to take them [two young women] both back and make a living for all three. She intended to live polygamously with the two. The companion [already] with her had agreed and I questioned her about the other girl. She stated she has written and told her friend and that she [the third woman] had agreed to the arrangement" (55).

Female case 5 also considered the possibility of a bisexual ménage à trois. This twenty-three-year-old nurse referred to the "vague possibility that she might indulge in hetero and homosexual relations simultaneously" (unnumbered page, dated 13 Nov. 1938). None of the gay men referred to living in ménage à trois relationships or having bisexual relationships simultaneously. That may reflect Berryman's inattention to gay male relationships or it may indicate that these gay men tended to be more conservative sexually than the lesbians of this study.

Among the most important contributions of Berryman's study are the statements of Utah women about their reactions to being lesbian during the early decades of the twentieth century. Thirty-seven-year-old female case 1 said that she "would not be happy in any other kind of a relationship than homosexual, [and] wouldn't change if she could, unless it were possible to become wholly masculine physically" (34). Twenty-year-old female case 3 said: "I know what I am and I'm not going on mak[ing] my life miserable trying to be what other people think I should be. . . . The sin is for a person like me to mess up someone else's life by marrying them and [then] hating them and myself because I married them." She added: "The only way I'd want to change would be to have a man's privilege and marry some girl I could love and [then] take care of her" (39).

Berryman interviewed a hospital nurse, twenty-three-year-old female case 5, about the question of lesbian and gay self-image:

Q. Do you believe homosexuality is wrong?
A. No, but I do believe it is abnormal.
Q. Would you marry and feel that you were doing the right thing?
A. No, I think it would be wrong for me to marry.
Q. What is your attitude in regard to the mentality of the homosexual?
A. I think in the beginning, the average homosexual is pure of mind and thought, their ideas and ideals are pure. But, when they awaken to the attitude of conventional society, they go haywire and take refuge in drink, drugs and loose habits of living.

This lesbian nurse added that many Utah lesbians and gay men "sacrifice their emotional life and chances of happiness in a harmonious homosexual relationship, and bury themselves in their work. Sometimes they may even conform to outward appearance and marry, but it is a mistake." Berryman indicated how much she valued this interview by providing two separate transcriptions of it (43, and unnumbered page dated 13 Nov. 1938).

Other lesbians shared a more negative view of themselves. Twenty-three-year-old female case 6 said: "I used to hate myself and the whole world because I am what I am. Now, I am going on and try to make a go of life. I've met someone and I think we can make a go of it. I love her and she does me and I've just quit bothering about what people think" (45). Twenty-seven-year-old female case 7 (who had her first lesbian relationship at age twenty-three): "refuses to acknowledge her homosexuality and yet cannot be happy in any other relationship" (46). Thirty-five-year-old female case 10 said: "In fact they [homosexuals] are all a little nuts, myself included. Senses are too keen; will-power pretty weak. There might be exceptions, but hardly. They want to absorb, but not be absorbed" (50).

The final lesbians in the study to comment on self-image gave the most positive responses. Forty-eight-year-old female case 11 "does not look upon her sexual variation as a crime or as abnormal" (51). Female case 20 "doesn't regard her sex variance as anything unusual and wonders why people make so much fuss about it." This twenty-nine-year-old woman added: "Because I love some one who has the same type of body as myself shouldn't be considered a crime, and I don't think I am a criminal" (58). The gay men may have had a similar range of self-concepts, but Berryman did not describe them.

However, one thing that both lesbians and gays talked about among themselves in Salt Lake City of the early 1900s was the general fear of being "discovered." Mildred Berryman blamed the publication of Radclyffe Hall's 1928 lesbian novel *The Well of Loneliness* for creating "a storm of talk" and a climate of homophobia in Salt Lake City. This book certainly created a national "storm of talk."[30] According to Berryman, this resulted in an "effort being made to classify" as homosexuals "every woman who wore a suit and was seen in the company of a girl companion more than once, and every man who had curly hair and might have a little more than feminine walk or a flair for bright colored ties" (57). However, if Utah Mormons gave such homophobic attention to external appearance in the late 1920s, then this homophobia coexisted with Mormon culture's acceptance of male cross-dressing for entertainment purposes.

For example, male students were performing openly as women at

Utah's two largest universities. In 1925, some Mormon students at Brigham Young University dressed as women for a comedy skit and also left prominent lipstick kisses on the cheeks of the one man who dressed as a man.[31] In March 1926, the Mormon community showed how fully it endorsed this kind of cross-dressing. For two consecutive nights, the LDS Church–owned Salt Lake Theatre performed a musical comedy "with an all-male cast" of fifty engineering students from the University of Utah. Photographs show half the male dancers as sleekly dressed women who had partners in tuxedos.[32] This transvestite dance musical opened a week after the University of Utah staged the play *Suppressed Desires* in which a young man learns after two years of marriage that he has "a suppressed desire to be freed from marriage."[33]

In fact, the Utah Mormon community repeatedly emphasized and praised the androgyny in these dozens of female impersonators of early 1926. Six separate issues of the university's newspaper published close-up photographs of what appeared to be glamorous young women from this male-only play. The editors even published a "Hot Scene" close-up photograph of one tuxedo-clad man in a passionate embrace with a remarkably authentic-looking female impersonator. Another photograph had the caption, "A Pair of Queens," then-current slang in the gay subculture for female impersonators.[34] "These [male] chorus beauties with their 'feminine' flutter," said the LDS Church's *Deseret News,* "made one forget for the moment that beneath the finery were—engineers."[35] These Utah examples were consistent with the general American acceptance of cross-dressing for entertainment purposes. For example, in 1923 the entertainment trade magazine *Variety* had reported that female impersonators were more common in vaudeville than ever before, with as many as three in a single night's program.[36]

Nevertheless, six of the Utah lesbians in Berryman's study (25 percent of the total) felt they were under the scrutiny of a homophobic society during this time period. Female case 4 had "fears of social ostracism" (40) and female case 5 "has forced herself to conform to conventional life, because she dislikes the trouble of gossip and scandal" ("45," should be p. 44). Berryman wrote that forty-three-year-old female case 8 was "conventionally minded and would suffer much if she were criticized for conduct" (48). Berryman commented about the "overwhelming fear of being known as an inter-sex" on the part of thirty-five-year-old female case 10: "It would seem at one time she was blackmailed by a quite 'normal' individual who threatened to expose her and thus obtained a considerable amount of her hard-earned money through pressure" (50). Female case 18 "feared social ostracism and used her feminine charms to keep men around in order to hide her homosexuality." Eventually this woman "cut [away] her homosexual or suspected homosexual friends and soon left [Salt Lake City], going to a foreign country and marrying" (57). Concerning the end of the lesbian relationship of female case 22 Berryman revealed: "I have heard it whispered it was gossip and family interference which caused the rupture between the two women and the woman in this case took refuge in marriage" (61).

About an equal percentage of the gay men in Berryman's study reported concern about Salt Lake City's homophobia during the twenties and thirties. Twenty-three-year-old male case 4 "lives in fear of legal persecution, although [he] has never been involved in any special sexual difficulty" (67). Also, twenty-six-year-old male case 7 is "extremely sensitive in regard to social criticism and makes every possible effort to cover up his sexual variance" (69).

Nevertheless, some Utah lesbians were open about their sexual orientation in the early 1900s. Twenty-two-year-old female case 14 "doesn't hide her homosexuality and feels it is quite normal to love a member of her own sex" (54). Prior to her death, female case 21's "attitude toward her homosexuality was clearly most normal. She did not feel ashamed of it, and when she knew she was talking with a person who understood and was sympathetic she made no effort to hide the fact. However, she did fear hostile gossip and people who had no sympathy with it" (60). Of her own lesbian relationship with a younger woman, thirty-six-year-old Mildred Berryman wrote: "Some of their friends are aware of the relationship and take it for granted, even occasionally making wise cracks to Z about her 'husband'" (64). These friends included "normal" husbands and wives. Undoubtedly that kind of self-confidence and support by heterosexual friends encouraged Berryman to begin her homosexual study at Westminster College at an unspecified date between 1916 and 1922. At the time she was less than twenty-one years old.

In fact shortly after she left the college, Westminster's students indicated they had a casual attitude toward homoerotic relationships. Sandwiched between photographs of bare-legged athletes on the men's track team, a photograph of two young men, each with one arm around the other's shoulders, appeared in the 1923 yearbook. Its caption was

"Adam at Evening."[37] Although her college adviser had discouraged Berryman's private study of same-sex relationships, some of her fellow students apparently didn't mind making such an emphasis publicly.

Eight years before she completed the study, she wrote as a nonstudent in the literary magazine of the University of Utah: "Love knows no law nor recognizes any man-made consecration. Love alone, that all-consuming fire that refuses to be quenched by half-measures, is a law unto itself." Berryman made no reference to homosexuality in this essay, but its lesbian subtext was indicated by an illustration of a female nude.[38]

Mildred J. Berryman's study provides an extraordinary window into the self-perceptions of lesbians and gay men in the early decades of the twentieth century. These people lived in a small city that had more in common with the values of America's heartland than a metropolis like New York City. Her study first of all demonstrates that even in such environments, lesbians and gays of that era had both self-identity and community identity as a sexual minority. They interacted sufficiently that Berryman referred to one hundred homosexuals of her own acquaintance.

While some of these lesbians and gay men felt self-loathing, others regarded their same-sex orientation as "abnormal" only from the perspective of the majority's experience. They saw homosexuality as potentially healthy and happy. A few regarded their homosexual desires as completely normal. Nearly all of these lesbians and gay men reported childhood awareness of their sexual orientation, although there were a few who became aware of same-sex attraction only in their midtwenties.

All accepted the bipolarity of gender behaviors and defined themselves and their sexual interests along strict lines of masculine/feminine. None described androgynous behaviors or interests, and few described the presently common pattern of feminine-acting lesbians who are attracted to feminine-acting women or masculine-acting gay men who are attracted to masculine-acting men.

Significant age differences were present only in lesbian couples, but age disparity was a potential for the gay men who indicated a preference for being "kept" by a male partner. Long-term relationships were common, especially among lesbians, but some lesbians chose to live alone and be celibate the rest of their lives after the breakup of their first same-sex relationship. Other lesbians followed the study's male pattern of transitory relationships, impersonal sexual encounters, and sexual adventures despite committed relationships. Nearly all the lesbians were passionate and amorous in their same-sex relationships, but the study was silent about whether those dynamics existed in gay male relationships.

Nevertheless, half of the lesbians and nearly half of the gay men had experienced heterosexual intimacy, often in marriage. While most of the lesbians and gay men expressed fear of being "discovered" within a homophobic society, a few were remarkably open with heterosexual friends about their sexual orientation. For lesbians and gay men today, this early study provides an opportunity to compare and contrast their own experiences with the self-perceptions of gay men and lesbians in America's heartland four generations ago.

NOTES

1. Mildred J. Berryman, "The Psychological Phenomena of the Homosexual," 64, rough-typed on the back of stationery of the American Red Cross, Salt Lake City, Utah, with the last page of the study dated 13 Nov. 1938, in the June Mazer Lesbian Collection, West Hollywood, Calif.

2. Vern Bullough and Bonnie Bullough, "Lesbianism in the 1920s and 1930s: A Newfound Study," *Signs: Journal of Women in Culture and Society* 2 (Summer 1977): 896; "Historian's Research Aimed at Learning about Living in Utah," *Salt Lake Tribune,* 5 May 1990, A-10; see also chap. 2. For the number of women and men, see note 10.

3. Bullough and Bullough, "Lesbianism in the 1920s and 1930s," 897; statement concerning enrollment of Mildred J. Berryman (b. 22 Sept. 1901) at age fifteen by Helen Olpin, Alumni Coordinator, Westminster College, photocopy in "History—Utah" Folder, Vertical Files, Library, Stonewall Center, Salt Lake City, Utah; *Westminster College Bulletin* 3 (May 1917): 51; *Westminster College Bulletin* 8 (May 1922): 51.

4. All citations are from Berryman, "The Psychological Phenomena of the Homosexual." To avoid creating repetitive source notes, the text discussion gives internal citations to the case and page number of each quotation or paraphrase. Because Berryman's manuscript was carelessly typed with little proofreading, my quotations in this chapter correct (without brackets) typographical errors, run-on sentences, unnecessary use of commas, capitalization, and missing punctuation. I use brackets to show my clarifications of her text.

5. Bullough and Bullough, "Lesbianism in the 1920s and 1930s," 896.

Although their 1977 article therefore indicated the study began about 1918, the Bulloughs have recently abandoned that dating. After a prepublication reading of my book manuscript's specific emphasis on 1918 as the beginning year, Vern L. Bullough wrote me on 22 Aug. 1995 that Berryman "did not start the study at 18" (2). His letter continued: "She really began the study when she lived with the social worker in the 1930's." Likewise, although Bullough and Bullough, "Lesbianism in the 1920s and 1930s," stated that "the [homosexual] community was located in Salt Lake City" (896) and referred to "the Salt Lake lesbians" (901), Vern Bullough's 22 Aug. 1995 letter states: "Second, we are not certain that all the people were from Salt Lake City or stayed there for any length of time" (2). The Bulloughs cited no new evidence to explain this change of their views from their 1977 article to their 1995 remarks after reading my independent interpretation of Berryman's manuscript. It is especially perplexing that the Bulloughs disputed in 1995 my restatements (cited above) of what they had published in 1977.

Nevertheless, I agreed to quote Vern L. Bullough's 1995 letter at various points of this chapter in order to incorporate their dissent from some of my conclusions. For example, during my telephone conversation with the Bulloughs on 22 August 1995, they added that Berryman began her study no earlier than 1928. However, I regard the Bulloughs's 1977 published estimate of a twenty-year study prior to the 1938 draft as completely consistent with Berryman's personal statement to them that she began her research in college. In addition, Berryman's 1938 draft said that female case 24 with whom she was living "has aspirations to an operatic career" (63), but mentioned nothing about female case 24 being a social worker, as claimed above by the Bulloughs.

6. Berryman's typed study has a title page that I regard as misleading: "A Thesis Prepared by M.J. Berryman for Doctor of Philosophy for the Temple Bar College, Seattle, Washington." During that period, there was no school by that name in Seattle according to the following sources: *American Universities and Colleges: A Handbook of Higher Education,* 3d and 4th eds. (Washington, D.C.: American Council on Education, 1936 and 1940); *Patterson's American Educational Directory,* 35th ed. (Chicago: Educational Directories, 1938); the 1938 Seattle telephone book; nor in the "Schools and Colleges" section of the Seattle Public Library's special files on the Pacific Northwest. Therefore, it is my conclusion that Berryman used the title page to disguise the fact that Salt Lake City was the location of the homosexual community she described. This is evidence of her concern about preserving the anonymity of her lesbian and gay friends, a preoccupation that Bullough and Bullough, in "Lesbianism in the 1920s and 1930s," 897 and 898 noted. I also view the "Temple Bar" reference as possibly an inside joke about the fact that the sexually active homosexuals of Berryman's study were barred from the temple of the LDS Church.

However, in his letter to me on 22 August 1995, Vern L. Bullough interprets this title page as indicating that Berryman "hoped to use one of the fly by night mail order houses to get a degree, something which she very much wanted, and which she sometime[s] pretended to have" (3). Although he cites no evidence for the existence of a correspondence school named Temple Bar College, Bullough concludes that "probably the school folded. I am not sure she could have succeeded if she finished. No graduate school in the United States would have accepted a Ph.D. dissertation on such a topic in the 1930s, even a mail order one. I do not think any journal would have published an article from it or any publisher would have accepted it."

The computer database WorldCat of thirty million publications allows one to search for publisher as well as author/title, but there is no entry for Temple Bar College. Nevertheless, WorldCat lists publications as small as one-page announcements for numerous U.S. correspondence schools before 1940, including American Correspondence School of Law, American School of Correspondence, Catholic Correspondence School, Central Correspondence College, Columbian Correspondence College, Correspondence Agricultural College, Correspondence School of Agriculture, Cosmopolitan Correspondence College, Elhanan Correspondence Bible School, Hadley Correspondence School for the Blind, Home Correspondence School, International Correspondence Schools, Interstate School of Correspondence, Metropolitan Correspondence Bible College, Nyack Correspondence Bible School, Pacific Horticultural Correspondence School, Palmer School of Correspondence, Sprague Correspondence School, Siegel-Myers Correspondence School of Music, and Western Correspondence School of Mining Engineering.

As noted below, medical journals had published studies of lesbians since 1895, while Harper and Brothers published a book that emphasized female-female sexuality in 1929. Also Bullough's claim that graduate schools in the thirties would not allow a student to emphasize homosexuality in a dissertation is not supported by Dawson Frank Dean, "Significant Characteristics of the Homosexual Personality" (Ph.D. diss., New York University, 1936), as contained in the computer index Dissertation Abstracts (1861–1981), with a correction of the author's name in my telephone conversation with the archivist of New York University.

7. Bullough and Bullough, "Lesbianism in the 1920s and 1930s," 901 for quotation; Celia Duel Mosher, *The Mosher Survey: Sexual Attitudes of Forty-Five Victorian Women,* ed. James MaHood and Kristine Wenburg (New York: Arno Press/New York Times, 1980); Carl N. Degler, *At Odds: Women and the Family in America from the Revolution to the Present* (New York: Oxford University Press, 1980), 262–65.

8. Havelock Ellis, "Sexual Inversion in Women," *Alienist and Neurologist* 16 (Apr. 1895): 141–58, and Ellis, "Sexual Inversion with an Analysis of Thirty

Three New Cases," *Medico-Legal Journal* 13 (Dec. 1895): 255–67, quoted and summarized in Jonathan Ned Katz, *Gay/Lesbian Almanac: A New Documentary* (New York: Harper and Row, 1983), 269–88.

9. Katharine Bement Davis, *Factors in the Sex Life of Twenty-Two Hundred Women* (New York: Harper and Brothers, 1929; reprint, New York: Arno Press/New York Times, 1972), 248, 298.

10. Bullough and Bullough, in "Lesbianism in the 1920s and 1930s," 890, calculated the median ages based on the erroneous total of twenty-five women and eight men (896). Including herself, Berryman's original study, "Psychological Phenomena," had twenty-four numbered cases of lesbians and nine numbered cases of gay men, each with different histories and ages, as follows: female case 1 (age 37); female case 2 (age 29); female case 3 (age 20); female case 4 (age 20); female case 5 (age 23); female case 6 (age 23); female case 7 (age 27); female case 8 (age 43); female case 9 (age 50); female case 10 (age 35); female case 11 (age 48); female case 12 (age 29); female case 13 (age 23); female case 14 (age 22); female case 15 (age 21); female case 16 (age 19); female case 17 (age 29); female case 18 (age 29); female case 19 (age 29); female case 20 (age 29); female case 21 (age 41); female case 22 (age 56); female case 23 (age 36); female case 24 (age 24); male case 1 (age 25); male case 2 (age 20); male case 3 (age 23); male case 4 (age 23); male case 5 (age 30); male case 6 (age 27); male case 7 (age 26); male case 8 (age 29); male case 9 (age 39). Therefore, to distinguish my calculations from those in the Bulloughs' article, I use the mean as an average. Also, if Berryman gave an estimated age interval instead of a single number (e.g., "20 to 21 years old"), I use the lower age.

Because my summaries of the Berryman study sometimes differ from the aggregate numbers given in the Bulloughs' article, I always cite the relevant case numbers for the lesbians and gay men to whom I refer. Some of these persons completed questionnaires, some Berryman interviewed formally, and others Berryman described only from her casual association with them. Therefore, in the topics for which Berryman wanted to gather data, there are gaps from one case to another, and case descriptions vary from detailed to superficial.

11. In a telephone interview on 22 August 1995, Bonnie Bullough expressed astonishment and disbelief that Mildred Berryman had ever been a Mormon, because this contradicted statements by Berryman during the thirty years she was in a lesbian relationship with Bullough's mother, Ruth Uckerman (Larsen Dempsey). Also Vern L. Bullough in his 22 August 1995 letter states that Mildred J. Berryman "was never a Mormon. . . . She regarded Mormons as inferior to her and was, to put in a word, a vile anti-Mormon" (1). However, the LDS Patriarchal Blessing Index (1833–1963) shows that Mildred Jessie Berryman (born to Richard Gordon Berryman Sr. and Mildred Stokes) received a patriarchal blessing on 11 September 1921 in Salt Lake City; the 1930 LDS Church Census also listed Mildred Berryman as a member of the Liberty Ward,

Liberty Stake in Salt Lake City, with a notation that Berryman had been "baptized [in] 31st Ward." Both sources were microfilmed decades ago and are located in the Family History Library of the Church of Jesus Christ of Latter-day Saints, Salt Lake City, Utah. See chap. 2, note 18 for the relationship between Mildred Berryman and Ruth Uckerman.

12. Robert S. Lynd and Helen Merrell Lynd, *Middletown: A Study in Contemporary American Culture* (New York: Harcourt, Brace, 1929); Dwight W. Hoover, *Middletown Revisited* (Muncie, Ind.: Ball State University Press, 1990).

13. "Elder Taylor's Talk," *Deseret Evening News,* 10 Oct. 1898, 2; Rudger Clawson diary, 10 July 1901, in Stan Larson, ed., *A Ministry of Meetings: The Apostolic Diaries of Rudger Clawson* (Salt Lake City: Signature Books/Smith Research Associates, 1993), 296; see also the discussion in chap. 10.

14. Harold T. Christensen, "Child Spacing Analysis via Record Linkage: New Data Plus a Summing Up from Earlier Reports," *Marriage and Family Living* 25 (Aug. 1963): 275; Daniel Scott Smith, "The Dating of the American Sexual Revolution: Evidence and Interpretation," in Michael Gordon, ed., *The American Family in Social-Historical Perspective,* 2d ed. (New York: St. Martin's Press, 1978), 429.

15. Francis M. Lyman statement, 29 Sept. 1914, photocopy of original typed document signed by Lyman, Folder 11, Box 12, Scott G. Kenney Papers, Manuscripts Division, J. Willard Marriott Library, University of Utah, Salt Lake City, Utah; also Anthon H. Lund diary, 29 Sept. 1914, microfilm, Archives, Historical Department of the Church of Jesus Christ of Latter-day Saints. The Lund diary microfilm is unrestricted to all researchers at LDS Archives by stipulation of its donor, and will be published in edited form by Signature Books, Salt Lake City.

16. Thomas G. Alexander, *Mormonism in Transition: A History of the Latter-day Saints, 1890–1930* (Urbana: University of Illinois Press, 1986), 260–69.

17. Vern L. Bullough to Quinn, 22 Aug. 1995, 4; also statements of Bonnie Bullough and Vern L. Bullough during telephone interview with Quinn, 22 Aug. 1995. However, this reflected Berryman's religious views as of the midforties when the Bulloughs first met her. Twenty years earlier, Berryman voluntarily obtained an LDS patriarchal blessing, a traditional indication of faith in Mormonism, particularly on the part of a twenty-year-old woman.

The preforties religious affiliation of Mildred Berryman is a matter about which the Bulloughs and I continue to disagree. They regard the LDS Church records showing Berryman's Mormon affiliation as "made up data" (Bullough to Quinn, 1), with Bonnie Bullough's more emphatic statement of that view in her telephone conversation with me on 22 August 1995. His letter also affirms: "We are certain, however, that not all people in the study were Mormons and that Barry [Mildred Berryman] herself certainly was not." He adds: "Bonnie feels that to call her a Mormon [at any point in her life] would be a disservice to the LDS Church and to what Barry stood for." Bullough to Quinn, 4. I have emphasized their views on this matter at the explicit request of Vern L. Bullough and Bonnie Bullough.

18. *Gold and Blue: Commencement Number, Published by the Senior Class of the L.D.S. University, May, 1909* (Salt Lake City: Skelton, 1909), unnumbered page. See chap. 1 for a discussion of cultural attitudes toward effeminate men and masculine women.

19. Bullough and Bullough, "Lesbianism in the 1920s and 1930s," 897, 900, and their statement in a preliminary draft, "The Salt Lake City Lesbian Community in the 1930s," 8, Berryman Papers, Mazer Collection, which the Bulloughs softened considerably on page 902 of its published form. In her telephone interview with me on 22 August 1995, Bonnie Bullough also said that Berryman "didn't like the men in her study."

20. Esther Newton, "The Mythic Mannish Lesbian: Radclyffe Hall and the New Woman," *Signs: Journal of Women in Culture and Society* 9 (Summer 1984): 566. For "butch-fem roles" before the 1940s, see Elizabeth Lapovsky Kennedy and Madeline D. Davis, *Boots of Leather, Slippers of Gold: The History of a Lesbian Community* (New York: Penguin Books, 1993), 323–26.

21. George Chauncey, *Gay New York: Gender, Urban Culture, and the Making of the Gay Male World, 1890–1940* (New York: Basic Books/HarperCollins, 1994), 99, 104, 101.

22. Kathleen Barry, *Female Sexual Slavery* (New York: New York University Press, 1984), 202.

23. Adrienne Rich, "Compulsory Heterosexuality and Lesbian Existence," *Signs: Journal of Women in Culture and Society* 5 (Summer 1980): 645, reprinted in Henry Abelove, Michele Aina Barale, and David M. Halperin, eds., *The Lesbian and Gay Studies Reader* (New York: Routledge, 1993), 237. I changed Rich's phrase from a question into a statement.

24. Newton, "The Mythic Mannish Lesbian," 575; emphasis in original.

25. Chauncey, *Gay New York*, 101, 102.

26. Ina Russell, ed., *Jeb and Dash: A Diary of Gay Life, 1918–1945* (Boston: Faber and Faber, 1993), 90–91 (4 Feb. 1927), quoted in Chauncey, *Gay New York*, 101.

27. Barry, *Female Sexual Slavery*, 203.

28. For a historical perspective on what Berryman meant by that phrase, see Michael Gordon, "From an Unfortunate Necessity to a Cult of Mutual Orgasm: Sex in American Marital Education Literature, 1830–1940," in James Heslin, ed., *Studies in the Sociology of Sex* (New York: Appleton, Century, Crofts, 1971), 53–77; Peter T. Cominos, "Innocent Femina Sexualis in Unconscious Conflict," in Martha Vicinus, ed., *Suffer and Be Still* (Bloomington:

Indiana University Press, 1972); Charles E. Rosenberg, "Sexuality, Class, and Roles in Nineteenth-Century America," *American Quarterly* 25 (May 1973): 131–53; Ronald G. Waters, *Primers for Prudery: Sexual Advice to Victorian America* (Englewood Cliffs, N.J.: Prentice-Hall, 1974); J. G. Barker-Benfield, *The Horrors of the Half-Known Life: Male Attitudes toward Women and Sexuality in Nineteenth-Century America* (New York: Harper and Row, 1976); Nancy F. Cott, "Passionless: An Interpretation of Victorian Sexual Ideology, 1790–1850," *Signs: Journal of Women in Culture and Society* 4 (Winter 1978): 219–36, reprinted in Nancy F. Cott and Elizabeth H. Pleck, eds., *A Heritage of Her Own: Toward a New Social History of American Women* (New York: Simon and Schuster, 1979), 162–81; Steven Seidman, "The Power of Desire and the Danger of Pleasure: Victorian Sexuality Reconsidered," *Journal of Social History* 24 (Fall 1990): 47–67; Robert M. Ireland, "Frenzied and Fallen Females: Women and Sexual Dishonor in the Nineteenth-Century United States," *Journal of Women's History* 3 (Winter 1992): 96.

29. See chap. 6, note 62 for a discussion of this term.

30. Radclyffe Hall, *The Well of Loneliness, with a Commentary by Havelock Ellis* (New York: Covici-Friede, 1928); Rebecca O'Rourke, *Reflecting on the Well of Loneliness* (London: Routledge, 1989); Jonathan Katz, *Gay American History: Lesbians and Gay Men in the U.S.A.* (New York: Thomas Y. Crowell, 1976), 397–405; Neil Miller, *Out of the Past: Gay and Lesbian History from 1869 to the Present* (New York: Vintage/Random House, 1995), 186–91.

31. Gary James Bergera and Ronald Priddis, *Brigham Young University: A House of Faith* (Salt Lake City: Signature Books, 1985), photo section.

32. "Utah Engineers, in Guise of 'Wimmen' Frolic in Comedy," *Deseret News,* 24 Mar. 1926, 3; *Utonian, 1927: A Record of the College Year, 1925–26* (Salt Lake City: Junior Class, University of Utah, 1926), 246, 306.

33. "'Moonshine' Is Production of Class in Plays: Dramatists to Offer One-Act Comedy and Two-Act Play Tuesday," *Utah Chronicle,* 5 Mar. 1926, 1. The performance of *Suppressed Desires* was postponed until the evening of March 15. Susan Glaspell and George Cram Cook, *Suppressed Desires: A Comedy in Two Episodes* (Boston: Walter H. Baker, 1924), 26, 28, with the closing lines on page 42: "What am I to do with my suppressed desire? . . . just keep right on suppressing it!"

34. "Speaking of Beauties!" *Utah Chronicle,* 2 Feb. 1926, 3; "Oo! Some Spanish Flapper!" *Utah Chronicle,* 9 Feb. 1926, 1; "Hot Scene from 'Mary Alice,'" *Utah Chronicle,* 16 Feb. 1926, 3; "Cuties Caper in 'Mary Alice,'" *Utah Chronicle,* 2 Mar. 1926, 1; "Another Beauty in Action," *Utah Chronicle,* 9 Mar. 1926, 1; "A Pair of Queens," *Utah Chronicle,* 16 Mar. 1926, 2. For *queen* as homosexual slang in the 1920s, see Chauncey, *Gay New York,* 101, and the list of homosexual slang in Aaron J. Rosanoff, *Manual of Psychiatry,* 6th ed. (New York: Wiley, 1927), as quoted in Katz, *Gay/Lesbian Almanac,* 439.

Elizabeth H. Bullard. "If I could sleep with you one night, [I] think we should not be very sleepy," her female friend and former college roommate wrote from LDS headquarters in 1839. (© *Utah State Historical Society. All rights reserved. Used by permission.*)

John C. Bennett, special counselor to Joseph Smith. A Mormon newspaper accused Bennett of "Buggery" after his excommunication in 1842. *(Courtesy of Manuscripts Division, University of Utah Libraries)*

Male-male dancing in the American West. The second LDS president, Brigham Young, hosted male-only dances from 1845 until the 1860s. *(Erwin E. Smith, "Dancing, Seemingly Not Hampered by Lack of Women," 1901–10, photograph, LC S6-058, courtesy of the Erwin E. Smith Collection of the Library of Congress on deposit at the Amon Carter Museum, Fort Worth, Texas)*

Bruce Taylor, son of the third LDS president. He was described in 1879 as *Aikane,* the Hawaiian name for a young man who was the sexual companion of an older man. *(Courtesy of Daughters of Utah Pioneers, Pioneer Memorial Museum, Salt Lake City, Utah)*

We'Wha, a Zuni berdache, in 1885. Functioning in women's traditional roles, the berdache were respected members of twenty-seven Native American tribes proselytized by Mormons. *(Photo no. 85-8666, National Anthropological Archives, Smithsonian Institution)*

Brigham Morris Young as "Madam Pattirini." After returning from a Hawaiian mission in 1885, Brigham Young's thirty-fifth child performed as a female impersonator in Utah for decades. *(Courtesy of Photographic Archives, Harold B. Lee Library, Brigham Young University, Provo, Utah)*

Thomas Taylor. Bishop of an LDS congregation, he was excommunicated in 1886 for "lewdness" with teenage boys.

Frank Smiley. At age seventeen he was sentenced to three years in the Utah penitentiary in 1894 for sodomy, apparently with a consenting teenager. *(Courtesy of Utah State Archives)*

Salt Lake City's prostitution district on Commercial Street. In 1897 apostles criticized the LDS Church's real estate company for leasing the upper floors as "whorehouses" where male prostitutes also worked. Such leasing continued for another forty-four years. *(© Utah State Historical Society. All rights reserved. Used by permission.)*

Kate Thomas. In 1903 the LDS *Young Woman's Journal* published her female-female love poetry, which used the word *gay,* while she was residing in Greenwich Village, where *gay* meant homosexual. *(© Utah State Historical Society. All rights reserved. Used by permission.)*

Willard E. Weihe. Solo violinist for the Tabernacle Choir, Weihe was also president in 1905 of the Salt Lake Bohemian Club, "with which many of the homosexuals in the city, male and female, had some affiliation." *(© Utah State Historical Society. All rights reserved. Used by permission.)*

Heber H. Thomas. Director of Utah's reform school, he was forced to resign because of a beating he administered in 1908 to teenage boys who engaged in "buggery" and group sex. *(© Utah State Historical Society. All rights reserved. Used by permission.)*

Caricature of effeminate males in the student magazine of LDS University (now LDS Business College) in 1909. Its caption: "A dandy is a thing that would / Be a young lady if he could, / But since he can't, does all he can / To let you know he's not a man." *(Courtesy of Manuscripts Division, University of Utah Libraries)*

Ada Dwyer Russell. Well known as a Utah Mormon actress, she entered a long-term relationship with Amy Lowell, a nationally prominent poet and lesbian, in 1912.

James Dwyer, father of Ada Dwyer Russell. In May 1913 the First Presidency learned that this cofounder of LDS University was "teaching young men that sodomy and kindred vices are not sins."

Andrew G. Johnson. In December 1913 the state supreme court overturned his sodomy conviction and freed him because oral sex was not a crime in Utah. *(Courtesy of Utah State Archives)*

Mildred J. Berryman. While a student at Westminster College (1916–22), she began a study of Salt Lake City's lesbians and gay men. *(Courtesy of June L. Mazer Lesbian Collection, West Hollywood, Calif.)*

Counselor May Anderson and Primary president Louie B. Felt. The LDS
Children's Friend in 1919 described these longtime roommates as "ardent
lovers," and labeled this photograph "THE 'DAVID AND JONATHAN' OF THE
GENERAL BOARD." *(Courtesy of Princeton University Library)*

Natacha Rambova. In 1922 this native Utahn became the wife of Rudolph Valentino, who was still married to the lesbian lover of his co-star, allegedly also Rambova's lesbian lover. *(Courtesy of the Academy of Motion Picture Arts and Sciences)*

In 1926 the University of Utah's newspaper titled this a "Hot Scene" from an all-male play at the LDS Church–owned Salt Lake Theatre. *(Courtesy of Manuscripts Division, University of Utah Libraries)*

Physical touch and Utah's male athletic teams. Although on the decline by the 1920s, such images persisted in yearbooks of Utah's high schools and colleges until the 1940s. (*Courtesy of Manuscripts Division, University of Utah Libraries*)

Patriarch Joseph F. Smith. Romantically involved with an LDS football player before marriage, Smith was forced to resign as Patriarch to the Church in 1946 after the discovery of his homosexual relationship with a navy veteran, also Mormon. (*© Utah State Historical Society. All rights reserved. Used by permission.*)

CHAPTER 8

The Coming Out of Three Prominent Mormons in 1919

"COMING OUT" was a far different experience for nineteenth-century Americans than it is today. Although the term has several meanings with reference to gay and lesbian issues, I use *coming out* here to indicate making a public reference to one's same-sex interests.[1] The homosocial, homopastoral, homotactile, and homoemotional dynamics in the nineteenth century made life somewhat easier and more secure for those Mormons who also felt the romantic and erotic side of same-sex relations. There was much that did not have to be hidden by the Mormons who felt sexual interest for those of their same gender.

It was socially and religiously acceptable for Mormon girls, boys, women, and men to walk arm-in-arm in public with those of their same gender. It was acceptable for same-sex couples to dance together at LDS Church socials. It was acceptable for Mormons to publicly or privately kiss those of their same sex, and it was okay to acknowledge that they dreamed of doing it. And as taught by the martyred prophet himself, it was acceptable for LDS "friends to lie down together, locked in the arms of love, to sleep and wake in each other's embrace." Like American culture of the time, nineteenth-century Mormonism approved and encouraged various levels of same-gender intimacy, which most Mormons experienced without an erotic response.

Of nineteenth-century society, the historian Peter Gay writes: "Passionate [same-gender] friendships begun in adolescence often survived the passage of years, the strain of physical separation, even the trauma of the partners' marriage. But these enduring attachments were generally discreet and, in any event, the nineteenth century mustered singular sympathy for warm language between friends." He adds that "the cult of friendship . . . flourishing unabated through much of the nineteenth [century], permitted men to declare their love for other men—or women for other women—with impunity."[2] Because nineteenth-century Americans almost never publicly referred to the obviously sexual side of their marital relationships, it was not necessary for Mormons (or any one else) of that era to acknowledge if there was an erotic side in their same-sex relationships.[3]

Therefore, it was possible for Americans to speak in the nineteenth-century vernacular of platonic love while actually announcing to the world their romantic and erotic attachments with persons of the same sex. Literary historians have observed this approach in the work of such nineteenth-century American writers as Emily Dickinson, Walt Whitman, Bayard Taylor, Herman Melville, William Dean Howells, Amy Lowell, George Santayana, Willa Cather, Henry James, and Mark Twain.[4] As Lowell's biographer has written, "those who had the eyes to see it or the antennae to sense it" would recognize the homoromantic and homoerotic subtexts of these works. Those who did not, would not.[5]

In such a manner, three prominent nineteenth-century Mormons apparently "came out" in public at the height of their LDS Church careers, and did so in an official LDS magazine of October 1919. Because even Berryman's study gave relatively little attention to the same-sex relationships of its anonymous Mormons, I give extended discussion to the same-sex relationships of these three prominent Mormons. The self-disclosures by Evan Stephens, Louie B. Felt, and May Anderson reveal a currently unrecognized dimension in the experience of nineteenth-century Mormons in Utah. At the very least their stories demonstrate that these prominent Mormons felt confident about expressing publicly their intensely homosocial, homoromantic, and homotactile relationships with their same-sex domestic partners.

Age sixty-five in 1919, Evan Stephens had been director of the Mormon Tabernacle Choir from 1890 until he retired in 1916. The *Contributor,* the LDS periodical for young men, had once praised Stephens as a man who in falsetto "could sing soprano like a lady, and baritone in his natural voice."[6] A tireless composer, Stephens wrote the words and music for nineteen hymns that remain in the official LDS hymn book today, more than any other single composer.[7]

The tightly knit Mormon community at church headquarters knew that Evan Stephens never married. A family who had known him for decades commented: "Concerning the reason he never married nothing could be drawn from him."[8] One biographer also observed: "Stephens' relations with women were paradoxical" and "he avoided relationships with women."[9]

Age sixty-nine in 1919, Louie B. Felt had been general president of the church's Primary organization for young children for nearly forty years. Many at church headquarters also knew that President Felt had lived with her unmarried first counselor, May Anderson, since 1889. Their live-in relationship began years before the death of Louie's husband, a polygamist who resided with his other wives after his legal wife, Louie, began living with Anderson. Even the city directory listed the co-residence of the Primary's president and counselor.[10]

Imagine such a situation today when Mormons begin to whisper about a young man's sexual orientation if he is not married by age twenty-six. Imagine the reaction of such whisperers to the description of the Tabernacle Choir director's same-sex relationships, and of the two leaders of the church's Primary organization as published in the same issue of the *Children's Friend.*

Beginning in January 1919, the magazine published monthly installments about the childhood of "Evan Bach," a play on the name of German composer J. S. Bach. Evan Stephens himself authored these third-person autobiographical articles that lacked a byline.[11] Starting with the October issue, the *Friend* devoted the three remaining issues of the year to the same-sex dynamics of his teenage life. During the next year, seven issues of this church magazine emphasized different aspects of Stephens's adult life, including his same-sex relationships. Because of the *Children's Friend*'s extensive coverage of his story, I also emphasize Stephens's experiences.

Of his arrival in Willard, Utah, at thirteen Stephens wrote: "The two great passions of his life seemed now to be growing very rapidly, *love of friendship* and *music*. His day dreams . . . were all centered around imaginary scenes he would conjure up of these things, now taking possession of his young heart." The article continued: "The good

[ward] choir leader was a lovable man who might have already been drawn to the blue-eyed, affectionate boy."[12] It was this choir leader "I most loved," Stephens wrote in the church's *Improvement Era,* and he was "crying his heart out at the loss" when the twenty-three-year-old chorister moved away. Stephens added: "I wanted to go with him."[13]

Stephens had close relationships with other members of the choir as well, who were young men in their teens and twenties: "Evan became the pet of the choir. The [young] men among whom he sat seemed to take a delight in loving him. Timidly and blushingly he would be squeezed in between them, and kindly arms generally enfolded him much as if he had been a fair sweetheart of the big brawny young men. Oh, how he loved these men, too."[14]

Stephens also acknowledged a physical dimension in his attraction to young men. He marveled at "the picturesque manliness with those coatless and braceless [suspenderless] costumes worn by the men. What freedom and grace they gave, what full manly outlines to the body and chest, what a form to admire they gave to the creature *Man.* . . . Those who saw the young men in their coatless costumes of early day, with their fine, free careless airs to correspond, [now] think of them as a truly superior race of beings."[15]

A continuation of this third-person autobiography in the *Friend* related that from age fourteen to sixteen, Stephens lived with the stonemason Shadrach Jones as his "loved young friend." Stephens gave no other reason for his decision to leave the home of his devoted parents in the same town. Evan's employment as Shadrach's helper did not require co-residence in the small town where they both lived.[16] At the time, Jones was in his late thirties and had never fathered a child by his wife.[17] After briefly returning to his family's residence in 1870, Stephens left them permanently. At age sixteen, Stephens moved in with John J. Ward, who was his same age and "dearest friend."[18]

Stephens explained, "Without 'John' nothing was worth while. With him, everything; even the hardest toil was heaven." He added, "What a treasure a chum is to an affectionate boy!"[19] The two friends were accustomed to sleeping in the same bed, since there were eight other children in the Ward family's house at the time.[20]

After three years of sharing a bed in the cramped family's house, the two young men moved out together. At nineteen, Stephens bought a two-room house (sitting room and bedroom) and began "batching it." Ward moved in and the *Children's Friend* said that this "was a happy time for Evan and John." A photograph of Stephens standing with his hand on Ward's shoulder is captioned: "WITH HIS BOY CHUM, JOHN [J.] WARD, WHEN ABOUT 21 YEARS OLD."[21]

After a total of six years of living with Stephens, Ward married in 1876, but Stephens remained close at hand. The census four years later showed him as a "boarder" just a few houses from Ward, his wife, and infant. After the June 1880 census, Stephens left their town of Willard to expand his musical career. Ward fathered ten children before Stephens's biography appeared in the *Children's Friend*. He named one of his sons Evan.[22]

That article did not mention several of Stephens's other significant "boy chums." Shortly after twenty-six-year-old Stephens moved to Logan in 1880, he met seventeen-year-old Samuel B. Mitton, organist of the nearby Wellsville Ward. Mitton's family later wrote: "From that occasion on their friendship grew and blossomed into one of the sweetest relationships that could exist between two sensitive, poetic musicians."[23] In 1882, Stephens moved to Salt Lake City to study with the Tabernacle organist, but "their visits were frequent, and over the years their correspondence was regular and candid, each bringing pure delight to the other with these contacts." Then in the spring of 1887 Samuel began seriously courting a young woman.[24]

According to Stephens, that was the same year "Horace S. Ensign became a regular companion [of mine] for many years." Ensign was not quite sixteen years old, and Stephens was thirty-three.[25] Stephens's former teenage companion, Samuel Mitton, married the next year at age twenty-five and later fathered seven children.[26] Still, Stephens and Mitton wrote letters to each other, signed "Love" during the next decades.[27]

As for Stephens and his new teenage companion, after a camping trip together at Yellowstone Park in 1889, Ensign lived next door to Stephens for several years. When Ensign turned twenty in 1891, he began openly living with thirty-seven-year-old Stephens.[28] In 1893, he accompanied the conductor on a two-week trip to Chicago. A few months later, they traveled to Chicago again when the Tabernacle Choir performed its award-winning concert at the 1893 World's Fair.[29] They were "regular companion[s]" until Ensign married in 1894 at age twenty-three. The two men remained close, however. Stephens gave Ensign a house as a wedding present and appointed him assistant conductor of the Tabernacle Choir. Eventually, Horace Ensign fathered four children and became an LDS mission president.[30]

Whenever Stephens took a long trip, he traveled with a younger male companion, usually unmarried. When the Tabernacle Choir made a ten-day concert tour to San Francisco in April 1896, Stephens traveled in the same railway car with Willard A. Christopherson, his brother, and father. The Christophersons had lived next to Stephens since 1894, the year Horace Ensign married.[31] In August 1897, forty-three-year-old Stephens took nineteen-year-old "Willie" Christopherson alone on a two-week camping trip to Yellowstone Park, but Stephens reassured Horace Ensign, who was married, in a letter from there: "you are constantly in my mind." Like Ensign, Christopherson was a member and soloist of the Tabernacle Choir.[32] During a visit to the East Coast in 1898, Stephens simply referred to his "accompanying friend," probably Christopherson.[33]

Stephens's primary residence was "State Street 1 north of Twelfth South" until a revision of the street-numbering system changed the address to 1996 South State Street. A large boating lake nearly surrounded this house, which stood on four acres of property. In addition to his house, Stephens also stayed in a downtown apartment.[34] Willard Christopherson had lived next to Stephens's State Street house from 1894 until mid-1899, when (at age twenty-two) he began sharing the same downtown apartment with forty-six-year-old Stephens.[35]

In early February 1900 Evan left for Europe with his "partner, Mr. Willard Christopherson."[36] After staying in Chicago and New York City for a month, Stephens and "his companion" boarded a ship and arrived in London on 22 March. They apparently shared a cabin room. In April, Stephens wrote the Tabernacle Choir that he and "Willie" had "a nice room" in London.[37]

He left Christopherson in London while he visited relatives in Wales, and upon his return they "decided on a fourteen days' visit to Paris." Stephens concluded: "My friend Willard stayed with me for about two months after we landed in England, and he is now in the Norwegian mission field, laboring in Christiania." Stephens returned to Salt Lake City in September 1900, too late to be included in the federal census.[38] City directories indicate that Stephens did not live with another male while Christopherson was on his full-time LDS mission.[39]

In March 1902, Stephens returned to Europe to "spend a large portion of his time visiting Norway, where his old friend and pupil, Willard Christopherson" was on a mission.[40] During his ocean trip from Boston to Liverpool, Stephens wrote: "I and Charlie Pike have a little room" aboard ship. Although he roomed with Stephens on the trip to Europe, twenty-year-old Charles R. Pike was en route to an LDS mission in Germany. Like most of Stephens's other traveling companions, Pike was a singer in the Tabernacle Choir.[41] While visiting Norway, Stephens also "had the pleasure of reuniting for a little while with my old—or young companion, Willard, sharing his labors, cares and pleasures while letting my own rest."[42]

Christopherson remained on this mission until after Stephens returned to the United States.[43] After Christopherson's return, he rented an apartment seven blocks from Stephens, where Christopherson remained until his 1904 marriage.[44]

That year, seventeen-year-old Noel S. Pratt began living with fifty-year-old Stephens at his State Street house. Like Ensign and Christopherson before him, Pratt was a singer in the Tabernacle Choir under the direction of Stephens. Pratt was also an officer of his high school's junior and senior class at the LDS University in Salt Lake City, where Stephens was professor of vocal music.[45] The LDS *Juvenile Instructor* remarked that Noel Pratt was one of Stephens's "numerous boys," and that the Stephens residence "was always the scene of youth and youthful activities."[46]

In 1907, Stephens traveled to Europe with Pratt and Stephens's loyal grandniece and housekeeper. Stephens and the twenty-year-old apparently shared a cabin room aboard ship during the two crossings of the Atlantic.[47] Before their trip together, Pratt had moved several miles south of Stephens's house. After their return in 1907, Pratt moved to an apartment a few blocks from Stephens. When the choir went by train to the West Coast for a several-week concert tour in 1909, Pratt shared a Pullman stateroom with Stephens. With them was Stephens's next boyfriend, Tom S. Thomas. Pratt became Salt Lake City's municipal judge, did not marry until age thirty-six, divorced shortly afterward, and died shortly after that.[48]

Stephens's most intense relationship with a male was only suggested by a photograph in a 1919 article in *Children's Friend*. The caption read "Tom S. Thomas, a grand-nephew and one of Professor Evan Stephens' dear boy chums." With this 1919 photograph Stephens skipped from his live-in boyfriend of the 1870s to his most recent, or as *Children's Friend* put it: "the first and last of his several life companions, who have shared his home life."[49]

Born in 1891, Tom S. Thomas Jr. was an eighteen-year-old inactive

Mormon when he began living with fifty-five-year-old Stephens. He moved in with Stephens near the time Thomas traveled to Seattle with the choir director in 1909.[50] They shared a house with the matronly housekeeper who was Thomas's second cousin and Stephens's grand-niece. The housekeeper remained a non-Mormon as long as Stephens lived.[51] Thomas had apparently stopped attending school while he lived in Idaho with his parents and did not attend during the first year he lived with Stephens. At age nineteen, with Stephens's encouragement, he began attending the LDS University in Salt Lake City as a freshman in high school. Another of Stephens's "boy chums" described Thomas as "a blond Viking who captured the eye of everyone as a superb spec-imen of manhood." The impressive and mature-looking Thomas be-came president of his sophomore class in 1911, and his final yearbook described him thus: "Aye, every inch a king," then added: "Also a 'Queener.'"[52]

During the last years they lived together in Utah, the city directory no longer listed an address for Thomas, but simply that he "r[oo]ms [with] Evan Stephens."[53] He accompanied Stephens on the choir's month-long trip to the eastern states in 1911, the same year Thomas was class president at the LDS high school. However, the choir's busi-ness manager, George D. Pyper, discreetly deleted Thomas's name from the passenger list of the choir and "tourists" as published by the church's official magazine, *Improvement Era*.[54] Pyper had apparently been uncomfortable about same-sex relationships since 1887, when he served as the judge in the first trial of a sensational sodomy case in-volving teenagers.[55]

After living with Stephens for seven years, twenty-five-year-old Thomas prepared to move to New York City to begin medical school in 1916. Stephens had put Thomas through the LDS high school and the University of Utah's premedical program and was going to pay for his medical training as well, but Stephens wanted to continue living with the younger man. He resigned as director of the Tabernacle Choir in July. He later explained that he did this so that he could "reside, if I wished, at New York City, where I was taking a nephew I was educat-ing as a physician, to enter Columbia University."[56] Stephens gave up his career for the "blond Viking" who had become the love of his life.[57]

In October 1916 the *Deseret Evening News* reported the two men's living arrangements in New York City: "Prof. Evan Stephens and his nephew, Mr. Thomas, are living at 'The Roland,' east Fifty-ninth street" and indicated this was "the same hostelry he [Stephens] used to patronize years ago when he was here for a winter with Mr. Willard Christopherson." Columbia University's medical school was located on the same street. The report added that Thomas intended to move into an apartment with eight other students near the medical school.[58] Stephens later indicated that Thomas's intended student-living arrangement did not alter his "desire" to be near the young man. A few weeks after the *Deseret News* article, the police conducted a well-publicized raid on a homosexual bathhouse in New York City.[59]

In November, Stephens wrote about his activities in "Gay New York." He referred to Central Park and "its flotsam of lonely souls—like myself—who wander into its retreats for some sort of companionship." For New Yorkers who defined themselves by the sexual slang of the time as "gay," Stephens's words would have appeared as a description of the common practice of seeking same-sex intimacy with strangers in Central Park.[60] Just days after the commemorative celebration in April 1917 that brought him back to Utah, Stephens said he had "a desire to return ere long to my nephew, Mr. Thomas, in New York."[61]

Stephens apparently returned later that spring and took up residence in the East Village of lower Manhattan, which is where the census indicated Thomas was living.[62] By then there were so many openly gay men and male couples living in Greenwich Village that a local song proclaimed: "Fairyland's not far from Washington Square."[63] Long before Stephens and Thomas arrived, New Yorkers used *fairy* and *fairies* as derogatory words for male homosexuals.[64] In fact, just before Stephens said he intended to return to Thomas in New York in 1917, one of the East Village's cross-dressing dances ("drag balls") was attended by two thousand people—"the usual crowd of homosexualists" according to one hostile investigator.[65]

Thomas apparently wanted to avoid the stigma of being called a New York "fairy," which had none of the light-hearted ambiguity of the "Queener" nickname from his school days in Utah.[66] Unlike the openness of his co-residence with Stephens in Utah, Thomas never listed his Village address in the New York City directories.[67] However, this relationship did not last long in Manhattan. "After some months," Stephens returned to Utah permanently, while Thomas remained in the Village. Thomas married within two years and fathered two children.[68]

Shortly after Stephens's final return from New York in 1917, he befriended thirty-year-old Ortho Fairbanks. Like most of Stephens's other Salt Lake City "boy chums," Fairbanks had been a member of the Tabernacle Choir since his late teens. Stephens once told him: "I believe I love you, Ortho, as much as your father does." In 1917, Stephens set up the younger man in one of the houses Stephens owned in the Highland Park subdivision of Salt Lake City. Fairbanks remained there until he married at nearly thirty-five years of age. He eventually fathered five children.[69]

However, during the five-year period after Stephens returned from New York City, Stephens did not live with Ortho Fairbanks or any other male.[70] No one had taken Thomas's place in Stephens's heart or home. Two years after Fairbanks began living in the Highland Park house, the *Children's Friend* identified Stephens's former "boy chum" Tom S. Thomas as the "last of his several life companions, who have shared his home life."[71] There is no record of the letters Stephens might have written during this period to his married "blond Viking" in the east.

However, neither Thomas nor Fairbanks was Stephens's last "boy chum." Three months after Fairbanks married in August 1922, Stephens (then sixty-eight) took a trip to Los Angeles and San Francisco with seventeen-year-old John Wallace Packham as "his young companion." Wallace Packham was a member of the Male Glee Club and in student government in high school at LDS University.[72] The Salt Lake City directory showed Packham living a few houses from Stephens as a student in 1924–25. At that time Stephens privately described Packham as the "besht boy I ish gott," although it is unclear why he imitated a drunkard's speech.[73]

After Wallace moved to California in 1926, Evan Stephens lived with no other male. From then until his death, Stephens rented the front portion of his State Street house to a succession of married couples in their thirties, while he lived in the rear of the house.[74]

When Stephens prepared his last will and testament in 1927, twenty-two-year-old Packham was still in California, where Stephens was supporting the younger man's education. Stephens's will divided the bulk of his possessions among the LDS Church, his brother, his housekeeper-niece, "and J. Wallace Packham, a friend." Packham eventually married twice and fathered two children.[75]

When Stephens died in 1930, one of his former "boy chums" confided to his diary: "No one will know what a loss his passing is to me. The world will never seem the same to me again."[76] Although Wallace

Packham received more of the composer's estate than any of Stephens's former "boy chums," Stephens also gave small bequests to John J. Ward, Horace S. Ensign, Willard A. Christopherson, the wife of deceased Noel S. Pratt, Thomas S. Thomas, and Ortho Fairbanks.[77]

As a teenager, Stephens had doubted the marriage prediction of his psychic aunt. "I see you married three times, two of the ladies are blondes, and one a brunette." She added: "I see no children; but you will be very happy."[78] Stephens fulfilled his aunt's predictions about having no children and being happy. However, beginning with sixteen-year-old John Ward a year later, Stephens inverted his aunt's prophecy about the gender and hair color of those described by the LDS magazine as "his several life companions." Instead of having more "blondes" as wives, Stephens had more "brunettes" as "boy-chums."[79]

The *Children's Friend* even printed Stephens's poem titled "Friends," which showed that each of these young men had shared his bed:

> We have lived and loved together,
> 　Slept together, dined and supped,
> Felt the pain of little quarrels,
> 　Then the joy of waking up;
> Held each other's hands in sorrows,
> 　Shook them hearty in delight,
> Held sweet converse through the day time,
> 　Kept it up through half the night.[80]

Whether or not Stephens intended it, well-established word usage allowed a sexual meaning in that last line of his poem about male bedmates. Since the 1780s, "keep it up" was common slang for "to prolong a debauch."[81]

Seventeen years before his poem "Friends" contained this possible reference to sexual intimacy with his youthful bedmates, Stephens indicated that there was a socially forbidden dimension in his same-sex friendships. In his introduction to an original composition, Stephens invoked the examples of Ruth and Naomi, David and Jonathan, Damon and Pythias, and then referred to "one whom we could love if we dare to do so." Indicating that the problem involved society's rules, Stephens explained that "we feel as if there is something radically wrong in the present make up and constitution of things and we are almost ready to rebel at the established order." Then the LDS high school's student magazine printed the following lines from Stephens's same-sex love song: "Ah, friend, could you and I conspire / To wreck this sorry scheme of things entire, / We'd break it into bits, and then— / Remold it nearer to the heart's desire."[82] The object of this desire may have been eighteen-year-old Louis Shaw, a member of the Male Glee Club at the LDS high school where Stephens was a music teacher. Shaw later became president of the Bohemian Club, identified as a social haven for Salt Lake City's lesbians and gay men.[83]

The words of this 1903 song indicate that Evan Stephens wanted to live in a culture where he could freely share homoerotic experiences with the young men he openly loved in every other way. Historical evidence cannot demonstrate whether he actually created a private world of sexual intimacy with his beloved "boy chums" who "shared his home life."

It can only be a matter of speculation whether Stephens had sex with any of the young men he loved, lived with, and slept with throughout most of his life. If there was any unexpressed erotic desire, it is possible that only Stephens felt it, since all his "boy chums" eventually married. Homoerotic desire could have been absent altogether or unconsciously sublimated or consciously suppressed. Of his personal experiences, Stephens once wrote: "some of it [is] even too sacred to be told freely[,] only to myself."[84]

Whether or not Stephens's male friendships were homoerotic, both published and private accounts showed that the love of the Tabernacle Choir director for young men was powerful, charismatic, reciprocal, and enduring. One biographer wrote that Stephens "attached himself passionately to the male friends of his youth, and brought many young men, some distantly related, into his home for companionship."[85]

With its emphasis on the love of a young man for other men, the Stephens third-person autobiography was a developmental introduction for the female-female emphasis in the same October 1919 issue of the *Children's Friend*. Two separate articles (also in the third person without a byline) used emotional and physical terms to describe the mature love between two Mormon women. The LDS magazine featured a photograph of May Anderson and Louie B. Felt, with Felt so close that her breast was touching Anderson's shoulder. The caption reads: "THE 'DAVID AND JONATHAN' OF THE GENERAL BOARD."[86] Rocky O'Donovan regards that as a virtual announcement that Felt and Anderson were lesbians.[87] In view of the *Friend*'s descriptions of these women and the linkage of their articles to the Stephens article, I agree that the entire October issue was an extraordinary affirmation of same-sex love and intimacy.

The two articles about the Primary presidency's "David and Jonathan" were filled with references to female love and intimacy. After eight years of childless marriage to her husband, Louie B. Felt "fell in love with Lizzie Mineer." Felt asked her husband to marry this "beautiful young lady" as a plural wife so that Felt could "share his love and her home with Lizzie." Through this polygamous marriage in 1875, "renewed love and happiness came to three instead of two." Six years later her husband married "another beautiful and faithful Latter-day Saint girl," and Felt also "shared her life and love." Each plural wife bore children to Felt's husband.[88]

O'Donovan regards this polygamous arrangement as a "medium for Lesbian expression among women, who could easily (albeit covertly) eroticize each other's bodies through the gaze of their shared husband."[89] That is not simply a projection of twentieth-century concepts on the nineteenth century, because courts in Illinois and Indiana during the 1870s granted several divorces to husbands who learned that their wives had married them only to be near a female "friend."[90] However, without a diary of her intimate thoughts, it is impossible to verify O'Donovan's claim that Louie Felt chose her husband's other wives as a covert "medium for Lesbian expression." Nevertheless, like the similar article on Stephens in the LDS magazine, homoemotional attachments dominated Felt's story as told by her live-in companion, Anderson.

A separate article on May Anderson in this October 1919 edition of *Children's Friend* described the meeting of the nineteen-year-old immigrant and the thirty-three-year-old president of the Primary: Anderson "looked up and saw a most beautiful woman. . . . She was so fascinated by [Felt's] blue eyes and lovely golden hair that she did not see the little girl who stood by her side." Those descriptive phrases indicated that physical attractiveness was part of what drew Anderson to Felt. The article noted: "This was the first meeting of those who are now known as 'The Primary David and Jonathan.'"[91]

The church magazine continued: "the friendship which had started when Sister Felt and Mary [Anderson] met on the train, ripened into love. Those who watched their devotion to each other declare that there never were more ardent lovers than these two. And strange to say during this time of love feasting, Mary changed her name to May because it seemed to be more agreeable to both."[92] In establishing their new relationship, the younger woman publicly took a different name, as would a new bride, rather than adopting a private nickname between close friends.

The article reported that after Anderson moved in with Felt the two had "never been separated unless duty called them away from each other." The article on Felt added that the two women shared the same bed: "When they were too tired to sit up any longer they put on their bathrobes and crawled into bed to work until the wee small hours of the night."[93] It is difficult to overlook the erotic dimension of that acknowledgment when coupled with the magazine's statement that "there never were more ardent lovers than these two." May Anderson was the editor when this publication described her relationship with Louie Felt.

Moreover, there was significance in the timing of this October 1919 *Children's Friend* affirmation of same-sex love. In mid-September 1919, the church's *Deseret Evening News* announced the beginning of the first International Conference of Women Physicians in New York City. The American women's magazine *Good Housekeeping* called this meeting "the most important conference held in this generation—perhaps in the history of the world."[94]

This conference included several positive views of homosexuality. Dr. Constance E. Long, president of the Federation of Medical Women of the British Isles, discussed "homosexual love" and concluded: "Justice demands that we must allow the genuine homo-sexual to express what is his normal sexuality in his own way."[95] Dr. Eleanor Bertine, who specifically endorsed Dr. Long's paper in advance, questioned whether there was any "moral difference between a deliberately childless, heterosexual marriage and a homosexual relationship." She was also on the national board of the Young Women's Christian Association (YWCA). Dr. Trigant Burrow began her discussion: "Sex is life. It is life in its deepest inherency." In this respect, she concluded that the only difference between normality and abnormality "lies merely in the greater weight of numbers."[96]

Still another paper at the conference endorsed the healthiness of masturbation. Prof. Horace W. Frink of Cornell University's medical school declared that "masturbation must be in essence a benign phenomenon" which "has occurred to some extent in the lives of about 90 per cent. of all people, the figure being somewhat over ninety for men, and somewhat, perhaps quite a little, below it for women."[97]

Dr. Ellen Brooke Ferguson, formerly staff physician of the Deseret Hospital of Utah, was living in New York City at the time of this conference of women physicians. Also another Mormon physician, a man, was an intern at the Brooklyn City Hospital.[98] Some of the other sixteen Mormon or Utah female physicians in 1919 may have attended this unprecedented medical meeting.[99]

One resident of Manhattan in September 1919 had medical interest in the conference of women physicians and a personal interest in its presentations about same-sex love. Tom S. Thomas, whose "boy chum" relationship with Evan Stephens was emphasized in the *Friend*, was starting his fourth year at Columbia University's medical school.

It is unclear when reports of the conference's presentations reached Utah, but the LDS *Relief Society Magazine* summarized the proceedings of the "sensible, cultured, and scientifically trained women" who spoke at this meeting of physicians.[100] A few weeks after that conference's statements about homosexuality, May Anderson, as editor, devoted most of the *Children's Friend* to same-sex love and particularly to her companionship with Louie Felt.

In October 1919 the *Relief Society Magazine* also featured a tribute to Rev. Anna Howard Shaw. Her relationship to the suffragist Susan B. Anthony was remarkably similar to the "ardent lover" relationship of May Anderson and Louie B. Felt as described in the *Children's Friend* of the same month.[101] Just as Felt was president of the LDS Primary organization when she met Anderson, Susan Anthony was president of the National Woman Suffrage Association when she met Anna Shaw. Just as Felt was significantly older than Anderson, Anthony was twenty-seven years older than Shaw. Just as Felt made Anderson her counselor, Anthony made Shaw her vice president.[102] In effect, the *Relief Society Magazine* in October 1919 offered its readers a secular role model whose female-female relationship paralleled the one emphasized in the *Children's Friend* of the same month.

Like Anderson and Felt, Shaw and Anthony were inseparable. Shaw's autobiography acknowledged that from 1888 "until Miss Anthony's death in 1906 we two were rarely separated."[103] Prior to the Relief Society tribute, Anthony's published biography also quoted Shaw's letter to her: "I miss you as a body must miss its soul when it has gone out . . . and I am yours with dearest love."[104] Susan B. Anthony wrote: "I give myself over entirely to Miss Shaw. Wherever she goes I shall probably go."[105]

Anthony's words echoed the Bible's most romantic vow between two women (now often quoted in heterosexual marriage ceremonies): "for whither thou goest, I will go; and where thou lodgest, I will lodge" (Ruth 1:16). One of the places where the two suffragists had spoken and lodged together was Salt Lake City.[106] Shaw was at the deathbed of Susan B. Anthony, whose last will and testament divided her estate equally between her sister, her niece, and her "friend Anna H. Shaw."[107]

A few years before the *Relief Society Magazine*'s tribute to Shaw, newspapers had also printed a "sensational full-page article" about the young women with whom Shaw surrounded herself in a secluded summer cottage. The newspaper article's title was "The Adamless Eden," and Shaw publicly referred to the implied lesbianism of the story as "almost libelous."[108] Reverend Shaw also told a young female friend that she said this prayer every night of her life: "I thank Thee for all good but for nothing more than I have been saved from the misery of marriage."[109]

It is possible to regard as sheer coincidence the fact that the LDS women's magazine featured a suffragist who was publicly rumored to be a lesbian during the same month that the LDS children's magazine told of the "ardent lovers" in the church's Primary presidency. However, under the circumstances, that strains the likelihood of mere coincidence.[110] There was not even a hint of same-sex dynamics in the pre-1919 autobiographies and biographies of Stephens, Felt, and Anderson.[111]

In 1919, the announced theme for October's churchwide Sunday school lessons for all fourteen-year-old Mormons was "What It Means to Be a Mormon." The goal of the October 12 lesson was "to have the class feel deeply in their hearts that no matter what the temptation, or the inducement, or the lure, they will remain honest."[112] Even though they were writing in the bilingualism of nineteenth-century homosexuals, Evan Stephens, Louie B. Felt, and May Anderson took a risk by telling of their same-sex relationships so honestly in October 1919.

Few, if any, other prominent Mormon bachelors had shared the same bed with a succession of "beloved" teenage boys for years at a time. The *Children's Friend* articles invited the conclusion that sexual intimacy was part of the personal relationship that Evan Stephens shared only with young men. Felt and Anderson risked a similar guilt-by-association conclusion by linking their own "ardent lovers" story with his.

At the least, these three prominent Mormons had announced themselves as role models for homosocial, homoromantic, and homotactile relationships. For Mormons who regarded themselves as gay, lesbian, or bisexual and had "the eyes to see it or the antennae to sense it," the *Children's Friend* of 1919 was also supportive of their own romantic and erotic same-sex relationships. About the time of this publication, Mildred Berryman began her study of homosexually identified Mormons in Salt Lake City.

However, for the vast majority of Mormons whose same-sex dynamics had no romantic or erotic dimensions, this publication passed by with no special notice. Certainly LDS president Heber J. Grant did not discern the implications of what the three had apparently done: Felt remained Primary general president until 1925, when Anderson succeeded her "ardent lover" in that position.[113] Even "coming out" in the *Children's Friend* did not require Mormon leaders to confront the reality of homoerotic behaviors. The nineteenth-century's "warm language between friends" covered a multitude of relationships.

NOTES

1. Wayne R. Dynes, ed., *Encyclopedia of Homosexuality*, 2 vols. (New York: Garland, 1990), 1:251–54; see also Barry M. Dank, "Coming Out in the Gay World," *Psychiatry* 34 (May 1971): 180–97; Rob Eichberg, *Coming Out: An Act of Love* (New York: Dutton, 1990); Gilbert Herdt, "'Coming Out' as a Rite of Passage: A Chicago Study," in Herdt, ed., *Gay Culture in America: Essays from the Field* (Boston: Beacon Press, 1992); Craig O'Neill and Kathleen Ritter, *Coming Out Within: Stages of Spiritual Awakening for Lesbians and Gay Men* (San Francisco: Harper, 1992); Stephen Likosky, ed., *Coming Out: An Anthology of International Gay and Lesbian Writings* (New York: Pantheon Books, 1992); Mary V. Borhek, *Coming Out to Parents: A Two-Way Survival Guide for Lesbians and Gay Men and Their Parents*, rev. ed. (Cleveland: Pilgrim Press, 1993); and George Chauncey, *Gay New York: Gender, Urban Culture, and the Making of the Gay Male World, 1890–1940* (New York: Basic Books/HarperCollins, 1994), 8n.

2. Peter Gay, *The Bourgeois Experience: Victoria to Freud*, vol. 2, *The Tender Passion* (New York: Oxford University Press, 1986), 217.

3. However, some readers apparently require that kind of explicit acknowledgment of sex between persons involved in demonstrably romantic, long-term relationships during which they shared a bed. See the responses to such a re-

quirement in Blanche Wiesen Cook, "The Historical Denial of Lesbianism," *Radical History Review* 20 (Spring–Summer 1979): 60–65; Leila J. Rupp, "'Imagine My Surprise': Women's Relationships in Historical Perspective," *Frontiers: A Journal of Women's Studies* 5 (Fall 1980): 61–62, 67; Walter L. Williams, *The Spirit and the Flesh: Sexual Diversity in American Indian Culture* (Boston: Beacon Press, 1986), 162.

4. By nineteenth-century authors, I mean those who reached adulthood in the nineteenth century, even if they published in the twentieth century. See chap. 4, notes 5, 46, 52, and 53 for sources on Dickinson and Whitman; Newton Arvin, *Herman Melville* (New York: William Sloan Associates, 1950), 128–30; Leslie A. Fiedler, *Love and Death in the American Novel* (New York: Criterion Books, 1960), 522, 531–38; Edwin Haviland Miller, *Melville* (New York: George Braziller, 1975), 234–50; Jeffrey Meyers, *Homosexuality and Literature, 1890–1930* (Montreal: McGill-Queens University Press, 1977), 20–31; Robert K. Martin, "The 'High Felicity' of Comradeship: A New Reading of Roderick Hudson," *American Literary Realism* 11 (Spring 1978): 100–108; Georges-Michel Sarotte, *Like a Brother, like a Lover: Male Homosexuality in the American Novel and Theater from Herman Melville to James Baldwin*, trans. Richard Miller (Garden City, N.Y.: Anchor Press/Doubleday, 1978), 12–13, 73, 78–83, 197–211; Robert K. Martin, "Bayard Taylor's Valley of Bliss: The Pastoral and the Search for Form," *Markham Review* 9 (Fall 1979): 13–17; Robert K. Martin, *The Homosexual Tradition in American Poetry* (Austin: University of Texas Press, 1979), 3–89, 97–114; Deborah Lambert, "The Defeat of a Hero: Autonomy and Sexuality in *My Antonia*," *American Literature* 53 (Jan. 1982): 676–90; Richard Hall, "Henry James: Interpreting an Obsessive Memory," *Journal of Homosexuality* 8 (Spring–Summer 1983): 83–97; Elizabeth Stevens Prioleau, *The Circle of Eros: Sexuality in the Work of William Dean Howells* (Durham: Duke University Press, 1983), 110; Sharon O'Brien, "'The Thing Not Named': Willa Cather as a Lesbian Writer," *Signs: Journal of Women in Culture and Society* 9 (Summer 1984): 576–99; Leon Edel, *Henry James: A Life* (New York: Harper and Row, 1985), 83, 245–46, 497, as condensed from his multivolume biography published decades earlier; John W. Crowley, *The Black Heart's Truth: The Early Career of W. D. Howells* (Chapel Hill: University of North Carolina Press, 1985), 89, 91, 97–99; Joanna Russ, "To Write 'Like a Woman': Transformation of Identity in the Work of Willa Cather," *Journal of Homosexuality* 12 (May 1986): 77–87; Timothy Dow Adams, "My Gay Antonia: The Politics of Willa Cather's Lesbianism," *Journal of Homosexuality* 12 (May 1986): 89–98; Robert K. Martin, *Hero, Captain, and Stranger: Male Friendship, Social Critique, and Literary Form in the Sea Novels of Herman Melville* (Chapel Hill: University of North Carolina Press, 1986), 6–7, 14–16, 26, 51–58, 63–64, 73–74, 105; Eve Kosofsky Sedgwick, "The Beast in the Closet: James and the Writing of

Homosexual Panic," in Ruth Bernard Yeazell, ed., *Sex, Politics, and Science in the Nineteenth Century Novel* (Baltimore: Johns Hopkins University Press, 1986), 148–86; Sharon O'Brien, *Willa Cather: The Emerging Voice* (New York: Oxford University Press, 1987), 127–46, 205–22, 357–69; John McCormick, *George Santayana: A Biography* (New York: Alfred A. Knopf, 1987), 49–52, 334; John W. Crowley, *The Mask of Fiction: Essays on W.D. Howells* (Amherst: University of Massachusetts Press, 1989), 56–82; Susan Gillman, *Dark Twins: Imposture and Identity in Mark Twain's America* (Chicago: University of Chicago Press, 1989), 34, 99, 119–22, 124; Robert K. Martin, "Knights-Errant and Gothic Seducers: The Representation of Male Friendship in Mid-Nineteenth-Century America," in Martin Bauml Duberman, Martha Vicinus, and George Chauncey Jr., eds., *Hidden from History: Reclaiming the Gay and Lesbian Past* (New York: New American Library, 1989), 169–82; Zan Dale Robinson, *Semiotic and Psychoanalytical Interpretation of Herman Melville's Fiction* (San Francisco: Mellon Research University Press, 1991), 53, 100; John Bryant, *Melville and Repose: The Rhetoric of Humor in the American Renaissance* (New York: Oxford University Press, 1993), 189–91, 217; Eve Kosofsky Sedgwick, *Tendencies* (Durham: Duke University Press, 1993), 73–103, 167–76; Mary W. Blanchard, "Boundaries and the Victorian Body: Aesthetic Fashion in Gilded Age America," *American Historical Review* 100 (Feb. 1995): 43–44; Neil Miller, *Out of the Past: Gay and Lesbian History from 1869 to the Present* (New York: Vintage/Random House, 1995), 64–67; Byrne R. S. Fone, *A Road to Stonewall, 1750–1969: Male Homosexuality and Homophobia in English and American Literature* (New York: Twayne, 1995), 41–55.

5. Jean Gould, *Amy: The World of Amy Lowell and the Imagist Movement* (New York: Dodd, Mead, 1975), 259.

6. Evan Stephens (b. 28 June 1854; d. 27 Oct. 1930); Andrew Jenson, *Latter-day Saint Biographical Encyclopedia*, 4 vols. (Salt Lake City: Deseret News Press and Andrew Jenson History, 1901–36), 1:740, 4:247; B. F. Cummings Jr., "Shining Lights: Professor Evan Stephens," *The Contributor, Representing the Young Men's Mutual Improvement Association of the Latter-day Saints* 16 (Sept. 1895): 655.

7. *Hymns of the Church of Jesus Christ of Latter-day Saints* (Salt Lake City: Church of Jesus Christ of Latter-day Saints, 1985).

8. Richard Bolton Kennedy, "Precious Moments with Evan Stephens, by Samuel Bailey Mitton and Others," Salt Lake City, 25 May 1983, 8, Family History Library of the Church of Jesus Christ of Latter-day Saints, Salt Lake City, Utah (hereafter LDS Family History Library). There is a brief discussion of Evan Stephens in Rocky O'Donovan, "'The Abominable and Detestable Crime against Nature': A Brief History of Homosexuality and Mormonism, 1840–1980," in Brent Corcoran, ed., *Multiply and Replenish: Mormon Essays on Sex and Family* (Salt Lake City: Signature Books, 1994), 142–43.

9. Ray L. Bergman, *The Children Sang: The Life and Music of Evan Stephens with the Mormon Tabernacle Choir* (Salt Lake City: Northwest, 1992), 182. In 1930 a woman claimed (185–86) that before her marriage (actually June 1869), Stephens told her his fiancée had just died. He would, however, have been only fourteen.

10. Sarah Louise ("Louie") Bouton Felt (b. 5 May 1850; d. 1928) married Joseph H. Felt as his first wife in 1866, had no children, and was general Primary President from 1880 to 1925. Mary ("May") Anderson (b. 8 June 1864; d. 1946) was Louie B. Felt's counselor in the Salt Lake City Eleventh Ward, then Primary general secretary (1890–1905), then first counselor to Felt (1905–25), then Felt's successor as general Primary President. Jenson, *Latter-day Saint Biographical Encyclopedia*, 4:271–72, 282–83; Susan Staker Oman, "Nurturing LDS Primaries: Louie Felt and May Anderson, 1880–1940," *Utah Historical Quarterly* 49 (Summer 1981): 262–76. Salt Lake City directories did not list May Anderson in co-residence with Louie B. Felt until 1896. From 1923 to Felt's death in 1928, the city directories show them residing in different parts of Salt Lake City. Available evidence does not indicate if the relationship of the two women intensified in 1896 or diminished in 1923. *Salt Lake City Directory, 1896* (Salt Lake City: R. L. Polk, 1896), 126, 292; *Salt Lake City Directory, 1922* (Salt Lake City: R. L. Polk, 1922), 77, 320. Despite apparent gaps in city directory listings, Carol Cornwall Madsen and Susan Staker Oman, in *Sisters and Little Saints: One Hundred Years of Primary* (Salt Lake City: Deseret Book, 1979), 36, observed that "the two women lived together for nearly three decades."

11. Bergman, *The Children Sang,* 219, 279.

12. [Evan Stephens], "Evan Bach: A True Story for Little Folk, by a Pioneer," *Children's Friend* 18 (Oct. 1919): 386, 387; for the acknowledgment of Stephens as the subject, see *Children's Friend* 18 (Dec. 1919): [468] (caption), "PROFESSOR EVAN STEPHENS, OUR 'EVAN BACH'"; Evan Stephens, "The Life Story of Evan Stephens," *Juvenile Instructor* 65 (Dec. 1930): 720.

13. Evan Stephens, "Going Home to Willard," *Improvement Era* 19 (Oct. 1916): 1090; "A Talk Given by Prof. Evan Stephens before the Daughters of the Pioneers, Hawthorne Camp, Feb. 5, 1930," typescript, Utah State Historical Society, Salt Lake City, published as "The Great Musician," in Kate B. Carter, ed., *Our Pioneer Heritage*, 20 vols. (Salt Lake City: Daughters of Utah Pioneers, 1958–77), 10:86; see also Cummings, "Shining Lights," 654; Bergman, *The Children Sang,* 49, 54.

14. Stephens, "Evan Bach" (Oct. 1919): 387. Although the phrasing of the sentence would lead the reader to expect the words "gently enfolded," the published article used "generally enfolded."

15. [Evan Stephens], "Evan Bach: A True Story for Little Folk, by a Pioneer," *Children's Friend* 18 (Nov. 1919): 432.

16. Ibid., 430; Cummings, in "Shining Lights," 655, noted that "Evan was employed by a stone mason, whose name was Shadrach Jones"; see also Bergman, *The Children Sang,* 57. Stephens, in "Life Story" (Dec. 1930): 720, observed that from 1868 to 1870, he "helped to build stone walls and houses in Willard."

17. Entry for Shadrach Jones (b. 17 Nov. 1832 in Wales; md. 9 July 1853, no children; d. 1883) in Ancestral File, LDS Family History Library (hereafter LDS Ancestral File); Jenson, *Latter-day Saint Biographical Encyclopedia,* 3:660–61; "In Box Elder County," in Kate B. Carter, ed., *Heart Throbs of the West,* 12 vols. (Salt Lake City: Daughters of Utah Pioneers, 1939–51), 11:22; Teddy Griffith, "A Heritage of Stone in Willard," *Utah Historical Quarterly* 43 (Summer 1975): 290–98. The U.S. 1870 Census of Willard, Box Elder County, Utah, sheet 78, microfilm, LDS Family History Library, mistakenly listed Jones by the first name "Frederick," as a stone mason, with wife Mary who "cannot write." The U.S. 1880 Census of Willard, Box Elder County, Utah, enumeration district 5, sheet 72–A, microfilm, LDS Family History Library, listed him as Shadrach, with consistent ages for him and wife Mary who "cannot write."

18. Quotation from Stephens, "Evan Bach" (Oct. 1919): 389; [Evan Stephens], "Evan Bach: A True Story for Little Folk, by a Pioneer," *Children's Friend* 18 (Dec. 1919): 470; see also Stephens, "Life Story" (Dec. 1930): 720; Bergman, *The Children Sang,* 56; see also O'Donovan, "'Abominable and Detestable Crime,'" 142–43, for the Stephens-Ward relationship.

19. Stephens, "Going Home to Willard," 1090; Bergman, *The Children Sang,* 56.

20. U.S. 1870 Census of Willard, Utah, sheet 78; see chap. 3 for the same-sex sleeping arrangements of children in early Mormon families.

21. Stephens, "Going Home to Willard," 1092, and Stephens, "Evan Bach" (Oct. 1919): 389 for "batching" references, (Dec. 1919): 471 for "happy time" quotation, and (Oct. 1919): 388 for photograph; see also [Evan Stephens], "Evan Bach: A True Story for Little Folk, by a Pioneer," *Children's Friend* 19 (Mar. 1920): 97; Bergman, *The Children Sang,* 64–65, for the Stephens-Ward living relationship. The *Children's Friend* mistakenly gave John Ward's middle initial as "Y."

22. U.S. 1880 Census of Willard, Utah, enumeration district 5, sheet 73–B; entry for John J. Ward (b. 23 Jan. 1854 in Willard, Utah; md. 1876, 10 children) in LDS Ancestral File. Stephens, in "Life Story" (Dec. 1930): 720, said that in "1879— Accepted a position in Logan as organist of the Logan Tabernacle." However, he accepted the position in 1880, remained a resident of Willard, and commuted to Logan as necessary. Bergman, *The Children Sang,* 69. The federal census of June 1880 showed him as a resident of Willard, not Logan. Some of the other dates in Evan's autobiography are demonstrably in error.

23. Samuel Bailey Mitton (b. 21 Mar. 1863; md. 1888, 7 children; d. 1954); Victor L. Lindblad, *Biography of Samuel Bailey Mitton* (Salt Lake City: by the author, 1965), 69, quotation from 293, copy in Utah State Historical Society; Jenson, *Latter-day Saint Biographical Encyclopedia,* 3:167–68.

24. Stephens, "Life Story" (Dec. 1930): 721; Bergman, *The Children Sang,* 75–76; Lindblad, *Mitton,* 7, quotation from 293.

25. Evan Stephens, "The Life Story of Evan Stephens," *Juvenile Instructor* 66 (Jan. 1931): 10; Horace S. Ensign Jr. was born 10 Nov. 1871 and was probably still fifteen years old when Stephens met him in 1887. See Jenson, *Latter-day Saint Biographical Encyclopedia,* 4:236.

26. La Rayne B. Christensen, Wilma J. Hall, and Ruth H. Maughan, *Windows of Wellsville, 1856–1984* (Providence, Utah: Keith W. Watkins and Sons, 1985), 619; Lindblad, *Mitton,* 322–60.

27. "From One Musician to Another: Extract from a letter written by Samuel B. Mitton, of Logan, to Evan Stephens of Salt Lake City," undated, but signed "Love to you," in *Juvenile Instructor* 65 (Oct. 1930): 599; Evan Stephens to Samuel B. Mitton, 7 December 1924, in Kennedy, "Precious Moments," 26–27; Stephens to Mitton, 14 Mar., 19 June 1921 in Bergman, *The Children Sang,* 236, 238.

28. *Salt Lake City Directory for 1890* (Salt Lake City: R. L. Polk, 1890), 274, 580, showed that Ensign had a room in a house next to Stephens's house. *Utah Gazetteer . . . 1892–93* (Salt Lake City: Stenhouse, 1892), 284, 676, and *Salt Lake City Directory, 1896,* 282, 654, showed them living together. Stephens referred to their trip "through the Park . . . seven or eight years ago" in his letter to Horace S. Ensign, 18 Aug. 1897, in *Deseret Evening News, 26* Aug. 1897, 5.

29. Evan Stephens, "The World's Fair Gold Medal, Continued from the September number of 'The Children's Friend,'" *Children's Friend* 19 (Oct. 1920): 420; "Making Ready to Go: Names of the Fortunate Four Hundred Who Will Leave for Chicago Tomorrow," *Deseret Evening News,* 28 Aug. 1893, 1; "The Choir Returns: Our Famous Singers Complete Their Tour," *Deseret Evening News,* 13 Sept. 1893, 1.

30. Evan Stephens, "The Life Story of Evan Stephens," *Juvenile Instructor* 66 (Mar. 1931): 133; *Salt Lake City Directory, 1898* (Salt Lake City: R. L. Polk, 1898), 272, 712; "Horace Ensign Is Appointed: New Leader for the Tabernacle Choir Chosen Last Night," *Deseret Evening News,* 19 Jan. 1900, 8; "Tabernacle Choir in Readiness for Tour of Eastern States," *Deseret Evening News,* 21 Oct. 1911, sect. 3, p. 1; Bergman, *The Children Sang,* 119, 214; Andrew Jenson, *Encyclopedic History of the Church of Jesus Christ of Latter-day Saints* (Salt Lake City: Deseret News, 1941), 374; entries for Horace S. Ensign and Mary L. Whitney in LDS Ancestral File; "H.S. Ensign Dies at Home," *Deseret Evening News,* 29 Aug. 1944, 9.

31. List of occupants of "Car No. 6" in "The Choir's Tour: Will Begin Monday Morning and Cover a Period of Ten Days," *Deseret Evening News,* 11 Apr. 1896, 8; *Salt Lake City Directory, 1894–5* (Salt Lake City: R. L. Polk, 1894), 219.

32. Stephens to Horace S. Ensign, 18 Aug. 1897, from Yellowstone Park, printed in full in "Evan Stephens' Bear Stories," *Deseret Evening News,* 26 Aug. 1897, 5; Bergman, *The Children Sang,* 203. See also Mary Musser Barnes, "An Historical Survey of the Salt Lake Tabernacle Choir of the Church of Jesus Christ of Latter-day Saints" (M.A. thesis, University of Iowa, 1936), 93, 136. For the biography of Christopherson (b. 15 Oct. 1877), see Noble Warrum, *Utah since Statehood,* 4 vols. (Chicago: S. J. Clarke, 1920), 4:736; and J. Cecil Alter, *Utah: The Storied Domain,* 3 vols. (Chicago: American Historical Society, 1932), 2:484.

33. "Stephens in Gotham," *Deseret Evening News,* 23 Dec. 1898, 4; Bergman, *The Children Sang,* 205.

34. Bergman, *The Children Sang,* 181, 215; "Famed Composer's Home Gone," *Deseret News "Church News,"* 28 May 1966, 6, noted that Stephens lived in this house when he wrote the song for Utah's statehood in 1896; see also Brigham H. Roberts, *A Comprehensive History of the Church of Jesus Christ of Latter-day Saints, Century I,* 6 vols. (Salt Lake City: Church of Jesus Christ of Latter-day Saints, 1930), 6:338.

35. *Salt Lake City Directory, 1894–5,* 219; *Salt Lake City Directory, 1896,* 214 (Willard Christopherson "bds e s State 2 s of Pearl av."), and 74 ("Pearl av, from State e to Second East, bet Eleventh and Twelfth South"); *Salt Lake City Directory, 1900* (Salt Lake City: R. L. Polk, 1900), 190, 678. Willard is listed erroneously as "Christensen" in the middle of the "Christophersen" entries on 189–90. His father and brother were also erroneously listed as "Christensen" with Willard, but were listed as Christophersen before and after the 1900 directory. See *Salt Lake City Directory, 1899* (Salt Lake City: R. L. Polk, 1899), 203; entry about Willard "Christophersen" in *Salt Lake City Directory, 1901* (Salt Lake City: R. L. Polk, 1901), 198. The 1899 directory was dated as of May 1; the 1900 directory gave no specific month for its completion but was based on Willard Christopherson's co-residence with Stephens prior to February 1900, when Willard moved to Europe. Therefore, Christopherson moved in with Stephens sometime between May 1899 and January 1900.

36. "Prof. Stephens' European Trip: Will Begin Next Month and Last for about One Year," *Deseret Evening News,* 2 Jan. 1900, 1.

37. "Evan Stephens Is Home Again," *Deseret Evening News,* 21 Sept. 1900, 8; Evan Stephens to Tabernacle Choir, 5 Apr. 1900, in "Evan Stephens on London," *Deseret Evening News,* 5 May 1900, 11; Bergman, *The Children Sang,* 206.

38. Evan Stephens to Tabernacle Choir, 24 Apr. 1900, from Paris, France, in "Evan Stephens in Wales," *Deseret Evening News,* 12 May 1900, 11; see also "Evan Stephens Is Home Again," *Deseret Evening News,* 21 Sept. 1900, 8; Bergman, *The Children Sang,* 209; the U.S. 1900 Census soundex has no entry for Evan Stephens (S-315), microfilm, LDS Family History Library.

39. My method in ascertaining this was to check the Salt Lake City directories for the residence addresses of every man named in the last will and testament of Evan Stephens, also of the members of the Male Glee Club at the LDS high school where Stephens was professor of vocal music at this time, and also the resident addresses of the male members of his music conductor's training class at the LDS high school during these years.

40. "Evan Stephens off to Europe," *Deseret Evening News,* 28 Mar. 1902, 2. Stephens claimed that Christopherson was "presiding over the mission," but he was only presiding over the Christiania Conference of the mission. See Alter, *Utah,* 2:485; Andrew Jenson, *History of the Scandinavian Mission* (Salt Lake City: Deseret News Press, 1927), 507.

41. "Evan Stephens to His Juvenile Singers," *Deseret Evening News,* 21 June 1902, sect. 2, p. 11. Although not published until June, this undated letter was written aboard ship in April after they "left Boston harbor." For Pike, see Frank Esshom, *Pioneers and Prominent Men of Utah, Comprising Photographs-Genealogies-Biographies* (Salt Lake City: Utah Pioneers Book, 1913), 1106; "Evan Stephens Music on Choir Program," *Deseret News "Church News,"* 16 Mar. 1957, 15. The city directories show that Pike lived with his parents during the years before his trip to Europe with Stephens.

42. "Prof. Stephens Home Again," *Deseret Evening News,* 29 July 1902, 2.

43. "No, I don't bring with me friend Willard. . . . And it is possible it may be another summer before he is released [from his full-time mission]," ibid.

44. *Salt Lake City Directory, 1903* (Salt Lake City: R. L. Polk, 1903), 234, 870; entry for Willard Christopherson (b. 15 Oct. 1877) in LDS Ancestral File.

45. Entry for Noel Sheets Pratt (b. 25 Dec. 1886; md. 1923; d. 1927) in LDS Ancestral File; *Salt Lake City Directory, 1904* (Salt Lake City: R. L. Polk, 1904), 679, 801; Barnes, "Historical Survey," 103; *Gold and Blue* 4 (July 1904): unnumbered page of third-year class officers; *Gold and Blue* 5 (1 June 1905): 8, page of fourth-year class officers; *Courses of Study Offered by the Latter-day Saints' University, Salt Lake City, Utah, 1901–1902* (Salt Lake City: Board of Trustees, 1901), [4]; *Gold and Blue* 2 (June 1902): 5.

46. Harold H. Jenson, "Tribute to Evan Stephens," *Juvenile Instructor* 65 (Dec. 1930): 722; see also Evan Stephens to Samuel B. Mitton, 2 May 1927, in Bergman, *The Children Sang,* 246. Jenson described himself as "one of numerous boys Professor Stephens' influence and life inspired to greater ambition."

47. Evan Stephens, Noel S. Pratt, and Sarah Daniels were among the LDS passengers on *Republic,* 17 July 1907, in LDS British Emigration Ship Registers (1901–13), 295, and (1905–9), unpaged, LDS Family History Library.

Bergman, in *The Children Sang*, 180, described Noel as "one of the Professor's 'Boys,'" and also examined the LDS passenger list for this 1907 trip (210). However, Bergman made no mention that Noel was listed as accompanying Evan and Sarah on this voyage.

48. *Salt Lake City Directory, 1906* (Salt Lake City: R. L. Polk, 1906), 727; *Salt Lake City Directory, 1907* (Salt Lake City: R. L. Polk, 1907), 857 (Noel S. Pratt "bds 750 Ashton av."), 48 ("ASHTON AVE—runs east from 7th to 9th East; 2 blocks south of 12th South"), 1004 (Evan Stephens "res State 1 n of 12th South); "Singers Will Leave Tonight: Two Hundred Members of Tabernacle Choir Ready for Trip to Seattle," *Deseret Evening News*, 21 Aug. 1909, 1; *Salt Lake City Directory, 1923* (Salt Lake City: R. L. Polk, 1923), 770. The entry for Noel S. Pratt in the LDS Ancestral File shows an undated divorce for his recent marriage, although there is no record of the divorce in Salt Lake County. He died only four years after his marriage.

49. "THE BEAUTIFUL LAKE MADE BY 'EVAN BACH,'" *Children's Friend* 18 (Nov. 1919): [428]; Stephens, "Evan Bach" (Dec. 1919): 473.

50. Entry for Thomas Thomas [Jr.] (b. 10 July 1891) in St. John Ward, Malad Stake, Record of Members (1873–1901), 36, 62, entry for Thomas S. Thomas Sr. (b. 1864) in LDS Ancestral File, and entries for Evan Stephens and Thomas S. Thomas in LDS Church census for 1914, all in LDS Family History Library; *Salt Lake City Directory, 1909* (Salt Lake City: R. L. Polk, 1909), 1038, 1076; "Singers Will Leave Tonight," 1. For Thomas's inactivity in the LDS Church, the church census for 1914 showed that he was still unordained at twenty-three years of age, LDS Family History Library.

51. Stephens, "Life Story" (Dec. 1930): 720; Bergman, *The Children Sang*, 179–82. Stephens's housekeeper and grandniece, Sarah Mary Daniels, joined the LDS Church after his death. She had herself sealed to him by proxy on 5 November 1931. See Kennedy, "Precious Moments," 28; Bergman, *The Children Sang*, 189. Kennedy mistakenly identified her as Stephens's cousin.

52. Jenson, "Tribute to Evan Stephens," 722; *The S Book: Commencement Number* (Salt Lake City: Associated Students of Latter-day Saints' University, 1914), 38 for photograph of Thomas. Born in 1895, Harold Jenson expressed regret that as a teenager he did not accept Stephens's invitation to leave his family and move in. Apparently he declined that invitation at age fourteen, shortly before Thomas became Stephens's live-in boyfriend. However, Stephens was no longer an instructor at the LDS high school when Thomas was a student there. See John Henry Evans, "An Historical Sketch of the Latter-day Saints' University," unnumbered page for "Teachers Who Have Taught at the School," typescript dated Nov. 1913, Special Collections, J. Willard Marriott Library, University of Utah, Salt Lake City, Utah.

53. *Salt Lake City Directory, 1915* (Salt Lake City: R. L. Polk, 1915), 966; *Salt Lake City Directory, 1916* (Salt Lake City: R. L. Polk, 1916), 832.

54. Thomas S. Thomas was listed in "Tabernacle Choir in Readiness for

Tour of Eastern States," *Deseret Evening News,* 21 Oct. 1911, sect. 1, p. 19, but deleted in [George D. Pyper], "Six Thousand Miles with the 'Mormon' Tabernacle Choir: Impressions of the Manager," *Improvement Era* 47 (Mar. 1912): 132–33; *The S Book,* 38.

55. "Before Justice Pyper," *Deseret Evening News,* 14 Jan. 1887, [3]; "PAY-ING THE PIPER: The Awful Accusation against the Boys," *Salt Lake Tribune,* 15 Jan. 1887, [4]; see also chap. 9.

56. Stephens, "Life Story" (Mar. 1931): 133; see also Stephens to Samuel B. Mitton, 28 July 1916, in Bergman, *The Children Sang,* 228; telephone statement to me on 14 September 1993 by Alumni Office of Columbia University's School of Medicine regarding the enrollment of Thomas S. Thomas in 1916. Stephens's autobiography claimed that he resigned in 1914, but his resignation occurred in 1916. See "Evan Stephens Resigns Leadership of Choir; Prof. A.C. Lund of B.Y.U. Offered Position," *Deseret Evening News,* 27 July 1916, 1–2.

57. This could be disputed, since Anthon H. Lund recorded in his diary on 13 July 1916 that the First Presidency and apostles decided to release Stephens as director of the Tabernacle Choir. Lund worried on 20 July that "Bro Stephens will take this release very hard." Instead, he recorded on 25 July that Stephens "seemed to feel alright." Lund diary, as quoted in Bergman, *The Children Sang,* 13–14. On the other hand, in the same letter in which Stephens acknowledged that he was personally offended that a "committee recommended my release," Evan privately described himself as "an old gye [guy] that deserted his job." Bergman, *The Children Sang,* 239. I believe the resolution of this apparent contradiction is that Evan Stephens deeply resented the LDS hierarchy's decision to release him, yet he had already planned to resign or ask for a leave of absence so he could move with Thomas to New York. Michael Hicks, in *Mormonism and Music: A History* (Urbana: University of Illinois Press, 1989), 157, described the conductor's abrasive relations with the LDS hierarchy, which led to this forced resignation. However, there is no indication that LDS leaders suspected any impropriety between Stephens and young men.

58. "Salt Lakers in Gotham," *Deseret Evening News,* 7 Oct. 1916, sect. 2, p. 7; entry for Columbia University's College of Physicians and Surgeons in *Trow General Directory of New York City, Embracing the Boroughs of Manhattan and the Bronx, 1916* (New York: R. L. Polk, 1916), 2047.

59. Chauncey, *Gay New York,* 217, 428n24, discussing a raid report dated 24 Oct. 1916. The well-known Ariston homosexual bathhouse was located on Broadway and Fifty-fifth Street, only a few blocks from the hotel where Stephens and his "boy chum" were staying. However, Chauncey doubts that "the Ariston continued to be a homosexual rendezvous after being raided [in 1903], given the notoriety of the trials and the severity of the sentences imposed on the patrons" (216).

60. "Stephens Writes of Musical Events in Gay New York," *Deseret Evening News,* 11 Nov. 1916, sect. 2, p. 3. For *gay boy* as American slang by 1903 for "a man who is homosexual," see J. E. Lighter, ed., *Random House Historical Dictionary of American Slang,* 3 vols. (New York: Random House, 1994–96), 1:872, also see chap. 4, note 55. For homosexual "cruising" in Central Park since the 1890s, see Chauncey, *Gay New York,* 98, 182, 423n58, and see 441n50 for *cruising* as a term used by nineteenth-century prostitutes; see also Lighter, *Random House Historical Dictionary of American Slang,* 1:531.

61. "Prof. Stephens Enlists as a Food Producer," *Deseret Evening News,* 21 Apr. 1917, sect. 2, p. 6. For the program, see "PROF. EVAN STEPHENS, Who Will Be Tendered a Monster Farewell Testimonial at the Tabernacle, Friday, Apr. 6th," *Deseret Evening News,* 31 Mar. 1917, sect. 2, p. 5; Stephens, "Life Story," (Mar. 1931): 133; Bergman, *The Children Sang,* 217–18. "Salt Lakers in Gotham," *Deseret Evening News,* 10 Mar. 1917, sect. 2, p. 7, reported that the two "well known Utah boys, Frank Spencer . . . and Tom Thomas, nephew of Prof. Evan Stephens" were still living together with six other students a few blocks from Columbia's medical school.

62. U.S. 1920 Census of New York County, New York, enumeration district 802 (enumerated in Jan. 1920), sheet 1, line 39, microfilm, LDS Family History Library.

63. Lyrics of a 1914 song, quoted in Steven Watson, *Strange Bedfellows: The First American Avant-Garde* (New York: Abbeville Press, 1991), 114.

64. Colin A. Scott, "Sex and Art," *American Journal of Psychology* 7 (Jan. 1896): 216; Havelock Ellis, *Sexual Inversion,* vol. 2 of *Studies in the Psychology of Sex* (Philadelphia: F. A. Davis, 1915), 299; Earl Lind [pseud.], *Autobiography of an Androgyne* (New York: Medico-Legal Journal, 1918; reprint, New York: Arno Press/New York Times, 1975), 7, 77–78, 155–56, 189; Jonathan Ned Katz, ed., *Gay/Lesbian Almanac: A New Documentary* (New York: Harper and Row, 1983), 235; Chauncey, *Gay New York,* 15, 190, 228; Lighter, *Random House Historical Dictionary of American Slang,* 1:718.

65. Chauncey, *Gay New York,* 235–36, 291, quotation from 431n28.

66. *Queen* was slang for male homosexual by the 1920s. See Chauncey, *Gay New York,* 101; see list of homosexual slang in Aaron J. Rosanoff, *Manual of Psychiatry,* 6th ed. (New York: Wiley, 1927), as quoted in Katz, *Gay/Lesbian Almanac,* 439. However, there is no published verification that it had this meaning as early as the 1914 usage in the LDS high school's yearbook. Nevertheless, I have verified other examples of historical citations in slang dictionaries being decades after Mormon and Utah slang usage, as in *sleeping with* in chap. 3 and *monkey with* in chaps. 9 and 10.

67. Thomas S. Thomas as a student does not appear in *Trow General Directory of New York City, 1916* (New York: R. L. Polk, 1916), 1660; *Trow*

General Directory of New York City, Embracing the Boroughs of Manhattan and the Bronx, 1917 (New York: R. L. Polk, 1917), 1915; *Trow General Directory of New York City, Embracing the Boroughs of Manhattan and the Bronx, 1919* (New York: R. L. Polk, 1919), 1874–75; *Trow General Directory of New York City, Embracing the Boroughs of Manhattan and the Bronx, 1920–21* (New York: R. L. Polk, 1920), 1783–84. Although the U.S. 1920 Census showed his residence address, Thomas apparently withheld that information from the city directory.

68. Stephens, "Life Story" (Mar. 1931): 133. Stephens erroneously dated this event as 1914. See also January 1920 U.S. Census of New York City, New York County, New York, enumeration district 802, sheet 1, microfilm, LDS Family History Library, for Thomas S. Thomas and wife Priscilla; *American Medical Directory, 1940* (Chicago: American Medical Association, 1940), 1126, for Thomas Stephens Thomas Jr., graduate of Columbia University School of Physicians and Surgeons, and practicing in Morristown, Morris County, New Jersey; "Dr. T.S. Thomas Dies at Seventy-Eight at Memorial," *Morris County's Daily Record,* 22 July 1969, 2.

69. Kathryn Fairbanks Kirk, ed., *The Fairbanks Family in the West: Four Generations* (Salt Lake City: Paragon Press, 1983), 318; *Salt Lake City Directory, 1917* (Salt Lake City: R. L. Polk, 1917), 301, for Ortho Fairbanks at 1111 Whitlock Avenue; *Salt Lake City Directory, 1919* (Salt Lake City: R. L. Polk, 1919), 35, for "WHITLOCK AVE (Highland Pk)"; entry for Ortho Fairbanks (b. 29 Sept. 1887) in LDS Ancestral File; *Salt Lake City Directory, 1923,* (Salt Lake City: R. L. Polk, 1923), 322; and Evan Stephens holographic Last Will and Testament, dated 9 Nov. 1927, Salt Lake County Clerk, Probated Will 16540, page 1, Utah State Archives, Salt Lake City, Utah, for Stephens's ownership of the Highland Park properties, and page 3 for Ortho Fairbanks as one of the persons to receive "a memento of my regards."

70. U.S. 1920 Census of Salt Lake City, Salt Lake County, Utah, enumeration district 88, sheet 12, microfilm, LDS Family History Library; and comparison of city directory listings with the names of all men mentioned in the last will and testament of Evan Stephens.

71. "THE BEAUTIFUL LAKE," [428]; Stephens, "Evan Bach" (Dec. 1919): 473.

72. "Los Angeles Entertains Veteran Composer: Prof Evan Stephens Guest of Musical Organization on Coast—A Most Enjoyable Occasion," *Deseret Evening News,* 3 Feb. 1923, sect. 3, p. 6; *The S Book of 1924: The Annual of the Latter-day Saints High School* (Salt Lake City: Associated Students of the Latter-day Saints High School, 1924), 106, 120; see also Bergman, *The Children Sang,* 222–23; entry for John Wallace Packham (b. 28 Dec. 1904; d. 1972) in LDS Ancestral File. Packham turned eighteen in the middle of his trip with Stephens.

73. *Salt Lake City Directory, 1924* (Salt Lake City: R. L. Polk, 1924), 741, 927; Evan Stephens to Samuel B. Mitton, 20 July 1924, in Bergman, *The Children Sang,* 242.

74. *Salt Lake City Directory, 1926* (Salt Lake City: R. L. Polk, 1926), 1003, 1035, 1443; *Salt Lake City Directory, 1927* (Salt Lake City: R. L. Polk, 1927), 424, 1044, 1495; *Salt Lake City Directory, 1928* (Salt Lake City: R. L. Polk, 1928), 1041, 1534; *Salt Lake City Directory, 1929* (Salt Lake City: R. L. Polk, 1929), 151, 1562; *Salt Lake City Directory, 1930* (Salt Lake City: R. L. Polk, 1930), 702, 1609; entries for occupants in LDS Ancestral File.

75. "Evan Stephens' Treasures Divided," *Salt Lake Telegram,* 9 Nov. 1930, sect. 2, p. 1; see also Bergman, *The Children Sang,* 214, 216; entry for John Wallace Packham (b. 28 Dec. 1904) in LDS Ancestral File and his obituary in *Salt Lake Tribune,* 17 Sept. 1972, E-19.

76. Samuel B. Mitton diary, 27 Oct. 1930, quoted in Lindblad, *Mitton,* 295. Despite Stephens's expressions of love for Mitton in correspondence as late as 1924, Stephens left Mitton out of his will in 1927. The reasons for that omission are presently unknown, but it must have been a bitter surprise for Mitton when he learned this fact after Evan's will was probated. Mitton and his wife had continued visiting Stephens up through the composer's final illness, and Mitton's diary entry showed the depth of the married man's love for Evan. Despite full access to his diaries, Mitton's biographer made no reference to his exclusion from the will that remembered all of Evan's other "boy chums" and no mention of Mitton's reaction to that omission. Either Mitton himself chose not to comment or his biographer chose not to tarnish his narrative of the loving relationship between Mitton and Stephens.

77. Stephens holographic Last Will and Testament, 1, 3.

78. Evan Stephens, "Evan Stephens' Promotion, as told by Himself," *Children's Friend* 19 (Mar. 1920): 96; Bergman, *The Children Sang,* 65.

79. Thomas S. Thomas was the only light blond "boy chum" of Evan Stephens as pictured in *Children's Friend* 18 (Nov. 1919): [428], and described in Jenson, "Tribute to Evan Stephens," 722. Photographs of his seven brunette "boy chums" (at least one of whom may have been dark blond as a younger man) are John J. Ward in *Children's Friend* 18 (Oct. 1919): 388; Samuel B. Mitton opposite page 6 in Lindblad, *Mitton;* Horace S. Ensign in Photo 4273, Item 1, Archives, Historical Department of the Church of Jesus Christ of Latter-day Saints, Salt Lake City, Utah (hereafter LDS Archives); Willard A. Christopherson in Photo 1700–3781, LDS Archives; Noel S. Pratt in Bergman, *The Children Sang,* 181; Ortho Fairbanks in Kirk, *Fairbanks Family,* 239; J. Wallace Packham in *Deseret Evening News,* 3 Feb. 1923, sect. 3, p. 6.

80. Evan Stephens, "Little Life Experiences," *Children's Friend* 19 (June 1920): 228.

81. John S. Farmer and W. E. Henley, *Slang and Its Analogues*, 7 vols. (London: Routledge and Kegan Paul, 1890–1904), 4:90; Eric Partridge, *A Dictionary of Slang and Unconventional English: Colloquialisms and Catch-Phrases, Solecisms and Catachreses, Nicknames, and Vulgarisms*, 8th ed., Paul Beale, ed. (London: Routledge and Kegan Paul, 1984), 638.

82. "Stephens's Day at School," *Gold and Blue* 3 (14 Jan. 1903): 5. Although some readers might question whether LDS student editors would knowingly print a sexual message of this kind, even more explicitly sexual items appeared in the student-edited publications of Brigham Young University. For example, the student editors included an obviously phallic cartoon in BYU's yearbook that depicted a man wearing a long, curved sword, the tip of which had been drawn as the head of a penis. The caption was "His Master's Vice," which was a multiple play on words, including "masturbate" and "secret vice," a euphemism for masturbation. See *Banyan, 1924,* 227; see also Gary James Bergera and Ronald Priddis, *Brigham Young University: A House of Faith* (Salt Lake City: Signature Books, 1985), 100–103, 255–57.

83. *Gold and Blue* 2 (1 Mar. 1902): 11; *Salt Lake City Directory, 1908* (Salt Lake City: R. L. Polk, 1908), 83; entry for Louis Casper Lambert Shaw Jr. (b. 17 May 1884) in LDS Ancestral File; and extended discussion in chap. 2. However, neither Shaw nor any other young man moved in with Stephens in 1903, but in 1904 fellow student Noel Pratt began living with the music director.

84. Stephens, "Going Home to Willard," 1093.

85. Bergman, *The Children Sang*, 182.

86. "Mary and May," *Children's Friend* 18 (Oct. 1919): 421.

87. Rocky O'Donovan, "Utah Gay and Lesbian History," official audiotape of paper presented at Conference on Sexuality and Homosexuality, 24 Apr. 1993, University of Utah; see also O'Donovan, "'Abominable and Detestable Crime,'" 127–28.

88. "Louie B. Felt," *Children's Friend* 18 (Oct. 1919): 407–8, 410–11; according to the entry in the LDS Ancestral File, Joseph H. Felt married Sarah Louise Bouton in 1866 and had no children, Alma Elizabeth Mineer in 1875 and had six children, and Elizabeth Liddell in 1881 and had seven children.

89. O'Donovan, "'Abominable and Detestable Crime,'" 127. However, without specific confirmation from the women involved, O'Donovan's statement can be no more than speculation. He also explains on page 163n1: "I capitalize Lesbian, Gay, and Bisexual as a way of affirming my belief that we have constructed an ethnic identity." His view is shared by some, but not all, writers who define themselves as lesbian, gay, or bisexual. Similar to O'Donovan, the feminist historian Maxine Hanks regards Utah's plural marriages as an "implied sealing of wives to wives in polygamy." Her conclusion derives from the well-known facts that "these women 'courted' other wives, placed their husband's hand on the new wife's, and were present at the seal-

ing ceremonies." She concludes that this "qualifies as a same-sex covenant of eternal companionship between women who were, in effect, sealed to other women in polygamy." Hanks to D. Michael Quinn, 4 Aug. 1995. While I see it as possible that some plural wives regarded themselves as joined together eternally through their shared husband, the ceremony's wording involved only the new bride and the already married groom.

90. James G. Kiernan, "Responsibility in Sexual Perversion," *Chicago Medical Reporter* 3 (May 1892): 208–9, summarized in Katz, *Gay/Lesbian Almanac*, 231.

91. "Mary and May," 420.

92. Ibid., 420–21.

93. Ibid., 421; "Louie B. Felt" (Oct. 1919): 414.

94. *Deseret Evening News*, 15 Sept. 1919, 1; Elizabeth O. Toombs, "In the Hands of Women," *Good Housekeeping*, Nov. 1919, 41.

95. Dr. Constance Long, "A Psycho-Analytic Study of the Basis of Character," *Proceedings of the International Conference of Women Physicians*, 6 vols., *Moral Codes and Personality* (New York: Woman's Press, 1920), 4:81, reprinted in *The Psychoanalytic Review* 7 (Jan. 1920): 13, in Long, *Collected Papers on the Psychology of Phantasy* (New York: Moffat, Yard, 1921), 142, and in Katz, *Gay/Lesbian Almanac*, 386.

96. Eleanor Bertine, "Health and Morality in the Light of the New Psychology," *Proceedings of Women Physicians*, vol. 4, *Moral Codes and Personality*, 12, with quote on 14; Trigant Burrow, "Psycho-Analysis in Theory and in Life," *Proceedings of Women Physicians*, vol. 4, *Moral Codes and Personality*, 15, 16. However, Christine Murrell disagreed with the view that homosexual conduct was "normal" for people who were also "normal." Murrell told the conference: "In some of the papers we have heard, an inference was made that because an occurrence was frequent, it was therefore normal; that is not a justifiable conclusion. It is perfectly possible that the circumstances are abnormal." See her "The Adaptation of the Young to Life," in *Proceedings of Women Physicians*, vol. 3, *The Health of the Child*, 126. The conference's official resolutions represented only the delegates in the health and legislative sections. Homosexuality was not included in the final resolutions because the delegates in the psychology section could not agree on resolutions for any topic, and therefore the "psychological section brought in no report." See *Survey* 43 (15 Nov. 1919): 110–11.

97. Horace W. Frink, "Masturbation," in *Proceedings of Women Physicians*, vol. 5, *Adaptation of the Individual to Life*, 82, 84. However, this physician regarded masturbation as healthy and inevitable only for adolescents. His views may have been influenced by the earlier publication of Havelock Ellis's *The Evolution of Modesty, the Phenomena of Sexual Periodicity, Auto-Eroticism*, vol. 2 of *Studies in the Psychology of Sex* (1915). However, Frink's

views and the multiple editions of Ellis's publication had no effect for many years on the diagnostic connection of masturbation with insanity in the physician commitments of persons to Utah's insane asylum (see chap. 10).

98. Ann Gardner Stone, "Ellen B. Ferguson," in Vicky Burgess-Olson, ed., *Sister Saints* (Provo, Utah: Brigham Young University Press, 1976), 336; "Utah News from Gotham," *Deseret Evening News,* 20 Sept. 1919, sect. 3, p. 4, regarding Dr. Ralph C. Pendleton.

99. Although "Utah News from Gotham" was usually a regular column in the Saturday issue of the *Deseret Evening News,* this report ceased during the weeks it might have provided information about Mormon physicians visiting New York to attend the conference of women physicians. Among LDS women physicians at the time were Hannah Sorenson Astlund, Martha Hughes Cannon, Belle Anderson Gemmell, Minnie F. Hayden Howard, Leah Jane Shaw Keeler, Caroline A. Mills, Romania Bunnell Pratt Penrose, Margaret Curtis Shipp Roberts, Sophie Ruesch, Ellis Reynolds Shipp, Jane Wilkie Manning Ballantyne Skolfield, and Helen Condie Thackeray. See "Pioneer Women Doctors," in Carter, ed., *Our Pioneer Heritage,* 6:364–421; also not listed by Carter were Drs. Claire Gouley, Mabel H. Parry, Wealthy Shefner, and Mrs. E. H. C. (Jerome) Tracy, who lived in Salt Lake City, Cedarville, and Woodrow, Utah, respectively. See *Utah State Gazetteer and Business Directory, 1918–1919* (Salt Lake City: R. L. Polk, 1918)344, 763–66. For their biographies, see Christine Croft Waters, "Romania P. Penrose," in Burgess-Olson, ed., *Sister Saints,* 341–60; Gail Farr Casterline, "Ellis R. Shipp," in Burgess-Olson, ed., *Sister Saints,* 363–81; Jean Bickmore White, "Martha H. Cannon," in Burgess-Olson, ed., *Sister Saints,* 383–97; Vicky Burgess-Olson, "Margaret Ann Freece," in Burgess-Olson, ed., *Sister Saints,* 399–413. Drs. Cannon, Penrose, Roberts, Skolfield, Shipp, and Thackeray were living in Salt Lake City during the year of this conference. See *Salt Lake City Directory, 1919,* 686, 743, 806, 1115; *Utah State Gazetteer and Business Directory, 1918–1919,* 210, 289.

100. "The Official Round Table," *Relief Society Magazine* 6 (Nov. 1919): 654–55.

101. "Anna Howard Shaw," *Relief Society Magazine* 6 (Oct. 1919): 596–97. Shaw had died in July 1919.

102. Angela Howard Zophy, ed., *Handbook of American Women's History* (New York: Garland, 1990), 401; *Who Was Who in America, Vol. 1, 1897–1942* (Chicago: Marquis Who's Who, 1962), 28, 1110. However, Shaw became vice president to Anthony in the NWSA's successor organization, the National American Woman Suffrage Association, from 1892 to 1900. After Anthony's retirement in 1900, Shaw was its president from 1904 to 1915.

103. Anna Howard Shaw, *The Story of a Pioneer* (New York: Harper and Brothers, 1915), 189; see also Dynes, *Encyclopedia of Homosexuality,* 2:924.

104. Ida Husted Harper, *The Life and Work of Susan B. Anthony*, 3 vols. (Indianapolis: Hollenbeck Press, 1898–1908), 3:1385.

105. Quoted in Kathleen Barry, *Susan B. Anthony: A Biography of a Singular Feminist* (New York: New York University Press, 1988), 350.

106. "Many Ladies Meet. Conference of the Woman's National Suffrage Association. SUSAN B. ANTHONY PRESIDES. Eloquent Speeches by the Rev. Anna Shaw and Others—Reception and Meeting Tonight," *Deseret Evening News*, 13 May 1895, 1; "At The Tabernacle. Rev. Anna Shaw and Miss Susan B. Anthony Speak," *Deseret Evening News*, 13 May 1895, 2; "Two Famous Women: Susan B. Anthony and Rev. Anna Shaw in the City," *Salt Lake Herald*, 13 May 1895, 8.

107. Harper, *Life and Work*, 3:1442–23, 1463.

108. Shaw, *Story of a Pioneer*, 267–68. Shaw did not identify the newspaper, and I have been unable to locate this story as originally published.

109. Anna Howard Shaw to Clara Osborne, 19 Aug. 1902, quoted in James R. McGovern, "Anna Howard Shaw: New Approaches to Feminism," *Journal of Social History* 3 (Winter 1969): 146.

110. In *Children's Friend* 18 (Dec. 1919): 483, which highlighted the live-in arrangement between Evan Stephens and his teenage "chum," there was also an article by Mrs. Jess Sweitzer Sheaffer. This may have been Henrietta Young Schweitzer, whose husband's name was unlisted in Susa Young Gates and Mabel Young Sanborn, "Brigham Young Genealogy," *Utah Genealogical and Historical Magazine* 12 (Jan. 1921): 31. Henrietta was the only daughter of Katherine Young Schweitzer, who had given the most financial support at the incorporation of the Salt Lake Bohemian Club for Mormon gays and lesbians (see chap. 2). Despite examining numerous genealogical and civil documents, I have been unable to verify the identity of author Mrs. Jess Sweitzer Sheaffer in order to determine if she was the daughter of Katherine Young Schweitzer. If such a relationship existed, then that would be added evidence of the intentional "coming out" in these October and December articles of the *Friend*.

111. Augusta Joyce Crocheron, *Representative Women of Deseret: A Book of Biographical Sketches . . .* (Salt Lake City: J. C. Graham, 1884), 57–59; Cummings, "Shining Lights," 651–63; Jenson, *Latter-day Saint Biographical Encyclopedia*, 1:740–46; *Biographical Record of Salt Lake City and Vicinity, Containing Biographies of Well Known Citizens of Past and Present* (Chicago: National Historical Record Company, 1902), 606–8; Orson F. Whitney, *History of Utah*, 4 vols. (Salt Lake City: George Q. Cannon and Sons, 1892–1904), 4:365–67; John Henry Evans, "Some Men Who Have Done Things: Evan Stephens, the Great Commoner in Music," *Improvement Era* 13 (Jan. 1910): 268–75; "Louie B. Felt," *Children's Friend* 13 (Nov. 1914): 597–605; May Anderson, "Louie B. Felt," *Young Woman's Journal* 26 (Mar. 1915): 145–46; Stephens, "Going Home to Willard," 1088–93.

The pre-October installments of "Evan Bach: A True Story for Little Folk, by a Pioneer," contained two references that appear significant only by comparison with the emphasis on male-male love in the October–December 1919 installments. The article in *Children's Friend* 18 (Feb. 1919): 47 referred to "an old schoolboy [in Wales] for whom he secretly cherished intense admiration and childish affection." Also the article in *Children's Friend* 18 (July 1919): 254 stated: "Most attractive of all to Evan Bach, were the merry smiling teamsters from the 'Valley.'"

112. Alfred C. Rees, "Lessons for October," *Juvenile Instructor* 54 (Aug. 1919): 433.

113. Jenson, *Latter-day Saint Biographical Encyclopedia,* 4:271–73, 282–83; Sarah Louise Bouton Felt (b. 5 May 1850; d. 13 Feb. 1928); Mary ("May") Anderson (b. 8 June 1864; d. 10 June 1946), LDS Ancestral File.

CHAPTER 9

Homoeroticism and Sex Crimes in Early Mormonism and Pioneer Utah

ON THE OCCASIONS when nineteenth-century LDS leaders had to actually confront homoerotic behaviors among other Mormons, there was no Latter-day revelation or teaching that either condemned or validated same-gender sexual acts. By definition, homoerotic activities were outside the bonds of marriage, whether they were consensual or coerced, monogamous or promiscuous, loving or indifferent, singular or continuing.[1]

Therefore, one would expect nineteenth-century Mormon leaders to have cited well-known Old Testament prohibitions and punishments for homoerotic activities.[2] However, in almost every instance Mormon leaders who served in the nineteenth century were more tolerant of homoerotic behaviors than they were of every other nonmarital sexual activity.

Restrained reactions to same-gender sexuality continued even for twentieth-century general authorities who had reached adulthood in the nineteenth century. A major part of the explanation for that tolerance is that as children and young adults those twentieth-century general authorities were accustomed to the pervasive same-sex dynamics of nineteenth-century Mormonism. Perhaps others will offer different explanations for this relative tolerance by Mormon leaders for homo-erotic behaviors down to the 1950s. In any event, I will illustrate that pattern with examples (see chap. 11).

Nevertheless, unlike the generally positive tone in the evidence cited by this study about other same-sex dynamics, there is a generally neg-ative tone in this chapter. That reflects the verifiable reactions toward actual sexual activities outside marriage by nineteenth-century Mor-mons and within the Mormon culture region. Utahns and Mormons did not want to confront sexual behavior of any kind by others. Also, despite the cases of Kate Thomas, Ada Dwyer Russell, Evan Stephens, Louie B. Felt, May Anderson, Mildred Berryman, and her study, there is far more evidence about exploitative same-sex behavior in the Mor-mon culture region than there is evidence of same-sex romance. That is particularly true in the legal prosecution of sodomy and homosexu-al rape in Utah.

Although this should be obvious, I must emphasize that men raping men is no more an indictment of all homosexual males than men rap-ing women is an indictment of all heterosexual males. The details in this chapter result from the available evidence. The sensational dimen-sion in some of the following examples of homoeroticism should be kept within the larger context of same-sex dynamics discussed previ-ously. However, even the negative reaction toward same-gender sexu-al acts was not uniformly severe among nineteenth-century Mormons.

The first known instance of homoerotic behavior in Mormon histo-ry involved John C. Bennett. An assistant counselor in the First Presi-dency since April 1841, Bennett was "disfellowshipped" (denied priv-ileges of LDS membership) in May 1842 and soon "excommunicated" (excluded from membership) for seducing a group of women whom he had also encouraged to have sex with anyone he sent to them.[3] The 27 July 1842 edition of the *Wasp,* a church newspaper at Nauvoo, Il-linois, detailed the charges against Bennett. First, the LDS newspaper claimed that Bennett had also engaged in sodomy. Second, it claimed that the Prophet Joseph Smith had tolerated Bennett's homoeroticism. Third, the church newspaper even printed one apostle's implication that Joseph Smith himself had also engaged in an "immoral act" with a man.

These are the actual words (written by Smith's brother William, an apostle): "Gen. [Joseph] Smith was a great *philanthropist* [in the eyes of Bennett] as long as Bennett could practice adultery, fornication, and—we were going to say (*Buggery,*) without being exposed."[4] At that time, the word *buggery* was a slang word and legal term for *sodomy,* or anal intercourse between men.⁵ Later statements by Brigham Young and Bennett himself indicate that this 1842 publication was not libeling Bennett.

Previous actions and statements by Joseph Smith could also be construed as his toleration for Bennett's various sexual activities. On motion of John C. Bennett on 5 October 1840, the general conference (presided over by Smith) voted that no one could be judged guilty of a crime unless proven "by two or three witnesses." Such a burden of proof helped shield Bennett's sexual exploits.⁶ In January 1841, Smith also dictated a revelation about Bennett: "his reward shall not fail, if he receive counsel; and for his love he shall be great, for he shall be mine if he do this, saith the Lord" (Doctrine and Covenants 124:17).

Later in 1841, the prophet further eroded the ability of anyone to investigate or punish Bennett's sexual conduct: "If you do not accuse each other, God will not accuse you. If you have no accuser you will enter heaven. If you will not accuse me, I will not accuse you." Then in words that must have warmed Bennett's heart, Smith continued his sermon by saying: "If you will throw a cloak of charity over my sins, I will over yours—for charity covereth a multitude of sins. What many people call sin is not sin."⁷

It must have seemed to Bennett and others that the LDS president put those charitable words into action when he appointed John C. Bennett as assistant counselor to the First Presidency in April 1841. That was a month after one of the bishops of the church privately reported to Smith his investigation at Bennett's former residence: "his wife left him under satisfactory evidence of his adulterous connections."⁸ If Joseph Smith had not heard that his new counselor was practicing "buggery," he at least knew of Bennett's reputation for adultery.

On the next page of the July 1842 *Wasp*, the church newspaper described Smith's reaction to Apostle Orson Pratt's vote against a resolution defending the prophet's chastity: "Pres. Joseph Smith spoke in reply [on July 22]—Question to Elder Pratt, 'Have you personally a knowledge of any immoral act in me toward the female sex, or in any other way?' Answer, by Elder O. Pratt, 'Personally, toward the female sex, I have not.'" Since this same issue of the *Wasp* had already raised the topic of Bennett's "buggery" and the prophet's alleged toleration of it, Smith's "or in any other way?" was an implicit challenge for Pratt to charge him with "buggery" as well. Pratt declined to answer whether

Joseph Smith had committed "any immoral act" with someone other than a woman, but also declined to exonerate the prophet from such a charge.[9] That indicates the depth of Pratt's disaffection, which resulted in his excommunication from the LDS Church within a month.[10]

Two years later, Nauvoo's two LDS newspapers printed Apostle Brigham Young's reference to John C. Bennett's bisexual conduct: "if he had let young men and women alone it would have been better for him." One of Bennett's "young men" was twenty-one-year-old Francis M. Higbee to whom Brigham's sermon specifically referred.[11]

Mormon newspapers also printed the startling confessions of the women Higbee seduced, printed testimony about Bennett performing abortions for the seduced women, referred to Bennett's patronizing of Nauvoo's brothel "on the hill," printed Associate President Hyrum Smith's statement that Higbee "had the P** [Pox, i.e., syphilis]," and printed Smith's testimony about another dissenter: "I have seen him put his hand in a woman's bosom, and he also lifted up her [under]-clothes."[12] Nevertheless, the LDS newspaper observed that it dropped other evidence about Francis Higbee that was "revolting, corrupt, and disgusting . . . [and] too indelicate for the public eye or ear." The earlier allegation of "buggery" was all that was left.[13]

Joseph Smith forgave Higbee in 1842, and homoerotic activities were not among the specific charges for which the thirty-seven-year-old Bennett was dropped from office and excommunicated that year.[14] In fact, the official *History of the Church* still prints Smith's confession that his "only sin" was in "covering up their (the Higbees', Fosters', Laws' and Dr. Bennett's) iniquities, on their solemn promise to reform."[15] Mormonism's founding prophet also revised the common interpretation that God destroyed Sodom because its inhabitants preferred sex between men. According to Smith, God destroyed Sodom "for rejecting the prophets."[16]

John C. Bennett left Nauvoo, but not Mormonism or his interest in young men. He later became counselor to Mormon schismatic leader James J. Strang. During a year-long stay at Strang's colony in Wisconsin, Bennett left his new wife back in Massachusetts. However, he was determined to have the company of a young physician. "He must not leave you until I come," Bennett wrote Strang in 1846, "and I hope we shall be able to persuade him to remain with us forever." Then more directly, he added, "I wish him for my sake to abide with you, at Voree."[17]

It was ten years before Mormons commented on another case of homoeroticism, and this time it was an allegation of attempted sex between women. While fulfilling a special preaching assignment from Brigham Young, Richard Ballantyne referred in December 1856 to an unnamed woman in Salt Lake City who "was trying to seduce a young girl." This married LDS woman admitted to adultery with a man, but she "denied having any hand in trying to seduce Brother West's daughter, though the testimony seems plain against her."[18] This was the first reference to female-female eroticism among nineteenth-century Mormons. However, it involved only an attempted seduction, rather than actual sexual acts between women.

It was not until twenty-two years after the 1842 Bennett scandal that Mormons commented on another case of actual sex between persons of the same gender. It is significant that during this period Brigham Young and other Mormon leaders repeatedly preached about the specific sins for which it was necessary to shed a person's blood. Although they included theft, apostasy, fornication, and adultery as sins requiring "blood atonement," these sermons made no reference to sodomy.[19]

Apostle Parley P. Pratt's 1853 sermon was the closest these early Mormon leaders came to associating sodomy with blood atonement. He warned the Mormons: "If we, like the Sodomites or Canaanites, were full of all manner of lawless abominations, holding promiscuous intercourse with the other sex, and stooping to a level with the brute creation . . . given to strange and unnatural lusts, appetites, and passions, would it not be a mercy to cut us off, root and branch, and thus put an end to our increase upon the earth? You all say it would."[20] Whether knowingly or not, Pratt had accepted the traditional Protestant claim that Sodom perished due to sexual sins, rather than Joseph Smith's statement ten years earlier that God destroyed Sodom for "rejecting the prophets."[21]

However, even in this justification for God's mass destruction of the people of Sodom, Pratt listed opposite-sex relations before "unnatural lusts." He did not suggest the death penalty as punishment for an individual who acted upon "unnatural lusts." Instead, his sermon lumped Sodomites with Canaanites as a cautionary warning to Mormons as an entire people. Likewise, Brigham Young warned Mormons in an 1855 sermon: "We *can* make the Territory of Utah . . . exceed the abominations of the ancient Sodomites, if we are so disposed."[22]

His earlier statements about Bennett's "young men" showed that Brigham Young was not shy about referring publicly to sodomy. In his sermons during these years, Young's catalog of blood-atonement sins seemed to come straight out of Leviticus in the Old Testament, but homoerotic activities were a glaring omission. If Young regarded homoerotic activities as sins (and I know of no evidence that he ever made such a statement), he apparently regarded sodomy as far less serious than fornication or adultery. Consistent with that view was the October 1857 comment by the LDS Church's *Deseret News* about the U.S. government's decision to send federal troops against Utah: "such conduct puts to blush that of the antediluvians, that of the inhabitants of Sodom and Gomorrah, and is nearly akin to that of the Jewish nation" in rejecting Jesus. Thus, to pioneer Mormons, the sin of Sodom was less serious than religious disbelief.[23]

On the other hand, earlier that year Brigham Young expressed approval for an LDS bishop who had castrated a man for committing a sex crime. On 31 May 1857, Bishop Warren S. Snow's counselor wrote that the twenty-four-year-old Welshman Thomas Lewis had "gone crazy" after being castrated by Bishop Snow for an undisclosed sex crime. When informed of Snow's action, Brigham Young said: "I feel to sustain him," even though Young's brother, a general authority, disapproved of this punishment. In July Young wrote a reassuring letter about the castration: "Just let the matter drop, and say no more about it," the LDS president advised, "and it will soon die away among the people."[24]

About October 1857, Cedar City's LDS bishop ordered the execution of a Mormon who had sexual intercourse with his stepdaughter. "Reputable eyewitnesses" reported that the man consented to this theocratic death penalty "in full confidence of salvation through the shedding of his blood."[25]

Even Brigham Young's counselor Daniel H. Wells ordered blood atonement in November 1857 for a sexual act. After Governor Young declared martial law for Utah at the approach of federal troops, Wells as commanding general ordered the execution of a Mormon soldier for "committing the sin of Sodomy or Bestiality [sexual intercourse with an animal—] one of the most heinous crimes." This court-martial occurred on 30 November, and Wells assembled all his troops the next day, requiring them to approve the judgment that twenty-one-year-old Willis Drake "be shot publicly & also the mare." However, despite the upraised right hands of the entire company, Wells delayed the execution long enough for Brigham Young to pardon Drake. Apparently his horse was not so lucky.[26]

This 1857 case was the first of its kind in several respects. It marked the first known use by Mormons of the word *sodomy,* although the term was equated with bestiality rather than same-sex intercourse. It was the first reported case of bestiality in Mormon culture, and this may have been the first time in American history when a court ordered the execution of a rape victim but freed the rapist.

In February 1858, Salt Lake City's police captain Hosea Stout, a devout Mormon, also described with no disapproval how Mormons "disguised as Indians" dragged a man "out of bed with a whore and castrated him by a square & close amputation." A few months later, the non-Mormon federal judge asked Stout to investigate and bring to justice those who had castrated another man for committing adultery with a Mormon's wife. That was the last reference in Stout's diary to the case, which he apparently ignored.[27]

Then in April 1858 the bishop of Payson, his brother (the sheriff), and several members of their LDS ward joined in shooting to death a twenty-two-year-old Mormon and his mother for committing incest. They also castrated the young man and killed the infant girl who was born of this incest.[28] A general authority resided in Payson at that time. Levi W. Hancock was a former member of the 1834 Zion's Camp, of the 1838 Missouri Danites, of the Nauvoo police, of the 1846–47 Mormon Battalion, a former member of the Utah Legislature, and a senior member of the First Council of Seventy. It is unlikely the bishop and sheriff would have committed this blood atonement without consulting with their prestigious uncle and fellow resident.[29] Thirty years later, the church's *Deseret News* expressed sympathy for those who had murdered "the brutal mother and son" because the Mormon community had been "disgusted and greatly incensed."[30]

On 12 September 1858 a clerk in the LDS Historian's Office also recorded that U.S. soldiers had discovered "this morning" a woman's decapitated head in Utah Valley. This Mormon woman had left her Provo ward only a week earlier to live in the camp of U.S. soldiers.[31] Six weeks before that, a dog in Utah Valley had found a different woman's decapitated head, "much dried and mummified."[32] This was consistent with First Presidency Counselor Heber C. Kimball's sermon that adulterers should be decapitated and his views of adulterous women:

"We wipe them out of existence."[33] These women had evidently received retributive blood atonement from Mormon zealots who took such sermons literally.

Aside from vigilante castrations for going to "bed with a whore," for adultery, and for incest, young Mormon men in the 1850s were also castrated for bestiality. In March 1859, a U.S. soldier's diary recorded that "two youths" fled to the U.S. army camp after being "castrated by the Mormons." One "handsome young Dane" had been courting a girl whom an LDS bishop wanted. To dispose of his rival, the bishop claimed the young man "had committed bestiality and had him castrated."[34]

Those bloody judgments in the 1850s contrasted dramatically with how nineteenth-century Utah Mormon leaders (including Wells) later treated Mormons who engaged in same-sex acts. If pioneer Mormon leaders had a hierarchy of sexual sins, then they viewed sodomy as far less serious than adultery, incest, bestiality, or fornication.

The next homoerotic act known to Mormon history occurred in October 1864. A non-Mormon soldier named Frederick Jones was arrested for sexually assaulting a nine-year-old Mormon boy in Salt Lake City. Jeter Clinton, the Mormon municipal judge, released the soldier because anal sex was not illegal in Utah.[35] By contrast, the Salt Lake County Court only a month before had sentenced a man to "20 years at hard labour in the Penitentiary" for "carnally knowing and abusing a Female child under ten years of age."[36] After the soldier's release by the court, someone (apparently the boy's father, Charles Monk) murdered Private Jones before he returned to the army fort. For lack of witnesses, Justice Clinton dismissed all charges against the father. As for the sexually assaulted boy, he married at age twenty-eight and fathered thirteen children.[37]

Mormon outrage in 1864 seemed directed more to the fact that the perpetrator was a non-Mormon than to the nature of his assault. Curiously, the *Deseret News* did not use this case as a warning against sodomy but instead as a warning against heterosexual acts already covered by Utah law: "there is always the risk that some one will be impatient of the law's delay in cases so outrageous and abominable, even when a statute covers the case."[38] For more than a decade, Mormons in Salt Lake City and its environs often murdered or castrated men for adultery and bestiality, after which police turned a blind eye or juries acquitted the Mormon perpetrators.[39] This 1864 case was also important for its public acknowledgment that sodomy was not illegal in pioneer Mormon Utah.

Despite this dramatic 1864 case, Utah legislators did not pass a sodomy law until January 1876. That legislative delay signifies Brigham Young's disinterest in criminalizing homoerotic activities. In response to the case of Private Jones, Brigham Young wrote in November 1864 that Utah had no sodomy law because "our legislators, never having contemplated the possibility of such a crime being committed in our borders had made no provision for its punishment."[40] The first problem with Young's explanation is that his claim of sodomy's inconceivability was not consistent with the reference to John C. Bennett's "buggery" in the Nauvoo *Wasp* or with Young's own remarks at that time about Bennett's "young men." Second, ten years before the Jones case, Apostle Parley P. Pratt and Brigham Young himself had publicly stated that it was possible for Utah Mormons to reenact the "unnatural lusts" of Sodom. If anything, Brigham's 1864 letter appears as a historically inaccurate excuse for the lack of a sodomy law in Utah.

Third, sodomy was certainly not inconceivable in Utah after the publicity of the 1864 Jones case, yet the legislature still did not criminalize sodomy for twelve years. This despite the fact that the LDS First Presidency controlled the Utah legislature every time it convened during this period. If Brigham Young had wanted a sodomy law in pioneer Utah, the legislature would have immediately passed one. The legislative process in pioneer Utah was that simple and direct.[41]

Ironically, passage of Utah's first sodomy law had nothing to do with homoeroticism. Utah's federally appointed non-Mormon governor had formally requested the Utah legislature to adopt California's Penal Code in full because Utah's criminal law, in effect since 1852, "omits to define or provide punishment for a large class of actions which in other communities are regarded as crimes and punished as such." Utah's legislature adopted the ordinance in 1876 against "every person who is guilty of the infamous crime against nature," but not because of any Mormon concern about same-sex intercourse. Mormon legislators enacted a sodomy law in 1876 only because it was part of the California code that Utah Territory adopted in its entirety.[42]

Less than a week after the Utah legislature began considering its first sodomy law, Mormon leaders demonstrated that they had no interest in prosecuting a Mormon for "the infamous crime against nature." On 23 January 1876, LDS leaders had to confront "the scandal and improper connexion between George Naylor and Frank Wells."[43] Used in that context, the word *connexion* in the 1870s meant sexual intercourse.[44]

There were three males who could have been this George Naylor in January 1876: a twelve year old, a seventeen year old, or the thirty-eight-year-old father of the youngest. LDS ward membership lists and the U.S. census show that there were two persons named Frank Wells living in Salt Lake County at the time: a nine-year-old boy in Salt Lake City and a forty-six-year-old husband and father living in Sandy. A third Frank Wells may have moved to Salt Lake City by 1876. Then twenty-eight years old, this unmarried Frank Wells had previously lived in Summit County with an unmarried salesclerk who was eight years his senior. While that living arrangement was consistent with the "improper connexion" of the 1876 scandal, the available documents do not show where this twenty-eight-year-old Frank Wells was living that year.[45]

The response by local LDS leaders helps to identify Naylor and Wells. It is unlikely that Frank Wells was the nine-year-old boy, since there was no talk of arrest, imprisonment, excommunication, or blood atonement for the older George Naylor. Daniel H. Wells was the father of the nine year old, and it is unlikely that he would have spared even a seventeen-year-old for performing a sexual act on his minor son. After all, Wells had ordered the execution of a young man for having sexual intercourse with a horse. Also, the son of Wells was known by his first name, Stephen, rather than by his middle name, Franklin.[46] Regardless the age of Frank Wells, church punishment would have been at least a matter of discussion if a thirty-eight-year-old married Mormon had been the George Naylor in question.

In fact, instead of any church punishment, Mormon authorities in Salt Lake sent the humiliated George Naylor on a special mission to Arizona in February 1876.[47] Exile is an unlikely punishment for a twelve year old, and this George Naylor was known by his middle name, Hamner, rather than by his first name.[48] This leaves the seventeen-year-old English immigrant as the most likely George Naylor who had "improper connexion" with Frank Wells, who was probably the twenty-eight-year-old non-Mormon. Therefore, LDS leaders simply decided to separate the two young men. After his face-saving mission to Arizona, Naylor married at age twenty-six and eventually fathered nine children.[49] In fact homoerotic conduct was not among the sex-related charges for which any Mormon was excommunicated between 1845 and Brigham Young's death in 1877.[50]

The year 1877 is also the earliest known reference to the possibility of male prostitution in Utah. In January 1877, the Salt Lake City Police Court fined "William Wright (alias Dick)" fifty dollars for "Prostitution at the Great Western on evidence of Mrs. Smith." That year "John Dix" and "John Doe" also paid similar fines for "prostitution." In contrast, this police court record distinguished other prostitution-related charges for men by such descriptions as "renting house to Prostitutes" and "renting house for Prostitution."[51] However, legal references to male prostitution did not become common in Utah for another fifteen years.[52]

Utah's first sodomy trial occurred in 1881 in Provo. According to the Provo newspaper, while jailed during the investigation of the death of one of his patients, Dr. Perry D. McClanahan, a thirty-eight-year-old married physician, committed sodomy on an unwilling "lad named Charles Henry Barrett, aged 15 years." Instead of *rape,* the criminal indictment used the equivalent word *ravish*. The newspaper added that the assault occurred while the victim (actually age seventeen) "was serving out 60 days for having committed an assault on a little girl of 5 years."[53]

The Mormon physician's published defense against this charge was the odd admission: "I hav'ent slept with two men for fifteen years."[54] Despite the fact that the sheriff testified he "discovered the scoundrel in the very act of his unnatural crime," this case resulted in two trials with hung juries of Mormons. In response, the judge simply kept this physician in prison for three months, without bail or retrial, before releasing him "on his own recognizance." Three months would become the average period of imprisonment for Utah men convicted of sodomy. Dr. McClanahan died a year later in Idaho. Barrett married at age twenty-four and fathered four children.[55]

Utah's first convictions for sodomy occurred in the summer of 1882. The two trials resulted in only a few months of imprisonment for each defendant. The first trial occurred in July of a thirty-five-year-old man accused of attempting to have sex with an unwilling ten-year-old boy. The prison record described his crime as an "Against Nature assault upon a Boy." The second case involved a seventeen-year-old who had just served nineteen months in prison for manslaughter. Three months after his release, the youth was arrested and tried in August for a crime "against nature," the details of which are presently unknown. Both the older man and this teenager (who was apparently LDS) were released from the Utah penitentiary after less than four months in prison.[56]

The harshest response of a nineteenth-century Mormon leader to homoeroticism occurred a month after the conclusion of these trials. In September 1882, First Presidency Counselor Joseph F. Smith instructed the stake presidency of Richfield, Utah: "Get the names of *all of them* & cut them off the church" for "obscene, filthy & horrible practices." He referred to a group of young LDS men who had engaged in "this monstrous iniquity, for which Sodom & Gomorrah were burned with fire sent down from heaven."[57] This was the first known instance in which teenagers were excommunicated from the LDS Church for homoeroticism.

In this statement, Joseph F. Smith made complete the reversal of his prophet-uncle's nonsexual interpretation of Sodom's destruction. Parley P. Pratt in 1853 had revised the founding prophet's view by saying God destroyed Sodom for its "promiscuous intercourse with the other sex" as well as the ancient city's "strange and unnatural lusts."[58] Now, Counselor Smith claimed that Sodom was destroyed only for "obscene, filthy & horrible practices" between men. His uncle Joseph had claimed God destroyed Sodom for "rejecting the prophets," and LDS leaders at Nauvoo had used the term "Buggery" to describe John C. Bennett's relationships with "young men," rather than the word *sodomy*.

It is possible that this Richfield case involved promiscuous homoeroticism, but evidence suggests that these young men were sexually intimate as couples. They seemed to be paired in age: two in their thirties, two aged nineteen and eighteen, and two fifteen year olds. The oldest was a thirty-two-year-old polygamist who had not fathered a child for four years and who fathered no more children after this homoerotic scandal. All but one of these excommunicated men remained unmarried the rest of their lives, and the oldest bachelor was apparently living with the former polygamist twenty years later.[59] However, despite the fact that Utah courts had recently tried an adult and a teenager for crimes "against nature," the First Presidency counselor made no suggestion of using Utah's sodomy law against these two adults and four teenagers for committing "this monstrous iniquity" with each other. That restraint may have been to avoid negative publicity.

Few Mormons learned of that 1882 farm town scandal, but four years later Utah's capital reeled at the news of homoerotic behavior by one of its elite. On 26 July 1886, his sixtieth birthday, the Salt Lake stake high council "suspended" Thomas Taylor as bishop of the Salt Lake City

Fourteenth Ward. He was not related to the LDS Church president.[60] Three teenagers testified that while each was alone in bed with Bishop Taylor, the bishop had used the young man's hand to masturbate himself and "had taught them the crime of Masturbation." They were ages fifteen to eighteen when the incidents occurred in Cedar City, several hundred miles south of the congregation over which the bishop presided. In addition, local LDS leaders in Cedar City wrote that a fourth "young man of this Ward has made a [verbal] statement similar to those contained herein," but he was out of town during the formal hearing.[61] There had been no homosexual sodomy cases in Utah courts since 1882. From shocked references in diaries and newspapers, the Thomas Taylor case was the first time most Mormons knew of a faithful Latter-day Saint man having homoerotic relations with teenagers.[62]

Thomas Taylor was a polygamist and had been arrested for polygamous cohabitation with his wives only a few months before. At the church trial, he denied the testimony of the two younger brothers, yet he had previously written a letter of apology to their father. He admitted the sexual incident with the oldest of the young men. Taylor said that it "was not the first one I practiced in my life, but was the first since I joined the Church [as a teenager]." In his autobiography, however, Taylor later described the charges as "trumped up slander."[63]

At the least, Taylor was vulnerable to prosecution for "indecent assault" on the minors. Newspapers reported that a grand jury in southern Utah considered "the charge against Thomas Taylor for an unmentionable crime" and "elicited some disgusting things of Taylor." However, despite the nearby residence of the young men involved, "there was no evidence of the crimes he was accused of," and the grand jury dropped the case in December 1886.[64]

By contrast, in May 1886 the district court in Ogden had sentenced a man to three years in prison for the "Crime Against Nature" of having "carnal intercourse" with "a certain bitch or female dog."[65] First, it is noteworthy that in 1886 the Utah court system regarded bestiality as more serious than a prominent Mormon's "indecent assault" on male teenagers. Second, conviction of sodomy with an animal resulted in several years of imprisonment, compared with the Utah sentencing pattern of several months in prison for those convicted of homosexual sodomy. This pattern existed before and after the 1886 case of bestiality. There continued to be a disparity in the sentencing for the two types of sodomy in Utah.

Thomas Taylor was excommunicated in 1886 for what the anti-Mormon *Tribune* and some contemporary Mormons called "sodomy," even though that term technically applied only to "unnatural" intercourse, either anal or bestial. *Sodomy* was not the legal term for Taylor's masturbatory conduct with the teenagers.[66] LDS authorities allowed him to be rebaptized into the LDS Church a few years later.[67] Despite the widespread knowledge of this scandal in southern Utah, Taylor moved there, where Mormons elected him to the Parowan City Council in 1888 and reelected him in 1890. The oldest of the three teenagers lived in Parowan at the time of their accusations. All three young men married between the ages of twenty-five and twenty-seven and fathered three or four children each.[68]

Mormons and non-Mormons reacted with even greater shock and revulsion at the next same-sex scandal only six months later. Because of this incident's special circumstances and publicity, I will describe it more fully here. Not quite thirteen years old, a Mormon farm boy arrived in Salt Lake City alone one Sunday evening. He had apparently run away from his home in Spanish Fork, Utah. With nowhere to stay on this freezing January night in 1887, he asked the police to help him. They said he could stay in the city jail, if he wanted. Instead of giving him a safe corner in a hallway on his own, the jailers locked the twelve year old in a room with a gang of teenagers already imprisoned for various offenses, including brutally kicking and beating a sixteen-year-old boy.[69]

After the jailers left, the young men spent the night repeatedly gang-raping the twelve year old and performing forcible oral sex on him. In the morning, the boy (who was described as "pale, sick and trembling") told the police what had happened.[70] His feelings were undoubtedly similar to another nineteenth-century teenage boy who testified that his Utah rapist made "a regular girl of me."[71] In 1887, Utah's community had to face crimes that had seemed inconceivable to many Mormons and non-Mormons—a boy had been raped, the rapists were teenagers, the oldest rapist was sixteen, and Salt Lake City police had allowed it all to happen.

The five teenagers attacked victims as a gang because of their own slight size. The tallest was 5 feet 2 inches and the heaviest weighed 100 pounds. Richard Buboltz was sixteen, Arthur Curtis was fifteen, William H. Paddock was fourteen, John Ledford was thirteen, and Daniel Hendry was twelve.[72]

The Mormon political newspaper *Salt Lake Herald* demanded immediate improvements in the conditions at Salt Lake City's jail. For city officials, it was bad enough that the defense of these teenage rapists was that "they had only done what the men prisoners had subjected them to when they were first turned in."[73] No one raised the possibility that the jailers had purposely locked that runaway boy in the cell for the sadistic sport of finding out what the teenage gang would do to him.

Unlike earlier instances of consensual sex involving male teenagers, no one could ignore Utah's sodomy statute in this sensational case. As a result, Judge George D. Pyper of Salt Lake City's municipal court convicted the two oldest perpetrators in January 1887 of what the Mormon newspaper called "an unmentionable crime against nature" and which the non-Mormon newspaper called "the infamous crime against nature." This twenty-year-old Mormon judge convicted the twelve and thirteen year olds only for "indecent assault," because they claimed "inability to carry the crime [of anal rape] into successful execution."[74]

However, they had joined the two older boys in performing oral sex on the twelve-year-old boy, which the Mormon political newspaper called "an additional and unnameable offense." The anti-Mormon *Salt Lake Tribune* caustically observed, "but as in the case with much other bestiality going on [such as polygamy], it is not a crime in this Territory." Judge Pyper's sentencing of the younger teenagers to one hundred days of imprisonment for "indecent assault" was apparently his way of compensating for the absence of a Utah law concerning oral sex.[75] Although newspaper accounts reported that the "unnameable" act of oral sex was not covered by Utah statutes, the Mormon-controlled legislature waited nearly fifty years to criminalize it.[76]

The municipal court's decision was reviewed by the district court with its federally appointed non-Mormon judge. Judge Charles S. Zane reconvicted the two older youths of sodomy but dismissed all charges against the twelve and thirteen year olds. Zane gave a three-month prison sentence to each of the two sodomy convicts.[77] One could argue that Zane's family situation predisposed him toward lenience in this case of teenage sodomy. At the time his twenty-three-year-old married son was an officer of the newly organized Bohemian Club, whose membership was verifiably homosexual within a few years. However, the Salt Lake Bohemian Club might not have been a social refuge this early for those who felt homoerotic interest.[78] Still, later developments indicate that both Mormons and non-Mormons regarded Zane's treatment of this case as lenient.

The Mormon newspapers (*Deseret News* and *Salt Lake Herald*) and the anti-Mormon *Salt Lake Tribune* all identified the five rapists by name, but none mentioned the religion of these criminals. Everyone in the religiously polarized city had reason to be embarrassed by this gang's religious backgrounds. The oldest, Richard Buboltz, was a sixteen-year-old Mormon. He had emigrated from the Swiss-German Mission to Salt Lake City six years earlier with his sister and widowed mother. The youngest gang member, Daniel Hendry, was a Scottish Mormon who sailed with Buboltz on the same ship to America.[79] The other imprisoned young men were American born, and at least one was also a Mormon.[80]

However, non-Mormons had the greatest reason to be embarrassed about William H. Paddock, a son of two of Utah's most prominent non-Mormons. Paddock led the gang rape of the twelve-year-old Mormon boy, in addition to being the ringleader in the gang's previous battery of a sixteen-year-old Mormon. Paddock was among the youngest of the accused, but his mother testified that he "never had the ordinary sense of right and wrong." Paddock led the gang rape on what was almost his fourteenth birthday, and the sodomy indictment listed him first among the accused.[81]

Paddock's parents had both been involved prominently in the anti-Mormon movement. His mother had written three books against the Mormons, and his father was clerk of the federally appointed Utah Commission, which was in charge of disfranchising all Mormon polygamists.[82] Although the *Deseret News* usually took every opportunity to ridicule members of the Utah Commission, the church's newspaper refrained from exploiting a family's tragedy.[83] Also the *Deseret News* articles changed the raped boy's first or last name, and the *Salt Lake Herald* never identified him in any way. On the other hand, the anti-Mormon *Tribune* fully identified the Mormon victim.[84] If the *Tribune* intended that to embarrass Mormons, the *Deseret News* did not respond by emphasizing the senior Paddock's federal position when the *News* reported that he committed his son to Utah's insane asylum. This was a few days after Paddock's conviction in the city court for sodomy, and it kept him out of prison temporarily.[85]

William Paddock was the first person whose commitment to the Utah insane asylum stemmed from homoerotic activities. However, the examining physician and the asylum admission records did not refer to Paddock's sexual activities. He remained there only until late July, when physicians judged him to be "not Insane" and sent him back to the penitentiary.[86] By then all the other gang members had been released from prison, Buboltz having served the most time (five months since his original arrest).[87] With Paddock out on bail in August, his parents again tried to have him declared mentally incompetent, apparently to avoid the possibility of imprisonment. The publisher of the *Tribune* joined as a friend of the family in testifying that Paddock was "of unsound mind and not morally responsible for his conduct."[88]

Whether or not William Paddock was "morally responsible," his conduct continued to be sociopathic, although not demonstrably homoerotic. In October, he led the older Arthur Curtis and younger Dan Hendry in stealing shotguns and burglarizing a store. Paddock evaded arrest, the charges were dropped against Curtis, and Hendry was sentenced to three months in county jail. Two years later, sixteen-year-old William Paddock was leading a different gang of "boy burglars."[89]

Like Paddock, most of the teenage perpetrators in the 1887 sodomy case continued a life of crime. The two youngest, Daniel Hendry (sometimes identified as David Hendry) and John Ledford, continued committing burglaries with a gang led by Arthur Curtis and his brothers for more than a decade.[90] Curtis, the next oldest and originally a Mormon, left the church, joined the U.S. Navy, and tattooed his left hand with a small cross or X on the fleshy webbing "bet thumb & finger [of] left hand." Sometimes a dot instead of a small cross, this left-hand tattoo was apparently a symbol during the 1890s to show interest in male-male sex.[91] However, Curtis returned to Utah, was imprisoned for burglary at age thirty, and eventually married.[92]

Conventional lifestyle characterized only two of those involved in the 1887 scandal. Buboltz, the oldest perpetrator and also a Mormon, avoided further arrest, settled down, married at age twenty-two, and fathered five children. The raped boy stayed with the LDS Church, married at age twenty-eight, but fathered only one child.[93]

These incidents of excommunication and imprisonment for same-sex acts from 1881 to 1887 occurred during the LDS presidency of John Taylor. Within days of his death, his counselors and the Mormon apostles expressed their dissent from the harsh response Taylor had required for all disapproved sexual conduct. On 12 August 1887, Lorenzo Snow told the other apostles that "Brigham Young was not so radical in his rulings on sexual crimes as John Taylor had been." And Taylor's first counselor George Q. Cannon added that "he had not been in full accord with the radical position taken by President Taylor regarding sexual crimes; and that he knew that President Taylor had changed very much in his feelings before the day of his death."[94] The apostles may have been thinking of the 1882 excommunication of the teenagers for consensual sodomy in Richfield when disapproving the "radical" punishments Taylor had required. In any event, five years after this meeting, Snow approved the complete exoneration of a polygamist accused of performing oral sex on his brothers, despite the testimony of multiple witnesses.

Ironically, two years after the Mormon hierarchy decided to return to a more lenient response for "sexual crimes," the federally appointed judges increased sodomy penalties dramatically in Utah. Before then, Utah's judges, both Mormon and non-Mormon, had treated "the infamous crime against nature" as no more serious than fornication by unmarried men or women. Until the late 1880s, Utah's judicial punishment for sodomy and fornication was usually from two to four months in prison, even though the sodomy convictions had always involved unwilling victims.[95] That is noteworthy, because Utah's 1876 sodomy law (copied from the California code) provided for a maximum imprisonment of five years.[96] Similarly, the state of New York did not criminalize consensual sodomy between adults until the end of the nineteenth century.[97]

However, in October 1889 (the first sodomy case since 1887), a non-Mormon judge in Provo sentenced forty-year-old Evan S. Thomas to a year in prison for sodomy. The judge remarked that "in all his practice in Tennessee he had never heard of such a case as this." Thomas was a believing Mormon who had received a patriarchal blessing the previous year.[98] In October 1890 another non-Mormon judge in Provo sentenced a twenty-three-year-old man to two years for "Assault with intent to commit Buggery."[99] Contrast those sodomy sentences with all the fornication sentences given by Utah courts in 1889–90: five days to one man convicted of fornication, fifty days to another, and six-month sentences to each of four men.[100]

In other words, two years after the 1887 sodomy case, the Utah judiciary suddenly began regarding sodomy as more serious than fornication. There is no obvious explanation for this in the circumstances and documents of Mormonism or of civil Utah. The judicial preoccupation in Utah from 1882 to 1890 was the vigorous federal indictments, arrests, prosecutions, and imprisonments of more than 1,300 polygamist Mormons. It is difficult to see any direct correlation of the so-called Polygamy Raid of the 1880s with the changes in judicial sentencing for sodomy cases in Utah during the same time period.[101]

Despite the lack of additional sodomy indictments from early 1887 to late 1889, a possible explanation for the increased severity is that Utah's judges regarded as too lenient the January 1887 judicial response to the teenage rapists. This is supported by an editorial in the *Deseret News* that was replying to the published complaints of Cornelia Paddock, mother of the ringleader in the 1887 case. In response to her claims that the Mormon police and judiciary were harassing her son, the *Deseret News* icily replied in May 1889: "His utterly vile and depraved conduct was condoned by sending him to the insane asylum, because there was then no reformatory in which he could be placed." While referring to her son's "natural depravity," the editorial continued: "And out of kindness to the parents who now seek to shield him and ungratefully spit out venom against the forebearing [Mormons], he has been dealt with gently and mercifully."[102]

It is possible to regard that May 1889 criticism of Mormon leniency toward Paddock's conviction as changing the judicial climate. A problem with that interpretation is that it was non-Mormon judges who began giving severe sentences for sodomy from 1889 onward, not the Mormon judges who may have resented Mrs. Paddock's "ingratitude" for the earlier mercy shown to the teenagers convicted of sodomy.

However, Sarah Barringer Gordon (a non-Mormon legal expert of Utah's criminal cases in the nineteenth century) has suggested another explanation. To the rest of America, Mormon polygamy made Utah into the "Sodom of the New World."[103] The virtual triumph of the judiciary over Mormon polygamy by 1889 left sodomy as a suddenly obvious target for Utah's federally appointed judges.[104] In any event, the change in sentencing patterns was remarkable.

Nevertheless, even though Utah's judges were increasing the sentences for homosexual sodomy, they still regarded that crime as less serious than sex with an animal. In September 1890, the Salt Lake County judge gave a three-year prison sentence to a sixty-year-old married Utahn who had "sexual intercourse with a certain animal, to wit with a certain bay mare." This was a month before the Provo judge gave a two-year sentence in the previous "buggery" trial. Also defined as a "Crime against Nature," bestiality was more serious than sodomy in the view of Utah's judges during the late nineteenth century.[105]

However, anal sex between consenting adults had a protected status in the eyes of some Mormons at the beginning of the 1890s. In the spring of 1891, five witnesses testified that James Hamilton, a thirty-five-year-old unmarried Mormon, "did make an assault" and used "his private part to penetrate" and "lie with the said William D. Burton as with a woman." The *Deseret News* added that this occurred "in the rear of the Keystone saloon, on Commercial street."[106] Burton was forty-three years old, of medium build, and had a "small Blue dot in India Ink between thumb and Forefinger on [his] left hand." As previously discussed, some men of the 1890s wore this tattoo to show interest in having sex with other men.[107]

While "W.D." Burton testified on behalf of the defendant that there was no assault, the LDS political newspaper still observed: "The facts of the case are of a most disgusting nature." This resulted in two trials. In the first, "after deliberating for five hours the jurors say they cannot agree and are discharged." In the second trial, the primarily Mormon jury in Salt Lake City took five minutes to acquit Hamilton on all charges. Although he had been imprisoned for six weeks, Hamilton and his alleged victim walked out of the courtroom as free men, despite the testimony of those who had discovered them engaging in anal intercourse. The *Deseret News* refused to publish the news of this acquittal, even though it noted the start of the second trial and gave the other verdicts for the day of Hamilton's exoneration. However, the LDS political newspaper, *Salt Lake Herald*, fully reported the acquittal.[108]

Before the next male sodomy case, Utahns got a sensational view of female-female passion, sexuality, same-sex marriage, jealousy, and female-female violence. Beginning 27 January 1892, the *Deseret News* gave front-page coverage to what a medical journal called "Lesbian Love and Murder."[109] The LDS Church newspaper told its Mormon readers that nineteen-year-old Alice Mitchell's girlfriend had agreed to a "proposed marriage" between the two young women, and the *News* explained that "the proposed marriage . . . was to be in the nature of an elopement." However, the girlfriend changed her mind and "returned the engagement ring." As a result, Mitchell murdered her girlfriend in Memphis, Tennessee, because "she loved her," and said: "I could not bear to be separated from her."[110]

The *Salt Lake Tribune*, a morning paper, had already reported the same quotations as appeared in the evening LDS newspaper. However, this sensational story was on page two of the non-Mormon paper, while it was front-page news in the Mormon newspaper. For the first time, these newspapers introduced the Utah community to the existence of female homoeroticism.[111]

A physician who testified at the trial wrote shortly afterward that the two young women "became lovers in the same sense of that relation between persons of different sexes," and that following the intended civil marriage ceremony, "Alice was to continue to wear man's apparel and meant to try and have a mustache."[112] The *Deseret News* indicated on February 6 that it would refuse to print "the *nature* of the evidence" contained in the correspondence between the two women.[113] Nevertheless, by comparison with the publication in the *Deseret News* of eight front-page, detailed stories, Salt Lake City's other dailies virtually ignored this tragic case of female-female passion.[114]

Curiously, even though it had stopped reporting the details of the female case, the *Deseret News* on 24 February 1892 gave front-page attention to a tragic example of male-male passion. Observing that the "peculiarities" of the Memphis case were "not confined to the feminine sex," the *News* headlined: "THE DOCTOR'S LOVE: His Strange Attachment to Isaac Judson Prompts Him to Kill Himself." Whereas the LDS newspaper had evaded homoeroticism when reporting on the Mitchell case, the *News* quoted the entire suicide note of the Baltimore physician. His words to his male friend clearly referred to the homoerotic: "We might have been happy together had it not been for . . . your high ideas of morality." The suicide note also complained that his friend valued parental approval more than the relationship the two men shared. The physician added: "Men of our natures and sins must have their punishment, and ours comes in terrible shape." This front-page story in the *Deseret News* added: "Judson says he has been an intimate friend of the suicide."[115]

The deceased man's reference to "men of our natures" indicates that by February 1892, some American men regarded their same-sex desires as distinguishing them from men who did not feel such passions. This preceded by a few months the first use of the terms *heterosexual* and *homosexual* in an American medical journal.[116] Thus, before homosexuality was a defined concept in the American medical community, those with intense (or exclusively) same-sex desires defined themselves as different. *Homosexual, lesbian,* and *gay* are culturally defined terms, yet it is demonstrable that some people regarded themselves as a sexual minority even though they lacked a common term to describe themselves.

Although the LDS Church newspaper had been reporting Utah cases of homosexual rape and sodomy for years, and continued to do so after 1892, the *Deseret News* added a different perspective that year. Its Mormon editors chose to reprint national news that brought a new dimension to the Utah media's treatment of homoeroticism. Same-sex eroticism could also be based on "love," a word the Mormon newspaper used without qualification in these stories about the two women and about the two men. This same-sex "love" had driven a woman to murder and a man to suicide, but the Mormon newspaper did not imply that this was unique to same-sex love.

In fact, during the same period in 1892, these two tragic stories of same-sex love shared the headlines with multiple reports of the equally tragic outcome of opposite-sex love. During these three weeks, the *Deseret News* reported that "unrequited" or "unhappy" love for women caused four men to commit suicide, one man to attempt suicide, one man to disfigure his former girlfriend with acid, one to beat his girlfriend, one to murder his wife, and another to murder his wife's male lover.[117] The *Deseret News* certainly did not endorse homoeroticism, but the Mormon newspaper in 1892 acknowledged that genuine "love"—even if tragic or "strange"—could be part of the "sin against nature."

Later that year, there were disparities in Utah's sodomy sentences for men within the same courtroom. In mid-September 1892 in Ogden, James A. Miner (a non-Mormon and also an associate justice of the Utah Supreme Court) sentenced an eighteen-year-old non-Mormon immigrant to six months in the Utah penitentiary for committing assault and "buggery" upon a seven-year-old boy.[118] Two weeks later, the same judge gave a two-year prison sentence to a twenty-eight-year-old man for what was apparently consensual sodomy. His alleged victim, then twenty-one years old, could not be located to testify at the trial, and four years later this alleged victim was himself convicted of sodomy in another case. That suggests that the 1892 sodomy "assault" was actually consensual intercourse between the two young men.[119] Age is the only conceivable explanation for why an eighteen year old's conviction of forcible sodomy on a child was one-fourth the length of imprisonment given during the same month by the same judge for consensual sex between men.

There were no sodomy cases in Utah's criminal courts during 1893. However, that year the town of Honeyville was rocked by a same-sex scandal that divided families and pitted local LDS leaders against each other. In October 1893, Box Elder Stake president Rudger Clawson rendered his decision concerning what he described as "one of the most extraordinary cases that ever arose in the church of Jesus Christ of Latter day Saints."[120] Two young men (then twenty-three and nineteen) accused their thirty-four-year-old, married half-brother Lorenzo Hunsaker of sexually fondling them and performing oral sex on them since "four years ago this fall," and as frequently as every two weeks. Twenty-three-year-old Peter Hunsaker said he woke up while his half-brother Lorenzo was "in the act of fingering me." He said his older brother also attempted to "ride him" (perform anal sex), and complained: "I did not want him to monkey with me." Peter added: "I do not think he would have intercourse with other women, but [he] is not virtuous with men."[121] A married twenty-five-year-old neighbor also testified that he awoke one night and discovered Lorenzo masturbating him while they slept together during a visit.[122]

The stake president decided that all charges against the respected high priest were lies and therefore reversed the previous decision of the bishop's court to disfellowship Lorenzo Hunsaker. Instead, Clawson excommunicated the two accusing brothers for the "gross wrong" of making "such a monstrous charge" against their married brother. A twenty-one-year-old half-brother escaped that fate by denying his previous statements that Lorenzo had repeatedly fondled him and attempted oral sex on him while they slept together. Apostle Lorenzo Snow was present and approved the decision to exonerate Lorenzo Hunsaker and to punish his brothers for claiming he sexually molested them.[123]

Stake President Clawson also released the ward bishop for encouraging dissent against this decision. Because most of the ward membership also protested these decisions, the stake president refused to allow the sacrament (communion) to be administered in that congregation's meetings for seven months. Apostle John Henry Smith restored that privilege in June 1894. However, Honeyville's residents refused to sustain their newly appointed bishop until November 1895.[124] This is the only instance in Mormon history when a specific community suffered the LDS equivalent of "the interdict"—a Roman Catholic practice of punishing a congregation or community by prohibiting the administration of the holy Sacraments. Homoeroticism was the background for this only known example of a Mormon congregation suffering such an interdict.[125]

Although his legal wife and plural wife were of child-bearing age, the accused Lorenzo Hunsaker fathered only one child after this Honeyville incident. Lorenzo's plural wife obtained a church divorce from him in 1897. His half-brothers (who were single at the times of the homoerotic incidents) married at twenty-one and twenty-two years of age. They and the other accusing brother, Peter (who was married at the time of the church court), all fathered eleven children each. Lorenzo moved to Arizona, where he served as an LDS bishop for many years, and at least one of the excommunicated brothers regained his LDS membership.[126]

This 1893 case is important for showing the existence of four diverse attitudes in nineteenth-century Mormon culture toward homoerotic behaviors. First, Lorenzo Hunsaker told his brothers that oral sex with him was a harmless way for them to avoid "bothering the girls." Second, he also advised them against "self-abuse" (masturbation).[127] Lorenzo's first statement mirrored the Mormon hierarchy's fifty years of regarding homoerotic behaviors as less serious than heterosexual intimacy outside marriage. His second statement indicated at least some Mormons also regarded masturbation as a more serious offense than homoerotic activities. The medical evaluations at the Utah insane asylum indicate that this was also the view of Utah's physicians during the same time period.[128]

Third, one of the accusing brothers also showed that some nineteenth-century Mormons had a negative judgment toward homoeroticism that seems identical to the views of many Americans today. In 1893 this twenty-three-year-old Mormon used the same slang term that is common in America now to describe the person who performs oral sex on a man.[129] Fourth, the reaction of the stake president to the church court evidence shows the power of denial that existed among some nineteenth-century Mormons regarding the reality of homoerotic activities.

In the next sodomy case of December 1894 the district court judge in Ogden gave another long prison sentence for what may have been consensual sex. This time, seventeen-year-old Frank Smiley was accused of "buggery" with "Willie" Clark, whose true name was unknown to the court and who seemed to be younger than the accused. Smiley pleaded guilty, apparently to avoid the necessity of requiring Clark to testify. Clark disappeared, and the non-Mormon judge sentenced Smiley to three years in the Utah penitentiary. However, this teenager's harsh punishment may have resulted from the fact that his sodomy conviction was less than a year after his release from the Utah prison for a burglary conviction.[130] As for the alleged victim, he may have been the "Willis" Clark who was being arrested monthly for prostitution nine years later.[131]

Four months after this Ogden trial for teenage sodomy, the Oscar Wilde case brought homoeroticism to the attention of Utah Mormons as never before. Wilde's crime was not "sexual assault," but "the Love that dare not speak its name." The evidence included love letters, love poems, casual sex between Wilde and young men, and his long-term relationship with Alfred Lord Douglas, sixteen years younger than Wilde.[132] Although the Wilde case occurred in England, its sensational publicity in the United States is often regarded as a turning point in both British and American attitudes toward same-sex relationships.[133] For example, one year after Wilde's conviction for sodomy, reports of "unnatural offenses" to London's police had more than doubled.[134] However, the effect of the Wilde case was quite different in Utah.

NOTES

1. This requires explanation. In prepublication review, Rocky O'Donovan criticized this chapter's inclusion of rape with consensual sexual activities and objected to my association of rape with *erotic,* from the Greek word *eros* (love). I agree that the rape of a female or a male is more an act of violence than an act of sex, and I believe that rape is never an act of love. However, emotional love may also be absent from someone's participation in sexual activities that are "erotic" by conventional definition. I choose to avoid the complexity of dividing this discussion topically into separate sections on coerced sex, consensual sex without affection, consensual sex with affection but no commitment, and committed sexual relationships of mutual affection. Instead, this discussion presents chronologically the occasions when Mormons learned about actual or attempted sexual activities between persons of the same gender.

2. Lev. 18:22, 20:13. For revisionist views, see Martin Samuel Cohen, "The Biblical Prohibition of Homosexual Intercourse," *Journal of Homosexuality* 19, no. 4 (1990): 3–20; Saul M. Olyan, "'And with a Male You Shall Not Lie the Lying Down of a Woman': On the Meaning and Significance of Leviticus 18:22 and 20:13," *Journal of the History of Sexuality* 5 (Oct. 1994): 179–206; see also Robin Scrogg, *The New Testament and Homosexuality* (Philadelphia: Fortress Press, 1984); George Edward, *Gay/Lesbian Liberation: A Biblical Perspective* (New York: Pilgrim Press, 1984); and John J. McNeill, "Scripture

and Homosexuality," *The Church and the Homosexual*, 4th ed. (Boston: Beacon Press, 1993), 36–64.

3. Lawrence Foster, *Religion and Sexuality: Three American Communal Experiments of the Nineteenth Century* (New York: Oxford University Press, 1981), 171, 316n147; Foster, *Women, Family, and Utopia: Communal Experiments of the Shakers, the Oneida Community, and the Mormons* (Syracuse: Syracuse University Press, 1991), 149–50; Richard S. Van Wagoner, *Mormon Polygamy: A History* (Salt Lake City: Signature Books, 1986), 24. For Bennett's biographical sketch, see D. Michael Quinn, *The Mormon Hierarchy: Origins of Power* (Salt Lake City: Signature Books/Smith Research Associates, 1994), 536–38.

4. "Bennettiana," *Wasp—Extra* (Nauvoo, Ill.), 27 July 1842, [2], emphasis in the original. For William Smith, see *Deseret News 1995–1996 Church Almanac: The Church of Jesus Christ of Latter-day Saints* (Salt Lake City: Deseret News, 1994), 51; Quinn, *Origins of Power*, 594–97.

5. James A. H. Murray, ed., *A New English Dictionary*, 14 vols. (Oxford: Clarendon Press, 1888–1928), 1:1160, cites published references from 1330 A.D. through 1861. For judicial responses to anal intercourse before the time of Joseph Smith, see Caroline Bingham, "Seventeenth-Century Attitudes toward Deviant Sex," *Journal of Interdisciplinary History* 1 (Spring 1971): 447–72; Louis Crompton, "Homosexuals and the Death Penalty in Colonial America," *Journal of Homosexuality* 1 (Spring 1976): 277–93; Robert F. Oaks, "'Things Fearful to Name': Sodomy and Buggery in Seventeenth-Century New England," *Journal of Social History* 12 (Winter 1978): 268–81; Robert F. Oaks, "Perceptions of Homosexuality by Justices of the Peace in Colonia Virginia," *Journal of Homosexuality* 5 (Fall 1979–Winter 1980): 35–41; Ed Cohen, "Legislating the Norm: From Sodomy to Gross Indecency," in Donald R. Butters, John M. Clum, and Michael Moon, eds., *Displacing Homophobia: Gay Male Perspectives in Literature and Culture* (Durham: Duke University Press, 1989), esp. 173–77.

6. Brigham H. Roberts, ed., *History of the Church of Jesus Christ of Latter-day Saints*, 7 vols., 2d ed., rev. (Salt Lake City: Deseret Book, 1978), 4:206.

7. Ibid., 4:445.

8. *Deseret News 1995–1996 Church Almanac*, 48–49; George Miller at McConnelsville, Morgan Co., Ohio, to Joseph Smith, 2 Mar. 1841, printed in full in *Wasp* (Nauvoo, Ill.), 25 June 1842, [3]; see Roberts, *History of the Church*, 4:286, and *Deseret News 1995–1996 Church Almanac*, 75, for Miller as bishop.

9. "Bennettiana," [2].

10. *Deseret News 1995–1996 Church Almanac*, 51; Breck England, *The Life and Thought of Orson Pratt* (Salt Lake City: University of Utah Press, 1985), 80–81; Quinn, *Origins of Power*, 569–71.

11. *Times and Seasons* 5 (15 May 1844): 539; *Nauvoo Neighbor,* 15 May 1844, [3]. As previously mentioned, *bisexual* was not a term that Bennett's contemporaries would have used. I use it here to describe Bennett's sexual activities as modern readers would understand them.

12. *Nauvoo Neighbor,* 15 May 1844, [3], 29 May 1844, [3], 19 June 1844, [2–3]; *Times and Seasons* 5 (15 May 1844): 538–42 (which censored some of what was printed in the *Neighbor*); "An Ordinance concerning Brothels and Disorderly Characters," *Wasp* (Nauvoo, Ill.), 14 May 1842, [3]; Roberts, *History of the Church,* 4:444, 5:8; Nauvoo City Council Minutes, 2 Oct., 1 Nov. 1841, 14 May 1842, Archives, Historical Department of the Church of Jesus Christ of Latter-day Saints, Salt Lake City, Utah (hereafter LDS Archives). For Hyrum Smith, see *Deseret News 1995–1996 Church Almanac,* 44; Quinn, *Origins of Power,* 583–85.

13. *Nauvoo Neighbor,* 15 May 1844, [3]. In his *Nightfall at Nauvoo* (New York: Macmillan, 1971), 118, 134, Samuel W. Taylor was the first modern writer to assert that Bennett had homoerotic relationships at Nauvoo. See also Rocky O'Donovan, "'The Abominable and Detestable Crime against Nature': A Brief History of Homosexuality and Mormonism, 1840–1980," in Brent Corcoran, ed., *Multiply and Replenish: Mormon Essays on Sex and Family* (Salt Lake City: Signature Books, 1994), 132–34.

14. Roberts, *History of the Church,* 5:49, 77–78.

15. Ibid., 6:360.

16. Scott G. Kenney, ed., *Wilford Woodruff's Journal, 1833–1898 Typescript,* 9 vols., plus index (Midvale, Utah: Signature Books, 1983–91), 2:213 (22 Jan. 1843); Roberts, *History of the Church,* 5:237; Joseph Fielding Smith, ed., *Teachings of the Prophet Joseph Smith* (Salt Lake City: Deseret News Press, 1938), 271; Andrew F. Ehat and Lyndon W. Cook, eds., *The Words of Joseph Smith: The Contemporary Accounts of the Nauvoo Discourses of the Prophet Joseph* (Provo, Utah: Religious Studies Center, Brigham Young University, 1980), 156; Joseph Fielding Smith, ed., *Scriptural Teachings of the Prophet Joseph Smith,* annotated by Richard C. Galbraith (Salt Lake City: Deseret Book, 1993), 6. For the traditional interpretation of Sodom's destruction, see Richard Davenport-Hines, *Sex, Death, and Punishment: Attitudes toward Sex and Sexuality in Britain since the Renaissance* (London: Collins, 1990), 101.

17. John C. Bennett to James J. Strang, 16 Apr. 1846, Research Library and Archives, Reorganized Church of Jesus Christ of Latter Day Saints, Independence, Mo. For Strang and Bennett's association with his movement, see Roger Van Noord, *King of Beaver Island: The Life and Assassination of James Jesse Strang* (Urbana: University of Illinois Press, 1988), esp. 43–65.

18. Richard Ballantyne, 1856–89 diary, 21 Dec. 1856, summary of the week's events, LDS Archives. For Ballantyne, see Andrew Jenson, *Latter-day*

Saint Biographical Encyclopedia, 4 vols. (Salt Lake City: Deseret News Press and Andrew Jenson History, 1901–36), 1:705.

19. Roberts, *History of the Church,* 5:296; *Journal of Discourses,* 26 vols. (Liverpool: Latter-day Saints Book Depot, 1854–86), 1:73 (Hyde/1853), 1:83 (Young/1853), 1:97 (G. A. Smith/1851), 1:108 (Young/1853), 3:246–47 (Young/1856), 4:49–51 (J. M. Grant/1856), 4:53–54 (Young/1856), 4:173–74 (Kimball/1857), 4:219–20 (Young/1857), 6:38 (Kimball/1857), 7:20 (Kimball/1854), 146 (Young/1859), 10:110 (Young/1863). For various explanations of early Mormon teachings about "blood atonement," see Charles W. Penrose, *Blood Atonement, as Taught by Leading Elders of the Church of Jesus Christ of Latter-day Saints* (Salt Lake City: Juvenile Instructor Office, 1884); Joseph Fielding Smith, *Blood Atonement and the Origin of Plural Marriage* (Salt Lake City: Deseret News Press, 1905); Ogden Kraut, *Blood Atonement* (Salt Lake City: Pioneer Press, 1981); Paul H. Peterson, "The Mormon Reformation of 1856–1857," *Journal of Mormon History* 15 (1989): 66–67, 73–75; Keith E. Norman, "A Kinder Gentler Mormonism: Moving beyond the Violence of Our Past," *Sunstone* 14 (Aug. 1990): 10–11. Typically, Mormon writers describe such sermons as limited to the religious enthusiasm and frenzy of the Utah reformation up to 1857. However, Brigham Young had been publicly and privately advocating immediate execution for various sins since 1846, and as late as August 1869, Apostle George Q. Cannon made the following statement: "We close the door on one side, and say that whoredoms, seductions and adulteries must not be committed among us, and we say to those who are determined to carry on such things[:] we will kill you." *Journal of Discourses,* 14:58. See later instances in the text when Mormons carried out that threat.

20. *Journal of Discourses,* 1:259 (P. P. Pratt/1853). For Parley P. Pratt, see *Deseret News 1995–1996 Church Almanac,* 51; Quinn, *Origins of Power,* 571–73.

21. Roberts, *History of the Church,* 5:237.

22. *Journal of Discourses,* 2:253 (Young/1855), emphasis in original.

23. *Deseret News,* 7 Oct. 1857, 244. For the Utah War, see Norman Furniss, *The Mormon Conflict, 1850–1859* (New Haven: Yale University Press, 1960); Eugene E. Campbell, *Establishing Zion: The Mormon Church in the American West, 1847–1869* (Salt Lake City: Signature Books, 1988), 233–52; Donald R. Moorman and Gene A. Sessions, *Camp Floyd and the Mormons: The Utah War* (Salt Lake City: University of Utah Press, 1992).

24. John A. Peterson, "Warren Stone Snow, a Man in Between: The Biography of a Mormon Defender" (M.A. thesis, Brigham Young University, 1985), 112–15, citing Thomas Pitchforth diary, 31 May 1857, and Brigham Young to Warren Snow, 7 July 1857; see also Kenney, *Wilford Woodruff's Journal,* 5:55 (2 June 1857), for Young's initial reaction.

Various LDS sources indicate that Thomas Lewis was age twenty-three, twenty-four, or twenty-five at this 1857 incident, so my text discussion uses the middle one. He was listed as age sixteen when his mother, Elizabeth, immigrated to Utah with her six children in 1849. The 1860 census listed Thomas as a twenty-eight-year-old bachelor living with his mother in Manti. The International Genealogical Index gives only the year 1833 as the birth date of Thomas Lewis, while the entry in the LDS Ancestral File for his father, David Thomas Lewis (who never came to Utah), gives Thomas Lewis's birth year as 1834 and indicates that the son died unmarried in 1854, the latter date being an obvious error. His actual death date is presently unknown, but Thomas Lewis lived long enough to join his younger brother Lewis Lewis and two friends in an attempt to castrate Warren Snow in revenge during March 1872. Snow used a pistol to shoot two of his attackers, and perhaps this was when Thomas Lewis actually died. See entry for Elizabeth Lewis and children in Utah Overland Immigration Index (1847–68) and the Manti Ward Record of Members (1850–75), 18, 19, 20, entry for David Thomas Lewis (b. 1809) in the Ancestral File (hereafter LDS Ancestral File), and entry for Thomas Lewis in International Genealogical Index for Wales, all in Family History Library of the Church of Jesus Christ of Latter-day Saints, Salt Lake City, Utah (hereafter LDS Family History Library); U.S. 1860 Census of Manti, Sanpete County, Utah, sheet 23–A (page 658 of entire census), microfilm, LDS Family History Library; Peterson, "Warren Stone Snow," 120–21. Some historians have also confused the castrated and never-married Welshman Thomas Lewis (born ca. 1832–34) with a decade-younger Englishman of the same name who married, fathered children, and first appeared with his wife and one-year-old child in the 1870 Utah census of Salt Lake City. Aside from the significant age disparity, the Utah census consistently distinguished Wales from England as a birthplace. See U.S. 1870 Census of Salt Lake City, Salt Lake County, Utah, sheet 724–B, microfilm, LDS Family History Library.

Some reminiscent accounts confused this 1857 incident involving a Welshman with an 1859 incident in which a diary referred to an unnamed bishop who had just castrated a young Danish man so that the bishop could marry his girlfriend (see below). The reminiscent accounts claimed the bishop was Warren Snow. This indicates either that Bishop Snow committed a second castration (not inconceivable in view of Brigham Young's approval of the 1857 castration) or that later accounts mistakenly blamed him for a castration performed by a different bishop two years later.

25. Gustive O. Larson, "The Mormon Reformation," *Utah Historical Quarterly* 26 (Jan. 1958): 62n39.

26. Ben Brown, ed., *The Journal of Lorenzo Brown, 1823–1900* ([St. George, Utah]: Heritage Press, n.d.), 92, 93 (1 Dec., 13 Dec. 1857), for first quotation; Frederick Kesler diary, 1 Dec. 1857, for second quotation, Manuscripts Division, J. Willard Marriott Library, University of Utah, Salt Lake City,

Utah (hereafter Marriott Library), describing the court-martial on 30 November and the general assembly and ratifying vote on 1 December; Daniel H. Wells general order, 28 November 1857, providing for a general court-martial on 30 November, Document 628, Folder 41, Box 1, Series 2210, Territorial Militia Records (1849–77), Utah State Archives, Salt Lake City, Utah. However, I was unable to locate the minutes or other reference to Drake's court-martial in this collection of military records. For Daniel H. Wells see *Deseret News 1995–1996 Church Almanac,* 47–48, and D. Michael Quinn, *The Mormon Hierarchy: Extensions of Power* (Salt Lake City: Signature Books/Smith Research Associates, 1995); see also Patriarchal Blessing Index (1833–1963) and entry for Willis Drake (b. 10 July 1836; no death date or marriage date listed), in LDS Ancestral File.

  27. Hosea Stout diary, in Juanita Brooks, ed., *On the Mormon Frontier: The Diary of Hosea Stout, 1844–1861,* 2 vols. (Salt Lake City: University of Utah Press, 1964), 2:635 (27 Feb. 1858), 663 (17 Aug. 1858), 692 (26 Mar. 1859); Jenson, *Latter-day Saint Biographical Encyclopedia,* 3:530–34.

  28. Indictment of People vs. George Washington Hancock, Lycurgus Wilson, James Bracken, Price Nelson, Alvin Crockett, Daniel B. Rawson, George Patten, Charles B. Hancock, filed on 26 August 1859, older document filed with the 1889 reindictment, Case 23, First District Court (Utah County), Criminal Case Files, Utah State Archives. The killing of the infant girl and the castration of her father-brother were reported in the trial testimony published in "The Payson Killing," *Salt Lake Herald,* 21 Mar. 1890, 5. The witnesses did not mention whether he was alive or dead when castrated.

  29. Entries for Thomas Hancock (b. 1763), his sons Solomon Hancock (b. 1793) and Levi W. Hancock (b. 1803), and their sons Charles B. Hancock (b. 1823), George W. Hancock (b. 1826), and Mosiah Lyman Hancock (b. 1834) in LDS Ancestral File. For Levi W. Hancock's various activities, see *Deseret News 1995–1996 Church Almanac,* 58; Quinn, *Origins of Power,* 550–51; Missouri General Assembly, *Document Containing the Correspondence, Orders, &c in Relation to the Disturbances with the Mormons* . . . (Fayette, Mo.: Boon's Lick Democrat, 1841), 106; Dennis A. Clegg, "Levi Ward Hancock: Pioneer and Religious Leader of Early Utah" (M.A. thesis, Brigham Young University, 1966). For the residence of Levi W. Hancock and his son Mosiah in Payson, see Payson Ward Membership Record (Early to 1871), 5, 24, LDS Family History Library; Mosiah Lyman Hancock autobiography, typescript, 52, 58, Utah State Historical Society, Salt Lake City; Bryan Lee Dilts, comp., *1856 Utah Census Index: An Every-Name Index* (Salt Lake City: Index, 1983), 109. The 1856 census of Utah was a name-and-place-only census authorized by Gov. Brigham Young.

  30. Editorial, "The Usual Dish of Sensations," *Deseret Evening News,* 22 Nov. 1889, [2]. The editorial claimed that the 1889 prosecution against "the

antiquated Payson homicide" was anti-Mormon and unnecessary since the evidence of incest "was clear and indisputable" (through the birth of a child), but the *Deseret News* editorial did not mention the murder of the infant.

31. Church Historian's Office Journal, 12 Sept. 1858, LDS Archives.

32. J. Cecil Alter and Robert J. Dwyer, eds., "Journal of Captain Albert Tracy, 1858," *Utah Historical Quarterly* 13 (1945): 32, for date of 31 July 1858. Like this discovery, a dog also found a woman's head in September. Nevertheless, these were two separate findings—the first head was "mummified" with age, whereas the second woman's head was found within days of when she was last seen alive in the army camp.

33. *Journal of Discourses,* 7:19–20 (Kimball/1854). For Kimball, see *Deseret News 1995–1996 Church Almanac,* 45; Quinn, *Origins of Power,* 556–59.

34. John W. Phelps diary, 28 Mar. 1859, Utah State Historical Society. Mormon apologists have disputed as unreliable the reminiscent accounts of this castration incident as found in John D. Lee, *Mormonism Unveiled; or, The Life and Confessions of the Late Mormon Bishop, John D. Lee . . .* (St. Louis: Bryan, Brand, 1877), 285–86, and Johanna Christina Neilson Averett History, 20, Elijah Averett History, Utah State Historical Society. Both Lee and Averett identified the castrating bishop as Warren Snow of Manti, Sanpete County, Utah, where many Danish immigrants settled. However, it seems difficult to dispute the daily diary of a soldier who recorded what the young man said on the day he told him about his being castrated. In addition, Brigham Young had approved Bishop Snow's castrating a non-Danish man two years earlier. Warren Snow may not have been the bishop involved in this 1859 castration, but the incident itself apparently occurred as described in the Phelps diary. See previous discussion.

35. In "A Horrid Assassination," the *Daily Union Vedette,* the military newspaper at Fort Douglas in Salt Lake City, reported on 31 Oct. 1864 that Private Jones committed "an unmentionable outrage on the person of a little son of Chas. Monk, a citizen" [2]. Charles Monk's oldest son was born on 10 March 1855 in Salt Lake City. See entry for Charles Monk (b. 1832) in LDS Ancestral File. For Clinton, see Frank Esshom, *Pioneers and Prominent Men of Utah, Comprising Photographs-Genealogies-Biographies* (Salt Lake City: Utah Pioneers Book, 1913), 246; Salt Lake City Court (Justice Jeter Clinton), Criminal Docket Books, Series 4671, Utah State Archives, has its earliest volume (1864–66) beginning 28 October 1864, with no reference to the Jones case.

Unless a newspaper or other publication has named the male victim of a sexual assault, I will not fully identify such victims, even when their names appear in publicly available court documents. However, in most of the criminal cases of homosexual rape, at least one Utah newspaper gave the name of the victim.

36. Salt Lake County Probate Court, Civil and Criminal Docket Book, page 240 for 13 Sept. and 19 Sept. 1864, Series 3944, Reel 3, Utah State Archives.

37. "A Heavy Case," *Salt Lake Daily Telegraph,* 27 Oct. 1864, [3]; "That Case," *Salt Lake Daily Telegraph,* 28 Oct. 1864, [3]; "The Death of a Sodomite," *Salt Lake Daily Telegraph,* 31 Oct. 1864, [3]; Frederick Jones inquest, 29 Oct. 1864, Salt Lake County Coroner's Inquest Book (1858–81), 6, Utah State Archives; entry for oldest son (b. 1855) of Charles Monk (b. 1832) in LDS Ancestral File.

38. "Police Report," *Deseret Weekly News,* 2 Nov. 1864, 36. See the somewhat different view of this Frederick Jones case in O'Donovan, "'Abominable and Detestable Crime,'" 138–39.

39. In addition to the sources already cited on these matters, see also Stout diary, in Brooks, *On the Mormon Frontier,* 2:393 (15 Feb. 1851), 396 (17 Mar. 1851), 404 (21 Sept. 1851), 407 (18 Oct. 1851), 514 (1–3 May 1854), 545 (14 Apr. 1856); Kenneth L. Cannon II, "'Mountain Common Law': The Extralegal Punishment of Seducers in Early Utah," *Utah Historical Quarterly* 51 (Fall 1983): 308–27; Robert M. Ireland, in "The Libertine Must Die: Dishonor and the Unwritten Law in the Nineteenth-Century United States," *Journal of Social History* 23 (Fall 1989): 31–32, 40, observes that Utah, Texas, New Mexico, and Georgia completely exonerated husbands for killing their wives' "paramours."

40. Brigham Young to Daniel H. Wells and Brigham Young Jr., 18 Nov. 1864, in "Correspondence," *Latter-day Saints' Millennial Star* 27 (7 Jan. 1865): 14.

41. For the role of the LDS hierarchy in the Utah legislature up to the 1870s, see Dale L. Morgan, "The State of Deseret," *Utah Historical Quarterly* 8 (Apr.–Oct. 1940): 65–239; Ronald Collett Jack, "Utah Territorial Politics, 1847–1876" (Ph.D. diss., University of Utah, 1970); Dale A. Bolingbrook, "A History of the Utah Territorial Legislature, 1851–1861" (M.A. thesis, Utah State University, 1971), 27; D. Michael Quinn, "The Mormon Hierarchy, 1832–1932: An American Elite" (Ph.D. diss., Yale University, 1976), 174–78, 206–8; and Quinn, *Extensions of Power.*

42. *Journals of the Legislative Assembly of the Territory of Utah, Twenty-Second Session, for the Year 1876* (Salt Lake City: Deseret News Steam Printing Establishment, 1876), 33–34, 59, 234; *Compiled Laws of the Territory of Utah . . .* (Salt Lake City: Deseret News Printing Establishment, 1876), 564, 598.

43. George Goddard diary, 23 Jan. 1876, LDS Archives.

44. Murray, *A New English Dictionary,* 2:839, cited published references as early as Boswell's 1744 biography of Samuel Johnson.

45. The possible males involved in this incident are George Hamner Duncan Naylor (b. 10 Mar. 1863), George Naylor (b. 25 Dec. 1858), George

Naylor (b. 26 Aug. 1837), Stephen Franklin Wells (b. 25 June 1867), Frank Wells (b. abt. 1848 in Illinois), L. Frank Wells (b. 1830). See Salt Lake City Thirteenth Ward Record of Blessing of Children, LDS Family History Library; Esshom, *Pioneers and Prominent Men of Utah*, 1063; Junius F. Wells, "The Wells Family Genealogy," *Utah Genealogical and Historical Magazine* 6 (Jan. 1915): 11; U.S. 1870 Census of Wasatch, Summit County, Utah, sheet 141–A, microfilm, LDS Family History Library; U.S. 1880 Census of Salt Lake County, Utah, enumeration district 56, sheet 255–A, microfilm, LDS Family History Library. I also examined the following sources for persons named George Naylor and Frank Wells: Salt Lake County Assessment Rolls, 1875–76, Utah State Archives; and Edward L. Sloan, *Gazetteer of Utah and Salt Lake City Directory* (Salt Lake City: Herald, 1874), 255, 292. Early membership records of several of the Salt Lake City wards do not extend back as far as 1876 at the LDS Family History Library.

46. See Esshom, *Pioneers and Prominent Men of Utah*, 1238, for "Stephen" born to Daniel H. Wells and Lydia Ann Alley; and compare this to his birth entry as Stephen Franklin Wells (b. 25 June 1867) in Salt Lake City Thirteenth Ward Record of Blessing of Children, LDS Family History Library.

47. Goddard diary, 2 Feb. 1876.

48. U.S. 1880 Census of Salt Lake City, Salt Lake County, Utah, enumeration district 52, sheet 194–B, microfilm, LDS Family History Library.

49. George Naylor (b. 25 Dec. 1858) and his parents arrived in Salt Lake City on 24 July 1872. See the LDS European Emigration Index (1849–1925), LDS Family History Library; Esshom, *Pioneers and Prominent Men of Utah*, 1063.

50. Record of Excommunicated Members, Book A (1845–78), LDS Archives, listed the following sex-related causes for which persons were actually excommunicated: adultery, attempted adultery, child sexual abuse, fornication, fornication with a non-Mormon, fornication with a Native American Indian woman, "being a whore with soldiers," keeping a brothel, adulterous "handling," incest, and attempted rape. See also Raymond T. Swenson, "Resolution of Civil Disputes by Mormon Ecclesiastical Courts," *Utah Law Review*, no. 3 (1978): 573–95; Mark P. Leone, "Ecclesiastical Courts: Inventing Labels and Enforcing Definitions," *Roots of Modern Mormonism* (Cambridge, Mass.: Harvard University Press, 1979), 111–47; C. Paul Dredge, "Dispute Settlement in the Mormon Community: The Operation of Ecclesiastical Courts in Utah," in Klaus-Friedrich Koch, ed., *Access to Justice*, vol. 4 of *The Anthropological Perspective: Patterns of Conflict Management: Essays in the Ethnography of Law* (Alphen aan den Rijn, Netherlands: Sijthoff and Noordhoff, 1979); Lester E. Bush Jr., "Excommunication and Church Courts: A Note from the General Handbook of Instructions," *Dialogue: A Journal of Mormon Thought* 14 (Summer 1981): 74–98; Edwin Brown Firmage and R. Collin

Mangrum, "The Ecclesiastical Court System in the Great Basin," *Zion in the Courts: A Legal History of the Church of Jesus Christ of Latter-day Saints, 1830–1900* (Urbana: University of Illinois Press, 1988), 263–370.

51. Salt Lake City Police Court Calendar (1875–78), 82 (5 Jan. 1877), 134 (27 Sept. 1877), Series 04632, Utah State Archives. For the other kinds of prostitution-related charges, see 63, 137. *Dick* was obviously not a nickname for William. Slang dictionaries traditionally cite *dick* as American slang for penis no earlier than 1880. See John S. Farmer and W. E. Henley, *Slang and Its Analogues,* 7 vols. (London: Routledge and Kegan Paul, 1890–1904), 2:280; Eric Partridge, *A Dictionary of Slang and Unconventional English: Colloquialisms and Catch-Phrases, Solecisms and Catachreses, Nicknames, and Vulgarisms,* 8th ed., Paul Beale ed. (London: Routledge and Kegan Paul, 1984), 304. However, its use in this Salt Lake City arrest of a man for prostitution may indicate that *dick* had a sexual meaning in Utah by the mid-1870s.

52. See chap. 10.

53. "A Base Wretch," *Territorial Enquirer* (Provo, Utah), 13 Oct. 1880, [3], which has a blurred age in the microfilm; indictment against Perry D. McClanahan, filed 23 Feb. 1881, Case 203, First District Court (Utah County) Criminal Case Files; entry for Charles Henry Barrett (b. 1 Feb. 1863) in LDS Ancestral File.

54. "A Mesh of Difficulties. 'Doc' McClanahan Finds No Bail Yet, but Fresh Charges of Criminality to Meet," *Territorial Enquirer* (Provo, Utah), 16 Oct. 1880, [2].

55. "A Base Wretch," [3]; First District Court (Utah County) Minute Book (1881–86), 16 (25 Feb. 1881), 25 (4 Mar. 1881), Series 1820, Utah State Archives; "District Court," *Territorial Enquirer* (Provo, Utah), 2 Mar. 1881, [3]; Utah Department of Corrections, Utah Territorial Prison Inmate Commitment Register (1875–86), 56, Series 80388, Utah State Archives; entries for Perry D. McClanahan (b. 1842; md. 1862, 1 child; d. 1882) and Charles Henry Barrett (b. 1863; md. 1887, 4 children; d. 1931) in LDS Ancestral File. The outcome of the second trial is missing from the court minute book, and Provo's *Territorial Enquirer* of 5 Mar. 1881 did not refer to McClanahan's second trial except to note that the district court jurors were discharged. There was no entry for McClanahan's conviction in the Utah prison record, which typically noted such matters.

56. "A Filthy Brute," *Ogden Daily Herald,* 15 July 1882, [3], gave a detailed account of the sexual assault by Charles Golden (age thirty-five); cases of Sidney Pickering (age seventeen) and Golden in Utah Territorial Prison Inmate Commitment Register (1875–86), 50, 89. The court documents for these two cases are missing, and I could find no newspaper reference to Pickering. The only Sidney Pickering in the 1880 census of Utah was a teenager, consistent with the prison records. The census for Parowan, Iron County, Utah,

enumeration district 21, sheet 8, listed Elizabeth Pickering with a thirteen-year-old son, "J. Sydne," and other children, including "E. Mary," Reuben, and "T. William." LDS membership records of the Parowan First and Second Wards listed the births of Mary E., Reuben, and William Thomas to John D. Pickering and Elizabeth Pickering. The ward records made no reference to the J. Sydne Pickering listed in the census, but he was undoubtedly Mormon like his parents and younger siblings. However, the June 1880 census listed this J. Sydne Pickering's age as thirteen, two years younger than the age in the prison record at the first conviction in August 1880 of Sidney Pickering, who was later imprisoned for a crime "against nature." It is possible that his birthday occurred between June and August, but that would still leave an error of one year in either the census or the prison records. The missing court records would verify Sidney Pickering's residence and possibly the names of his parents. However, in the absence of those documents, there is only a strong possibility that Elizabeth Pickering's son (a Mormon) was the teenager imprisoned for manslaughter in 1880 and sodomy in 1882.

57. Joseph F. Smith to Presidents F. Spence and W. H. Seegmiller of Richfield, Utah, 15 Sept. 1882, my narrative reconstruction of the abbreviated notes in Folder 22, Box 5, Scott Kenney Papers, Manuscripts Division, Marriott Library. For Smith, see *Deseret News 1995–1996 Church Almanac,* 42–43; Quinn, *Extensions of Power.*

58. *Journal of Discourses,* 1:259 (P. P. Pratt/1853).

59. I did not examine the minutes of the actual court cases of the Richfield Ward for the excommunicated males, but instead identified them through entries in the membership record, which listed their excommunication about the time of Smith's letter. Unlike the other notations for excommunicated persons, the Richfield Ward membership records give no cause for the excommunication of these young men. Smith's 1882 letter specifically named only the married and endowed participant, Soren Madsen (b. 1850). Because of my tentative identification of the others in this incident, I do not fully identify them here. The other young men apparently involved were P—— A—— L—— (b. 1852), A—— B—— (b. 1863), F—— C—— M—— (b. 1864), J—— C—— S—— (b. 1867), and N—— J—— (b. 1867); see Membership Record of Richfield First Ward (1878–91) and Membership Record of Richfield Second Ward (1878–91), LDS Family History Library; LDS Ancestral File; and LDS European Emigration Index (1849–1925). Soren Madsen did not appear in the U.S. 1900 Census soundex for Utah, but the above P—— A—— L—— was living with "Robert" Madsen in the male-dominant mining town of Eureka, Utah, enumeration district 102, sheet 3, microfilm, LDS Family History Library. Of the others, only F—— C—— M—— was living in Utah in 1900, and he was residing alone as a bachelor in West Jordan, Salt Lake County, enumeration district 67, sheet 16, microfilm, LDS Family History Library.

60. Thomas Taylor (b. 26 July 1826; LDS baptism 16 May 1840; d. 8 Dec. 1900), as in LDS Ancestral File, and Jenson, *Latter-day Saint Biographical Encyclopedia,* 2:366–67.

61. John Henry Smith diary, 22 June 1886, George A. Smith Family Papers, Manuscripts Division, Marriott Library; "Minutes of an Investigation Held in the Tithing Office, Cedar City, Iron Co., Utah, July 6th 1886, in the Case of Bishop Thomas Taylor, of Salt Lake City," with concluding statement by Francis Webster and R. W. Heubourne, copied into the Salt Lake Stake High Council Minutes, 1882–89 (26 July 1886), LDS Archives; entries for Richard Williams (b. 12 Nov. 1865), Simeon W. Simkins (b. 3 Feb. 1868), and William W. Simkins (b. 13 Aug. 1870) in LDS Ancestral File. The testimony of William Simkins is in the original minutes but is missing from the partial transcription of this case in William H. Holyoak to John Taylor, 9 October 1886, Folder 1, Box 1–B, and Folder 10, Box 4–B, John Taylor Family Papers, Western Americana, Marriott Library. Although they claimed to be unwilling victims, I fully identify these teenagers because they were named in O'Donovan's published essay "'Abominable and Detestable Crime,'" 135.

62. "City and Neighborhood," *Salt Lake Tribune,* 22 Aug. 1886, [4], regarding Thomas Taylor's release as bishop for an unnamed reason; "Judge Them by Their Works," *Salt Lake Tribune,* 29 Aug. 1886, [2]; "City and Neighborhood," *Salt Lake Tribune,* 29 Aug. 1886, [4], that "Brother A has been guilty of a horrible and beastly sin—Brother A, who is a polygamist," and continued later: "Indeed an editorial notice was given that Bishop Taylor had been excommunicated from the Mormon Church. . . . And should he be prosecuted in the courts? Or is there no law against sodomy, either, in this most lawless of Territories?"

63. Andrew Jenson, *Church Chronology: A Record of Important Events Pertaining to the History of the Church of Jesus Christ of Latter-day Saints,* 2d ed., rev. (Salt Lake City: Deseret News, 1914), for 24 Mar. 1886; Thomas Taylor to James Simkins, 14 June 1886, in Salt Lake Stake High Council Minutes, 1882–89 (26 July 1886); Thomas Taylor statements in "Minutes of an Investigation Held in the Tithing Office"; Thomas Taylor autobiography, 12, Manuscripts Division, Marriott Library.

64. "Our Beaver Letter," *Salt Lake Tribune,* 24 Dec. 1886, [4]. The grand jury convened in the jurisdiction of the district court for southern Utah, where the alleged crimes had occurred.

65. Indictment against Charles D. Thomas, filed 10 May 1886, Case 862 (marked "First District Court" on all filings), Second District Court (Weber County), Criminal Case Files, Utah State Archives; First District Court (Weber County) Minute Book (1885–87), 285, 288, 290–91, Series 5062, Utah State Archives; Utah Territorial Prison Inmate Commitment Register (1875–86), 222.

66. "Excommunicated," *Deseret Evening News,* 28 Aug. 1886, [2]; "City and Neighborhood," *Salt Lake Tribune,* 29 Aug. 1886, [4]; Abraham H. Cannon diary, 29 Aug. 1886, Manuscripts Division, Marriott Library; Seymour B. Young diary, 16 Sept. 1886, LDS Archives. Young was a physician and an LDS general authority at this time. For another study that includes this incident, see Brent D. Corcoran, "'My Father's Business': Thomas Taylor and Mormon Frontier Economic Enterprise," *Dialogue: A Journal of Mormon Thought* 28 (Spring 1995): 105–41, esp. 125–29. He observes (128) that despite the August announcement of the excommunication, Taylor was not actually excommunicated in southern Utah until October. The Salt Lake City newspaper announcement mistakenly used the word *excommunicated* with reference to the fact that the Salt Lake Stake High Council had dropped Taylor as bishop and disfellowshipped him from church privileges.

67. Cannon diary, 21 Mar. 1892, referred to this rebaptism as having occurred, but did not give a date for it.

68. It was Taylor's son Thomas who served as sexton of the cemetery from 1898 through 1906. Luella Adams Dalton, *History of the Iron County Mission, Parowan, Utah* ([Parowan, Utah?]: n.p., [1972?]), 104–5; entries for Richard Williams, Simeon W. Simkins, and William W. Simkins in LDS Ancestral File; and Elmo Orton and Glenis S. Orton, *Simkins Family History* (Austin, Tex.: Historical Publications, 1987), 17, 320, 369.

69. "Loathsome Depravity," *Deseret News,* 11 Jan. 1887, [3], and "Local Briefs," *Salt Lake Herald,* 11 Jan. 1887, 8, described the other boy's arrival in Salt Lake City and his placement in the city jail, but the press mistakenly described him as fourteen years old. For the gang's beating of sixteen-year-old George W. Riter, see "Before Justice Pyper," *Deseret Evening News,* 14 Jan. 1887, [3]. For gang member Arthur Curtis's stoning of a Chinese man, see "City and Neighborhood," *Salt Lake Tribune,* 29 Oct. 1886, [4].

70. "Local Briefs," *Salt Lake Herald,* 11 Jan. 1887, 8; "The Jail Horrors," *Salt Lake Herald,* 12 Jan. 1887, 8; The People vs. William Paddock, Richard Bubbles, Arthur Curtis, Dan Henry, and John Leadford, indictment by the grand jury, filed 23 Feb. 1887, Case 1096 (originally Case 388), Third District Court (Salt Lake County), Criminal Case Files, Utah State Archives. Buboltz and Hendry were mistaken listed with different surnames. "Leadford" was the spelling in most court documents, but "Ledford" was the spelling in the prison record, which contained detailed biographical information about the convicts.

71. Testimony of fifteen-year-old Gustave Albert Peterson, transcript of the preliminary examination in the case of the State of Utah vs. J. F. Harrington, before Municipal Judge J. A. Howell on 10 Jan. 1903, 2, Case 291, Second District Court (Weber County) Criminal Case Files. I identify Peterson because he was named in "Guilty of Revolting Crime," *Ogden Standard,* 18 Feb. 1903, 5. Born 3 April 1887, Peterson died unmarried in 1963. LDS Ancestral File.

72. Utah Territorial Prison Inmate Commitment Register (1886–88), 40, 49, 84, Series 80388, Utah State Archives. The prison register listed "D. Hendry," which was the correct spelling of his surname, whereas court documents spelled his name "Henry." The prison register described Richard "Bubbles" as fifteen years old, but he was sixteen. Although the register listed the "complexion" of Arthur Curtis and William Paddock as "dark," the racial listing for them and their parents was "W" (white) in the U.S. 1880 Census of Salt Lake County, Utah, enumeration district 42, sheet 34–B, enumeration district 58, sheet 286–A. The prison register also described John Ledford's complexion as "dark," and identified his occupation as "Boot Black." I have been unable to locate Ledford or his family in a census, which would verify his race. However, very few boot blacks in Salt Lake City were African American at this time. For example, of the seventeen young men in Salt Lake City's union local for boot blacks in 1907, only one was African American. See their Labor Day 1907 photograph in the Utah State Historical Society.

73. "The Jail Horrors," 8.

74. Salt Lake City Court, Criminal Docket Book of George D. Pyper (Jan.–Dec. 1887 volume, unpaged), entries for 13–14 Jan. 1887, and Salt Lake City Court, Criminal Docket Book of George D. Pyper (1886–90), 74, 82, 83, both in Series 4671, Utah State Archives; "PAYING THE PYPER: The Awful Accusation against the Boys," *Salt Lake Tribune,* 15 Jan. 1887, [4]; "Fragments," *Deseret Evening News,* 13 Jan. 1887, [3]. For Pyper, see Jenson, *Latter-day Saint Biographical Encyclopedia,* 1:685–86 (incorrect printed pagination; actual pagination for this entry is 669–70).

75. "Local Briefs," *Salt Lake Herald,* 15 Jan. 1887, 8; "PAYING THE PYPER," [4]. It is my conclusion that the "additional and unnameable offense" was oral sex. Since it was "unnameable," no newspaper named it, and since "it is not a crime in this Territory," court documents did not refer to it.

76. *Laws of the State of Utah* (Kaysville, Utah: Inland, 1923), sect. 1, chap. 13, page 21, 17 Feb. 1923; see also chap. 10 for a discussion of the Utah Supreme Court's decision about oral sex in the Andrew G. Johnson case of 1913.

77. Third District Court (Salt Lake County) Minute Book (1886–88), 194, 201, Series 1649, Utah State Archives; "THE THIRD DISTRICT COURT, Motions Disposed of Yesterday by Judge Zane—Boys Convicted," *Salt Lake Tribune,* 23 Apr. 1887, [4]; Utah Territorial Prison Inmate Commitment Register (1886–88), 40, 49; see also Thomas G. Alexander, "Charles S. Zane, Apostle of the New Era," *Utah Historical Quarterly* 34 (Fall 1966): 290–314; *The National Cyclopaedia of American Biography,* 63 vols. (New York: James T. White, 1893–1984), 12:128.

78. "The Bohemians," *Salt Lake Tribune,* 2 Nov. 1886, [4]; marriage entry on 25 Mar. 1884 for John M. Zane (b. 26 Mar. 1863) in International Genealogical Index and Zane's entry in U.S. 1920 Census of Chicago, Cook

County, Illinois, microfilm, both in LDS Family History Library. See chap. 2 for a discussion of Salt Lake City's Bohemian Club and chap. 7 for Mildred J. Berryman's study of its self-defined homosexual members.

79. Entry for Richard L. Buboltz (b. 3 Apr. 1870 in Westfalia, Germany; md. 1892, 5 children; d. 1963) in LDS Ancestral File; passenger list of Mormon emigrants from Europe who departed Liverpool on the USS *Nevada* on 4 Sept. 1880 and arrived in Salt Lake City on Sept. 25, Emigration Ship Registers of the British Mission (1849–1925), LDS Family History Library. The emigrating Mormons included Julia "Bubolz," with her children Richard and Martha, and Sarah "Hendry," with her children Sarah and Daniel. Julia Buboltz was listed in the city directories as "Buballs" or "Bubols," which was phonetically misspelled as "Bubbles" in the court documents, prison records, and newspapers of 1887. See *The Utah Directory for 1883–84* (Salt Lake City: J. C. Graham, 1883), 41; *Salt Lake City Directory, for the Year Commencing Aug. 1, 1885* (New York: U.S. Directory, 1885), 91; *Utah Gazetteer and Directory of Salt Lake, Ogden, Provo, and Logan Cities for 1888* (Salt Lake City: Lorenzo Stenhouse, 1888), 92.

80. The parents of the accused Arthur Curtis were Mormon, even though their son Arthur, at age thirty, claimed "no religion" when he registered for a later imprisonment. I have been unable to find anyone by the name of Ledford or Leadford in Esshom, *Pioneers and Prominent Men of Utah*, in the U.S. 1880 Census of Utah, Salt Lake County Assessment Rolls (1885–86), or Salt Lake City directories (1885–86). The prison register showed that the convicted John Ledford was born in Pennsylvania, but I was unsuccessful in tracing him there, either. John Ledford was born after 1869, when the LDS Church stopped recording native-born Americans who moved to Utah.

81. "Before Justice Pyper," *Deseret Evening News,* 14 Jan. 1887, [3]; Cornelia Paddock affidavit, 26 Sept. 1887, in Case File 1096, People vs. Wm Paddock, filed 26 Sept. 1887, Third District Court (Salt Lake County) Criminal Case Files; The People vs. William Paddock, Richard Bubbles, Arthur Curtis, Dan Henry, and John Leadford, indictment by the grand jury, filed 23 Feb. 1887, also in Case 1096 (originally Case 388), Third District Court (Salt Lake County) Criminal Case Files. His mother testified that William Paddock was born in January 1873.

82. Mrs. A. G. [Cornelia] Paddock, *In the Toils; or, Martyrs of the Latter Days* (Chicago: Dixon and Shepard, 1879); *The Fate of Madame La Tour: A Tale of Great Salt Lake* (New York: Fords, Howard, and Hulbert, 1881); *Saved at Last from among the Mormons* (Springfield, Ohio: Farm and Fireside, 1881); George A. Crofutt, *Salt Lake City Business Directory, 1885–6* (Salt Lake City: by the author, 1885), 140; U.S. 1880 Census of Salt Lake County, eunumeration district 42, sheet 34–B (original page 20). For the history and significance of the Utah Commission at this time, see Brigham H. Roberts, *A Comprehen-*

sive History of the Church of Jesus Christ of Latter-day Saints, Century I, 6 vols. (Salt Lake City: Church of Jesus Christ of Latter-day Saints, 1930), 6:58–60, 111–13, 137; Stewart Lofgren Grow, "A Study of the Utah Commission, 1882–96" (Ph.D. diss., University of Utah, 1954); Edward Leo Lyman, *Political Deliverance: The Mormon Quest for Utah Statehood* (Urbana: University of Illinois Press, 1986), 46–47, 114–15, 134–36, 175, 260.

83. "Before Justice Pyper," *Deseret Evening News,* 8 Jan. 1887, [3]; "Before Justice Pyper," *Deseret Evening News,* 13 Jan. 1887, [3].

84. "Loathsome Depravity," *Deseret Evening News,* 11 Jan. 1887, [3], called him "Jenkinson"; *Deseret Evening News,* 15 Jan. 1887, [3], gave the victim's correct last name, but changed his first name to Daniel and changed the spelling of his last name to "Pryor." On the other hand, "City and Neighborhood," *Salt Lake Tribune,* 14 Jan. 1887, [4], identified the Mormon victim accurately as "David Prior," and later as "Pryor" in "Three Little Boys Brought into Court in a Shameful Condition—Investigation Ordered," *Salt Lake Tribune,* 2 Mar. 1887, [4]. The *Salt Lake Herald* never identified the victim by name in its various articles: "Local Briefs," 11 Jan. 1887, 8; "The Jail Horrors," 12 Jan. 1887, 8; "Local Briefs," 14 Jan. 1887, 8; "Local Briefs," 15 Jan. 1887, 8; "Local Briefs," 23 Apr. 1887, 8. See also entry for David Prior (b. 10 Mar. 1874) in LDS Ancestral File.

85. "Going to the Asylum," *Deseret News,* 20 Jan. 1887, [3], reported only that "A.G. Paddock" committed his son to the asylum.

86. William H. Paddock (admitted 22 Jan. 1887, discharged 22 July 1887), Case 94, Utah Territorial Asylum Admission Record Book (1885–91), and his patient records in Medical Records Section, Heninger Administration Building, Utah State Hospital, Provo, Utah. I am confident that Paddock was the first because I examined all patient commitment records of Utah's insane asylum from its establishment in 1885 to Paddock's internment and cross-referenced them to the records of criminal indictments for sodomy. See chap. 10 for a discussion of patients committed to the Utah insane asylum.

87. Utah Territorial Prison Inmate Commitment Register (1886–88), 40, 49, 84.

88. P. H. Lannan affidavit, 26 Sept. 1887, File 1096, People vs Wm Paddock, Third District Court (Salt Lake County) Criminal Case Files; O. N. Malmquist, *The First One Hundred Years: A History of the* Salt Lake Tribune, *1871–1971* (Salt Lake City: Utah State Historical Society, 1971), 74, 135.

89. Salt Lake City Court, Criminal Docket Book of George D. Pyper (1886–90), 216 (24–26 Oct. 1887); George D. Pyper, "Record of Cases Originating in Salt Lake County outside of Salt Lake City" (1885–90), 85–87 (24–28 Oct. 1887), Utah State Archives; "The Boy Burglars: Paddock, Fisher, and Rooney Held to the Grand Jury," *Deseret News,* 17 May 1889, [3].

90. Arrest of Norton Curtis, John Ledford, and five others for burglary in

Salt Lake City Court Record (Apr.–June 1890), 41 (10 Apr. 1890), filed with Salt Lake City police blotters at Utah State Archives in 1994; indictment against Norton Curtis, Daniel Henry, Henry Stewart, and Raymond Curtis, filed 13 Feb. 1895, People vs. Norton Curtis, et. al, File 1235 and File 1239, Third District Court (Salt Lake County) Criminal Case Files; entries for "David Hendry" and Norton Curtis, 23 Feb. 1895, Utah Department of Corrections, Utah Territorial Prison Inmate Commitment Register (1891–95), 450, Series 80388, Utah State Archives.

91. Entries for Arthur Curtis (including a description of his left-hand tattoo and Navy tattoo) and for his brother Norton Curtis, Utah Department of Corrections, Utah Territorial/State Prison Inmate Commitment Register (1892–1908), 150, Series 80388, Utah State Archives. For a similar left-hand tattoo on other Utah men involved in cases of sodomy, see the William D. Burton case of 1891 later in this chapter; see also chap. 10 for this tattoo on male prostitutes of the 1890s to early 1900s and on Mike McCormick in a sodomy case of 1900.

There is an ironic history for this small cross (or x) tattoo on the webbing between the left thumb and forefinger of Anglo-American homosexuals in the 1890s. Half a century later, Mexican-American gangs in Los Angeles made this type of tattoo their trademark. The Chicano gangs claimed to have invented this "pachuco mark," which in turn was adopted in the 1950s by some homosexuals who had no knowledge of the previous use of that tattoo by Anglo homosexuals. See Samuel M. Steward, *Bad Boys and Tough Tattoos: A Social History of the Tattoo with Gangs, Sailors, and Street-Corner Punks, 1950–1965* (New York: Haworth Press, 1990), 55, 67. Steward was not aware of the decades-earlier use of this tattoo by men engaging in same-gender sexual acts.

92. Complaint against Jack Richards, B. Y. Lamb, Arthur Curtis, and Norton Curtis for burglary, filed 10 Jan. 1899, File 418, Third District Court (Salt Lake County) Criminal Case Files. There are conflicts in birth information for Arthur Curtis in both the prison records and genealogical records. The 1899 prison admission record stated the age of Arthur Curtis as "30", (born ca. 1869) instead of the equivalent age of 27 (born ca. 1872) shown for his earlier imprisonments. Likewise the 1899 prison record lists his birthplace as Utah, instead of Nevada as indicated for his earlier imprisonments. However, the physical descriptions are consistent with the Arthur Curtis imprisoned for sodomy in 1887, for burglary in 1888, and for burglary in 1899 with his brother Norton. See Utah Territorial Prison Inmate Commitment Register (1886–88), 49, 144, and Utah Territorial/State Prison Inmate Commitment Register (1892–1908), 150. Likewise, the obituary for Arthur Curtis lists his birth date as 15 August 1870 in Utah, whereas other genealogical records give his birth date as 1870 in Nevada or 1873 in Nevada. His obituary also listed a wife. I

have not verified their marriage date, but it was after Curtis was sentenced as an unmarried man to ten years of imprisonment in 1899. See *Deseret Evening News,* 26 Mar. 1948, 23, and *Salt Lake Tribune,* 26 Mar. 1948, 24; 1880 U.S. Census of Salt Lake County, enumeration district 58, sheet 286; LDS Ancestral File.

93. Entry for Richard Buboltz (b. 3 Apr. 1870) and David Prior (b. 10 Mar. 1874) in LDS Ancestral File. Although Prior was a victim, I name him because newspapers identified him by name.

94. Heber J. Grant journal sheets, 365, 368, (12 Aug. 1887), LDS Archives. For John Taylor, Lorenzo Snow, and George Q. Cannon, see *Deseret News 1995–1996 Church Almanac,* 42, 45; Quinn, *Origins of Power,* 597–99; Quinn, *Extensions of Power.*

95. Concerning this sentencing pattern for fornication, see Utah Territorial Prison Inmate Commitment Register (1886–88), 89, 95, 126, 129, 139. See text and notes 55, 56, and 77 for the sentencing in previous sodomy convictions.

96. *Compiled Laws of the Territory of Utah* (1876), 598.

97. John D'Emelio and Estelle B. Freedman, *Intimate Matters: A History of Sexuality in America* (New York: Harper and Row, 1988), 123. This citation also noted that from 1796 to 1873, New York City courts prosecuted only twenty-two sodomy cases, most involving coercion or cases of adult men having sex with prepubescent boys or young adolescents.

98. Entry for Evan Thomas, Utah County Jail Register of Prisoners (1884–91), 55 (19 Sept. 1889), Series 5044, Utah State Archives; First District Court (Utah County) Minute Book (1888–90), 301, 330; "Crime against Nature" subheading in "First District Court," *Utah Enquirer* (Provo, Utah), 1 Oct. 1889, [3]; Utah Department of Corrections, Utah Territorial Prison Inmate Commitment Register (1888–96), 71, Series 80388, Utah State Archives; Patriarchal Blessing Index (1833–1963) and entry for Evan S. Thomas (b. 6 Apr. 1849) in LDS Ancestral File; judge's quotation from "Court at Provo," *Deseret Evening News,* 12 Oct. 1889, 3; "One Year for a Heinous Crime," subheading in "First District Court," *Utah Enquirer* (Provo, Utah), 15 Oct. 1889, [3]. Although all the criminal records involved the same man, there were discrepancies in statements about his age and marital status. I could not locate the criminal file for the specifics of the complaint and indictment against Thomas. Although also Welsh, Evan Thomas was apparently no relation to the forty-years-younger Thomas S. Thomas (of Welsh parentage) involved with Evan Stephens, nor a relative of Stephens (see chap. 8). This Evan Thomas was also no relation to the twenty-years-younger Kate Thomas, whose same-sex poetry was discussed in chap. 4. This convicted Evan Thomas was also apparently no relation to the twenty-years-younger, Welsh-born Heber H. Thomas who brutally punished seven teenagers for a sodomy incident at the Utah state re-

form school in 1908 (see chap. 10). For Judge John W. Judd as a non-Mormon, see Jenson, *Church Chronology*, for 9 July 1888; *Utah: Her Cities, Towns and Resources* (Chicago: Manly and Litteral, 1891), 149.

99. Utah County Jail Register of Prisoners (1884–91), 69; Complaint against Frank Devine by John A. Brown [deputy sheriff], dated 26 Aug. 1890, grand jury indictment of Devine, filed 3 October 1890, both in Case 74, First District Court (Utah County) Criminal Case Files; First District Court (Utah County) Minute Book (1888–90), 619, 628, 635; Utah Territorial Prison Inmate Commitment Register (1888–96), 150; "First District Court," *Provo Daily Enquirer*, 8 Oct. 1890, [3]. For Judge John W. Blackburn as a non-Mormon, see "Judge Blackburn's Death," *Deseret Evening News*, 6 Jan. 1894, 3.

100. Utah Territorial Prison Inmate Commitment Register (1888–96), 31, 82, 98, 115, 117.

101. Paul Wilbur Tappan, "Mormon-Gentile Conflict: A Study of the Influence of Public Opinion on In-Group versus Out-Group Interaction, with Special Reference to Polygamy" (Ph.D. diss., University of Wisconsin, 1939); Richard D. Poll, "The Political Reconstruction of Utah Territory, 1866–1890," *Pacific Historical Review* 27 (May 1958): 111–26; Leonard J. Arrington, "The Raid," *Great Basin Kingdom: An Economic History of the Latter-day Saints, 1830–1900* (Cambridge, Mass.: Harvard University Press, 1958), 353–79; Mark Wilcox Cannon, "The Mormon Issue in Congress, 1872–1882, Drawing on the Experience of Territorial Delegate George Q. Cannon" (Ph.D. diss., Harvard University, 1960); Thomas G. Alexander, "Federal Authority versus Polygamic Theocracy," *Dialogue: A Journal of Mormon Thought* 1 (Autumn 1966): 85–100; Gustive O. Larson, *The "Americanization" of Utah for Statehood* (San Marino, Calif.: Huntington Library, 1971); Charles A. Cannon, "The Awesome Power of Sex: The Polemical Campaign against Mormon Polygamy," *Pacific Historical Review* 43 (Feb. 1974): 61–82; Joseph H. Groberg, "The Mormon Disfranchisements of 1882 to 1892," *Brigham Young University Studies* 16 (Spring 1976): 399–408; James B. Allen and Glen M. Leonard, *The Story of the Latter-day Saints*, 2d ed., rev. (Salt Lake City: Deseret Book, 1992), 399–421; James L. Clayton, "The Supreme Court, Polygamy, and the Enforcement of Morals in Nineteenth-Century America: An Analysis of *Reynolds vs. United States*," *Dialogue: A Journal of Mormon Thought* 12 (Winter 1979): 46–61; Rosa Mae McClellan Evans, "Judicial Prosecution of Prisoners for LDS Plural Marriage: Prison Sentences, 1884–1895" (M.A. thesis, Brigham Young University, 1986); Sarah Barringer Gordon, "'The Twin Relic of Barbarism': A Legal History of Anti-Polygamy in Nineteenth-Century America" (Ph.D. diss., Princeton University, 1994).

102. Editorial, "Falsehood Added to Ingratitude," *Deseret Evening News*, 17 May 1889, [2], which was responding to Mrs. Paddock's statements pub-

lished that morning in "Judicial and Criminal: The Paddock Case before Commissioner Norrell," *Salt Lake Tribune,* 17 May 1889, [4].

103. Reverend DeWitt Talmage, quoted in B. Carmon Hardy, *Solemn Covenant: The Mormon Polygamous Passage* (Urbana: University of Illinois Press, 1992), 43.

104. Telephone interview on 25 May 1994 with Professor Sarah Barringer Gordon, School of Law, University of Pennsylvania.

105. Indictment against Frank Wilson, filed 11 Sept. 1890, Case 654, Third District Court (Salt Lake County) Criminal Case Files; Third District Court (Salt Lake County) Minute Book (1889–91), 418, 450, 468; Utah Territorial Prison Inmate Commitment Register (1888–96), 133. See also note 65 for a bestial sodomy case in 1886.

106. Complaint against James Hamilton, filed 7 Mar. 1891, and indictment against James Hamilton for "the Infamous crime against nature," filed 11 Apr. 1891, Case 743, Third District Court (Salt Lake County) Criminal Case Files; personal information about James Hamilton in Utah Territorial Prison Inmate Commitment Register (1888–96), 187; James Hamilton in LDS European Emigration Index (1849–1925). Because Burton's testimony (as a defense witness) undermined the claim of witnesses and the police that he was an unwilling victim of sexual assault, I have identified him here. See notes 107, 108.

107. Entry for W. D. Burton, 106 in alphabetical section, Salt Lake City Police, Criminal Register (1892–97), Series 4658, Utah State Archives. Burton was arrested for robbery in 1892, but died before he went to trial. For the tattoo, see note 91.

108. Third District Court (Salt Lake County) Minute Book (1891–92), 204, 255, Series 1649, Utah State Archives; "DEMANDING JURIES. The Effect of the Recent Ruling in the District Court. HAMILTON IS DECLARED INNOCENT," *Salt Lake Herald,* 28 May 1891, 8; also "Third District Court," *Salt Lake Tribune,* 28 May 1891, 5, compared with "Third District Court," *Deseret Evening News,* 27 May 1891, 8; "Third District Court," *Deseret Evening News,* 28 May 1891, 8. There was no male with the initials W. D. among the known relatives of Robert T. Burton, a counselor in the LDS Presiding Bishopric at the time of this trial. See entry for Robert T. Burton in LDS Ancestral File; *Deseret News 1995–1996 Church Almanac,* 77.

109. "A Young Murderess: She Cuts the Throat of a Friend from Ear to Ear," *Deseret Evening News,* 27 Jan. 1892, 1; *Medical Record* (23 July 1892), quoted in Jonathan Ned Katz, *Gay/Lesbian Almanac: A New Documentary* (New York: Harper and Row, 1983), 204.

110. "VERY STRANGE: Why Alice Mitchell Killed Her Friend," *Deseret Evening News,* 29 Jan. 1892, 1.

111. "SHE WANTED TO MARRY HER: Strange and Fatal Infatuation of Two Girls for Each Other," *Salt Lake Tribune,* 29 Jan. 1892, 2.

112. Dr. F. L. Sim, "Forensic Psychiatry: Alice Mitchell Adjudged Insane," *Memphis Medical Monthly* 12 (Aug. 1892): 379–89, as quoted in Jonathan Katz, *Gay American History: Lesbians and Gay Men in the U.S.A.* (New York: Thomas Y. Crowell, 1976), 54–55; see also other testimony quoted in Katz, *Gay/Lesbian Almanac*, 223–27.

113. "The Girl Slayer: Alice Mitchell Visited by a Doctor to Examine Her Mental Condition," *Deseret Evening News*, 6 Feb. 1892, 1, emphasis in original.

114. See notes 109, 110, and 113, and "Alice Mitchell," *Deseret Evening News*, 16 Feb. 1892, 1; see also "The Two Girls Indicted," *Deseret Evening News*, 1 Feb. 1892, 1; "Is She Crazy?: The Memphis Murderess Pleads Insanity," *Deseret Evening News*, 2 Feb. 1892, 1; "Miss Mitchell," *Deseret Evening News*, 12 Feb. 1892, 1; and "Alice Mitchell," *Deseret Evening News*, 16 Feb. 1892, 1, compared with coverage in "Maiden Murderers in Memphis," *Salt Lake Tribune*, 27 Jan. 1892, 1; "The Maiden Murderers Indicted," *Salt Lake Tribune*, 31 Jan. 1892, 1; "She Pleads Insanity," *Salt Lake Tribune*, 2 Feb. 1892, 1. By contrast, "Lily Johnson Arrested," *Salt Lake Herald*, 27 Jan. 1892, 1, was the *Herald*'s only coverage of the case from 26 Jan. through 31 Mar. 1892.

115. "THE DOCTOR'S LOVE: His Strange Attachment to Isaac Judson Prompts Him to Kill Himself," *Deseret Evening News*, 24 Feb. 1892, 1.

116. James G. Kiernan, "Responsibility in Sexual Perversion," *Chicago Medical Reporter* 3 (May 1892): 185–210, quoted in Katz, *Gay/Lesbian Almanac*, 232 and 232n.

117. See the following stories in the *Deseret Evening News:* "CUT HIS THROAT: A Bountiful Poultry Dealer Severs His Throat with a Razor," 27 Jan. 1892, 5; "Suicide of a Lawyer," 28 Jan. 1892, 1; "A STRANGER SUICIDES on Capitol Hill at an Early Hour This Morning: A LOVE LETTER TELLS WHY. His Name was Otto Nagel and His Fiance Lives in Chicago," 28 Jan. 1892, 8; "A JILTED LOVER: His Revenge Upon His Former Sweetheart," 9 Feb. 1992, 1; "SHOT HIMSELF," 10 Feb. 1892, 5; "Insanely Jealous though over Seventy Years Old," 13 Feb. 1892, 1; "A HUMAN BRUTE ARRESTED," 15 Feb. 1892, 1; "AN OLD, OLD STORY: Mrs. Deacon Betrays Her Husband at a Fashionable Hotel in France. THE HUSBAND ARRIVES HOME UNEXPECTEDLY. Finds the Paramour in a Compromising Situation and Kills Him," 19 Feb. 1892, 1.

118. Complaint and indictment against James Warren, filed 9 Sept. 1892, Case 252, Fourth District Court (Weber County), Criminal Case Files, Utah State Archives; Fourth District Court (Weber County) Minute Book (1892–95), 10, 19, Series 3588, Utah State Archives; Utah Territorial Prison Inmate Commitment Register (1888–96), 282; entry for victim H—— P. S—— (b. 1 Dec. 1884; md. 1910; d. 1917) in LDS Ancestral File; "In the Fourth District Court," *Ogden Standard*, 11 Sept. 1892, 3; *Biographical Record of Salt Lake City and Vicinity* (Chicago: National Historical Record, 1902), 25–26. War-

ren did not appear in the LDS European Emigration Index (1849–1925) and was therefore a non-LDS immigrant to Utah.

119. Complaint against John Mack for a "crime against nature" committed "with one Frank Howard," filed 10 Aug. 1892, and indictment against John Mack, filed 9 Sept. 1892, subpoena for Frank Howard and others, filed 20 Sept. 1892, Case 254, Fourth District Court (Weber County) Criminal Case Files; Utah Territorial Prison Inmate Commitment Register (1888–96), 288; complaint against Frank Howard, 1 May 1896, Case 5 (originally Case 46 in First District Court), Fourth District Court (Utah County) Criminal Case Files; entry for Frank Howard in Utah Territorial Prison Inmate Commitment Register (1888–96), 490; "First District Court News," *Ogden Standard*, 28 Sept. 1892, 1; "Sentences in the Fourth District Court," *Ogden Standard*, 1 Oct. 1892, 5.

120. Beginning statement on 30 Jan. 1894 of a sixty-four-page summary of the case from October 1893 to Jan. 1894 in Rudger Clawson's 1893–94 diary, 83–146, Manuscripts Division, Marriott Library. Clawson's diary reads as though he simply copied the minutes of the church court. For Clawson's appointment as an LDS apostle in 1898 and as second counselor in 1901, see *Deseret News 1995–1996 Church Almanac*, 48.

121. Quotations of Hans Peter Hunsaker in Clawson's 1893–94 diary, 98, 106, 108, 113, and testimony of Weldon Hunsaker on 84–85, 92–96. David S. Hoopes and Roy Hoopes, *The Making of a Mormon Apostle: The Story of Rudger Clawson* (Lanham, Md.: Madison Books, 1990), 163–67, and O'Donovan, "'Abominable and Detestable Crime,'" 136–37, discussed this case and named two of the younger brothers who were involved. In my discussion of this case, I fully identify only those named in the Hoopes book and by O'Donovan, and I follow the ages given in the Hunsaker family's published history. Hoopes and Hoopes and O'Donovan indicate that the charge of homoerotic activity was secondary to the financial and personal disputes among the polygamous families of the recently deceased Abraham Hunsaker, father of the Hunsaker brothers involved in this scandal. Despite those family disputes, the testimony of several non-Hunsaker witnesses established that during the previous two years the three younger brothers had told others that their brother Lorenzo was performing oral sex on them or was attempting to do so.

Aside from this sexual use of the word *monkey* in Utah in 1893, there was a similar homoerotic use of *monkeying* fifteen years later in testimony about anal sex among teenage boys at the Utah state reform school (see chap. 10). As a verb with sexual meaning, however, *monkey* does not appear in Farmer and Henley, *Slang and Its Analogues*, in Partridge, *Dictionary of Slang and Unconventional English*, or in the *Oxford English Dictionary*. It does appear in Hugh Rawson, *Wicked Words: A Treasury of Curses, Insults, Put-Downs*, *and Other Formerly Unprintable Terms from Anglo-Saxon Times to the Present* (New York: Crown, 1989), 254, as the generally nonsexual "to monkey around," which Rawson notes has sexual overtones only because "*monkey* also is a nineteenth century Americanism for the vulva" (255). This indicates that national dictionaries of slang do not always pick up regional vulgarisms such as Utah's homoerotic use of *monkey* during the late nineteenth century.

122. Quotation from testimony of J—— M. G—— (b. 7 May 1868), who used the phrase "skinning my 'dick'" in Clawson's 1893–94 diary, 119. As discussed in note 51, *dick* became American slang for penis during the nineteenth century. Although the exact wording of this Utah vulgarism did not appear in national dictionaries of American slang, variations of *skin* as a verb for masturbation appeared in Farmer and Henley, *Slang and Its Analogues* 6:228, and Partridge, *Dictionary of Slang and Unconventional English*, 1079.

123. B—— Hunsaker statement to one of the neighbor witnesses at the trial that "he had to hold to the bed to keep Lorenzo from turning him over that he might play with his penis" (96), and other information in Clawson's 1893–94 diary, 85, 144–45, 155–56. I do not fully identify this brother because he has not previously been identified in print as one of the alleged victims.

124. Clawson diary, 29 Jan., 17 June 1894, 3 Nov. 1895; Hoopes and Hoopes, *The Making of a Mormon Apostle*, 163–67.

125. *New Catholic Encyclopedia*, 15 vols. (New York: McGraw-Hill, 1967), 7:567–68. However, for nonspecific sinfulness, Brigham Young prohibited the entire Mormon population from receiving the sacrament (communion) during five months of the Utah reformation. See Peterson, "The Mormon Reformation of 1856–1857," 77.

126. The case involved Lorenzo Hunsaker (b. 21 Mar. 1859), Hans Peter Hunsaker (b. 9 July 1870), and half brothers B—— Hunsaker (b. 5 July 1872) and Weldon Hunsaker (b. 20 Nov. 1875) in Q. Maurice Hunsaker and Gwen Hunsaker Haws, *History of Abraham Hunsaker and His Family* (Salt Lake City: Hunsaker Family Organization, 1957), 216–17, 236–38, 239–41, 253–56. Birth dates in the family history do not always agree with the stated ages of the brothers in the 1893 church minutes. Although the published family history acknowledges only one wife for Lorenzo Hunsaker, the LDS Ancestral File shows that he was also married to Sarah Alice Nye, by whom he had one child, and that she divorced him and married another man in 1898. For the 1897 date of the divorce, see Wilford Woodruff Record of Divorces (1889–98), 228, Box 2, Wilford Woodruff Collection (donated by Carolyn Woodruff Owen), MsD 5506, LDS Archives.

127. Testimony of Weldon Hunsaker and another brother at the trial of Lorenzo Hunsaker in Clawson's 1893–94 diary, 94, 130.

128. See chap. 10.

129. Hans Peter Hunsaker statements in Clawson's 1893–94 diary, 106,

110. In his diary on 15 November 1885, Frederick S. Ryman likewise used "c---sucker" as a derogatory term, which was also the nickname for a male house of prostitution in New York City. See Martin Duberman, *About Time: Exploring the Gay Past,* rev. ed. (New York: Meridian Books/Penguin, 1991), 62; George Chauncey, *Gay New York: Gender, Urban Culture, and the Making of the Gay Male World, 1890–1940* (New York: Basic Books/HarperCollins, 1994), 42. Partridge, *Dictionary of Slang and Unconventional English,* 233, dates this vulgarity as originating in the United States, no earlier than the nineteenth century. As an example of the time lag between actual usage and an entry in slang dictionaries, J. E. Lighter, ed., *Random House Historical Dictionary of American Slang,* 3 vols. (New York: Random House, 1994–96), 1:447, gives 1891 as the earliest use of this vulgarism, which Ryman had recorded in 1885.

130. Indictment against Frank Smiley, filed 11 Dec. 1894, Case 452, Fourth District Court (Weber County) Criminal Case Files, and Fourth District Court (Weber County) Minute Book (1892–95), 366, 369, 371; entries for Frank W. T. Smiley in Utah Territorial Prison Inmate Commitment Register (1888–96), 310, 439; entries for Willis Clark in Park City, Utah, Police Department, Register of Arrests (1892–1904), 159, 161–62, 166–67, Microfilm A-797, Utah State Historical Society; Park City Justice's Court Docket (1902–4), 1306, 1323, 1355, 1395, 1465, Microfilm A-760, Utah State Historical Society; "FOURTH DISTRICT COURT: Frank Smily [*sic*] Changes His Plea and Says He Is Guilty," *Ogden Standard,* 14 Dec. 1894, [4]. For the non-Mormon background of Judge Harvey W. Smith, see "Judge Smith Dead," *Deseret Evening News,* 23 Nov. 1895, 8. He had successfully argued the disincorporation of the LDS Church before the U.S. Supreme Court in 1890.

131. Park City Justice's Court Docket (1902–4), 1306 (14 May 1903), 1323 (12 June 1903); Park City, Utah, Police Department, Register of Arrests (1892–1904), 159 (13 July 1903), 161–62 (13 Aug. 1903), 166–67 (13 Oct. 1903).

132. Upon his release from prison, Wilde resumed living with his former lover, Alfred Lord Douglas, for a few months, until both their families threatened to cut off their financial support unless they separated. Douglas came to comfort Wilde upon his wife's death, was the chief mourner at Wilde's funeral, and tried to throw himself onto the coffin after it was lowered into the grave. See Richard Ellman, *Oscar Wilde* (New York: Vintage Books, 1988), 435–524, 544, 566, 584, 588; see also Clifford Allen, "Homosexuality and Oscar Wilde: A Psychological Study," in Hendrik Ruitenbeek, ed., *Homosexuality and Creative Genius* (New York: Astor-Honor, 1967), 61–83; Linda Dowling, *Hellenism and Homosexuality in Victorian England* (Ithaca: Cornell University Press, 1994), 140–52; Neil Miller, *Out of the Past: Gay and Lesbian History from 1869 to the Present* (New York: Vintage/Random House, 1995), 45–54; Gary Schmidgall, *The Stranger Wilde: Interpreting Oscar Wilde* (New York: Dutton, 1995), 169–294.

133. Jeffrey Weeks, *Sex, Politics, and Society: The Regulation of Sexuality since 1800* (London: Longman, 1981), 103; Michael Bronski, *Culture Clash: The Making of Gay Sensibility* (Boston: South End Press, 1984), 63–64.

134. A. D. Harvey, *Sex in Georgian England: Attitudes and Prejudices from the 1720s to the 1820s* (New York: St. Martin's Press, 1994), 147.

CHAPTER 10

Utah's Judicial and Medical Responses: The Wilde Case to 1918

THE OSCAR WILDE sodomy case of 1895 was of particular interest to Mormons because he had visited Utah. LDS president John Taylor even gave him a personal tour of Salt Lake City in 1882. The flamboyant Wilde also impressed some of the city's youth. Dressed in lace and velvet tights, he walked on the stage of the Salt Lake Theatre to lecture and was greeted by an "array of young men on the front row, each adorned with an enormous sunflower."[1] The names and religious identity of Wilde's sunflower boys in Utah are unknown, but their garish presence was consistent with the *Washington Post*'s report that Wilde's conspicuous admirers at his lectures were young men "with unmistakable rouge upon their cheeks."[2]

Beginning in April 1895 the LDS Church's *Deseret News* featured eighteen front-page stories and two editorials about the Wilde trial. Still, the *News* refused to quote the testimony or even identify the crime for which Wilde was accused.[3] On the other hand, the LDS political newspaper *Salt Lake Herald* used the word *sodomy* in the headline of its first report about Wilde. However, after two long articles (each more than one column) about the trial's sensational testimony, the *Herald* stopped printing such details. This was undoubtedly at the request of LDS leaders, since Apostle Heber J. Grant was vice president of the Herald Publishing Company at this time. The few stories about the

Wilde case that subsequently appeared in the *Herald* were similar to the restrained reports in the *Deseret News*.[4]

Although equally restrained about the Wilde case, the non-Mormon *Salt Lake Tribune* printed less than half as many articles as the *Deseret News* did.[5] However, coverage of the Wilde scandal in twenty issues of the *News* was typical for the nation at large. The *New York Times* ran articles on it in twenty-one separate issues.[6]

Contrary to what one might expect, the sensational publicity of Wilde's trial was followed by a lessening of penalties in Utah's sodomy convictions. There was no sodomy case in Utah's courts in 1895, but in May 1896, Jacob Johnson (whose parents and wife were Mormon) as acting judge in Utah County sentenced two men (ages twenty-five and twenty-six) to one year's imprisonment each for using "force and arms" to "perpetrate that infamous crime against nature" on three unwilling teenagers as young as thirteen. The Provo newspaper reported that the two "brutal tramps" had committed "the offense of sodomy" on the three young Mormons, who had recently run away from their homes in Salt Lake City.[7] During the 1890s, about 10 percent of America's male tramps and hobos engaged in sex with other men.[8]

In June 1896, a Mormon judge in Weber County sentenced a twenty-two year old to only nine months for sodomy, despite the fact that he had been previously imprisoned for burglary and despite the fact that he had raped a "boy."[9] When Henry H. Rolapp gave this nine-month sentence for homosexual assault in 1896, the Mormon judge again made forcible sodomy no more serious an offense than consensual fornication. For example, a few months after Rolapp's decision, another district court gave a six-month sentence to an eighteen-year-old man for "having [consensual] Carnal knowledge of a female person over 13 and under 18 years of age."[10]

These sentences for homosexual assault in the first half of 1896 were two-thirds shorter than the punishment decreed by the non-Mormon federal judge in Weber County in the previous case of sodomy in 1894. That case had apparently been consensual, and its harsher punishment was before the publicity of the Wilde sodomy trial. Again, there is no obvious explanation for this apparent contradiction, except that the two lenient judges in 1896 were of Mormon background, while the harsh judge in 1894 was non-Mormon.

In fact, religion appeared to be the crucial factor in a sensational case that received full newspaper coverage in Provo in September 1896.

Thomas H. Clark, an eighteen-year-old non-Mormon from Los Angeles, claimed that sixteen "tramps" had gang-raped him during a drunken party at Spanish Fork in Utah County. He personally identified nine males who had performed "buggery, to the great disgrace and scandal of all human kind." The arrested "tramps" included six Mormons. From seventeen to thirty years of age, they were members of various LDS wards in Utah County and Salt Lake County.[11]

Despite the victim's recognition of nine of his attackers, the non-LDS "committing magistrate" Charles DeMoisey dismissed all charges against the six Mormons without explanation. In reporting the dismissal of those defendants, Provo's Mormon newspaper claimed on 18 September that the victim identified only three men. However, Clark had personally identified all nine, and the newspaper on 17 September even named one of the identified attackers, who was released the next day. Although the magistrate's court record is unavailable, county prosecutor Samuel A. King (a Mormon) was apparently the one who asked DeMoisey to drop the charges against the accused Mormons. Available records show that King also asked the district court to drop all charges against the six Mormons.[12]

The trial proceeded for only the three non-Mormons (including one Catholic). They were aged twenty-four to fifty-one, and district judge Warren N. Dusenberry (also a Mormon) gave each of them a three-year prison sentence. Dusenberry, at prosecutor King's request, also dropped the charges against the Mormon perpetrators who had been identified by the victim. No factor besides religious affiliation separated the freed men from the tried and convicted.[13] These were the last sodomy convictions in Utah during the 1890s.[14]

America's Gay Nineties was also the period in which male prostitution first became significant nationally. New York City, Boston, Philadelphia, Chicago, St. Louis, New Orleans, and San Francisco had "boy houses," or houses of prostitution filled only with young men in their teens and twenties. There were also traditional houses of prostitution that included at least one young man for customers interested in male-male sex. Manhattan had eight such male brothels in the 1890s.[15] There had undoubtedly always been some male prostitution in America,[16] but evidence of it became extensive during the 1890s.

In addition, one experienced investigator wrote before 1910 that some female prostitutes preferred having sex with women: "in almost all large brothels, there is at least one."[17] That observation was consistent with the living arrangements of several Salt Lake City prostitutes. The 1900 census showed that twenty-three-year-old Jennette Henry was the domestic "partner" of twenty-five-year-old Raffella Lee. The two women had been regularly arrested for prostitution during the previous three years. Also, "Madge" Daniels, arrested monthly as a "keeper of a house" during 1899, appeared in the census as a twenty-four-year-old householder with twenty-three-year-old "Lou" Miller, a woman, as her only "lodger."[18]

For decades LDS leaders had commented about Salt Lake City's female prostitutes. In 1896 General Authority J. Golden Kimball preached: "There are 500 girls who are public prostitutes in Salt Lake City. Some of these are daughters of Latter-day Saints."[19] The city had nearly thirty-five houses of prostitution in the 1890s.[20]

Utah apparently even had a male brothel in the mining town of Eureka in Juab County. In February 1897, Eureka's police arrested three men for "Resideing in a House of Prostitution," including one known Mormon: David Baum, age fifteen. He later married and fathered one child. During the same raid the police arrested Harry Mason for "Keeping a House of Ill Fame." Mason's wife was also the "keeper" of a brothel and was arrested on separate occasions with her female prostitutes. This suggests that the husband and wife ran two separate houses of prostitution. A year later, Harry Mason no longer managed what was apparently Eureka's male house of prostitution, and the police arrested Thomas Downey for "Keeping a Disorderly House."[21] In the 1900 census, males were 55.9 percent of Eureka's population of 3,085, not as male-dominant a population as one might expect of a mining town.[22]

Elsewhere in the state, the major houses included young men for interested customers, although Utah's cities did not have an exclusively male house of prostitution. In addition to arresting men for "resorting" to prostitutes or for "gambling" in a brothel, police also arrested a few males as "inmate[s] of house of Ill fame" in raids on brothels in Salt Lake City, Park City, and Ogden during the 1890s.[23] It is unlikely that these male "inmates" were young "cadets" or "pimps," because, as the historian Ruth Rosen observed, "madams never permitted [their] pimps to live in the brothels" in the early 1900s.[24]

Utah's police also arrested males for street "Prostitution," which the judge often reduced to the lesser charge of "Vagrancy."[25] Several males arrested in Utah as vagrant or "hobo" in the 1890s also had the left-hand tattoo common among other men convicted of sodomy in Utah.[26]

One case of sodomy and prostitution also indicated that by 1890, at least some Utah men regarded men who had sex with other men as fundamentally different. Witnesses testified that they saw Otto Venson (age unknown) lying naked, face down on a bed as another man withdrew from anal intercourse. Venson said he was too drunk to remember what happened. Besides, he claimed, "I'm not that kind of a man." Venson said he had no idea why the accused man gave him money after getting dressed. This occurred on Commercial Street, Salt Lake City's prostitution district. It is possible that Venson claimed he was "not that kind of a man" only because he anticipated that the judge and jury viewed men who engaged in anal intercourse as fundamentally different from other men. Apparently his testimony succeeded, because the charges were dropped against both men.[27]

Misdemeanor arrests and fines for prostitution rarely described the persons, but details survive about some male prostitutes in Utah during this period. In 1892, the Salt Lake City police arrested George Raymond for "vagrancy" one night, and described the seventeen-year-old as a "Call boy."[28] Alias "George Conley," this brown-haired, brown-eyed boy was a slender 104 pounds for his height of 5 feet 3¾ inches. He escaped from the city jail in Salt Lake, only to be killed by a train in Ogden.[29]

In April 1898, Park City police arrested "Fred Stephenson" as an "Inmate [of a] house [of] ill fame." This was apparently a twenty-three-year-old returned missionary of the LDS Church. He never married but was ordained a high priest thirty-one years after this arrest. In 1904 Park City's police arrested Ray Lewis as a prostitute. He was apparently a twenty-one-year-old Mormon who married at age twenty-seven.[30]

In the June 1900 federal census, Ray (or Roy) E. Osborne was a nineteen-year-old male "servant" at a rooming house in the "Gentile" town of Corinne, Utah. A year later, he was arrested with fourteen female prostitutes as an "inmate [of a] house [of] ill fame" in the mining town of Park City. During the next two years, this town's police arrested and fined Osborne seven times for "prostitution" or for being a male "inmate" of a brothel.[31] The Utah state historian John S. McCormick observes that those police raids on houses of prostitution—usually scheduled on the same day each month—were "not so much to suppress prostitution as to produce revenue for the city."[32]

In Salt Lake City of the 1890s, most male prostitutes were in their twenties when arrested for street prostitution or for being an "inmate" in one of the city's houses of prostitution.[33] The church's *Deseret News* may even have invented a euphemism for male prostitute when the newspaper listed "the male parasite" among inhabitants of Commercial Street's prostitution district.[34]

A little-known irony is that the LDS Church had a long-term relationship with several of Salt Lake City's houses of prostitution on Commercial Street since 1891.[35] This created conflict within the Mormon hierarchy. Because the Brigham Young Trust Company's officers had "elected to let [i.e., lease] buildings to whores," Apostle Brigham Young Jr. angrily resigned in January 1897 as vice president of this LDS company that bore his father's name.[36] At a meeting in the Salt Lake temple four months later, the First Presidency and apostles discussed Young's resignation and "the matter of the Brigham Young Trust Co. having fitted up a first class whore-house and President [George Q.] Cannon being President of the company was brought up."[37] The First Presidency persuaded Young to return to the corporate responsibility of his church position.

At another apostolic meeting in the Salt Lake temple in 1900, Apostle Brigham Young Jr. recorded that there was "much talk about B.Y. Trust Co running a whore house on Commercial Street. Pres. G.Q.C. president & B.Y. Vice president [with] Jos. F S[mith]. director on BY board." The consensus of the LDS First Presidency and apostles in 1900 was that "we all disapprove of it." Young "expressed myself as determined to get out of it," and the two members of the First Presidency and the Twelve's president resigned as trustees by 1901.[38] In fact, the LDS Church holding company leased more buildings to prostitutes, and the arrest records indicate that some male prostitutes lived and worked in these houses.

There may have been a connection between this June 1900 temple meeting and a change in the arrest procedures for male prostitutes shortly thereafter. Salt Lake City's police stopped charging men with prostitution or for residing in a house of prostitution and simply charged those arrested with "vagrancy," a term that included many nonsexual activities. For example, the *Salt Lake Tribune* reported in April 1901: "Victor LaGrasselle, Victor Pinto and Charles Dubois, who are charged with being vagrants, because they had lived in and around houses of prostitution, were yesterday discharged by Judge Timmony, on motion of Prosecutor Diehl. The Judge said there was a very grave doubt in his mind whether the defendants could be convicted under the ordinance."[39] Although the LDS Church's *Deseret News* had a regular column titled "Judge Timmony's Court," it did not publish it on the day of this decision.[40] These males may have been living in the "whore house on Commercial Street," which Young said the church's holding company was "running," but arrest and court documents were not detailed enough to verify that. The hierarchy's documents on this situation are also too sketchy to determine whether LDS leaders had quietly encouraged that change in the arrest procedures for prostitutes, both male and female, in 1900–1901.

Nevertheless, Salt Lake City's police continued to charge young men with "vagrancy" rather than prostitution, as was formerly the arrest procedure.[41] That change was also reflected in the arrest records of Park City.[42] The effect of this change was to obscure the extent of Utah's prostitution by submerging it into the nonsexual categories "vagrancy" and "disorderly conduct." Not until its annual report of 1916 did the Salt Lake City Police Department publicly acknowledge the existence of male prostitutes, twelve of whom were arrested that year. That was the first published report since 1893 to identify the gender of arrested prostitutes.[43]

The LDS Church's connection with houses of prostitution remained an uncomfortable secret until 1908 when the *Salt Lake Tribune* proclaimed that the Brigham Young Trust Company "filled these houses on Commercial Street." This article noted that the church-owned Clayton Investment Company continued to lease these houses of prostitution and that the LDS Church's annual rent was $2,400 from just one of these brothel leases. At that time $2,300 was the purchase price for a "12–room modern house, 3 blocks from the Temple."[44] The *Tribune*'s description of the situation was not as harsh as the views of Counselor Anthon H. Lund, who had previously written as an apostle that the general authorities on the company's board had "fitted up a first class whore-house" or Young's charge that they were "running a whore house." Although the LDS Church was technically and legally only the lessor of the buildings, some general authorities regarded the church's leadership as morally implicated in brothel management.[45]

As an apostle, Heber J. Grant had also complained that "Brigham Young Trust Co. kept a Whorehouse." By invitation in 1897, Grant attended a late-night reception at what he thought was a newly opened business of the LDS Church, only to discover that he was "in a regular whore-house."[46] However, as church president after 1918 Grant did not require the church's Clayton Investment Company to change things. Commercial Street ceased to be a prostitution district in 1908,[47] but the LDS Church continued to lease the relocated houses of prostitution.

This LDS holding company did not divest its houses of prostitution until 1941, when its president told First Presidency Counselor J. Reuben Clark that the church still "has 'whorehouses' on Clayton Investment." Because Clayton Investment was merging with the higher-profile Zion's Securities Corporation, Clark ordered the Clayton leadership to "clean or close all Clayton Investment houses of shoddy character." He added that the First Presidency "cared nothing about the money involved." To the First Presidency's financial secretary, Counselor Clark reaffirmed, "Money is not the primary objective but morality and cleanliness."[48]

However, the First Presidency had declined to accept the loss of the revenues from its leased houses of prostitution throughout the presidencies of Wilford Woodruff, Lorenzo Snow, Joseph F. Smith, and most of the presidency of Heber J. Grant. During that same period Grant had waged public and private campaigns to prohibit the use of alcohol and tobacco in Utah.[49] In all, four general authorities of the LDS Church were officers or directors of the two LDS holding companies while they leased houses of prostitution. In addition, the First Presidency's financial secretaries were also board members during those years.[50] A similar, though lesser, conflict of business income and religious values during the same time involved the sale of alcohol at the church-owned resort, Saltair.[51]

Nevertheless, it was an example of cognitive dissonance for LDS leaders to even grudgingly allow houses of prostitution to operate on church-owned properties for decades. That contradiction is both perplexing and inconsistent with the personalities of the general authorities who knew of this situation. The clinical social worker Marybeth Raynes, a Mormon, has suggested that such discordant views and behaviors within an individual are consistent with Post-Traumatic Stress Disorder (PTSD). She noted that for decades the federal government's antipolygamy campaign had forced LDS leaders to battle for survival on issues of disapproved sexuality and endangered finances. Raynes explains: "Repeated trauma often results in reactions that numb or blunt a person's awareness of conflicts and incongruities in their life, particularly when these conflicts and incongruities occur in the area of life in which the trauma occurred." She sees this as a possible explanation for the apparent compartmentalization of conflicting values when disapproved sexuality and endangered finances intersected again in the LDS Church's income from the houses of prostitution.[52]

For example, Heber J. Grant constantly lived in fear of arrest following his polygamous marriages in 1884, was repeatedly on the verge of bankruptcy for decades as an apostle, was arrested for polygamous cohabitation in 1907, and as LDS president struggled to keep church corporations solvent from the 1920s through the 1930s.[53] Raynes suggests that PTSD would explain why Grant and other turn-of-the-century LDS leaders were psychologically unable to disengage the financially struggling LDS Church from the income derived from its houses of prostitution. In any case, after fifty years, the LDS Church finally severed its connection with Salt Lake City's houses of prostitution, which had also housed some male prostitutes since the 1890s.[54]

Utah's male prostitutes of the 1890s and early 1900s left no record of their feelings about participating in the world's oldest profession. However, the sociologist Nels Anderson interviewed a male prostitute in Ogden during the summer of 1921. He found the fourteen year old "had a pleasant disposition" and was "strong, active and mentally alert." The "witty" boy told a group of adult tramps that "he would 'do business' with anyone in the crowd for fifty cents."[55] Fifty cents might not seem like much money, but fifty cents was the cost of a night's rent for a furnished room with bath in downtown Salt Lake City in 1921.[56] Ten years later in New York City, with its higher cost of living, a sixteen-year-old male prostitute "charged 50 cents for oral sex and 75 cents for anal sex."[57]

The morning after the young Utah prostitute had gone with a man for the night, this Mormon sociologist interviewed the "talkative" teenager: "In brief this was his philosophy [about being a prostitute]. It was an easy way to get by. He didn't hurt anyone. He minded his own business and paid his way. He didn't steal or beg. It wasn't any worse than many other things people did. No, he didn't work; he didn't have to. He never traveled with a man."[58] The views of this male prostitute in Utah during 1921 are remarkably similar to views expressed by America's young "hustlers" and male prostitutes (including one Mormon) in recent decades.[59] Therefore, this fourteen year old's remarks were probably consistent with the self-image of his fellow male prostitutes in Utah during the 1890s and early 1900s.

Youthful male prostitution in Utah at the turn of the century also had a parallel in the state's juvenile court records. However, there are problems with the Utah statistics of juvenile prostitution, because it was defined as a female crime. The juvenile courts of Utah used the label "vagrancy" to describe what was actually the prostitution of male teenagers. For example, Salt Lake City's juvenile court was probably describing male prostitution in the following cases at the turn of the century. All but one of these young men was seventeen years old. Sam was a "delinquent child by immoral conduct." Walter was "wandering about the streets in the night time without any lawful business occupation." Roy was "immoral in his conduct, stays out late at night, associates with people of bad repute" and "commit[s] immoral acts." Howard was "immoral in his conduct and habits, and he keeps bad company and stays out late at nights."[60] When described in that way by court documents, female juveniles were typically labeled "prostitutes," whereas the courts never used that label for male juveniles whose behavior was described in the same way.[61] This reflected the practice of Utah's police after 1900 in charging men with vagrancy rather than prostitution, which had the effect of obscuring the amount of male prostitution.

One curious development in Utah's juvenile courts during the early 1900s was the criminalizing of a homosocial activity that had survived unscathed throughout the era of Victorian prudishness. *The Swimming Hole* by Thomas Eakins gave classic visual expression in 1883 to the universal practice of nude swimming outdoors by adolescent American boys. The United States even included this canvas in the 1939 world's fair exhibit "Life in America." This was the official exhibit's caption for this naturalistic painting of nude teenage boys in the nineteenth century: "No American community was complete without its swimming hole and no river, stream, or creek was ever too muddy, small, or contaminated to keep the boys away."[62]

Mormon legislators did not share that nostalgia for nude swimming outdoors by young men. There is no obvious explanation for this, since these legislators were teenagers during the nineteenth century when the nude swimming hole was as common in Utah as elsewhere in America. Nevertheless, this activity became a crime in the Mormon culture region during the early 1900s.

Therefore, some young nineteenth-century Mormons suddenly found that their previously noncriminal homosocial activity was now erotic by definition. In 1907, for example, Salt Lake City's police arrested two teenage boys (ages fourteen and seventeen) for swimming nude out-doors. The judge found each guilty of "taking off his clothing and exposing himself in nude condition, near Jordan River" and sentenced them to report weekly to the probation officer of the juvenile court. In the nineteenth century, nude swimming outdoors by adolescent boys had been an exception to laws that prohibited "indecent exposure."[63]

During a heat wave in July 1909, the *Salt Lake Herald* could not resist mocking such a policy for actually creating more "indecent exposure" in public than it was intended to prevent. The newspaper reported that "about a dozen youngsters made a wild dash from the [makeshift] swimming pool at First South and the Salt Lake Route tracks yester-day afternoon, and leaving their clothes on the bank, ran for several blocks [naked] to escape the police."[64]

One case also demonstrated that Salt Lake City's juvenile court did not define every homoerotic activity as a "crime against nature." One evening in 1909, six young men (between the ages of thirteen and sev-enteen) entered the grounds of the Emerson public school, where they were discovered acting together "in an indecent manner." Whatever "indecent" acts the three pairs of Mormon boys had committed, they did with each other, because the court records made no mention of any female involvement.[65] By contrast, the same Salt Lake City juvenile court routinely named girls as young as eleven and seven who partici-pated in sexual activities with twelve- and thirteen-year-old boys who appeared before the court.[66] Despite the homoerotic dimensions of this case, the juvenile court judge merely required the six young men to meet weekly with a probation officer.[67]

On the other hand, of 709 young men (under age twenty-one) com-mitted to the Utah state reform school from 1897 through 1902, 5 percent (35) were confined for such crimes as sodomy, attempted rape, and rape. Only 1.3 percent (9) were charged with the "crime against nature."[68] Actual "penetration" was apparently why the juvenile courts defined these "against nature" crimes as more serious than the night-time "indecent" acts among the young men at the Emerson School in 1909.

Ironically, although the Utah state reform school housed young men who were committed for sodomy, the school's sleeping arrangements actually encouraged erotic contact among its inmates. One of the school's employees testified that overcrowding required young men over the age of twelve to sleep by twos in beds that were two-feet wide. When a nineteen-year-old former inmate was asked, "is there much vulgarity in the bedroom at night after you go to bed?" he replied: "There are some that lay close together."[69] One employee also testified that for severe infractions, three or four teenage boys had to share a single bed in underground "cells" where they were left unattended for days.[70] This testimony was part of an investigation that resulted from the disclosure of the Utah reform school's violent response to an incident of anal intercourse.

During a July 1908 campout in Ogden Canyon for the residents of the Utah reform school, the administrators discovered seven teenagers between the ages of nineteen and sixteen engaged in "that unmentionable crime" of "buggery" on "small boys" as young as eleven at a secluded spot.[71] All but the two oldest of the perpetrators were Mormons, and one of the non-Mormons was an eighteen-year-old African American.[72] During this time period, juveniles remained in the reform school until age twenty-one. This was the earliest-known reference in Utah to what has been called "the situational homosexuality" of incarcerated people.[73]

In this study's terms, homoeroticism was the only possibility for sexual intimacy in a homoenvironmental prison or reform school. The records of Utah's reform school during this period made no reference to homoerotic activities between females, but a national periodical observed that sexual acts between young women were "well known among workers in reform schools and institutions for delinquent girls."[74]

Other testimony clarified that the "small boys" involved in this group sex incident of 1908 were not as young as the phrase suggested. Concerning previous testimony about the Utah reform school's housing, assistant superintendent William E. Kneass explained that the term *small boys* referred to inmates who were about twelve years of age.[75] Some of these "small" sex partners may have been teenagers only a few years younger than the sixteen to nineteen year olds who engaged in sex with the younger boys. None of the testimony about this incident indicated that the physically smaller young men were raped.

Nevertheless, forty-six-year-old Superintendent Heber H. Thomas (a Mormon) said that "it simply made your blood run cold,—it was a revolting affair." In contrast, a nineteen year old (whom the superintendent regarded as an inmate of superior behavior and attitude) described the incident as just some teenagers "monkeying with the other boys."[76] Several witnesses, including Superintendent Thomas, acknowledged that the 1908 incident was only the most recent occurrence of anal sex and group sex among the reform school's teenage boys.[77] However, Heber H. Thomas (b. 1862) demonstrated that some nineteenth-century Mormons reacted with cold fury when confronted with same-sex acts by young men also born in that century.

Assistant Superintendent Kneass described the punishment that the reform school's superintendent gave to the older youths involved in this incident. The two administrators and three other adult employees of the reform school took turns beating each young man from twenty to twenty-five times on the shoulders and back with a leather strap attached to a wooden handle. The room filled with their screams of pain, pleas for mercy, promises never to do "it" again, and admissions that they deserved their punishment. Between beatings, Thomas and Kneass lectured the young men about "the vileness of the offense which they committed." All this continued for forty-five minutes, accompanied by music from the reform school's band, which the superintendent had ordered to perform outside the room in which he conducted the beatings.[78]

Although the scene was reminiscent of Dante's *Inferno,* the reform school's superintendent administered this punishment by permission of Utah's governor. According to Superintendent Thomas, Governor John C. Cutler (also a Mormon) said that "strapping was no punishment at all,—they were fit for the pen." Thomas also got individual authorization from several members of the reform school's board of trustees to whip these teenagers. Thomas himself was a counselor in the LDS bishopric of the Ogden Fifth Ward.[79]

Before their beating, the teenagers had been confined in underground cells for two weeks on a diet of only bread and water. One youth fainted after receiving twenty lashes, was taken out to be revived, and then was given more lashes. An employee later acknowledged that he "strapped" the young men as hard as he could on this occasion. The beating gouged out a chunk of flesh the size of a cork from one boy's back and from another's arm and left bloody welts on all of the young men. An employee who examined one of these teenagers the day after the beating said "his back was like a roast of a piece of meat . . . was blue and black and blood stains." Some of the young men were unable to walk upright for a week.[80]

The aftereffects of this incident and the teenagers' punishment haunted Utah's reform school for the next year. The day after the beating, the superintendent refused to let a Mormon mother see her badly bruised son. Superintendent Thomas said that he had "given Stanley a whipping and that he would get something worse in the near future." Fearful of that greater punishment, eighteen-year-old Stanley Rasmussen and seventeen-year-old fellow Mormon William Buchanan escaped the next night. On 5 August 1908, the school's board of trustees voted to approve "the punishment given by direction of the Superintendent to the inmates named" and offered a reward for their capture. During his effort to evade arrest, Rasmussen died in a railroad accident, but Buchanan remained free and unmarried until his death in San Francisco.[81] In addition, other teenage boys died of scarlet fever or typhoid at the reform school shortly after being beaten or after being put on a diet of bread and water for various infractions.[82]

In the aftermath of newspaper reports, the reform school's board voted to forbid "corporal punishment except as a last resort." A newly elected governor ordered an official inquiry in June 1909.[83] At the investigation's conclusion, the *Salt Lake Herald* reported that the attorney for the complainants said the "orgy" did not occur during the sodomy incident in the canyon but occurred during the punishment of the teenagers by Superintendent Thomas. On the other hand, the superintendent's attorney replied that the young men were "burly brutes who had outraged smaller boys" and that "whipping is much too good for them."[84]

In demanding the resignation of Thomas, the *Salt Lake Herald* editorialized that the reform school's residents "were beaten, starved and kept in solitary confinement in narrow, unsanitary cells. That some of them died under the treatment received was to be expected." The editor was so furious that he even implied that Superintendent Thomas should commit suicide.[85]

After this investigation, Heber H. Thomas was forced to resign less than two months after he was reelected to another four-year term by the reform school's board. The punishments Thomas had ordered for the sodomy incident were the catalyst for his downfall.[86]

During the first decade of the twentieth century, there was also a significant increase in the length of punishment that Utah's judges gave to those convicted of sodomy. Every case involved sexual assault by adult males on minors as young as thirteen, and there was no indication of consensual sex.

In 1900, one man received a ten-year sentence, another received eight years' imprisonment, and a court sentenced two others to six years each. Sentenced to eight years for sodomy despite his lack of a criminal record, twenty-nine-year-old Mike McCormick also had the significant tattoo: "Dot of india ink bet thumb & first finger [of] left hand."[87]

That sentencing pattern continued through the decade. In the only Utah sodomy cases of 1901 the two convicted men received four years each. In the next case in 1903 the man received a four-year sentence. In the next case in 1906 the court sentenced the man to fifteen years. In the next sodomy conviction of 1909, the man received a ten-year sentence.[88] By comparison, three years was the severest sentence in nineteenth-century Utah for sodomy, even forcible sodomy. Sentences of less than six months had once been the norm for forcible sodomy in Utah.

As of 1900, Utah's judges seemed to turn the cold fury of the law against those who crossed the line into same-sex intercourse. Rocky O'Donovan partially attributes such growing homophobia to the sensational newspaper coverage of Oscar Wilde's sodomy trial in 1895.[89] However, as previously discussed, there appears to have been a reduction of homophobia in the Utah judiciary during the closing years of the 1890s. A more significant factor may have been the collective awareness by 1900 of Utah's police, judges, juvenile court officers, and reform school officials that there were widespread homoerotic activities among Utah's males—whether teenagers or adults, Mormons or non-Mormons. Likewise, the historian David F. Greenberg gave a similar explanation for the fact that in the United States as a whole, imprisonments for "unnatural crimes" increased by 350 percent between 1880 and 1890.[90]

However, there also seemed to be a religious dimension in the severe sentencing for convictions of sodomy in Utah during the early 1900s. Of the nine Utah men convicted of sodomy from 1900 through 1909, all were non-Mormons—six Protestants and three Catholics. Every one of the young men they assaulted was Mormon. Before receiving jail terms as long as fifteen years for sodomy, these Catholic and Protestant defendants were held in prison without bail.[91]

Things were different for the one Mormon charged with sodomy during the same decade. Utah's former governor Heber M. Wells and the current clerk of the district court (both LDS) paid the bail for forty-four-year-old Edward Burke, who was accused in 1907 of committing "the infamous crime against nature" on a fifteen-year-old boy. After several court delays, the Mormon skipped bail and avoided both trial and punishment.[92] Salt Lake City's police chief Tom D. Pitt apparently cooperated in concealing this case by claiming in his published report for 1907 that there had been no arrest that year for attempted sodomy, for the "Crime Against Nature," or for sodomy.[93] A year later, Pitt was forced to resign because he opposed requiring prostitutes to leave the houses of prostitution of Commercial Street and elsewhere in order to move to Salt Lake City's "Stockade" of legally supervised prostitution.[94]

However, a non-Mormon could win an acquittal during this period. In 1909, the Salt Lake City municipal judge acquitted a thirteen-year-old Greek Orthodox immigrant for sodomy with another young man. The *Deseret News* reported that "Nick P[o]ulos, a foreigner, was arraigned on the charge of committing a crime against nature against a youth named Lashaway [Lackaway], a foreigner." In this article, the double emphasis of *foreigner* identified two non-Mormons whom the *Deseret News* expected to be of little interest to its readers. The non-Mormon judge acquitted the accused Poulos despite the testimony of three prosecution witnesses. The age of the accused may have been the reason for his acquittal.[95]

In 1911, a twenty-nine-year-old Catholic also plea-bargained his way into a relatively light sodomy sentence for non-Mormons in Utah during this period. Indicted for actually having "carnal knowledge of the body" of an eleven-year-old Mormon boy, the man pleaded guilty to the lesser crime of "AN ATTEMPT TO COMMIT THE INFAMOUS CRIME AGAINST NATURE." The Mormon judge sentenced him to "eighteen months at hard labor." Nine non-Mormon convicts of the previous decade could envy that sodomy sentence, yet Frank Sweeney shortened his imprisonment even further by successfully escaping from the Utah penitentiary.[96]

Utah's supreme court also upheld a similar sentence for the state's only sodomy case in 1912. Joseph Morasco, an Italian Catholic, received a two-year sentence for "Assault with intent to commit Sodomy." He was released after serving eighteen months in the Utah State Prison.[97]

Nevertheless, the religious disparity in Utah's sodomy convictions was starkest during 1913. Municipal judge Nathaniel H. Tanner (a Mormon) tried the forcible sodomy case of forty-one-year-old William Payne, a Mormon who was discharged by the district court.[98] The sodomy case of another Mormon remained at the municipal level, and Judge Tanner sentenced twenty-three-year-old John Randolph to forty-five days in the Salt Lake County Jail.[99] By contrast, that same year two Protestants and a Catholic convicted of sodomy received state prison sentences for three years, five years, and four years, respectively.[100]

Religion had been a noticeable factor in several of Utah's sodomy cases since 1896. That year statehood allowed a resurgence of Mormon influence in Utah's judiciary. Separate study is required to determine whether religion played a factor in the conduct and outcome of other criminal cases in the state of Utah from 1896 to the early 1900s.

Nevertheless, one of those three non-Mormon sodomy convicts received good news from the Utah Supreme Court in December 1913. In his twenties, Andrew G. Johnson was the first African American convicted of sodomy in Utah, and he appealed to the state supreme court on the day of his sentencing for performing oral sex on an apparently willing man.[101] The state's high court reversed Johnson's conviction because oral sex was not covered by Utah's sodomy statute. William McCarty, the non-Mormon chief justice of the Utah Supreme Court, wrote: "While we, from the standpoint of decency and morals, fully concur . . . regarding the loathsome and revolting character and enormity of the act charged, yet we cannot, in the absence of legislative enactment making such acts criminal and punishable, denounce and punish them as crimes."[102] This was almost thirty years after the 1887 sodomy case, during which the *Salt Lake Tribune* also complained that Utah's statute did not cover oral sex. Nearly ten years after this court decision, the Mormon-dominated legislature made oral sex a crime in Utah.[103]

None of the four daily newspapers in Salt Lake City reported the Utah Supreme Court's decision of 16 December 1913 about oral sex. Nor did they report Johnson's release from prison a week later. This was an intentional news blackout. The *Salt Lake Herald-Republican* (the organ of apostle and senator Reed Smoot's political organization) had already typeset the news article headlined "Supreme Court Upholds District Bench's Contention, But Reverses Decision." Ironically, the *Herald-Republican* substituted photographs of two young men in the place of the sodomy decision. However, in their last-minute rush, the editors of this LDS Church–owned newspaper forgot to remove the title of the deleted article from the front-page index of that issue's major stories.[104]

Even in a 1901 case with non-Mormon perpetrators and a Mormon victim, one Mormon judge was willing to apply a very narrow definition of the sodomy statute and a very broad definition of homoerotic consent. Judge Samuel W. Stewart instructed the jury:

> If you find from the evidence that the complaining witness was of such an age as to understand the nature of the crime, and consented to its commission, then it is immaterial that he is under the age of fourteen years, and I charge you that under such circumstances the said John Langenbecker is an accomplice. If you find that said John Langenbecker was an accomplice, I further charge you that if the corroborating testimony of other witnesses is not in itself sufficient to justify you in finding a verdict against the defendant, that you should find the defendant Not Guilty.

As it turned out, the jury found the Methodist and Catholic defendants guilty of forcible sodomy upon the thirteen-year-old Mormon. The LDS judge gave each man a four-year sentence.[105]

In fact, Utah had a high rate of conviction for men who were indicted for sodomy from 1900 to 1917. Of the twenty-five sodomy indictments during that period, three men were acquitted, three were dismissed for insufficient evidence, one avoided trial by skipping bail, and one served eight months in Utah's insane asylum in lieu of trial. Utah's courts convicted the other seventeen men (68.0 percent), and the state supreme court reversed only one of those convictions. Therefore, Utah had a net conviction rate of 64.0 percent of the men who were indicted for sodomy. By contrast, during the same period in New York City, "less than half of the indictments for sodomy (and in some years less than a quarter) resulted in conviction."[106]

However, the judiciary and organized religion were not the only social institutions that had to confront sexuality in Utah. In its own way Utah's medical community responded more leniently to homoerotic behaviors and for a longer time period than Utah's judiciary. Beginning in 1885, physicians throughout Utah wrote the medical evaluations of persons committed to the Utah insane asylum by county courts. From then through 1918, there was no reference to homoerotic behaviors in the physician evaluations of more than 3,500 patient commitments.[107]

Of that number, only seven men and women were described as "sexual perverts" at their commitment to the Utah insane asylum. In three of those cases, the physicians specified that the "perversion" was the masturbation practiced by these men and women.[108] In one case, the physician specified that a male patient was a "sexual pervert" because he "committed rape on a little girl."[109] In three cases, the medical evaluations gave no stated reason for the "pervert" description.[110]

In contrast to this medical evidence of masturbation by heterosexual women in Utah, all the Salt Lake City lesbians in Mildred Berryman's study during the first decades of the twentieth century said they avoided masturbation. Either Berryman did not ask the question of the gay men, or they declined to discuss it.[111] The Utah lesbians described masturbation as "degenerating" or "repulsive." One lesbian teacher reported that "she has a horror of masturbation and watches for evidence of it among her pupils closely."[112]

Two other cases at the Utah insane asylum from 1885 to 1918 show that even the unexplained "pervert" labels in a few commitment documents did not necessarily refer to homoerotic behaviors. Two young men were committed to the asylum after the police accused them of committing sodomy. The first was the 1887 case of fourteen-year-old William H. Paddock. Paddock's medical evaluation made no mention of his criminal indictment for sodomy or of any homoerotic behavior, but indicated that he was "dangerous to commit an assault upon any person."[113]

The other case was sixteen-year-old Joseph Flaherty, who was accused by the Salt Lake City police of sodomy in 1901. Despite the seriousness of the charge, the *Salt Lake Tribune* gave an almost laudatory account of the previously "docile" teenager's attempted escape from the custody of the police and into the crowds of Main Street: "the youth suddenly assumed the position of a football player preparing for a touchdown run, and bolted forward with the speed of a startled antelope." Flaherty's medical evaluation at the Utah insane asylum described him as a "Moral degenerate" but made no reference to homoerotic behavior or the sodomy charge. Instead, the physician described Flaherty as a "degenerate" because he "will not obey parents, has a violent temper. Has not religious impressions."[114]

In other words, down to at least 1918, Utah's physicians did not regard verified homoerotic behavior as significant for any patient's mental history. The physicians simply ignored the evidence of homoerotic behavior in patients committed to the asylum. This was not due to any reticence to describe disapproved sexual activities, because Utah's physicians wrote graphic descriptions of the masturbatory and heteroerotic activities of committed patients. In fact, Utah physicians listed masturbation as a cause for the mental illness of 143 patients during the same period. The two patients with verified homoerotic experiences spent only a few months in the Utah insane asylum, while patients diagnosed as masturbators were typically confined in the asylum for a minimum of several years, and often until death.[115] According to the thinking of the time, masturbation could lead to insanity, but a mental patient's sexual experiences with a person of their same gender were not of interest to Utah physicians or to the Utah insane asylum as late as 1918 and perhaps later.

However, the U.S. military paid more attention to homoerotic activities among Utahns during this same period. After several U.S. servicemen were arrested in a police raid on a gay bar in San Francisco, a California psychiatrist wrote in September 1918: "From a military viewpoint the homosexualist is not only dangerous, but an ineffective fighter." The military added sodomy to its list of military crimes, and "perverts" were among the twenty-six Utahns who received dishonorable discharges during World War I.[116]

In a few years, judges, attorneys, and accused were all born too late to remember the thirty years of pioneer Utah when heterosexual fornication was a crime but homosexual sodomy was not. Or that after sodomy was criminalized, most Utah judges for decades treated the "crime against nature" no more harshly than fornication. Likewise, new generations of Mormon physicians and mental-health specialists would not remember the decades in Utah when homoerotic behavior was unimportant in the evaluation of a patient's mental health.[117]

The French philosopher Michel Foucault was correct in asserting that during the nineteenth century, certain European-American writers created the view that "the homosexual was now a species," not just a regular person who happened to engage in sex with someone of the same gender.[118] As a result, the historian E. Anthony Rotundo concluded: "Romantic friendship disappeared [between same-sex persons in the twentieth century], as the sharp line was drawn between homosexual and heterosexual."[119]

However, it always takes time for new views of society's opinion makers in any field to become the settled view of the specialists. It often takes decades for views of a society's elite to become the worldview of the general population—even of the highly educated. A national pattern of belief can also vary widely from city to town, region to region, national culture to subculture, middle class to working class, and from person to person.[120] This was certainly true for the views of the judicial, medical, and religious elites of Utah concerning homoerotic behaviors. Moreover, the religious views and cultural practices of nineteenth-century Mormonism tended to impede the growth of homophobia within the Mormon culture region.

So how extensive were homoerotic behaviors among nineteenth-century Mormons? I have found relatively few instances of homoerotic activities among Mormons born before 1900. These homoerotic cases involved fifty-two LDS men and twenty-four primarily Mormon women as willing participants from 1842 onward. For an additional fifty-five men, their religious background is unknown.[121] That compares to a total Mormon population of about 400,000 to the end of that century, divided about equally between males and females.[122]

For comparison, there are the published results of sex surveys of Mormon students at Brigham Young University from the 1950s to the 1970s. During those three decades, 10 percent of BYU's Mormon male students reported homoerotic experiences, and 2 percent of BYU's Mormon women reported homoerotic experiences.[123] Applied to the nineteenth-century Mormon population, this indicates my historical evidence is about 20,000 examples short for homoerotic activities among LDS men and about 4,000 examples short for homoerotic activities among Mormon women.

The existence of so few examples of homoeroticism among nineteenth-century Mormons allows for two possible explanations.

1. Modern Mormons and nineteenth-century Mormons had extraordinarily different sexual needs or extraordinarily different ways of expressing those sexual needs. Therefore, as indicated by BYU's sex surveys of the 1950s to 1970s, homoerotic experiences were 400 times more prevalent among even the most conservative modern Mormon men than among Mormon men born in the nineteenth century. Correspondingly homoerotic experiences were 175 times more prevalent among midtwentieth-century LDS women than among Mormon women born in the nineteenth century.

2. Modern Mormons and nineteenth-century Mormons had similar sexual needs and ways of expressing those sexual needs. Therefore, the incidence of homoeroticism among midtwentieth-century BYU students was no greater than that among earlier Mormons. Therefore, the actual homoerotic experiences of nineteenth-century Mormon males were 400 times greater than available historical evidence indicates. Likewise,

the prevalence of female-female sexual activities was 175 times greater among nineteenth-century Mormon women than mentioned in existing documents.

There is no way historically to prove or disprove either suggestion. However, two factors are significant in explaining the lack of homoerotic examples among nineteenth-century Mormons. First, there was an unwillingness in many Mormons to recognize the existence of homoerotic behaviors. Second, there was an unwillingness among nineteenth-century Mormons to acknowledge the full extent of any nonmarital sexual activity.

Here is an example of the unwillingness or inability of early Mormons to recognize homoerotic behaviors. In 1887 the married president of the young men's organization tried to explain why LDS leaders wanted to prohibit the waltz as "a dangerous temptation."[124] To demonstrate this to the assembled Mormon youths, the man grabbed a teenage boy and began waltzing on the dance floor with him. As he held the teenager in a tight embrace, the man rubbed his groin against his partner's body until the young man had a erection. Then the older man stepped aside so that the others could see the result of waltzing.

Apparently no one there (except possibly the teenager) recognized this incident as a homoerotic, sexually abusive act. One Mormon woman later demonstrated her lack of recognition by publishing this incident as a humorous anecdote of the tightly knit Mormon community. Nearly seventy years later, her description captured much of the homoerotic dimension of this 1887 incident: "A few awkward whirls with the young man clasped tightly in his arms, a few waddles and twists as he pumphandled and shoved him about seemed to induce the favorable reaction he sought." The LDS Church's Deseret Book Company published this book in 1954 as an "intimate account of a Mormon village."[125]

Of the general unwillingness to acknowledge the extent of nonmarital sex among nineteenth-century Mormons, let us return to those BYU sex surveys. During a twenty-year period from the 1950s to 1970s, no more than 52 percent of BYU's female students said they had premarital sexual intercourse.[126] That was below the reported rates of premarital intercourse among non-Mormon women of the same age during the same period.[127]

However, look how the results of BYU's sex surveys compare to premarital sexual intercourse among nineteenth-century Mormon women. In 1884 Apostle Wilford Woodruff preached to a stake conference in Sanpete County, Utah, "against the liberty the young people are taking during their engagement period, to have sexual intercourse with each other before marriage." The evidence was "the fact that the first baby in so many families is born a few months too early."[128] Apostle John W. Taylor told the general conference in 1898 that he was astounded by the report that the couples in 80 percent of LDS marriages in another of Utah's valleys engaged in premarital sex.[129] In 1901, Apostle Anthon H. Lund reported to the apostles that during a six-month period, 58 percent of LDS marriages in still another rural Utah area were "forced."[130]

However, extensive premarital intercourse occurred in Mormon communities outside Utah as well. In 1915 Lund (then a counselor in the First Presidency) wrote that he was "astonished" at the widespread prevalence of premarital sex in the Mormon settlements of the Big Horn Valley, Wyoming. The pattern there was that LDS women initiated sexual relations with their Mormon boyfriends.[131]

In a more precise illustration, a high of 14.8 percent of new brides were pregnant in the first decades of twentieth-century Provo (home of BYU), and bridal pregnancy there was never lower than 11.9 percent.[132] Yet bridal pregnancy is a conservative measure of premarital sex, since a significant portion of the sexually active women do not get pregnant before marriage. However, references to such extensive premarital sexual activity of Mormon women rarely showed up in the diaries of persons living in Provo or other Mormon communities where bridal pregnancy was common.[133]

Therefore, it seems clear that most nineteenth-century Mormons declined to make references in diaries or other sources about their knowledge of the extent of something so obvious as bridal pregnancy occurring for large numbers of the LDS couples in various wards and stakes of Utah. There was a widespread reticence to acknowledge erotic behavior of any kind except in the most general terms.

Another option is also obvious. Either nineteenth-century Mormon women had far more premarital sex than modern BYU college students, or female students at BYU from the 1950s to 1970s underreported the extent of their premarital sexual experiences on those questionnaires. The underreporting option is supported by research in the 1990s that 58 percent of Mormon women admitted to engaging in premarital sexual intercourse. This research indicates that Mormon women since

1945 have been no more or less sexually active before marriage than Mormon women born in the nineteenth century.[134] Extrapolating backward, this indicates there is justification for assuming that nineteenth-century Mormons engaged in sexual activities in similar percentages as demonstrated in the BYU sex surveys of the 1950s through the 1970s.

Likewise it is unlikely that homoeroticism was hundreds of times more prevalent among the conservative BYU students who filled out those surveys in the midtwentieth century than same-sex activities were among the nineteenth-century men and women who followed Mormonism. Despite the two era's different cultural norms regarding same-sex behaviors, the 10 percent reporting of homoeroticism among BYU's male students from the 1950s to the 1970s was consistent with the earliest known estimate of "unnatural intercourse" in a nineteenth-century group of Americans: "every tenth man practises it."[135]

Therefore, it seems legitimate to extrapolate backward from the findings of homoerotic experiences among BYU's students during the twenty-year study. Homoerotic activities were probably experienced by thousands of LDS women and by tens of thousands of Mormon men who were born in the nineteenth century. Diaries, letters, LDS Church documents, Utah's court records, and Berryman's interviews therefore account for only a small fraction of the homoerotic experiences of nineteenth-century Mormons.

NOTES

1. Helen L. Warner, "Oscar Wilde's Visit to Salt Lake City," *Utah Historical Quarterly* 55 (Fall 1987): 330–31; see also Rocky O'Donovan, "'The Abominable and Detestable Crime against Nature': A Brief History of Homosexuality and Mormonism, 1840–1980" in Brent Corcoran, ed., *Multiply and Replenish: Mormon Essays on Sex and Family* (Salt Lake City: Signature Books, 1994), 144.

2. *Washington Post*, 22 Jan. 1882, 2, quoted in Mary W. Blanchard, "Boundaries and the Victorian Body: Aesthetic Fashion in Gilded Age America," *American Historical Review* 100 (Feb. 1995): 40.

3. "Oscar Wilde's Suit, Libel Case Brought against the Marquis of Queensbury, SENSATIONAL DEVELOPMENTS, 'Poetic' Love Letters to a Boy—Morality in Literature—Crowds Enjoy the Court Proceedings," *Deseret Evening News*, 3 Apr. 1895, 1; "The Wilde Infamy. Testimony in the Suit against the Mar-

quis of Queensberry. NOT SUITABLE FOR PUBLICATION. The English Public Now Involved in One of the Orgies of Indecency, Says a London Paper," *Deseret Evening News*, 4 Apr. 1895, 1; "For the Marquis. Verdict in the Wilde Libel Case. OSCAR ARRESTED AT A HOTEL. He Will Probably Be Given an Opportunity to Explain Further the 'Poetry' of His Letters," *Deseret Evening News*, 5 Apr. 1895, 1; "No Bail for Oscar. Wilde Listens to Damaging Testimony against Him. CROWDS THRONG THE COURT ROOM. The Social Lion Caught in the Trap Set for the Marquis of Queensberry," *Deseret Evening News*, 6 Apr. 1895, 1; "Wilde Suffering from Insomnia," *Deseret Evening News*, 8 Apr. 1895, 1; editorial, "The Wilde Case," *Deseret Evening News*, 10 Apr. 1895, 4; "Wilde and Taylor Formally Committed for Trial—Bail Refused," *Deseret Evening News*, 19 Apr. 1895, 1; "Wilde's Home Sold," *Deseret Evening News*, 24 Apr. 1895, 1; "Wilde Pleads Not Guilty," *Deseret Evening News*, 26 Apr. 1895, 1; "Wilde and Taylor," *Deseret Evening News*, 27 Apr. 1895, 1; "Wilde's Defense. The Prisoner Denies Everything—Cheered by His Friends," *Deseret Evening News*, 30 Apr. 1895, 1; "Wilde Admitted to Bail," *Deseret Evening News*, 3 May 1895, 1; "Oscar Wilde," *Deseret Evening News*, 4 May 1895, 1; "Wilde Released on Bail," *Deseret Evening News*, 7 May 1895, 1; "The Wilde Trial," *Deseret Evening News*, 20 May 1895, 1; "Wilde Taken Ill," *Deseret Evening News*, 22 May 1895, 1; "The Wilde Trial," *Deseret Evening News*, 23 May 1895, 1; "The Wilde Trial," *Deseret Evening News*, 24 May 1895, 1; "Oscar Wilde Guilty: Sentenced to Two Years' Imprisonment with Hard Labor," *Deseret Evening News*, 25 May 1895, 1; editorial, "Wilde Sentenced," *Deseret Evening News*, 26 May 1895, 4.

4. "Oscar Wilde's Libel Suit: One of the Most Peculiar Cases Ever Heard. LOVE LETTERS TO A BOY. Knight of the Sunflower Shows Up Very Badly. Accused of Intimacy with Lord Alfred Queensbury and Another Youth—His Book Wherein Sodomy Appears to Be Justified—The Poet Draws a Large Audience, and Admission Is Had by Ticket Only," *Salt Lake Herald*, 4 Apr. 1895, 2; "Evidence Too Vile to Repeat. Life of the 'Apostle of the Pure, the Good and the Beautiful.' AFTERNOON TEA PARTIES. Suspected Intimacy with Various Youths," *Salt Lake Herald*, 5 Apr. 1895, 2; "Is No Meaner Thing Than He: Wilde One of the Lowest Creatures That Now Disgrace the Earth," *Salt Lake Herald*, 6 Apr. 1895, 1; "Caught in the Marquis' Trap. The Apostle of Purity Denied the Privilege of Bail. DAMAGING EVIDENCE GIVEN," *Salt Lake Herald*, 7 Apr. 1895, 10; "Oscar's Remorse," *Salt Lake Herald*, 8 Apr. 1895, 2; "Oscar Wilde's Wife: She Leaves the Brute and Seeks Freedom by a Divorce," *Salt Lake Herald*, 30 Apr. 1895, 1; "Wilde Once More," *Salt Lake Herald*, 24 May 1895, 2; "Those Famous Letters: Once More Brought Out in the Wilde Trial," *Salt Lake Herald*, 25 May 1895, 1; "Two Years in Prison Garb. Sentence Pronounced on Oscar Wilde and Alfred Taylor. THE JUDGE VERY SEVERE. Poetry and Bestiality Were Synonymous," *Salt Lake Herald*, 26 May 1895,

1. See *Salt Lake Herald*, 4 Apr. 1895, 4, for Apostle Grant as vice president of the newspaper when it used the word *sodomy* in the headline about the Wilde case. For Grant's church service, see *Deseret News 1995–1996 Church Almanac: The Church of Jesus Christ of Latter-day Saints* (Salt Lake City: Deseret News, 1994), 43; D. Michael Quinn, *The Mormon Hierarchy: Extensions of Power* (Salt Lake City: Signature Books/Smith Research Associates, 1995).

5. "Oscar Wilde as Witness," *Salt Lake Tribune*, 4 Apr. 1895, 3; "Wilde Was in Bad Company: Admits Evil Associations," *Salt Lake Tribune*, 5 Apr. 1895, 2; "Oscar Wilde Arrested," *Salt Lake Tribune*, 6 Apr. 1895, 1–2; "Wilde Held without Bail: Strong Evidence Upsets His Counsel," *Salt Lake Tribune*, 7 Apr. 1895, 2; "Wilde and Taylor's Case. Sent Back to Jail for a Week's Postponement—No Bail," *Salt Lake Tribune*, 12 Apr. 1895, 1; "Wilde Jury Disagreed," *Salt Lake Tribune*, 2 May 1895, 2; "For and against Wilde," *Salt Lake Tribune*, 25 May 1895, 1; "Wilde Up for Two Years: Hard Labor in Prison for the Poet," *Salt Lake Tribune*, 26 May 1895, 1.

6. *The New York Times Index for the Published News of 1894–1898* (New York: R. R. Bowker, 1966), 350. This extensive coverage of the Wilde trials in newspapers from Utah and New York conflicts with Jonathan Katz, *Gay American History: Lesbians and Gay Men in the U.S.A.* (New York: Thomas Y. Crowell, 1976), 577n60: "I have found few American references to Wilde's troubles [of 1895]."

7. Complaint against Frank Howard by Rex Holden, filed 1 May 1896, Case 5 (originally Case 46 in First District Court), Fourth District Court (Utah County), Criminal Case Files; complaint against Daniel Reynolds by Frank Howland, filed 1 May 1896, Case 6 (originally Case 47 in First District Court) Fourth District Court (Utah County), Criminal Case Files; Fourth District Court (Utah County) Minute Book (1894–98), 62, 64, located in First District Court (Utah County) Minute Book, Series 1820, Reel 60012; Utah Department of Corrections, Utah Territorial/State Prison Inmate Commitment Register (1892–1908), 39, Series 80388, all in Utah State Archives, Salt Lake City, Utah; "BRUTAL TRAMPS: They Make a Beastly Assault on Little Boys," *Provo Daily Enquirer*, 1 May 1896, 1; "A Dastardly Crime," *Provo Daily Enquirer*, 2 May 1896, 1; obituary for Rex Holden (b. 17 Dec. 1882; md. May 1914, 1 child) in *Deseret News*, 9 Sept. 1958, B-9; entry for Frederick James Wardrobe (b. 24 May 1882; LDS baptism 1890; md. 1907, no children; d. 1957), Ancestral File, Family History Library of the Church of Jesus Christ of Latter-day Saints, Salt Lake City, Utah (hereafter LDS Ancestral File and LDS Family History Library); with no genealogical record yet found for victim Frank Howland or Holland. Although Jacob Johnson had enforced the law against polygamous Mormons, his parents, brother, and two civilly married wives were all Mormons, and the LDS Church magazine memorialized

him at his death. See Andrew Jenson, *Church Chronology: A Record of Important Events Pertaining to the History of the Church of Jesus Christ of Latter-day Saints,* 2d ed., rev. (Salt Lake City: Deseret News, 1914), for 10 July 1892; "Passing Events," *Improvement Era* 28 (Oct. 1925): 1195–96; and Ardath E. Johnson, "Judge Jacob Johnson" (Bachelor of Independent Studies Project, Brigham Young University, 1989), 5, 14–15, 17. Again, I name the victims because the Provo newspaper identified them.

8. Josiah Flynt [Josiah Flint Willard], "Homosexuality among Tramps," in Havelock Ellis and John Addington Symonds, *Sexual Inversion* (London: Wilson and Macmillan, 1897; reprint, New York: Arno Press/New York Times, 1975), 253–54; see also the discussion in chap. 6. This coauthored book was an early version of what later appeared as a volume by the same title in multiple editions of *Studies in the Psychology of Sex* with Ellis as sole editor and author. After his death, Symonds's heirs withdrew permission to use his name.

9. "Information" (indictment) against William Brown, dated 12 June 1896, Case 28, Second District Court (Weber County), Criminal Case Files, Utah State Archives; Second District Court (Weber County) Minute Book (1896–97), 234, Series 5062, Utah State Archives; Utah Territorial/State Prison Inmate Commitment Register (1892–1908), 41; "Wm. White Sentenced—Wm. Brown Pleaded Guilty and Got Nine Months," *Ogden Standard,* 14 July 1896, 3. For the Mormon background of Judge Henry H. Rolapp, see Andrew Jenson, *Latter-day Saint Biographical Encyclopedia,* 4 vols. (Salt Lake City: Deseret News Press and Andrew Jenson History, 1901–36), 3:501–2. The prison record described William Brown, born in Philadelphia, as age twenty in 1896, but he was actually born there in 1874 according to the International Genealogical Index, LDS Family History Library, which lists his LDS baptism date as 1907. However, that could be a rebaptism, following an excommunication in the 1890s for his criminal convictions.

10. Utah Territorial/State Prison Inmate Commitment Register (1892–1908), 55. If heterosexual relations with underage females were forced, the Utah judicial records and prison register used the terms *rape* or *assault.* Otherwise, the records used *carnal knowledge* for consensual sex with minor females.

11. "BEASTLY TRAMPS. Crime Committed by Them against Nature," *Provo Daily Enquirer,* 16 Sept. 1896, 1; "Notes," *Deseret Evening News,* 17 Sept. 1896, 2; complaint against Thomas Rogers, James Owens, Patsey Calvey, Frank Merrill, Charles W. Merrill, Samuel Bennett, Hugh Nicholes, James Woods, and William Foster, filed 15 September 1896, Case 18 (originally Case 127 in First District Court), Fourth District Court (Utah County), Criminal Case Files, Utah State Archives. I name the victim because the newspapers fully identified Clark. I do not go beyond the court documents to give the birth dates or middle names of the discharged Mormon defendants (Rogers, C. W. Merrill, Bennett, Nicholes, Woods, and Foster) because in some cases there was

more than one Mormon with the same name who could have been an identified perpetrator in this rape. See Spanish Fork Ward Membership Record (early-1891), 47; Spanish Fork Second Ward Membership Record (1892–1940), 20; 1880 Census of Provo, Utah County, Utah, enumeration district 81, sheet 149–A, and of Spanish Fork, Utah County, Utah, enumeration district 83, sheet 186–B, microfilm, LDS Family History Library; LDS Ancestral File, LDS Patriarchal Blessing Index (1833–1963), and Deceased LDS Members File (1941–74), all in LDS Family History Library; *Deseret News,* 15 Sept. 1921, 2; *Deseret News,* 29 Sept. 1947, 8; see also *Deseret News,* 22 Oct. 1963, B-8, for comparison with the indicted men.

12. Utah County Jail Register of Prisoners (1891–98), 60–62, Series 5044, Utah State Archives; *Provo Daily Enquirer,* 17 Sept. 1896, [4]; "TRAMPS HELD. Three Identified by the Young Man Abused," *Provo Daily Enquirer,* 18 Sept. 1896, [4]; "City and County Jottings," *Provo Daily Enquirer,* 14 Oct. 1896, [4]; Fourth District Court (Utah County) Minute Book (1894–98), 265.

13. "TRAMPS HELD, [4]; "DISTRICT COURT. Roylance Divorce Suit—Tramps Get Three Years," *Provo Daily Enquirer,* 17 Oct. 1896, [4]; Fourth District Court (Utah County) Minute Book (1894–98), 149, 153, 169, 171, 176, 178, 265; religious descriptions of Peter ("Patsey") Calvey, Frank Merrill, and James Owens in Utah Territorial/State Prison Inmate Commitment Register (1892–1908), 51; biographies of magistrate DeMoisey, prosecutor King, and Judge Dusenberry are in "Veteran Utah Barrister Dies in Ogden," *Salt Lake Tribune,* 17 May 1940, 12; Noble Warrum, *Utah Since Statehood,* 4 vols. (Chicago: S. J. Clarke, 1920), 3:366–67; T. Earl Pardoe, *The Sons of Brigham* (Provo, Utah: BYU Alumni Association, 1969), 62.

14. A thirty-five-year-old man named J. W. Bonner was arrested in June 1899 upon a formal complaint that he had sexually assaulted a seven-year-old Mormon boy. However, there is no record of any court proceedings in this case, and no record of his imprisonment upon a conviction. I did not find a newspaper reference to the final disposition of his case, so the charges may have been dropped. Entry for J. W. "Boller" on 8 June 1899 in Salt Lake City Police Arrest Register (1896–99), Series 4611, Utah State Archives; complaint against J. W. Bonner, dated 9 June 1899, Case 465, Third District Court (Salt Lake County), Criminal Case Files, Utah State Archives; "In Police Circles," *Salt Lake Tribune,* 9 June 1899, 5; "Bonner Is Held," *Salt Lake Tribune,* 15 June 1899, 2; entry for H—— F—— Y—— (b. 6 Apr. 1892) in LDS Patriarchal Blessing Index (1833–1963).

15. Xavier Mayne [Edward Irenaeus Prime Stevenson], *The Intersexes: A History of Similisexualism as a Problem in Social Life* (Rome: n.p., [1909?]; reprint, New York: Arno Press/New York Times, 1975), 430–32; Vern L. Bullough, *Sexual Variance in Society and History* (New York: John Wiley and Sons, 1976), 608–9; Katz, *Gay American History,* 44–47; Jonathan Ned Katz,

Gay/Lesbian Almanac: A New Documentary (New York: Harper and Row, 1983), 297–99; Wayne R. Dynes, ed., *Encyclopedia of Homosexuality*, 2 vols. (New York: Garland, 1990), 1:166–68. In his *Autobiography of an Androgyne*, 125, Earl Lind referred to New York City's male houses of prostitution in 1891 when he was seventeen: "in some public houses of the better class . . . [the male prostitutes] suggested to me to become an inmate of such a house." Dynes, *Encyclopedia of Homosexuality*, 2:899, and George Chauncey, *Gay New York: Gender, Urban Culture, and the Making of the Gay Male World, 1890–1940* (New York: Basic Books/HarperCollins, 1994), 34–35, 67–68, 73, list the following male houses of prostitution in New York City during the 1890s: the Golden Rule Pleasure Club, Manilla Hall, Columbia ("Paresis") Hall, the Palm, Black Rabbit, Little Bucks, the Artistic Club, and the Slide, as well as the back rooms of saloons. For a cross-cultural perspective of the same time period, see Jeffrey Weeks, "Inverts, Perverts, and Mary-Annes: Male Prostitution and the Regulation of Homosexuality in England in the Nineteenth and Early Twentieth Centuries," *Journal of Homosexuality* 6 (Fall 1980–Winter 1981): 113–34, reprinted in Jeffrey Weeks, *Against Nature: Essays on History, Sexuality, and Identity* (London: Rivers Oram Press, 1991), 46–67. For a modern description of the "call boys" in an American male house of prostitution and of its operation, see David J. Pittman, "The Male House of Prostitution," *Trans-Action* 8 (Mar.–Apr. 1971): 21–27.

16. For male prostitution in New York City as early as 1812, see Timothy J. Gilfoyle, *City of Eros: New York City, Prostitution, and the Commercialization of Sex, 1790–1920* (New York: W. W. Norton, 1992), 136–38, 220, 369n42.

17. Mayne, *Intersexes*, 523, see also 524–25.

18. Entries for Lee and Henry in Salt Lake City Police, 1896–99 Arrest Record (15 Apr., 15 June 1897; 23 July, 22 Aug., 22 Sept., 22 Oct. 1898; 21 Jan., 21 Feb., 23 Feb., 21 Mar., 20 Apr., 20 May, 20 June, 19 July, 19 Aug., 19 Sept., 18 Oct., 18 Nov., 19 Dec. 1899); entry for Lee and Henry in U.S. 1900 Census of Salt Lake City, Salt Lake County, Utah, enumeration district 54, sheet 2–A, microfilm, LDS Family History Library; entries for Daniels on 19 Sept., 18 Oct., 18 Nov., and 26 Dec. 1899 in Salt Lake City Police Arrest Register (1896–99); and for Daniels and Miller in U.S. 1900 Census of Salt Lake City, enumeration district 55, sheet 3–B. Like many arrested prostitutes in Utah, Raffella Lee, Jennette Henry, and Madge Daniels stated their ages differently at each arrest, varying the age from the twenties to the forties. Although "Lou" Miller had a nickname in the census typical of arrested prostitutes, she did not appear in the arrest records of Salt Lake City.

19. Quoted in Levi J. Taylor diary, 20 Sept. 1896, Archives, Historical Department of the Church of Jesus Christ of Latter-day Saints, Salt Lake City, Utah (hereafter LDS Archives). For Kimball, see *Deseret News 1995–1996*

Church Almanac, 61; and Quinn, *Extensions of Power.* For earlier comments
by LDS leaders on Utah's prostitution, see *Journal of Discourses,* 26 vols. (Liverpool, England: Latter-day Saints Book Depot, 1854–86), 3:234 (J. M. Grant/
1856), 11:202 (A. M. Lyman/1866), 24:196 (J. Taylor/1883), 25:88 (J. Taylor/1884). Recent studies of female prostitution in Utah are Helen Williams,
"'The Stockade': An Experiment in Controlled Prostitution in Salt Lake City,
1908–1911" (undergraduate research paper, History 400, University of Utah,
May 1969), Vertical Files, Special Collections, J. Willard Marriott Library,
University of Utah, Salt Lake City, Utah (hereafter Marriott Library); John S.
McCormick, "Red Lights in Zion: Salt Lake City's Stockade, 1908–11," *Utah
Historical Quarterly* 50 (Spring 1982): 168–81; Raye C. Ringholz, "The Giddy
Girls of Deer Valley Gulch," *Park City Lodestar* 7 (Summer 1984): 9–13.

20. Thomas G. Alexander and James B. Allen, *Mormons and Gentiles: A
History of Salt Lake City* (Boulder, Colo.: Pruett, 1984), 118.

21. Eureka City Arrest Book (1893–99), 94–95, 111, 128, 192, Utah State
Archives, also Microfilm A-670 in Utah State Historical Society, Salt Lake City;
entry for David Wallace Baum (b. 25 Feb. 1882; md. 1902, 1 child; d. 1918)
in LDS Ancestral File, with no other David Baum listed in the U.S. 1900 Census soundex. David Baum, Thomas Paramore, and William Holmes were arrested with Harry Mason in February 1897, and Oscar Patter (Patten?) had
been arrested the previous August. Utah's arrest records sometimes used "Disorderly House" instead of "House of Ill Fame" in arrests of prostitutes.

22. U.S. Department of the Interior, Census Office, *Twelfth Census of the
United States, Taken in the Year 1900, Population,* 2 vols. (Washington: United States Census Office, 1901–2), 1:644; see also Philip F. Notarianni, *Faith,
Hope, and Prosperity: The Tintic Mining District* (Eureka, Utah: Tintic Historical Society, 1982) for photographs and descriptions of Eureka at the turn
of the century.

23. Salt Lake City Police Arrest Register (1891–94), 28–29, 57, 69, 79, 110–
11, 115, 271, 326, 339, 354, Series 4611, Utah State Archives; Salt Lake City
Police Arrest Register (1894–96) for 24 July 1895, 15 Jan. 1896, Series 4611,
Utah State Archives; Park City, Utah, Police Department, Register of Arrests
(1892–1904), 118, 120, 121, 122, 124, 127, 129, 130, 159, 161–62, 166–67,
185, Utah State Archives, and Microfilm A-797, Utah State Historical Society; Case 280 (5 Mar. 1896), Ogden City Justice Dockets, Utah State Archives.

Unless I could verify their gender, my citations omit arrested prostitutes with
names that sound like male nicknames, which female prostitutes often adopted in this era. Also, I exclude names that are probably misspellings by the police
of feminine names and nicknames. Therefore, without some evidence of gender, I exclude such names in the prostitution arrest records as Alex, Bernie,
Bert, Bill (as misspelling of Belle), Cecil, Claud, Claudie, Clyda, Davie, Dean
(for Deanne), Eugene, Frankie, Francis, Fred, Freddie, Gene, George, Harry,

Jas (for Jasmine), Jos (for Josephine), Leo or Leon (for Leonora or Leona), Lou, Ollie (for Olivia), Pat, Pet (for Petra), Vern or Vernie (for Verna), Vic, Virg, Virgie, Will or Willie (for Wilhelmina or William). I also omitted a prostitute named Alma, which is a male name among Mormons but a female name among non-Mormons.

My imprecise gender identification of arrested prostitutes is necessary because there were no photographs, and rarely any gender identifications, in the arrest records I examined. The Salt Lake City Police Department Museum has the booking registers (with arrest photos) from 1892 to 1920, but these registers are presently unavailable for research according to a letter from Lt. Steve Diamond to me on 7 June 1994. However, the police booking registers apparently excluded prostitutes. Jeff Nichols, a University of Utah graduate student who is writing a dissertation on Salt Lake City prostitution, was allowed to skim through the 1892–1920 registers in his search for photos from the monthly raids of brothels. In an interview on 9 March 1995, Nichols said he found no female mug shots in the booking registers. If Salt Lake City's police department did not photograph women arrested for prostitution in 1892–1920, male prostitutes were probably not photographed either. The tax-revenue purpose of these prostitute round-ups is evident from the fact that those arrested were fined but neither booked nor photographed.

Also, I could seldom cross-reference prostitute arrests with the U.S. 1900 Census because Utah's census takers did not include houses of prostitution. That significant omission was apparently based on the rationale that houses of prostitution were places of employment, not places of residence. This may have been simply an adroit way to avoid requiring entry into brothels by Utah's census takers, who included many women and actively Mormon men. Houses of prostitution were included in the federal censuses of other American cities.

24. Ruth Rosen, in *The Lost Sisterhood: Prostitution in America, 1900–1918* (Baltimore: Johns Hopkins University Press, 1982), 76, notes that during this period, the brothel's pimp was a "young man, averaging from eighteen to twenty-five years of age." It was his responsibility to recruit male customers from the streets and saloons and bring them to the house of prostitution. The meaning and significance of pimps later changed as they became independent managers of street prostitutes rather than employees of brothels.

25. William Barnes, Case 769 (9 Jan. 1897), and William Barry, Case 967 (1 June 1897), Ogden City Justice Dockets.

26. Joseph Banks (age fifty), James Brooks (age twenty-three, previously arrested as "Hobo" in San Francisco), James Carnell (age twenty-seven), George Ennis (age twenty-three), William H. Ford (alias George Earl, age seventeen), James Watson (age thirty) in Salt Lake City Police Criminal Register (1892–97), alphabetical sections, Series 4658, Utah State Archives. Other men also had that left-hand tattoo at their arrests for robbery or burglary. See chap.

9 for a discussion of the tattoo worn by Arthur Curtis in the 1887 case of sodomy.

27. Territory vs. Thomas Hanrahan, Salt Lake City Court record book (Apr.–June 1890), 16 (21 Mar. 1890), filed with Salt Lake City Police blotters, uncataloged documents, Utah State Archives as of 1994; "Police Items," *Deseret Evening News,* 22 Mar. 1890, [3]. Charges were apparently dismissed against Hanrahan, who did not appear in the jail or prison records. I could not find Otto Venson or variant spellings of his name in LDS records or in the U.S. census, and therefore cannot state his age at the time of this court case.

28. According to *The Oxford English Dictionary,* 2d ed., 20 vols. (Oxford: Clarendon Press, 1989), 2:789, *call boy* meant a young man who was employed to transmit messages and also meant "a young male prostitute." By 1903 its female equivalent, *call girl,* appeared in print as American slang for prostitute. See J. E. Lighter, ed., *Random House Historical Dictionary of American Slang,* 3 vols. (New York: Random House, 1994–96), 1:350. As previously indicated, the actual usage of slang terms in Utah preceded their publication by years, sometimes decades. Utah arrest records also describe the occupation of some prostitutes as "prostitute" or "sport."

29. Salt Lake City Police Arrest Register (1891–94), 99, arrest of seventeen-year-old George Raymond, occupation "Card Cutter," for petty larceny on 18 January 1892, cross-referenced to page 158 arrest of "Geo Conley (Raymond)" for vagrancy, occupation "Call boy," on 19 Sept. 1892; Raymond's physical description appeared in Salt Lake City Police Criminal Register (1892–97), "R" section.

30. Park City, Utah, Police Department, Register of Arrests (1892–1904), 104 (16 Apr. 1898), 185 (12 Aug. 1904); entries for Alfred Franklin Stevenson (b. 22 Dec. 1874) in the Deceased LDS Members File (1941–74), and in the LDS Ancestral File, and see obituary in *Deseret News,* 1 July 1964, D-3, for Ray Coleman Lewis. Again, my identification must be tentative because it is based on name similarity, since there are no detailed personal data in the arrest record.

31. U.S. 1900 Census of Weber County, Utah, enumeration district 205, sheet 8, line 25, microfilm, LDS Family History Library; Park City, Utah, Police Department, Register of Arrests (1892–1904), 118, 120, 121, 122, 124, 127, 129, 130; Park City, Police Justice's Court Docket (1898–1902), 898, 913, 919, 954, 992, 1013, Microfilm A-759, Utah State Historical Society. For Corinne as a wild exception to the surrounding Mormon culture, see Brigham D. Madsen, *Corinne: The Gentile Capital of Utah* (Salt Lake City: Utah State Historical Society, 1980).

32. McCormick, "Red Lights in Zion," 173. Also, Utah's police usually reduced the likelihood of arresting the male customers by raiding houses of prostitution between midmorning and midafternoon. It was rare to find a raid

on a Utah house of prostitution that occurred in the early evening, and I never found an arrest in a house of prostitution that occurred late at night or in the early morning hours. This undoubtedly was an intentional way to avoid public embarrassment for some of Utah's prominent men who patronized these establishments. The only exception to this pattern occurred in 1885, when Salt Lake City's Mormon police arrested prominent "anti-Mormon" patrons of brothels. The arrested men included the assistant U.S. district attorney for Utah, deputy U.S. marshals, and one of the federally appointed members of the Utah Commission. The Mormons intended this as a public demonstration of the hypocrisy of "Gentiles" who arrested Mormons for having plural wives. The federally appointed, non-Mormon judges in 1885 dismissed the charges against the non-Mormons and instead convicted and imprisoned some of the Mormon policemen for conspiracy to operate houses of prostitution. See "Tables Turned," *Salt Lake Herald,* 22 Nov. 1885, 12; Brigham Young Hampton journal, 167–68 (1885), LDS Archives; Jenson, *Church Chronology,* 21 Nov., 23 Nov., 27 Nov., 30 Nov., 4 Dec., 7–8 Dec., 11–12 Dec., 14 Dec., 18 Dec., 24 Dec., 30 Dec. 1885.

33. For example, see entries for William Barker (age twenty-two), John Field (age thirty), Murry Jones (age nineteen), Amos Peterson (age twenty), John Smith (age twenty-five), Paul Slater (age twenty-six), Peter Williams (age twenty-five), Frank Wilson (age twenty-seven), with no ages given for Larry Benjamin, Arthur Hawley, Charles Harris, John Jenkins, and Spencer Meader (whose ages I have not been able to identify from other sources) in Salt Lake City Police Arrest Register (1891–94), 79, 111, 115, 201, 271, 354, 357; and entries for 24 July 1895 and 15 Jan. 1896, Salt Lake City Police Arrest Register (1894–96); Salt Lake City Police blotter (1897–98), 179 (2 Dec. 1897). In our youth-oriented culture, many readers might assume that there would be no male prostitutes in their thirties either in the 1890s or at present. However, *Salt Lake Tribune,* 3 May 1995, B-2, headlined the arrest of a Utah male prostitute, age thirty-one.

34. "Evolution of Commercial St.: All the Old Notorious Landmarks Are Now Steadily Being Obliterated," *Deseret Evening News,* 24 June 1909, 2.

35. Brigham Young Hampton journal, 240–42, LDS Archives. According to his account, he had protested about these leases, but had been brushed off by the officers of the Brigham Young Trust Co. When Judge Charles S. Zane in 1891 threatened to prosecute the owners of houses of prostitution, the officers of the Brigham Young Trust Company decided to make Hampton the scapegoat, due to his previous conviction in 1885 for operating a Mormon spy ring in a Salt Lake City house of prostitution for the purpose of entrapping federal officials with prostitutes (167–68). Hampton was indicted on 15 November 1891 for operating a house of prostitution, but the charges were dropped on 26 March. As evidence of the truthfulness of Hampton's statements about these

operations, the First Presidency and Quorum of the Twelve agreed on 14 June 1900 to pay Hampton $3,600 for his previous work in the house of prostitution. See Journal History of the Church of Jesus Christ of Latter-day Saints, 14 June 1900, 1–2, microfilm, Special Collections, Marriott Library. Hampton originally presented his claim for this "detective work" on 7 June 1900, the same day that the First Presidency and apostles discussed the situation of LDS-leased houses of prostitution. See Journal History, 7 June 1900, 4; Brigham Young Jr. diary, 7 June 1900, LDS Archives.

36. Young diary, 15 Jan., 21 Jan. 1897. For his biographical sketch, see *Deseret News 1995–1996 Church Almanac,* 49; Davis Bitton, "The Ordeal of Brigham Young, Jr.," *The Ritualization of Mormon History and Other Essays* (Urbana: University of Illinois Press, 1994), 115–49; Quinn, *Extensions of Power.*

37. Anthon H. Lund diary, 8 Apr. 1897, microfilm, LDS Archives. The Lund diary microfilm is unrestricted to all researchers at LDS Archives by stipulation of its donor, and will be published in edited form by Signature Books, Salt Lake City. John Henry Smith diary, 8 Apr. 1897, in Jean Bickmore White, *Church State and Politics: The Diaries of John Henry Smith* (Salt Lake City: Signature Books/Smith Research Associates, 1990), 369; J. Golden Kimball diary, 7 May 1897, Manuscripts Division, Marriott Library. For Cannon's biographical sketch, see *Deseret News 1995–1996 Church Almanac,* 45; Quinn, *Extensions of Power.*

38. Young diary, 7 June 1900; corporation documents and trustee bonds of Brigham Young Trust Co., File 737, Corporation Files, Salt Lake County Clerk, Utah State Archives.

39. "Vagrancy Cases Dismissed," *Salt Lake Tribune,* 9 Apr. 1901, 5.

40. "Judge Timmony's Court," *Deseret News,* 8 Apr. 1901, 2, and 10 Apr. 1901, 2, but not in the 9 Apr. 1901 issue.

41. See, for example, the vagrancy charge against five men arrested with nineteen female prostitutes in a 2:00 P.M. raid on a house of prostitution in Salt Lake City Police Blotter (Jan.–June 1902), entry for 22 Apr. 1902. The Salt Lake City arrest records for 1900–1901 are missing at the Utah State Archives, so I could not verify if police had stopped charging men with prostitution before the April 1901 newspaper story.

42. Park City Justice's Court Dockets (1904–6, 1906–8), Microfilms A-761 and A-762, Utah State Historical Society.

43. *Annual Reports of the Officers of Salt Lake City, Utah for the Year 1916* (Salt Lake City: Grocer, [1917]), 355 and compare with the annual reports for 1893–1915. There were no men arrested for prostitution in the police department's report of 1893.

44. "Pages from the History of Zion: Something about the Brigham Young Trust Company and Its Stockholders. TRUST OWNED PROPERTY IN TENDERLOIN

OF ZION. Buildings of Company Rented by the Officers for Immoral Purposes," *Salt Lake Tribune*, 26 Sept. 1908, 14; "Compelled to Sell," *Deseret Evening News*, 12 Sept. 1908, 11.

45. *Deseret News 1995–1996 Church Almanac*, 45.

46. Translation of Danish entry in Lund diary, 6 August 1897, second quotation from English language entry of 8 April 1897. The brothel reception's announced hours were 8:00 P.M. to 4:00 A.M.

47. Williams, "'The Stockade'"; McCormick, "Red Lights in Zion."

48. J. Reuben Clark office diary, 10 Mar., 18 Aug. 1941, Department of Special Collections and Manuscripts, Harold B. Lee Library, Brigham Young University, Provo, Utah; Frank Evans diary, 18 Aug. 1941, LDS Archives. For Clark, see *Deseret News 1995–1996 Church Almanac*, 46; D. Michael Quinn, *J. Reuben Clark: The Church Years* (Provo, Utah: Brigham Young University Press, 1983). In 1944, Frank Evans, financial secretary to the First Presidency, was one of the incorporators at the reincorporation of the Clayton Investment Company. See File 14390, Corporation Files, Salt Lake County Clerk, Utah State Archives.

49. *Deseret News 1995–1996 Church Almanac*, 42–43. For Heber J. Grant's long involvement in campaigns for alcohol and tobacco prohibition, see John S. H. Smith, "Cigarette Prohibition in Utah, 1921–23," *Utah Historical Quarterly* 41 (Autumn 1973): 358–72, esp. 362; Francis M. Gibbons, *Heber J. Grant: Man of Steel, Prophet of God* (Salt Lake City: Deseret Book, 1979), 154–62; Brent G. Thompson, "'Standing between Two Fires': Mormons and Prohibition, 1908–1917," *Journal of Mormon History* 10 (1983): 35–52; Thomas G. Alexander, *Mormonism in Transition: A History of the Latter-day Saints, 1890–1930* (Urbana: University of Illinois Press, 1986), 262–67.

50. See George Q. Cannon, David A. Smith, Joseph F. Smith, and Brigham Young Jr. in the bonds of officers and directors for Brigham Young Trust Company and Clayton Investment Company, File 737, Corporation Files, Salt Lake County Clerk, Utah State Archives; see also *Deseret News 1995–1996 Church Almanac*, 42, 45, 49, 77; and Quinn, *Extensions of Power*. As church president after 1918, Heber J. Grant had his interests in the Clayton Investment Company represented on its board by the First Presidency's financial secretaries Arthur Winter and Frank Evans, by Grant's sons-in-law Willard R. Smith and Robert L. Judd, and by John F. Bennett, all of whom were also in the above bonds of directors.

51. Alexander, *Mormonism in Transition*, 260–61.

52. Statements of Marybeth Raynes to me on 1 May, 19 May 1994. A clinical survey of PTSD is Charles R. Marmar and Mardi J. Horowitz, "Diagnosis and Phase-Oriented Treatment of Post-Traumatic Stress Disorder," in John P. Wilson, Zev Harel, and Boaz Kahana, eds., *Human Adaptation to Extreme Stress: From the Holocaust to Vietnam* (New York: Plenum Press, 1988), 81–103.

102–20; Donald W. Cory and John P. LeRoy, "The Hustlers," *The Homosexual and His Society: A View from Within* (New York: Citadel Press, 1963), 92–104; John O'Day and Leonard A. Loway, *Confessions of a Male Prostitute* (Los Angeles: Sherbourne Press, 1964); Harry Benjamin and Robert E. L. Masters, "Male Prostitution on the West Coast," *Prostitution and Morality: A Definitive Report on the Prostitute in Contemporary Society and an Analysis of the Causes and Effect of the Suppression of Prostitution* (New York: Julian Press, 1964), 286–337; Donald E. J. MacNamara, "Male Prostitution in American Cities: A Socioeconomic or Pathological Phenomenon?" *American Journal of Orthopsychiatry* 35 (Mar. 1965): 204; Kenneth N. Ginsburg, "The 'Meat-Rack': A Study of the Male Homosexual Prostitute," *American Journal of Psychotherapy* 21 (Apr. 1967): 170–85; Robert W. Deisher, Victor Eisner, and Stephen I. Sulzbacher, "The Young Male Prostitute," *Pediatrics* 43 (June 1969): 936–41; Dennis Drew and Jonathan Drake, *Boys for Sale: A Sociological Study of Boy Prostitution* (New York: Brown Books, 1969); Donald Hayes Russell, "From the Massachusetts Court Clinics: On the Psychopathology of Boy Prostitutes," *International Journal of Offender Therapy* 15, no. 1 (1971): 49–52; Martin Hoffman, "The Male Prostitute," *Sexual Behavior* 2 (Aug. 1972): 16–21; Neil R. Coombs, "Male Prostitution: A Psychosocial View," *American Journal of Orthopsychiatry* 44 (Oct. 1974): 782–89; Sivan E. Caukins and Neil R. Coombs, "The Psychodynamics of Male Prostitution," *American Journal of Psychotherapy* 30 (July 1976): 441–51; Robin Lloyd, *For Money or Love: Boy Prostitution in America* (New York: Vanguard Press, 1976); John Rechy, *The Sexual Outlaw: A Documentary, A Non-Fiction Account, with Commentaries, of Three Days and Nights in the Sexual Underground* (New York: Grove Press, 1977); Donald M. Allen, "Young Male Prostitutes: A Psychosocial Study," *Archives of Sexual Behavior* 9 (Oct. 1980): 399–426; Sparky Harlan, Luanna L. Rodgers, Brian Slattery, *Male and Female Adolescent Prostitution: Huckleberry House Sexual Minority Youth Services Project* (Washington, D.C.: Youth Development Bureau, U.S. Department of Health and Human Services, 1981); Jennifer James, *Entrance into Juvenile Male Prostitution* (Washington, D.C.: National Institute of Mental Health, 1982); Urban and Rural Systems Associates, *A Report on Adolescent Male Prostitution* (Washington, D.C.: Youth Development Bureau, U.S. Department of Health and Human Services, 1982); David Scott Wilson, "Night Acts: An Analysis of the Street Working Male Prostitutes of Denver, Colorado" (M.A. thesis, University of New Mexico, 1983); Avedis Y. Panajian, "Psychological Study of Male Prostitutes" (Ph.D. diss., United States International University, 1983); D. Kelly Weisberg, *Children of the Night: A Study of Adolescent Prostitution* (Lexington, Mass.: Lexington Books, 1985), 20–83; David F. Luckenbill, "Entering Male Prostitution," *Urban Life* 14 (July 1985): 131–53; Jim A. Cates, "Adolescent Male Prostitutes by Choice," *Child and Adolescent Social Work Journal* 6 (Summer 1989): 151–56; Samuel M. Steward, *Understanding the Male Hustler* (New York: Haworth Press, 1991); Cudore L. Snell, *Young Men in the Street: Help-Seeking Behavior of Young Male Prostitutes* (Westport, Conn.: Praeger, 1993); Donald J. West and Buz de Villiers, *Male Prostitutes* (New York: Haworth Press, 1993); Robert McNamara, *The Times Square Hustler: Male Prostitution in New York City* (Westport, Conn.: Praeger, 1994).

60. See Salt Lake City Juvenile Court, Case 594, Case 814, Case 986, Case 996, Case Files, Box Z213A5, Utah State Archives; I have withheld the surnames from the text.

61. This information is based on my examination of the juvenile court files of Box Elder, Cache, Davis, Salt Lake, Utah, and Weber Counties for hundreds of young men and women from 1880 through 1918.

62. *Life in America: A Special Loan Exhibition of Paintings Held during the Period of the New York World's Fair, April 24 to October 29* (New York: Metropolitan Museum of Art, 1939), 184. Although the Metropolitan Museum of Art was the publisher of the catalog, various galleries and art museums throughout the United States loaned the paintings (on request) for this exhibit.

63. Salt Lake City Juvenile Court, Case 1047 and Case 1048, each complaint filed on 3 Sept. 1907. However, until the 1970s nude swimming indoors by males continued in such conservative American organizations as the YMCA. See John Donald Wrathall, "American Manhood and the Y.M.C.A., 1868–1920" (Ph.D. diss., University of Minnesota, 1994), 224–25. Also, I personally know that the YMCA even sponsored summer camps where clothing was optional and nude swimming outside was the norm at such locations as Catalina Island, offshore from Los Angeles, California. Prepubescent boys, teenagers, and adult advisers participated together in these nude outings of the YMCA. Also, nude swimming was routine in Yale University's gymnasium until Yale began admitting female students in 1969.

64. "Youngsters Go Home without Their Clothes," *Salt Lake Herald,* 3 July 1909, 16.

65. Salt Lake City Juvenile Court, Case 1737 through Case 1742, each complaint filed on 1 March 1909. I verified their LDS Church membership through various sources at the LDS Family History Library.

66. Salt Lake City Juvenile Court, Cases 1300, 1301, 1768, for sexual activities occurring between 1907 and 1909.

67. Salt Lake City Juvenile Court, Cases 1300, 1301, 1737–42, 1768, and "Thirteen Bad Children," *Salt Lake Tribune,* 2 Mar. 1909, 2.

68. *First Biennial Report of the Board of Trustees of the State Industrial School of Utah and Accompanying Documents, Ending December 31st, 1898* (Salt Lake City: Deseret News, 1899), 36–37; *Second Biennial Report of the*

Board of Trustees of the State Industrial School of Utah and Accompanying Documents, Ending December 31st, 1900 (Salt Lake City: Deseret News, 1901), 30–31; *Third Biennial Report of the Board of Trustees of the State Industrial School of Utah and Accompanying Documents, Ending December 31st, 1902* (Salt Lake City: Star Printing, 1903), 42–44. Utah's territorial Reform School was renamed the State Industrial School in 1896. Youths were confined there by order of juvenile court judges. See Martha Sonntag Bradley, "Reclamation of Young Citizens: Reform of Utah's Juvenile Legal System, 1888–1910," *Utah Historical Quarterly* 51 (Fall 1983): 328–45.

Contrast the 5 percent rate of sexual offenders among Utah's male juvenile delinquents (to age twenty-one) during 1897–1902 with the pattern nearly a century later. Of 335 males (ages twelve-eighteen) who received psychological evaluations by order of Salt Lake City's juvenile court from 1985 to 1988, more than one-third were sex offenders. Either the rate of criminal sexual behavior of Utah's juvenile males had increased more than 600 percent in a century, or earlier juveniles committed such sex crimes without discovery or arrest, or there was a dramatic change in the procedures of the police and juvenile court system. See Patricia E. Kunke, "Personality Characteristics of Adolescent Sexual Offenders" (Ph.D. diss., University of Utah, 1988), 32–33.

69. Testimony of John Harold Scott (carpentry instructor), of W. E. Kneass (assistant superintendent), and of Lorenzo Farley (former inmate) in "Investigation of the State Industrial School of Utah. June 14th, 17th, 18th, 21st, 23rd, 24th, 25th and 29th, and July 17th, 1909," 486, 674, and 1030, transcript of 1,234 typed pages in Industrial School Reports, Department of Public Welfare, Box XC24G6, Utah State Archives, also copy in Claude Pratt Papers, Special Collections, Weber State University, Ogden, Utah.

70. Testimony of John Borger (employee) in "Investigation of the State Industrial School of Utah," 251–52; "Fate of Thomas with Committee," *Salt Lake Herald*, 30 June 1909, 3; "Declare School in Bad Condition: Citizens' Committee Report Is Filled with Strong Censure," *Salt Lake Herald*, 9 July 1909, 3.

71. Testimony of Kneass in "Investigation of the State Industrial School of Utah," 605, 663.

72. According to age, the seven perpetrators were Perry Bacon (b. 20 June 1889), Roswell Hudson ("a colored boy," b. 18 Feb. 1890), Stanley Rasmussen (b. June 1890), William Buchanan (b. 10 Apr. 1891), Niels August Emer Pearson Jr. (b. 28 May 1891), Bird (Burt) Hughes (b. 11 Oct. 1891), and Edward W. Wells (b. 18 Dec. 1891). After the public disclosure in June 1909 of the beatings at the reform school, one of Bacon's relatives requested his immediate release upon her affidavit, which claimed (falsely) that Bacon had turned twenty-one. Although records of the court and reform school showed that he would not be twenty-one until 1910, the school's trustees acquiesced

to the family affidavit in the midst of the public scandal and released Bacon in 1909. See Utah State Industrial School admission card file, administration building, Millcreek Youth Center, Ogden, Utah; Utah State Industrial School Minute Book (1906–9), 152 (4 Sept. 1908), 237 (5 June 1909), Department of Public Welfare, Utah State Archives; testimony of employees Borger, Kneass, Evan Carlsen, W. H. Ackaret, and Thomas Myers and former inmate Farley in "Investigation of the State Industrial School of Utah," 262, 290–92, 602, 672, 1016, 1036, 1082–83, 1090, 1094–95, 1142; entry for Stanley Rasmussen in U.S. 1900 Census of Salt Lake City, enumeration district 20, sheet 4; entries for William Buchanan and Niels August Pearson in LDS Ancestral File; see also their obituaries in *Deseret News*, 19 July 1926, sect. 2, p. 1, 14 Jan. 1932, sect. 2, p. 7, 20 July 1960, B-7, and 20 Jan. 1963, B-8. Sources did not always agree on the birth year of each young man, but this note is my best effort to reconcile the discrepancies.

73. See Dynes, *Encyclopedia of Homosexuality*, 2:1197–98, and chap. 6 for a discussion of sexual activities in homoenvironmental situations. For a study of sexual behavior after leaving a homoenvironmental situation, see Edward Sagarin, "Prison Homosexuality and Its Effect on Post-Prison Sexual Behavior," *Psychiatry* 39 (Aug. 1976): 245–57.

74. Margaret Otis, "A Perversion Not Commonly Noted," *Journal of Abnormal Psychology* 8 (June–July 1913): 113. The subject of her article was interracial sex between young women in America's reform schools.

75. In "Investigation of the State Industrial School of Utah," employee Scott testified that "the small boys slept in the cottage . . . which Mr. Kneass occupies" (486), but Kneass explained that the "boys" in the cottage were actually over twelve (674).

76. Entry for Heber H. Thomas (b. 17 Nov. 1862) in LDS Ancestral File; testimony of Heber H. Thomas and Farley in "Investigation of the State Industrial School of Utah," 1202, 1036. Farley was so favorable about his experience at the reform school that he was called as a defense witness for Superintendent Thomas. See chap. 9, note 121 for a discussion of the homoerotic meaning of the verb *monkey*.

77. Testimony of Parley N. Griffin and Thomas in "Investigation of the State Industrial School of Utah," 1154–55, 1200–1201; "Close of Inquiry at Ogden School," *Salt Lake Herald*, 26 June 1909, 3. Of the sodomy incidents before the appointment of Thomas in 1905, Griffin testified that staff members "used to whip them just the same and worse" than they did in the 1908 incident. Assistant Superintendent Kneass also testified that he "strapped" Niels Pearson for committing a "crime against nature with a calf" (672–73). Pearson later was one of the perpetrators in the group sex incident.

78. Testimony of Kneass in "Investigation of the State Industrial School of Utah," 593, 601–3, 605–6, 608, 628; "KNEASS TELLS TORTURE STORIES: In-

dustrial School Boys Whipped until Unconscious—Others Wore Oregon Boots," *Salt Lake Herald,* 24 June 1909, 3; "Investigation Continues at the Industrial School," *Ogden Morning Examiner,* 24 June 1909, 8; "MEAT TAINTED, SYRUP SOURED, FOOD TOO OLD, Otherwise the Inmates of the State Industrial School Fare Well under Thomas. BOYS SEVERELY BEATEN AND PUT IN DAMP CELLS, Otherwise Are Kindly Treated by a Beneficent Management," *Salt Lake Herald,* 22 June 1909, 3; "Superintendent Thomas on Witness Stand Yesterday," *Ogden Morning Examiner,* 26 June 1909, 1, 8.

79. Testimony of Thomas in "Investigation of the State Industrial School of Utah," 1201–2; "Investigation at State Industrial School Ends," *Ogden Morning Examiner,* 30 June 1909, 8; "Ogden News. Fifth Ward Reorganized: John Watson Chosen Bishop, Heber H. Thomas and Thos. A. Shreeve Counselors," *Deseret Evening News,* 5 Nov. 1900, 5. For Governor Cutler as a Mormon, see Jenson, *Latter-day Saint Biographical Encyclopedia,* 3:360–62. Although Heber H. Thomas was born in Wales, he was apparently no relation to the previously discussed Thomas S. Thomas, whose father was born in a different Welsh county and town, and no relation to Kate Thomas, whose father was born in England.

80. Testimony of Borger, testimony and quotation of Evan Carlsen (employee), testimony of Scott, testimony of Kneass, testimony of W. H. Ackaret (who helped beat the teenagers) in "Investigation of the State Industrial School of Utah," 251, 263, 293, 504, 626, 1086, 1089; "Joseph Acting as if on Trial," *Salt Lake Herald,* 19 June 1909, 3; "MEAT TAINTED," *Salt Lake Herald,* 22 June 1909, 1; "KNEASS TELLS TORTURE STORIES: Industrial School Boys Whipped until Unconscious—Others Wore Oregon Boots," *Salt Lake Herald,* 24 June 1909, 3; "Investigation Continues at the Industrial School," *Ogden Morning Examiner,* 24 June 1909, 8; "Investigation at State Industrial School Ends," *Ogden Morning Examiner,* 30 June 1909, 8; "Fate of Thomas with Committee," *Salt Lake Herald,* 30 June 1909, 3. In another incident, a runaway boy was whipped after being on bread and water rations in the basement cell for twenty-one days. Also, on other occasions and for different infractions, some young men received up to seventy-five lashes with the leather strap. Some defense witnesses disputed the testimony about chunks of flesh being torn from the young men during this 1908 beating, but all witnesses described similar beatings administered to teenage boys at the reform school for attempted escapes, fighting with each other, destroying school property, theft, showing disrespect to employees, urinating in unauthorized places (the teenager in question had a bladder infection), or even "turning out the light in the playroom." Young women were not beaten but sometimes received solitary confinement in an underground cell for two weeks on bread and water rations.

81. "Grieved Mother Blames Officers: Mrs. Caroline Olson Says Stanley Rasmussen Was Not Treated Kindly," *Deseret Evening News,* 26 Aug. 1908,

5; Utah State Industrial School Minute Book (1906–9), 141 (5 Aug. 1908); U.S. 1900 Census of Salt Lake City, enumeration district 20, sheet 4; entry for William Buchanan (b. 10 Apr. 1891) in LDS Ancestral File and "Native of Salt Lake Dies in San Francisco," *Deseret News,* 19 July 1926, sect. 2, p. 1. Newspapers claimed Rasmussen was age twenty when he died, but he was born in June 1890 and died in August 1908. Aside from Buchanan, Edward W. Wells also remained unmarried. Bird Hughes married and fathered six children, while Niels Pearson fathered four children by his wife. Pearson also joined the U.S. Marine Corps in World War I and served two years with the notation: "Character: Excellent." I have been unable to find the later marital status of the two remaining perpetrators in the 1908 sodomy incident, Perry Bacon and Roswell Hudson. See *Deseret News,* 14 Jan. 1932, sect. 2, p. 7, 20 July 1960, B-7, and 20 Jan. 1963, B-8; LDS Ancestral File; LDS Church census for 1914–35, LDS Family History Library; Niels Pearson in Military Service Cards (1898–1975), Reel 31, Series 85268, Utah State Archives.

82. "Victim of Scarlet Fever," *Deseret Evening News,* 15 Aug. 1908, 3; "Fever Claims Another Boy from State Industrial School," *Deseret Evening News,* 20 Aug. 1908, 3; "Investigators Look into Alleged Mismanagement by H.H. Thomas," *Ogden Morning Examiner,* 15 June 1909, 1; "Reform School Inquiry Begins," *Salt Lake Herald,* 15 June 1909, 3; "Effort Made to Prove Graft at Industrial School," *Ogden Morning Examiner,* 22 June 1909, 8; "Fate of Thomas with Committee," *Salt Lake Herald,* 30 June 1909, 3.

83. Utah State Industrial School Minute Book (1906–9), 153 (4 Sept. 1908), 158 (5 Oct. 1908); "State Industrial School under Fire of Federated Club of Women: Largely Attended Meeting—Superintendent Thomas Charged with Mismanagement—Inmates Poorly Fed: Sensational and Unprintable Charges Made—Punishment Alleged to Have Been Inflicted—Superintendent Declared to Be Manifestly Unfit—Resolution to Governor Asks for Removal," *Ogden Morning Examiner,* 8 June 1909, 1; "Ask Removal of H.H. Thomas: Mass Meeting Appeals to Governor for Discharge of Superintendent of School," *Salt Lake Herald,* 8 June 1909, 3.

84. See "Fate of Thomas with Committee," 3, compared with "Investigation at State Industrial School Ends," 8.

85. Editorial, "The Investigation Ended," *Salt Lake Herald,* 1 July 1909, 4.

86. Utah State Industrial School Minute Book (1906–9), 241 (5 June 1909), 260–61 (2 Aug. 1909); "Supt. Thomas to Be Removed: This Is Said to Be Logical Result of Committee's Report," *Salt Lake Herald,* 29 July 1909, 5; "Report Says Supt. Thomas Will Not Do: Recommends More Competent Person Be Given Charge at Industrial School," *Salt Lake Herald,* 30 July 1909, 1, 5; "Thomas Goes Out, Gowans Goes In," *Salt Lake Herald,* 3 Aug. 1909, 3. The state inquiry also resulted from allegations that Superintendent Thomas had asked detailed sexual questions of female teenagers who were confined

for prostitution. However, most of the 1,200–page "Investigation of the State Industrial School of Utah" emphasized the punishments given routinely to disorderly male inmates and the 1908 sodomy incident, in particular.

87. Complaint against Mike McCormick, Fred Wilson, and George Powers, filed 29 June 1900, Case 165, Second District Court (Weber County) Criminal Case Files; Second District Court (Weber County), Minute Book (1899–1900), 507; complaint against Frank Billings, filed 23 July 1900, Case 599, Third District Court (Salt Lake County) Criminal Case Files; Third District Court (Salt Lake County), Minute Book (1900–1901), 426, Series 1649, Utah State Archives; Utah Territorial/State Prison Inmate Commitment Register (1892–1908), 186, 189, esp. 186 for McCormick's tattoo; "The Two Found Guilty: McCormick and His Two Pals to Be Sentenced Monday. Convicted of Sodomy Committed upon the Person of Three Boys—Are Hard Cases," *Ogden Standard,* 20 July 1900, 5; "On Trial for Serious Crime," *Deseret Evening News,* 18 Sept. 1900, 2; "Billings Found Guilty," *Salt Lake Tribune,* 20 Sept. 1900, 3; see also the discussion of the tattoo in chap. 9. O'Donovan, in "'Abominable and Detestable Crime,'" 140, claims that sentencing for sodomy in Utah did not increase beyond three years until 1907, an assertion contradicted by the judicial records from 1900 onward.

88. Complaint against William Dean, filed 9 Apr. 1901, Case 721, Third District Court (Salt Lake County) Criminal Case Files; complaint against Frank Brown, 9 Apr. 1901, Case 722, Third District Court (Salt Lake County) Criminal Case Files; entries for William Dean and Frank Brown in Utah Territorial/State Prison Inmate Commitment Register (1892–1908), 206; "Vile Crime Is Charged: Two Men Accused of Committing a Beastly Offense," *Salt Lake Tribune,* 9 Apr. 1901, 8; "Guilty of Infamous Crime: Verdict of the Jury against William Dean," *Salt Lake Tribune,* 1 May 1901, 5; complaint against J. F. Harrington, filed 7 Jan. 1903, Case 291, Second District Court (Weber County) Criminal Case Files; Second District Court (Weber County), Minute Book (1896–97), 612; "Guilty of Revolting Crime," *Ogden Standard,* 18 Feb. 1903, 5; entry for James Burns in Utah Territorial/State Prison Inmate Commitment Register (1892–1908), 404; "TWO RECEIVE SENTENCE: Judge Howell Gives Doman and Burns Fifteen Years Each in the Penitentiary," *Salt Lake Herald,* 6 July 1906, 1; complaint against Thomas La Cross[e], dated 15 Feb. 1909, Case 2084, Third District Court (Salt Lake County) Criminal Case Files; entry for Thomas La-Crosse, Utah Department of Corrections, Utah State Prison Inmate Commitment Register (1908–17), 31, Series 80388, Utah State Archives. One sodomy case was dismissed in 1901 because of insufficient evidence that a man had sex with his ten-year-old stepson, despite the testimony of the boy. See entry for John Shaw in Salt Lake County Jail Register of Prisoners, Book (1901–5), Series 4372, Utah State Archives; "Unnatural Crime Charged," *Salt Lake Tribune,* 2 Nov. 1901, 8; "Evidence Not Sufficient," *Salt Lake Tribune,* 9 Nov. 1901, 8.

89. Rocky O'Donovan, "Historical Highlights of Mormon Attitudes toward Homosexuality," Utah State Historical Society.

90. David F. Greenberg, *The Construction of Homosexuality* (Chicago: University of Chicago Press, 1988), 401.

91. See also previous discussion of the 1896 rape of Thomas H. Clark. Court documents on bail were not always available, but the prison records showed whether the accused were admitted to bail before final sentencing.

92. Complaint against Edward Burke, filed 25 Nov. 1907, Case 1871, Third District Court (Salt Lake County), Criminal Files; Salt Lake County Jail Register of Prisoners, Book (1907–9), 1, Series 4372, Utah State Archives; Third District Court (Salt Lake City) Criminal Register (1907–9), Case 1871, Utah State Archives; "Judge Diehl's Court," *Deseret Evening News*, 29 Nov. 1907, 5; "Judge Diehl's New Record. Disposes of Five Felony Charges in Twenty Eight Seconds," *Deseret Evening News*, 23 Jan. 1908, 1. Former governor Wells and Joseph U. Eldredge paid the bonds. See Jenson, *Latter-day Saint Biographical Encyclopedia*, 1:722; J. Cecil Alter, *Utah: The Storied Domain*, 3 vols. (Chicago: American Historical Society, 1932), 2:54; entry for bachelor Edward Burke (b. Sept. 1863) in U.S. 1900 Census of Parley Park Precinct, Summit County, Utah, enumeration district 140, sheet 3, microfilm, LDS Family History Library.

93. *Message of the Mayor with the Annual Reports of the Officers of Salt Lake City, Utah for the Year 1907* (Salt Lake City: Century Printing, 1908), 380, for "Total Arrests and Offenses."

94. "Tom D. Pitt Called by Death Today," *Deseret Evening News*, 20 Dec. 1909, 1; "Evolution of Commercial St.," 2; Williams, "'The Stockade'"; McCormick, "Red Lights in Zion," 174–75.

95. Entry for Nick Poulos in Salt Lake County Jail Register of Prisoners, Book (1907–9), 160, and for Poulos case 2421 in Salt Lake City Police Blotter of Trials (Oct. 1908–Feb. 1910), 58, 67, 69, which did not list crimes, but gave case number and disposition of the case; "Given a Chance to Go," *Deseret Evening News*, 19 Jan. 1909, 2; obituary for Nick Poulos in *Deseret News*, 1 July 1938, 18. Frank Lashaway (Lackaway in the criminal records) was not an LDS "foreigner" because there is no reference to him or his family in the LDS European Emigration Index (1849–1925), LDS Family History Library. For Judge John M. Bowman as a non-Mormon, see *Biographical Record of Salt Lake City and Vicinity: Containing Biographies of Well Known Citizens of the Past and Present* (Chicago: National Historical Record, 1902), 205–6.

Utah's only sodomy case in 1910 resulted in an acquittal because the fourteen-year-old victim could not "positively" identify the accused. Because religion was not a possible factor, I do not include this case in the text discussion, and because of the witness's uncertainty I do not include Fairchild in this study's statistical summaries. See entry for "H. D." Fairchild in Salt Lake County Jail Register of Prisoners, Book (1909–11), 52, Series 4372, Utah State Archives; "F. D." Fairchild in "In Police Court," *Salt Lake Tribune,* 9 Feb. 1910, 12; and "D.H. Fairchild Acquitted," *Salt Lake Herald-Republican,* 14 July 1910, [5].

96. Complaint against Frank Sweeney, filed 31 Mar. 1911, and sentence of Judge Thomas D. Lewis on 5 May 1911, Case 2667, Third District Court (Salt Lake County) Criminal Case Files; Utah State Prison Inmate Commitment Register (1908–17), 142; entry for victim W—— C—— C—— (b. 15 Oct. 1899; d. 1972) in LDS Ancestral File; Alter, *Utah: The Storied Domain,* 2:371–72.

97. Remittitur document of the Utah Suprème Court, 4 Dec. 1912, in State of Utah vs. Joseph "Marasco," Case 109, Seventh District Court (Emery County), Criminal Case Files, Utah State Archives; entry for Joseph "Morasco," Utah State Prison Inmate Commitment Register (1908–17), 192.

98. Complaint against William Payne, dated 19 August 1913, transcript of action before Salt Lake City Judge N. H. Tanner on 29 August 1913 in State vs. William Payne, File 3336, Third District Court (Salt Lake County), Criminal Files, Series 1471, Utah State Archives; Salt Lake County Jail Register of Prisoners, Book (1913–14), 80, Series 4372, Utah State Archives; Third District Court (Salt Lake County) Criminal Register (1913–14) for Case 3336, State of Utah vs. William Payne, Utah State Archives; entry for William Richard Payne (b. 25 Sept. 1871) in LDS Patriarchal Blessing Index (1833–1963).

99. Entry for John Randolph, Salt Lake County Jail Register of Prisoners, Book (1913–14), 30. No entry for his sodomy case appeared in the Third District Court (Salt Lake County), Criminal Register (1912–13), Utah State Archives. The Salt Lake City judge over the criminal division in 1913 was Nathaniel H. Tanner, a Mormon. See John A. Randolph in Military Service Cards (1898–1975), Reel 33, Series 85268, Utah State Archives; Maurice Tanner, comp., *Descendants of John Tanner: Born August 15, 1778 at Hopkingtown, R.I. Died April 15, 1850, at South Cottonwood, Salt Lake County, Utah* (n.p.: Tanner Family Association, 1942), 148–49; C. C. Goodwin, *History of the Bench and Bar of Utah* (Salt Lake City: Interstate Press Association, 1913), 208–9.

100. Descriptions of G. W. Clark, Andrew G. Johnson, and John Oscar in Utah State Prison Inmate Commitment Register (1908–17), 261, 265, 279. The register gave little information about Johnson, whose conviction was reversed by the Utah Supreme Court. However, he did not appear in LDS records and because he was an African American, I have assumed he was Protestant.

101. "Court Notes," *Weekly Press* (Beaver, Utah), 17 Oct. 1913, 1. The incomplete prison record did not state Johnson's age, but he appeared to be

in his twenties in his prison photograph. I was unable to locate Johnson's criminal indictment, which would have clearly indicated whether the other male claimed this was an assault.

102. Utah v. Johnson, 44 Utah 18 (137 Pac. 632), 19, decision on 16 Dec. 1913. According to the decision sodomy "does not include copulation by one male person in the mouth of another, the definition being dependent on the common law" (18). Justice McCarty cited similar decisions about oral sex by courts in Kentucky, California, Texas, and Nebraska (22). Also, Lawrence R. Murphy, in "Defining the Crime against Nature: Sodomy in the United States Appeals Courts, 1810–1940," *Journal of Homosexuality* 19, no. 1 (1990): 55, demonstrated that appellate courts had made similar rulings about oral sex cases in Texas, California, and Arizona since 1873. For Justice McCarty's biography, see Warrum, *Utah since Statehood*, 2:76–80.

103. *Laws of the State of Utah* (Kaysville, Utah: Inland Printing, 1923), sect. 1, chap. 13, p. 21 (17 Feb. 1923).

104. Index, *Salt Lake Herald-Republican* (23 Dec. 1913): 1, compared with actual contents of page 14; also *Deseret News,* 16 Dec.–23 Dec. 1913; *Salt Lake Telegram,* 16 Dec.–23 Dec. 1913; *Salt Lake Tribune,* 16 Dec.–23 Dec. 1913; Utah State Prison Inmate Commitment Register (1908–17), 265, that Johnson was released on 22 December 1913 by "Order of Court." For the *Herald-Republican* as the LDS Church–owned organ of the "Smoot Machine" or "Federal Bunch," see Alexander, *Mormonism in Transition,* 28–29, 41, 53. For Smoot, see *Deseret News 1995–1996 Church Almanac,* 54; and Milton R. Merrill, *Reed Smoot: Apostle in Politics* (Logan: Utah State University Press, 1990).

105. Handwritten instructions of Judge Samuel W. Stewart to the jury on 30 Apr. 1901, in People vs. William Dean, File 721, and the case of codefendant Frank Brown, File 722, Third District Court (Salt Lake County) Criminal Case Files; entries for Dean and Brown in Utah Territorial/State Prison Inmate Commitment Register (1892–1908), 206; entry for John Paul Langenbacker (b. 20 Sept. 1887; LDS baptism 1895; md.; d. 1952) in LDS Ancestral File. This study identifies the victim because he was named in "Vile Crime Is Charged: Two Men Accused of Committing a Beastly Offense," *Salt Lake Tribune,* 9 Apr. 1901, 8; and "Guilty of Infamous Crime," *Salt Lake Tribune,* 1 May 1901, 5. For Judge Stewart as a Mormon, see Jenson, *Latter-day Saint Biographical Encyclopedia,* 1:786.

106. Chauncey, *Gay New York,* 419n19.

107. The staff in Medical Records Division, Utah State Hospital, informed me in November 1993 that all patient records for 1918 and earlier were available for public research and published study. I personally examined the admission records of every patient admitted to Utah's insane asylum from 1885 through 1918.

108. Admission Record Book (1896–99), Case 722 (21 Oct. 1897), with patient's case file in Reel 99; Admission Record Book (1899–1902), Case 925 (2 Dec. 1899), with patient's file in Reel 33; Patient Commitment Book (Cases 1440–2929), Case 2130 (11 Nov. 1910), with patient's case file in Reel 607, Utah State Hospital.

109. Admission Record Book (1899–1902), Case 975 (2 June 1900), with patient's case file in Reel 604.

110. Admission Record Book (1896–99), Case 767 (26 Mar. 1898), with patient's case file in Reel 604; Admission Record Book (1896–99), Case 891 (15 July 1899), with patient's case file in Reel 605; Admission Record Book (1902–5), Case 1324 (7 Jan. 1904), with patient's case file in Reel 611, Utah State Hospital.

111. For example, Berryman wrote that she was "unable to give any information in regard to masturbation or early sexual habits" concerning male case 1 in Berryman, "The Psychological Phenomena of the Homosexual," 66, rough-typed on the back of stationery of the American Red Cross, Salt Lake City, Utah, with the last page of the study dated 13 Nov. 1938, in the June Mazer Lesbian Collection, West Hollywood, Calif. See chap. 7 for analysis of her study.

112. Quotations from female case 2, female case 4, female case 20 in Berryman, "Psychological Phenomena," 36, 41, 58. In addition, Berryman made such statements as "has never practised masturbation" concerning female cases 3, 4, 14, on 39, 54, and unnumbered page (dated 13 Nov. 1938).

113. Admission Record Book (1885–91), Case 94 (22 Jan. 1887), with patient's case file in Reel 605, Utah State Hospital. See the discussion of the 1887 sodomy case in chap. 9.

114. Entry for J. Flaherty on 18 May 1901 in Salt Lake County Jail Register of Prisoners, Book (1901–5); "Flaherty Became Desperate: Boy Charged with Crime Broke Away from Officer, but Was Overtaken and Knocked Down before He Surrendered," *Salt Lake Tribune,* 19 May 1901, 5; "Taken to the Asylum," *Salt Lake Tribune,* 1 June 1901, 5; entry for Joseph Flaherty, Admission Record Book (1899–1902), Case 1067 (31 May 1901), with patient's case file in Reel 609-B, Utah State Hospital. The police thought Flaherty was twenty years old, but his medical records showed he was actually sixteen, and the newspaper reported his age as seventeen.

115. Admission records for Case 1 through Case 3541, Utah State Hospital. For the historical development of this diagnostic connection between masturbation and insanity, see Thomas S. Szasz, "The New Product—Masturbatory Insanity," *The Manufacture of Madness: A Comparative Study of the Inquisition and the Mental Health Movement* (New York: Harper and Row, 1970), 180–206.

116. Randy Shilts, *Conduct Unbecoming: Lesbians and Gays in the U.S.*

Military, Vietnam to the Persian Gulf (New York: St. Martin's Press, 1993), 15; Noble Warrum, *Utah in the World War: The Men behind the Guns and the Men and Women behind the Men behind the Guns* (Salt Lake City: Utah State Council of Defense, 1924), 449.

117. Szasz gave a slashing evaluation of what became the orthodox psychoanalytic view of homosexuality (especially by Sigmund Freud and Karl Menninger). See "The Product Conversion—From Heresy to Illness," and "The Model Psychiatric Scapegoat—The Homosexual," *Manufacture of Madness,* 160–79, 242–59. In 1973, the American Psychiatric Association officially stopped defining homosexuality as a mental illness. For a historical perspective and evaluation of critiques by Szasz and others, see George Chauncey Jr., "From Sexual Inversion to Homosexuality: The Changing Conceptualization of Female Deviance," *Salmagundi: A Quarterly of the Humanities and the Social Sciences,* nos. 58–59 (Fall 1982–Winter 1983): 114–46, reprinted in Kathy Peiss, Christiana Simmons, and Robert A. Padgug, eds., *Passion and Power: Sexuality in History* (Philadelphia: Temple University Press, 1989), 87–117; Henry Abelove, "Freud, Male Homosexuality, and the Americans," *Dissent* 33 (Winter 1986): 59–69; Ronald Bayer, *Homosexuality and American Psychiatry: The Politics of Diagnosis* (Princeton, N.J.: Princeton University Press, 1987); Kenneth Lewes, *The Psychoanalytic Theory of Homosexuality* (New York: Simon and Schuster, 1988). For contemporary Freudian and Jungian perspectives, see Richard C. Friedman, *Male Homosexuality: A Contemporary Psychoanalytic Perspective* (New Haven: Yale University Press, 1988); Robert H. Hopche, *Jung, Jungians, and Homosexuality* (Boston: Shambhala, 1989).

118. Michel Foucault, *The History of Sexuality: Volume I: An Introduction,* trans. Robert Hurley (New York: Random House, 1978), 43; see also E. Anthony Rotundo, *American Manhood: Transformations in Masculinity from the Revolution to the Modern Era* (New York: Basic Books, 1993), 275–76.

119. Rotundo, *American Manhood,* 278. He adds that because of this "homosexual stigma" and consequent homophobia, all American males have lost "the opportunity for the open intimacy of the romantic male friendships that were common in the nineteenth century; more broadly, the fear of homosexuality can block men's access to tender feelings and the skills that humans need in order to build connections with one another" (292).

120. Chauncey, in *Gay New York,* 26–27, 34–45, 58–127, 190–204, 243–67, examines differences in attitude between medical specialists and the general population, between middle-class culture and working-class culture during the same time period. In particular, he analyzes the stark differences between middle-class males and working-class males regarding their social acceptance of "obvious" homosexuals and regarding their views about the significance of participating in homoeroticism.

121. I omit the previously discussed 1856 case of LDS women because it involved an attempted seduction, not actual sexual contact. Also, these numbers omit the following groups of Mormons: those in same-sex co-residence without "proof" of sexual intimacy (the same-sex couples in the 1880 and 1900 censuses noted in chap. 6) and those whose homoeroticism was only implied by the sources (Kate Thomas, Ada Dwyer Russell, Natacha Rambova, Louie B. Felt, May Anderson, James Dwyer, and Evan Stephens and his several "boy-chums" noted in chaps. 4, 6, and 8). However, I include all males who were positively identified and charged with sexual assault or forcible sodomy by their alleged victims, even if charges were eventually dropped against the accused or even if the sodomy trial resulted in an acquittal. There were probably more Mormons among the other males convicted of sodomy or prostitution, even though I could not verify their religious background (such as Sidney Pickering, a teenager convicted of sodomy in 1882).

The following is a list of nineteenth-century Mormons who chose to have homoerotic experiences (from church records, court records, diaries, the Berryman study to 1938 [most, if not all, of the persons in her study were of Mormon background], and chaps. 9–11), according to the date of the first known incident:

> 1842—John C. Bennett (age 37, separated from wife, consensual)
> 1842—Francis M. Higbee (age 21, single, consensual)
> 1876—George Naylor (age 17, consensual)
> 1881—Perry D. McClanahan (age 38, married, assaulted a male)
> 1882—Soren Madsen (age 32, polygamist, consensual)
> 1882—P—— A—— L—— (age 30, single, consensual)
> 1882—A—— B—— (age 19, consensual)
> 1882—F—— C—— M—— (age 18, consensual)
> 1882—J—— C—— S—— (age 15, consensual)
> 1882—N—— J—— (age 15, consensual)
> 1886—Thomas Taylor (age 60, polygamist, imposed himself on males)
> 1887—Richard Buboltz (age 16, assaulted a male)
> 1887—Arthur Curtis (age 15, assaulted a male)
> 1887—Daniel Hendry (age 12, assaulted a male)
> 1889—Evan S. Thomas (age 40, single, assaulted a male)
> 1891—James Hamilton (age 35, single, consensual)
> 1893—Lorenzo Hunsaker (age 33, polygamist, imposed himself on brothers)
> 1896—William Brown (age 22, single, earliest LDS baptism shown as 1907—probably a rebaptism following excommunication for sexual acts—assaulted a male)
> 1896—Thomas Rogers (assaulted a male)

1896—Charles W. Merrill (assaulted a male)
1896—Samuel Bennett (assaulted a male)
1896—Hugh Nicholes (assaulted a male)
1896—James Woods (assaulted a male)
1896—William Foster (assaulted a male)
1897—David Baum (age 15, prostitute, Eureka)
1898—Fred "Stephenson" (Stevenson, age 23, prostitute, Park City)
1901—John Shaw (age 50, imposed himself on stepson)
1904—Ray Lewis (age 21, prostitute, Park City)
1907—Edward Burke (age 44, single, assaulted a male)
1908—Stanley Rasmussen (age 18, consensual)
1908—William Buchanan (age 17, consensual)
1908—Niels Pearson Jr. (age 17, consensual)
1908—Bird (Burt) Hughes (age 16, consensual)
1908—Edward W. Wells (age 16, consensual)
1909—M——— C——— C——— (age 13, consensual)
1909—M——— J——— C——— (age 14, consensual)
1909—L——— G——— A——— (age 14, consensual)
1909—F——— C. D——— (age 15, consensual)
1909—I——— D——— (age 16, consensual)
1909—R——— H——— J——— (age 17, consensual)
1913—John Randolph (age 23, single, assaulted a male)
1913—William Payne (age 41, single, assaulted a male)
1918—Female case 1 (age 37, consensual, in Berryman study)
1918—Female case 2 (age 29, consensual, in Berryman study)
1918—Female case 3 (age 20, consensual, in Berryman study)
1918—Female case 4 (age 20, consensual, in Berryman study)
1918—Female case 5 (age 23, consensual, in Berryman study)
1918—Female case 6 (age 23, consensual, in Berryman study)
1918—Female case 7 (age 27, consensual, in Berryman study)
1918—Female case 8 (age 43, consensual, in Berryman study)
1918—Female case 9 (age 50, consensual, in Berryman study)
1918—Female case 10 (age 35, married, consensual, in Berryman study)
1918—Female case 11 (age 48, consensual, in Berryman study)
1918—Female case 12 (age 29, consensual, in Berryman study)
1918—Female case 13 (age 23, consensual, in Berryman study)
1918—Female case 14 (age 22, consensual, in Berryman study)
1918—Female case 15 (age 21, consensual, in Berryman study)
1918—Female case 16 (age 19, consensual, in Berryman study)
1918—Female case 17 (age 29, married, consensual, in Berryman study)
1918—Female case 18 (age 29, married, consensual, in Berryman study)
1918—Female case 19 (age 29, married, consensual, in Berryman study)

1918—Female case 20 (age 29, consensual, in Berryman study)
1918—Female case 21 (age 41, consensual, in Berryman study)
1918—Female case 22 (age 56, married, consensual, in Berryman study)
1918—Female case 23 (age 36, married, consensual, in Berryman study)
1918—Female case 24 (age 24, consensual, in Berryman study)
1918—Male case 1 (age 25, consensual, in Berryman study)
1918—Male case 2 (age 20, consensual, in Berryman study)
1918—Male case 3 (age 23, consensual, in Berryman study)
1918—Male case 4 (age 23, consensual, in Berryman study)
1918—Male case 5 (age 30, consensual, in Berryman study)
1918—Male case 6 (age 27, consensual, in Berryman study)
1918—Male case 7 (age 26, consensual, in Berryman study)
1918—Male case 8 (age 29, consensual, in Berryman study)
1918—Male case 9 (age 39, married, consensual, in Berryman study)
1926 and 1946—Joseph F. Smith (age 27, age 47, married, consensual)

122. *Deseret News 1995–1996 Church Almanac,* 419, reports the total number of living LDS members in 1900 as 283,765. I estimate an additional 116,235 Mormons between 1830 and 1899 who died, defected, or were excommunicated. When presented with the rounded-off estimate of 400,000 nineteenth-century Mormons on 14 Mar. 1995, Mormon demographer Dean L. May, professor of history at the University of Utah, said he regarded it as reasonable and probably conservative.

123. Wilford E. Smith, "Mormon Sex Standards on College Campuses, Or Deal Us out of the Sexual Revolution," *Dialogue: A Journal of Mormon Thought* 10 (Autumn 1976): 77. This was the finding of questionnaires that Smith distributed during a twenty-year period to BYU sociology students, whom he identified on page 77 as "Mormons in a large church university." While I was enrolled in a BYU sociology course during those years, I took this survey, which was identified as Wilford E. Smith's on the day my class received it. See also the text of chap. 1 and its notes 53–55 for comparative perspectives on these BYU findings.

124. "This style of dance has been taken advantage of by many impure persons," the First Presidency instructed all Mormons in April 1887, "and respectable people have been annoyed and grieved thereat, and have felt that it should be entirely prohibited." See James R. Clark, ed., *Messages of the First Presidency of the Church of Jesus Christ of Latter-day Saints, 1833–1964,* 6 vols. (Salt Lake City: Bookcraft, 1965–75), 3:122.

125. Nellie Spilsbury Hatch, *Colonia Juarez: An Intimate Account of a Mormon Village* (Salt Lake City: Deseret Book, 1954), 266n2; see also stake president Rudger Clawson's unwillingness to acknowledge homoeroticism in the Honeyville case of 1893, as described in chap. 9.

126. Smith, "Mormon Sex Standards on College Campuses," 77.

127. Morton Hunt, *Sexual Behavior in the 1970s* (Chicago: Playboy Press, 1974), 150 (81 percent of surveyed American women had premarital intercourse by age twenty-four); Carol Tavris and Susan Sadd, *The Redbook Report on Female Sexuality: 100,000 Married Women Disclose the Good News about Sex* (New York: Delacorte Press, 1975), 34 (96 percent of surveyed young women under age twenty had premarital intercourse; 91 percent of surveyed women between twenty and twenty-four years old had premarital intercourse); John DeLamater and Patricia MacCorquodale, *Premarital Sexuality: Attitudes, Relationships, Behavior* (Madison: University of Wisconsin Press, 1979), 95 (63 percent of nonstudent women and 50 percent of female college students had premarital intercourse); Paul H. Gebhard and Alan B. Johnson, *The Kinsey Data: Marginal Tabulations of the 1938–1963 Interviews Conducted by the Institute for Sex Research* (Philadelphia: W. B. Saunders, 1979), 267 (77.1 percent of college-educated women had premarital intercourse by age twenty-four).

128. Hans Dinesen diary, 121, retrospective entry in early 1885, translated from Danish, complete typescript in my possession; Scott G. Kenney, ed., *Wilford Woodruff's Journal: 1833–1898 Typescript*, 9 vols. (Murray, Utah: Signature Books, 1983–85), 8:286 (15 Nov. 1884) for date Woodruff spoke.

129. "Elder Taylor's Talk," *Deseret Evening News*, 10 Oct. 1898, 2.

130. Rudger Clawson diary, 10 July 1901, in Stan Larson, ed., *A Ministry of Meetings: The Apostolic Diaries of Rudger Clawson* (Salt Lake City: Signature Books/Smith Research Associates, 1993), 296. The actual numbers were seven out of twelve marriages.

131. Lund diary, 26 Nov. 1915.

132. Harold T. Christensen, "Child Spacing Analysis via Record Linkage: New Data Plus a Summing Up from Earlier Reports," *Marriage and Family Living* 25 (Aug. 1963): 275; Daniel Scott Smith, "The Dating of the American Sexual Revolution: Evidence and Interpretation," in Michael Gordon, ed., *The American Family in Social-Historical Perspective*, 2d ed. (New York: St. Martin's Press, 1978), 429.

133. Even Dinesen made reference in his diary to this fact of his community only because an apostle publicly criticized this pattern of premarital intercourse.

134. "Of LDS Women, 58% Admit Premarital Sex," *Salt Lake Tribune*, 9 Aug. 1991, B-2.

135. Flynt, "Homosexuality among Tramps," 253–54.

CHAPTER 11

From Relative Tolerance to Homophobia in Twentieth-Century Mormonism

EVEN NATIONALLY, the transition from tolerance to homophobia was uneven during the early decades of twentieth-century America. Longer than other segments of society, religious leaders tended to retain previously positive views of same-sex dynamics.[1] This was also true of Mormonism. Sometimes serving to the midtwentieth century, LDS leaders who reached adulthood in the nineteenth century were remarkably restrained or tolerant when they confronted homoeroticism or homosexuality among Latter-day Saints.

A personal example is the response of LDS general authority J. Golden Kimball (b. 1853) to the discovery in 1902 that his twelve-year-old son had been "teaching" a cousin "self abuse." In a letter that apparently referred to the young men practicing mutual masturbation, Kimball wrote: "Children are begotten in passion and their very souls are eaten up with passion," and he advised his brother that they should not confront either of their sons about these practices: "The thing for us to do is to keep mum and fight the devil in a quiet way."[2] To better understand the poignant resignation of those words, it is necessary to recognize that J. Golden Kimball had long struggled with "false appetites or passions" of his own.

Despite a time and eternity marriage and his position as a general authority, Kimball began writing in his diary about his own sexual conflict five years before he discovered his son's playful sexuality with a cousin. In 1897, J. Golden Kimball wrote: "my father and mother are in no wise respo[n]sible for any of my false appetites or passions." A year later he wrote: "Unhappiness reigns supremely in our home. It is needless for me to say more, than to write that I am unhappy." Six months before his letter concerning the sexual activities of his son and nephew, Kimball wrote: "I frankly confess that my anger[,] passions and appetites are such that I seem not able to live any where near the requirements of the Gospel."[3] It is unknown whether same-sex attraction was part of the "false appetites or passions" that discouraged J. Golden Kimball and contributed to his marital unhappiness. In any event, his own struggles predisposed this LDS Church leader to be restrained when he learned of his son's sexual experiences with a male cousin.

In the first administrative example of similar restraint toward homoeroticism, the First Presidency learned in May 1913 that "Prof. Dwyer" had been "teaching young men that sodomy and kindred vices are not sins, [but] only the [sexual] connection with a woman is sinful."[4] Then in his eighties, James Dwyer had the honorary title of "Professor" due to his being one of the founders of the LDS University (now LDS Business College) in Salt Lake City. A father of eight children, he remained unmarried after his wife's death in 1897.[5] Dwyer's views reflected those of other nineteenth-century Mormons, who looked upon sodomy as less serious than other sexual sins. A year before Dwyer came to the attention of Mormon leaders as an advocate of "sodomy and kindred vices," his daughter Ada Dwyer Russell began her long-term relationship with the lesbian poet Amy Lowell.[6]

In 1911 the church's *Improvement Era* had described James Dwyer as "a sign-post pointing the way to thousands of young men of promise and capacity." As the principal bookseller for college texts in Utah since the 1870s, he became closely associated with "literally thousands of young persons." He gave some university students "books on credit" because "he knew, from experience, what a book may mean to a boy." The *Era* had added that there was "never a young man in need of sympathy and encouragement that did not get it" from James Dwyer.[7]

Anthon H. Lund's diary shows that he regarded the Dwyer case as noteworthy, but the First Presidency counselor indicated neither shock nor revulsion.[8] Although Dwyer's stake president and bishop wanted to excommunicate him, the First Presidency instead allowed Dwyer to voluntarily "withdraw his name" from LDS Church membership.[9] During Mormonism's first century, it was virtually unknown to give Mormons this option rather than for them to endure an excommunication trial. Not until later that year did LDS headquarters issue instructions allowing a Mormon to request "that his name be stricken from the records . . . to have his membership cancelled."[10]

That forbearance was not simply due to Dwyer's advanced age, life's work, or out of consideration to his children. Only three years earlier the same First Presidency had authorized the *Deseret News* to make a front-page announcement of the excommunication of eighty-four-year-old Judson Tolman. A year after the Dwyer case, the LDS hierarchy gave front-page publicity to its excommunication of eighty-two-year-old John W. Woolley. The error of these ordained patriarchs and Utah pioneers was in secretly performing plural marriages unauthorized by the LDS hierarchy. LDS leaders obviously regarded private performance of unauthorized polygamy as more serious than encouraging young men to engage in "sodomy and kindred vices."[11]

The option of voluntary withdrawal from church membership was not the last evidence of the First Presidency's restrained response toward Dwyer. When he died in 1915, the *Improvement Era* (of which LDS president Joseph F. Smith was the editor) described Dwyer as "a man of sterling character."[12] Either President Smith's views had mellowed since 1882 (see chap. 9) or someone else wrote this editorial tribute to a Mormon who had been "teaching young men that sodomy and kindred vices are not sins."

Mildred J. Berryman may have begun her decades-long study of Salt Lake City's lesbians and gay men before President Joseph F. Smith died in November 1918. Some prominent Utah Mormons were among the self-defined lesbians and gay men in Berryman's study during the 1920s, and she concealed their identities.[13] Nevertheless, the family background of an LDS social worker seems to match the description of a similar-aged "nurse" who was one of the lesbians in Berryman's study.[14] Born in Ogden, Utah, of Dutch immigrant parents in 1897, Cora Kasius undoubtedly knew Mildred Berryman. Other Utah lesbians described Kasius as a Mormon lesbian, and both she and Berryman were connected with the Salt Lake City office of the American Red Cross.[15]

Cora Kasius had been a staff member at the LDS Relief Society's headquarters since 1920 and an assistant secretary to its general president since 1923. She authored the *Relief Society Magazine*'s description of a twelve-week institute on social work in 1925 during which year she also became executive secretary of the local American Red Cross.[16] In 1927 Kasius moved to New York City, where she was a faculty member of the all-female Barnard College and a staff member with the Family Welfare Association of America. At the end of World War II, Kasius served as the United Nations liaison officer to Holland for relief work and later became the UN's displaced persons representative to Sweden. She also authored several books about social work, was a Fulbright lecturer, and served as the editor of the journal *Social Casework* for seventeen years.[17]

However, Berryman was probably unaware in the 1920s of the same-sex experiences of one young man who would later become an LDS general authority. Grandson of LDS president Joseph F. Smith and oldest son of Apostle Hyrum M. Smith, Joseph F. Smith (b. 1899) entered into a relationship with another young man during the mid-1920s. It is possible that while an instructor at the University of Utah Joseph F. Smith began his relationship with Norval Service while the teenager was a high school athlete at the Latter-day Saint University in Salt Lake City.[18]

One odd coincidence was that Service was in school with Wallace Packham during the time Packham was the "boy chum" of retired Tabernacle Choir director Evan Stephens. During 1924 Packham was in student government and the Male Glee Club, while Service was on the football team.[19] They undoubtedly knew each other in this small school, but there is no evidence they were sufficiently close friends for Packham to tell Service of his relationship with Stephens.

However, the relationship between Smith and Norval probably began in the fall of 1926, when Service was a twenty-one-year-old student at the University of Utah, where Smith had just been reappointed as an instructor.[20] Then a twenty-seven-year-old bachelor, Smith had just returned to Utah after a two-year absence in England and Illinois for a master's degree in speech and drama.[21] The two young men lived in separate residences in Salt Lake City, but apparently maintained their private relationship until Smith married in 1929. His six-years-younger friend Service married a year later, but fathered no children.[22]

In October 1942, LDS president Heber J. Grant appointed Joseph F. Smith as Patriarch to the Church. Decades later, one member of the extended Smith family claimed that the new patriarch's homoerotic activities with college students were even known to Salt Lake City's police at that time. Grant "put this man in," according to the relative, "knowing that he was a homosexual."[23] That seems unlikely and Grant's personal diary made no reference to his knowing about the new patriarch's orientation, but other Mormons certainly did. A female friend of Norval Service was aware of his relationship with Smith, and she said that the professor's appointment as a church patriarch stunned her and others who knew of his homosexuality.[24]

Nevertheless, from the appointment of Patriarch Smith in 1942 until 1946, no one in the Mormon hierarchy indicated they had the slightest suspicion of his same-sex interests.[25] The Mormons who knew otherwise remained silent because of their assumptions that Patriarch Joseph F. Smith had abandoned homosexual conduct and that President Grant had accepted his repentance for the previous relationship(s).[26] Then on 6 October 1946, more than a year after Grant's death, the First Presidency publicly released the former president's namesake and grandson as Patriarch to the Church. The hierarchy explained that they had released Patriarch Joseph F. Smith due to illness, but it was actually for the discovery of his same-sex activities.[27]

At the time, the forty-seven-year-old patriarch was involved with another young man, a twenty-one-year-old Mormon who had been serving in the U.S. Navy. Members of the First Presidency consistently called this sailor "the boy," which is understandable in view of his boyish appearance even two years later.[28] It is not known if the patriarch and the young man were intimate during his first attendance at the University of Utah from fall 1942 until he joined the navy in March 1943. After he turned eighteen that month, the sailor shipped out for wartime duty in the Pacific and apparently did not return to Utah until after his release from the navy on 4 May 1946.[29] If the patriarch and the sailor had begun their relationship after the young man's return to Salt Lake City, then it lasted no more than two months and perhaps only a few weeks.

Whether this same-sex relationship was of long or short duration, the young man's local LDS leaders caused a crisis in July 1946 by asking him to go on a proselytizing mission. When his father asked why he declined to serve a mission, the young man admitted he was in an intimate relationship with the patriarch. The father immediately complained to the First Presidency.[30] On 10 July 1946 LDS president George

Albert Smith wrote that he was "heartsick," when he told the apostles about the "bad situation" of the patriarch (his distant cousin). Apostle Joseph Fielding Smith (the patriarch's uncle) wrote that this information "brought a shock to me and my brethren, [and] this was of a nature which I do not feel at liberty or capable of discussion."[31]

The First Presidency of George Albert Smith, J. Reuben Clark, and David O. McKay (all born in the 1870s) required no ecclesiastical court for this general authority. Instead, they released Joseph F. Smith as patriarch for this same-sex activity and instructed him not to perform religious ordinances or accept church assignments.[32] According to instructions published by LDS headquarters since 1928, this was a very informal and mild response to one of the "other infractions of the moral law."[33] The First Presidency was far more lenient with Patriarch Joseph F. Smith in 1946 than his grandfather had been with the endowed Mormon involved in the 1882 Richfield case of homoeroticism.[34]

After this private crisis of 1946, the former patriarch moved with his family to Hawaii. The First Presidency instructed the stake president there to prohibit him from speaking in church or from having other church privileges. President George Albert Smith continued the monthly allowance to the former patriarch until the end of 1947 and then again beginning in March 1948. The church president also met with him in Hawaii in 1950 for a compassionate talk "with reference to his problems."[35]

George Albert Smith's successor, David O. McKay, authorized the Hawaii stake president to rehabilitate the former patriarch in 1957. By then, the young man involved in the 1946 incident had married and fathered two children. His approval was necessary for the restoration of the former patriarch to full church privileges that year. McKay authorized his full rehabilitation on 10 July 1957, exactly eleven years to the day since the First Presidency had learned of the patriarch's homoeroticism.[36] Joseph F. Smith soon became a member of his stake high council. He lived the remaining years of his life with the full opportunity to perform priesthood functions and with the devotion of his wife and seven children (all born before his release).[37]

Compare the hierarchy's restrained response to homoerotic behaviors in one "prophet, seer, and revelator" with the way the same LDS leaders responded to heterosexual misconduct by another general authority. On 2 November 1943, First Presidency Counselor J. Reuben Clark (equally involved in the patriarch's case less than three years later) received word that Apostle Richard R. Lyman was having an extramarital affair. Clark assigned two apostles and some others to follow Lyman at night to verify this and ascertain where the couple spent the night. Clark asked the compliant chief of Salt Lake City's police department to stage a smashed-door raid on the apartment the night of 11 November. The police and two apostles found the nearly seventy-three-year-old Lyman in bed with his seventy-one-year-old female companion. The next day, the Quorum of Twelve excommunicated Lyman and announced to the world that the apostle had committed a "violation of the Christian law of chastity." Although the hierarchy allowed Lyman to be baptized eleven years later, they declined to restore priesthood to him.[38]

In all, the harsh punishments upon one general authority for extramarital heterosexuality were totally absent in the LDS hierarchy's response to extramarital homosexuality in another general authority. Yet the two incidents occurred within three years of each other during the 1940s, and J. Reuben Clark was prominently involved in the response to both cases.

A Brigham Young University student's reminiscence (both unpublished and published) describes an incident in which President George Albert Smith also encouraged two young men to "live their lives as decently as they could" within their homosexual companionship. Both were BYU students and one was the son of a stake president. This father arranged for them to see the church president because the young men "were lovers and felt concerned and guilty because of their sexual activities."[39] According to the published account by one of their gay friends at BYU, this is what happened during the interview at LDS headquarters: "They stated their case to him and acknowledged their love for each other. President Smith treated them with great kindness and told them, in effect, to live the best lives they could. They felt they had gambled and could have been excommunicated right then and there; instead they went away feeling loved and valued."[40] According to their friend this occurred in 1948, "perhaps in the spring."[41] In the section for 11–12 April in President Smith's 1948 appointment book, there is an unexplained entry, "Homo Sexual," which he did not include in his diary for this period.[42] The reminiscent account is also consistent with George Albert Smith's compassionate response to others whose circumstances and behavior did not conform to official LDS standards.[43]

The First Presidency's relative tolerance for homoerotic activities continued into the 1950s. In 1950, an Idaho stake presidency asked whether to disfellowship or excommunicate a Mormon professor who was fired by church-owned Ricks College in Rexburg, Idaho, for homoerotic conduct. The professor's homosexual relationship "had been going on for several years." J. Reuben Clark, counselor in the First Presidency, replied, "thus far we had done no more than drop them from positions they held."[44] This was less than a year before church president George Albert Smith died and was consistent with the previous restraint of both Smith and Clark toward the church patriarch's homosexuality. This 1950 case of the Ricks College professor also demonstrates that the lenient response toward Patriarch Joseph F. Smith in 1946 was part of an unwritten policy of the First Presidency toward homoeroticism, and not an isolated example of restraint.

However, despite his nineteenth-century origins, J. Reuben Clark certainly did not condone homoerotic behaviors. In his talk to the women of the Relief Society in October 1952, he was the first LDS leader to publicly warn that "the homosexuals are today exercising great influence," and the first to publicly acknowledge the existence of lesbianism and of sex with animals. Clark was also the first LDS leader to discuss masturbation and homosexuality in a general church meeting. His sermon assumed that all these behaviors existed among the Mormons. Clark was also the first LDS leader to warn LDS women against allowing a gay man to use them as a substitute male in dating or marriage: "I wonder if you girls have ever reflected on the thought that was in the mind of the man who first began to praise you for your boyish figures."[45] However, after Clark's death, it became LDS Church policy to encourage homosexually oriented men to marry and thus substitute a woman in place of their primary sexual interests.

Apostle Spencer W. Kimball (b. 1895) was the principal advocate of marriage as a remedy for same-sex desires, and he was the most influential example of a crucial transition in Mormon attitudes toward same-sex desires and homoeroticism. Nephew of J. Golden Kimball, Spencer W. Kimball in 1947 began a life's work of counseling young men about their same-sex desires.[46]

Later to become church president, Kimball retained the nineteenth-century's views of same-sex dynamics, manifested the twentieth-century's homophobia, but rejected the twentieth-century's medical view that homosexuality was a condition of some humans. Similar to the segregated-gender emphasis of nineteenth-century America,[47] Kimball's own statements were almost exclusively male-oriented regarding same-sex issues.

Like his father's generation, Spencer W. Kimball valued homoemotional expressions of love between males. He even became known for hugging and kissing other males publicly, a practice virtually unknown among more recent generations of Mormons.[48] Kimball also retained the nineteenth century's views on homosexuality. Steadfastly rejecting the twentieth-century's medical findings that a small minority of humans have felt same-sex desires as long as they could remember, Kimball maintained the nineteenth-century's emphasis on sexual activities. He regarded homosexual desires as a "habit" caused primarily by masturbation.[49] For Kimball, people were not homosexual, only acts were.

Kimball publicly acknowledged: "Some say marriage has failed" as a cure for homosexuality. However, he encouraged every homosexually oriented Mormon man to "force himself to return to normal pursuits and interests and actions and friendships with the opposite sex." Kimball did not comment about the effect on a Mormon woman's self-esteem to be a therapeutic sex object in a marriage her husband had "force[d] himself" to enter as a religious obligation. Spencer W. Kimball indicated that the potential unhappiness of such marriages was worthwhile because "the Lord makes clear that only through the eternal union of man and woman can they achieve eternal life."[50] However, in the years following the widespread adoption of Kimball's marriage remedy for homosexual men, Mormon wives recounted a consistent pattern of despair and self-loathing at their inability to achieve reciprocal intimacy (both emotional and sexual) with their homosexually oriented husbands.[51]

Contemporary with Kimball's counseling of Mormon men with homoerotic experiences, the First Presidency did not add "homo-sexual acts" as grounds for excommunication for sixteen years after Clark's 1952 talk. It was nearly thirty years after Clark's talk before "lesbianism" joined the list of causes for which an LDS Church member could be excommunicated.[52] This is one indication that the LDS presidents and their counselors who reached adulthood in the nineteenth century shared less stringent views than Kimball, who was assigned to counsel homosexually oriented men.

Instead, the First Presidency's approach of relative toleration for homoeroticism continued into the presidency of David O. McKay. In October 1951, Stephen L Richards, a counselor in the First Presidency, instructed a mission president that a full-time missionary elder was only "guilty of a great indiscretion" for fondling the sexual organs of three boys, ages twelve to thirteen. Without "proof of actual penetration," Richards explained, this was "a superficial charge." Therefore, the counselor recommended against excommunicating the missionary for this homoerotic incident.[53]

Increase of Homophobia in Mormonism after the 1950s

Reaching adulthood in the twentieth century seemed to be the crucial factor in the decline of tolerance among LDS leaders for homoerotic behaviors and the rise of homophobia within the Mormon hierarchy since the early 1950s. For example, Joseph Fielding Smith (an uncle of the released patriarch) made no reference to homosexual conduct during fifty years of doctrinaire writing and speaking as an LDS apostle.[54] Smith reached adulthood in the nineteenth century.

However, in 1958 his son-in-law Bruce R. McConkie (born in 1915) published *Mormon Doctrine,* which listed "sodomy, onanism, and homosexuality" among the types of "lewdness, lasciviousness, and licentiousness." Although he typically cited his father-in-law or the earlier church president Joseph F. Smith in support of his book's definitions, McConkie could find no early Mormon leader to quote against homosexuality or homoerotic behaviors. In addition, citing Leviticus, McConkie observed wistfully that "anciently the death penalty was invoked for adultery and for many other offenses against God and man." Because "modern governments do not take the life of the adulterer," this general authority concluded that such leniency "is further evidence of the direful apostasy that prevails among the peoples who call themselves Christians."[55]

In fact, 1958 was apparently a crucial turning point for the attitudes of LDS leaders toward homosexuality. The year had begun with a series of highly publicized arrests of men in Salt Lake City for same-sex crimes. This was the result of the police department's new strategy of using decoys and surveillance at gay meeting places.[56] In response, the Catholic editor of the *Salt Lake Tribune* urged judicial restraint. In September 1958, John F. Fitzpatrick expressed strong support for giv-

ing suspended sentences and professional counseling to men convicted of homosexual activities: "Homosexuality is a social evil which must
be fought. But experience proves that confinement in jail or prison is
no answer." Fitzpatrick's editorial acknowledged that "rehabilitation
through medical treatment is not sure," but he still affirmed that "some
are helped thereby."[57]

McConkie's 1958 reference to homosexuality and his endorsement
of "the death penalty" for sex crimes may have been specific responses to the publicity about the arrests in Salt Lake City. In fact, the Catholic editor's advocacy of no imprisonment for homosexual activities
may have been part of what impelled McConkie in 1958 to equate
Catholicism with the "CHURCH OF THE DEVIL," to claim that "in this
world of carnality and sensuousness, the great and abominable church
will continue its destructive course," and to insist that "justice" required
that whenever "the Lord's law has been given, punishment always follows disobedience."[58]

The David O. McKay presidency privately condemned McConkie's
Mormon Doctrine as "full of errors and misstatements . . . (some 1,067
of them)" and stopped the book's distribution.[59] However, the First
Presidency disputed only two of the above cited passages. When the
hierarchy allowed McConkie to issue a revised edition, *Mormon Doctrine* had dropped the specific statements about Catholicism and about
capital punishment for sex crimes. However, McConkie left unchanged
the 1958 references to homosexuality, to the "carnality and sensuousness" of "the great and abominable church" (which was originally
cross-referenced to "Catholicism"), and to the absolute requirement
of punishment.[60]

Because McKay was repulsed by the very thought of same-sex intimacy,
it was not necessary to change McConkie's statement on homosexuality. As reported by Apostle Spencer W. Kimball, McKay said "that in his
view homosexuality was worse than [heterosexual] immorality; that it
is a filthy and unnatural habit." Kimball later published that "the sin of
homosexuality is equal to or greater than that of fornication or adultery."
In this respect, he departed significantly from the view of LDS leaders in
the nineteenth century, when homoerotic activities were clearly regarded as far less serious than adultery (see chap. 9).[61]

Thus, the LDS general authority most often described as having
"David-and-Jonathan" friendships[62] was also homophobic by the late
1950s, despite the fact that David O. McKay reached adulthood in the

nineteenth century. Likewise, a Roman Catholic journalist (who reached adulthood in the early twentieth century) was the least homophobic community leader in the face of publicized acts of homoeroticism in Salt Lake City in 1958. This demonstrates that the homocultural attitudes in the nineteenth century were not accepted by all Americans or Mormons of that era, nor was homophobia a characteristic of all who reached adulthood in the early decades of the twentieth century. These diverse reactions in 1958 serve as a useful reminder that trends and exceptions coexist in society.

McKay's personal attitudes toward homosexuality encouraged increased activism by younger general authorities who were demonstrably homophobic. This did not occur while McKay was second counselor in the First Presidency during the 1930s and 1940s because his position then was subordinate and deferential to the LDS president and first counselor, who demonstrated greater leniency toward homoeroticism. However, Apostle Spencer W. Kimball had been counseling homosexually oriented Mormons for a decade before Salt Lake City's police began their mass arrests of gay men in 1958. A year later, Apostle Mark E. Petersen (b. 1900) joined him in this "special assignment."[63] In regard to the LDS Church's position toward homosexuality, after 1958 the balance shifted dramatically toward the viewpoint of general authorities who had reached adulthood in the twentieth century.

After 1958 there was increased discussion and activism at LDS headquarters about same-sex orientation (even without homoerotic activities). In May 1959, Brigham Young University's president, Ernest L. Wilkinson, reported that the apostles on the executive committee of the Church Board of Education discussed "the growing problem in our society of homosexuality."[64] This was two days after the death of First Presidency Counselor Stephen L Richards, who had been so lenient concerning the homoerotic activities of a full-time missionary.[65]

Later that year a best-selling novel brought national attention to Mormons and homoeroticism. A central character of Allen Drury's *Advise and Consent* was Brigham Anderson, who had a homosexual affair in the military a decade before this fictitious Mormon was elected a U.S. senator from Utah. During four weeks with an eighteen year old in Hawaii, Anderson had experienced "a perfectly genuine happiness," but abruptly ended the sexual relationship due to jealousy about his boyfriend. Despite his subsequent marriage and devoted love for his wife and child, Anderson kept a photograph of the young man and never again experienced "happiness" equal to that in their brief relationship. After a decade, their only contact was an unanswered letter and one telephone call, both from the younger man. When political opponents discovered evidence of the senator's homosexual activities, they blackmailed him. Admitting the former incident to his wife, he reaffirmed his love for her, downplayed the emotional significance of his homosexual affair, yet expressed no regret. However, faced with public humiliation, the fictitious Utah senator committed suicide. Grief stricken for contributing to his former lover's downfall and death, the young man also killed himself.[66]

Mormons objected to the storyline of *Advise and Consent* because of the "bad light it places on a good, clean-cut Utah boy"[67] and were concerned about the novel's popularity. On 4 October 1959, the book joined the *New York Times* best-seller list, where it remained as number one for thirty weeks and in second place for a year. As the best-selling novel of 1960, Drury's book sold 4.4 million copies and earned its author the Pulitzer Prize.[68]

LDS leaders were appalled to learn that the influential Hollywood director Otto Preminger planned to make a "quality" film of the novel. Mormon millionaire J. Willard Marriott complained that such a "movie would do inestimable damage to the image of our people." Marriott joined with Utah senator Wallace F. Bennett in asking non-LDS friends to "get to Preminger on a person-to-person basis" to "at least make sure that there is no identification of this character with the Mormon Church." Apostle Richard L. Evans, a director of Rotary International, used his contacts in the broadcast industry in a similar way.[69]

This lobbying by prominent Mormons failed because Preminger was using *Advise and Consent* to end Hollywood's self-censorship code against portrayals of homosexuality. He even publicly advised that youths under sixteen "should not be permitted to see this film except in the company of their parents," because "there is a homosexual theme throughout the picture."[70] He added a scene to the film in which the Utah senator entered a nightclub for gay men, the first time Americans saw a gay bar in a Hollywood film. This scene occurred immediately after a gay character referred to Brigham Anderson as one of "the Mormons." Consistent with the character's image as "a good, clean-cut Utah boy," the film also showed the senator drinking soft drinks instead of alcohol.[71]

It is beyond the scope of this study to examine issues regarding lesbians and gay men in the Mormon culture region after the 1950s.[72] That requires separate discussion and analysis. Nevertheless, I will mention some developments in LDS Church policy.

Shortly after that 1959 meeting of the Church Board of Education, BYU began "aversion therapy" to "cure," "repair," or "reorient" the same-sex desires of Mormon males. These young men were referred to this program by BYU's mental health counselors, by LDS bishops and stake presidents, by BYU's office to enforce student standards, or by referrals from outside BYU (such as mission presidents and general authorities). The staff of this BYU program showed increasingly erotic images of women and men to each young man in a dark room. Therapists implied or indicated that the Mormon youth should fantasize of sex or masturbate while looking at images of women. The punishment for getting an erection at the sight of a male body was a 1,600–volt impulse to the LDS client's arm for eight seconds.[73] It is unknown if this was consistent with the kind of medical "rehabilitation" the *Salt Lake Tribune*'s Catholic editor had in mind. This aversion therapy was certainly *not* consistent with Kimball's view that masturbation led to homosexual desires or with his sermons against encouraging lustful thoughts of any kind.

In connection with this aversion therapy program, Apostles Spencer W. Kimball and Mark E. Petersen informed Wilkinson in 1962 that "no one will be admitted as a student at the B.Y.U. whom we have convincing evidence is a homosexual."[74] That same year, Petersen required full-time missionaries to sleep in separate beds in Britain and western Europe, while he presided over the missions there.[75] General authorities had long since stopped sleeping together during travel assignments, and he now prohibited young missionaries from doing so in their apartments. In Petersen's view, this prevented homoerotic incidents, but his ruling did not become churchwide practice.[76] Petersen's ruling also denied his missionaries the opportunity to fulfill the founding prophet's words that "it is pleasing for friends to lie down together, locked in the arms of love, to sleep and wake in each other's embrace and renew their conversation."[77]

However, LDS presidents David O. McKay (b. 1873) and Joseph Fielding Smith (b. 1876) may have had no knowledge of some of these changes, particularly the aversion therapy program at BYU. From the late 1950s until his death in 1970, McKay was in a weakened physical and mental condition. This was also true of Smith throughout his entire presidency from 1970 to his death in 1972. After the 1950s, LDS administrative initiative and active decision-making were in the hands of First Presidency counselors and apostles who had reached adulthood after the nineteenth century.[78]

Nevertheless, during these years McKay and Smith did sign First Presidency statements that showed increased concern about homoerotic behaviors. In February 1964, the McKay presidency issued a letter to LDS stake presidents and mission presidents that prospective missionaries "found guilty of fornication, of sex perversion, of heavy petting, or of comparable transgressions should not be recommended until the case has been discussed with the bishop and stake president and the visiting [general] Authority."[79] In 1968, the *General Handbook of Instructions* added "homo-sexual acts" to the list of sins for which excommunication was appropriate.[80]

That change at LDS headquarters may have resulted from the discovery that gay men had organized a schismatic Mormon group in Denver, Colorado. In 1966 David-Edward Desmond formed the United Order Family of Christ, which involved only young men. Six years later he wrote: "The ages of our Order are from 18 to 30. Only one member of the Family is over 25." Because of the group's economic communalism ("We hold everything in common"), Desmond acknowledged that his organization was "not for the great majority of the Gay LDS." However, as the spiritual leader, or "First Key," of this little-known group, he may have performed commitment ceremonies for gay male couples.[81]

In March 1970, the Smith presidency sent a letter to stake presidents and mission presidents: "There is much concern on the part of the brethren concerning the apparent increase in homosexuality and other deviations, and we call to your attention a program designed . . . to counsel and direct them back to total normalcy and happiness." The letter designated Apostles Spencer W. Kimball and Mark E. Petersen to "send material and give counsel." In a follow-up letter of December 1970, the Smith Presidency instructed local leaders to "ask direct questions" about homosexuality in pre-mission interviews because one mission president had discovered that a newly assigned missionary elder "admitted to having masturbated in groups with other college students at the BYU which implies possible homosexual activities."[82]

Ironically, during the same time LDS leaders were warning about homoeroticism among missionaries, missionary preparation books were emphasizing same-sex intimacy and instructing young men in particular to love their male missionary companions. A 1968 book referred to the challenge of young missionaries "living so intimately" with their companions and compared this twenty-four-hour-a-day relationship with marriage.[83] Every mission preparation book emphasized that missionaries must feel love for their companions and express this love verbally to the companion. One book titled *The Effective Missionary,* published by the LDS Church's Deseret Book Company, affirmed: "Four of the sweetest words that every mission president likes to hear are: 'I love my companion.'"[84]

This same book also drew a stark comparison between the homoemotionalism of missionary companionships and the emotionally distant relationships between most young men in midtwentieth-century America. The book noted one young man's words during a meeting: "I love you missionaries. When I was home I never had a friend. Nobody loved me. Here in the mission field I feel that I have true friends, and I know that you love me."[85] An LDS mission was rarely the first introduction of a young man to male-male love in the nonhomophobic nineteenth century, when teenage friends and adult men held hands in public, called each other "David and Jonathan," kissed on the lips publicly, and followed their prophet's counsel to sleep with a same-sex friend "locked in the arms of love."[86]

Moreover, by comparison with the Mormon leadership's fear of homoerotic situations among missionaries in the late twentieth century, there has been greater fear of allowing a companion any opportunity to find opposite-sex intimacy. "If your companion goes to the restroom," one book stated, "you go and stand outside the restroom."[87] This joined-at-the-hip emphasis was an extreme reformulation of earlier missionary policy. Until the midtwentieth century, Mormon leaders raised in the nineteenth century had emphasized the importance of staying with one's assigned companion, but allowed missionaries to make exceptions if one "is fulfilling an assignment which makes it necessary to travel alone."[88]

Then in July 1972, Harold B. Lee (b. 1899) became president of the LDS Church. He was the first LDS president who reached adulthood in the twentieth century. His presidential tenure lasted barely seventeen months before his sudden death of a coronary. However, during that brief time, Lee issued two public documents about homosexuality. In

February 1973, the *Priesthood Bulletin* published a First Presidency statement that "homosexuality in men and women runs counter to . . . divine objectives and, therefore, is to be avoided and forsaken. . . . Failure to work closely with one's bishop or stake president in cases involving homosexual behavior will require prompt Church court action." Before Lee's death in December 1973, LDS headquarters also published *Homosexuality: Welfare Services Packet*.[89]

Consistent with his decades of behind-the-scenes emphasis, Spencer W. Kimball increased the public discourse about homosexuality after he became LDS president in December 1973. By fall 1974 non-Utah newspapers were reporting Kimball's talks against homosexuality, which eventually gained the attention of the *New York Times*.[90]

Kimball even issued a First Presidency statement in apparent response to the publication of Utah's first newspaper for lesbians and gay men. On 30 May 1975, he and his counselors wrote "about the unfortunate problem of homosexuality which occurs from time to time among our people" and referred to the length of time it took "to conquer the habit." Three days earlier Salt Lake City's *Gayzette* had published its first issue, to which the Kimball letter seemed a rushed response.[91]

In fact, beginning in October 1976 homosexuality was a central argument of the Kimball presidency against ratification of the proposed Equal Rights Amendment to the U.S. Constitution.[92] That same year LDS headquarters replaced "homo-sexual acts" with "homosexuality" as grounds for excommunication. This seemed to make Mormons vulnerable to church punishment for their homosexual orientation, even if they had not engaged in sexual activities.[93] During the next year's bitter conflicts at state meetings of the International Women's Year, preconvention lectures at LDS chapels in Utah and other states even accused pro-ERA women of being lesbians.[94]

The low point in the Mormon hierarchy's homophobia since the 1950s was Apostle Boyd K. Packer's talk at the general priesthood meeting in October 1976. Born in 1924, Packer encouraged young men to physically assault any male who tried to "entice young men to join them in these immoral acts." As an example, Packer told about a full-time missionary who knocked his assigned companion to the floor for showing a sexual interest in him. "Somebody had to do it," the apostle told the young men of the LDS Church. Packer said that his position as a general authority was all that kept him from striking homosexual missionaries. Packer told the young man to feel no regret about beating up the missionary who demonstrated a same-sex interest.[95] There are no available statistics to measure whether "gay bashings" increased in Utah after Packer's 1976 sermon.[96] He is now the "acting-president" of the Quorum of the Twelve Apostles,[97] but it is beyond the scope of this study to examine more recent developments of same-sex issues within Mormonism.

Boyd K. Packer's 1976 talk is a convenient stopping point for this summary of the decline of nineteenth-century Mormon attitudes toward same-sex dynamics and homoeroticism. Packer's sermon about beating up homosexually oriented missionaries was one hundred years after LDS leaders in Salt Lake City sent a young man on a special mission because of his "improper connexion" with another man. The Mormon worldview had changed dramatically, and same-sex relationships were part of that change.

NOTES

1. For example, see George Chauncey Jr., "Christian Brotherhood or Sexual Perversion?: Homosexual Identities and the Construction of Sexual Boundaries in the World War One Era," *Journal of Social History* 19 (Winter 1985): 189–212; John Donald Wrathall, "American Manhood and the Y.M.C.A., 1868–1920" (Ph.D. diss., University of Minnesota, 1994), esp. 58, 65–66.

2. J. Golden Kimball to Elias S. Kimball, 14 July 1902, in J. Golden Kimball 1888–1902 letterbook, 466, Archives, Historical Department of the Church of Jesus Christ of Latter-day Saints, Salt Lake City, Utah (hereafter LDS Archives); entry for J. Golden Kimball in Ancestral File, Family History Library of the Church of Jesus Christ of Latter-day Saints, Salt Lake City, Utah (hereafter LDS Ancestral File and LDS Family History Library). The cousin was *not* Spencer W. Kimball, who has central importance later in this chapter.

3. J. Golden Kimball diary, 14 June 1897, 6 Nov. 1898, 23 Dec. 1901, photocopies of original holographs, Manuscripts Division, J. Willard Marriott Library, University of Utah, Salt Lake City, Utah (hereafter Marriott Library).

4. Anthon H. Lund diary, 9 May 1913, microfilm, LDS Archives. The Lund diary microfilm is available to all researchers at LDS Archives by stipulation of its donor, and will be published in edited form by Signature Books, Salt Lake City. For this well-established use of *connexion* and *connection* to mean sexual intercourse, see James A. H. Murray, ed., *A New English Dictionary*, 14 vols. (Oxford: Clarendon Press, 1888–1928), 2:839, which cited published references as early as 1744.

5. "James Dwyer, Pioneer Bookman of West, Goes to Last Reward," *Deseret Evening News,* 13 Jan. 1915, 2; see also John Henry Smith, "An Historical Sketch of the Latter-day Saints' University," 7, bound typescript, Nov. 1913, Special Collections, Marriott Library.

6. Jean Gould, *Amy: The World of Amy Lowell and the Imagist Movement* (New York: Dodd, Mead, 1975), 123, 194–95, 258; C. David Heymann, *American Aristocracy: The Lives and Times of James Russell Lowell, Amy, and Robert Lowell* (New York: Dodd, Mead, 1980), 211; Thomas Cowan, *Gay Men and Women Who Enriched the World* (New Canaan, Conn.: Mulvey Books, 1988), 131; see also chap. 6.

7. John Henry Evans, "Some Men Who Have Done Things," *Improvement Era* 14 (June 1911): 696, 701, 702.

8. Lund diary, entry for 9 May 1913, which lacked the exclamation points, shorthand, or foreign-language entries that Lund used for entries he regarded as shocking or sensational; see also biographical entries for Lund in *Deseret News 1995–1996 Church Almanac: The Church of Jesus Christ of Latter-day Saints* (Salt Lake City: Deseret News, 1994), 45; D. Michael Quinn, *The Mormon Hierarchy: Extensions of Power* (Salt Lake City: Signature Books/Smith Research Associates, 1995).

9. Lund diary, 9 May 1913. James Dwyer was not listed as a church member in the LDS Church census for 1914, LDS Family History Library.

10. Lester E. Bush Jr., "Excommunication and Church Courts: A Note from the *General Handbook of Instructions,*" *Dialogue: A Journal of Mormon Thought* 14 (Summer 1981): 79.

11. Andrew Jenson, *Latter-day Saint Biographical Encyclopedia,* 4 vols. (Salt Lake City: Deseret News Press and Andrew Jenson History, 1901–36), 2:78, 3:285–86; "Excommunication," *Deseret Evening News,* 3 Oct. 1910, 1; "Excommunication," *Deseret Evening News,* 31 Mar. 1914, 1.

12. "James Dwyer," *Improvement Era* 18 (Feb. 1915): 374. For Smith, see *Deseret News 1995–1996 Church Almanac,* 42–43; Quinn, *Extensions of Power.*

13. Mildred J. Berryman, "The Psychological Phenomena of the Homosexual," rough-typed on the back of stationery of the American Red Cross, Salt Lake City, Utah, with the last page of the study dated 13 Nov. 1938, in the June Mazer Lesbian Collection, West Hollywood, Calif.; see also the analysis of her study in chap. 7, its notes 3 and 5 for discussion of when she began the study, and its note 11 for her Mormon affiliation.

14. Berryman, in "Psychological Phenomena," 43–44, said that female case 5 was born "of Dutch parentage who came to America for religious reasons. . . . There are several children in the family and Z is about in the middle of the group. Z. suspects her brother who is a twin to a girl of being homosexual." As the second of six or seven children, Cora Kasius was not quite "in

the middle," but her brother Sam (whose birth date is presently unknown) may have been the twin of her sister Effie M. Kasius. See 1910 U.S. Census of Ogden, Weber County, Utah, enumeration district 231, sheets 8–A, 8–B, microfilm, LDS Family History Library, for Andrew Kasius and wife Effie (both born in Holland) and six of their children; entry for Andrew Kasius, 1920 LDS Church census, LDS Family History Library; 1920 U.S. Census of Ogden, Weber County, Utah, enumeration district 163, sheet 13, microfilm, LDS Family History Library; "Merchant Dies after Lingering Illness," *Deseret News,* 18 Nov. 1921, 6, the only source to mention her brother Sam, who was listed among the siblings in the chronological place of her sister Effie. The lack of an entry for Cora Kasius in the LDS Patriarchal Blessing Index (1833–1963), LDS Family History Library, is also consistent with Berryman's description of female case 5: "She has been more or less a source of worry to her father because she could not accept the chosen faith" ("45," should be 44). If Cora Kasius was female case 5, this indicates that her prominent association with the LDS Relief Society was motivated by her interest in social work, not by her personal faith in Mormonism.

15. "Interview with L.H. on 8 Aug. 1988, and interview with J.B.B. on 7 January 1990," as cited in Rocky O'Donovan, "'The Abominable and Detestable Crime against Nature': A Brief History of Homosexuality and Mormonism, 1840–1980," in Brent Corcoran, ed., *Multiply and Replenish: Mormon Essays on Sex and Family* (Salt Lake City: Signature Books, 1994), 165n30, for discussion of Cora Kasius as "another Mormon Lesbian" (131); "Utah Woman to Join Dutch Welfare Group," *Deseret News,* 8 Mar. 1945, 11; Berryman, "Psychological Phenomena."

16. *Salt Lake City Directory, 1920* (Salt Lake City: R. L. Polk, 1920), 497; *Salt Lake City Directory, 1923* (Salt Lake City: R. L. Polk, 1923), 520; *Salt Lake City Directory, 1925* (Salt Lake City: R. L. Polk, 1925), 680; Cora Kasius, "The Relief Society Social Service Institute," *Relief Society Magazine* 12 (June 1925): 345–49; *Salt Lake City Directory, 1927* (Salt Lake City: R. L. Polk, 1927), 663; "Utah Woman to Join Dutch Welfare Group," 11; Jill Mulvay Derr, Janath Russell Cannon, and Maureen Ursenbach Beecher, *Women of Covenant: The Story of Relief Society* (Salt Lake City: Deseret Book, 1992), 236.

17. Cora Kasius, "Searching for Unwritten Manuscripts," *Highlights: Family Welfare Association of America* 1 (1941): 158–59; "To Take UNRRA Training before Going to Holland: Miss Cora Kasius," *New York Times,* 8 Mar. 1945, 5; "A Change in Leadership," *Journal of Social Casework* 28 (Jan. 1947): 35; Cora Kasius, "Casework Developments in Europe," *Social Casework* 32 (July 1951): 281–88; Margaret E. Rich, *A Belief in People: A History of Family Social Work* (New York: Family Service Association of America, 1956), 150; "A Change in Leadership," *Social Casework* 45 (Dec. 1964): 610; "1965

NCSW Awards," *Social Casework* 46 (June 1965): 363. The publications by Cora Kasius include *Relief Practice in a Family Agency: Family Service, Community Service Society of New York* (New York: Family Welfare Association of America, 1942); *Nancy Clark, Social Worker* (New York: Dodd, Mead, 1949); *A Comparison of Diagnostic and Functional Casework Concepts: A Report* (New York: Family Service Association of America, 1950); *Principles and Techniques in Social Casework: Selected Articles, 1940–1950* (New York: Family Service Association of America, 1950); *New Directions in Social Work* (New York: Harper, 1954); and *Social Casework in the Fifties: Selected Articles, 1951–1960* (New York: Family Service Association of America, 1962).

18. Jenson, *Latter-day Saint Biographical Encyclopedia,* 4:246; entry for Norval M. Service (b. 8 Jan. 1905) in Deceased LDS Members File (1941–74), LDS Family History Library. The identity of Patriarch Joseph F. Smith's "young man," Norval Service, was revealed in an interview with LDS Church Patriarch Eldred G. Smith on 18 June 1977, 28, transcript in my possession, also my handwritten notes of Eldred Smith's statements at his home in Salt Lake City. O'Donovan, in "'Abominable and Detestable Crime,'" 167n75, also refers to "N***** S*******" as "the boy" involved with Patriarch Joseph F. Smith in 1946, apparently without recognizing that Norval was forty-one years old then. For Eldred Smith and basketball player Norval Service as graduating seniors in a small high school, see *The S Book, Nineteen Twenty-Five* (Salt Lake City: Associated Students of the Latter-day Saints University, 1925), 68, 70, 149, and the above interview; for Joseph F. Smith's position in 1923–25 as an instructor at the University of Utah, see *Salt Lake City Directory, 1923,* 883; *University of Utah Official Directory of the Student Body, 1923–24* (Salt Lake City: University of Utah, 1923), 10; *Catalogue of the University of Utah: The School of Arts and Sciences, the School of Education, the State Schools of Mines and Engineering, the School of Medicine, the School of Law, the School of Commerce and Finance, the Extension Division, Announcements for 1924–25 with Lists of Students during 1923–24* (Salt Lake City: University of Utah, 1924), 25.

19. *The S Book of 1924: The Annual of the Latter-Day Saints High School* (Salt Lake City: Associated Students of Latter-day Saints High School, 1924), 106, 120, 122, 157; see chap. 8 for the Stephens-Packham relationship.

20. For Joseph F. Smith's arrival as an instructor at the University of Utah in 1926, the only year Norval Service attended there, see *University of Utah Official Directory of the Student Body, 1926–1927* (Salt Lake City: University of Utah, 1926), 11, 57.

21. Joseph Fielding Smith, "Joseph F. Smith, Patriarch to the Church," *Improvement Era* 45 (Nov. 1942): 694–95; *Champaign and Urbana City Directory, 1926* (Champaign, Ill.: Flanigan-Pearson, 1926). Whether by coincidence or possibly as the professor's first introduction to the Service fami-

ly, Norval's older brother Clyde R. Service was a full-time missionary in England while Smith attended London University in 1924–25. However, Clyde's missionary assignment was in northern England that year, which would have limited the possibility of his becoming acquainted with Smith in London. Like Smith on 5 September 1925, Clyde also booked passage from Liverpool to Chicago instead of to Salt Lake City like the other LDS passengers sailing with Clyde Service on 6 November 1925. However, all missionaries traveling with Clyde Service likewise booked their passage to Chicago. The reason for that Chicago booking is unclear, but Clyde Service was not the "Clyde C. Servis" living in Urbana at the same time as Professor Joseph F. Smith in 1925–26. The Champaign and Urbana directories show that various members of the Servis family had also lived at the same address in 1924 while the unrelated Service was a missionary in England. Clyde Service's parents resided in Salt Lake City during his mission, and he returned to live with them on 18 November 1925 at which time Professor Smith was in Illinois. Therefore, during 1924–25 Smith may have never met the brother of his future boyfriend. Despite the name coincidence, the Servis living in Urbana was not the young man with whom Smith was sexually involved. See "Branch Conferences," *Latter-day Saints Millennial Star* 87 (17 Sept. 1925): 608; "Branch Conferences," *Latter-day Saints Millennial Star* 87 (8 Oct. 1925): 655; "Socials," *Latter-day Saints Millennial Star* 87 (12 Nov. 1925): 735; "Departures," *Latter-day Saints Millennial Star* 87 (12 Nov. 1925): 733; LDS Passenger Lists of British Mission (1914–25), 94, 95, and Ensign Ward Form E report for missionaries in 1925, LDS Family History Library.

22. See Deceased LDS Members File (1941–74) and Norval M. Service's obituary in *Deseret News,* 11 Aug. 1971, B-11; Smith, "Joseph F. Smith, Patriarch to the Church," 694–95; *Salt Lake City Directory, 1926* (Salt Lake City: R. L. Polk, 1926), 952, 977; *Salt Lake City Directory, 1927,* 989, 1016, 1278; *Salt Lake City Directory, 1928* (Salt Lake City: R. L. Polk, 1928), 1014, 1043, 1314.

23. Ralph G. Smith interview, 17 June 1977, 16, transcript in my possession and also my handwritten notes of the interview at his apartment in Salt Lake City. His full statement was that Joseph F. Smith "was known to be a homosexual [in 1942]. My brother, John [Gibbs Smith], was very, very upset because he was Captain of the anti-vice squad at the Salt Lake Police Department. Why, he says, the man's got a record. He says, we've had many women call in and complain about him molesting their little boys [over eighteen years old, actually] at the school at the University of Utah." For the patriarchal appointments of Joseph F. Smith and his successor, Eldred G. Smith, see *Deseret News 1995–1996 Church Almanac,* 57–58

24. Statement of Freda Hammond as reported in Eldred G. Smith interview, 28; compare with references to Joseph F. Smith (b. 1899) in Heber J. Grant

typed journal, 14 Sept., 17 Sept., 1–2 Oct., 10 Oct. 1942, 27 Feb. 1943, LDS Archives. Eldred Smith's reference to "Freda Hammond" blended the names of Winnifred Haymond and Freda Tiemersma, two young women who graduated with him and Norval Service from the LDS high school. Freda Tiemersma did not marry a man named Hammond, and it is presently uncertain which of the two young women knew about the sexual relationship between her friend Norval Service and Joseph F. Smith. See *The S Book, Nineteen Twenty-Five,* 60, 68, 70, 72.

25. Based on my research in the diaries of Presidents Heber J. Grant and George Albert Smith, of Counselors J. Reuben Clark and David O. McKay, and of Apostles Joseph Fielding Smith, George F. Richards, Richard R. Lyman, Sylvester Q. Cannon, and Spencer W. Kimball. However, based on "Eldred G. Smith Personal Records," Irene M. Bates and E. Gary Smith in *Lost Legacy: The Mormon Office of Presiding Patriarch* (Urbana: University of Illinois Press, 1996), 200n49, state: "In 1944 Ralph [G. Smith] went with his brother John, a police inspector, to tell President Grant about Joseph F. Smith II's alleged homosexual activity." While it is very difficult to believe that Heber J. Grant would simply ignore such an alleged report, from 1932 to 1942 the church president's diary indicated that these brothers were bitter about his decision not to appoint their nephew Eldred G. Smith as the church's patriarch. That being the case, it is conceivable that Grant could have dismissed such a report in 1944 as malicious and not worth investigating.

The above quote's use of "II" (sometimes "III" in other sources), reflects the inaccurate designation many Mormons gave to Patriarch Joseph F. Smith (b. 1899) to distinguish him from his grandfather, church president Joseph F. Smith, his uncle Apostle Joseph Fielding Smith (formerly Joseph F. Smith Jr.), and his first cousin Joseph Fielding Smith Jr. (not a general authority). Patriarch Joseph F. Smith was neither Jr., nor II, nor III, having been born as the son of Hyrum M. Smith.

26. Reported by Norval Service's friend Freda in Eldred G. Smith interview, 28. See note 24.

27. "Patriarch to the Church: Released from Duties," *Improvement Era* 49 (Nov. 1946): 685, 708, with his letter of resignation dated 3 Oct. 1946. Previous references to the homosexual background for Patriarch Smith's 1946 release have appeared in "Grey Matters: The Office of Patriarch," *Seventh East Press* (Provo, Utah) 2 (17 Nov. 1982): 15, 17; Irene May Bates, "Transformation of Charisma in the Mormon Church: A History of the Office of Presiding Patriarch, 1833–1979" (Ph.D. diss., University of California at Los Angeles, 1991), 328–29; O'Donovan, "'Abominable and Detestable Crime,'" 145–46; Bates and Smith, *Lost Legacy,* 195–96, 200n54.

28. Concerning B—— D—— B—— (twenty-one years old) in the 1946 homosexual scandal are *Salt Lake City Directory (Salt Lake County, Utah), 1946* (Salt Lake City: R. L. Polk, 1946), 129; George Albert Smith diary, 10

July, 16 Sept. 1946, George A. Smith Family Collection, Manuscripts Division, Marriott Library; J. Reuben Clark office diary, 16 Sept., 25 Oct. 1946, Department of Special Collections and Manuscripts, Harold B. Lee Library, Brigham Young University, Provo, Utah (hereafter Lee Library); *Utonian 1948* (Salt Lake City: Junior Class, University of Utah, 1948), 78; David O. McKay office diary, 10 Apr. 1957, 10 July, 9 Dec. 1957, and statement in undated (Apr. 1957) document in "Joseph F. Smith of Honolulu" File, David O. McKay Papers, LDS Archives. O'Donovan, in "'Abominable and Detestable Crime,'" 167n75, suggested another male ("A******** R***** B********") as "the boy" in the 1946 scandal, due to circumstantial evidence. However, B——— D——— B——— was specifically identified as "the boy" in the First Presidency Papers connected with the former patriarch's restoration to full church privileges in 1957. Also, O'Donovan's letter to me on 17 June 1991 stated that A——— R——— B——— was a thirty-three-year-old non-Mormon in 1946. However, "the boy" in the 1946 crisis was a Mormon who disclosed his relationship with the patriarch when the young man was asked to become an LDS missionary, all of which contradicts A——— R——— B———'s biographical information. See the following discussion.

29. B——— D——— B——— was enrolled at the University of Utah in the fall 1942 quarter and the winter 1943 quarter, according to a statement to me by the Registrar's Office, University of Utah, 8 July 1994; see also *Official Directory of the University of Utah, 1942–1943* (Salt Lake City: University of Utah, 1943), 32; University of Utah Board of Regents Minute Book (1942–43), 73 (11 Dec. 1942), Manuscripts Division, Marriott Library, for appointment of Joseph F. Smith as "Part-time instructor—Winter and Spring Quarters," due to his recent appointment as church patriarch; B——— D——— B——— in Military Service Cards (1898–1975), Reel 57, Series 85268, Utah State Archives, Salt Lake City, Utah.

30. Eldred G. Smith interview, 27. As early as February 1946, this young man's LDS father had been visiting Joseph F. Smith due to the patriarch's being bedridden with back pain. The patriarch's back problems during this period appeared in George Albert Smith diary, 26 Feb. 1946; "'Pygmalion' Highlights Theater's Jubilee," *Daily Utah Chronicle*, 9 May 1946, 1; Frank Evans (financial secretary of the First Presidency) diary, 27 May 1946, LDS Archives; Clark office diary, 29 May 1946; and Joseph Fielding Smith diary, 29 June 1946, LDS Archives. In his office diary on 16 Sept. and 25 Oct. 1946, Clark also indicated that the young man's father was the one who brought this matter to the First Presidency's attention in 1946 and was the parent with whom the Presidency continued to consult.

31. George Albert Smith diary, 10 July 1946; Joseph Fielding Smith diary, 10 July 1946. For these two Smiths, see *Deseret News 1995–1996 Church Almanac,* 43; Quinn, *Extensions of Power.*

32. Bates, "Transformation of Charisma in the Mormon Church," 328–29;

George Albert Smith diary, 10–11 July, 16 Sept. 1946; Joseph Fielding Smith diary, 10 July 1946; Clark office diary, 16 Sept., 25 Oct. 1946; George F. Richards diary, 6 Dec. 1947, LDS Archives. For McKay and Clark, see *Deseret News 1995–1996 Church Almanac*, 43, 46; Quinn, *Extensions of Power*; D. Michael Quinn, *J. Reuben Clark: The Church Years* (Provo, Utah: Brigham Young University, 1983), 83–86, 114–30.

33. Bush, "Excommunication and Church Courts," 80.

34. Joseph F. Smith to Presidents F. Spence and W. H. Seegmiller of Richfield, Utah, 15 Sept. 1882, notes in Folder 22, Box 5, Scott Kenney Papers, Manuscripts Division, Marriott Library; see also chap. 9.

35. George F. Richards diary, 6 Dec. 1947; Frank Evans diary, 19 Mar., 23 Sept. 1947, 15 Mar. 1948; George Albert Smith diary, 16 Aug. 1950.

36. Statements regarding B—— D—— B—— and his father in undated (Apr. 1957) document in "Joseph F. Smith of Honolulu" File; McKay office diary, 10 July 1957.

37. David O. McKay office diary, 9 Dec. 1957; Ruth Pingree Smith to David O. McKay, 13 Apr. 1958; Irene M. Bates to D. Michael Quinn, 22 Jan. 1991; Bates, "Transformation of Charisma in the Mormon Church," 329; LDS Church census for 1960, LDS Family History Library; "Smith Rites Held in S.L.," *Deseret News*, 31 Aug. 1964, A-10; Lawrence Flake, *Mighty Men of Zion: General Authorities of the Last Dispensation* (Salt Lake City: K. D. Butler, 1974), 313.

38. Clark office diary, 2 Nov. 1943; Joseph Fielding Smith diary, 2 Nov., 4 Nov., 11 Nov., 12 Nov. 1943; George Albert Smith diary, 9 Nov., 12 Nov. 1943; George F. Richards diary, 12 Nov. 1943; "Notice of Excommunication," *Deseret Evening News*, 13 Nov. 1943, 1; Richard R. Lyman to Stephen L Richards, 12 Nov. 1949, 10 Apr. 1956, LDS Archives; Edward L. Kimball and Andrew E. Kimball Jr., *Spencer W. Kimball: Twelfth President of the Church of Jesus Christ of Latter-day Saints* (Salt Lake City: Bookcraft, 1977), 209, 346; L. Brent Goates, *Harold B. Lee: Prophet and Seer* (Salt Lake City: Bookcraft, 1985), 183; John R. Sillito, "Enigmatic Apostle: The Excommunication of Richard R. Lyman," paper given at Sunstone Symposium, Salt Lake City, Aug. 1991. For Lyman, see *Deseret News 1995–1996 Church Almanac*, 54; Quinn, *Extensions of Power*.

39. Earl Baird Kofoed, "President George Albert Smith's Stand on Homosexuality," unpublished typescript, with Kofoed's attached note dated 8 February 1995, photocopy in my possession; my telephone interview on 17 May 1995 with Kofoed, who repeated the same details about the incident and gave further information about the two young men and their gay male associates at BYU.

40. Earl Kofoed, "Memories of Being Gay at BYU," *Affinity: Official Publication of Affirmation/Gay and Lesbian Mormons* (Apr. 1993): 9. Kofoed

discussed several of the self-identified gay men at BYU in 1946–48, many of whom met and socialized through French language classes and the French Club: "All of my roommates at BYU were gay. We lived off-campus so we could be independent and have parties and meals with our gay friends. And we were quite a crowd. There was one whose father was a department head at the university and another whose father was an instructor. One friend's brother-in-law later became president of BYU. Another's father was a local stake president. Then there was the handsome young man who later became student body president [actually, president of the sophomore class]" (7). See also *Directory of the Brigham Young University Student Body, 1946–1947* (Provo, Utah: White Keys, Brigham Young University, 1947), 59; *Directory of the Brigham Young University Student Body, 1947–1948* (Provo, Utah: White Keys, Brigham Young University, 1948), 79; *Banyan, 1948* (Provo, Utah: Brigham Young University, 1948), 45, 315, 348, 363.

41. "Earl" to "Dear Jay," 12 March 1995, photocopy in my possession.

42. For the interview reference see George Albert Smith 1948 appointment book, Folder 5, Box 78, Smith Family Papers, Marriott Library. The interview had to occur before his departure from Salt Lake City on the afternoon of 12 April for a trip to Los Angeles. See diary, 12 April 1948, Box 75. However, there are some additional aspects to this entry in the appointment book. Written neatly in black ink with a fountain pen, the words "Homo Sexual" followed the phrase "Meet Stake Pres of St al Jan 17.[19]48 2 pm," yet his diary for January shows neither such a meeting nor such a topic. In blue ink with a ballpoint pen at a later date (possibly much later, due to the shaky handwriting), Smith wrote the word "Psychology" immediately after "Homo Sexual." At the top of the page, this subsequent blue-ink handwriting also added the words "Communists, Sodomites, Valentine." His 1948 diary does not help to explain these fragmentary entries in the appointment book.

43. Glen R. Stubbs, "A Biography of George Albert Smith, 1870 to 1951" (Ph.D. diss., Brigham Young University, 1974), 278–82; Merlo J. Pusey, *Builders of the Kingdom: George A. Smith, John Henry Smith, George Albert Smith* (Provo, Utah: Brigham Young University Press, 1981), 301.

44. Clark office diary, 11 Sept. 1950, quoted in Quinn, *J. Reuben Clark,* 155; see also O'Donovan, "'Abominable and Detestable Crime,'" 146, who specifies that the professor had "sexual relations with several male students," a statement that was not in the Clark diary and is not otherwise substantiated in O'Donovan's source notes.

45. This section of J. Reuben Clark, "Home and the Building of Home Life," *Relief Society Magazine* 39 (Dec. 1952): 793–94, reads in full:

"There are other abominations that go along with this. With genuine apologies, I will mention some by way of warning.

"The person who teaches the non-sinfulness of self-pollution [masturbation] is in the same class with the teachers who prostitute the sex urge [by saying "that the sex urge is like hunger"].

"So also the person who teaches or condones the crimes for which Sodom and Gomorrah were destroyed—we have coined a softer name for them than came from old; we now speak of homosexuality, which, it is tragic to say, is found among both sexes. I wonder if you girls have ever reflected on the thought that was in the mind of the man who first began to praise you for your boyish figures. Not without foundation is the contention of some that the homosexuals are today exercising great influence in shaping our art, literature, music, and drama.

"I forebear to more than mention that abomination of filth and loathsomeness of the ancients—carnal knowledge with beasts."

Since the 1870s, LDS leaders had spoken about masturbation in nongeneral church meetings such as stake priesthood meetings.

46. Kimball and Kimball, *Spencer W. Kimball,* 271, 381–83. However, Spencer W. Kimball was *not* the nephew of J. Golden Kimball, as discussed in the beginning of this chapter.

47. Peter Gay, *The Bourgeois Experience: Victoria to Freud,* vol. 2, *The Tender Passion* (New York: Oxford University Press, 1986), 215.

48. Kimball and Kimball, *Spencer W. Kimball,* 393; Edward L. Kimball and Andrew E. Kimball Jr., *The Story of Spencer W. Kimball: A Short Man, A Long Stride* (Salt Lake City: Bookcraft, 1985), 114, 125. In June 1980 after a dinner at the Lion House in Salt Lake City, for several minutes without interruption Spencer W. Kimball embraced me, repeatedly kissed me, hugged me, and told me he loved me.

49. "Crime against Nature" chapter in Spencer W. Kimball, *The Miracle of Forgiveness* (Salt Lake City: Bookcraft, 1969), esp. 76, 84; see also Kimball, *New Horizons for Homosexuals* (Salt Lake City: The Church of Jesus Christ of Latter-day Saints, 1971); "President Kimball Speaks Out on Morality," *Ensign* 10 (Nov. 1980): 97. For an analysis of Kimball's views and their sources in American popular magazines and medical publications, see O'Donovan, "'Abominable and Detestable Crime,'" 147–49. Also see Vern L. Bullough and Martha Voght, "Homosexuality and Its Confusion with the 'Secret Sin' in Pre-Freudian America," *Journal of the History of Medicine and Allied Sciences* 28 (Apr. 1973): 143–55.

50. Kimball, *The Miracle of Forgiveness,* 86, 81, also 84. However, less than two years after Kimball's death, First Presidency Counselor Gordon B. Hinckley (appointed LDS Church president in 1995) instructed the church's general conference: "Marriage should not be viewed as a therapeutic step to solve such problems as homosexual inclinations or practices." "Reverence and Morality," *Ensign* 17 (May 1987): 47. Although not announced as a policy change, this reversed Spencer W. Kimball's decades of encouragement for homosexu-

ally oriented men to "force" themselves to marry women. In backpedaling from the frequently published counsel of the deceased president Kimball for homosexuals to marry, Apostle Dallin H. Oaks (former Utah Supreme Court judge) had already announced on national television that "he did not know whether individual priesthood leaders have given such advice." See "LDS Policy on Homosexuality Reaffirmed during CBS TV Interview," *Deseret News "Church News,"* 14 Feb. 1987, 12.

51. Bush, "Excommunication and Church Courts," 84–85.

52. A warning of that outcome was announced by a BYU professor and published by the LDS Church newspaper during Kimball's presidency in "Y. Expert Says Marriage Won't Cure Homosexuals," *Deseret News,* 13 Apr. 1979, D-1; see also Carol Lynn Pearson, *Good-Bye, I Love You* (New York: Random House, 1986), 25–27, 30–32, 46–47, 75–82, 91–95; Debra A. Fairchild, "An Exploratory Study of Women Divorced from Homosexual Men Compared to Women Divorced from Heterosexual Men" (M.S. thesis, Brigham Young University, 1988); "Divorce from Gays Called Especially Painful," *Deseret News,* 24 Aug. 1988, B-6; Karen Brown, "One View of a Troubled Relationship," and "A Wife's Story," in Ron Schow, Wayne Schow, and Marybeth Raynes, eds., *Peculiar People: Mormons and Same-Sex Orientation* (Salt Lake City: Signature Books, 1991), 96–102, 103–6; "Why's a Nice Mormon Girl like Me Married to a Gay Man?" *Student Review* (Provo, Utah), 28 Oct. 1992, 13–14; "A Wife's Account," in Dwight Cook, Rob Killian, and Karen Swannack, eds., *Decisions of the Soul: LDS Personal Accounts of Same-Sex Orientation and Opposite-Sex Marriage,* Series 1 of Family Fellowship History Project (Salt Lake City: Intermountain Conference on Sexuality and Homosexuality, 1995), 1–9: Jan Yonally, "Jan's Journey," in Cook, Killian, and Swannack, eds., *Decisions of the Soul,* 132–35; Susan Fullmer, "Lessons from My Gay/Straight Marriage," in Cook, Killian, and Swannack, eds., *Decisions of the Soul,* 164–67; "Homosexuality Comes Out Despite Mormon Doctrine," *Salt Lake Tribune,* 20 May 1995, D-1, D-4. Also, for an unmarried LDS woman's view of the problems involved in dating or pseudo-dating with gay males, see Maxine Hanks, "Guilt: The Gift That Keeps on Giving," unpublished paper, 1987, revised in 1992, copy in Special Collections, Marriott Library.

53. Stephen L Richards office diary, 29 Oct. 1951, LDS Archives; see also *Deseret News 1995–1996 Church Almanac,* 46; Quinn, *Extensions of Power;* see also Gordon B. Hinckley, "An Appreciation of Stephen L Richards," *Improvement Era* 54 (July 1951): 499, for his David-and-Jonathan relationship with David O. McKay.

54. See for example, Joseph Fielding Smith, *Doctrines of Salvation,* 3 vols. (Salt Lake City: Deseret Book, 1955); Joseph Fielding Smith, *Answers to Gospel Questions,* 5 vols. (Salt Lake City: Deseret Book, 1957–66).

55. Bruce R. McConkie, *Mormon Doctrine* (Salt Lake City: Bookcraft, 1958), 104, 639; see also *Deseret News 1995–1996 Church Almanac*, 56. He was obviously unaware of Joseph F. Smith's 1882 letter about the sin of Sodom. See the discussion in chap. 9 of this 1882 letter. See also the earlier discussion in this chapter for Smith's possible modification of that condemnation by 1915.

56. "Suspect Held in Boys Morals Ring," *Salt Lake Tribune*, 13 Feb. 1958, 10; "Police Nab Twenty-Three in Twenty-Seven-Day Morals Drive," *Salt Lake Tribune*, 29 May 1958, 10.

57. "A Wise Court Policy," *Salt Lake Tribune*, 30 Sept. 1958, 12; O. N. Malmquist, *The First One Hundred Years: A History of the* Salt Lake Tribune, *1871–1971* (Salt Lake City: Utah State Historical Society, 1971), 269, 384.

58. McConkie, *Mormon Doctrine* (1958), 108, 130, 549.

59. McKay office diary, 8 Jan., 27 Jan. 1960. This precise number of doctrinal errors was based on a word-for-word examination of the 1958 edition of *Mormon Doctrine* by Apostles Mark E. Petersen and Marion G. Romney.

60. Bruce R. McConkie, *Mormon Doctrine*, 2d ed., rev. (Salt Lake City: Bookcraft, 1966), 111 (for missing entry on capital punishment), 115 (for missing entry on Catholic Church), 139 (for unchanged reference to "carnality"), 611 (for unchanged entry about "justice"), and 708 (for unchanged entry about "sodomy, onanism, and homosexuality").

61. Ernest L. Wilkinson diary, 21 May 1959, photocopy, Manuscripts Division, Marriott Library; Kimball, *Miracle of Forgiveness*, 81–82. Because of Spencer W. Kimball's well-known emphasis that homosexuality was a "habit" rather than a condition, his retelling of McKay's views may have introduced Kimball's own preferred term to a statement that originally lacked the word *habit*.

62. Gordon B. Hinckley, "An Appreciation of Stephen L Richards," *Improvement Era* 54 (July 1951): 499; see also the discussion in chap. 4.

63. Kimball and Kimball, *Spencer W. Kimball*, 381; for Petersen's position, see *Deseret News 1995–1996 Church Almanac*, 55.

64. Wilkinson diary, 21 May 1959.

65. See the previous discussion of Richards and this case.

66. Allen Drury, *Advise and Consent* (Garden City, N.Y.: Doubleday, 1959), 288–89, 419, 431–33, 436–37, 447, 448; see also James Levin, *The Gay Novel in America* (New York: Garland, 1991), 167–68.

67. J. Willard Marriott to Wallace F. Bennett, 25 Sept. 1961, Folder 8, Box 16, Bennett Papers, Manuscripts Division, Marriott Library.

68. Alice Payne Hackett and James Henry Burke, *Eighty Years of Best Sellers, 1895–1975* (New York: R. R. Bowker, 1977), 16, 41, 177, 178, 180; John Bear, *The #1 New York Times Bestseller* (Berkeley, Calif.: Ten Speed Press, 1992), 79; Gita Siegman, *World of Winners: A Current and Historical Perspective on Awards and Their Winners* (Detroit: Gale Research, 1992), 777.

69. Marriott to Bennett, 25 Sept. 1961; Wallace F. Bennett to J. Willard Marriott, 2 Oct. 1961, for reference to Evans's activity regarding *Advise and Consent,* both in Folder 8, Box 16, Bennett Papers; see Leonard J. Arrington, *Service above Self: A History of Salt Lake Rotary Club 24, 1911–1981* (Salt Lake City: Publishers Press, 1981), 46–47, for the role of Evans at this time in Rotary International, over which he would become president in five years. During the same period, in a related effort to prevent the dramatization of Irving Wallace's *Twenty-Seventh Wife,* Evans reported that "the Presidency and all the brethren" had considered purchasing "the stage and screen rights to it [Wallace's book] through a secondary source." See Richard L. Evans to Wallace F. Bennett, 18 Aug. 1961, Folder 20, Box 18, Bennett Papers.

70. Vito Russo, *The Celluloid Closet: Homosexuality in the Movies,* rev. ed. (New York: Harper and Row, 1987), 120–22, 141–43; see Gerald Pratley, *The Cinema of Otto Preminger* (London: A. Zwemmer; New York: A. S. Barnes, 1971), 140, for the interview released by Columbia Pictures.

71. In this added scene, the Utah-Mormon senator entered the gay bar reluctantly in an effort to find his former lover, was repelled by the environment, and ran out. Preminger's attention to detail was so exact that in one scene of the film the Utah senator's LDS temple undergarment (with its distinctively low-cut neckline and thick collar) was clearly visible beneath the Mormon's white shirt as he entered the bedroom of his home. However, in a continuity error of filming, there was no undershirt whatever as the Utah senator reentered the bedroom while taking off his shirt. This was probably an intentional lapse to avoid cinematic display of a garment sacred to Mormons. However, this 1962 film portrayed the Utah senator as revolted by homoeroticism and also included a scene in which Anderson angrily rejected his former lover. By contrast, the novel showed this fictitious Mormon's fond memory of the homosexual relationship, his lingering affection during the young man's apology for being the cause of the senator's downfall, and the young man's suicide after learning of the senator's suicide. Compare Drury, *Advise and Consent,* 288–89, 433, 437, 448, with the commercially available videotape of the Hollywood film, which showed the Utah senator drinking a soft drink at home, shortly before the scene showing his temple undergarment.

72. For an analysis of this time period in Mormonism from the perspective of a self-proclaimed "Gay" radical (who insists on the capitalization), see O'Donovan, "'Abominable and Detestable Crime,'" 123, 147–63; see also chap. 1 and chap. 10 for discussions of homosexual and lesbian issues at Brigham Young University and this chapter's note 96 on violence in Utah against gays and lesbians.

73. Max Ford McBride, "Effect of Visual Stimuli in Electric Aversion Therapy" (Ph.D. diss., Brigham Young University, 1976), 42–60, esp. 46, 48, 58; Elizabeth C. James, "Treatment of Homosexuality: A Reanalysis and Synthe-

sis of Outcome Studies" (Ph.D. diss., Brigham Young University, 1978); B. Roy Julian, "Male Homosexuality: A Theoretical and Philosophical Analysis and Integration of Etiology" (Ph.D. diss., Brigham Young University, 1978); Gary James Bergera and Ronald Priddis, *Brigham Young University: A House of Faith* (Salt Lake City: Signature Books, 1983), 83–89, 122, 126–27, 324, 422n71; Pearson, *Good-Bye, I Love You*, 98–99.

74. Wilkinson diary, 12 Sept. 1962.

75. Mark E. Petersen made this ruling soon after his appointment in 1962 to preside over the LDS missions in Great Britain, Ireland, and parts of western Europe. I was told of this change by British missionaries, who commented on the financial difficulties it caused British widows who had housed missionaries for years, but had to dispose of a double bed and purchase two single beds.

76. For example, one former missionary reports that due to overcrowding at the Language Training Mission in July–August 1974, LDS missionaries were housed at hotels in Provo, Utah. Four missionaries were assigned to a room with two queen-sized beds. This overcrowding continued until the completion of the first stage of the dormitory-like Missionary Training Center in 1976. Author's interview with Gary James Bergera, 6 Mar. 1995.

77. Joseph Smith statement, 16 Aug. 1843, in Brigham H. Roberts, ed., *History of the Church of Jesus Christ of Latter-day Saints*, 7 vols., 2d ed., rev. (Salt Lake City: Deseret Book, 1978), 5:361.

78. Quinn, *J. Reuben Clark*, 128, 141–42; Edwin B. Firmage, ed., *An Abundant Life: The Memoirs of Hugh B. Brown* (Salt Lake City: Signature Books, 1988), 141–43; Eugene E. Campbell's typed draft of Hugh B. Brown biography, chapter titled, "Responsibility Without Authority—The 1st Counselor Years," 13, Eugene E. Campbell Papers, Department of Special Collections and Manuscripts, Lee Library; Goates, *Harold B. Lee*, 410–12; D. Michael Quinn, *The Mormon Hierarchy: Origins of Power* (Salt Lake City: Signature Books/ Smith Research Associates, 1994), 256–58.

79. Circular letter of David O. McKay, Hugh B. Brown, and N. Eldon Tanner to "All Stake Presidents and Mission Presidents," 12 Feb. 1964, photocopy in my possession, obtained through a local LDS officer.

80. Bush, "Excommunication and Church Courts," 84.

81. David-Edward Desmond to David C. Martin in *Restoration Reporter* 2 (Feb. 1973): 2, reprinted in Steven L. Shields, *Divergent Paths of the Restoration: A History of the Latter Day Movement*, 3d ed. (Bountiful, Utah: Restoration Research, 1982), 175–76; see also *Restoration Reporter* 2 (Nov. 1972): 1, for information that "a 'homosexual Church of Jesus Christ' has been organized in Denver." "David-Edward Desmond" was apparently an alias, since no one by either of those first names appears in the LDS Ancestral File, LDS Patriarchal Blessing Index (1833–1963), or LDS Church censuses for 1950–60. Because

so little is known about Desmond's group, there is no estimate of its highest membership level. Nor is it certain that the male couples received an equivalent of the LDS ordinance of "marriage for time and all eternity."

82. Circular letters from Joseph Fielding Smith, Harold B. Lee, and N. Eldon Tanner to "ALL STAKE PRESIDENTS AND MISSION PRESIDENTS," 19 Mar. 1970, and from Joseph Fielding Smith, Harold B. Lee, and N. Eldon Tanner to "Stake Presidents, Bishops, and Branch Presidents," 23 Dec. 1970, photocopies in my possession, obtained through a local LDS officer.

83. Barbara Tietjen Jacobs, *So You're Going on a Mission?* (Provo, Utah: Press Publishing, 1968), 101.

84. Rulon G. Craven, *The Effective Missionary* (Salt Lake City: Deseret Book, 1982), 56; see also Jack Stephan Bailey, *Inside a Mormon Mission: The Candid Story of a Faithful Mormon Missionary* (Salt Lake City: Hawkes, 1976), 68–69; G. Hugh Allred and Steve H. Allred, *How to Make a Good Mission Great* (Salt Lake City: Deseret Book, 1978), 15; Elaine Cannon and Ed. J. Pinegar, *Called to Serve Him: Preparing Missionaries to Bring People to Christ* (Salt Lake City: Bookcraft, 1991), 93.

85. Craven, *The Effective Missionary,* 54.

86. Roberts, *History of the Church,* 5:361; see also chaps. 3 and 4.

87. Cannon and Pinegar, *Called to Serve Him,* 93; see also the similar emphasis in *Missionary Handbook Supplement* (Provo, Utah: Missionary Training Center, 1976), [1].

88. Heber J. Grant, J. Reuben Clark, David O. McKay, the First Presidency of the Church of Jesus Christ of Latter-day Saints, *The Missionary's Hand Book* (Independence, Mo.: Zion's Printing and Publishing, 1937), 26.

89. *Priesthood Bulletin* (Salt Lake City: Church of Jesus Christ of Latter-day Saints, Feb. 1973); *Homosexuality: Welfare Services Packet* (Salt Lake City: Church of Jesus Christ of Latter-day Saints, 1973). For Lee, see *Deseret News 1995–1996 Church Almanac,* 43; Goates, *Harold B. Lee.*

90. Spencer W. Kimball, *President Kimball Speaks Out* (Salt Lake City: Deseret Book, 1981), 10–12; Edward L. Kimball, ed., *The Teachings of Spencer W. Kimball, Twelfth President of the Church of Jesus Christ of Latter-day Saints* (Salt Lake City: Bookcraft, 1982), 274–78, 282; "Mormon President Raps Homosexuals," *Advocate* 150 (6 Nov. 1974): 15; "Mormon President Kimball Demands Homosexuals Avoid Their Obscene Past and Conform to Church," *Vanguard, Portland State University* 31 (28 Oct. 1975): 3; "Mormon Church Elder Calls Homosexuality an Addiction," *New York Times,* 6 Apr. 1981, A-12.

91. Circular letter of Spencer W. Kimball, N. Eldon Tanner, and Marion G. Romney, 30 May 1975, photocopy in my possession, obtained through a local LDS officer; *Gayzette,* 27 May 1975, copy in Special Collections, Marriott Library.

92. "LDS Leaders Oppose ERA," *Deseret News,* 22 Oct. 1976, B-1; "Church Leaders Reaffirm ERA Stand," *Deseret News "Church News,"* 26 Aug. 1978, 2; Peter James Caulfield, "Rhetoric and the Equal Rights Amendment: Contemporary Means of Persuasion" (D.A. diss., University of Michigan, 1984), 136–37; D. Michael Quinn, "The LDS Church's Campaign against the Equal Rights Amendment," *Journal of Mormon History* 20 (Fall 1994): 138–39.

93. Bush, "Excommunication and Church Courts," 84.

94. "Honolulu Stake Workshop Assignments," July 1977, Folder 1, Collection of Conservative Women Opposed to the Equal Rights Amendment," Department of Special Collections and Manuscripts, Lee Library; "Bitter Battle Expected at Women's Meeting," *Honolulu Star-Bulletin,* 8 July 1977; Linda Sillitoe, "Women Scorned: Inside the IWY Conference," *Utah Holiday* 6 (Aug. 1977): 63; transcript of an untitled talk by LDS Assemblywoman Karen Hayes at the Las Vegas Second and Eighth Wards meetinghouse, 15 Feb. 1978, 4–6, Folder 7, Box 7, Sonia Johnson Papers, Manuscripts Division, Marriott Library; Dixie Snow Huefner, "Church and Politics at the Utah IWY Conference," *Dialogue: A Journal of Mormon Thought* 11 (Spring 1978): 64; Lisa Bolin Hawkins, "Report on the Utah International Women's Year Meeting," 7–8, Folder 5, Box 2, Collection of Utah Women's Issues, Manuscripts Division, Marriott Library; Quinn, "Church's Campaign against the Equal Rights Amendment," 113, 118; Martha Sonntag Bradley, "The Mormon Relief Society and the International Women's Year Conference," *Journal of Mormon History* 21 (Spring 1995): 139–40.

95. *Conference of the Church of Jesus Christ of Latter-day Saints, October 1, 2, 3, 1976 with Report of Discourses* (Salt Lake City: Church of Jesus Christ of Latter-day Saints, 1976), 101. The First Presidency deleted this entire sermon from the publication of conference talks in the church's official magazine, the *Ensign.* However, the talk was officially printed by the LDS Church in 1976 as the pamphlet *To Young Men Only,* which was reprinted in 1980. Packer's October 1976 talk may have been a response to publicity at the University of Utah, Utah State University, and in a Mormon independent journal about gays and lesbians in Mormon society and at Brigham Young University. See "Homosexuals Discuss 'Gayness' and Society," *Daily Utah Chronicle,* 19 Jan. 1976, 1–2; "Utah 'Blue Laws' Are Unenforced," *Daily Utah Chronicle,* 19 Jan. 1976, 3; "Support Gays," *Daily Utah Chronicle,* 22 Jan. 1976, 5; "Graduate Student Studies Lesbian Lifestyle," *Daily Utah Chronicle,* 23 Jan. 1976, 1–2; "God Hates Gays," *Daily Utah Chronicle,* 27 Jan. 1976, 2; "A Jackass," *Daily Utah Chronicle,* 28 Jan. 1976, 3; "Not Sinful," *Daily Utah Chronicle,* 29 Jan. 1976, 5; "Psychological Help," *Daily Utah Chronicle,* 29 Jan. 1976, 5; "Falls Short," *Daily Utah Chronicle,* 3 Feb. 1976, 4–5; Anon., "Lovesong for David," *Crucible* (Utah State University), Spring 1976,

16; Anon., "Solus," *Dialogue: A Journal of Mormon Thought* 10 (Summer 1976): 94–99; Wilford E. Smith, "Mormon Sex Standards on College Campuses, Or Deal Us out of the Sexual Revolution," *Dialogue: A Journal of Mormon Thought* 10 (Autumn 1976): 77 for homoerotic experiences of 10 percent of male students and 2 percent of female students, "Mormons in a large church university" (BYU) during the previous twenty years.

96. Concerning violence against lesbians and gays in Utah, see "Gays Claim Lack of Protection," *Salt Lake Tribune,* 14 Dec. 1978, B-6; "Murder Suspect in Mental Ward: Alarms Gays," *Salt Lake Tribune,* 15 Dec. 1978, B-4; "Violence Charges Mostly Paranoia," *Deseret News,* 15 Jan. 1979, A-5; "'Gay Bashing?' Utahn Guilty of Assault," *Salt Lake Tribune,* 24 Nov. 1988, B-3; Two Men Get Zero-Five Years for Near Fatal Beating," *Deseret News,* 28 Dec. 1988, D-5; "Death of Hitchhiker in Utah Is Linked to a Similar Slaying in Pennsylvania," *Deseret News,* 9 Dec. 1989, B-5; "Hatch Criticized in Hate-Crimes Bill," *Deseret News,* 11 Feb. 1990, B-12; "Jury Finds Wood Guilty of 1988 Torture-Slaying," *Salt Lake Tribune,* 11 Mar. 1990, B-1; "Police Accused of Failing to Aid Gay Crimes Victims," *Deseret News,* 21 Mar. 1990, B-1; "Hate Crimes Prompt Gays to Form Patrols," *Salt Lake Tribune,* 10 Apr. 1990, B-1; "Jury Acquits Salt Lake Men in Slaying," *Deseret News,* 14 Apr. 1990, G-5; "Three Face Assault Charges in 'Gay-Bashing' Incidents," *Deseret News,* 1 Aug. 1990, B-3; "Three Supremacists Sentenced, Fined," *Deseret News,* 14 Jan. 1991, D-6; "Democratic Leader Wants State to Keep Track of Hate Crimes," *Salt Lake Tribune,* 22 Jan. 1991, A-4; "Utah Group Notes 377 Assaults on Gays," *Deseret News,* 22 Jan. 1991, B-5; "Inmate Gets Probation in '88 Beating," *Deseret News,* 25 Jan. 1991, B-10; "S.L. Policeman May Be Linked to Gay-Bashing," *Deseret News,* 14 Mar. 1991, B-1, B-2; "Gay Bashing? Lawman on Suspension: Police Chief, Officer Offer Apologies," *Salt Lake Tribune,* 29 Mar. 1991, B-1; "Hate Crimes Do Occur on WSU's Campus" *Signpost* (29 Jan. 1992): 7, 9; "377 Anti-Gay/Lesbian Acts of Violence in Utah," *Signpost* (29 Jan. 1992): 8–9; "Hate-Crime Bill Opponents Lash Out at Homosexuality during Capitol Hill Debate," *Deseret News,* 29 Jan. 1992, B-12; "Hate-Crimes Bill Now Excludes Gays," *Salt Lake Tribune,* 1 Feb. 1992, B-11; "Reason Falls by Wayside in Fight over Hate Crimes," *Deseret News,* 2 Feb. 1992, A-1; editorial, "Pass Utah 'Hate Crimes' Bills," *Deseret News,* 2 Feb. 1992, A-14; "Diluted Hate-Crimes Bill Will Condone Violence against Gays, Say Activists," *Salt Lake Tribune,* 3 Feb. 1992, B-1; "Angels in America? Not in Utah, Where Book Ban Generates Gay-Bashing," *Salt Lake Tribune,* 19 June 1993, A-7; "Was Car Shooting Directed at Gays?" *Deseret News,* 17 Aug. 1993, B-2; "Was Slaying in Park City a Hate Crime? Sources Close to Probe Say Killer May Have Believed Victim Was Gay," *Deseret News,* 27 Aug. 1993, B-1, B-2; "Gang Rapes of Two Men Spark S.L. Fears of Gay-Bashing Attacks," *Salt Lake Tribune,* 28 Aug. 1993, B-1; "Incidents of Hate Crime Cast

Shadow over Salt Lake," *Deseret News,* 28 Aug. 1993, B-3; "220 Call for an End to Hate Crimes in Utah," *Deseret News,* 2 Sept. 1993, B-13; "Was August Shooting a Hate Crime?" *Deseret News,* 12 Sept. 1993, B-6; "Boy, Sixteen, Will Stand Trial for Capital Murder in Shooting," *Salt Lake Tribune,* 16 Oct. 1993, D-3; "5 Murders, 11 Attempted Murders, 18 Rapes, 31 Acts of Vandalism, 35 Chasings, 43 Death Threats by Mail or Telephone, 104 Beatings, 195 Acts of Verbal Harassment," in Christian P. Brown, "Anti-Gay and Anti-Lesbian Violence," *Pillar of the Gay and Lesbian Community for Utah* (Salt Lake City), Oct. 1993, 7; Mark Jensen, "Gordon," *Sunstone* 17 (June 1994): 20; "Killer's Sentence Too Light, Says Family of Gay Victim," *Salt Lake Tribune,* 16 Aug. 1994, C-1; "Driver Gets Probation for Role in Park City Slaying," *Salt Lake Tribune,* 23 Aug. 1994, C-1; "Utah Hate-Crime Law Sees Its First Case: S.L. Man Who Admits Beating Women Says Lifestyle Wasn't Issue," *Salt Lake Tribune,* 23 Oct. 1994, B-1; *Anti-Violence Project Newsletter* (Salt Lake City) 1994– ; "Man Averts Hate-Crime Prosecution for Assault," *Salt Lake Tribune,* 13 Dec. 1994, C-1; "Officer's Beat: Protect Gays, Lesbians," *Salt Lake Tribune,* 11 Mar. 1995, B-3. For an analysis and statistical profiles of those involved in hate crimes, see Gary David Comstock, *Violence against Lesbians and Gay Men* (New York: Columbia University Press, 1991).

97. *Deseret News 1995–1996 Church Almanac,* 17. In 1996 Packer was also second in line to become LDS president.

Conclusion

ALTHOUGH IT IS ONE of the most significant religious cultures in the United States, Mormonism is still not very far removed in time from its pioneer origins. Because Mormonism originated amidst conflict with the larger American society, many people today overlook the similarities that pioneer Mormonism had with nineteenth-century America. Among those cultural similarities were attitudes toward same-sex dynamics and manifestations of those relationships between persons of the same gender.

Despite its many peculiarities, nineteenth-century Mormon culture was thoroughly American in its same-sex dynamics. Like other Americans of that time, Mormons valued and manifested extensive social interaction, emotional bonding, and physical closeness of males with males and of females with females. Also, like other Americans of that time, the shared religious fervor of individual Mormons intensified their same-sex friendships to the degree that they were indistinguishable from what Americans today call "romantic love." There was a "homocultural orientation" of pre-1900 American society of which Mórmon culture was simply one example. For the vast majority of Americans and Mormons of that era, those same-sex relationships were nonerotic, at least at the conscious level, which is the only level that leaves evidence for historians to examine.

Nevertheless, for some Americans and some Mormons the erotic was part of their same-sex social, emotional, and physical relationships in the nineteenth century and beyond. Unsurprisingly, most nineteenth-century Americans, Mormons, and their institutions expressed disapproval when required to confront homoerotic behaviors. Looking from the twentieth century we expect this disapproval in an age we regard as sexually repressed and religiously defined. However, strange as it may seem to us, even jurists, church leaders, and physicians one hundred years ago did not regard homoerotic behaviors with the same significance most Americans and Mormons presently do.

Because they had a pervasively nonerotic homoculture and because they did not have categories to define "sexuality," nineteenth-century Americans and Mormons responded to homoeroticism in ways that often seem restrained, even tolerant, today. That impression of restraint grows as we compare those nineteenth-century responses to homoeroticism with responses of that era to other nonmarital sexual activities. For many Americans and Mormons today, it is jarring (almost disorienting) to discover such differences in worldview in a culture that is otherwise so familiar. Since we know the general history of that period and since we know what it is like to live in the same country in the twentieth century, we assume that those people thought the same way we think today.

It is in this regard that a cross-cultural perspective is helpful. When we discover that the meaning of same-sex intimacy in Melanesia today differs vastly from ours, that makes it easier for us to understand the contrasts between past and present of both America and of Mormonism. Likewise, our understanding of the homocultural contrasts within America and Mormonism during the past 150 years can also help us to accept that other cultures define sexual identity and same-sex behaviors in ways that are alien to our own. Those differences do not always involve absolutes of approved/disapproved, normal/abnormal, right/wrong, or even defined/undefined. It gives pause to discover that some cultures do not even have words for their accepted same-sex behaviors that many Americans and Mormons consider inappropriate.

In matters of sexual identity and in definitions of sexual behaviors, we grow up expecting every culture and time period to mirror our own views—both individual and cultural. We do not expect to find alien sexualities in foreign cultures, but that is what we encounter when we look at other cultures on their own terms. And in our own culture—American or Mormon—the past sometimes seems alien when compared with behaviors and definitions we have regarded as the norm. The benefit in all this, it seems to me, is to recognize that our personal experience, understanding, and cultural values have limits that can isolate us from our own heritage and alienate us from the diversity of human experience. That perspective is beneficial whether we are responding to past or present, our culture or foreign cultures, our experience or the experience of those who are different from us.

Chronology of Same-Sex Issues in American and Mormon Culture

1610 (24 May)	The colony at Jamestown, Virginia, decreed the death penalty for any "man [who] shall commit the horrible, detestable sin of Sodomie." Several men were executed for sodomy during the following decades.
1636	The Puritan minister John Cotton recommended the death penalty for "carnal fellowship of . . . woman with woman." The Massachusetts Bay Colony did not enact this.
1642 (5 Dec.)	The Massachusetts Bay Colony sentenced Elizabeth Johnson to be "severely whipped" and fined "for unseemly practices betwixt her and another maid."
1649 (6 Mar.)	Judges of the colony at Plymouth, Massachusetts, gave only a stern warning to Sarah Norman (married, age unknown) and Mary Hammon (newly married, age fifteen) "for lewd behavior each with [the] other upon a bed."
1656 (1 Mar.)	The colony at New Haven, Connecticut, decreed the death sentence for female-female acts of "Sodomitical filthiness," as well as for those between men.

1707 (9 Feb.)   A political opponent recommended the replacement of Edward Hyde as governor of New York and New Jersey because of "his dressing publicly in woman's clothes every day." An official portrait shows the governor in women's clothes.

1778 (10 Mar.)   Gen. George Washington ordered the court-martial of Frederick Gotthold Enslin, a lieutenant in the Continental Army, for sodomy.

1778 (19 Mar.)   General von Steuben conducted the first drill of the Continental Army. Unknown to the Americans, he was forced to leave Europe because of a complaint about his same-sex relationships—"having taken familiarities with young boys and which the law forbids and punishes severely." General von Steuben reported to General Washington with a seventeen-year-old Frenchman as his live-in companion and lived with a young American soldier during the latter part of the Revolution.

1779 (18 June)   Thomas Jefferson wrote Virginia's law that decreed castration as the punishment for all men convicted of rape, sodomy, bestiality, or polygamy.

1779   The American John Ledyard commented about the Hawaiian practice of "of sodomy . . . between the chiefs and the most beautiful males they can procure about 17 years old." Young men in this relationship were called *Aikane*. An LDS president's son was later described with this designation.

1798   A visiting writer remarked that some women in Philadelphia were "willing to seek unnatural pleasure with persons of their own sex."

1804 (3 Apr.)   "I don't see how I can live any longer without having a friend near me, I mean a male friend," wrote Daniel Webster, later a U.S. senator. The twenty-two year old explained to his same-aged friend: "Yes, James, I must come; we will yoke together again; your little bed is just wide enough."

1826 (25 Apr.)	Louis Dwight reported his visits to prisons from Massachusetts to Georgia: "THE SIN OF SODOM IS THE VICE OF PRISONS AND BOYS ARE THE FAVORITE PROSTITUTES."
1830 (6 Apr.)	Joseph Smith Jr. organized a new church in which he was "a prophet, a seer, and a revelator." This was less than two weeks after he published the *Book of Mormon* as a new book of holy scripture.
1832 (27 Dec.)	Joseph Smith announced a revelation that included a covenant between men "to be your friend . . . forever and ever."
1833 (24 Jan.)	The male-only School of the Prophets commenced in accordance with a revelation on 27 December 1832.
1835 (Aug.)	Joseph Smith's revelations and commandments were published as *The Doctrine and Covenants,* which included the male-male covenant of 1832.
1836 (30 Mar.)	Joseph Smith washed the feet of the members of the Quorum of the Twelve Apostles, "and then the Twelve proceeded to wash the feet of the Presidents of the several quorums."
1837 (Mar.)	A nineteen-year-old student at Yale wrote of his friend: "Often too he shared my pillow—or I his, and then how sweet to sleep with him, to hold his beloved form in my embrace, to have his arms around my neck, to imprint upon his face sweet kisses!" Albert Carrington was the only early Mormon man to live at an eastern boarding college. Carrington graduated from Dartmouth in 1834 but left no record of his feelings about college roommates or their experiences together.
1837 (8 July)	Mary Fielding Smith, wife of Joseph Smith's counselor Hyrum, wrote: "Some of the Sisters while engaged in conversing in toungues their countenances beaming with joy, clasped each others hands & kissd in the most affectinate manner."
1839 (24 Feb.)	Twenty-seven-year-old Elizabeth Haven wrote her second

cousin Elizabeth Bullard: "If I could sleep with you one night, [I] think we should not be very sleepy," and added, "at least I could converse all night and have nothing but a comma between the sentences, now and then." The two Mormons had been roommates at Amherst College.

1840

Richard Henry Dana's *Two Years before the Mast* referred to his young Hawaiian boy "friend and *aikane*."

1840 (3 Oct.)

The general church conference appointed twenty-nine-year-old Robert B. Thompson as General Church Clerk. His wife later said that he and the church president "truly loved each other with fervent brotherly affection." Joseph Smith told her: "Sister Thompson, you must not feel bad towards me for keeping your husband away from you so much, for I am married to him."

1840 (5 Oct.)

On motion of John C. Bennett, the general conference (presided over by Joseph Smith) voted that no one could be judged guilty of a crime unless proven "by two or three witnesses." This was Bennett's way of shielding his own sexual activities with both women and men.

1841 (19 Jan.)

Joseph Smith announced a revelation containing this statement concerning John C. Bennett: "his reward shall not fail, if he receive counsel; and for his love he shall be great, for he shall be mine if he do this, saith the Lord." Smith appointed John C. Bennett as the assistant counselor to the First Presidency in April.

1841 (27 Oct.)

Joseph Smith married a plural wife who was living with her legal husband at the time. Zina D. Huntington Jacobs's husband gave his permission to Smith and later to Brigham Young to marry her.

1841 (7 Nov.)

Joseph Smith preached: "If you do not accuse each other, God will not accuse you. If you have no accuser you will enter heaven. If you will not accuse me, I will not accuse you. . . . What many people call sin is not sin. I do many things to break down superstition, and I will break it down."

1842 (15 Mar.)	Joseph Smith was initiated into the new organization the Nauvoo Lodge of Freemasonry, a brotherhood for Mormon men.
1842 (17 Mar.)	Joseph Smith organized the Female Relief Society as a sisterhood for Mormon women, and he installed his wife Emma as its president.
1842 (1 Apr.)	The LDS Church's *Times and Seasons* published Joseph Smith's description of himself between the ages of fourteen and seventeen: "I frequently fell into many foolish errors and displayed the weakness of youth and the corruption of human nature, which I am sorry to say led me into divers temptations, to the gratification of many appetites offensive in the sight of God. In consequence of these things I often felt condemned for my weakness, and imperfections."
1842 (25 May)	Assistant Counselor John C. Bennett was "disfellowshipped" (denied church privileges) and later "excommunicated" (removed from church membership). His homoerotic activities were publicly revealed two months later.
1842 (16 July)	The Mormon political newspaper *Wasp* published Brigham Young's phrenological chart: "Amativeness—7 [Fair]" and "Adhesiveness—10 [Large]." Phrenological writings (which nineteenth-century Mormons even used as textbooks in Sunday school classes) regarded a person with low scores in Amativeness and high scores in Adhesiveness as subject to "unnatural," "improper," or "disease[d]" same-sex friendships.
1842 (27 July)	The *Wasp* claimed that the excommunicated John C. Bennett had committed "adultery, fornication, and—we were going to say (*Buggery*)." This is the first known reference to homoeroticism in Mormon history.
1843 (22 Jan.)	Joseph Smith preached that God destroyed Sodom "for rejecting the prophets," a revision of the traditional sexual interpretation of Sodom's destruction.
1843 (16 Apr.)	Joseph Smith preached that "two who were vary friends

indeed should lie down upon the same bed at night locked in each other['s] embrace talking of their love & should awake in the morning together." The official *History of the Church* still renders this as "it is pleasing for friends to lie down together, locked in the arms of love, to sleep and wake in each other's embrace and renew their conversation." Smith used this common practice to illustrate the doctrine of resurrection.

1843 (17 Sept.)   Joseph Smith criticized the Nauvoo congregation for having "men among women, and women among men." Mormon meetings were segregated by gender throughout most of the nineteenth century.

1844 (11 Mar.)   The male-only theocratic Council of Fifty was organized.

1844 (8 May)   Joseph Smith confessed that his "only sin" was in "covering up their (the Higbees', Fosters', Laws' and Dr. Bennett's) iniquities, on their solemn promise to reform."

1844 (15 May)   Nauvoo's two LDS newspapers printed Apostle Brigham Young's reference to John C. Bennett's bisexual conduct: "if he had let young men and women alone it would have been better for him."

1844 (25 June)   After kissing his wife and children good-bye, Joseph Smith began the journey to surrender himself to hostile anti-Mormons. On the way he told forty-two-year-old George W. Rosecrans: "If I never see you again, or if I never come back, remember that I love you."

1844 (26 June)   Joseph Smith shared a bed with thirty-two-year-old Dan Jones, "and lay himself by my side in a close embrace."

1844 (27 June)   A mob killed Joseph Smith at Carthage, Illinois.

1844 (8 Aug.)   A special Nauvoo conference voted for the Quorum of the Twelve Apostles, with Brigham Young as its president, to be the acting church presidency for the Mormons.

1845 (10 May)   James M. Monroe, an unmarried twenty-three year old at Nauvoo, gave the earliest Mormon description of a struggle with the "habit" of masturbation: "I am determined no longer to be a slave to my own passions. I have been in subjection long enough."

1845 (15 May) James M. Monroe wrote that Apostle William Smith (Joseph Smith's only surviving brother) "slept with me last night and will to night."

1845 (29 Nov.) LDS general authorities Brigham Young, Heber C. Kimball, Joseph Young, and Levi W. Hancock "danced a French four together" accompanied by the Nauvoo Brass Band.

1846 (2 Jan.) In the Nauvoo temple, "President B. Young then invited some one to join him in the dance and found a partner in Brother Chase."

1846 (1 June) Philip C. Van Buskirk enlisted in the U.S. Marines. In his diary of his twenty-three years of service aboard ship he stated that "ninety percent of the white boys of this day" were "sodomites."

1846 (25 Jan.) Brigham Young began the adoption ceremony ("sealing of men to men") in the Nauvoo Temple. Rank-and-file Mormons were adopted to prominent Mormons, especially apostles, who became the spiritual "fathers" of these adopted men and their families. No current apostle was adopted to another apostle. Because this "sealing of men to men" was the last ordinance Brigham Young introduced in the Nauvoo Temple, some have interpreted it as higher in importance than the sealing of women to men, and higher than the second anointing of husband and wife.

1846 (16 Apr.) John C. Bennett wrote Mormon schismatic leader James J. Strang in Wisconsin concerning a young physician: "He must not leave you until I come, and I hope we shall be able to persuade him to remain with us forever." Bennett left his wife in Massachusetts during the year he was Strang's counselor in Wisconsin.

1847 (23 Jan.) At Winter Quarters, Nebraska, "The persons that took the [dance] floor to set the pattern were as follows:

Brigham Young, Heber C. Kimball, Wilford Woodruff & Ezra Taft Benson of the Twelve, & Joseph Young & A. P. Rockwood of the Seventies."

1847 (23 Feb.)   Brigham Young dreamed that he met the deceased Joseph Smith and "kissed him many times."

1847 (24 July)   Brigham Young entered the Salt Lake Valley and proclaimed it as the new headquarters of the LDS Church.

1851 (14 Feb.)   The first LDS convert in Hawaii was a sixteen-year-old young man who spoke English and who may have been the *Aikane* of a previous American visitor to the island.

1852 (29 Aug.)   The Mormons of Utah officially announced that they lived in polygamy, despite their public denials extending back to 1835.

1853 (10 Apr.)   Apostle Parley P. Pratt preached that God destroyed Sodom due to its "lawless abominations, holding promiscuous intercourse with the other sex, and stooping to a level with the brute creation . . . given to strange and unnatural lusts, appetites, and passions." This reversed the Mormon founder's nonsexual interpretation of Sodom's destruction.

1855 (16 Oct.)   "How I wish you were mine, as you once were, when I had you in the morning, and when the sun went down, and was sure I should never go to sleep without a moment from you," wrote poet Emily Dickinson to a young woman. She added: "Let us love with all our might, Jennie, for who knows where our hearts go, when this world is done?"

1855   Female cross-dresser Elsa J. Guerin ("Mountain Charley") traveled through Utah's mountain passes on the way to California.

1856 (28 July)   The Martin company of handcart pioneers began walking from Iowa City, Iowa, to Salt Lake City. The close association of forty-five-year-old widower Luke Carter and fifty-six-year-old bachelor Charles Edmonds caught the attention of one of their fellow pioneers. He wrote that the two unmarried Englishmen "slept in the same tent, cooked and bunked together," and that the more "tender" of the two men died on the overland journey.

1856 (21 Dec.) A Mormon's diary referred to an unnamed LDS woman in Salt Lake City who "was trying to seduce a young girl." This is the first known reference to female homoeroticism in Mormon history.

1857 (2 Aug.) Brigham Young preached: "There are probably but few men in the world who care about the private society of women less than I do." Several of his plural wives agreed with that assessment and wrote of his emotional distance and indifference. One of his daughters also acknowledged that Brigham Young ignored some of his wives sexually.

1857 (7 Oct.) The LDS Church's *Deseret News* editorialized that disbelief in Jesus and attacking the Mormon people were more serious sins than the "conduct" of Sodom and Gomorrah.

1857 (30 Nov.) Brigham Young's first counselor Daniel H. Wells ordered the firing squad execution of a twenty-one-year-old Mormon man for having sexual intercourse with a horse while on duty in the Utah militia. Young pardoned the man, but apparently allowed the mare to be shot for "the sin of Sodomy or Bestiality[,] one of the most heinous crimes." This is the first known Mormon use of the word *sodomy*.

1858 (20 May) "Prest. Young said he dreamed last night, of seeing [non-Mormon] Gov. [Alfred] Cumming. He appeared exceedingly friendly, and said to Prest. Young we must be united, we must act in concert; and commenced undressing himself to go to bed with him."

1858 (5 Aug.) Apostle Erastus Snow told one Mormon man that "he want[e]d me to Stay with him where ever he tarried" at night.

1859 (2 Jan.) Brigham Young instructed that all Mormon congregations have the following seating arrangement: women sitting to the north (or right) of the center aisle, and men sitting to the south (or left), with children on the front benches. This gender segregation continued for decades.

1860 (13 Feb.)   At Salt Lake City, "the Twelve [apostles] and others" danced together until two in the morning, when they returned home to their wives.

1862 (6 Apr.)   Brigham Young preached: "With the introduction of the Priesthood upon the earth was also introduced the sealing ordinance. By this power men will be sealed to men back to Adam." This referred to the early Mormon ordinance of adult men adopting other adult men.

1862 (8 July)   The Morrill Act was enacted, which prohibited "bigamy" in U.S. territories and disincorporated the LDS Church. This was the first congressional law regarding sexual conduct.

1864 (19 Sept.)   The Salt Lake County Court sentenced a man to "20 years at hard labour in the Penitentiary" for "carnally knowing and abusing a Female child under ten years of age."

1864 (28 Oct.)   The Mormon municipal judge of Salt Lake City dismissed all charges against U.S. Army private Frederick Jones, who had been arrested for sexually assaulting a nine-year-old Mormon boy. Sodomy was not illegal in Utah, but someone (apparently the boy's father) murdered the soldier later that day.

1866 (19 Mar.)   The Unitarian church of Boston charged Reverend Horatio Alger Jr. with "the abominable and revolting crime of unnatural familiarity with boys." Alger moved to New York City, where he became the author of nationally famous "rags-to-riches" books for boys.

1868 (12 Feb.)   The *Deseret News* editorial "Marry and Be Happy" said that if Mormon men continued to refuse to marry, the paper "would be inclined to favor the revival of the Spartan custom of treating bachelors [by flogging]."

1869 (Aug.–Sept.)   The *Deseret News* praised "*The Overland Monthly,* which, as usual, is full of good things" when the *Over-land Monthly* published Charles Warren Stoddard's story of his erotic experiences in a bed "big enough for a Mormon" with his "beloved" sixteen-year-old Tahitian, after "an immense amount of secrecy and many vows." Stoddard had Utah and Mormon connections.

1870 (2 May)   The term *lesbian* was used as the equivalent of *sodomy* for the first known time in English. It appeared in a man's diary, which indicates that the word was probably in common usage.

1871 (11 Sept.)   First Presidency Counselor Daniel H. Wells told the Grantsville School of the Prophets that "a great many of our young men, [are] abusing themselves by the habit of self-pollution: or self-abuse, or as the Bible terms it Onanism, and was satisfied that, that was one great cause why so many of our young men were not married, and it was a great sin, and would lead to insanity and a premature grave." As an extension of such views, Spencer W. Kimball, later an apostle and LDS president, taught that masturbation "would lead" to homosexuality.

1873 (15 Apr.)   The Mormon suffragist magazine *Woman's Exponent* reprinted a non-Mormon woman's essay, "Women Lovers," which began: "Perhaps you do not know it, but there are women who fall in love with each other."

1873 (4 Sept.)   Brigham Young preached that "we can seal women to men [without a temple], but not men to men, without a Temple."

1875 (15 Oct.)   The *Woman's Exponent* published an essay by a Utah Mormon calling herself "Old Maid" who wrote about men: "I have such an utter detestation for the whole sex that it is with the greatest difficulty that I can treat the men with common civility."

1876 (17 Jan.)   At the request of the non-Mormon governor, Utah's Mormon legislators prepared to adopt the entire Criminal Code of California, which included punishment of five years' imprisonment for "every person who is guilty of the infamous crime against nature." The governor signed it into law on 18 February.

1876 (23 Jan.)   LDS leaders in Salt Lake City discussed "the scandal and improper connexion between George Naylor and Frank Wells." They decided to separate the young men by sending seventeen-year-old Naylor on a special mission outside Utah on 2 February.

1876 (8 Feb.)   Local LDS leader Francis M. Lyman wrote about sleeping with another LDS leader: "He was so dirty that it made me crawl whenever he touched me."

1877 (5 Jan.)   Salt Lake City's police court fined "William Wright (alias Dick)" fifty dollars for "Prostitution." This is the first reference to male prostitution in Utah.

1877 (29 Aug.)   Brigham Young died. His last words were: "Joseph! Joseph! Joseph!"

1879 (6 Jan.)   The U.S. Supreme Court issued its *Reynolds v. the United States* decision, which upheld the constitutionality of the 1862 Morrill Anti-Bigamy Act, the court's first ruling about sexual conduct.

1879 (19 Aug.)   Apostle Wilford Woodruff visited the pueblo of the Zuni (population 1,500). Like twenty-six other Native American tribes among whom Mormons lived and proselytized, the Zuni had berdache—men who dressed as women and took the wife's role in same-sex marriages. Seven years later, a Zuni berdache visited the nation's capital and met with the U.S. president.

1879 (24 Oct.)   Apostle Wilford Woodruff wrote: "Brother Hatch . . . Staid & slept with me over night."

1879 (16 Nov.)   First Presidency Counselor Joseph F. Smith described Arthur Bruce Taylor (son of the LDS president) as an *Aikane*. Smith had been an LDS missionary in Hawaii and apparently knew its *Aikane* custom of young men who were sexual companions of older men.

1880 (13 Oct.)   The *Territorial Enquirer* of Provo, Utah, reported that Dr. Perry D. McClanahan had been caught in the act of raping a male teenager. The Mormon physician's published defense was "I hav'ent slept with two men for fifteen years." This first sodomy trial in Utah resulted in two hung juries of Mormons, and McClanahan was released after three months in prison.

1881 (24 July)   First Presidency Counselor George Q. Cannon preached: "Men may never have beheld each other's faces and yet they will love one another, and it is a love that is greater than the love of woman. It exceeds any sexual love that can be conceived of, and it is this love that has bound the [Mormon] people together."

1882 (12 Mar.)   After an investigation of America's private colleges for women, Alice Blackwell wrote about the "unnatural & fantastic" friendships between female students who were "violently in love with each other, and suffering all the pangs of unrequited attachment, desperate jealousy etc. etc., with as much energy as if one of them were a man."

1882 (10 Apr.)   Dressed in lace and velvet tights, Oscar Wilde walked on the stage of the Salt Lake Theatre to lecture and was greeted by an "array of young men on the front row, each adorned with an enormous sunflower." Earlier that day the LDS Church president had given Wilde a private tour of Salt Lake City.

1882 (17 July)   A thirty-five-year-old man was convicted of sodomy in Utah. The defendant received a sentence of three to four months in prison for Utah's first sodomy conviction, which was a sentence equivalent to that for fornication in the territory.

1882 (15 Sept.)   First Presidency Counselor Joseph F. Smith instructed local LDS leaders in Richfield, Utah, to "Get the names of *all of them* & cut them off the church" for "obscene, filthy & horrible practices." He referred to a group of young LDS men who had engaged in "this monstrous iniquity, for which Sodom & Gomorrah were burned with fire sent down from heaven." The oldest was a thirty-two-year-old polygamist, his apparent partner was an unmarried thirty year old, and the others were two pairs of teenagers. This was the first excommunication of young men for homoerotic activities.

1883 (27 May)   Sarah Edmunds Seelye, a cross-dresser who served as a Union soldier during the Civil War, was interviewed in the *Detroit Post and Tribune*.

1883 (9 Oct.)   In several hours of meetings with stake presidents, the First Presidency and apostles spoke about "Masturbation . . . self-pollution of both sexes & excessive indulgence in the married relation." This is the first known Mormon reference to female masturbation.

1884 (20 June)   The fifty-year-old Mormon bachelor Henri Edouard Desaules wrote that he "lay awake early dreaming lasciviously" in Utah, while he was reading a boy's magazine, *Youth's Companion*.

1885 (4 July)   Without referring to the gender of the people in his sexual fantasies, Henri Edouard Desaules wrote about his "terrible weakness" of masturbation since he was age fourteen: "I have tried over and over again to overcome it. I have never been able to be fifteen days without succumbing to it."

1885 (19 July)   In a Mormon community in Grass Valley, Utah, "The boys had a Dance last night, on the occasion of young Johny Wilcox leaving for a trip to Colorado." This apparently was a male-only dance.

1885   Brigham Morris Young, the thirty-fifth child of Brigham Young, returned with his wife from an LDS mission to Hawaii. Shortly afterward he began performing as Lady Pattirini, a female impersonation act he continued for decades in various wards (congregations) and stakes (dioceses) of Utah.

1886 (13 May)   The district court in Ogden sentenced a man to three years in prison for the "Crime Against Nature" of having "carnal intercourse" with "a certain bitch or female dog." This was the first imprisonment in Utah for bestial sodomy.

1886 (26 July)   Sixty-year-old Thomas Taylor was removed as bishop of the Salt Lake City Fourteenth Ward because he had masturbated individually with three male teenagers. He was later excommunicated, but a grand jury dropped criminal charges against him. Two years later, Mormons elected him to public office in southern Utah, where these homoerotic incidents had occurred.

1886 (14 Aug.)   Dr. Randolph Winslow published his study of the widespread anal and oral sex practiced by the young men in a Baltimore reform school.

1886 (Aug.)   "I am certain that the thought of the least demonstration of unmanly & abnormal passion would have been as revolting to him as it is & ever has been to me," wrote a twenty-eight-year-old non-Mormon about his affectionate sleeping companion. Then he added: "yet I do love him & love to hug & kiss him."

1886 (27 Oct.)   The Bohemian Club of Salt Lake City was organized as a male-only social club modeled on San Francisco's Bohemian Club, whose publications celebrated the presence of "slender young Bohemians, clad in economical bathing suits" at secret retreats by the Russian River. When incorporated five years later, Salt Lake City's Bohemian Club included both women and men as members.

1887 (11 Jan.)   The *Deseret News* reported the "Loathsome Depravity" of six male teenagers who raped a twelve-year-old boy and performed oral sex on him. The perpetrators were both Mormon and non-Mormon, and the oldest was sixteen. The court sentenced the oldest defendants to a three-month sentence for sodomy, but dismissed the charges against the younger defendants because oral sex was not a crime in Utah.

1887 (22 Jan.)   William H. Paddock, age fourteen, was the first person whose commitment to Utah's insane asylum stemmed from homoerotic activities. However, even though he had been arrested and indicted for sodomy, the examining physician and the asylum admission records made no reference to his sexual activities. The asylum discharged him as "not Insane" on 22 July, and within weeks the prison released him as well.

1887 (12 Aug.)   Within days of the death of LDS president John Taylor, his counselors and the apostles expressed their dissent from the harsh response Taylor had required for sex crimes.

1887 (Fall)   To demonstrate the evils of waltzing to the assembled youths of the Juarez Ward in Mexico, a married Mormon man began waltzing with a teenage boy and induced an erection by rubbing his groin against the young man's body.

1889 (17 May)   A *Deseret News* editorial accused the parents of William H. Paddock of ingratitude for criticizing the Mormons who "gently and mercifully" responded to their son's "utterly vile and depraved conduct [of gang-raping a boy] . . . by sending him to the insane asylum, because there was then [in 1887] no reformatory in which he could be placed."

1889 (7 Sept.)   The American physician G. Frank Lydston published that there was "in every community of any size a colony of male sexual perverts; they are usually known to each other, and are likely to congregate together."

1889 (11 Oct.)   A non-Mormon judge in Provo sentenced forty-year-old Evan S. Thomas, an active Mormon, to a year in prison for sodomy. The judge remarked that "in all his practice in Tennessee he had never heard of such a case as this." This was the first time that non-Mormon Utah judges began giving sentences for sodomy that were more harsh than those for fornication.

1890 (21 Mar.)   Otto Venson told the Salt Lake City Court: "I'm not that kind of a man," when witnesses testified that he had allowed another man to penetrate him anally. This occurred on Commercial Street, Salt Lake City's prostitution district, but Venson said he had no idea why the man gave him money afterward.

1890 (24 Sept.)   LDS president Wilford Woodruff published the Manifesto, which advised all LDS Church members to obey the antipolygamy laws.

1891 (29 Jan.)   Apostle Heber J. Grant wrote about First Presidency Counselor George Q. Cannon: "he leaned over and kissed me and I felt the tears of gratitude coming to my eyes as I returned the kiss."

1891 (24 Mar.)   Utah's chief justice wrote: "Polygamy has demoralized the people of Utah. I presume there are more sexual crimes here in proportion to the population than anywhere else."

1891 (2 Apr.)   Apostle Anthon H. Lund wrote that he "slept with" Apostle John Henry Smith during a trip from Salt Lake City to nearby Ogden, Utah.

1891 (27 May)   A Mormon jury in Salt Lake City took five minutes to acquit two men of consensual sodomy despite the testimony of five witnesses who caught them in the act. At least one of the two men was a Mormon.

1891 (19 July)   L. John Nuttall, the First Presidency's secretary, wrote: "I found Bro. F.M. Lyman in my bed at the Gardo & we slept together." Over the next several months, Nuttall sometimes recorded that the two LDS leaders slept together, even though their wives were also in Salt Lake City at the time.

1891 (9 Nov.)   The Bohemian Club of Salt Lake City was incorporated with three life-long bachelors as its directors. Brigham Young's granddaughter Katherine Young Schweitzer was its principal incorporator and benefactor. Decades later, Mildred J. Berryman began a study of thirty-three lesbians and gay men, many of whom were members of the Bohemian Club.

1892 (27 Jan.)   The *Deseret News* began reporting the details of a Memphis, Tennessee, murder case in which nineteen-year-old

Alice Mitchell killed her girlfriend "because she loved her" and could not accept the fact that the girlfriend had ended their same-sex relationship. For the first time, this publicly introduced the Mormon community to the existence of female homoeroticism.

1892 (16 Feb.)   The *Deseret News* headline read: "THE DOCTOR'S LOVE: His Strange Attachment to Isaac Judson Prompts Him to Kill Himself." The article quoted the suicide note, which indicated the homoerotic relationship of the two men.

1892 (7 Mar.)   Dr. James G. Kiernan, who had published articles on "sexual perversion" for a decade, made the first American use of the words *heterosexuals* and *homosexuals* in his address to the Chicago Medical Society. His remarks were published in a medical journal in May.

1892 (12 Sept.)   Non-Mormon judge James A. Miner sentenced an eighteen-year-old non-Mormon immigrant to six months in the Utah penitentiary for committing assault and "buggery" upon a seven-year-old boy. Two weeks later, Judge Miner gave a two-year prison sentence to a twenty-eight-year-old man for what was apparently consensual sodomy.

1893 (16 May)   L. John Nuttall, the First Presidency's secretary, wrote: "At [my wife] Sophia's. Bro & Sister R also staid with us. He slept with me." The two wives shared a separate bedroom.

1893 (24 Oct.)   With the approval of Apostle Lorenzo Snow, local LDS leader Rudger Clawson completely exonerated Lorenzo Hunsaker from the charges of performing oral sex on his brothers while sleeping with them. Despite corroborating testimony from neighbors, Clawson excommunicated two of the brothers for not withdrawing their "monstrous" charge against the respected high priest.

1894 (15 Dec.)   A non-Mormon judge gave a three-year prison sentence to seventeen-year-old Frank Smiley for what was apparently consensual sex with a male teenager.

1895 (27 Jan.)   Apostle Abraham H. Cannon wrote that a local LDS leader "slept with me at night, as it was extremely cold."

1895 (3 Apr.)   The LDS Church's *Deseret News* printed the first of eighteen front-page stories about the Oscar Wilde sodomy trial. The *News* refused to use the word *sodomy,* even though that appeared in the headline of the first story by the *Salt Lake Herald,* of which Apostle Heber J. Grant was vice president.

1895 (Apr.)   Dr. Havelock Ellis published "Sexual Inversion in Women" in the *Alienist and Neurologist.* The historian Jonathan Ned Katz calls this study "the most detailed, wide-ranging, and sympathetic to have appeared in a U.S. medical journal up to that time." Unlike the Kinsey studies fifty years later, Ellis published his findings about women before he published his study of male "sexual inversion" in December. Ellis criticized previous studies that depended on "inverts" in asylums and prisons because such sampling caused earlier researchers "to overestimate the morbid or vicious elements in such cases."

1896 (4 Jan.)   Utah became a state in the Union, and Mormons again entered the Utah judiciary, where they resumed a lenient response to men accused of sodomy or convicted thereof.

1896 (24 Jan.)   Polygamist and stake president Charles O. Card wrote: "I dreamed that president Woodruff & I met & embraced each other & Kissed each other in a very affectionate manner & I remarked he was the sweetest man I ever kissed. I thought in our embraces it was from the pure love of the Gospel."

1896 (13 June)   Mormon judge Henry H. Rolapp gave a nine-month sentence for homosexual assault, thus again making forcible sodomy no more serious an offense than consensual fornication.

1896 (17 Sept.)   At the urging of Mormon prosecutor Samuel A. King, all charges of sodomy were dropped against six Mormons, even though the eighteen-year-old non-Mormon victim had personally identified them as his rapists. This Provo trial proceeded only for three non-Mormons, all of whom were convicted by the Mormon judge and sentenced to three years in prison.

1896
An official history of the Young Men's Christian Association stated that the YMCA was organized due to "the craving of young men for companionship with each other."

1897 (15 Jan.)
Apostle Brigham Young Jr. angrily resigned as vice president of the Brigham Young Trust Co. because the other general authority board members had "elected to let [i.e., lease] buildings to whores." Male prostitutes were also being arrested during raids on these Commercial Street houses of prostitution. The First Presidency persuaded Young to resume his position on April 8.

1897 (26 Feb.)
The owner of a male house of prostitution was arrested in the mining town of Eureka, Utah, and so were three male prostitutes residing there, including a fifteen-year-old Mormon. This was apparently Utah's only all-male house of prostitution, but large cities throughout the United States had them during this period.

1897
Havelock Ellis and John Addington Symonds published *Sexual Inversion.* This included Josiah Flynt's "Homosexuality among Tramps," which was based partly on his experience and interviews in Salt Lake City. Flynt estimated that "every tenth man" experienced "unnatural intercourse" with other men, which was the first American estimate that 10 percent of men engaged in homoeroticism.

1898 (3 Jan.)
Apostle Abraham Owen Woodruff told Arizona stake president Andrew Kimball that "he had learned to love me from our first meeting."

1898 (21 Apr.)
Lucy Jane Brimhall and Inez Knight arrived in Liverpool, England, as the first LDS women to serve as missionary companions, a twenty-four-hour-a-day homosocial and emotional relationship that Mormons often compare to marriage. Mormon men had experienced such missionary companionship since 1830.

1898 (May)
Mormon suffragist Emmeline B. Wells publicly praised

the last same-sex relationship in Frances Willard's life: "She has lived much of the time with Lady [Isabel] Somerset . . . a congeniality between these two women has held them fast in a sublime and sacred friendship." President of the national Women's Christian Temperance Union (WCTU), Willard had already published an autobiography of her "heart affair[s]" with fifty women.

1898 (10 Sept.)   Apostle Anthon H. Lund wrote that Apostle Heber J. Grant "kissed me when he saw me."

1989 (1 Oct.)   In "Queer Love Affair," St. Anthony, Idaho's newspaper told its rural LDS readers that "Miss Densmore is given to wearing male attire" and that her "sweetheart is another girl, 18 years old." They lived in Missouri.

1900 (5 May)   Dr. William Lee Howard published "Effeminate Men and Masculine Women" in the *New York Medical Journal.*

1900 (7 June)   At the temple meeting of the First Presidency and apostles, there was "much talk about B.Y. Trust Co running a whore house on Commercial Street. Pres. G.Q.C. president & B.Y. Vice president [with] Jos. F S[mith]. director on BY board." Male prostitutes continued to be arrested at these houses of prostitution for "vagrancy."

1900 (June)   The U.S. census allowed unrelated persons to describe themselves as domestic "partners." There were more than two thousand same-sex partner households in the combined New York City boroughs of the Bronx and Manhattan, which included Greenwich Village's homosexual "Fairyland." In Salt Lake City, fifty same-sex couples defined themselves as domestic partners.

1901 (31 May)   Joseph Flaherty was the second person whose commitment to the Utah insane asylum stemmed from homoerotic activities. Even though the Salt Lake City Police arrested him for sodomy, the examining physician and the asylum admission records made no reference to sixteen-year-old Flaherty's sexual activities. The asylum discharged him on 2 February 1902.

1902 (14 July)   Upon discovering that his son and a teenage male cousin were masturbating together, General Authority J. Golden Kimball wrote: "The thing for us to do is to keep mum and fight the devil in a quiet way."

1903 (14 Jan.)   The LDS high school's student magazine published music teacher Evan Stephens' encouragement for same-sex friends to "rebel at the established order," and "dare" to love according to their "heart's desire." Within a year one of the male students moved in with Stephens.

1903 (Jan.)   The LDS *Young Woman's Journal* published one of Kate Thomas's same-sex love poems about "the one in all the world I love best." In the next line, Thomas used the word *gay* and continued: "From her lips I take Joy never-ceasing." Thomas, a devout Mormon who never married, published this while she was living in New York City's Greenwich Village, where *gay* was a code word for homosexual at that time.

1903 (7 July)   Apostle Rudger Clawson told the other apostles: "the practice of self-abuse [masturbation] existed to an alarming extent among the boys in our community who attended the district schools, and also, he doubted not, the church schools. He felt that the boys and girls should be properly instructed in regard to this evil."

1903 (28 Sept.)   General Authority J. Golden Kimball wrote that when he met Apostle Heber J. Grant on the street, he "not only shook me by the hand, but kissed me."

1904   At age twenty-one, Charles Badger Clark began four years as a cowboy in Arizona's cattle industry. He later wrote of his cowboy companion: "we loved each other . . . more than any woman's kiss could be." After the death of his "Pardner," Clark (who never married) longed to "feel his knee rub mine the good old way." Clark published this in 1915.

1905   Willard E. Weihe, violin soloist for the Mormon Tabernacle Choir, announced himself as president of the Bohemian Club.

1907 (1 Aug.)   Apostle David O. McKay wrote that he "kissed Elder John Henry [Smith] good bye, after a mutual expression of pleasure at each other's company." Nevertheless, recently appointed McKay wrote his wife that he would rather sleep on the floor than sleep with another man, even though that was the policy for LDS leaders on church assignments away from home.

1907 (3 Sept.)   Salt Lake City's juvenile court sentenced two male teenagers to probation for swimming nude in the Jordan River. In the nineteenth century, this homosocial activity had been regarded as harmless, but it became erotic by definition in Utah during the early 1900s.

1908 (July)   Superintendent Heber H. Thomas of the Utah reform school and four staff members spent forty-five minutes beating seven male teenagers for participating in anal and group sex. As a result of the publicity about this punishment, the superintendent (who was a member of an Ogden ward bishopric) was forced to resign a year later.

1909 (17 Feb.)   First Presidency Counselor Anthon H. Lund wrote that LDS president Joseph F. Smith "kissed me good-bye."

1912 (Mar.)   The Mormon actress Ada Dwyer Russell met Amy Lowell, a lesbian poet, at a Boston party, and they began their relationship shortly afterward.

1912 (Sept.)   The *Young Woman's Journal* paid tribute to "Sappho of Lesbos" and made the first reference to lesbianism in an LDS magazine.

1913 (30 Apr.)   Nathaniel H. Tanner, a Mormon and Salt Lake City municipal judge, sentenced a Mormon to forty-five days in jail for sodomy. That same year, state courts found two Protestants and a Catholic guilty of sodomy and sentenced them respectively to three years, five years, and four years in the Utah State Prison.

1913 (9 May)   The First Presidency learned that James Dwyer, cofounder of Salt Lake's LDS University (now LDS Business College), had been "teaching young men that sodomy and kindred vices are not sins." A year earlier Dwyer's daughter had begun a relationship with the lesbian poet Amy Lowell. Dwyer's stake president and bishop wanted to excommunicate him, but the First Presidency allowed Dwyer, then in his eighties, to voluntarily "withdraw his name" from LDS Church membership.

1913 (16 Dec.) The Utah Supreme Court reversed the sodomy conviction of Andrew G. Johnson, an African American, on the basis that oral sex was not covered by Utah's sodomy statute. Salt Lake's four daily newspapers failed to refer to this decision or Johnson's release from prison.

1914 (29 Sept.) The Quorum of the Twelve learned that a mission president "had discovered that 15% of the [missionary] Elders in the Netherlands during the past two years, have been guilty of immoral practices, and that a much greater percentage of Elders has been exposed to these evils." The report did not specify whether this referred to opposite-sex or same-sex activities or both.

1915 (Feb.) At the death of James Dwyer, the LDS Church's *Improvement Era* described him as "a man of sterling character," despite the First Presidency's knowledge that he had been "teaching young men that sodomy and kindred vices are not sins."

1916 (20 Aug.) Edward Carpenter's *My Days and Dreams* was published in the United States as the first autobiographical statement of homosexuality using the author's real name.

1916 (11 Nov.) The *Deseret News* published Evan Stephens's letter describing his activities in "Gay New York," including his practice of going to the "retreats" of Central Park "for some sort of companionship." In New York at that time, Central Park was a well-known place for men to meet for sexual encounters.

1917 (23 Mar.) One of the East Village's cross-dressing dances ("drag balls") was attended by two thousand people—"the usual crowd of homosexualists," according to one hostile investigator in New York City.

1917 (21 Apr.)   Back in Utah for his retirement celebration, Evan Stephens said he wanted to "return ere long" to the young man he was supporting in Manhattan. He and his "blond Viking" moved to the East Village, which New Yorkers called a homosexual "Fairyland" at that time.

1917 (10 Oct.)   The 145th Field Artillery regiment departed Utah for duty in World War I. Nearly all of its officers and enlisted men were LDS, so the unit was nicknamed "the Mormon regiment." Of the 21,000 Utahns (primarily Mormons) who served in World War I, twenty-six received dishonorable discharges, including "Perverts."

1918 (June)   Dr. E. A. Shepherd wrote in the *American Journal of Urology and Sexology:* "Our streets and beaches are overrun by male prostitutes (fairies)."

1918 (19 Oct.)   Signing himself as "Jonathan," Apostle Orson F. Whitney wrote to "Dear Brother David," his fellow apostle David O. McKay.

ca. 1918–22   Following her "disasterous" attempt to "escape her homosexuality" by marrying at age sixteen (ca. 1917–18), Mildred J. Berryman began a study of her homosexual friends before she left Westminster College in May 1922. Many of the twenty-four lesbians and nine gay males in this decades-long study were members of the Salt Lake Bohemian Club. At age twenty, Berryman obtained her prophetic LDS "patriarchal blessing" in 1921.

1919 (15 Sept.)   The *Deseret News* announced the beginning of the first International Conference of Women Physicians in New York City. Mormon physicians apparently attended this conference that presented positive views of homosexuality, including: "Justice demands that we must allow the genuine homo-sexual to express what is his normal sexuality in his own way." The LDS *Relief Society Magazine* praised the "sensible, cultured, and scientifically trained women" who spoke at this conference, but did not mention their endorsement of same-sex love.

1919 (Oct.)   The LDS *Children's Friend* published accounts of the same-sex relationships of Tabernacle Choir director Evan Stephens and of "ardent lovers" Louie B. Felt and May Anderson, respectively Primary general president and her first counselor. This same month, the *Relief Society Magazine* featured a tribute to Rev. Anna Howard Shaw, a suffragist who was publicly rumored to be a lesbian after the death of her long-time companion Susan B. Anthony.

1920 (June)   The *Children's Friend* published Evan Stephens's poem that indicated that all his youthful boyfriends had shared his bed, and "Held sweet converse through the day time, / Kept it up through half the night."

1920 (July)   The YMCA's official publication stated: "The friend of boys should be a lover of boys—should have suffered because of boys until he has purged himself without pity of the lustful desires that come storming, whether he will or not, to take possession of him."

1920 (20 Dec.)   First Presidency Counselor Anthon H. Lund wrote: "Prest. Grant came and kissed me when we shook hands."

1921 (30 June)   A Tongan young man wrote Apostle David O. McKay about "my love for you," and concluded: "I thank the Lord that I have lived to see you, to hear your voice and to touch your hand."

1921 (June)   The Mormon sociologist Nels Anderson conducted the first known interview of a Utah male prostitute, who was fourteen.

1922 (13 May)   Natacha Rambova (born as Winifred Kimball Shaughnessy in Salt Lake City) married silent film actor Rudolph Valentino. He had previously married the lesbian lover of his costar Alla Nazimova, who was also rumored to be Rambova's lesbian lover. Rambova was the granddaughter and great-granddaughter of prominent Mormons Heber P. Kimball and Heber C. Kimball.

1922 (Nov.)   Sixty-eight-year-old Evan Stephens began a trip to Los

Angeles and San Francisco with his last "young companion," seventeen-year-old John Wallace Packham.

1923 (17 Feb.)   Utah added oral sex to the definition of sodomy. This was more than nine years after the Utah Supreme Court threw out a sodomy conviction because there was no provision for oral sex in the statute.

1923 (June)   Sandwiched between photographs of bare-legged athletes on the men's track team, a photograph of two young men, each with one arm around the other's shoulders, appeared in Westminster College's yearbook. Its caption was "Adam at Evening."

1923 (June)   The yearbook of Salt Lake City's East High School included a track team photograph showing one young man whose right hand held the bare leg of one teammate, his left hand rested on the bare knee of another, while his own shoulders were embraced by a third teammate kneeling above him. Such images continued in Utah's school yearbooks until the 1940s, while physical touch had disappeared from the YMCA's publications by the 1920s.

1924 (20 July)   Seventy-year-old Evan Stephens described nineteen-year-old Wallace Packham, a student at the LDS University, as the "besht boy I ish gott." Six years later, "J. Wallace Packham, a friend" was a principal beneficiary in the will of the Tabernacle Choir's retired conductor, who wrote a poem indicating that such "boy chums" had shared his bed.

1924 (10 Dec.)   Incorporation in Chicago, Illinois, of the Society for Human Rights, the first homosexual emancipation organization in the United States. Its officers were all arrested in 1925, ending the organization.

1925 (June)   Cora Kasius published an article in the *Relief Society Magazine*. Born in 1897 in Utah, she had been a staff member at the Relief Society's headquarters since 1920 and an assistant secretary to its general president since 1923. Known as a Mormon lesbian to other Utah lesbians, she was apparently one of the participants in Mildred

Berryman's study. Cora Kasius moved to New York City in 1927, where she soon became a faculty member of Barnard College. She served as a liaison officer between the United Nations and the Netherlands in 1945 and wrote several books about social work.

1925   A Brigham Young University "social unit" (nonnational fraternity) performed a comedy burlesque in which male students dressed as women and left prominent lipstick marks on the face of the only male dressed as a man.

1926 (23 Mar.)   An "all-male-cast musical comedy" had its first performance at the LDS Church–owned Salt Lake Theatre. The male dancers looked remarkably authentic as sleekly dressed women with partners in tuxedos, and for two months the University of Utah's newspaper featured close-up photographs of the most authentic looking "beauties," including one cross-dresser in a passionate embrace with a male student.

1926 (28 Sept.)   The University of Utah school year began, during which twenty-one-year-old student Norval Service began a relationship with twenty-seven-year-old professor Joseph F. Smith, the unmarried son of deceased Apostle Hyrum M. Smith.

1928 (27 July)   Radclyffe Hall's lesbian novel *The Well of Loneliness* was published. Mildred J. Berryman, a lesbian, claimed that this book caused the Salt Lake City community to gossip about "masculine-acting" women and "feminine-acting" men. As a result, some of Utah's self-defined lesbians entered into heterosexual marriages.

1929   Katharine Bement Davis published *Factors in the Sex Life of Twenty-Two Hundred Women,* which showed that 26 percent of unmarried college graduates "admitted overt homosexual practices," and 31.7 percent of married female college graduates had engaged in homoerotic activities.

1930 (1 Apr.)   The *New York Times* reported the self-censorship standards of the Hays Commission of the Motion Picture

Producers and Distributors Association, including: "Sex perversion or any inference of it is forbidden on the screen."

1930 (27 Oct.)   A former "boy chum" of Evan Stephens confided to his diary: "No one will know what a loss his passing is to me. The world will never seem the same to me again."

1931 (Jan.)   The LDS *Juvenile Instructor* published the autobiography of Tabernacle Choir conductor Evan Stephens, who stated that in 1887, fifteen-year-old "Horace S. Ensign became a regular companion for many years."

1936 (Spring)   Dawson Frank Dean submitted "Significant Characteristics of the Homosexual Personality" for his Ph.D. degree at New York University. More than five hundred pages long, this was the first U.S. doctoral dissertation on homosexuality.

1937 (Jan.)   Dr. George Henry presented a report to the Payne Whitney Psychiatric Clinic of New York City in which he studied "100 socially well adjusted men and women whose preferred form of libidinous gratification is homosexual."

1938 (13 Nov.)   Mildred J. Berryman completed her two-decade study of lesbians and gay men in Salt Lake City, but decided not to publish it.

1941 (10 Mar.)   The president of the LDS Church's holding company informed First Presidency Counselor J. Reuben Clark that the church had "'whorehouses' on Clayton Investment." At Clark's prodding, the First Presidency decided five months later to "clean or close all Clayton Investment houses of shoddy character." This ended fifty years of the LDS Church's connection with houses of prostitution, which had also housed male prostitutes.

1942 (8 Oct.)   Joseph F. Smith (b. 1899) was appointed a general authority and Patriarch to the Church. A female friend of Smith's earlier male companion remarked that his appointment as patriarch stunned her and others who knew of his homosexuality.

1945 (6 Apr.)   S. Dilworth Young became a general authority, and short-
                  ly after visiting officially with an LDS mission president
                  he wrote: "I slept in the same bed with him for three
                  weeks, nearly, and he told me a lot of things about the
                  brethren, good and bad of his own experiences."

1946 (10 July)   From the father of a twenty-one-year-old Mormon sail-
                  or, the First Presidency learned that Patriarch Joseph F.
                  Smith had been in a relationship with the young man. The
                  patriarch was allowed to resign for "illness" in October.
                  Without an LDS Church court or public announcement,
                  the former patriarch was deprived of church privileges.
                  He was fully restored to church privileges eleven years
                  later.

1946 (Winter)   The University of Utah's literary magazine, the *Pen*, pub-
                  lished Robert Shelley's "Streak of Lavender," which rid-
                  iculed "the inverted Libido" of male ballet dancers who
                  "shrilly lisped" and were "more graceful than the wom-
                  en." A Navy ROTC student, Shelley also published in the
                  same issue a poem that referred to "Niggerboys" at a
                  public swimming pool.

1947 (17 Jan.)   William Tilden, formerly world tennis champion, was
                  sentenced to nine months in the Los Angeles County Jail
                  for having consensual sexual relations with a fourteen-
                  year-old boy.

1947   Apostle Spencer W. Kimball received the special assign-
                  ment to counsel with young men who had homosexual
                  desires or homoerotic experiences. Many of these were
                  seeking to become full-time missionaries.

1948 (11–12 Apr.) In his appointment book, George Albert Smith wrote the
                  words: "Homo Sexual" without explanation. Decades
                  later a Brigham Young University student's autobiogra-
                  phy explained that the church president had a private
                  interview at this time with two students who were in a
                  sexual relationship as male "lovers." President Smith told
                  them to "live their lives as decently as they could" with-
                  in their homosexual companionship.

1948   The Radio City bar opened in Salt Lake City to a clientele of heterosexuals. However, it evolved into a gay bar, in 1996 the oldest in continuous operation in Utah.

1948   Dr. Alfred Kinsey published *Sexual Behavior in the Human Male,* which gained immediate notoriety for its announcement of unexpectedly high statistics of homoerotic experiences.

1949 (Aug.)   A University of Utah sociology student submitted a master's thesis about the sexual experiences of two hundred male students. In this first publicly available study of Utah's diverse sexuality, John A. Pennock found that 16.5 percent of these men reported they had homoerotic experiences. Sixty-nine percent were Mormons, and 80 percent were actively LDS. All planned to marry.

1950 (19 Apr.)   The *New York Times* reported that the national chairman of the Republican party declared that the "sexual perverts who have infiltrated our Government in recent years" were "perhaps as dangerous as the actual Communists."

1950 (11 Sept.)   First Presidency Counselor J. Reuben Clark replied, "thus far we had done no more than drop them from positions they held," when a stake president asked if a Ricks College professor should be excommunicated for a homosexual relationship. It "had been going on for several years."

1950 (11 Nov.)   The Mattachine Society held its first informal meeting in Los Angeles. The first national organization of American homosexuals, it was formally organized on 1 Apr. 1951.

1951 (July)   Gordon B. Hinckley (later appointed an apostle and LDS president) wrote that in their late twenties, LDS president David O. McKay and his counselor Stephen L Richards "commenced a David-and-Jonathan friendship which has lasted and strengthened."

1951 (29 Oct.)   First Presidency Counselor Stephen L Richards instructed a mission president not to excommunicate a missionary elder for the "superficial charge" of fondling the genitals of three young men, ages twelve to thirteen. Richards said the missionary was only "guilty of a great indiscretion."

1952 (2 Oct.)   First Presidency Counselor J. Reuben Clark was the first LDS leader to publicly warn about the "great influence" nationally of gay men and the first to publicly acknowledge the existence of lesbianism and of sex with animals. Clark was also the first LDS leader to discuss masturbation and homosexuality in a general church meeting, in this case an address to the women's Relief Society.

1953 (Jan.)   *One Magazine,* the first openly homosexual periodical in the United States, published its first issue in Los Angeles.

1953 (2 July)   The *Los Angeles Herald-Examiner* headlined, "State Department Fires 531 Perverts, Security Risks." The *Deseret News* headlined the same story as "107 Fired in State Department," and its text used only the word *homosexuality* in referring to the sexual orientation issue.

1953   Dr. Alfred Kinsey published *Sexual Behavior in the Human Female.*

1955 (21 Sept.)   The Daughters of Bilitis, "the oldest lesbian organization of America and the world," was organized in San Francisco.

1955 (2 Nov.)   "Three Boise Men Admit Sex Charges" was the headline of the *Idaho Daily Statesman.* This began the public disclosure of sexual relationships in Boise between men and boys and male prostitution, which included some Mormons.

1956 (Oct.)   The *Ladder,* the first openly lesbian periodical in the United States, published its first issue in San Francisco.

1957 (10 July)   LDS president David O. McKay authorized the Honolulu stake president to restore all church privileges to Joseph F. Smith, the former patriarch. This was eleven years to the day since the Mormon hierarchy had learned of the patriarch's homoeroticism. Smith would later serve on the high council of his Honolulu stake.

1958 (12 Feb.) The Salt Lake City Police Department made the first arrest after instituting the policy of using decoys and surveillance at gay meeting places.

1958 (30 Sept.) The *Salt Lake Tribune*'s Catholic editor opposed prison sentences for men arrested for homosexual activities and urged local courts to give suspended sentences and professional counseling to all those convicted of homosexual conduct.

1958 General Authority Bruce R. McConkie published *Mormon Doctrine*, which condemned "sodomy, onanism, and homosexuality" and supported the death penalty for all sex crimes.

1959 (21 May) The apostles instructed Brigham Young University's president about "the growing problem in our society of homosexuality." Spencer W. Kimball reported that President McKay had said "that in his view homosexuality was worse than [heterosexual] immorality; that it is a filthy and unnatural habit."

1959 (4 Oct.) Allen Drury's *Advise and Consent* entered the *New York Times* best-seller list, where it remained for more than a year. The Pulitzer Prize–winning novel told about the downfall of fictitious Utah senator Brigham Anderson due to this Mormon's brief homosexual affair while in the military.

1960 (Fall) The University of Utah's literary magazine, the *Pen*, published Utah's first nonjudgmental description of same-sex persons in a homoerotic relationship: "He just said, Lawrence and I are in love and we will probably go away to Paris together. In fact he was sure. I did not know what to do. I did not feel like running, or being surprised, or anything. I just felt like saying all right. The two of them never kissed in front of me or touched. I just walked along with them and they took me with them most places." The "A Corner of Winter" story's author, Robert Foster, was an undergraduate student who also published poetry about his romantic love for women.

1961 (3 Oct.) The Motion Picture Association of America announced that it would permit homosexuality to be "treated with care, discretion, and restraint" in feature films. This was in response to the public announcement by influential director Otto Preminger that he expected the MPAA to cooperate with his intention to film the homosexual scenes involving the Mormon character of *Advise and Consent.* Thus a fictional story of Mormon homoeroticism ended Hollywood's self-censorship code regarding homosexuality. When released a year later, the film added a scene not in the novel that introduced America's filmgoers to a gay bar for the first time.

1962 (12 Sept.) In connection with Brigham Young University's program of electric shock aversion therapy for homosexually oriented men, Apostles Spencer W. Kimball and Mark E. Petersen informed BYU's president that "no one will be admitted as a student at the B.Y.U. whom we have convincing evidence is a homosexual." Shortly afterward, as newly appointed president of the West European Mission, Petersen ruled that missionaries there had to sleep in separate beds.

1964 (12 Feb.) The First Presidency issued a letter stating that prospective missionaries "found guilty of fornication, of sex perversion, of heavy petting, or of comparable transgressions should not be recommended until the case has been discussed with the bishop and stake president and the visiting [general] Authority."

1966 David-Edward Desmond organized Mormonism's first schismatic group of homosexuals. Comprised of gay men between eighteen and thirty years of age, the United Order Family of Christ was economically communal: "We hold everything in common." As the group's spiritual leader Desmond apparently also solemnized male-male relationships. Located in Denver, Colorado, this group disbanded within eight years.

1967 (16 Jan.) The Louisiana Supreme Court confirmed the conviction of Mary Young and Dawn DeBlanc for "unnatural carnal copulation" with each other. Each woman served thirty months in prison.

1968 (22 Apr.)	Juliet Hulme was baptized in California despite her confession to LDS authorities that she had been convicted and imprisoned at age fifteen for helping to murder her girlfriend's mother. Court documents, her girlfriend's diary, and the 1994 film *Heavenly Creatures* described the homoerotic friendship that led to the bludgeoning murder of the mother for trying to separate the girls. Active in LDS women's organizations, Juliet Hulme became internationally famous as Anne Perry, author of murder mysteries. In 1995 she told a reporter for the *Village Voice* that she could "love" a woman, but never be "in love" with one.
1968 (19 Nov.)	An article in the University of Utah's student newspaper made the first public acknowledgment that Salt Lake City has "gay bars."
1968	The *General Handbook of Instructions* added "homosexual acts" to the list of sins for which a person could be excommunicated from the LDS Church.
1969 (26 Feb.)	Brigham Young University's president instructed all bishops and stake presidents of BYU's student stakes to report to campus authorities any students who confessed unacceptable conduct. This was a way of "eliminating students who do not fit into the culture of BYU so that those [who] would fit into it might be admitted to the institution." This policy also ended the confidentiality of confessions to LDS leaders.
1969 (Spring)	Utah State University in Logan published the first student poem with a subtle lesbian theme, "Modigliani's Gypsy," in the literary magazine the *Crucible*.
1969 (28 June)	Gay men rioted as the police tried to arrest patrons of the Stonewall Bar in Greenwich Village, New York City, which began the gay liberation movement.
1969 (22 Sept.)	Brigham Young University's administration privately agreed to curtail aversion therapy (by electric shock) for homosexually oriented BYU students. However, the program continued for another decade.

1969   Apostle Spencer W. Kimball published *The Miracle of Forgiveness.* Its chapter titled "Crime against Nature" encouraged homosexually oriented men to "force" themselves to marry women.

1970 (19 Mar.)   A First Presidency letter stated: "There is much concern on the part of the brethren concerning the apparent increase in homosexuality and other deviations, and we call to your attention a program designed . . . to counsel and direct them back to total normalcy and happiness." The letter designated Apostles Spencer W. Kimball and Mark E. Petersen to "send material and give counsel." Apostle Kimball's *New Horizons for Homosexuals* (later titled *A Letter to a Friend*) had sections titled "It Is Curable" and "Multiply and Replenish," which recommended that homosexually oriented young men should get married and father children as signs of overcoming their same-sex desires.

1970 (23 Dec.)   A First Presidency letter instructed that those being interviewed for missions should be asked "direct questions" concerning "fornication, adultery, homosexuality, masturbation, heavy petting, or drug abuse." The First Presidency itemized examples of what one mission president found after carefully interviewing a group of newly assigned missionaries, including: "One Elder admitted to having masturbated in groups with other college students at the BYU which implies possible homosexual activities."

1971 (12 May)   Five students at the University of Utah organized a Gay Rap Group that later became the officially recognized Gay and Lesbian Student Union on the Salt Lake City campus.

1971 (13 May)   The University of Utah student newspaper ran a front-page story about a local "Gay Lib" group. The editorial page endorsed the group on May 24. Similarly, on 18 May 1993, the University of Utah's student editors officially endorsed the legalization of same-sex marriages throughout the United States.

1971 (18 May)   The University of Utah's student newspaper recommended *Boys in the Band,* the first openly gay play to be performed in Utah.

1973 (17 Feb.)   Joe Redburn opened the Sun Tavern, Utah's first gay-owned bar to be homosexually oriented at its opening in Salt Lake City. As Utah's largest gay bar, it was still in operation as of 1996.

1973 (Feb.)   The First Presidency made a statement in *Priesthood Bulletin* that "homosexuality in men and women runs counter to . . . divine objectives and, therefore, is to be avoided and forsaken. . . . Failure to work closely with one's bishop or stake president in cases involving homosexual behavior will require prompt Church court action."

1973 (30 Oct.)   University of Utah's newspaper *Daily Chronicle* featured the story "Gay Church Welcomes Community Unwanted" about the Metropolitan Community Church in Salt Lake City, founded in 1972.

1973 (15 Dec.)   The American Psychiatric Association dropped homosexuality as "a psychiatric disorder," advocated laws to protect lesbians and gay men from discrimination in employment, housing, transportation, and licensing, and encouraged "the repeal of all legislation making criminal offenses of sexual acts performed by consenting adults in private."

1973 (30 Dec.)   Spencer W. Kimball became LDS Church president, the first time that office was filled by a man who was already known for his statements about homosexuality. While on an airplane not long afterwards, President Kimball engaged in conversation with a young man in his twenties and repeatedly kissed this non-Mormon, who became overwhelmed with emotion and shed tears freely.

1973   The LDS Church published *Homosexuality: Welfare Services Packet.*

1974 (6 Nov.)   The national gay and lesbian magazine the *Advocate* headlined, "Mormon President Raps Homosexuals." The *Advocate*'s editor, Robert I. McQueen, had been a full-time missionary for the LDS Church. He was excommunicated in 1979 after publishing several other articles critical of the LDS position toward gay men and lesbians.

1975 (Jan.) Brigham Young University began an effort to expel all homosexual male students. BYU security officers interrogated students majoring in fine arts or drama. Security operatives also took down license plate numbers of cars parked outside Salt Lake City's gay bars and cross-checked them with cars registered with BYU by current students. BYU's president Dallin H. Oaks acknowledged these activities in general terms in the *Salt Lake Tribune* on March 22. The *Advocate* published three articles about this "purge," beginning with the issue of 18 June.

1975 (27 May) *Gayzette,* Utah's first newspaper for gays and lesbians, published its first issue.

1975 (30 May) The First Presidency issued a letter "about the unfortunate problem of homosexuality which occurs from time to time among our people" and referred to the length of time it took "to conquer the habit." The letter encouraged church leaders "not to label people as homosexual because this both discourages and tends to make the matter seem beyond solving."

1975 (8 Sept.) The cover of *Time* headlined, "I Am a Homosexual: The Gay Drive for Acceptance," with a photograph of Sgt. Leonard Matlovich Jr. in full uniform. A Mormon convert, Matlovich had served three tours of duty in Vietnam, where he received the Bronze Star, a Purple Heart, and an Air Force Meritorious Service Medal. Although he had not mentioned his LDS membership in media interviews about his court challenge against the U.S. military's ban against gay men and lesbians, his local LDS leaders excommunicated him in November.

1976 (Spring) Utah State University's student literary magazine, the *Crucible,* published the first male-male love poem by a Utah student (anonymous), "Lovesong for David."

1976 (Summer) *Dialogue: A Journal of Mormon Thought* published "Solus," the first personal essay by an acknowledged homosexual in a Mormon publication. He was celibate.

1976 (Fall) *Dialogue: A Journal of Mormon Thought* published a

BYU sociologist's results of sex surveys he had administered to thousands of students during the previous twenty years. Ten percent of Mormon male students reported homoerotic experiences and 2 percent of LDS female students reported homoerotic experiences.

1976 (2 Oct.)   Apostle Boyd K. Packer encouraged young men of the LDS Church to physically assault men (including missionary companions) who showed sexual interest in them. This was one hundred years after LDS leaders sent a young man on a special mission outside Utah because of his homoerotic relationship with another young man in Salt Lake City.

1976 (22 Oct.)   The First Presidency issued a statement against ratification of the Equal Rights Amendment to the U.S. Constitution: "We fear it will even stifle many God-given feminine instincts." This was Spencer W. Kimball's first allusion to lesbianism in the LDS Church's campaign against the ERA. In a longer message, the First Presidency stated as its first objection to passage of the Equal Rights Amendment: "an increase in the practice of homosexual and lesbian activities, and other concepts which could alter the natural, God-given relationship of men and women."

1976   The *General Handbook of Instructions* dropped "homosexual acts" and added "homosexuality" to the list of sins for which a person could be excommunicated from the LDS Church. This implied that Mormons could be punished for their homosexual orientation even if they were celibate. By removing the burden of proof, this allowed overly zealous bishops and stake presidents to excommunicate Mormons who admitted their homosexual orientation but denied accusations of homoerotic behavior.

1976 (31 Dec.)   The *Salt Lake Tribune*'s newspaper index lacked a separate heading for same-sex topics. The following year's index added "Gay Rights" as a subject heading, which had entries for twenty-two separate articles. A national movement had gained official recognition in the Mormon culture region.

Index

"Abdicating Fathers/Homosexual Sons."
See Fallacies
Abel, Elijah, 189n84
Abnormal/normal, 4, 93, 218, 219, 221,
244, 261n96, 402, 419, 429. See also
Cultural relativism; Deviance; Natural/
unnatural; Perversion
Abolitionists, 109
Absolute definitions/values. See Cultural
relativism; Mormons: ethical relativism
Acosta, Mercedes de. See De Acosta, Mer-
cedes
"Adamless Eden," 246
Adams, Barry D., 42
Adams, Marian, 168
Adams, Maude, 135
"Adhesiveness." See Phrenology
Adoption ceremony, 136–38, 149n38, 411,
414
Adultery, 266, 267, 269, 271–72, 297n50,
372, 376, 380, 409, 440
Advise and Consent, 377–78, 395n71,
437, 438
Advocate (Los Angeles), 441, 442
Affirmation (organization for gay and les-
bian Mormons), 138
Africa, 42, 131–32, 182n28
African Americans: excluded from interra-
cial marriage, 166; excluded (1852–
1978) from LDS priesthood, 189n84;
first sodomy conviction was reversed,
330, 428; mentioned, 302n72, 325,
352n72, 358n100, 434; not subordinate

among Utah's interracial same-sex partners, 167–68; as same-sex partners in
Salt Lake City, 166–68, 170; viewed as
the equal of "whites" by Joseph Smith,
189n84; viewed as inherently inferior by
Brigham Young, 168
"Against nature." See Bestiality; Natural/
unnatural; Sodomy
Age differences: female-female, 78–79, 161,
171, 172, 215, 222, 243–44, 246; male-
male, 93, 103n51, 131–32, 161, 165,
168, 182n28, 187n62, 215, 222, 235–43,
275, 276–78, 279, 286, 287, 289,
292n19, 306n97, 335, 370, 375, 387n23,
414, 419, 434, 436, 441. See also Inter-
generational relationships; "Kept boys"
"Age-structured homosexuality," 142n13,
182n28
Aikane, 38–41, 54n29, 140, 406, 408,
412, 416
Aleuts, 131
Alexander the Great, 36
Alger, Horatio, Jr., 414
Alienist and Neurologist (St. Louis), 423
"Alien sexualities," 402
"Amativeness." See Phrenology
Amazon River region, 38
Amazons/berdache, 133–34, 143n15, 144,
145n16, 416
American Journal of Urology and Sexology
(New York City), 429
American Psychiatric Association,
361n117, 441

American Red Cross, 368, 369

America's heartland, 196, 222, 223

Amherst College, 87, 156, 408

Anal sex, 34, 41, 54*n*32, 58*n*51, 94, 132, 141*n*7, 154, 156, 266–67, 268, 279, 284, 287, 318, 322, 325–26, 353*n*77, 419, 420, 427. *See also* "Buggery"; Homoerotic acts, voluntary; Sodomy

Animals, sex with. *See* Bestiality; Blood atonement; Castration; Death penalty; Sodomy

Anderson, Brigham. *See Advise and Consent*

Anderson, Cora, 174*n*1

Anderson, George E., 135

Anderson, Lavina Fielding, 115, 127*n*50

Anderson, Mary, 174*n*1

Anderson, May, 125*n*41, 232, 242–47, 250*n*10, 266, 429

Anderson, Nels, 157, 182*n*31, 322, 349*n*58, 430

Androgyny, 220, 222

Anger, 107, 155, 204–5, 212, 213, 241. *See also* Homoemotional

Anson, James H., 83*n*32

Anthony, Susan B., 245–46, 262*n*102, 430

Anti-female attitudes. *See* Misogyny

Anti-male attitudes, 108, 120*n*8, 121*n*8, 202, 228*n*19, 415

Anti-Mormons, 70, 226*n*11, 279, 280, 282–83, 294*n*30

Apache, 133

Apostles, 40, 86, 89, 90, 91, 101*n*36, 113, 114, 134, 137, 138–40, 149*n*38, 173, 199, 256*n*57, 267, 269, 281–82, 287, 292*n*19, 310*n*120, 314, 319, 320, 322, 336, 347*n*35, 348*n*50, 369, 371–80, 382–83, 388*n*25, 394*n*59, 407, 410–16, 418, 420–30, 432, 434, 435, 437, 438, 440, 443

Apperson, Louise Behrens, 26*n*19

Arabic cultures, 144, 182*n*28

Argentina, 156

Arizona, 15*n*5, 158, 174*n*1, 274, 288, 359*n*102, 424, 426

Army. *See* Soldiers

Assault, sexual. *See* Child sexual abuse; Rape

Athenian Bachelors' Club, 71, 72

Athletic teams, 66, 95–96, 106*n*63, 221, 431. *See also* Same-sex dynamics: photographs depicting

Atlantic Monthly (Boston), 56*n*37

Aversion therapy. *See* Brigham Young University; Homoerotic desire; Homosexuality

Azande, 131–32, 141*n*7

Bach, Evan (pseud.), 233. *See also* Stephens, Evan

Bachelors. *See* Unmarried

Bacon, Perry, 352*n*72, 355*n*81

Baker City, Oregon, 15*n*5, 57*n*43

Ballantyne, Richard, 269

Baltimore, 154, 285, 419

Banguia, 132

Banks, Joseph, 344*n*26

Bannock tribe, 133

Bantu, 141*n*9

Barker, William, 346*n*33

Barnard College, 369, 432

Barnes, Lorenzo D., 138–39, 150*n*43

Barrett, Charles Henry, 275

Barry, Kathleen, 205, 206

Baseball. *See* Athletic teams

Basketball. *See* Athletic teams

Baum, David, 317, 343*n*21, 363

Beaver, Utah, 88, 300*n*64

Beaver Island, Michigan, 15*n*5

Bedmates, same-sex, 1, 39, 40, 42, 72, 85, 86–91, 92, 93, 94, 99*n*19, 100*n*26, 110, 117–18, 153, 155, 156, 231, 234–35, 235–36, 237, 238, 241, 242, 244, 246, 247*n*3, 277, 287, 324–25, 379, 381, 396*n*76, 406, 407, 408, 409–10, 410–11, 413, 416, 419, 421, 422, 423, 427, 430, 431, 434, 438. *See also* Homotactile; Siblings; "Sleeping with"

Beehive House, 100*n*26

Benjamin, Larry, 346*n*33

Benkert, Karoly Maria, 33

Bennett, John C., 266–68, 273, 291*nn*11 and 13, 362*n*121, 408, 409, 410, 411

Bennett, John F., 348*n*50

Bennett, Samuel, 363

Bennett, Wallace F., 378

Benson, Ezra T., 86, 412

Berbers, 42

Berdache. *See* Amazons/berdache

Bering Strait, 131

Berryman, Mildred J., 35, 69, 73, 77*nn*16, 17, and 18, 78, 120*n*8, 135, 171–72, 187*n*62, 191*nn*92 and 94, 192*n*95, 195–

222, 224*n*6, 225*n*6, 226*nn*10 and 11,
   227*n*17, 228*n*19, 247, 266, 332,
   360*nn*111 and 112, 362*n*121, 363–64,
   368–69, 421, 429, 431, 432, 433
Bertine, Eleanor, 244
Bestiality (humans having sex with animals), 35, 270–71, 272, 277, 279, 283,
   353*n*77, 373, 392*n*45, 413, 418–19, 436
Bestial sodomy. *See* Bestiality; Sodomy
Bias: beliefs, 4, 7; compartmental, 37, 94,
   108–9; cultural, 36, 37, 41, 43–44, 45,
   73, 193*n*102, 285, 402; environmental,
   37; "feminine" behavior/"masculine"
   behavior, 6, 35–36, 202, 205–6; gender,
   36; heterosexual, 62*n*57, 159, 165; in
   language, 4, 37–38, 45, 144–45, 285,
   402; male, 76*n*6, 323, 354*n*80, 374;
   male-identified, 202, 205–6; of opinion
   makers, 333; in presentation of evidence,
   8, 197, 266, 289*n*1; presentist, 3, 402;
   religious, 37, 198–99; right-handed, 4;
   scholarly toward "deviant" groups,
   23*n*12, 26*n*19, 27*nn*20 and 22, 244,
   429; and self-identity, 36, 37, 45, 402;
   and sexual orientation, 4, 36, 159; and
   social class, 37; specialists, 333,
   361*n*120; and time period, 37, 45, 402
Bible, 34, 46*n*5, 51*n*19, 112–13, 124*n*31,
   148*n*32, 246, 289*n*2. *See also* Old Testament
Bieber, Irving, 5, 28*n*22
Big Horn Valley, Wyoming, 336
Big Nambas, 141
Bilingualism of nineteenth-century homosexuals, 232, 246. *See also* Double en-
   tendre/double meaning; Homosexual
   subtext
Billings, Frank, 356*n*87
Bisexuality: as ambidextrous sexuality, 4,
   52; ancient, 36; and bias, 36, 42; cultural approval of, 38, 41–42, 109; early
   twentieth-century meaning of, 51*n*20,
   291*n*11; as ethnic identity to some,
   260*n*89; examples of, 174, 194*n*111,
   209, 210, 211, 212, 218, 268, 269,
   291*n*11, 408, 410; self-defined, 104*n*51,
   138, 247, 268; sexual imperative of,
   121*n*8; sources of, 52–53
Blackburn, John W., 307*n*99
Blackmail, 220–21, 378

Blackwell, Alice, 111, 417
Blanc, Dawn de. *See* De Blanc, Dawn
Blessing (a formal ceremony). *See* Men performing blessing for males; Patriarchal
   blessing; Women: performing blessing
   for females
Blood atonement: for adultery, 271–72,
   295*n*32, 375; for bestiality, 270–71;
   defined, 269–70, 292*n*19; for incest,
   271, 294*n*30; instead of legal proceed-
   ings, 272, 375; for sexual intercourse
   with stepdaughter, 270
Blunt, Frank (pseud.). *See* Morris, Anna
Boarder/renter in homes, 160, 169–70,
   184*n*44
Boarding schools, 153, 155–56, 196,
   180*n*15, 407–8, 417
Bogoras, Waldemar, 130
Bohemian Club. *See* Salt Lake Bohemian
   Club; San Francisco's bohemian club
Bohemian enclaves/subcultures, 116–17,
   196. *See also* Greenwich Village; New
   York City; San Francisco
Boise, Idaho, 436
Bonding: female, 107, 108, 111, 401;
   male, 102*n*51, 107, 109, 110, 139,
   148*n*31, 401. *See also* Homoemotional
Bonner, J. W., 341*n*14
Book of Mormon, 2, 66, 148*n*32, 407
Boston, 56*n*37, 163, 166, 236, 316, 414,
   427
"Boston marriages." *See* Couples, same-
   sex; Women: "Boston marriages"
Boswell, John, 130
Bowman, John M., 357*n*95
"Boy chum." *See* "Chum"; Stephens, Evan
Boys in the Band, 440
Brain, Robert, 89, 100*n*28
Brazil, 6
Bridal pregnancy, 199, 336
"Bride wealth." *See* Male-wives; Marriage,
   same-sex
Brigham Young Trust Company, 319–20,
   346*n*35, 348*n*50, 424, 425
Brigham Young University: and aversion
   therapy, 379, 438, 439; homosexual is-
   sues at, 60–61, 120–21, 372, 377, 379,
   380, 390*nn*39 and 40, 398*n*95, 434,
   437, 438, 440, 442; mentioned, 83*n*37,
   94, 95, 106*n*63, 157, 199, 220, 230*n*37,

260*n*82, 432; "purge" of suspected ho-
mosexuals, 442; sex surveys at, 42,
59*n*54, 334, 336–37, 364*n*123, 399*n*95,
439, 442–43
Brimhall, Lucy Jane, 424
Britain, 66, 379, 396*n*75
Bronx, 162, 425. *See also* New York City
Brooklyn, New York, 245
Brooks, James, 344*n*26
Brothel. *See* Prostitution: house of
Brothers. *See* Siblings
Browe, William C., 80*n*20
Brown, Frank, 356*n*88, 359*n*105
Brown, Victor L., Jr., 30*n*29
Brown, William, 340*n*9, 362*n*121
Buboltz, Richard, 278–81, 301*n*70,
302*n*72, 303*n*79, 362*n*121
Buchanan, William, 327, 352*n*72, 363
Buck, Irving A., 153
"Buggery," 266–67, 268, 273, 276, 282,
283, 286, 288, 316, 325, 409. *See also*
Anal sex; Sodomy
Bullard, Elizabeth, 87, 408
Bullock, Thomas, 149*n*38
Bullough, Bonnie, 77*n*17, 78, 195, 202,
226*n*11, 227*n*17, 228*n*19
Bullough, Vern L., 77*n*17, 115, 135, 195,
202, 224*n*5, 225*n*6, 226*n*11, 227*n*17
Burke, Edward, 328–29, 363
Burns, James, 356*n*88
Burrow, Trigant, 244
Burton, Robert T., 308*n*108
Burton, William D., 284, 305*n*91,
308*nn*106, 107, and 108
"Butch-fem" roles, 228*n*20. *See also* Gen-
der: behaviors; Lesbians: masculine-fem-
inine dichotomy in relationships of
Byrd, A. Dean, 64*n*63
BYU. *See* Brigham Young University

Cahoon, Brent F., 88
California, 90, 134, 240, 273, 282,
359*n*102, 412, 415, 439
"Call boy," 318, 342*n*15, 345*n*28. *See also*
Prostitution
Cameron, Deborah, 18*n*7
Cameroon, 132, 142*n*12
Camille, 174
Canada, 15*n*5, 89, 92
Canandaigua, New York, 174*n*1

Cannon, Abraham H., 90, 423
Cannon, George Q., 40, 72, 91, 113, 139,
281, 292*n*19, 319, 348*n*50, 417, 421,
425
Cannon, Sylvester Q., 388*n*25
Card, Charles O., 92, 102*n*51, 104*n*51,
423
Card, Orson Scott, 2, 102–4*n*51
Cardston, Alberta, Canada, 15*n*5
"Carnal knowledge," 340*n*10. *See also*
Fornication
Carnell, James, 344*n*26
Carpenter, Edward, 428
Carrington, Albert, 71, 155
Carrington, Calvin S., 70–71, 82*n*26, 109
Carter, Luke, 153, 178*n*5, 412–13
Carthage Jail, 113, 410
"Casa Lesbiana," 171–72
Cashinahua, 53*n*24
Castration: for adultery, 271, 272; for bes-
tiality, 35, 272, 295*n*34, 406; for forni-
cation, 271, 272; for polygamy, 35, 406;
for rape, 35, 406; for sodomy, 35, 406;
for undisclosed sexual act, 270, 293*n*24
Cather, Willa, 232
Catholics. *See* Roman Catholics
Cedar City, Utah, 270, 277
Celibacy, 67, 132, 137, 140, 214–15, 222,
381, 442, 443. *See also* Homoerotic desire: unexpressed sexually; Same-sex intimacy without homoeroticism
Censorship, 284, 285, 291*n*12, 295*n*35,
314, 320, 330, 351*n*60, 378, 395*n*69,
423, 428, 432–33, 438
Census, LDS, 78, 81*n*25, 83*n*32, 125*n*34,
194*n*109, 226–27, 255*n*50, 384*n*9
Census, U.S.: failed to identify certain
kinds of co-residence, 159; limits of
present analysis, 160–61; possibly provided way to identify same-sex couples
in boarding houses and hotels, 184*n*43;
underreported same-sex couples, 160,
163
Census, U.S. (1860), 293*n*24
Census, U.S. (1870), 251*n*17, 274, 293*n*24
Census, U.S. (1880): mentioned, 160–62,
235, 251*nn*17 and 22, 299*n*56, 302*n*72;
religious affiliation provided only for
Utah residents, 162
Census, U.S. (1890): manuscript acciden-

tally burned, 160; statistical summary published before accident, 166, 188*n*69

Census, U.S. (1900): allowed homosexuals to claim domestic partnership, 162, 425; mentioned, 162–71, 185*n*51, 236, 254*n*38, 317, 343*n*21, 344*n*23. *See also* Couples, same-sex: as domestic partners

Census, U.S. (1910), 83*n*32, 385*n*14

Census, U.S. (1920), 83*n*32, 258*n*68

Census, U.S. (1990), 162

Census, Utah (1856), 294*n*29

Central Park (New York City), 239, 257*n*60, 428

Champaign, Illinois, 387*n*21

Chapman, Arvis Scott, 191*n*93

Chapman, Edith Mary, 78, 171–72, 191*n*94

Chapman, Sarah Ann Briggs, 171, 172, 191*n*94

Chase, "Brother" (Ezra or Isaac), 85, 411

Chauncey, George, Jr., 76*n*14, 116, 166, 205, 206, 256*n*59, 361*n*120

Chicago, 166, 235, 236, 316, 387*n*21, 431

Chicago Medical Society, 422

Chickasaw, 133

Children's Friend (Salt Lake City), 233, 234, 235, 237, 240, 241, 242, 243, 244, 245, 246–47, 263*n*110, 264*n*111, 429–30

Child sexual abuse, 272, 275, 278, 286, 297*n*50, 306*n*97, 315, 341*n*14, 356*n*88, 414, 422

China, 130, 165–67, 182*n*28, 188*nn*70 and 71. *See also* Immigrants

Choctaw, 133

Choir. *See* Salt Lake Tabernacle Choir

Christiania, Norway, 236

Christopherson, Willard A., 190*n*86, 236–37, 239, 241, 253*n*35, 254*n*40

"Chum" (term for close friend), 40, 83*n*33, 115, 234, 235, 237, 238, 240–42, 245, 259*n*76, 369, 431, 433

Church activity, 70, 198, 200

Church affiliation: of persons engaging in homoerotic activities, 42, 59*n*53, 60, 247, 362*n*121; of self-identified homosexuals and lesbians, 59*n*54, 78, 79*n*18, 138, 151*n*48, 197–200, 226*n*11, 227*n*17, 247, 368

Church Board of Education. *See* LDS Church Board of Education

Church courts. *See* LDS Church courts

Church of Jesus Christ of Latter-day Saints, 2, 9*n*3, 287. *See also* First Presidency

Civil War, U.S., 134, 146*n*21, 153, 418

Clark, Charles Badger, 158, 426

Clark, Hiram, 39

Clark, J. Reuben, 321, 371, 372, 373, 374, 388*n*25, 391*n*45, 433, 435, 436

Clark, Thomas H., 316

Clark, Willis, 288–89

Classes. *See* Middle-class culture; Privileged society; Working-class culture

Clawson, Rudger, 287, 310*n*120, 364*n*125, 422, 426

Clayton Investment Company, 320–21, 348*nn*48 and 50, 433

Cleburne, Patrick Ronayne, 153, 179*n*6

Cleveland, Ruth, 94

"Cleveland Street Scandal," 128*n*55

Cline, Walter, 42

Clinton, Jeter, 272

"Closet, the," 41. *See also* Heterosexual cover; Marriage, opposite-sex

Cluff, Lehi E., 82*n*28

Cognitive dissonance, 321

Colonia Juarez, Chihuahua, Mexico, 15*n*5, 335, 420

Colorado, 86, 15*n*5, 175*n*1, 380, 418, 438

Columbia University, 238–39, 245, 257*n*61

"Coming out," 231, 246–47

Commercial Street (Salt Lake City), 284, 318, 319–21, 329, 420, 424, 425

Commitment ceremonies, same-sex, 380, 397*n*81, 438. *See also* Female-female: covenants; Male-male covenants; Marriage, same-sex

Communists, 435

Companionship. *See* Couples, same-sex; Missionary companionship

"Compulsory heterosexual orientation," 17*n*7, 23*n*12, 120*n*8. *See also* Rich, Adrienne

Confederate States of America, 94, 153

Confidentiality of confession to LDS leaders as inapplicable to homoerotic acts, 60, 439

Congregational life: segregated by gender, 67, 410, 413–14

Conley, George (pseud.). *See* Raymond, George
Connecticut, 34, 109, 405
Conrad, Susan, 138, 150*n*42
Consensual. *See* Fornication; Homoerotic acts, voluntary; "Sexual acts performed by consenting adults in private"
Constitution Building, 72
Contributor (Salt Lake City), 232
Convents, 153
Cook, Blanche Wiesen, 6–7, 121*n*9, 159
Coolbrith, Ina (pseud.), 40, 57*n*40. *See also* Smith, Josephine
Copenhagen, 42–43
Corcoran, Brent D., 301*n*66
Co-residence of same-sex persons: examples, 82, 142*n*13, 152–53, 154, 155, 156, 158–74, 233–47, 250*n*10, 274; not in itself "proof" of homoerotic relationship, 158, 159, 161, 162, 163, 169–70, 186*nn*58 and 59. *See also* Census, U.S.; Couples, same-sex; Denial of homosexuality/lesbianism
Co-residence of unmarried heterosexuals, 159
Corinne, Utah, 318, 345*n*31
Cornell University, 156, 244
"Corner of Winter," 437
Cotton, John, 34, 405
Cottrell, Emily, 186*n*59
Council Bluffs, Iowa, 15*n*5
Council of Fifty, 66, 173, 410
Couples, same-sex: as American families, 162, 425; "Boston marriages," 163; as domestic partners, 71, 112, 82*n*25, 158, 162–71, 185*nn*51 and 52, 186*n*59, 232, 234–47, 250*n*10, 276, 312*n*132, 317, 425; and financial support, 142*n*13, 152, 164–65, 168, 187*n*62, 211, 212, 213, 217, 235, 238, 240, 380, 429; instructed by LDS president to live their homoerotic relationship "as decently as they could," 372, 434; mentioned, 112, 152–53, 154, 156, 157, 158–74, 234–47, 276, 284–85, 312*n*132, 369, 370–71, 372, 377–78, 380, 412–13, 425, 427, 429–30, 433. *See also* Marriage, same-sex; Missionary companionship
Cousins: as homoerotic sex partners, 216, 366

Covenants. *See* Commitment ceremonies, same-sex; Doctrine and Covenants; Female-female: covenants; Male-male covenants; Marriage, same-sex
Cowboys, 85, 154, 158, 426
Creek tribe, 133
"Crime against nature." *See* Anal sex; Bestiality; "Infamous crime against nature"; Natural/unnatural; Sodomy
Criminalization of same-sex acts, 34, 47*n*8, 272–73, 279, 282, 290*n*5, 300*n*62, 302*n*75, 330, 414, 415–16, 419, 427, 428, 431, 438, 441. *See also* Castration; Death penalty; Mormons: and jury decisions; Sodomy; Swimming, nude; Utah's criminal sentencing patterns; Utah's juvenile courts; Utah's penitentiary
Cross-cultural comparisons, 3, 6, 35, 37–44, 342*n*15, 402
Cross-dressing, 38, 41, 43, 54*nn*28 and 29, 85, 131, 132, 133–36, 146*n*21, 147*n*22, 148*n*31, 152, 175*n*2, 206–7, 219–20, 285, 406, 412, 418, 432. *See also* "Drag dances"/"drag balls"; Masquerade of one's gender from sex partners
Crucible (Logan, Utah), 439, 442
Cultural relativism: erotic, 37, 43–44, 73, 92, 132, 323, 402, 427; and femininity/masculinity, 35–36; and gender, 35; and heterosexuality, 33, 37, 41–42, 43–44, 285, 402; and homophobia, 44, 361*n*120, 402; and homosexuality, 6, 22*n*11, 35, 37, 38, 41–42, 43–44, 73, 83*n*37, 92, 285, 402; and sexual orientation, 6, 37, 41–42, 44, 83*n*37, 285, 402. *See also* Bias; Mormons: and ethical relativism; Social construction: controversy about
Cumming, Alfred, 87, 413
Curtis, Arthur, 278–81, 301*n*69, 302*n*72, 303*n*79, 305*n*92, 345*n*26, 362*n*121
Curtis, Norton, 305*n*91
Customary practices, 38, 91
Cutler, John C., 326

Daily Utah Chronicle (Salt Lake City), 441. *See also* University of Utah: student newspaper
Dakota tribe, 144

Damon, S. Foster, 192*n100*

Damon and Pythias, 39, 241

Dana, Richard Henry, 39, 408

Dancing, same-sex, 85–86, 135, 231, 335, 411–12, 414, 418. *See also* Homotactile

Daniels, "Madge," 317

Daniels, Sarah Mary, 255*n51*

Danites, 66, 271

Dante's *Inferno,* 326

"Dark Age"/"Golden Age." *See* Fallacies

Dartmouth College, 155, 407

Daughters of Bilitis, 436

Davenport-Hines, Richard, 47*n6*

David (biblical), 112, 241

David-and-Jonathan friendship: defined, 112–13; females in, 114, 125*n41*, 242, 243; males in, 112, 113–14, 241, 242, 376, 381, 393*n53*, 429, 435; Mormon leaders in, 112, 113–14. *See also* Friendship; Homoemotional; Same-sex intimacy without homoeroticism

Davis, Katharine Bement, 196, 432

Day, Frances, 146*n21*

Deacon, A. Bernard, 131

De Acosta, Mercedes, 194*n111*

Dean, Dawson Frank, 433

Dean, William, 356*n88,* 359*n105*

Death penalty: for adultery, 271–72, 292*n19,* 296*n39,* 375, 437; for bestiality, 35, 270–71, 413; for fornication, 292*n19;* for incest, 271, 294*n30;* for intercourse with stepdaughter, 270; for same-sex acts between women, 34–35, 405; for sodomy between men, 34, 405. *See also* Blood atonement; Criminalization of same-sex acts

De Blanc, Dawn, 438

Decapitation, 271–72. *See also* Blood atonement

Delta, Utah, 79*n18*

D'Emelio, John, 86

De Moisey, Charles, 316

Dempsey, Harry I., 78. *See also* Uckerman, Ruth

Denial of erotic meaning, 113, 116, 124*n31,* 128*n52,* 260*n82,* 335, 336

Denial of homosexuality/lesbianism: ecclesiastical, 21–22, 30*n30,* 51*n19;* historical, 109, 121*n9,* 159, 165, 188*nn70* and *71,* 194*n111,* 247*n3,* 393*n50;* news

blackout, 320, 330, 428; personal, 115, 127*n47,* 173, 175*n2,* 246, 439; police, 320, 329; psychological, 31*n30,* 41, 42, 43, 174, 219, 247, 287, 288, 335, 364*n125,* 422; silence about, 8, 36, 173, 188*n71,* 329, 335

Denmark, 31*n30,* 42–43, 148*n31*

Denver, 166, 380, 396*n81,* 438

De Raylan, Nicholas (pseud.), 174*n1*

Desaules, Henri Edouard, 67–69, 86, 418

Deseret Book Company, 335, 381

Deseret News (Salt Lake City), 40, 87, 220, 238, 239, 244, 262*n99,* 270, 271, 272, 279, 280, 283, 284, 285, 286, 294*n30,* 314–15, 319, 320, 329, 368, 393*n52,* 413, 414, 419, 420, 421–22, 423, 428, 429, 436

Desmond, David-Edward, 380, 396*n81,* 438

Detroit Post and Tribune, 418

Deviance: concept based on majority's experience, 4, 26*n19,* 38, 41, 244, 261*n96.* *See also* Abnormal/normal; Homoerotic acts, voluntary: declared unimportant in evaluating mental health of Americans; Natural/unnatural; Perversion

Devine, Frank, 307*n99*

De Wolfe, Elsie, 174

Dialogue: A Journal of Mormon Thought (Salt Lake City), 442–43

Diamond, Steve, 344*n23*

Diaries and sexual activities, 35, 38, 68–69, 92, 93, 128*n52,* 154, 367–68, 384*n8,* 411, 413, 415

Dickinson, Emily, 107–8, 115, 116, 126–27, 232, 412

Diehl, Christopher B., 319

Disciplinary council. *See* LDS Church courts

Disfellowshipped status, 266, 301*n66,* 409. *See also* LDS Church courts

"Disorderly house," 343*n21.* *See also* Prostitution: house of

Disraeli, Benjamin, 155, 181*n16*

Dix, John (pseud.), 275, 298*n51.* *See also* Prostitution, male; Slang, sexual

Doctrine and Covenants, 136, 138, 267, 407

Dodd, Albert, 93–94, 109

Domestic partners. *See* Couples, same-sex

Donoghue, Emma, 34

Dormitories. *See* Boarding schools; Reform schools; Utah's reform school; Young Men's Christian Association

Double entendre/double meaning, 54*n*32, 116, 221–22, 239, 241, 260*n*82, 298*n*51, 428. *See also* Denial of erotic meaning; Homosexual subtext; Slang, sexual

Douglas, Alfred Lord, 54*n*26, 289, 312*n*132

Downey, Thomas, 317

Dowries. *See* Male-wives; Marriage, same-sex

"Drag dances"/"drag balls," 135, 239, 428. *See also* Cross-dressing; Dancing, same-sex

Drake, Willis, 270–71

Dreams of same-sex intimacy, 87, 92, 412, 413, 423

Drury, Allen, 377–78, 437

Duberman, Martin B., 93

Dubois, Charles, 319

Due, Oliver, 165

Duke, Harry T., 80*n*20

Duponceau, Pierre Etienne, 179*n*8

Dusenberry, Warren N., 316

Dwight, Louis, 154, 407

Dwyer, Ada. *See* Russell, Ada Dwyer

Dwyer, James, 173, 367–68, 384*n*9, 427

Dwyer, "Miss," 174*n*1

Eakins, Thomas, 323

Earl, George (pseud.). *See* Ford, William H.

East High School. *See* Salt Lake City's East High School

East Village. *See* Greenwich Village

Edmonds, Charles, 153, 179*n*5, 412–13

Edwards, Harriet, 179*n*5

Edwards, Harry, 79*n*19

Edwards, William, 178*n*5, 179*n*5

Effective Missionary, 381

"Effeminate" males, 6, 35–36, 38, 41, 129*n*55, 131, 133, 135, 158, 202–6, 432, 434. *See also* Bias; Gender: behaviors; Homosexuals: masculine-effeminate dichotomy in relationships of

"Effeminate Men and Masculine Women," 35–36, 425

Eldredge, Grata P. Willis. *See* Fern, Fanny

Eldredge, Joseph U., 357*n*92

Elites. *See* Privileged society

Ellis, Havelock, 196, 181*n*24, 261*n*97, 340*n*8, 423, 424

Emotional distance between males, 96, 113–14, 333, 361*n*119, 381. *See also* Homoemotional; Homophobia; Homoromantic; Homosexual angst/panic

Endowment, temple, 84–85

England, 34, 92, 155, 289, 293*n*24, 387*n*21. *See also* Britain

Ennis, George, 344*n*26

Ensign, Horace S., Jr., 235, 236, 237, 241, 433

Enslin, Frederick Gotthold, 406

Episcopalians. *See* Protestants

Equal Rights Amendment, proposed, 382, 443

Erotic meaning: differs from culture to culture, 37, 43–44, 73, 402; differs over time, 323, 402, 427

Essentialism. *See* Homoerotic desire: biological/genetic causation of; Homosexuality: biological/genetic causation of; Social construction: controversy about

Eton, 155

Eureka, Utah, 299*n*59, 317, 343*n*22, 424

European-American culture, 33–36, 41, 43–44, 142*n*13

Evans, Frank, 348*nn*48 and 50

Evans, Richard L., 378, 395*n*69

Evans-Pritchard, E. E., 131–32

Exceptionalism. *See* Mormons

Excommunication, 266, 268, 274, 276, 278, 281–82, 287, 288, 297*n*50, 299*n*59, 301*n*66, 368, 372, 373, 374, 375, 380, 382, 409, 417–18, 422, 435, 439, 441, 442, 443. *See also* LDS Church courts; LDS Church membership

Factors in the Sex Life of Twenty-Two Hundred Women, 196, 432

Faderman, Lillian, 17*n*7, 162–63, 192*n*100

Fairbanks, Ortho, 240, 241, 258*n*69

Fairchild, "H. D.," 357–58

"Fairy," 162, 205, 206, 239, 425, 429

Fallacies: "Abdicating Fathers/Homosexual Sons," 5–6; "Dark Age"/"Golden Age," 3; minorities not historically relevant, 8

Family: same-sex couples as, in U.S. census, 162, 425
Family Welfare Association of America, 369
Farley, Lorenzo, 325–26, 352n69, 353n76
Farrer, Eliza Ware, 86
Farrer, William, 39
"Father hunger" of heterosexual sons throughout life, 24
Father-mother-daughter relationships, 22n12, 43, 201
Fathers: homosexually oriented men as. *See* Homosexuals
Father-son estrangement: and heterosexual sons, 4–6, 23n14, 25nn15, 16, and 17, 27nn20 and 22; and homosexual sons, 5–6, 28–29, 29n25, 204
Faust, James E., 22n8
Federation of Medical Women of the British Isles, 244
Feil, Daryl K., 59n52
Feliz, Antonio A., 138, 139, 150nn40, 41, and 42, 151n48
Felt, Joseph H., 250n10, 260n88
Felt, Sarah Louise "Louie" Bouton, 125n41, 232, 242–47, 250n10, 260n88, 266, 429
Female-female: covenants, 156, 243–44, 246, 260n89, 261n89; seduction, 117, 269, 413; violence, 211–12, 284, 286, 421–22, 439. *See also* Bonding; Commitment ceremonies, same-sex; Homoemotional; Homoerotic desire; Homoromantic; Homosocial; Homotactile; Lesbians; Marriage, same-sex; Mormons; Women
Female-husbands: masculine-acting, 133, 285; mentioned, 221; as seers, 144; as shamans, 133, 144; sources about, 141n9, 143n15; warriors, 133. *See also* Amazons/berdache; Cross-dressing; Gender: behaviors; Male-wives
Female impersonation, 134–35, 152, 154, 175n2, 418, 432. *See also* Cross-dressing; Male impersonation
"Female World of Love and Ritual," 45. *See also* Smith-Rosenberg, Carroll
"Feminization of American religion." *See* Religion, American
Ferguson, Ellen Brooke, 245

Ferguson, James, 86
Fern, Fanny (pseud.), 108
Field, Gertrude, 174n1
Field, John, 346n33
Field, Percy H., 82n28
Film industry. *See Advise and Consent*; Hays Commission; Hollywood film industry; Preminger, Otto
First Presidency: defined, 40; denials of "inborn homosexual orientation," 21n8, 51n19; formal statements about homosexuality, 21n8, 51n19, 380, 381–82, 438, 440, 441, 442, 443; mentioned, 72, 171, 256n57, 266, 267, 271, 273, 276, 319, 321, 347n35, 364n124, 366–68, 370, 371, 373–77, 389n28, 395n69, 408, 417, 418, 421, 422, 424, 425, 427, 428, 430, 433
Fitzpatrick, John F., 375–76
Flaherty, Joseph, 332, 360n114, 425
Flashman, Willard J., 70–71
Flynt, Josiah (pseud.), 156–57, 181n24, 424
Ford, William H., 344n26
Fornication, 39, 199, 266, 269, 271–72, 282, 297n50, 306n95, 315, 333, 340n10, 376, 380, 409, 423, 438, 440
Foster, Robert, 437
Foster, William, 363
Foucault, Michel, 333
Fowler, Charles H., 82n26
Fowler, Orson S., 110
Fox tribe, 133
Fraternities, 71, 432
Freedman, Estelle B., 86
Freemasonry, 66, 409
Freud, Sigmund, 361n117
Friendship: cult of, 232; mentioned, 87, 89, 92, 96, 109–11, 112, 117, 119n4, 129n60, 132, 136, 155, 160, 165–66, 173, 179n6, 188n70, 232, 233, 235, 241, 243, 333, 361n119, 374, 381, 406, 408, 409, 417, 425, 435; "warm language" of, 232, 247, 407. *See also* David-and-Jonathan friendship; Same-sex intimacy without homoeroticism
Frink, Horace W., 244

Gagnon, John H., 63n61
Gardo House, 90, 421

Garland, Jack Bee (pseud.). *See* Mugarrieta, Elvira Virginia

Gates, Susa Young, 111

Gay, Peter, 66, 109, 232

Gay and Lesbian Student Union (GLSU), 440

"Gay" as older term meaning "light-hearted," 116, 316. *See also* Double entendre/double meaning; Homosexual codes

"Gay" as recent term for homosexual: difficulties of cross-cultural application of either "gay" or "homosexual," 33, 37, 41, 42, 45, 83n37; as ethnic identity to some, 260n89, 395n72; inapplicable to some behaviors within a culture, 44, 100n28; later used in academic studies and popular media, 19, 20, 21, 197; rejected by some, 30n29, 64n63; this study accepts as a conventional term, 30n29, 33; use by Anglo-American homosexuals from 1880s onward, 116, 128n55, 157, 239, 257n60, 426, 428; use by current Mormons concerning homoerotic experiences, 59n54, 61n54, 391n40; use by *Deseret News*, 20, 21, 393n52, 399n96; used by this study most often to indicate people's self-definition in twentieth-century European-American culture, 45, 285. *See also* Bisexuality: self-defined; Homosexuals: self-defined; Lesbians: self-defined; "Non-gay homosexual"

Gay bar, 77n14, 333, 378, 435, 438, 439, 441, 442

"Gay bashing," 104n51, 383. *See also* Violence against lesbians and gays

"Gay Church Welcomes Community Unwanted," 441

Gay liberation, 77n14, 129n60, 431, 435, 436, 439, 440, 441, 443

Gay Rap Group, 440

Gayzette (Salt Lake City), 382, 442

Gender: behaviors, 35, 131, 132–33, 135–36; and cultural definitions, 35; imbalance in population, 85, 166, 188nn69 and 71, 317; segregation, 67, 111, 410, 413–14. *See also* Amazons/berdache; Bias; "Butch-fem" roles; Cross-dressing; "Effeminate" males; Homoenvironmental; "Masculine" females; "Soft men"

General authorities: definition of, 82n31;

individual examples of, 2, 22n8, 40, 66, 67, 70, 71, 72, 85, 86, 87, 89, 90, 91, 92, 110–11, 112–14, 125n40, 266–74, 276, 281–82, 287, 292n19, 293n24, 295n34, 301n66, 308n108, 310n120, 311nn125 and 126, 314, 317, 319, 320, 321, 322, 336, 348n50, 366–67, 368, 369–83, 388n25, 394nn55 and 59, 407–18, 420–27, 429–30, 432–38, 440, 443; Mormon adoration for, 113, 430; once regarded homoerotic acts as less serious than fornication or adultery, 270, 288, 368, 376; recently regarded homoerotic acts as more serious than fornication or adultery, 376; rental of brothels, 319–22, 346n35, 347n35, 348n50, 349n54, 424; restraint/tolerance toward homoerotic acts, 265–66, 267, 268, 270, 272, 274, 281–82, 287, 366–68, 371–73, 374–75, 377, 402, 434, 435–36; revulsion toward homoerotic acts, 276, 376; significance of reaching adulthood in nineteenth century, 265, 366, 373–74, 375, 376–77, 380, 381–82. *See also* Apostles; First Presidency; Patriarch to the Church; Seventy, the

General Handbook of Instructions, 380, 439, 443

"Gentiles" (non-Mormons), 162

Georgia, 154, 296n39, 407

Germany, 154, 237

Ghana, 132, 142n12

Gibson, James, 163–64

Glossolalia, 67, 91, 407

God and the origin of homosexuality, 51n19, 103n51

Golden, Charles, 275, 298n56

Gomorrah. *See* Sodom

Good Housekeeping (New York City), 244

Gordon, Sarah Barringer, 283

Gosiute, 133

Gossip, 68–69, 219, 220, 221, 233, 388n25, 432

Graham, Dorothy, 171–72

Grant, Heber J., 91–92, 95, 114, 247, 314, 320–22, 348nn49 and 50, 369–70, 388n25, 421, 423, 425, 426, 430

Grantsville, Utah, 415

Grass Valley, Utah, 86, 418

Graupe, William, 168–69, 190n89

Great Britain. *See* Britain
Greece, 36, 71, 82*n27*, 130, 154, 182*n28*
Greek Orthodox, 329
Green, George (pseud.), 174*n1*
Green, Richard, 5, 28*n22*
Greene, Louise L. *See* Richards, "Lula" Greene
Greenwich Village (New York City), 116–17, 162, 239, 425, 426, 428–29, 439
Grief, 107, 131, 158, 240, 312*n132*. *See also* Homoemotional
Griffin, Parley N., 353*n77*
Groin groping, 34, 287, 375, 435. *See also* Homoerotic acts, involuntary
Group sex, 324, 326, 327, 353*n77*, 427. *See also* Homoerotic acts, voluntary
Guatemala, 6
Guerin, Elsa J., 134, 147*n21*, 412
Guilt. *See* Mormons: and ethical relativism; Social construction: of guilt
Gulf of same-sex desire, 7
Gulik, R. H., 166

Hall, Murray (pseud.). *See* Anderson, Mary
Hall, Radclyffe, 219, 432
Halperin, David M., 6
Hamilton, James, 284, 362*n121*
Hammon, Mary, 34, 405
"Hammond, Freda," 388*n24*
Hammond, James H., 94
Hammond, William A., 154
Hampton, Brigham Young, 346*n35*, 349*n54*
Hancock, Levi W., 85, 271, 411
Handcart pioneers, 153, 412
Hanks, Maxine, 108, 120*n8*, 260*n89*
Hanrahan, Thomas, 318, 345*n27*
Hanson, Ralph O., 82*n28*
Harrington, J. F., 356*n88*
Harris, Charles, 346*n33*
Harrow, 155
Harvey, A. D., 34
Hatch, Lorenzo, 89, 416
Hatfield, Charles (pseud.). *See* Guerin, Elsa J.
Haven, Elizabeth, 87, 156, 407–8
Hawaii, 15*n5*, 38–40, 54*n29*, 140, 147*n26*, 371, 377, 406, 408, 412, 416, 418, 436
Hawley, Arthur, 346*n33*

Haymond, Winnifred. *See* "Hammond, Freda"
Hays Commission, 432–33. *See also* Hollywood film industry
Heavenly Creatures, 439
Hebrew Bible. *See* Old Testament
"Hegemonic masculinity," 62*n57*
Hendry, Daniel, 278–81, 301*n70*, 302*n72*, 303*n79*, 362*n121*
Henry, George, 433
Henry, Jennette, 167, 189*n82*, 317
Herdt, Gilbert, 42, 44, 142*n13*, 182*n28*
Hermaphroditism, 35, 48*n18*. *See also* Intersexuality
Hess, John W., 112
Heterosexism, 62*n57*, 159
Heterosexual: as a term, 33, 44, 422
Heterosexual cover, 70, 207, 211, 221, 243. *See also* "Closet, the"; Marriage, opposite-sex
Heterosexual eroticism. *See* Adultery; Bestiality; Fornication; Incest; Marriage, opposite-sex; Onanism; Polyandry; Polygamy; Premarital intercourse and bridal pregnancy; Prostitution; Rape
Heterosexuality: "compulsory," 17*n7*, 23*n12*, 120*n8*; "deviant" in some cultures, 41; "institution of," 4, 16*n7*; as recent concept in European-American culture, 33, 37, 43, 285, 402, 422; as right-handed sexuality, 4
Heterosexual relationships of heterosexually identified persons. *See* Co-residence of unmarried heterosexuals; Marriage, opposite-sex; Polyandry; Polygamy
Heterosexual relationships of homosexually identified persons, 174, 207–11, 374. *See also* Bisexuality; "Closet, the"; Marriage, opposite-sex; Unmarried
Heterosexuals: association with homosexuals and lesbians, 73, 221; defined by primary or exclusive sexual attraction for opposite-sex, 4, 36; nicknamed "straights," 7, 37; share many responses with homosexuals, 7, 286; some as nonjudgmental toward homosexuals and lesbians, 221, 437. *See also* Bias
Hickok, "Wild Bill," 35
Higbee, Francis M., 268, 362*n121*
Higginson, Thomas Wentworth, 116, 128*n52*

Highland Park (Salt Lake City), 240, 258*n*69

Hilton, Robert J., 80*n*20

Hinckley, Gordon B., 114, 392*n*50, 435

Hirschfeld, Magnus, 166

Historical denial of homosexuality/lesbianism. *See* Cook, Blanche Wiesen; Denial of homosexuality/lesbianism

Historical silence on sexuality. *See* Denial of homosexuality/lesbianism

History: and minority experience, 8; differences of interpretation, 8, 16*n*7, 22*n*11, 23*n*12, 27*n*19, 29*n*23, 30*n*29, 34, 64*n*62, 78, 79*n*19, 99*n*19, 120*n*8, 124*n*30, 129*n*60, 136–37, 138–39, 142*n*13, 144–45, 150*n*40, 179*nn*5 and 6, 182*n*28, 188*n*70, 192*n*100, 194*n*111, 224*n*5, 225*n*6, 226*n*11, 227*n*17, 242–43, 247*n*3, 255*n*47, 256*n*57, 260*n*89, 261*n*89, 295*n*34, 296*n*38, 339*n*6, 356*n*87, 386*n*18, 389*n*28; presentation of evidence, 8, 185*n*52, 186*n*59, 197, 226*n*10, 254*n*39, 190*n*89, 191*n*92, 192*n*95, 253*n*35, 258*n*70, 266, 289*n*1, 295*n*35, 299*n*59, 304*n*86, 334–35, 340–41, 343*n*23, 351*n*60, 353*n*72, 386*n*21, 394*n*61, 397*n*81. *See also* Bias; Denial of homosexuality/lesbianism; Social history

History of the Church, 87, 99*n*19, 110, 122*n*15, 268, 410

Hite, Shere, 62*n*58

Hobo. *See* Tramp/hobo

Holden, Rex, 339*n*7

Holding hands publicly, 1, 95. *See also* Homocultural orientation; Homotactile

Holland. *See* Netherlands

Hollywood film industry, 174, 378, 432–33, 438

Holmes, William, 343*n*21

Homoaffectionalism, 107. *See also* Homoemotional; Homoromantic

Homocultural orientation, 1, 2, 3, 41, 45, 231, 265–66, 377, 401, 402

Homoemotional, 1, 45, 87, 91, 93, 95, 96, 103*n*51, 107–18, 142*n*13, 152, 154, 155, 156, 157, 158, 213, 215, 231, 232, 240, 243, 244, 245, 259*n*76, 284, 285, 286, 289*n*1, 333, 361*n*119, 374, 379, 381, 401, 416, 417, 419, 421, 424, 430, 441. *See also* Emotional distance between males; Homoromantic; "Love that dare not speak its name"; Platonic love; Same-sex "love" acknowledged in LDS publications

Homoenvironmental, 45, 64*n*62, 111, 153–58, 325, 353*n*73, 411

Homoerotic acts, involuntary: classifying as erotic, 289*n*1; examples not involving forcible rape, 277, 287, 310*n*121, 311*n*123, 329, 335; Mormon perpetrators of, 275, 276–77, 280, 287, 316, 328, 329, 335, 362*n*121, 375, 417, 419, 423; naming victims, 295*n*35, 300*n*61, 308*n*106, 310*n*121, 311*n*123; non-Mormon or religiously unidentified perpetrators of, 272, 275, 280, 284, 286, 315, 316, 328, 329, 419; not an indictment of all homosexuals, 266; physician indifference toward, in evaluation of mental health of Utahns, 280–81, 419–20; restraint/tolerance toward, 279, 282, 288, 366–68, 371–73, 374–76, 377, 402, 419, 420, 434, 435–36. *See also* Child sexual abuse; Criminalization of same-sex acts; Rape: homosexual

Homoerotic acts, voluntary: among American Mormons, 42, 59*nn*53 and 54, 60, 103*n*51, 152, 200–201, 265–68, 272, 273–74, 276, 281, 282, 284, 289*n*1, 291*n*13, 299*n*56, 317–18, 324, 325, 327, 328, 334, 337, 362*n*121, 366, 369–70, 372, 373, 409, 413, 417–18, 421, 425–26, 430, 434, 435, 436, 442–43; caused revulsion, 93, 125*n*40, 276, 277, 278, 284, 301*nn*69 and 71, 325–26, 330, 376, 419, 437; condemned by some homosexually oriented people, 155; considered "habit," 376, 382, 394*n*61, 437, 442; declared unimportant in evaluating mental health of Americans, 244, 361*n*117, 429, 433, 441; under false pretenses, 175*n*2; between females, 33, 34–35, 42–43, 44, 63*n*58, 92, 109, 132, 133, 153, 155, 156, 182*n*25, 200, 269, 316–17, 334, 337, 363–64, 405, 406, 438; first experience of, 200–201, 219; higher incidence of reported by females than males, 42–43, 61*n*55; honored in some cultures, 38, 41, 130–31, 133; light-hearted views toward, 54*n*32, 94, 104*n*51, 155, 221–22, 431;

between males, 33–34, 36, 38, 40, 41–42, 44, 89, 94, 103–4*n51*, 131–32, 133, 144, 152, 154–55, 156–58, 182*n25*, 201, 265–68, 272, 273–74, 276–77, 284–85, 288–89, 314–15, 317–20, 324, 325–26, 334, 337, 362*n121*, 366, 369–70, 372, 405, 406, 407; mentioned, 1, 45, 188*n72*, 265, 289*n1*; monogamous versus promiscuous, 215–16, 217, 222–23, 265, 276, 289, 289*n1*; among Mormon converts in tribal cultures, 38, 39, 41, 58*n49*, 131, 132, 412; among non-Mormon or religiously unidentified Americans, 34–35, 44, 63*n58*, 94, 133, 154–55, 156–58, 196, 275, 284–85, 286, 288–89, 316–22, 325, 328, 334, 337, 353*n74*, 405, 406, 407, 415, 421–22, 430, 432, 434, 435, 438, 439; percentage of nineteenth-century Americans who experienced, 154, 156, 157, 158, 315, 334, 337, 411, 424; physician indifference toward, in evaluating mental health of Utahns, 280–81, 331–33, 419–20, 425; punishable by excommunication, 276, 278, 380, 382, 417–18, 419, 440, 441; regarded differently by individuals in same culture, 44, 244, 429; regarded differently by various cultures, 43, 44, 73, 92, 132, 402; regarded differently by working class and middle class, 361*n120*; regarded as less serious than fornication or adultery, 270, 288, 315, 367, 368, 376; regarded as more serious than fornication or adultery, 376; regarded as separating people into two different categories, 34, 35, 318, 333, 420; between relatives, 41, 88–89, 216, 282, 287–88, 310*n121*, 311*n123*, 366, 422, 425; required by some cultures, 41, 57*n44*, 58*n47*, 182*n28*; restraint/tolerance toward, 2, 125*n40*, 244, 265–66, 267, 270, 272, 273–74, 277, 279, 282, 284, 288, 325–26, 366–68, 371–73, 374–75, 377, 402, 421, 429, 434, 435–36, 437; among same-sex persons in co-residence, 152–53, 161, 163; and self-definition, 44, 94, 104*n51*, 109; as sign of masculinity in some cultures, 41–42, 57*n44*, 58*n47*, 131–32; universally experienced in some cultures, 38, 41, 42, 58*n51*. *See also* Anal

sex; Criminalization of same-sex acts; Groin groping; Group sex; Homoerotic desire; Intercrural intercourse; Mutual masturbation; Oral sex; Prostitution: male; Same-sex dynamics; Sodomy
Homoerotic desire: aversion therapy for, 379, 438, 439; biological/genetic causation of, 4, 5, 18*n8*, 21–22, 26*n18*, 36, 42, 51*n19*, 103*n51*; childhood/youthful awareness of, 121*n8*, 155, 196, 200–201, 222, 374; commented on by LDS leaders, 269, 276; considered "habit," 374, 382, 394*n61*, 437, 442; efforts to change or "cure," 5, 23*n12*, 27*n20*, 30*n29*, 156, 196, 208, 210, 379, 440; and female-female violence, 211–12, 284, 286, 421–22; gulf of, 7, 285, 429; in heterosexual marriage, 73, 103–4*n51*, 127*n47*, 131, 159, 192*n95*, 196, 208–10, 275, 276, 277, 281, 287–88, 371; as minority experience, 4, 22*n8*, 31, 69, 85, 89, 285, 401; not part of most people's same-sex dynamics, 1, 64*n62*, 69, 85, 89, 92, 93, 96, 109, 113, 114, 231, 247, 401; phrenological views of, 110; probable existence in prehistoric times, 4, 36, 285; punishable by excommunication, 374, 382, 443; regarded as common by YMCA's leaders, 160, 165, 430; regarded as effeminate for males in European-American culture, 93, 205, 278, 419; regarded as masculine for males outside European-American culture, 35, 41–42, 57*n44*, 131–32; regarded as nonfeminine for females in European-American culture, 205; regarded as separating people into two different categories, 34, 35, 36, 104*n51*, 285, 333; as sexual imperative, 4, 121*n8*, 196; as somewhat easier to cope with in nineteenth century, 231, 232; unexpressed sexually, 68–69, 160, 165, 212, 214–15, 216, 222, 242, 418, 430; as widespread in America's male subcultures, 154, 158, 160, 165, 407. *See also* Celibacy; Homoerotic acts; Homosexuality; Lesbianism; Sexual repression
Homoerotic in literature, 40, 55*n37*, 103–4*n51*, 117, 127*n51*, 129*n60*, 158, 219, 232, 248*n4*, 377–78, 432, 437, 440. *See also* Homosexual subtext

Homomarital, 45, 130–33, 136, 152, 174*n1*. *See also* Marriage, same-sex

Homopastoral, 45, 84–85, 89–90, 231

Homophobia: defined, 62*n57*; and general authorities, 373, 375, 376–77, 379, 382–83, 438; referred to, 1, 22*n8*, 44, 95–96, 100*n28*, 103–4*n51*, 115, 129*n60*, 166, 174, 175*n2*, 188*n70*, 219, 220, 289, 333, 361*n119*, 432, 434; religion as moderating influence on, 95–96, 315, 334, 366, 436; varies between cultures, 44, 402; varies between individuals, 376–77; varies between social classes, 361*n120*. *See also* Emotional distance between males; Homosexual angst/panic; Physical distancing between males; Self-loathing

Homoromantic, 45, 93, 103*n51*, 109, 110, 111, 112, 114–18, 154, 155, 156, 157, 158, 173, 181*n22*, 213, 215, 231, 232, 240–42, 243–44, 245, 247, 266, 284–85, 286, 289*n1*, 333, 361*n119*, 372, 379, 401, 407, 410, 412, 415, 425, 426, 439, 442. *See also* Homoemotional; Romantic love

Homosexual: as a term, 33, 41–42, 44, 45, 100*n28*, 422, 442

Homosexual angst/panic, 103–4*n51*, 115, 166, 188*n70*, 249*n4*. *See also* Homophobia; Sexual repression

Homosexual bathhouse, 239, 256*n59*

Homosexual codes, 116, 239, 314, 417, 426, 428. *See also* Homosexual subtext; Slang, sexual; Tattoo

Homosexual "cruising," 257*n60*

Homosexual emancipation. *See* Gay liberation; Society for Human Rights

"Homosexual societies": term used by some anthropologists but disputed by others, 42, 59*n52*

Homosexual subtext, 54*n32*, 55*n37*, 116, 127*n51*, 220, 221–22, 232, 239, 246, 247, 260*n82*, 428, 439. *See also* Homosexual codes; Slang, sexual

Homosexuality: age-structured, 142*n13*; in America's heartland, 196, 222, 223; aversion therapy for, 379, 438, 439; biological/genetic causation of, 4, 5, 18*n8*, 21–22, 26*n18*, 36, 42, 51*n19*, 103*n51*; cultural meanings of, 6, 22*n11*, 35, 37,

41–42, 43, 44, 73, 83*n37*, 92, 285, 402; defined by gender behavior rather than gender of sex partner in some cultures, 35; does not exist as a concept in some cultures, 41–42, 83*n37*, 285, 402; environmental influences on, 4, 6, 42–43; ethnic identity to some, 260*n89*; first acknowledged by LDS hierarchy, 373, 392*n45*, 436; first doctoral dissertation on, 433; "latent" in Mormonism, 137; as left-handed sexuality, 4; marriage used to remedy, 373–74, 429, 440; as more than erotic activities, 6–7, 103*n51*, 188*n72*; not caused by poor relationship with father, 4–6, 29*n22*; as recent concept in European-American culture, 33, 36, 37, 46*n3*, 285, 333, 402, 422; regarded as psychologically healthy, 218, 219, 222, 244, 361*n117*, 429, 441; regarded by some as defect to be repaired, 23*n13*; rejected by some as term, 30*n29*, 373, 374; reparative therapy for, 5, 23*n12*, 27*n20*; ritualized, 41, 58*n47*; situational, 64*n62*, 154–55, 158, 325, 353*n73*, 411, 419; studies on skewed by selecting subjects from insane asylums or prisons, 27*n19*, 196, 423. *See also* Bisexuality; Denial of homosexuality/lesbianism; Heterosexuality; Homoerotic acts; Homoerotic desire; Lesbianism; Same-sex dynamics

"Homosexuality among Tramps," 156, 424

Homosexuality: Welfare Services Packet, 382, 441

Homosexuals: age differences in relationships of, 222; as fathers, 104*n51*, 127*n47*, 159, 213; associating as subculture, 69, 73, 76*n14*, 116–17, 171–72, 195–96, 220, 382, 391*n40*, 420, 421, 440, 441, 442; avoiding relationships with women, 211; celibacy of, 442; and coming out, 231; community identity of, 222, 382, 391*n40*, 431, 435, 436, 440, 441; and cross-dressing, 135, 207; defined by primary or exclusive sexual attraction for same sex, 4, 36; domestic "partner" option in census, 162, 425; fear of being discovered, 196, 219, 221, 223; first covert Utah organization of, 69–70, 421; first national organization of, 435; first national periodical for, 436; first openly gay and lesbian Utah organization of, 440; first Utah publication for, 382, 442; heterosexual intimacy of, 103–4*n51*, 210–11, 223; included in U.S. census definition of "family," 162; isolating their experience from general experience, 5, 22*n12*, 26*n19*, 27*n20*, 196; left-handedness in at higher rates than in heterosexuals, 26*n18;* long-term relationships of, 176*n3*, 201, 216–17, 222, 265, 289, 434, 435; masculine-effeminate dichotomy in relationships of, 204–6, 222, 432; mass arrests of by police, 77*n14*, 239, 256*n59*, 333, 375, 377, 431, 437, 439; mental processes of differ from those of heterosexuals, 26*n18;* Mormon support group for, 138; "myth of isolation," 76*n14;* national influence of, 373, 392*n45*, 435, 436; not defined by instances of rape, 266; nurturing, 213; opposition to their imprisonment, 376; parental relationships and, 5–6, 28–29, 204; "philandering" and sexual fidelity among, 216; rejected as term by some, 30*n29*, 108–9, 374, 442; relationship dynamics of, 156–58, 213–14; religious background of, 197–98; schismatic Mormon group of, 380; self-defined, 45, 59*n54*, 63*n58*, 64–65, 69, 70, 71, 73, 103–4*n51*, 135, 138, 151*n48*, 195–223, 247, 364*n121*, 368, 382, 391*n40*, 433; self-image of, 201; as sexual minority, 197, 285, 318, 401; some satisfied in both heterosexual and homosexual relationships, 103–4*n51*, 210; suicide attempts of, 201–2; and use of alcohol and tobacco, 199–200; and using females as substitute for males, 210, 373, 440; "well adjusted," 433. *See also* "Closet, the"; Couples, same-sex; Denial of homosexuality/lesbianism; "Fairy"; "Gay" as recent term for homosexual; Homosexuality; Heterosexual cover; Lesbians; Lovers; Male-male covenants; Marriage, same-sex; "Queer"; Same-sex dynamics

Homosocial, 16*n7*, 45, 63*nn61* and *62*, 66–73, 100*n28*, 107, 153, 163, 164, 231, 232, 247, 401, 407, 409, 410, 419, 424, 427, 432

Homosociality, 64*n62*, 69

Homotactile, 1, 45, 84–96, 98*n7*, 104*n51*, 107, 108, 113, 152, 179*n6*, 231, 232, 234, 247, 250*n14*, 324, 379, 381, 392*n48*, 401, 408, 410, 411, 416, 419, 423, 426, 430, 431, 432, 441. *See also* Bedmates, same-sex; Dancing, same-sex; Holding hands publicly; Homopastoral; Kissing; Same-sex dynamics: photographs depicting

Honeyville, Utah, 286–87

Honolulu, Hawaii, 436

Hopi, 133

"House of ill fame," 317, 318, 343*n21*. *See also* Prostitution

Howard, Frank, 286, 310*n119*, 339*n7*

Howard, William (pseud.), 174*n1*

Howard, William Lee, 425

Howe, William, 170

Howells, William Dean, 56*n37*, 232

Howland, Frank, 339*n7*

Hsu, Francis, 166, 188*n70*

Hudson, Roswell, 352*n72*, 355*n81*

Hughes, Bird (Burt), 352*n72*, 355*n81*, 363

Hughes, Thomas, 170

Hulme, Juliet, 439

Hunsaker, Abraham, 310*n121*

Hunsaker, Hans Peter, 287–88, 311*n126*

Hunsaker, Lorenzo, 286–88, 310*n121*, 311*n126*, 362*n121*, 422

Hunsaker, Weldon, 311*n126*

"Hustler," male, 187*n62*. *See also* Prostitution

Hyde, Edward, 406

"I Am a Homosexual: The Gay Drive for Acceptance," 442

Idaho, 15*n5*, 238, 275, 373, 421, 436

Idaho Daily Statesman (Boise), 436

Illinois, 15*n5*, 66, 138, 173, 175*n1*, 243, 266–68, 387*n21*

Immigrants: Chinese, 165–67, 170–71, 186*n59*, 187*n67*, 188*nn69*, *71*, and *72*; European, 153, 161, 163–64, 165, 167, 170–71, 178*n5*, 185*n49*, 187*n67*, 188*n70*, 197, 274, 280, 286, 295*n34*, 303*n79*, 329, 368, 384*n14;* Japanese, 170

Imperial Russian Ballet, 174

Improvement Era (Salt Lake City), 234, 238, 367, 428

"Inactive" Mormons. *See* Church activity
Incest, 271, 272, 295*n*30, 297*n*50
Incidence of homoeroticism. *See* Homo-
    erotic acts; Mormons; Sex surveys
"Indecent exposure." *See* Swimming, nude
Independence, Missouri, 15*n*5
Indiana, 243
Individuality, 37, 333–34. *See also* Bias
"Infamous crime against nature," 273,
    315, 329, 415–16. *See also* Anal sex;
    Natural/unnatural; Sodomy
Insanity. *See* Homoerotic acts, voluntary:
    declared unimportant in evaluating men-
    tal health of Americans; Homoerotic
    acts, voluntary: physician indifference
    toward, in evaluating mental health of
    Utahns; Homosexuality: regarded as
    psychologically healthy; Masturbation;
    Utah's insane asylum
Intercrural intercourse, 141*n*7. *See also*
    Homoerotic acts, voluntary
Interdict, 287. *See also* Roman Catholics;
    Sacrament
Intergenerational relationships: defined,
    142*n*13, 182*n*28; dynamics of, 142*n*13,
    156–57, 182*n*31; female-female, 132,
    161, 171, 243–44, 246; female-male,
    110, 171; male-male, 38–41, 55*n*37,
    56*n*39, 109, 117–18, 131–32, 141*n*7,
    154, 156–57, 159, 161, 165, 179*n*8,
    182*n*28, 187*nn*62 and 65, 235–42, 246,
    255*n*52, 289, 306*n*97, 370, 387*n*23,
    406, 407, 415, 416, 426, 430–31, 434;
    preserving heterosexual subordination,
    132–33, 142*n*13; warning about, 165.
    See also "Kept boys"; Mentor-protégé
    relationships
Intermediate sex: as early term for "homo-
    sexuals," 51*n*20
International Conference of Women Physi-
    cians, 105*n*56, 244–45, 261*n*96,
    262*n*99, 429
International Women's Year, 382
Intersex: as early term for "homosexuals,"
    51*n*20, 197
Intersexuality, 36, 48*n*18, 49–51
Inuit, 131
Iowa City, Iowa, 412
Iowa tribe, 133
Irish in America, 153

Islamic countries, 182*n*28
Isleta, 133

Jackson, James C., 88
Jacobs, Zina D. Huntington, 408
James, Henry, 232
Jamestown, Virginia, 405
Janus, Cynthia L. and Samuel S., 63*n*58
Japan, 182*n*28. *See also* Immigrants
Jargon, 64*n*62, 144. *See also* Language
Jealousy, 107, 110, 111, 131–32, 155, 171,
    196, 212, 213, 214, 284, 377, 417. *See
    also* Homoemotional
Jefferson, Thomas, 35, 406
Jeffreys, Sheila, 159
Jenkins, John, 346*n*33
Jensen, Bruce, 175*n*2
Jensen, Leasa (pseud.). *See* Urioste, Felix
Jenson, Harold H., 254*n*46, 255*n*52
Jessee, Dean C., 99*n*19, 147*n*26
Jewish affiliation, 70, 80*n*22, 168, 270
"Jocker," 157. *See also* Intergenerational
    relationships; Tramp/hobo
Johnson, Andrew G., 302*n*76, 330,
    358*n*100, 428
Johnson, Elizabeth, 405
Johnson, Jacob, 315, 339*n*7
Johnson, Sonia, 121*n*8
Johnson, William, 150*n*43
Jonathan (biblical), 112, 241. *See also*
    David-and-Jonathan friendship
Jones, Dan, 87, 410
Jones, Frederick, 272, 414
Jones, Shadrach, 234, 251*n*17
Jordan River (Utah), 323–24, 427
Juab County, Utah, 317
Juarez. *See* Colonia Juarez, Chihuahua,
    Mexico
Judd, John W., 307*n*98
Judd, Robert L., 348*n*50
Judson, Isaac, 285, 422
Jung, Karl, 361*n*117
Juvenile Instructor (Salt Lake City), 237,
    433

Kamehameha the Great, 38
Kana-ana, 55*n*37
Kasius, Andrew, 385*n*14
Kasius, Cora, 368–69, 384*n*14, 385*n*15,
    431–32

Kasius, Effie, 385*n14*
Katz, Jonathan Ned, 33, 44, 339*n6*, 423
Kentucky, 359*n102*
Kenya, 141*n9*, 142*n12*
"Kept boys," 187*n62*, 211, 213, 222
Kerwinieo, Ralph (pseud.). *See* Anderson, Cora
Kesinger, Kenneth M., 53*n24*
Keystone saloon, 284
Kiernan, James G., 422
Kimball, Andrew, 424
Kimball, Heber C., 85, 86, 173, 271–72, 411, 412, 430
Kimball, Heber P., 173, 430
Kimball, J. Golden, 114, 317, 366–67, 373, 383*n2*, 392*n46*, 426
Kimball, Spencer W., 124*n33*, 373–74, 376, 377, 379, 380, 382, 383*n2*, 388*n25*, 392*nn46, 48, 49*, and *50*, 394*n61*, 415, 434, 437, 438, 440, 441, 443
King, Samuel A., 316, 423–24
Kinsey, Alfred, 423, 435, 436
Kirtland, Ohio, 15*n5*, 66, 91, 136
Kissing: among American same-sex friends, 1, 92, 93, 109, 231, 374, 381, 392*n48*, 407, 412, 419, 423; between brothers, 91; between David and Jonathan, 112; between females, 86, 91, 116, 117, 231, 407; between LDS general authorities, 91–92, 114, 374, 412, 421, 425, 426, 427, 430, 441; between males, 91–92, 93, 109, 114, 220, 231, 374, 381, 407, 412, 419, 421, 423, 425, 426, 427, 430, 432; between Protestant ministers, 92, 102*n48*, 109. *See also* Homoemotional; Homotactile
Klenke, Henry, 70–71
Klenowski, Dorothy, 174*n1*
Kneass, William E., 325, 326, 353*n77*
Knight, Inez, 424
Knight, Joseph, Jr., 87
Kodiaks, 131
Kofoed, Earl Baird, 390*n40*
Kosloff, Theodore, 174

Lackaway, Frank, 329, 357*n95*
LaCrosse, Thomas, 356*n88*
Ladder (San Francisco), 436
LaGrasselle, Victor, 319

Laguna tribe, 133
Laie, Hawaii, 15*n5*
Lakota. *See* Sioux
Lambourne, Alfred, 172, 193*n102*
Lamoni, Iowa, 15*n5*
Lang, Sabine, 144
Langenbacker, John Paul, 331, 359*n105*
Langenbecker, John. *See* Langenbacker, John Paul
Language. *See* Bias; Bilingualism of nineteenth-century homosexuals; Double entendre/double meaning; Homosexual subtext; Jargon; Literary conventions; Platonic love; Slang, sexual
Language, lack of: for homoerotic acts, 37–38, 402; for sexuality, 33, 94, 285, 415
Larsen, Francis E., 78. *See also* Uckerman, Ruth
Las Vegas, Nevada, 15*n5*
Lashaway, Frank. *See* Lackaway, Frank
LDS Business College, 367, 427
LDS Church. *See* Church of Jesus Christ of Latter-day Saints
LDS Church Board of Education, 377, 379
LDS Church courts, 267, 268, 276, 281–82, 287, 297*n50*, 299*n59*, 300*n61*, 310*n120*, 368, 371, 373, 382, 408, 417, 422, 434, 435, 441. *See also* Disfellowshipped status; Excommunication
LDS Church membership: voluntary withdrawal of, 368, 428
LDS Church's holding company: rental of brothels, 319–22, 346*n35*, 347*n35*, 348*n50*, 349*n54*, 424, 433
LDS high school. *See* LDS University
LDS Primary, 233, 242–43, 245, 247, 429
LDS publications. *See Children's Friend; Contributor; Deseret News; General Handbook of Instructions; Improvement Era; Juvenile Instructor; Priesthood Bulletin; Relief Society Magazine; Salt Lake Herald; Salt Lake Herald-Republican; Times and Seasons; Wasp; Woman's Exponent; Young Woman's Journal*
LDS Relief Society, 66, 368–69, 373, 385*n14*, 409, 431, 436
LDS University: mentioned, 72, 95, 202, 237, 238, 240, 367, 369, 427, 431; student magazine, 241–42, 426

LDS Young Women's Mutual Improvement
  Association (YMMIA), 127*n*49, 168
Ledford, John, 278–81, 301*n*70, 302*n*72,
  303*n*79
Ledyard, John, 38, 406
Lee, Harold B., 381–82
Lee, John D., 89, 137, 149*n*38
Lee, Raffella, 167, 189*n*82, 317
Left-handedness, 4, 22*n*8, 26*n*18, 51*n*19.
  See also Bias
Lesbianism: in America's heartland, 196,
  223, 284; as ethnic identity to some,
  260*n*89; as "feminist choice" or resistance to patriarchy, 108, 120*n*8, 121*n*8,
  206; and heterosexual marriage, 78,
  208–10, 215, 217, 221, 243; and heterosexual polygamy, 243, 260*n*89; LDS hierarchy acknowledges, 373, 382,
  392*n*45, 436, 441, 443; as more than
  sexual activities, 6–7, 17*n*7, 109; parental relationship and, 22*n*12; punishable
  by excommunication, 374, 382; as recent concept, 33, 34, 35, 108, 173,
  193*n*102, 197, 415, 422; referred to in
  LDS publications, 172, 284–85, 427; as
  sexual imperative, 121*n*8, 156. *See also*
  Bisexuality; Denial of homosexuality/les-
  bianism; Female-female; Heterosexuality; Homoerotic acts; Homoerotic desire;
  Homosexuality; Lesbians; Lesbos; Same-
  sex dynamics; Women
Lesbians: age differences in relationships
  of, 171, 172, 215, 222; amorous, 172,
  203, 205, 212, 215, 223; as mothers, 44,
  77*n*17, 78, 202, 209, 212; associating as
  subculture, 69, 117, 171–72, 174, 195–
  96, 220, 368, 382, 421, 431, 440, 441;
  avoiding masturbation, 332; avoiding
  relationships with men, 207; blackmailed, 220–21; and celibacy, 109, 214–
  15, 222; and coming out, 231; community identity of, 222, 382, 436, 440,
  441; and cross-dressing, 207, 285; cousins as homoerotic lovers, 216; and fear
  of being discovered, 196, 219–21, 223,
  432; first national organization and periodical, 436; first study of in America,
  225*n*6; first Utah covert organization,
  69–70, 421; first Utah openly gay and
  lesbian organization, 440; first Utah

publication for, 442; and heterosexual
  intimacy, 207–10, 223; homosexuality of
  siblings, 201; imprisoned, 438; included
  in U.S. census definition of "family,"
  162; labeled on basis of feminist support, 382; long-term relationships of,
  172, 176*n*3, 200, 209, 214, 216–17,
  222, 265, 427; and male identification,
  205; masculine-feminine dichotomy in
  relationships of, 202–6, 222, 228*n*20,
  432; as a minority of feminists, 121*n*8;
  Mormon support group for, 138; nationally prominent, 172, 173, 174, 367,
  431–32; open about sexuality, 221, 223;
  and parental relationships, 22*n*12, 201,
  216; "philandering" and sexual fidelity
  of, 215–16; rejected by some as term,
  30*n*29; relationship dynamics of, 211–
  16; religious background of, 197–98,
  368–69, 385*n*15, 431; and sadism, 211–
  12; in Salt Lake City's "Casa Lesbiana,"
  171–72; self-defined, 44, 45, 59*n*54,
  63*n*58, 69, 73, 109, 171–72, 174,
  194*n*111, 195–223, 247, 285, 363–64,
  368, 382, 432, 433; self-image of, 200,
  201, 202, 218–19, 221, 222; as sexual
  adventurers, 208, 212, 215–16, 217–18,
  222; as sexual minority, 197, 401; some
  satisfied in both heterosexual and lesbian
  relationships, 209, 210; suicide attempts
  of, 201–2; using males as substitute for
  females, 208–9, 243; "well adjusted,"
  433. *See also* "Closet, the"; Couples,
  same-sex; Denial of homosexuality/lesbi-
  anism; Female-female; Heterosexual cover; Homoerotic acts; Homoerotic desire;
  Homosexuals; Lesbianism; Lesbos; Lovers; Marriage, same-sex; Same-sex dynamics; Women
Lesbian subtext. *See* Homosexual subtext
Lesbos, 33, 172, 173, 427
Lesotho, 132, 142*n*12
Letter to a Friend, 440
Letter writers, 86, 87, 92, 94, 107–8, 109,
  113, 114, 115, 155, 181*n*22, 235,
  259*n*76, 268, 285, 289
Leviticus. *See* Old Testament
Lewis, Ray Coleman, 318, 363
Lewis, Thomas, 270, 292–93
Libya, 42

Liddell, Elizabeth, 260*n88*
"Life in America," 323
Limericks, cowboy, 158. *See also* Poetry, same-sex
Lind, Earl (pseud.), 342*n15*
Lipman-Blumen, Jean, 16*n7*
Lister, Anne, 92
Literary conventions, 115, 247. *See also* Homoerotic in literature; Homosexual subtext
Livermore, Mary A., 146*n21*
Liverpool, England, 236, 387*n21*, 424
Lobell, Lucy Ann, 175*n1*
Lodgers. *See* Boarder/renter in homes
Logan, Utah, 235, 251*n22*
Logging camps, 154, 158
London, England, 128*n55*, 172, 236, 289, 387*n21*
Long, Constance E., 244
Los Angeles, 174, 240, 316, 430–31, 434, 435, 436
Los Angeles Herald-Examiner, 436
Louisiana, 438
Lovers: female, 172, 285; male, 130, 138, 141*n7*, 165, 285, 372, 434. *See also* Couples, same-sex; "Women Lovers"
"Love that dare not speak its name," 38, 54*n26*, 72, 241, 289, 426. *See also* Homoromantic; Homosexuality; Lesbianism; Unmentionable crime; Same-sex "love" acknowledged in LDS publications
Lowell, Amy, 118, 172–73, 192*n100*, 232, 367, 427, 428
Lumbermen. *See* Logging camps
Lund, Anthon H., 90, 256*n57*, 320, 336, 367, 421, 425, 427, 430
Lydston, G. Frank, 420
Lyman, Francis M., 90, 101*n36*, 416, 421
Lyman, Richard R., 372, 388*n25*
Lyman, Stanford M., 166, 167
Lynch, Michael, 110

MacArthur, J'Wayne "Mac," 158
Macintosh, William W., 70, 80*n22*
Mack, John, 286, 310*n119*
Macnish, Robert, 110
Madsen, Soren, 276, 299*n59*, 362*n121*
Mahu (Mahoo), 54*n29*
Male bias. *See* Bias
Male bonding. *See* Bonding; Homoemo-

tional; Homoromantic; Homosocial; Homotactile
Male dominance. *See* Gender: imbalance in population; Misogyny; Patriarchy
Male Glee Club, 72, 240, 242, 254*n39*, 369
Male identification, 205, 206. *See also* Bias
Male impersonation, 134–35, 152, 174*n1*, 175*n2*, 207. *See also* Cross-dressing
Male-male covenants, 40, 132, 136, 407, 415. *See also* Commitment ceremonies, same-sex; Marriage, same-sex; Mormons
Male-wives: feminine-acting, 131, 133; masculine-acting, 131, 132; as seers, 144; as shamans, 130–31, 133, 144; their families received dowries or "bride wealth," 130, 131; as warriors, 131–32. *See also* Amazons/berdache; Cross-dressing; Female-husbands; Gender: behaviors
Man-boy marriage, 131, 141*n7*. *See also* Intergenerational relationships; Marriage, same-sex
Manhattan, 162, 316, 425. *See also* Greenwich Village; New York City
Manhood, 41, 94, 57*n44*
Manti, Utah, 270, 293*n24*, 295*n34*
Marbury, Elisabeth, 174
Maricopa tribe, 133
Marines, U.S., 154, 355*n81*, 411
Marks, Jeannette, 156
Marriage, Mormon: as sealing for "time and eternity," 136, 138, 149*n36*, 151*n48*, 411
Marriage, opposite-sex: dynamics of, 10–13, 115, 413; "excessive" sexual intercourse in, 418; of homosexually identified persons, 44, 73, 78, 127*n47*, 159, 174, 192*n95*, 196, 208–11, 214–15, 217, 219, 221, 223, 243, 363–64, 374, 393*n52*, 429, 432; not regarded as superior to same-sex relationships, 130–31, 133, 244; of persons engaging in homoerotic activity (who were possibly not homosexually identified), 34, 36, 38, 41–42, 73, 131, 132, 174, 267, 269, 275, 276, 277, 287–88, 300*n62*, 318, 355*n81*, 362, 369–71, 374, 377–78, 393*n52*, 405; used as LDS remedy for homosexually oriented males, 373–74, 392*n50*, 393*n52*, 440. *See also* Bi-

sexuality; "Closet, the"; Heterosexual cover

Marriage, same-sex: ancient Greek, 130; celibate, 132, 137, 140; Chinese, 130, 188n70; desire for, 139, 218, 284; dowries or "bride-wealth" for male-wife, 130, 131; early Christian, 130; under false pretenses, 152, 173, 174n1, 175n2, 284; female-female, 130, 132, 133, 141n9, 173, 174n1, 284; and figurative reference to Mormon founder, 136, 408; formally recognized, 38, 130–34, 148n31, 151n48; gender roles in, 132–33, 136, 416; among the Inuit, 131; legalized, 130–31, 148n31; male-male, 130–33, 152, 175n1, 188n70, 416; Mormon possibilities for, 136–40, 260n89, 397n81; mourning and, 131; Native American, 133–34, 416; not regarded as inferior to opposite-sex marriage, 130–31, 133, 244; recently banned in Utah, 162; recently endorsed by University of Utah student newspaper, 440; Siberian, 130–31; South Pacific, 131; sub-Saharan African, 131–32, 137; without formal ceremony, 141n2. *See also* Couples, same-sex; Intergenerational relationships; Lovers

Marriott, J. Willard, Sr., 378
Marshall, John A., 80n20
Martin, Robert K., 64n62
"Masculine" females, 35–36, 135, 202–4, 425, 432. *See also* Bias; "Butch-fem" roles; Gender: behaviors; Lesbians: masculine-feminine dichotomy in relationships of
Mason, Harry, 317, 343n21
Mason, H. P., 80n20
Masonry. *See* Freemasonry; Nauvoo Masonic Lodge
Masquerade of one's gender from sex partners, 147n22, 175n2. *See also* Cross-dressing; Female impersonation; Male impersonation
Massachusetts, 34, 87, 154, 405, 407
Masturbation: linked with homosexuality, 374, 392n50, 415; linked with insanity, 262n97, 332–33, 360n115, 415; mentioned, 68–69, 76n11, 230n37, 244, 260n82, 261n97, 277, 278, 287, 288, 331–33, 360nn111, 112, and 115, 373,

374, 379, 391n45, 409, 410–11, 415, 418, 426, 440; warnings to women about, 418, 426, 436
Matlovich, Leonard, Jr., 442
Mattachine Society, 435
Ma'u, Jione, 113, 124n34
May, Dean L., 364n122
Mayne, Frank (pseud.). *See* Day, Frances
McAddo, W. George, Jr., 26n19
McCarty, William, 330, 359n102
McClanahan, Perry D., 275, 298n55, 362n121, 417
McConkie, Bruce R., 375–76, 394nn55 and 59, 437
McCormick, John S., 318
McCormick, Mike, 305n91, 328, 356n87
McCullough, Ellen Mar, 68
McKay, David O., 90, 91, 113, 114, 125n40, 371, 375, 376–77, 379–80, 388n25, 427, 429, 430, 435, 436, 437
McQueen, Robert I., 441
Meader, Spencer, 346n33
Melanesia, 41, 96, 132, 182n28, 402. *See also* Papua New Guinea
Melville, Herman, 39, 54n32, 232
Memphis, Tennessee, 284–85, 421–22
Ménage à trois, 131, 164, 174, 217–18
Menninger, Karl, 361n117
Men performing blessing for males, 84
Mental health. *See* American Psychiatric Association; Homoerotic acts, voluntary: declared unimportant in evaluating mental health of Americans; Homoerotic acts, voluntary: physician indifference toward, in evaluating mental health of Utahns; Homosexuality: regarded as psychologically healthy; Insanity; Masturbation; Utah's insane asylum
Mentor-protégé relationships, 131, 132, 137, 165, 254n46. *See also* Intergenerational relationships; "Kept boys"
Meredith, William, 181n16
Merrill, Charles W., 363
Methodists. *See* Protestants
Metropolitan Community Church, 441
Metropolitan Museum of Art (New York City), 351n62
Mexico, 15n5, 89, 420
Middle-class culture, 92, 94, 107, 163–64, 333, 361n120

"Middletown, U.S.A.," 199

Military, U.S., 154, 333, 442. *See also* Marines; Sailors; Soldiers

Military academies. *See* Boarding schools

Miller, "Lou," 317, 342*n18*

Mineer, Alma Elizabeth "Lizzie," 243, 260*n88*

Miner, James A., 286, 422

Mining camps, 85, 154, 317

Minorities, sexual. *See* Homoerotic desire; Homosexuals; Intersexuality; Lesbians; Transsexuality

Minorities as not historically relevant. *See* Fallacies

Miracle of Forgiveness, 440

Misogyny, 62*n57*

Missionary companionship, 39, 66, 67, 76*n6*, 113–14, 153, 199, 379, 381, 382–83, 387*n21*, 396*n76*, 424, 434, 438, 443

Missouri, 15*n5*, 66, 421

Mitchell, Alice, 284–85, 421–22

Mitton, Samuel B., 235, 259*n76*

Moberly, Elizabeth R., 29*n23*

Moby Dick, 54*n32*

"Modigliani's Gypsy," 439

Moisey, Charles de. *See* De Moisey, Charles

Monasteries, 154

Monk, Charles, 272, 295*n35*

Monroe, James M., 89, 410–11

Monson, Caroline "Carline," 171–72, 191*n92*, 192*n95*

Monson, Thomas S., 171

Montalvo, Tasha "Joe," 175*n2*

Morasco, Joseph, 329

Morgan, Anne, 174

Morgan, J. P., 174

"Mormon" (nickname). *See* Book of Mormon

Mormon Battalion, 271

Mormon Choir. *See* Salt Lake Tabernacle Choir

Mormon Church. *See* Church of Jesus Christ of Latter-day Saints

Mormon culture region, 2, 15*n5*, 266, 323, 334, 379, 443

Mormon Doctrine, 375–76, 394*nn55* and 59, 437

"Mormon President Raps Homosexuals," 441

Mormons: early history of, 2, 9*n3*; early references to lesbianism among, 172, 392*n45*, 427; and ethical relativism, 267, 271, 294*n30*, 321–22, 367–68, 408, 427–28; as exception to U.S. society in opposite-sex polygamy, 1–2, 9*n4*; female-female covenants among, 151*n48*, 243–44, 260*n89*, 261*n89*; homophobic contrasts between past and present, 95–96, 102–4*n51*, 376, 381, 383, 402; instructed by LDS president to live their homoerotic relationships "as decently as they could," 372, 434; and jury decisions, 272, 275, 277, 284, 417, 419, 421; lower incidence of nonmarital sex among than among other surveyed groups, 42–43, 335, 365*n127*; as mainly typical of U.S. society's same-sex dynamics, 2, 69, 71, 85, 86–87, 92, 93, 94, 107, 114, 265, 401; male-male covenants among, 136, 137–38, 140, 151*n48*; as mirror of early America's homocultural orientation, 2, 401; often examined in isolation, 3; opposite-sex monogamy among, 10*n4*, 139; organization of schismatic homosexual group, 380; percentage of who experienced homoerotic acts, 42–43, 59*nn53* and 54, 334, 337, 428, 435, 442–43; and phrenology, 109–11, 409; premarital sex and bridal pregnancy among early, 199, 336, 428; previously regarded homoerotic acts as less serious than fornication or adultery, 270, 288, 315, 367, 368, 376, 423; and public expression of homoerotic desire, 241–42; recently regarded homoerotic acts as more serious than fornication or adultery, 376; regarded masturbation as more serious than homoerotic acts, 288; and restraint/tolerance toward homoerotic acts, 2, 103*n51*, 125*n40*, 265–66, 267, 270, 272, 273–74, 276, 277, 278, 283, 284, 315, 325–26, 366–68, 371–73, 374–75, 402, 419, 420, 421, 434, 435–36; revulsion of toward homoerotic acts, 125*n40*, 276, 277, 278, 284, 288, 301*n71*, 316, 325–26, 376, 437; sometimes an exception to U.S. society in same-sex dynamics, 86, 289; support group for gay and lesbian, 138; suppos-

edly committed "more sexual crimes
here in proportion to the population
than anywhere else," 421; and time lag
in adopting the homophobia of U.S. society, 95–96, 289, 315, 328, 334; total in
nineteenth century, 334, 364*n*122; unmarried experience of, 13*n*4, 68–69, 71,
153, 178*n*5, 233, 241, 246, 276, 284,
299*n*59, 301*n*71, 327, 355*n*81, 369,
407–8, 410, 412–13, 414, 415, 418,
426; "What It Means to Be a Mormon,"
246. *See also* Church activity; Church of
Jesus Christ of Latter-day Saints
Morrill Act, 414, 416
Morris, Anna, 174*n*1
Morris, Robert J., 38
Mosher, Celia Duel, 93, 105*n*56, 196
Mother-daughter relationships, 22*n*12,
201, 216
Mothers, lesbians as. *See* Lesbians
Mother-son relationships, 5, 23*n*14,
25*n*16, 29*n*22
Motion Picture Association of America
(MPAA), 438. *See also* Hollywood film
industry; Preminger, Otto
Motion Picture Producers and Distributors
Association. *See* Hays Commission; Hol-
lywood film industry
"Mountain Charley," 134, 412. *See also*
Guerin, Elsa J.
Mount Holyoak College, 156
Mourning. *See* Grief; Homoemotional;
Marriage, same-sex
Mugarrieta, Elvira Virginia, 147*n*22
Muncie, Indiana, 199
Murrell, Christine, 261*n*96
Mutual admiration, 107, 109, 158. *See
also* Homoemotional
Mutual masturbation, 155, 158, 277, 278,
366, 380, 425–26, 440. *See also* Homo-
erotic acts
My Days and Dreams, 428
"Myth of isolation." *See* Homosexuals

Nandi, 141*n*9
Naomi. *See* Ruth and Naomi
Nash, Mrs., 154
Nash, S. C., 80*n*20
Natural/unnatural: concept of, 4; desire,
269, 276, 283, 286, 324, 412; friend-

ship, 110, 111, 409, 417; sex acts, 4,
16*n*7, 33, 109–11, 269, 286, 289,
299*n*56, 308*n*106, 376, 414, 424, 437.
See also Abnormal/normal; Cultural relativism; Deviance; Perversion
National American Woman Suffrage Asso-
ciation, 262*n*102
National Woman Suffrage Association, 245
Native American tribes, 133–34
Nature-nurture controversy, 4, 36, 51*n*19.
See also Homoerotic desire: biological/
genetic causation of; Homosexuality: bi-
ological/genetic causation of; Lesbian-
ism; Sexual attraction, primary; Social
construction: controversy about
Nauvoo, Illinois, 15*n*5, 66, 138–39, 266–
68, 271, 276, 291*n*13
Nauvoo Legion, 66
Nauvoo Lyceum, 66
Nauvoo Masonic Lodge, 66, 409
Nauvoo temple, 85, 411
Navajo, 133
Navy, 154, 411. *See also* Marines, U.S.;
Sailors
Naylor, George, 274, 296*n*45, 297*n*46,
362*n*121, 416
Nazimova, Alla Lavendera, 174, 430
Nebraska, 86, 175*n*2, 359*n*102, 411
Neff, Lillian Estelle, 168
Nelson, William, 80*n*20
Netherlands, 148*n*31, 369, 428, 432
Nevada, 15*n*5
New Guinea. *See* Papua New Guinea
New Haven, Connecticut, 34, 405
New Hebrides, 131
New Horizons for Homosexuals, 440
New Jersey, 406
New Mexico, 15*n*5, 133, 296*n*39
New Orleans, 316
New Testament, 91
Newton, Esther, 16*n*7, 205, 206
New York City, 115, 116–17, 157, 160,
162, 166, 169, 172, 174*n*1, 185*n*52,
196, 205, 206, 236, 238–39, 240, 244–
45, 306*n*97, 312*n*129, 316, 322, 331,
342*nn*15 and 16, 369, 414, 425, 426,
428–29, 432, 433, 439
New York Colony, 406
New York Medical Journal (New York
City), 425

New York State, 15n5, 91, 93, 282

New York Times, 315, 378, 382, 432–33, 435, 437

New York University, 433

New York World's Fair, 323, 351n62

Nez Perce, 133

Nicholes, Hugh, 363

Nichols, Jeff, 344n23

Nicolosi, Joseph, 27n20

Nimkoff, Meyer F., 4–5

"Non-gay homosexual": self-definition of former activist with Queer Nation, 64–65; term used by reparative therapists, 64n63

Non-Mormons, 185n50. *See also* "Gentiles"

Norman, Sarah, 34, 405

North, William, 179n8

Norway, 148n31, 237

Nudity. *See* Swimming, nude

Nuttall, L. John, 90–91, 421, 422

Nuttall, Sophia Taylor, 91, 422

Nyakyusa, 42

Nyasa, Lake, 42

Nye, Sarah Alice, 311n126

Nzema, 132

Oakland, California, 172

Oaks, Dallin H., 393n50, 442

Oberndorfer, Joseph, 80n20

O'Donovan, Rocky, 69, 77n17, 79n19, 80n19, 121n8, 129n62, 179n5, 194n111, 242, 243, 260n89, 289n1, 296n38, 328, 356n87, 385n15, 386n18, 389n28, 391n44, 395n72

Ogden, Utah, 90, 96, 277, 286, 288, 317, 318, 322, 325–27, 368, 418, 421

Ohio, 15n5, 66, 91, 136, 138, 160

Oil, consecrated, 84, 85

Oklahoma, 158

"Old Maid," 108, 415. *See also* Unmarried

Old Testament, 2, 46n5, 112–13, 124n31, 246, 265, 270, 289n2, 375. *See also* Bible

Omaha, Nebraska, 86

Omaha tribe, 133

Onanism (technically coitus interruptus, but often equated with masturbation), 375, 415, 437. *See also* Masturbation

One Magazine (Los Angeles), 436

Oral sex, 41, 55–56, 132, 158, 278, 279, 287, 288, 302n75, 322, 330, 359n102, 419, 428, 431. *See also* Homoerotic acts

Orbison, James, 167

Oregon, 15n5, 40, 57n43

Orientation. *See* Homocultural orientation; Left-handedness; Right-handedness; Sexual orientation

Osborne, Ray (Roy) E., 318

Oto, 133

Ottinger, George M., 120n7

Out of the Bishop's Closet, 138, 151n48

Overland Monthly (San Francisco), 40, 55n37, 414–15

Oviatt, James Z., 83n32

Pachuco mark, 305n91

Packer, Boyd K., 382–83, 398n95, 443

Packham, John Wallace, 240–41, 369, 430–31

Paddock, Cornelia, 280, 283

Paddock, William H., 278–81, 302n72, 303n81, 332, 419–20

Paiute, 133

Palmyra, New York, 15n5

Panic. *See* Homophobia; Homosexual angst/panic

Papago, 133

Papua New Guinea, 41, 182n28. *See also* Melanesia

Paramore, Thomas, 343n21

Paris, France, 236

Park City, Utah, 317–18, 320

Parkhurst, Charles Durkee (pseud.), 147n22

Parowan, Utah, 278, 298n56

Partners, same sex. *See* Couples, same-sex; Marriage, same-sex

Parton, Grata P. Willis Eldredge. *See* Fern, Fanny

Patriarchal blessing, 69, 84, 226n11, 227n17, 282, 385n14, 429

Patriarch to the Church, 83n31, 369–71, 387n23, 388n25, 433

Patriarchy, 84, 108, 120n8, 206

Patter (Patten?), Oscar, 343n21

Pattirini, Madam (pseud.). *See* Young, Brigham Morris

Pawnee, 133

Payne, William Richard, 329, 363

Payne Whitney Psychiatric Clinic, 433

Payson, Utah, 271

Pearson, Niels August Emer, Jr., 352*n72*, 353*n77*, 355*n81*, 363

Pen (Salt Lake City), 434, 437. *See also* University of Utah: student literary magazine

Pendergast, M. S., 80*n20*

Penis holding as conversational mode, 37

Pennock, John A., 435

Percentage who have experienced homoeroticism. *See* Homoerotic acts, voluntary; Mormons; Sex surveys

Perry, Anne (pseud.). *See* Hulme, Juliet

Peru, 53*n24*

Perversion, 38, 69, 110, 122*n15*, 157, 331–32, 380, 420, 422, 435, 436, 438. *See also* Abnormal/normal; Bias; Deviance; Homoerotic acts, voluntary: declared unimportant in evaluating mental health of Americans; Natural/unnatural

Petersen, Mark E., 377, 379, 380, 394*n59*, 396*n75*, 438, 440

Peterson, Amos, 346*n33*

Peterson, Gustave Albert, 301*n71*

Philadelphia, 35, 166, 316, 406

Philippines, 6

Phoenix, 15*n5*

Photographs. *See* Same-sex dynamics

Phrenology, 109–11, 122*n15*, 409

Physical distancing between males, 96, 379, 438. *See also* Emotional distance between males; Homophobia

Physical touch. *See* Athletic teams; Bedmates; Homotactile; Same-sex dynamics

Pickering, Sidney, 275, 298*n56*, 362*n121*

Pike, Charles R., 236–37, 254*n41*

Pike, Edward, 80*n20*

Pillow talk, same-sex, 89. *See also* Bedmates

Pima, 133

Pinto, Victor, 319

Pitt, Tom D., 329

Plato, 124*n30*

Platonic love, 113, 115, 124*n30*, 160, 165, 232, 417. *See also* Same-sex intimacy without homoeroticism

Play on words, 55*n33*, 224*n6*, 241, 260*n82*. *See also* Denial of erotic meaning; Double entendre/double meaning

Plural marriage. *See* Polyandry; Polygamy

Plural wives: homosocial co-residence, 67; loving relationship with each other, 243; mentioned, 276; passionate response to husbands, 110, 112, 115; possible relationships, 243, 260*n89*; sexually neglected by husbands, 111, 122–23, 131, 413; turning to homoeroticism, 121*n8*, 132. *See also* Marriage; Polygamy; Women

Plymouth, Massachusetts, 34

Poetry, same-sex, 115–18, 126*n46*, 158, 173, 193*nn102* and *107*, 241–42, 289, 426, 430, 439, 442. *See also* Double entendre/double meaning; Homosexual subtext

Police: concealment of extent of male prostitution, 320, 329, 347*n43*; cooperation with LDS headquarters, 346*nn32* and *35*, 372; raids on homosexual meeting places, 77*n14*, 239, 256*n59*, 317–18, 319, 333, 375, 377, 437, 439; raids on Utah brothels as form of taxation, 318, 344*n23*; raids on Utah brothels designed to protect prominent men, 346*n32*, 347*n41*

Political correctness, 8

Polyandry: heterosexual, 408; male-male, 131

Polygamy: opposite-sex, 2, 9*n4*, 67, 159, 197–98, 233, 243, 260*n89*, 276, 277, 279, 280, 282, 283, 287, 300*n62*, 307*n101*, 310*n121*, 321–22, 368, 412, 414, 416, 421; same-sex, 131, 133, 217–18, 260*n89*. *See also* Marriage; Ménage à trois; Plural wives; Polyandry

Ponca, 133

Post, Aaron, 165

Post-Traumatic Stress Disorder (PTSD), 321

Potawatomi, 133

Poulos, Nick, 329

Powers, George, 356*n87*

Pratt, Noel S., 72, 83*n32*, 237, 241, 255*n48*, 260*n83*

Pratt, Orson, 267–68

Pratt, Parley P., 269, 273, 276, 412

Premarital intercourse and bridal pregnancy, 199, 335–36, 365*n127*

Preminger, Otto, 378, 395*n71*, 438

Prep schools. *See* Boarding schools

Presentist bias. *See* Bias

Presidency. *See* First Presidency

Priesthood, 84, 189*n84*, 371, 372, 414
Priesthood Bulletin, 382, 441
Primary organization for children. *See* LDS
   Primary
Prior, David, 304*n84,* 306*n93*
Prisons, 153, 154, 407. *See also* Homoen-
   vironmental; Homosexuality: situational
Pritt, Ann F., 27*n19*
Pritt, Thomas E., 25*n15,* 27*n19*
Privacy, 87
Privileged society, 1, 88, 91, 100*n26,*
   148*n31,* 155, 198, 276–77, 333
Prophet: Mormon definition, 2, 112,
   148*n32*
Prophet, seer, and revelator: Mormon male
   leaders as, 113, 371, 407; women as, 84
Prostitution: female, 34, 117, 166,
   188*n71,* 189*n82,* 316–23, 329, 342*n18,*
   343*n23,* 345*n28,* 355*n86;* house of, 34,
   117, 128*n55,* 268, 275, 297*n50,*
   312*n129,* 316–22, 329, 342*n15,*
   344*nn23* and 24, 345*n32,* 346*n35,*
   348*nn46* and *50,* 424, 425, 433; legally
   supervised, 329; male, 117, 128*n55,*
   154, 187*n62,* 257*n60,* 275, 289,
   298*n51,* 305*n91,* 316–20, 322, 323,
   342*nn15* and *16,* 345*n28,* 349*n59,* 363,
   407, 416, 420–21, 424, 425, 429, 430,
   433, 436; Mormon female, 317; Mormon male, 317, 318, 322, 349*n59,* 363,
   424, 436; pimp's role changed over time,
   344*n24;* "Stockade," 329. *See also*
   "Hustler," male; "Kept boys"; Police
Protestants, 67, 70, 95, 114, 134,
   193*n104,* 200, 269, 328, 330, 331,
   358*n100,* 414, 427
Provo, Utah, 199, 275, 282, 315–16, 336,
   396*n76,* 417, 420, 423–24
"Prushuns," 157. *See also* Intergenerational relationships; Tramp/hobo
Public awareness. *See* Publicity
Publicity, 70, 73, 86, 87, 95–96, 108, 110–
   11, 111–12, 113, 114, 116–17, 153,
   154, 155, 156–58, 160, 163, 172–73,
   196, 219–20, 232, 237, 239, 241–42,
   242–43, 244–45, 247, 266–68, 272–73,
   275, 276, 278–80, 284–86, 289,
   295*n35,* 300*nn61* and 62, 314–16, 320,
   327, 330, 382, 407, 409, 415, 417, 418,
   419, 421–22, 423, 427, 428, 429, 430,

432, 433, 434, 435, 436, 437, 438, 439,
   440, 441, 442
Pulitzer Prize, 378, 437
Puritans, 34, 405
Pye, Hannah, 178*n5*
Pyper, George D., 238, 279

"Queen," 220, 238, 239, 257*n66*
"Queer": early meaning as "different,"
   205; midtwentieth-century meaning as
   "homosexual," 158
Queer Nation, 64–65
Quorum (holders of specific LDS priesthood office, organized numerically), 66,
   85, 407
Quorum of the Twelve: defined, 40. *See
   also* Apostles

Radio City, 435. *See also* Gay bar
Rambova, Natacha (pseud.), 173–74,
   194*n111,* 430
Randolph, John A., 330, 363
Rape: heterosexual, 35, 266, 272, 275,
   289*n1,* 297*n50,* 324, 340*n10;* homosex-
   ual, 117, 156, 266, 272, 275, 277, 278–
   81, 282, 285, 286, 289*n1,* 315, 316,
   325, 327–31, 417, 419, 423–24; naming
   victims of, 295*n35,* 340*n7. See also*
   Child sexual abuse; Homoerotic acts, in-
   voluntary
Rasmussen, Stanley, 327, 352*n72,* 355*n81,*
   363
"Ravish." *See* Rape
Raylan, Nicholas de. *See* De Raylan,
   Nicholas
Raymond, George, 318
Raynes, Marybeth, 53*n22,* 321–22
Reality, perceptions of, 36, 37. *See also*
   Bias; Cultural relativism
Redburn, Joe, 441
Rees, Robert A., 30*n29*
Reform schools, 153, 154, 283, 306–7,
   310*n121,* 324–27, 353*n74,* 419. *See
   also* Homoenvironmental; Homosexuali-
   ty: situational; Utah's reform school
Relativism. *See* Cultural relativism; Mor-
   mons: and ethical relativism
Relief Society. *See* LDS Relief Society
Relief Society Magazine (Salt Lake City),
   245, 246, 391*n45,* 430, 431

Religion, American: encouragement of same-sex intimacy in, 92, 102*n48,* 109, 334; feminization of, 67

Renter. *See* Boarder/renter in homes

Reorganized Church of Jesus Christ of Latter Day Saints, 15*n5*

Reparative therapy of homosexuals, 5, 23*n12,* 27*n20. See also* Homoerotic Desire; Homosexuality; Lesbianism

Repression. *See* Sexual repression

Republican party, 435

Restoration Church of Jesus Christ, 151*n48*

Restraint/tolerance toward homoerotic acts. *See* General authorities; Homoerotic acts; Mormons; Utah's criminal sentencing patterns

Revelations, LDS, 136, 148*n32,* 265, 267, 407, 408

Revolutionary War, 154, 406

Rexburg, Idaho, 373

Rich, Adrienne, 16*n7,* 120*n8,* 121*n8,* 205. *See also* "Compulsory heterosexual orientation"

Richard of Devizes, 187*n62*

Richards, George F., 388*n25*

Richards, "Lula" Greene, 108, 120*n7*

Richards, P. Scott, 64*n63*

Richards, Stephen L., 114, 125*n40,* 375, 377, 393*n53,* 435–36

Richards, Willard, 139–40, 149*n38,* 151*n48*

Richfield, Utah, 276, 282, 299*n59,* 371, 417

Ricks College, 373, 435

Right-handedness, 4, 5. *See also* Bias

Riter, George W., 301*n69*

RLDS Church. *See* Reorganized Church of Jesus Christ of Latter Day Saints

Roberts, Bolivar, Jr., 80*n20*

Robinson, Jeremiah L., 100*n25*

Robinson, Lorenzo, 88, 100*n25*

Rockwood, Albert P., 86, 412

Rogers, Thomas, 362*n121*

Rogerson, Josiah, 178*n5,* 179*n5*

Rolapp, Henry H., 315, 423

Role models: mentioned, 8, 205; self-announced, 247

Roman Catholics, 22*n8,* 130, 173, 316, 328, 329, 330, 331, 375–76, 427, 437

Roman Empire, 130

Romantic love, 114, 401. *See also* Homoromantic

Romney, Marion G., 394*n59*

Rosecrans, George W., 113, 410

Rosen, Ruth, 317

Rossiter, Shamira Young, 161

Rotary International, 378, 395*n69*

Rotundo, E. Anthony, 94, 333, 361*n119*

Rupp, Leila J., 108–9, 121*n8*

Russell, Ada Dwyer, 118, 172–73, 192*n100,* 266, 367, 427, 428

Russia, 130

Russian River (California), 70, 419

Ruth and Naomi, 241, 246

Ryman, Frederick S., 93, 312*n129*

Sacrament (LDS equivalent of Communion), 287, 311*n125*

Sacraments (Roman Catholic), 287

Sadism, 211–12

Sage College, 156

Sailors: and homoerotic tattoo, 281, 305*n91;* homophobia of, 434; percentage involved in homoerotic acts, 154, 411; homoerotic activities while in Utah, 281, 370, 434. *See also* Homosexuality: situational; Shipboard life

St. Louis, Missouri, 316

Salome, 174

Saltair, 321

Salt Lake Bohemian Club, 69–73, 77*n17,* 79*n19,* 80*nn20* and *22,* 82*n28,* 83*nn32* and *33,* 195, 242, 263*n110,* 279, 419, 421, 426, 429

Salt Lake City, 42–43, 57*n41,* 66, 86, 90, 91, 95–96, 120, 135, 152, 157, 160–72, 173, 184*n43,* 187*n62,* 195–223, 235–47, 269, 271–81, 284–86, 298*n51,* 314–15, 317–24, 329–30, 332, 344*n23,* 346*n35,* 367–70, 375–77, 387*n21,* 391*n42,* 392*n48,* 412, 414, 416, 417, 419, 420, 421, 424, 425, 429–33, 435, 437, 439, 440, 441

Salt Lake City directory, 70–72, 78, 82, 233, 236, 238, 240, 250*n10,* 251*n35,* 254*nn39* and *41,* 303*n79*

Salt Lake City's East High School, 95, 431

Salt Lake City's social clubs: for females, 71; for males, 72

Salt Lake City's Stonewall Center, 138

Salt Lake County, Utah, 274, 283, 316, 414

Salt Lake Herald, 278, 279, 280, 284, 314–15, 324, 327, 423

Salt Lake Herald-Republican, 330

Salt Lake Philharmonic Orchestra, 71

Salt Lake Tabernacle, 67, 235

Salt Lake Tabernacle Choir, 70, 72, 117, 190*n*86, 232, 235–38, 240, 242, 256*n*57, 369, 426, 430, 431

Salt Lake temple, 100*n*26, 349*n*54

Salt Lake Theatre, 220, 314, 417, 432

Salt Lake Tribune, 80*n*20, 103*n*51, 138, 162, 178*n*5, 278, 279, 280, 281, 300*n*62, 315, 319, 320, 330, 332, 375–76, 379, 437, 442, 443

Salt Lake Valley, Utah, 412

Sambia, 41, 57*n*44

Same-sex couples. *See* Census; Couples, same-sex; Marriage, same-sex; Partners, same-sex

Same-sex dynamics: photographs depicting, 85, 94–96, 106*n*63, 221–22, 235, 242, 431; regarded differently by various cultures, 37, 44, 73, 402; why the preferred term, 33, 44–45. *See also* Celibacy; Homocultural; Homoemotional; Homoenvironmental; Homoerotic; Homomarital; Homopastoral; Homoromantic; Homosocial; Homotactile; Marriage, same-sex; Mutual admiration; Platonic love

Same-sex intimacy without homoeroticism, 1, 69, 85, 89, 92, 93, 96, 103*n*51, 109, 113, 114, 231, 247, 401. *See also* Celibacy; David-and-Jonathan friendship; Friendship; Platonic love

Same-sex "love" acknowledged in LDS publications, 72, 87, 108, 112, 113, 114, 116–17, 234, 241, 243, 284–85, 286, 381, 415, 421–22, 426. *See also* Homoemotional; Homoromantic; "Love that dare not speak its name"; Platonic love

Samoa, 15*n*5

San Francisco, 40, 157, 196, 236, 240, 316, 327, 333, 344*n*26, 430–31, 436

San Francisco's Bohemian Club, 70, 419

Sanpete County, Utah, 336

Santayana, George, 232

Sappho, 172–73, 193*n*102, 427

Scannell, R. L., 80*n*20

School of the Prophets, 66, 84, 136, 140, 407, 415

Schweitzer, Henrietta Young, 263*n*110

Schweitzer, Henry B., 70, 80*n*22

Schweitzer, Katherine Young, 70, 80*n*22, 81*n*23, 263*n*110, 421

Schweitzer, Leopold, 80*n*22

Schweitzer, Louis, 80*n*22

Sealing. *See* Marriage, Mormon

Sealing of men to men, 137, 415. *See also* Adoption ceremony

Seattle, 172, 196, 224*n*6, 238

Second anointing, 411

"Secret vice," 260*n*82. *See also* Masturbation

Seduction. *See* Female-female: seduction

Seelye, Sarah Edmunds, 146–47, 418

Segregation. *See* Congregational life; Gender: segregation

"Self-abuse," 288, 415, 426. *See also* Masturbation

Self-definition versus society's definition, 44, 64–65, 109

Self-image, positive, 200, 218, 219, 221, 222

Self-loathing, 109, 174, 201, 202, 219, 222, 374, 409. *See also* Guilt; Homophobia; Homosexual angst/panic

"Self-pollution," 391*n*45, 415, 418. *See also* Masturbation

Semen transactions in Melanesia, 41, 57*n*44, 182*n*28

Seminole, 133

Separate spheres of females and males, 66, 107. *See also* Bias; Homosocial; Victorian cultural values; Women

Service, Clyde R., 387*n*21

Service, Norval, 369, 386*nn*18 and 20, 388*n*24, 432

Servis, Clyde C., 387*n*21

Settle, Burton G., 82*n*28

Settle, Francis E. M., 82*n*28

"Seven Sisters" colleges, 111, 417

Seventh Cavalry, 154

Seventy, the (general authority office), 82*n*31, 86, 271, 412

Sex surveys, 5, 30*n*30, 42–43, 44, 59*n*53, 62*n*58, 93, 156, 157, 182*n*25, 195–223,

334, 364*n123*, 365*n127*, 399*n95*, 432, 435, 442–43

Sexual activities. *See* Heterosexual eroticism; Homoerotic acts

"Sexual acts performed by consenting adults in private," 441. *See also* Criminalization of same-sex acts; Homoerotic acts, voluntary

Sexual assault. *See* Rape

Sexual attraction, primary, 4, 16*n7*, 36. *See also* Bisexuality; Heterosexuality; Homoerotic desire; Lesbianism; Nature-nurture controversy; Sexual orientation

Sexual Behavior in the Human Female, 436

Sexual Behavior in the Human Male, 435

Sexual identity, 34, 94, 115

Sexual Inversion, 157, 196, 424

"Sexual Inversion in Women," 423

Sexual minorities. *See* Homoerotic desire; Homosexuals; Intersexuality; Lesbians; Transsexuality

Sexual orientation: concept adopted recently, 6, 33–34, 37, 94, 115, 244, 402, 422; concept led to American homophobia, 96, 333, 361*n119*; culturally defined, 6, 37, 41–42, 44, 83*n37*, 285, 402; involves more than erotic activities, 6–7; mentioned, 443. *See also* Bias; Heterosexuality; Homocultural orientation; Homoerotic desire; Lesbianism; Sexual attraction, primary

Sexual repression, 93, 105*n55*, 107, 118*n4*, 124*n30*, 160, 165, 212, 215, 218, 220, 228*n28*, 229*n33*, 242, 381, 430. *See also* Celibacy; Homosexual angst/panic

Sharp, Ronald A., 117, 129*n60*

Shaughnessy, Winifred Kimball. *See* Rambova, Natacha

Shaw, Anna Howard, 245–46, 262*n102*, 430

Shaw, John, 356*n88*, 363

Shaw, Louis C. L., Jr., 72–73, 83*n32*, 242, 260*n83*

Sheaffer, Mrs. Jess Sweitzer, 263*n110*

Shelley, Mary Wollstonecraft, 125*n42*

Shelley, Percy B., 114–15, 125*n42*

Shelley, Robert, 434

Shepherd, E. A., 429

Sheridan, Philip, 146*n21*

Shilts, Randy, 179*n6*

Shipboard life: homoenvironmental, 154; percentage of sailors with homoerotic experience, 154, 411. *See also* Homosexuality: situational

Shoshone, 133

Siblings: bedmates, 87–88, 100*n25*; as homoerotic sex partners, 88–89, 282, 287, 310*n121*, 311*n123*, 422

"Significant Characteristics of the Homosexual Personality," 433

Simkins, Simeon W., 277, 300*n61*

Simkins, William W., 277, 300*n61*

Simon, William, 63*n61*

Sin. *See* Mormons: and ethical relativism

Sioux, 133, 144

Sisters. *See* Siblings

Situational homosexuality. *See* Homosexuality

Siwa, 42, 58*n51*

Slang, sexual, 89, 94, 101*n29*, 116, 127*n51*, 128*n55*, 158, 173, 187*n62*, 193*n106*, 220, 238, 241, 257*n66*, 287, 288, 298*n51*, 310–11, 312*n129*, 325–26, 345*n28*, 383*n4*. *See also* Denial of erotic meaning; Double entendre/double meaning; Homosexual subtext

Slater, Paul, 346*n33*

Slavery, 109, 189*n84*

"Sleeping with" as term, 89, 101*n29*. *See also* Bedmates

"Smashes," 111. *See also* Homoemotional; Homoenvironmental; Homoromantic; "Seven Sisters" colleges

Smiley, Frank, 288, 422

Smith, David A., 348*n50*

Smith, Eldred G., 387*n23*, 388*nn24* and 25

Smith, Emma Bidamon, 409

Smith, George Albert, 370–71, 372–73, 388*n25*, 391*n42*, 434

Smith, Harvey W., 312*n130*

Smith, Hyrum, 160, 184*n44*, 268, 407

Smith, Hyrum M., 369, 388*n25*, 432

Smith, John, 346*n33*

Smith, John Gibbs, 387*n23*, 388*n25*

Smith, John Henry, 90, 91, 287, 421

Smith, Joseph, Jr., 2, 67, 87, 89, 91, 92, 99*n19*, 110, 112, 113, 136, 138, 139,

148*n*32, 189*n*84, 266–68, 269, 276, 379, 407, 408, 409, 410, 412

Smith, Joseph F. (1838–1918, First Presidency counselor and LDS president), 40, 92, 276, 319, 321, 348*n*50, 368, 369, 375, 388*n*25, 394*n*55, 416, 417, 427

Smith, Joseph F. (1899–1964, Patriarch to the Church), 364*n*121, 369–71, 373, 386*nn*18 and 20, 387*nn*21, 23, and 24, 388*n*25, 389*nn*28, 29, and *30*, 432, 433, 434, 436

Smith, Joseph F., Jr. (1876–1972). *See* Smith, Joseph Fielding

Smith, Joseph F., "II" (erroneous nickname for Joseph F. Smith, b. 1899), 388*n*25

Smith, Joseph F., III (1913–74). *See* Smith, Joseph Fielding, Jr.

Smith, Joseph F., "III" (erroneous nickname for Joseph F. Smith, b. 1899), 388*n*25

Smith, Joseph Fielding (1876–1972), 371, 375, 379–80, 388*n*25

Smith, Joseph Fielding, Jr. (1913–74), 388*n*25

Smith, Josephine, 57*n*40. *See also* Coolbrith, Ina

Smith, Mary Fielding, 91, 407

Smith, Orson, 90

Smith, Ralph G., 387*n*23, 388*n*25

Smith, Wilford E., 59*n*54, 364*n*123

Smith, Willard R., 348*n*50

Smith, William, 89, 266, 411

Smith-Rosenberg, Carroll, 45, 63*n*61, 100*n*28

Smoot, Reed, 330

Snow, Erastus, 89, 413

Snow, Lorenzo, 281–82, 287, 311*n*123, 321, 422

Snow, Warren S., 270, 293*n*24, 295*n*34

"Snuggling," same-sex, 86–87, 88. *See also* Bedmates; Homotactile

Social Casework (New York City), 369

Social class differences among same-sex partners, 142*n*13, 163, 170. *See also* Middle-class culture; Privileged society; Working-class culture

Social construction: controversy about, 22*n*11; of guilt, 94–95, 109, 372; of sexual views and experience, 4, 6, 22*n*11, 31*n*30, 37. *See also* Cultural relativism; Homoerotic desire: biological/genetic causation of; Homosexuality: biological/genetic causation of

Social history, 83*n*37, 159

Social isolation, 67–69

Society for Human Rights, 431

Sodom: as reason for biblical destruction, 268, 269, 270, 276, 291*n*16, 392*n*45, 409, 412, 413, 417

"Sodomites," 34, 154, 269, 391*n*42, 411

"Sodom of the New World," 283

Sodomy: "beastly" or bestial, 270–71, 277, 283, 413; oral, 330, 428, 431; same-sex, 34, 38, 42, 154, 159, 173, 238, 266, 269, 271, 272–74, 275, 276, 282–83, 286, 288, 289, 305*n*91, 306*n*97, 314–16, 317–18, 324, 327–33, 345*n*26, 356*n*88, 359*n*102, 362*n*121, 366, 368, 405, 406, 407, 417, 419, 420, 422, 423, 425, 427–28, 431, 441. *See also* Anal sex; Bestiality; "Buggery"; Castration; Criminalization of same-sex acts; Death penalty; Homoerotic acts; "Sexual acts performed by consenting adults in private"; Utah's criminal sentencing patterns

"Soft men," 130–31, 141*n*3. *See also* Gender: behaviors

Soldiers, U.S., 154, 272, 406, 414, 429, 442

"Solitary vice," 76*n*11, 260*n*82. *See also* Masturbation

"Solus," 442

Somerset, Isabel, 112, 425

Song of Solomon, 113, 124*n*31. See also Denial of erotic meaning

Sorensen, Arthur P., 38

Sororities, 71

South Africa, 85, 142*n*12

South America, 37–38, 182*n*28

South Carolina, 94

"South-Sea Idyl," 40, 55*nn*33 and 37

Spanish Fork, Utah, 278, 316

Speaking in tongues. *See* Glossolalia

Spencer, Frank, 257*n*61

Stake (similar to diocese), 89, 135, 276, 287, 379, 380, 418, 424, 435, 436, 438, 439, 443. *See also* Congregational life

Steed, Henry L., 82*n*28

Stein, Gertrude, 173

Stephens, Evan, 72, 83*n*33, 117, 168, 190*n*86, 232–42, 246–47, 251*n*22, 253*nn*34 and 35, 255*n*51, 256*n*57, 259*n*76, 264*n*111, 266, 369, 426, 428–29, 429–30, 430–31, 433
Stephenson, Fred. *See* Stevenson, Alfred Franklin
Steuben, General von. *See* Von Steuben, General
Stevenson, Alfred Franklin, 318, 363
Stevenson, Charles L., 80*n*20
Stevenson, Isabella, 186*n*59
Steward, Samuel M., 305*n*91
Stewart, Samuel W., 331, 359*n*105
"Stockade." *See* Prostitution
Stoddard, Charles Warren, 40, 55*nn*33 and 37, 56*n*39, 57*n*41, 415
Stonewall Bar, 77*n*14, 439. *See also* Gay bar; Gay liberation
Storey, James, 163–64, 187*n*60
Stout, Hosea, 271
Stout, Jan, 29*n*23
"Straights." *See* Heterosexuals
Strang, James J., 15*n*5, 268, 411
"Streak of Lavender," 434
Stuart, Charles, 109
Subcultures: female, 155–56, 171–72, 174, 195–96, 222; homosexually identified, 69, 73, 76*n*14, 117, 171–72, 174, 195–96, 222, 420; male, 153–58, 195–96, 222; variations in national patterns of belief, 333, 361*n*120
Sub-Saharan Africa, 131–32, 140, 142*n*12
Suicide, 201–2, 285–86, 327, 378, 422
Sun Tavern, 441. *See also* Gay bar
Suppressed Desires, 220, 229*n*33
Suppression. *See* Sexual repression
Sweden, 369
Sweeney, Frank, 329
Swenson, Paul, 103*n*51
Swimming, nude, 323–24, 351*n*63, 427. *See also* Criminalization of same-sex acts; Homosocial
Swimming Hole, 323
Swim teams. *See* Athletic teams
Symonds, John Addington, 115, 127*n*47, 155, 181*n*24, 340*n*8, 424
Symposium, 124*n*30
Syndergaard, Hyrum F., 82*n*28

Syrett, "Father," 68
Szasz, Thomas S., 360*n*115, 361*n*117

Tabernacle. *See* Salt Lake Tabernacle
Tahiti, 38, 39–40, 55*n*37, 140, 415
Talmage, DeWitt, 308*n*103
Tanner, Nathaniel H., 329–30, 427
Tattoo: as homoerotic code in nineteenth century, 281, 284, 305*n*91, 317, 328, 344*n*26. *See also* Homosexual codes
Taylor, Alfred. *See* Douglas, Alfred Lord
Taylor, Arthur Bruce, 40–41, 57*n*43, 416
Taylor, Bayard, 232
Taylor, John, 40, 112, 281, 314, 420
Taylor, John W., 336
Taylor, Samuel W., 291*n*13
Taylor, Thomas, 276–77, 278, 300*n*62, 301*n*68, 362*n*121, 419
Taylor, William, 112
Teena, Brandon, 175*n*2
Temple Bar College, 224*n*6, 225*n*6
Temples, 137, 149*n*38, 152, 224*n*6, 395*n*71, 415. *See also* Endowment, temple; Nauvoo temple; Salt Lake temple
Tennessee, 282, 284–85, 420, 421–22
Territorial Enquirer (Provo, Utah), 417
Texas, 296*n*39, 359*n*102
Third gender/third sex, 35, 47*n*14, 144. *See also* Bias: gender; Gender; Intersexuality; Transsexuality
Thomas, Arthur L., 80*n*20
Thomas, Evan S., 127*n*49, 282, 306*n*98, 362*n*121, 420
Thomas, Heber H., 127*n*49, 306*n*98, 325–27, 353*n*76, 354*n*79, 355*n*86, 427
Thomas, Kate, 115–17, 127*n*49, 129*n*62, 266, 306*n*98, 354*n*79, 426
Thomas, M. Carey, 156
Thomas, Samuel, 150*n*42
Thomas, Thomas S., Jr., 127*n*49, 237–40, 241, 245, 255*n*50, 256*n*57, 257*nn*61 and 67, 258*n*68, 306*n*98, 354*n*79
Thompson, Frank (pseud.). *See* Seelye, Sarah Edmunds
Thompson, Robert B., 136, 408
Tiermersma, Freda. *See* "Hammond, Freda"
Tilden, William, 434
Time (New York City), 442
Times and Seasons (Nauvoo, Illinois), 409
Timmony, John B., 319–20

Todd, Mabel Loomis, 92, 128*n52*
Toklas, Alice B., 173
Tolerance/restraint toward homoerotic acts. *See* General authorities; Homoerotic acts; Mormons; Utah's criminal sentencing patterns
Tolman, Judson, 368
Tonga, 15*n5*, 113, 430
Tongues. *See* Glossolalia
Track and field. *See* Athletic teams
Tramp/hobo, 156–57, 182*n31*, 315, 316, 317, 322, 344*n26*
Transsexuality (emotional and surgical), 36, 49–51, 152, 175*n2*. *See also* Bias: gender; Gender; Intersexuality
Transvaal, 85
Transvestism. *See* Cross-dressing
Tribal societies, 1, 37–38, 130–34
Twain, Mark (pseud.), 232
Twelve. *See* Quorum of Twelve
Twenty-seventh Wife, 395*n69*
"Two Loves," 54*n26*
Two Years before the Mast, 39

Uckerman, Ruth, 77*n17*, 78, 79*n18*, 226*n11*
Unitarians. *See* Protestants
United Nations, 369, 432
United Order Family of Christ, 380, 438
U.S. Congress, 414
U.S. News and World Report (Washington, D.C.), 94
U.S. Supreme Court, 416
University of Southern California, 159
University of Utah: homosexual issues at, 437, 439, 440; mentioned, 83*n33*, 88, 95, 168, 171, 369, 370, 386*nn18* and 20, 387*n23*, 389*n29*, 398*n95*, 432; sex surveys, 5, 42–43, 59*n53*, 344*n23*, 364*n122*, 435; student literary magazine, 222, 434, 437; student newspaper, 220, 432, 439, 440, 441
Unmarried: men, 13–15, 68–69, 70, 71, 73, 89, 153, 157, 158, 166, 233, 246, 276, 284, 299*n59*, 301*n71*, 355*n81*, 369, 406, 410, 412–13, 414, 421, 426; women, 13–15, 108, 112, 233, 245–46, 407–8, 415, 426
"Unmentionable crime," 279, 302*n75*. *See also* Anal sex; "Love that dare not speak its name"; Oral sex; Sodomy

Upper class. *See* Privileged society
Urbana, Illinois, 387*n21*
Urioste, Felix, 175*n2*
Utah, 2, 15*n5*, 40, 42–43, 66–73, 86–92, 95–96, 108, 110, 114, 115–17, 134, 135, 136, 138, 152, 154, 156, 157, 158, 160–74, 189*n84*, 195–223, 232–47, 253*n34*, 257*n66*, 260*n89*, 266, 269–89, 298*n51*, 310–11, 311*n122*, 314–37, 345*n28*, 366–83, 412–43
Utah Commission, 280
Utah County, Utah, 315, 316
Utah legislature, 273, 296*n41*, 323, 330, 415–16
Utah pioneer day, 68, 113, 412
Utah reformation, 292*n19*, 311*n125*
Utah's criminal sentencing patterns: mentioned, 277, 279, 282–83, 286, 296*n39*, 306*n95*, 315–16, 327–31, 333, 356*n87*, 417, 418–19, 420, 422, 423–24, 427; religious factors in, 282–83, 315–16, 328–31, 334, 352*n68*, 420, 423–24, 427. *See also* Criminalization of same-sex acts; Mormons: and jury decisions; Utah's juvenile courts
Utah's insane asylum, 262*n97*, 280–81, 288, 304*n86*, 331–33, 359*n107*, 419–20, 425
Utah's juvenile courts, 323–24, 351*nn60* and 61, 352*n68*, 427
Utah's medical community. *See* Brigham Young University: and aversion therapy; Homoerotic acts: physician indifference toward; Reparative therapy of homosexuals; Utah's insane asylum
Utah's penitentiary, 275, 281, 282, 286, 288, 326, 328, 329, 427
Utah's reform school, 154, 283, 306–7, 310*n121*, 324–27, 352*nn68* and 72, 354*n80*, 355*n86*, 427
Utah State Band, 71
Utah State Hospital. *See* Utah's insane asylum
Utah State Industrial School, 352*n68*. *See also* Utah's reform school
Utah State Prison. *See* Utah's penitentiary
Utah State University, 398*n95*, 439, 442
Utah Supreme Court, 329, 330, 359*n102*, 428
Utah Territorial Prison. *See* Utah's penitentiary

Utah Valley, 271
Ute, 133

Vagrancy, 317, 318, 319–20, 323, 347n41,
    425. See also Prostitution
Valentino, Rudolph (pseud.), 174,
    194n111, 430
Van Buskirk, Philip C., 154, 411
Vance, Carole S., 37
Vanuatu, 131
Variety (New York City), 220
Venereal disease, 268
Venson, Otto, 318, 345n27, 420
Victorian cultural values, 92–93, 107,
    119n5, 209, 228n28, 323
Village Voice (New York City), 439
Violence against lesbians and gays,
    103n51, 175–76, 382–83, 399n96, 443
Virginia, 35, 174n1, 405, 406
Von Steuben, General, 154, 179n8, 406
Voree, Wisconsin, 15n5, 268
Vosbaugh, Katherine, 175n1
Vulgarities. See Slang, sexual

Wales, 264n111, 293n24, 306n98
Wallace, Irving, 395n69
Waltz, 335, 364n124, 420
War. See Civil War; Revolutionary War;
    World War I; World War II
Ward, John J., 234–35, 241
Ward (congregation, similar to parish), 89,
    135, 276–77, 287, 316, 326, 418, 419,
    427. See also Congregational life
Wardrobe, Frederick James, 339n7
Warren, James, 286, 309–10
Washing of feet as religious ceremony, 84,
    407
Washington, George, 154, 406
Washington, D.C., 134
Washington Post (Washington, D.C.), 314
Washington Square (New York City), 239.
    See also Greenwich Village
Wasp (Nauvoo, Ill.), 111, 266, 267–68,
    273, 409
Watson, James, 344n26
Watters, William G., 168–69, 190nn88
    and 89
Weber County, Utah, 315
Webster, Daniel, 92, 406
Weeks, Jeffrey, 6

Weihe, Willard E., 70–71, 426
Weir, John, 64–65
Weld, Theodore Dwight, 109
Wellesley College, 156
Well of Loneliness, 219, 432
Wells, Anna Mary, 181n22
Wells, Daniel H., 270–71, 272, 274, 413,
    415
Wells, Edward W., 352n72, 355n81, 363
Wells, Emmeline B. Woodward, 111–12,
    424–25
Wells, Frank, 274, 297nn45 and 46, 416
Wells, Heber M., 328, 357n92
Wellsville, Utah, 235
Welter, Barbara, 67
Werner, Teresa Kimball, 194n109
Westminster College, 69, 77, 78, 95,
    106n63, 195–96, 221–22, 429, 431
West Valley City, Utah, 175n2
We'Wha (We'Wa), 133–34
"What It Means to Be a Mormon," 246
Whipple, Evangeline, 94
Whitman, Walt, 115, 117, 126n46,
    127n47, 129n60, 232
Whitney, Orson F., 114, 429
Wilcox, "Johny," 86, 418
Wilde, Oscar, 38, 46n3, 54n26, 115, 159,
    183n38, 289, 312n132, 314–15, 328,
    417, 423
"Wild Nights," 116, 128n53
Wilkinson, Ernest L., 377, 379
Wilkinson, William B., 150n42. See also
    Conrad, Susan
Willard, Frances E., 111–12, 425
Willard, Josiah Flint, 181n24. See also
    Flynt, Josiah
Willard, Utah, 233–35
Williams, Peter, 346n33
Williams, Richard, 277, 300n61
Williams, Steven, 167
Williams, Walter L., 144, 159
Willis, Grata P. See Fern, Fanny
Wilson, Amanda, 138
Wilson, Frank, 308n105, 346n33
Wilson, Fred, 356n87
Winkte, 144. See also Amazons/berdache
Winn, Alma H., 80n20
Winslow, Randolph, 419
Winter, Arthur, 348n50
Winter Quarters, 86, 411

Wisconsin, 15*n*5, 174*n*1, 268, 411
Withers, Jeffrey, 94
Wolfe, Elsie de. *See* De Wolfe, Elsie
Woman's Exponent (Salt Lake City), 108, 111, 120*n*7, 415
Women: amorous, 92–93, 107, 111, 112, 115, 117, 119*n*4, 156, 172, 181*n*22, 203, 205, 212, 223, 244, 336; "Boston marriages," 163; heterosexuals masturbated but lesbians did not, 418, 332, 360*n*112; orgasmic emphasis of, 92, 119*n*4, 212, 228*n*28; performing blessing for females, 84, 85, 98*n*7; and physical education class, 94; and physicians, 84, 105*n*56, 244–45, 262*n*99, 429; as prophetesses, seers, and revelators, 84, 144; punished for homoerotic acts, 34, 438; as soldiers/warriors, 133, 134, 146*n*21; used as therapeutic sex objects to reform homosexually oriented LDS men, 374, 392*n*50, 440; women-committed, 109. *See also* Bonding; Female-female; Female-husbands; Gender; Lesbians; Plural wives; Separate spheres of females and males
"Women Lovers," 108, 415. *See also* Lesbians; Lovers
Women's Christian Temperance Union (WCTU), 71, 111–12, 425
Woodruff, Abraham Owen, 113, 424
Woodruff, Wilford, 86, 87, 88, 89, 92, 134, 138, 146*n*18, 150*n*42, 311*n*126, 321, 412, 416, 421, 423
Woods, James, 363
Woolf, Isaac (b. 1841), 81*n*22
Woolf, Isaac or "Ike" (b. 1850), 70, 80*n*22, 81*n*22
Woolf, Simon, 70, 80*n*22
Woolley, John W., 368
Woolley, Mary, 156
Word of Wisdom, 199–200, 378
Words. *See* Bilingualism of nineteenth-century homosexuals; Denial of erotic meaning; Double entendre/double meaning; Language; Play on words; Slang, sexual
Working-class culture, 1, 333, 361*n*120
World War I, 174, 333, 355*n*81, 429

World War II, 369, 370
World We Have Lost, 3
Wrathall, John D., 73, 83*n*37, 100*n*28
Wright, William, 275, 416
Wyoming, 15*n*5, 336

Yacovone, Donald, 109, 115
Yale University, 93, 109, 130, 351*n*63, 407
Yee, John M., 167
Yellowstone Park, 235, 236
Young, Brigham, 2, 66, 67, 70, 75*n*3, 85, 86, 87, 92, 100*n*26, 111, 122*n*19, 135, 136–37, 140, 168, 173, 189*n*84, 267, 268, 269–70, 271, 273, 274, 293*n*24, 295*n*34, 311*n*125, 349*n*54, 408, 409, 410, 411, 412, 413, 415, 416, 418, 421
Young, Brigham, Jr., 86, 319, 320, 348*n*50, 424
Young, Brigham Morris, 135, 147*n*26, 418
Young, Bryant S., 70, 80*n*22
Young, Galen S., 135
Young, Harriet Cook, 123*n*20
Young, Joseph, 85, 86, 411, 412
Young, Kimball, 136–37
Young, Mary, 438
Young, S. Dilworth, 90, 434
Young, Seymour B., 301*n*66
Young Lady's Friend, 86
Young Men's Christian Association (YMCA), 1, 71, 72, 95, 107, 159–60, 165, 184*n*43, 351*n*63, 424, 430, 431
Young Woman's Journal (Salt Lake City), 115–16, 168, 172, 426
Young Women's Christian Association (YWCA), 244
Young Women's Mutual Improvement Association. *See* LDS Young Women's Mutual Improvement Association
Youth's Companion (Boston), 68, 418

Zane, Charles S., 279, 346*n*35
Zane, John M., 80*n*20, 279, 302*n*78
Zimmerman, Bonnie, 17*n*7
Zion: as Mormon ideal, 109
Zion's Camp, 66, 271
Zion's Securities Corporation, 321
Zuger, Bernard, 29*n*25
Zuni, 133–34, 146*n*18, 416

D. MICHAEL QUINN holds a Ph.D. in history from Yale University. He has received awards from Yale University, the American Council of Learned Societies, the National Endowment for the Humanities, the American Academy of Arts and Sciences, the Mormon History Association, the John Whitmer Historical Association, and Dialogue Foundation. He has been a fellow of the Mrs. Giles Whiting Foundation, the Henry E. Huntington Library, the Giles Mead Foundation, the National Endowment for the Humanities, the Glen W. Irwin Foundation, and Indiana University–Purdue University. His publications include *J. Reuben Clark: The Church Years*, *Early Mormonism and the Magic World View*, *The Mormon Hierarchy: Origins of Power*, and *The Mormon Hierarchy: Extensions of Power*. He was a professor of American social history at Brigham Young University for twelve years and is now an independent scholar.

Mormon Studies from the University of Illinois Press

Mormonism in Transition: A History of the Latter-day Saints, 1890–1930
Thomas G. Alexander

Trials of Discipleship: The Story of William Clayton, a Mormon
James B. Allen

Brigham Young: American Moses   *Leonard J. Arrington*

The Mormon Experience: A History of the Latter-day Saints (2d ed.)
Leonard J. Arrington and Davis Bitton

Building the City of God: Community and Cooperation among the Mormons
(2d ed.)   *Leonard J. Arrington, Feramorz Y. Fox, and Dean L. May*

Lost Legacy: The Mormon Office of Presiding Patriarch
Irene Bates and E. Gary Smith

Sisters in Spirit: Mormon Women in Historical and Cultural
Perspective   *Edited by Maureen Ursenbach Beecher and
Lavina Fielding Anderson*

The Ritualization of Mormon History and Other Essays   *Davis Bitton*

Joseph Smith and the Beginnings of Mormonism   *Richard L. Bushman*

Contemporary Mormonism: Social Science Perspectives
Edited by Marie Cornwall, Tim B. Heaton, and Lawrence A. Young

Mormon Odyssey: The Story of Ida Hunt Udall, Plural Wife
Edited by Maria S. Ellsworth

Zion in the Courts: A Legal History of the Church of Jesus Christ of Latter-day
Saints   *Edwin Brown Firmage and R. Collin Mangrum*

Nauvoo: Kingdom on the Mississippi   *Robert Bruce Flanders*

Religion and Sexuality: The Shakers, the Mormons, and the Oneida Community
Lawrence Foster

Letters of Catharine Cottam Romney, Plural Wife
Edited by Jennifer Moulton Hansen

Solemn Covenant: The Mormon Polygamous Passage   *B. Carmon Hardy*

Mormonism and Music: A History   *Michael Hicks*

When Truth Was Treason: German Youth against Hitler
Edited by Blair R. Holmes and Alan F. Keele

The Latter Day Saints: A Study of the Mormons in the Light of Economic Conditions *Ruth Kauffman and Reginald Wright Kauffman*

Heber C. Kimball: Mormon Patriarch and Pioneer *Stanley B. Kimball*

Historic Sites and Markers along the Mormon and Other Great Western Trails
Stanley B. Kimball

Prisoner for Polygamy: The Memoirs and Letters of Rudger Clawson at the
Utah Territorial Penitentiary, 1884–87 *Edited by Stan Larson*

Joseph Smith III: Pragmatic Prophet *Roger D. Launius*

Kingdom on the Mississippi Revisited: Nauvoo in Mormon History
Edited by Roger D. Launius and John E. Hallwas

Differing Visions: Dissenters in Mormon History
Edited by Roger D. Launius and Linda Thatcher

Political Deliverance: The Mormon Quest for Utah Statehood
Edward Leo Lyman

The Angel and the Beehive: The Mormon Struggle with Assimilation
Armand L. Mauss

The Journals of William E. McLellin, 1831–1836
Edited by Jan Shipps and John W. Welch

Mormon Enigma: Emma Hale Smith (2d ed.)
Linda King Newell and Valeen Tippets Avery

Carthage Conspiracy: The Trial of the Accused Assassins of Joseph Smith
Dallin H. Oaks and Marvin S. Hill

Science, Religion, and Mormon Cosmology *Robert Erich Paul*

Same-Sex Dynamics among Nineteenth-Century Americans: A Mormon
Example *D. Michael Quinn*

Mormon Thunder: A Documentary History of Jedediah Morgan Grant
Gene A. Sessions

Prophesying upon the Bones: J. Reuben Clark and the Foreign Debt Crisis,
1933–39 *Gene A. Sessions*

Mormonism: The Story of a New Religious Tradition *Jan Shipps*

Mormon Lives: A Year in the Elkton Ward *Susan Buhler Taber*

Victims: The LDS Church and the Mark Hofmann Case *Richard E. Turley, Jr.*

The Millenarian World of Early Mormonism *Grant Underwood*